THE

LYLE
OFFICIAL
ANTIQUES
REVIEW · 1982

While every care has been taken in the compiling of information contained in this volume the publishers cannot accept any liability for loss, financial or otherwise, incurred by reliance placed on the information herein.

All prices quoted in this book are obtained from a variety of auctions in various countries during the twelve months prior to publication and are converted to dollars at the rate of exchange prevalent at the time of sale.

DRAWINGS BY

PETER KNOX
PETER TENCH
JOHN MARTIN
DENISE FREEMAN
ELAINE HARLAND
NICOLA PARK
CARMEN MILIVOYEVICH
JOANNE BROWN

THE
LYLE
OFFICIAL
ANTIQUES
REVIEW · 1982

COMPILED BY MARGOT RUTHERFORD
EDITED by ANTHONY CURTIS

The publishers wish to express their sincere thanks
to the following for their kind help and assistance
in the production of this volume:

JANICE MONCRIEFF
SHONA BROWN
JENNIFER KNOX
MAY MUTCH
KAREN KILGOUR
EILIDH MARTIN
CHRISTINE O'BRIEN
JOSEPHINE McLAREN
TANYA BLACK
MARION McKILLOP

The Library of Congress Cataloged This Serial as Follows:

The Lyle official antiques review.

[Galashiels, Scot.]
v.   Illus.   23 cm.   annual.
Began with 1971/72 issue. Cf. new serial titles.

1. Art objects—Collectors and collecting—Catalogs.
NK1133.L9   745.1   74-640592
MARC-S

ISBN 0-698-11119-2 hardcover
ISBN 0-698-11120-6 flexible binding
Printed in the United States of America
Distributed in the United States by Coward, McCann & Geoghegan,
200 Madison Avenue, New York, N.Y. 10016

INTRODUCTION

Beyond its purely aesthetic appeal, an article of a bygone age frequently has one great advantage over that which is produced at the present time: it generally appreciates in value as each year passes and few people in this day and age would disagree with the proposition that a beautiful piece, whose investment potential may be as high as that of property, is an asset indeed.

This year tens of thousands of Antique Dealers and Collectors will make full and profitable use of their Lyle Official Antiques Review. They know that only in this one volume will they find the widest possible variety of goods – illustrated, described and given a current market value to enable them to BUY RIGHT AND SELL RIGHT throughout the year of issue.

They know, too, that by building a collection of these immensely valuable volumes year by year, they will equip themselves with an unparaleled reference library of facts, figures and illustrations which, properly used, cannot fail to help them keep one step ahead of the market.

In its twelve years of publication, Lyle's has gone from strength to strength and has become without doubt the pre-eminent book of reference for the antique trade throughout the world. Each of its 672 fact filled pages contains a treasure for someone and descriptions, prices and illustrations are given for over 10,000 collectable items.

You will find illustrations for almost every category of antique and curio, together with a corresponding price collated during the twelve months prior to publication from the best established and most highly respected auction houses in Europe and the U.S.

ANTHONY CURTIS

THE

LYLE

OFFICIAL

ANTIQUES

REVIEW · 1982

CONTENTS

10

Acknowledgements

Ball & Percival, *132 Lord Street, Southport.*
Banks & Silvers, *Worcester Street, Kidderminster.*
T. Bannister & Co., *Market Place, Haywards Heath, Sussex.*
Bermondsey Auctions Ltd., *Newnham Row, London, S.E.1.*
Biddle & Webb, *Five Ways, Edgbaston, Birmingham.*
Boardman's, *Station Road Corner, Haverhill, Suffolk.*
Bonham's, *Montpelier Galleries, Montpelier Street, London.*
Richard A. Bourne Co. Inc., *P.O. Box 141, Hyannis Port, Massachusetts.*
Bowers and Ruddy Galleries, *Suite 600, 6922 Hollywood Boulevard, Los Angeles.*
Brackett's, *27-29 High Street, Tunbridge Wells, Kent.*
Bradley & Vaughan, *52 Perrymount Road, Haywards Heath, Sussex.*
Wm. Bragdon Galleries, *311 South Broad Street, Philadelphia.*
Brogden & Co., *38-39 Silver Street, Lincoln.*
Wm. H. Brown, *31 St. Peter's Hill, Grantham, Lincs.*
Brown & Merry, *9 High Street, Woburn Sand, Milton Keynes.*
Bruton Knowles & Co., *Upton on Severn, Worcs.*
Buckell & Ballard, *1a Parsons Street, Banbury, Oxon.*
Burrows & Day, *39-41 Bank Street, Ashford, Kent.*
Burtenshaw Walker, *66 High Street, Lews, Suffolk.*
Butler & Hatch Waterman, *86 High Street, Hythe, Kent.*
Butterfield's, *1244 Sutter Street, San Francisco, California.*
Capes, Dunn & Co., *The Auction Galleries, 38 Charles Street, Manchester.*
Chancellor's & Co., *31 High Street, Ascot, Berks.*
H. C. Chapman & Sons, *North Street, Scarborough, Yorks.*
Christie's, *8 King Street, St. James's, London.*
Christie's, *8 Place de la Taconnerie, 1204 Geneva.*
Christie's, *502 Park Avenue, New York, N.Y. 10022.*
Christie's S. Kensington, *85 Old Brompton Road, London.*
Christie's & Edmiston's, *164-166 Bath Street, Glasgow.*
Churchman's Auction Galleries, *Church Street, Steyning, W. Sussex.*
Coles, Knapp & Kennedy, *Palace Pound, Ross-on-Wye, Hereford.*
Jose Collins & Harris, *29 Coinage Hall Street, Helston, Cornwall.*
Cooper Hirst, *Goldlay House, Parkway, Chelmsford.*
T. W. Arnold Corby, *30-32 Brook Street, Raunds, Northants.*
Cubitt & West, *Millmead, Guildford, Surrey.*
Dacre, Son & Hartley, *1-5 The Grove, Ilkley, Yorks.*
Clifford Dann & Partners, *43 South Street, Eastbourne.*
Davis & Sons, *Chepstow, Wales.*
Alonzo Dawes & Hoddell, *Sixways, Clevedon, Avon.*
Dickinson, Davy & Markham, *10 Wrawly Street, Brigg.*
Wm. Doyle Galleries, *175 East 87th Street, New York.*
Drewatt, Watson & Barton, *22 Market Place, Newbury, Berks.*
Hy. Duke & Son, *40 South Street, Dorchester, Dorset.*
Edwards, Bigwood & Bewlay, *78 Colmore Row, Birmingham.*
Ekins, Dilley & Handley, *The Salerooms, Market Road, St. Ives, Cambs.*
R. H. Ellis & Sons, *44-46 High Street, Worthing, Sussex.*
Clive Emson & Co., *16 High Street, Hythe, Kent.*
H. Evans & Sons, *Hull, Yorks.*
Frank H. Fellows, *Bedford House, 88 Hagley Road, Edgbaston.*
Flick & Son, *Old Bank House, Saxmundham, Suffolk.*

Fox & Sons, *1 Cranbury Terrace, Cranbury Place, Southampton.*
John Francis, Thomas Jones & Sons, *Queen Street, Carmarthen, Dyfed.*
Galerie Koller Zurich Inc., *30 Rockefeller Plaza, Suite 1929, New York.*
Ronald J. Garwood, *55 Mill Street, Ludlow, Shrops.*
Geering & Colyer, *Highgate, Hawkhurst, Kent.*
Andrew Grant, *Cookshill, Salwarpe, Droitwich, Worcs.*
Graves, Son & Pilcher, *38 Holland Road, Hove, Sussex.*
Grays Antique Market, *58 Davies Street, London.*
Grays Antique Mews, *1-7 Davies Mews, London.*
Gribble, Booth & Taylor, *West Street, Axminster, Devon.*
Hall, Wateridge & Owen, *Welsh Bridge Salerooms, Shrewsbury, Shrops.*
Harrods Auction Galleries, *Arundel Terrace, Barnes, London.*
Heathcote Ball & Co., *Bradgate Hall, Newtown Linford, Leics.*
Honiton Galleries, *High Street, Honiton, Devon.*
Edgar Horn, *47 Cornfield Road, Eastbourne, Sussex.*
Humberts, King & Chasemore, *Magdalene House, Taunton, Somerset.*
Raymond P. Inman, *35-40 Temple Street, Brighton.*
Irelands, *2 Upper King Street, Norwich, Norfolk.*
Jackson-Stops & Staff, *Town Hall, Chipping Camben, Glos.*
Jacobs & Hunt, *Lavant Street, Petersfield, Hants.*
W. S. Johnson & Co., *10 Market Square, Buckingham.*
Lacy Scott, *3 Hatter Street, Bury St. Edmunds.*
Laidlaw's, *Crown Court, Wakefield, Yorks.*
Lalonde Bros. & Parham, *Station Road, Weston-Super-Mare, Avon.*
Lambert & Symes, *Paddock Wood, nr. Tonbridge, Kent.*
W. H. Lane & Son, *Morrab Road, Penzance, Cornwall.*
Langlois, *Don Street, Jersey.*
Lawrence Fine Arts, *South Street, Crewkerne, Somerset.*
James & Lister Lea, *11 New Hall Street, Birmingham.*
Locke & England, *1-2 Euston Place, Leamington Spa, Warwicks.*
R. L. Lowery & Partners, *24 Bridge Street, Northampton.*
R. J. Lucas & Son, *9 Victoria Place, Haverfordwest.*
Mallam's, *24 St. Michael's Street, Oxford.*
Manchester Auction Mart, *3-4 Atkinson Street, Manchester.*
Frank R. Marshall, *Marshall House, Church Hill, Knutsford.*
May, Whetter & Grose, *Cornubia Hall, Par, Cornwall.*
McCartney, Morris & Barker, *25 Corve Street, Ludlow, Shrops.*
Messenger, May & Baverstock, *93 High Street, Godalming.*
Milwaukee Galleries, *4747 West Bradley Road, Milwaukee, Wisconsin.*
Moore, Allen & Innocents, *38 Castle Street, Cirencester, Glos.*
Morphet's, *The Mart, 4-6 Albert Street, Harrogate.*
Morris, Martin & Poole, *Newton.*
Morton's Auction Exchange, *643 Magazine Street, New Orleans, U.S.A.*
Alfred Mossop & Co., *Kelswick Road, Ambleside.*
Neales of Nottingham, *192 Mansfield Road, Nottingham.*
D. M. Nesbit & Co., *7 Clarendon Road, Southsea, Hants.*
Nottingham Auction Mart, *Byard Lane, Bridlesmith Gate, Nottingham.*
Olivers, *23-24 Market Hill, Sudbury, Suffolk.*
Osborne, King & Megran, *14 Montgomery Street, Belfast.*
Osmond Tricks & Son, *The Auction Rooms, Regent Street, Bristol.*
Outhwaite & Litherland, *Kingsway Galleries, Fontenoy Street, Liverpool.*
J. R. Parkinson, Son & Hamer, *14 Bolton Street, Bury, Lancs.*
Parsons, Welch & Cowell, *129 High Street, Sevenoaks, Kent.*
Pearson's, *Walcote Chambers, High Street, Winchester.*

Phillips, *7 Blenheim Street, New Bond Street, London.*
Phillips Brooks, *39 Park End Street, Oxford.*
Phillips & Jolly, *The Auction Rooms, Old King Street, Bath.*
Phillips Jacoby, *480 St. Francis Xavier Street, Montreal, Canada.*
Phillips, Son & Neale Inc., *867 Madison Avenue, New York.*
Phillips Ward-Price, *67 Davenport Road, Toronto, Canada.*
John H. Raby & Son, *21 St. Mary's Road, Bradford.*
Samuel Rains & Sons, *17 Warren Street, Stockport.*
Renton & Renton, *16 Albert Street, Harrogate, Yorks.*
Ernest R. de Rome, *12 New John Street, Westgate, Bradford.*
Russell, Baldwin & Bright, *Ryelands Road, Leominster.*
M. Phillip H. Scott, *East View, Langthorne, Bedale.*
Scott & Muirhead, *Alnwick, Northumberland.*
Selkirk Galleries, *4166 Olive Street, St. Louis, Missouri.*
Shoulder & Son, *43 Nottingham Street, Melton Mowbray.*
Simmons & Lawrence, *Henley on Thames.*
Robert W. Skinner Inc., *Bolton Gallery, Massachusetts, U.S.A.*
C. G. Sloan & Co. Inc., *715 Thirteenth Street, Washington D.C.*
Smith-Woolley & Perry, *43 Castle Hill Avenue, Folkestone.*
Sotheby's, *34-35 New Bond Street, London.*
Sotheby Bearne, *3 Warren Road, Torquay, Devon.*
Sotheby's Belgravia, *19 Motcomb Street, London.*
Sotheby Beresford Adams, *The Cross, Chester.*
Sotheby's Boston, *232 Clarendon Street, Boston, Massachusetts.*
Sotheby's, *24 Rue de la Cite, Geneva.*
Sotheby, King & Chasemore, *Station Road, Pulborough, Sussex.*
Sotheby's, *7660 Beverley Boulevard, Los Angeles, U.S.A.*
Sotheby's, *Sporting d'Hiver, Monte Carlo.*
Sotheby's, *980 Madison Avenue, New York.*
Sotheby's Philadelphia, *1630 Locust Street, Philadelphia.*
Sotheby's San Francisco, *210 Post Street, San Francisco.*
Sotheby's Vancouver, *2321 Granville Street, Vancouver, Canada.*
Spear & Sons, *The Hill, Wickham Market, Suffolk.*
H. Spencer & Sons, *20 The Square, Retford, Notts.*
Stanilands, *28 Nether Hall Road, Doncaster.*
Stockholms Auktionsverk.
Stride & Son, *Southdown House, St. John's Street, Chichester.*
Swetenham's, *5 St. Werburgh Street, Chester.*
David Symonds, *High Street, Crediton.*
Taylor Lane & Creber, *Central Auction Rooms, Trelawney Lane, Plymouth.*
Theriault, *P.O. Box 151, Annapolis, MD 21404.*
Turner, Rudge & Turner, *29 High Street, East Grinstead, Surrey.*
V. & V.'s, *The Memorial Hall, Shiplake on Thames.*
Vernon's, *1 Westgate, Chichester.*
Vincent & Vanderpump, *24 Greyfriars Road, Reading, Berks.*
Walker, Walton & Hanson, *The Salerooms, Byard Lane, Nottingham.*
Warren & Wignall, *113 Towngate, Leyland, Lancs.*
Thomas Watson & Son, *Northumberland Street, Darlington, Co. Durham.*
J. M. Welch & Son, *The Town Hall, Dunmow, Essex.*
Whitehead's, *34 High Street, Petersfield.*
Whitton & Laing, *Exeter.*
Peter Wilson & Co., *50 Hospital Street, Nantwich, Cheshire.*
Woolley & Wallis, *The Castle Auction Mart, Salisbury, Wilts.*
Worsfolds, *40 Station Road West, Canterbury, Kent.*

ANTIQUES REVIEW

'Boom!' That is the only word to describe the take-off rate of the antiques market in America. In the last couple of years the market has literally boomed and observers of the trade say that there has never been an acceleration rate like it since the halcyon days of the 1960's in London. The growth rate has been phenomenal and though the London end of the trade like to produce arguments against it, the fact is that New York seems to have taken over as the antiques centre of the world.

What has made America turn to antiques buying at a time of world-wide recession? The answer, many people believe, lies in the fact that the public is growing more knowledgeable about antiques and have more confidence in their own judgement. A significant number of customers crowding into auction rooms, antiques shows and sales are young, first time buyers who know what they want and can select what is good. Their parents were in the habit of employing decorators when they wanted to do over their homes and some of

the older generations still do this, but younger, more enterprising buyers now trust their own judgement.

It only takes a quick look through the numerous trade papers to appreciate what a big business antique buying and selling has become. Antique markets, flea markets, shows, sales and shops appear everywhere with catchy ads and cheeky slogans — 'Buy a money box like this and be the only kid in your street to own one!' was written beneath the picture of a 1920's thrift box. The auction houses too have been cashing in on the boom time and none of them more than the London based salerooms — Sothebys, Christies and to a lesser extent Phillips, Bonhams, and coin dealer Spinks.

It was Sothebys and Christies who brought antiques to the notice of Europe's mass market and now in America they are continuing their 'hard sell' tactics. So much so that the PR lady of one of their rivals, Phillips, complained 'Sothebys and Christies hype the hell out of everything.' But 'hyping the hell' out of antiques is a money making formula and the big two have excellent returns to show for their trouble. Sothebys' North American total turnover for the past year was $130 million of which $116 million was generated in New York. Their Los Angeles outlet, Sotheby Parke Bernet, turned over a total of $9.7 million and Canada brought in another $4 million.

During the fall of 1980, the combined North American total for Sothebys' and Christies' sales turnover was about $180 million while the equivalent figure for the United Kingdom was only $140 million. Both companies increased their turnovers by significant percentages – Sothebys by 43% and Christies by 42%. Moreover by taking the lion's share of the New York market Sothebys have fulfilled one of their initial predictions when they first moved to New York that the U.S. market would eventually outsell London.

Following the two big timers, Phillips, who established themselves in New York three years ago are also making a significant niche in the market for themselves. They run 'speciality' sales because they had to think of something new in a fast moving and cut throat market. The sales concentrate on individual items – lead soldiers, or the work of painter Louis Icart . . . Phillips have zeroed in on small categories of specific items and their tactics are a lesson in promotion. Not long ago they held a sale of one weathervane from Lexington, which, they said, might have witnessed the ride of Paul Revere. The

18th century gilded copper weathervane was attributed to Shem Drowne (1683-1774) and, according to Phillips original publicity material it was the one mentioned in Longfellow's poem, 'The Midnight Ride of Paul Revere.' These claims were later toned down a little because of trade criticism and the final estimate for the weathervane fell to between $60,000 and $90,000. In the event the hype fell flat and the weathervane was withdrawn unsold at only $34,000. However the specialist sale idea is not a bad one and collectors turn out to pay good prices for such items as military miniatures and Lalique glass.

Another of the big London auction houses to establish themselves in New York is Bonhams of Knightsbridge in London, a long established family firm. They opened their New York auction house in 1981 and their chairman Nicholas Bonham also gives valuation and advice sessions. This year too, Spink and Son, the London coin specialists, have launched a Manhattan base to sell mainly coins but also works of art and antiques.

Because of the dynamism of the New York market, Sothebys in a blaze of publicity in 1980 opened their enormous new facility on the corner of York Avenue and 72nd Street – over 160,000 square feet of space that some trade rivals predicted they would never be able to utilise to the full. Indeed Sothebys themselves planned to let off one of the floors but in the event that plan has never materialised and all the space is being used for their own trading.

The building they took over was the old Kodak building and their total costs in renovating it and turning it over to auctioneering was in excess of $15 million — a figure that made wiseacres shake their heads even more. However the new building has lived up to Sotheby's expectations by turning over a figure in excess of the $100 million predicted for their first year and success seems secured. The out of the way location of the York Avenue site was also used as an argument for its possible failure but Sotheby's took care of that by providing a free shuttle service between their Madison headquarters and the new facility — the shuttle runs every half hour and takes both Sotheby's staff and their clients back and forward. They are also pulling in custom by operating late night and Sunday afternoon viewing sessions and they aim for seven day selling eventually. There is a pavement cafe on the site and parts of the building are used for lectures and seminars on art and antiques while other departments dealing with conservation and renovation for clients have also been established. 'It's a cradle to the grave operation for our customers,' said a Sotheby's man, 'We sell them the goods, look after them for the clients and then we sell their collections for their heirs.'

Sothebys have found that their business is divided down the middle into Fine Arts which they base at 980 Madison and Decorative pieces which they turn over at York Avenue.

In the Decorative class the most keenly attended sales are the Americana which is perhaps the most significant growth area in all the antique scene.

A mixture of fierce national pride and a nostalgic hankering after the rural past of our ancestors seem to be the two forces that have made folk art the most popular area of the antique world for collectors. Every antiques magazine and newspaper have pages and pages of adverts showing items of interest from the folksy past — weathervanes, whirlgigs, samplers, duck decoys, kitchen cupboards, quilts, children's toys . . . anything typical of the life of homestead America.

Mid 19th century metal rooster weathervane. $1,500 (Robert W. Skinner Inc.)

The Americana craze really took off in 1979 when Sothebys set the pace by holding a sale of the collection of the late Stewart E. Gregory at which many price records were set up — perhaps because the items on sale had been little regarded before. That sale raised

*Late 19th century crazy quilt with matching shams. $1,000
(Robert W. Skinner Inc.)*

$1.3 million and was epoch making at the time. Since then many of the records have been broken and re-broken.

The folk art market is really an East Coast phenomenon and it is one that demands a great deal of care from people prepared to dabble in it because the simplicity of the pieces so sought after has meant that many fakes have appeared for sale. Who is to tell with certainty whether a weathervane has stood on a barn for twenty years or for over a century? The market hazards have meant that really keen Americana enthusiasts have become very sophisticated and knowledgeable and they more and more show their discrimination, often turning away with open scorn suspicious items that come up for sale. This happened on more that one occasion this year and not only with the Lexington weathervane. The keynote of a good piece of folk art is quality and it takes a practised eye to pick it out. When quality items do appear for sale however the prices they make reflect their rarity.

Middle to lower quality items have stayed pretty constant in price for some time but the more unique items have forged ahead. For example even the Sothebys auctioneers were surprised when a carved wooden eagle wall plaque which they had estimated at $12,000 was knocked down for $39,000 and when a hooked rug estimated at $3,500 made $12,000.

Samplers are very highly prized and Sothebys sold a very fine Pennsylvania example in January for $38,000 which was between seven and eight times the expected figure and was a record price for a needlework sampler – the previous record having been only $5,700. At the same sale a 1776 sampler stitched by a 12 year-old girl called Lucy Low sold for $22,000 against an estimate of $2,000 to $3,000. What would little Lucy have thought about that!

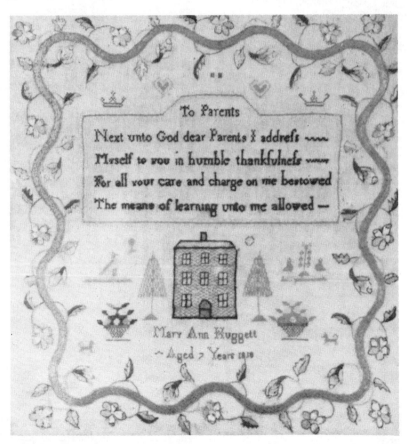

American needlework sampler by 'Mary Ann Hugget, aged 7 years, 1810.' $210 (Robert W. Skinner Inc.)

A Boston school needlework picture this year made the exceptional price of $28,500 when it was sold at Robert W. Skinner Galleries in Boston. The Sewing bees that made old quilts too would be amazed at the prices their handiwork fetches today in auction rooms and antique shops. Included in the category of Americana are pieces made by American Indians though this is still only a developing area of the market and could be one in which to specialise. At Waddingtons in Toronto recently there was a well attended sale where examples of the handiwork of various Indian tribes like the Iroquois, Navajo, Bella Coola and Haidai tribes came up for auction.

A Haida wood bear dance mask with a large circular handle, 20in. tall. $1,215 (Sotheby's)

A Sioux Indian hide jacket decorated with geometric motif beadwork. $1,580 (Sotheby's)

19

Chippendale mahogany games table, Boston, circa 1760, 33½in. wide.
$21,000 (Robert W. Skinner Inc.)

Younger buyers have shown a strong preference for American furniture which has also shown a rapid escalation of price for any item that is good and clean and without a 'cruddy' finish. At a spring sale of Americana, Christies recorded excellent prices for authentic items but they withdrew a few lots in the sale when authenticity was questioned. More than in other areas of the market is it important to 'look before you leap' with Americana. What have been going well however are items of painted furniture, Shaker furniture and chairs – a good example of an elegant Shaker rocker can cost over $1,000. Milliners' wooden heads, cigar store figures and even old trade boards also make good prices. The most up to date home decorators today are looking to the past for their household furnishings.

Sharing this folk-art craze are naive pictures which are also having a vogue at the moment. American pictures always sell well — look at the astonishing prices that Norman Rockwell's pictures are making today — but buyers are also out in force looking for more primitive pictures done by untaught painters of the past. These men who would do a trade sign one day and paint a rich man's family the next have at last been recognised for the genuine talents they possessed, a talent that combined charm with humor and a fresh lack of self consciousness.

So keen is the enthusiasm for naive art that British dealer Andras Kalman brought his personal collection of 65 pictures by British folk artists to show in New York in the summer of 1980 because he reckoned that it was only there that they would attract a sufficiently knowledgeable public.

'They are as excited about folk art here as they are about Turner in England,' said Mr Kalman who runs the Crane Kalman Gallery in London, and who has been collecting naive art for many years in spite of the predominant indifference on the part of his compatriots and fellow dealers. Mr Kalman thinks that folk art is a genuine art form because it shows the indigenous talent of a people and he admires American collectors for appreciating it — 'There is no market in Britain for folk art,' he

Wooden clothier trade sign, 84in. high, Hartford, Connecticut, circa 1900. $1,600 (Robert W. Skinner Inc.)

said. When he finds a good example of naive painting, Mr Kalman ships it across the Atlantic to New York for sale.

Of course the world of collecting and antiques is a many splendored thing and nowhere is the variety more marked than here in America. Different regions all have their individual preferences. The distinctive quality of American taste was first noticed by French auction house Didier Aaron of Paris who arrived in New York with a stock of the sort of items that would have gone down very well in Paris, only to discover that New York buyers gave them a marked thumbs down. New Yorkers have little interest in French furniture which they consider too classical. Nor do they like 'prissy' porcelain — delicately printed Sevres is not for them.

'It's too dainty,' said a New York dealer, 'People aren't living dainty lives today.'

New York likes folk art, it also likes Art Nouveau and Art Deco and any of the more way out idiosyncratic items that come on the market from time to time . . . Icart prints which are young and funky, wearable Edwardian jewelry, Galle glass, early cameras, Oriental and Japanese inro. New Yorkers are keen specialist collectors and they are

A selection of Galle glass , most sought after by specialist collectors. (Christie's)

usually first into a new craze. The centre of the Oriental art world too is New York.

In the South however tastes are different. There they like Victorian furniture and dealers can sell so much of it that they have trouble finding stock. In Florida the buyers love anything that is florid, gilded, and the more rococo the better. Pieces of furniture held up by gilded cupids will easily find a Florida buyer. Texans go for Art Nouveau and good quality early English furniture, people in Chicago like folk art, quilts, trunks and old sledges and San Francisco goes for silver.

There are also however certain categories of antiques that have a universal appeal for collectors and these fall into the high class and specialised categories.

One of the fastest growing areas is good quality English furniture. At a Christies' sale in New York in the spring most of the lots on offer went to American buyers many of whom were private collectors. English dealers who attended the sale were also able to take back to their own country some high quality items that discriminating American customers had bought several years and several price rises ago. Typical of the pieces were a pair of George I giltwood mirrors that went to a private New York buyer for well over the $28,000 estimate. A George III giltwood settee by Robert Adam sold for $28,000. This upward rise in the price of English furniture has been going on steadily for the past couple of years and was most marked when Christies sold the collec-

tion of the late Marjorie Wiggin Prescott last year. There a George I burr-walnut bureau tripled its estimate to sell at $230,000 and a George III mahogany and ormolu tambour writing table which was bought in London in 1953 for $465 was sold for $85,000. The Prescott sale prices made dealers go away shaking their heads and puzzling over the question of whether the sales estimates were wrong or whether the market had risen so much that their own goods were priced too low. Whatever the answer it is certain that prices will continue to rise for top grade English furniture, especially for walnut which is a great favorite. The taste for this sort of furniture also appears to be spread throughout all parts of the U.S.A. Mortons in New Orleans are always sure of excellent prices when a good example of English furniture comes up for sale. A Texan buyer recently paid $14,000 for a pair of George II marble topped console tables. Among the more interesting items to appear in the New Orleans saleroom was also a tea caddy made of applewood and carved in the shape of a big apple sold for $550 and a Victorian sewing box inlaid with ivory, bought for $800.

While buyers seem to concentrate mainly on the better items of the English furniture scene, there is also a thriving market for medium quality 18th and early 19th century furniture and many of the buyers are English dealers who are exporting container loads of this sort of furniture back to Britain because it can be found in greater quantity and at lower prices in America than in England.

The sort of thing the English dealers regard as bargains are items of Regency or satinwood furniture — especially dumb waiters, library steps, pedestal desks, sofa tables and partners' desks. There is a bigger selection of things like that, they say, in New York than there is in London.

If Americans collect English furniture however they are also enthusiastic about the pieces produced by native furniture makers as well. Particularly popular is the opulent furniture made by the Belter company — ornately carved items made from rosewood which often fetch amazing prices in sales. A record for a Belter piece was made this year when a carved rosewood table dating from around 1855 sold for $60,000. The rise in the price of Belter furniture has been sudden because pieces which were selling for around $3,000 in the early '70's are making as much as $40,000 today. Many of the people buying Belter now are doing so as investments. Another American piece to make good money this year was a New York Empire style table of about 1815 made by an emigre French craftsman and which sold to a New York collector for $190,000. Buyers are also on the look out for good examples of tall case clocks and another home-made product fetching high prices is American pewter. A private buyer at Christies in New York set a new record for any piece of pewter ever sold at auction when he paid $15,000 for a flat top quart tankard by William Bradford Junior of New York City, dating from around the early part of the 18th century. The previous record for a piece of pewter was $13,000 which was paid in

A George III satinwood sofa table crossbanded with rosewood and tulipwood. (Christie's)

England in 1973 for a charger engraved with the figures of King Charles II and his Queen, Catherine of Braganza.

There is also growing interest in American glass — a term that is used to describe everything from old bottles to decorative glass. Examples from the 19th century are most highly priced. Also popular with glass collectors is English pressed glass, and of course paperweights, especially examples from Clichy, Baccarat and St. Louis. The prices of these are rising by a steady 20% a year in the U.S.A.

Collectors looking for a new growth area might do well to consider European ceramics, an area that has been fairly quiet in America till now. Many of the choice lots that come up for sale are taken back across the Atlantic especially to Germany because Germans think that prices asked in the U.S.A., for Meissen in particular, are very attractive. At a

Clichy faceted scattered millefiori weight with pink central rose, 7.2cm. diam. $960 (Christie's)

sale of Rockefeller effects two 18th century Meissen swans dated around 1747 were the top lot sellers at $130,000. Sevres too is sought after in America where native collectors tend to undervalue it. Examples of English porcelain are also often snapped up by London dealers, particularly pieces of Derby, Chelsea, Bow and salt glaze Leeds and Whieldon pottery.

Pair of Derby figures of a recumbent stag and hind, circa 1765, about 17cm. wide. $1,170 (Christie's)

A small Strohmenger Art Deco grand piano. $12,500 (Sotheby's)

The big, big markets in America at the moment however are Art Deco, Art Nouveau and Orientalia.

Art Deco and Art Nouveau is a wide spectrum covering such diverse items as silver, jewelry, posters and pictures, decorative items and furniture. Phillips in New York recently had considerable success with a jewelry sale which included a crystal and diamond bracelet that made $11,000. The silver market which took such a shaking because of the activities of the Hunt brothers a couple of years ago is still show-ing strength for better quality pieces – Paul Storr and Lamarie pieces sell any-where at any time and rise in price by 25% every year, but collectors are now looking for pieces of Tiffany silver especially those made in the Japanese style that was fashionable between 1870 and 1890.

A sale worth its name is not complete without a Tiffany style lamp at the moment and these have cropped up all over the place during the year. There must have been a tremendous output of these when they were first made

*A Tiffany Favrile leaded and stained glass window, circa 1890.
(Robert W. Skinner Inc.)*

*Tiffany bronze and leaded Favrile glass table lamp, early 20th century.
$20,000 (Robert W. Skinner Inc.)*

because hundreds still exist after years of wear and tear. At one time they were sold for the value of the lead holding together the stained glass shades: last year Christies notched up a record price of $360,000 for a Tiffany spiderweb lamp which makes the price paid for the lead look pretty small. Collectors have also been eagerly hunting for Galle lamps and several of those too appeared for sale – Christies again sold one for $82,000. Daum, Legras and Muller are also becoming popular names in the lamp-hunters' world.

Other names that knowledgeable collectors have been searching for include Lalique glass, Rhulmann and Jean Dunand furniture, Rookwood pottery and Stickley chairs. Art Nouveau jewelry is very popular because it is prettier and easier to wear than the ponderous Victorian suites of jewelry that often appear on the market. Art Deco pieces of jewelry that come on the market are even more modern but are very, very expensive.

The star of the antiques world however is the Oriental market. New York is now without doubt the centre of the Oriental art world with Los Angeles not far behind. Prices recorded over the year for items of Oriental art recall the insanity prices of 1972 and 1973 and values are still rising with a great deal of investment buying. The whole mood of the market is one of heady optimism.

Japanese inros are typical of the things that have been selling well. At Sothebys in New York a 19th century piece signed by Oyama Saku sold for $56,000 which was seven times its estimate. The inro, which was bought by a New York dealer, set a new record because the previous best price was $27,000 paid in London. There is also a boom in Chinese ceramics with prefered periods being the Ming and Ching dynasties which ranged from the 14th to 19th century. The American buyers turned their attention to Chinese ceramics after President Nixon's visit to China in the '70's and since then they have become a passion with many discriminating collectors. They often have to vie for good examples with buyers from the East, particularly from Hong Kong. Japanese buyers are also strong in the market. When they buy Chinese items they prefer those of the Sung as well as the Ming and Ching dynasties but they are particularly eager to buy examples of their own native artists — particularly cloisonne, lacquer work and ivory. Gold lacquer items are most sought after but prices for all Japanese pieces, particularly those of the Meigi period, are higher than ever before. So strong is the interest in the Oriental art market that Robert C. Eldred, the Massachusetts dealer and auction house was able to hold a week long sale of Orientalia recently. Most of the lots went to American buyers and the remainder went to Hong Kong and Japan.

With the expansion of the antiques market, dealers are flooding into America from all over the world. Many long established London dealers are following their auction houses across the Atlantic and in America itself thousands of first time buyers are entering the market. It is a buoyant world where everyone interested is very aware that knowledge is all important.

In a market rising so fast there are still bargains to be picked up but buyers have to know what to look for — and how to tell if it is a treasure when they find it.

LIZ TAYLOR

29

Hawker Hurricane 11B, 1942, 1,635 H.P. engine, wingspan 40ft. (Christie's) $488,800

Miles M38 Messenger 155 H.P. engine plane, wingspan 36ft.2in. (Christie's) $2,445

Bristol (Fairchild) Bolingbroke IVT plane, 1942, two 920 H.P. engines, wingspan 56ft.4in. (Christie's) $33,840

Hunting Percival Provost T1, 1953, 550 H.P. engine, wingspan 35ft.2in. (Christie's) $30,080

DH 80 A Puss Moth, 1930, 130 H.P. engine, wingspan 36ft.9in. (Christie's) $14,100

De Havilland DH 85 Leopard Moth, 1934, 130 H.P. engine, wingspan 37ft.6in. (Christie's) $52,640

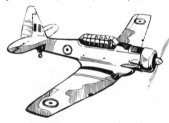

North American Harvard 11B, 1943, 600 H.P. engine, wingspan 42ft. (Christie's) $37,600

Short Scion I twin engine plane with two 90 H.P. engines, 42ft. wingspan, 1934. (Christie's) $18,800

De Havilland DH 87B Hornet Moth plane, 1936, 130 H.P. engine, wingspan 31ft.11in. (Christie's) $11,280

De Havilland DH 94 Moth Minor, 1939, 80 H.P. engine, wingspan, 36ft.7in. (Christie's) $31,960

Lockheed Hudson IV twin engine plane, 1942, 1,200
H.P., wingspan 65ft.6in.(Christie's)$30,080

Grumman Avenger TBM-3WS, 1945, 1,850 H.P.
engine, wingspan 54ft.2in. (Christie's)$14,665

De Havilland DH 98 Mosquito B35, 1946, two 1,710
H.P. engines, wingspan 54ft.2in. (Christie's)
$188,000

De Havilland DH 82A Tiger Moth, 1942, 130 H.P.
engine, wingspan 29ft.4in. (Christie's)
$35,720

Miles M18 Mark II, 1939, 155 H.P. engine, wingspan 31ft.
(Christie's) $6,580

General Aircraft GAL 24 Cygnet, 1941,
150 H.P. engine, wingspan 34ft.6in.
(Christie's) $13,160

Miles M17 Monarch, 1938, 145 H.P. engine, wingspan
35ft.7in. (Christie's) $4,890

De Havilland DH 98A Dominoe T1 (Dragon Rapide),
1944, two 200 H.P. engines, wingspan 48ft.
(Christie's) $15,040

Reid and Sigrist BS3/4 Desford (Bobsleigh), 1945,
two 145 H.P. engines, 34ft. wingspan. (Christie's)
$10,340

Avro Anson Mark 19 Series II plane, two 420 H.P.
engines, wingspan 57ft.6in., 1950. (Christie's)
$1,130

Egyptian alabaster cylinder jar, of Dynasty III, 7in. high. (Christie's) $300

Mid 15th century Malines alabaster pieta, 32cm. high. (Christie's) $6,910

Old Kingdom Egyptian alabaster cylinder jar, with everted rim, 8in. high. (Christie's) $230

16th century Malines alabaster relief of Faith, Hope and Charity, 10.5 x 13cm. (Christie's) $935

Egyptian alabaster vase of open chalice form, 5in. high, of Dynasty XVIII. (Christie's) $695

16th century Malines alabaster relief of Moses striking the rock, 15.5 x 12cm. (Christie's) $1,405

15th century Hispano-Flemish alabaster group of the Virgin and Child, 74.5cm. high. (Christie's) $6,550

Nottingham alabaster fragment of St. Christopher, early 15th century, 10¾in. high. (Sotheby's) $2,225

6th-4th century B.C. alabaster conical-shaped vessel with two handles, 4in. high. (Christie's) $230

One of a pair of 14th century Nottingham alabaster reliefs of St. Thomas, 39 x 24cm. (Christie's) $11,700

Fine 15th century Flemish alabaster relief of the Last Supper, 53 x 57cm. (Christie's) $6,550

Mid 15th century Nottingham polychrome alabaster relief of the Ascension, 37 x 23.5cm. (Christie's) $8,890

1st century South Arabian alabaster funerary plaque carved with the head of a woman, 7¼in. high. (Christie's) $615

Early 20th century enamel and alabaster bell-push by G. A. Scheid, Vienna, 7.5cm. high. (Sotheby's Belgravia)$285

Alabaster jar of deep rounded form with twin vestigial handles, 5½in. high. (Christie's) $800

1st. century B.C./1st. century A.D. South Arabian alabaster plaque, 13.7cm. wide. (Sotheby's) $1,755

Egyptian alabaster canopic jar, barrel-shaped with human headed lid. (Christie's) $800

1st. century South Arabian funerary plaque in alabaster, carved with the head of a man, 6½in. high. (Christie's) $520

2nd/3rd. century A.D. Roman alabaster figure of Diana of Ephesus, 11¾in. high, restored. (Sotheby's) $2,845

17th century Malines alabaster relief in ebonised frame, 12½in. high. (Sotheby's)$4,740

Early 15th century Nottingham alabaster figure of St. James, 18½in. high. (Sotheby's) $9,955

Malines alabaster relief of the Communion of Judas, signed HVH, circa 1600, 7in. high. (Sotheby's) $1,660

Alabaster bust entitled Mignon, by Prof. G. Besji, circa 1890, 37cm. high. (Sotheby's Belgravia) $1,270

Malines alabaster relief by Tobias Tissenaken, circa 1600, in wood frame, 5¼in. high. (Sotheby's) $1,660

33

AMUSEMENT MACHINES

Bijou Pickwick clown-type halfpenny amusement machine, circa 1915, 30in. high. (Sotheby's Belgravia)$350

J. Kindsbuber Monaco bar-top gambling machine, German circa 1915, 14½in. high. (Sotheby's Belgravia)$260

Clown-type Zeppelin amusement machine in oak case with glazed window, circa 1915, German, 27in. high. (Sotheby's Belgravia) $290

English penny-in-the-slot amusement machine ' 'The Twins', circa 1935, 66in. high. (Sotheby's Belgravia) $955

Amusement machine by the International Muto-scope Reel Co. Ltd., America, circa 1915, 69½in. high, with two spare reels of stills. (Sotheby's Belgravia) $995

American jewel box crane penny-in-the-slot amusement machine, by Buckley & Co., circa 1935, 70½in. high. (Sotheby's Belgravia) $310

An Ahrens automatic palmistry amusement machine, 193cm. high. (Sotheby's Belgravia) $730

'Marco the Mystic' amusement machine in painted metal and wood cabinet, circa 1935, 69½in. high. (Sotheby's Belgravia)$1,140

English penny-in-the-slot amusement machine by E.A.M. Co. Ltd., circa 1915, 44½in. wide. (Sotheby's Belgravia) $1,195

American totalisator one-armed bandit decorated with War Eagle, circa 1931, 27in. high. (Sotheby's Belgravia)$660

34

Mills American War Eagle slot machine finished in black on stained wooden base, 25½in. high, circa 1932.(Sotheby's Belgravia) $870

English Fireman and Ladders amusement machine on cast-iron legs, circa 1925, 74in. high. (Sotheby's Belgravia)$455

Sega bell fruit machine in full working condition. (Alfie's Antique Market) $280

English Pussy Shooting Gallery amusement machine, circa 1935, 76in. high. (Sotheby's Belgravia) $580

Mill's Perfect Muscle-Developing Owl Lifter amusement machine with cast-iron base, circa 1904, 67½in. high. (Sotheby's Belgravia) $1,760

'The Miser's Dream' working model automaton, circa 1935, 71½in. high. (Sotheby's Belgravia) $785

An Ahrens test-your-strength machine, circa 1920, 6ft.7in. high. (Sotheby's Belgravia) $800

Bunny Shooter amusement machine, stained oak cabinet with glazed upper section, circa 1935, 68in. high. (Sotheby's Belgravia)$185

English Football amusement machine operated by handle below, circa 1925, 55in. high. (Sotheby's Belgravia) $725

American stereoscopic viewer amusement machine in stained oak case, circa 1915, 42in. high. (Sotheby's Belgravia)$540

Very rare passenger pigeon, mounted on branch, 22in. high, in glass dome. (Sotheby's Belgravia) $1,200

Pacific Island turtle shell mask. (Woolley & Wallis) $2,150

Crocodile handbag with stuffed crocodile on the front flap. (Sotheby's Belgravia)$800

Victorian silver mounted table snuff mull. (Christie's & Edmiston) $2,035

Lion skin rug, of a male African lion with snarling head, 120in. long. (Sotheby's Belgravia) $785

Leopard skin rug, mounted on felt backcloth, 72in. long, nose to tail tip. (Sotheby's Belgravia) $900

One of a pair of English shell decorations, with glass domes, circa 1880, 23in. high. (Sotheby's Belgravia) $325

Tiger skin rug, mounted on felt with oilskin backing, 91in. long. (Sotheby's Belgravia) $495

Unusual Barbedienne gilt bronze mounted lacquered ostrich egg, 23cm. high, circa 1870. (Sotheby's Belgravia)$490

Stuffed barn owl. (Alfie's Antique Market) $105

Stuffed and mounted barn owl on a stump, within glazed case, 49.5cm. high. (Sotheby's Belgravia)$105

One of a pair of stuffed puffins. (Phillips) $45

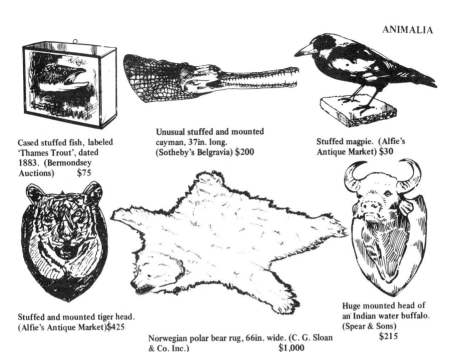

Cased stuffed fish, labeled 'Thames Trout', dated 1883. (Bermondsey Auctions) $75

Unusual stuffed and mounted cayman, 37in. long. (Sotheby's Belgravia) $200

Stuffed magpie. (Alfie's Antique Market) $30

Stuffed and mounted tiger head. (Alfie's Antique Market)$425

Norwegian polar bear rug, 66in. wide. (C. G. Sloan & Co. Inc.) $1,000

Huge mounted head of an Indian water buffalo. (Spear & Sons) $215

Stuffed and mounted barn owl on a stump, within glazed case, 49.5cm. high. (Sotheby's Belgravia)$105

Late 19th century dome of stuffed and mounted exotic birds on ebonised base, 66cm. high. (Sotheby's Belgravia) $260

Stuffed and mounted tawny owl, within glazed case, 56cm. high. (Sotheby's Belgravia) $130

Tiger skin rug with glass eyes and chipped teeth, 121½in. long. (Sotheby's Belgravia) $630

White-tailed sea eagle and chick in glass case, 36in. high. (Sotheby's Belgravia) $270

One of a pair of beaded and quilted buffalo hooves. (Phillips) $3,840

North Italian half-armour of Pisan type, circa 1560-70, comprising one-piece cabaset with pear stalk finial. (Wallis & Wallis) $5,075

Pair of French 19th century Cuirassier breast and backplates, with original brass shoulder chains and attachment fittings. (Wallis & Wallis) $410

Asagi-Ito-Odoshi yoko-hagi okegawa-do, signed Myochin Muneysahi saku, 19th century. (Christie's) $4,680

Kabuto with fine russet iron hoshi-bachi of tenkokuzan, signed Nagamichi, mid Edo period.(Christie's) $3,510

Scarce 18th or 19th century Japanese russet face-guard mempo in red and black lacquer. (Wallis & Wallis) $235

18th century O-Boshi hoshi no kabuto with twenty-four-plate russet iron hachi, signed Masuda Myochin no Kami Ki Munemasa. (Christie's) $4,680

Black lacquered Kon-Ito-Sugake odoshi yokohagi-do of the Edo period, with Hineno style san-mai-bachi. (Christie's) $1,640

Well made and detailed miniature suit of 16th century armour, fully articulated, 27in. high, in good condition. (Wallis & Wallis) $935

Mid Edo period Moegi-Ito-Odoshi dangaie-do, kabuto with black and brown lacquered Hineno style san-mai-bachi, unsigned. (Christie's) $5,615

19th century French Cuirassier Trooper's breast and backplate with original leather backed chain mountings. (Wallis & Wallis) $600

Mid 17th century Cromwellian armour comprising a lobster tail helmet, breast and backplates of siege weight. (Wallis & Wallis) $740

Pair of late 19th century French Cuirassier's breast and backplates, with original shoulder chains. (Wallis & Wallis) $440

Cromwellian period siege weight breastplate, ribbed neck section and arm cusps, medial ridge terminating at flared skirt in small beak. (Wallis & Wallis)$290

Pair of mid 17th century Cromwellian elbow gauntlets, fully articulated. (Wallis & Wallis) $430

Late 18th century russet iron yukinoshita-do of five main plates, signed Miochin Ki Munemasu. (Christie's) $750

Edo period brown lacquered Kon-Ito-Kebiki-Odoshi do-maru, upper part laced in yellow, orange and green. (Christie's) $2,455

Fine Aka-Shiro-Ito-Odoshi Nimai-do gusoku, hachi 17th century, mounting 19th century. (Christie's)$8,190

Interesting Kawazutsumi-Hotoke-do, signed Boshu Iwakuni Haruta Masatoki, Edo period. (Christie's) $2,340

AUTOMATONS

'Revolving Clown' automaton, circa 1925, 16in. high. (Sotheby's Belgravia) $310

German piano-player musical automaton, circa 1900, 14in. wide. (Sotheby's Belgravia) $670

Automaton conjuror in good condition. (Christie's S. Kensington) $9,520

American cast-iron automaton clock in the form of a Negress, circa 1870, 16¼in. high. (Sotheby's Belgravia) $835

French monkey fisherman automaton by J. Phalibois, circa 1880's. (Sotheby's Belgravia) $2,890

French singing bird automaton in domed gilt cage, circa 1890, 44.5cm. high. (Sotheby's Belgravia) $435

American 'dancing dolls' automaton, circa 1880's, 10in. high, slightly damaged. (Sotheby's Belgravia) $355

Spice box automaton by Nicholas Engleheart, circa 1830's, 34.5cm. wide. (Sotheby's Belgravia) $725

French fan-waving musical doll automaton, circa 1910, 49.5cm. high. (Sotheby's Belgravia) $965

French singing bird automaton beneath a gilt cage, 47cm. high, circa 1895. (Sotheby's Belgravia) $845

Late 19th century French knitting woman automaton by Theroude, 63.5cm. high. (Sotheby's Belgravia) $1,445

French 'seated dandy' musical automaton by Decamps, circa 1880's, 61cm. high. (Sotheby's Belgravia) $1,325

Late 19th century German shaped rectangular singing bird box with two keys
and case. (Sotheby's Belgravia)
$1,010

Swiss musical picture automaton,
circa 1870, 46 x 43cm.
(Sotheby's Belgravia) $875

Late 19th century shaped rectangular
singing bird box, 9.6cm. long.
(Sotheby's Belgravia) $1,050

Mechanical bird automaton in
domed brass cage, 23cm. high.
(Sotheby, King & Chasemore)
$240

Late 19th century French bisque-headed
'swimming doll' automaton by E. Martin.
42cm. long. (Sotheby's Belgravia)
$770

French 'kitten-in-a-milk-churn'
automaton, circa 1920, 10in. high.
(Sotheby's Belgravia) $540

French musical picture automaton,
signed Berthoud, Paris, circa 1900,
46cm. high. (Sotheby's Belgravia)
$950

French automaton of a bird in a gilded cage with gold leaf and gesso
base, 26cm. high. (C. G. Sloan &
Co. Inc.) $525

French musical automaton showing
two monkeys, circa 1890, 59cm.
high. (Phillips) $1,880

Large French musical automaton,
1920, 45in. high. (Sotheby's
Belgravia) $835

Two musicians automaton, 9¾in. wide,
circa 1900. (Sotheby's Belgravia)
$995

Large French musical clock automaton, movement by Japy Fils,
circa 1860-70, 86cm. high.
(Sotheby's Belgravia)$1,105

BAROMETERS

George III mahogany baro-
meter inlaid with boxwood
stringing, circa 1820, 98cm.
high. (Sotheby's)
$385

Mahogany stick barometer
with silvered register plate
signed M. Woller, Birmingham, 98.5cm. high.
(Lawrence Fine Art)
$725

Mahogany wheel barometer,
silvered dial signed G.
Kalabergo, Banbury, 97.8cm.
high. (Lawrence Fine Art)
$4,680

Georgian mahogany and
chequered line banded
stick barometer by
Berrenger, London, 38in.
high. (Geering & Colyer)
$865

George III style inlaid mahogany banjo barometer/
thermometer, 38in. high, by
A. Tori & Pozzi & Co.
(C. G. Sloan & Co. Inc.)
$600

George III mahogany
stick barometer, signed
Ramsden, London, 97cm.
high. (Christie's)
$2,870

Mahogany veneered stick
barometer, inscribed
Manticha Fecit, London,
98.5cm. high. (Lawrence
Fine Art) $515

19th century mahogany cased
mercurial banjo wheel barometer inlaid with marquetry,
signed G. Broggi. (Sotheby,
King & Chasemore)
$510

Rosewood barometer with
onion cresting, circa 1840,
104.5cm. high. (Sotheby's
Belgravia) $455

Mahogany stick baro-
meter with ivory
register plates, signed
Pastorelli & Co.,
London, 96.5cm.
high. (Lawrence Fine
Art) $560

Early 20th century
'George III' mahogany
banjo barometer, dial
signed Maple & Co.,
London, 112cm. high.
(Sotheby's Belgravia)
$420

Unusual bow front
thermometer by
Dolland. (Phillips)
$1,350

Late 19th century mahogany barometer by Langford, London, 107cm. high. (Sotheby's Belgravia) $860

George III mahogany wheel barometer in banjo-shaped case. (Capes, Dunn & Co.) $580

18th century wheel barometer by J. Whitehurst, Derby. (James & Lister Lea) $9,600

Brass and copper 'Windmill' clock and barometer with revolving sails, German, circa 1870. (Alfie's Antique Market) $690

George III mahogany stick barometer by H. Frodsham, Liverpool, 97cm. high. (Christie's) $1,910

Late George III mahogany wheel barometer, signed Jno. Russell, Falkirk, 120cm. high. (Sotheby's) $8,280

George III mahogany stick barometer by Ramsden, London, with silver register plate, 97cm. high. (Christie's) $2,150

19th century banjo barometer/thermometer by H. Andrews of Royston (W. H. Lane & Son) $385

19th century mahogany banjo barometer inlaid with boxwood and ebony stringing, by Stiegelhalder, Exeter. (May Whetter & Grose) $250

Mahogany stick barometer, signed Tagliabue, Holborn, London, 99cm. high. (Lawrence Fine Art) $1,545

Mahogany wheel barometer with silvered dial, signed Grassi & Fontana, Exeter, 95.2cm. high. (Lawrence Fine Art) $175

18th century stick barometer in mahogany case. (Bradley & Vaughan) $1,935

BAROMETERS

Walnut stick barometer by Spencer Browning & Co., London, 38½in. high. (C. G. Sloan & Co. Inc.) $1,000

French carved giltwood barometer with octagonal body, dial signed J. Colleno, Paris, 36in. high. (C. G. Sloan & Co. Inc.) $600

Admiral Fitzroy barometer by Negretti and Zambra in carved oak case. (Hobbs Parker) $822

George III rosewood stick barometer by L. Casella & Co. (Olivers) $723

Mahogany and ebony strung bow-fronted barometer. (Phillips) $1,880

Victorian mahogany wheel barometer and thermometer. (Capes Dunn & Co.) $620

George III mahogany stick barometer with open arched brass register plate, 36½in. high. (Sotheby, King & Chasemore) $870

Mahogany wheel barometer, signed Wagner, Cape Town, circa 1860, 100cm. high. (Sotheby's) $1,835

Early Victorian wheel or banjo barometer, circa 1850, 40in. high. (Christopher Sykes) $553

Mid 19th century mahogany stick barometer by B. Martin, London, 90cm. high. (Sotheby, King & Chasemore) $1,252

Wheel barometer in rosewood case, circa 1830, 43in. high. (Christopher Sykes) $621

Charles II marquetry stick barometer. (Boardman's) $7,344

Double column barometer marked H. A. Clum, Rochester, New York, circa 1860, 37½in. high. (Robert W. Skinner Inc.) $800

Mid 19th century stick barometer by D. E. Lent, Rochester, New York, 37¾in. high. (Robert W. Skinner Inc.) $525

Rare angle barometer in walnut case by Charles Orme, 1736, Ashby-de-la Zouch. (Irelands) $7,080

Gimbal style cherry barometer by C. Wilder, New Hampshire, circa 1860, 39½in. long. (Robert W. Skinner Inc.) $425

Mahogany wheel barometer, dial signed Lione & Somalvico, London, 38in. high. (Lawrence Fine Art) $260

Rosewood stick barometer with ivory register plate, 35¼in. high. (Lawrence Fine Art) $315

Rosewood wheel barometer with silvered dial, 38¼in. high. (Lawrence Fine Art) $160

Walnut stick barometer by Charles Wilder, 1860, 38in. high. (Robert W. Skinner Inc.) $800

Walnut stick barometer with shaped crest and three turned brass finials, 39in. high. (C. G. Sloan & Co. Inc.)$1,300

19th century banjo barometer and spirit level in mahogany case, by Giobbio & Co., Devizes.(Edgar Horn) $475

Fine early 18th century walnut veneered stick barometer by John Patrick, distressed. (Osmond Tricks) $3,510

Sheraton mahogany banjo barometer by J. & A. Cetti & Co., London.(C. G. Sloan & Co. Inc.) $450

Boehm bronze and ivory figure with Egyptian hairstyle, 1920's, 33cm. high. (Sotheby's Belgravia) $2,690

Large Chiparus bronze and ivory group of a pierrot and pierrette, 1920's, 36.5cm. long. (Sotheby's Belgravia)　$2,105

Fayral patinated metal lamp cast as a Grecian girl, 1930's, 42cm. high. (Sotheby's Belgravia)　$1,285

Kratina bronze figure of a young woman, signed, circa 1900, 15cm. high. (Sotheby's Belgravia) $620

Large cold-painted bronze and ivory figure of a fencer, 13.4cm. high, 1920's, marked R. Lange. (Sotheby's Belgravia)　$515

Art Nouveau patinated metal lamp, circa 1900, 61.8cm. high. (Sotheby's Belgravia)$585

Bronze and ivory dancing girl, 1920's, 37.4cm. high, on marble base. (Sotheby's Belgravia) $1,910

Bronze and ivory group of three dancers, signed Chiparus on base, 1920's, 41.7cm. (Sotheby's Belgravia)　$7,955

Uriano gilded metal group, 1920's, 70cm. high. (Sotheby's Belgravia)　$350

Stylish bronze figure of a dancer on black marble plinth, 1920's, 44cm. high. (Sotheby's Belgravia) $585

Chiparus bronze and ivory group 'Les Amis de Toujours', 1920's, 63cm. wide. (Sotheby's Belgravia)　$8,890

Preiss cold-painted bronze and ivory figure 'The Torch Dancer', 1930's, 43.2cm. high.(Sotheby's Belgravia)$3,980

Preiss bronze and ivory figure of a mandolin player, 59cm. high, 1920's. (Sotheby's Belgravia) $6,085

Bronze figure 'The Dying Gaul', by F. Barbedienne (Moore, Allen & Innocent) $305

Poertzel cold-painted bronze and ivory figure of a young woman wearing trousers, 1930's, 17cm. high. (Sotheby's Belgravia) $585

Menneville & Rochard gilded metal and ivory group of a girl and a dog, 1930's, 48cm. high. (Sotheby's Belgravia) $1,050

Bronze group of two eagles, 55cm. high, circa 1900. (Sotheby's Belgravia) $630

Preiss bronze and ivory figure of a flautist, on marble base, 1920's, 46.3cm. high. (Sotheby's Belgravia) $5,615

Preiss bronze and ivory figure of a dancer wearing a short dress, 38.8cm. high, 1920's. (Sotheby's Belgravia) $2,805

Polished bronze and ivory figure by D. H. Chiparus, 1920's, 57.5cm. high, on marble base. (Sotheby's Belgravia) $13,570

Chiparus bronze and ivory figure of an Egyptian dancer, 1920's, signed, 73.2cm. high. (Sotheby's Belgravia) $3,275

Chiparus bronze figure of an Egyptian dancer in skirt and bikini top, 1920's, 40.5cm. high. (Sotheby's Belgravia) $1,590

Bronze study of a stallion by G. Garrard, signed and dated 1821, 9¼in. high. (Sotheby, King & Chasemore) $580

Lorenzl cold-painted bronze and ivory figure of a young woman, 23.5cm. high, 1920's. (Sotheby's Belgravia) $445

47

BRONZE

Bronze and ivory group of a skating couple, 33.5cm. high, 1930's. (Sotheby's Belgravia) $1,195

19th century Chinese bronze figure of Ho-Tei, 10in. high. (Robert W. Skinner Inc.) $250

Silvered and gilt metal group of a huntress and hind, 1930's, 49cm. high. (Sotheby's Belgravia) $405

Large Godard bronze and ivory figure of a girl and a bubble, 1920's, 53.5cm. high. (Sotheby's Belgravia) $3,210

19th century American or European bronze statue of a man and a stag, 29in. wide, unsigned. (Robert W. Skinner Inc.) $1,400

Gilt bronze figure of a young woman in trousers, by Bruno Zack, 1930's, 73cm. high. (Sotheby's Belgravia) $3,585

Bronze and ivory dancer by Prof. V. Poertzel, 1930's, 32cm. high. (Sotheby's Belgravia) $1,075

Le Faguays bronze and ivory figure of a girl running, 1930's, 22.5cm. high. (Sotheby's Belgravia) $1,435

Colinet bronze and ivory dancing girl, signed, 1920's, 36cm. high. (Sotheby's Belgravia) $3,210

19th century French bronze figure of the Mussel Gatherer, signed G. Leroux, 21in. high. (Robert W. Skinner Inc.) $1,500

Late Ming dynasty bronze standing figures of the Daoist Immortals, 17cm. high. (Sotheby's) $315

One of a pair of George IV gilt-metal candelabra, circa 1820, 2ft. 8½in. high. (Sotheby's) $945

Late 19th century French bronze statue of a reaper, signed A. Larroux, 10½in. high. (Robert W. Skinner Inc.) $650

Early 17th century Nuremberg nest of weights with swing handle, 8½in. high. (Sotheby's) $5,450

Late 19th century French bronze statuette of a seated goddess, signed Leon Pillot, 12in. high. (Robert W. Skinner Inc.) $325

Chiparus bronze and ivory dancing girl on a brown marble base, 1920's, 40cm. high.(Sotheby's Belgravia) $2,995

1st century Roman bronze cauldron with tapering body, 7in. high. (Christie's) $285

Chiparus gilt bronze figure of a young girl, 1920's, marked, 31.2cm. high. (Sotheby's Belgravia) $1,285

Late 19th century Chinese bronze floor lamp, 68in. high. (Robert W. Skinner Inc.) $850

Preiss bronze and ivory figure 'The Torch Dancer', 41.5cm. high, 1930's. (Sotheby's Belgravia) $3,825

Bouraine gilt bronze figure of a young girl, 35.5cm. high, marked, 1920's. (Sotheby's Belgravia) $810

19th century French bronze statue of a nude woman, 25½in. high. (Robert W. Skinner Inc.) $750

Chinese bronze figure of a raven, 30cm. high. (V. & V.)$375

Limousin gilt bronze nude figure on black marble base, 1920's, 43.5cm. high. (Sotheby's Belgravia) $450

Bronze African nude study by Hagenauer, Austrian, circa 1910-20, 41.75cm. high. (Sotheby's Belgravia) $1,435

17th century European bronze Sabbath lamp, 12½in. high. (Robert W. Skinner Inc.) $1,600

Chiparus bronze figure of a woman, reclining on a black slate base, 1920's, 24.5cm. high. (Sotheby's Belgravia) $640

Large Netherlandish bronze mortar with twin dolphin handles, dated 1567, 15in. high. (Sotheby's) $3,790

20th century American relief bronze wall fountain, signed H. Burton, 29¾in. wide. (Robert W. Skinner Inc.) $575

19th century Chinese two-handled vase with gilt and polychrome lights, 18in. high. (Robert W. Skinner Inc.) $450

Bronze and gilt-bronze candelabrum on marble base, 1870's, 109cm. high. (Sotheby's Belgravia) $660

Bronze and ivory figure of a skater by F. Preiss, 1930's, 35.5cm. high. (Sotheby's Belgravia) $2,390

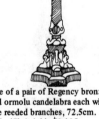

One of a pair of Regency bronze and ormolu candelabra each with five reeded branches, 72.5cm. high. (Christie's) $2,195

18th century Italian bronze figure of a putto holding a goose, 14½in. high. (Sotheby's) $1,420

16th century Japanese patinated bronze menpo of a Ten Gu, 9½in. high. (Robert W. Skinner Inc.) $500

North Italian gilt bronze hand bell, handle covered in velvet, 6¾in. high. (Sotheby's) $1,300

Mid 19th century French bronze statue of a mare and stallion by P. J. Mene, 12¾in. long. (Robert W. Skinner Inc.) $900

19th century Chinese incense burner with animal decoration, 12.5cm. high. (Robert W. Skinner Inc.) $60

Lalique bronze plaque cast with the head and shoulders of a girl, 47.5cm. wide, circa 1900. (Sotheby's Belgravia)$1,910

Late 19th century French bronze inkwell 'Salamander', by G. Flamand, 10½in. diam. (Robert W. Skinner Inc.) $1,550

European lamp in the form of a bronze statue, 38in. high. (Robert W. Skinner Inc.) $1,100

Bronze statue of swallows, signed Arson, circa 1870, 7½in. high. (Robert W. Skinner Inc.) $500

Philippe bronze and ivory dancing girl, 1920's, 58.5cm. high. (Sotheby's Belgravia)$3,585

Large bronze figure by Bruno Zack, 67cm. high, 1930's. (Sotheby's Belgravia) $8,125

Chiparus bronze and ivory dancing girl, marked D. H. Chiparus, 1920's, 53.5cm. high. (Sotheby's Belgravia) $5,990

Late 19th century European bronze figure of a young woman, 34in. high. (Robert W. Skinner Inc.)$2,100

Early 17th century Venetian bronze inkwell, 7½in. high. (Sotheby's) $4,620

Bronze lamp figure of a woman, light fitting within her dress, 31cm. high, circa 1900. (Sotheby's Belgravia)$855

BRONZE

Bronze figure of a crane, 97cm. long, with bowed neck and open mouth. (Christie's)$2,820

Rare 19th century bronze fire curb with pierced center panel, 62½in. long. (Taylor Lane & Creber) $690

One of a pair of ormolu wall lights of Louis XV style, 17in. high. (Christie's) $500

Sino-Shan drum with double strap handles, 63cm. diam. (Christie's) $1,175

A fine Benin bronze cockerel standing on a square base with raised guilloche decoration around the sides. (Sotheby's) $98,280

One of a pair of late 19th century bronze vases, engraved and overlaid in green enamel. (H. C. Chapman & Sons) $860

19th century French Art Nouveau bronze figure of a nude female, 35cm. high. (C. G. Sloan & Co. Inc.) $800

One of a pair of early 20th century bronze Marley horses, signed Coustou, 49cm. high. (Sotheby's Belgravia) $1,145

Bronze torso by Gutzon Borglum, 31cm. high. (C. G. Sloan & Co. Inc.) $800

One of a pair of ormolu wall lights with scrolled pierced back plates, 25in. high. (Christie's)$905

Porcelain and gilt bronze encrier, circa 1880, 15cm. wide. (Sotheby's Belgravia) $355

Bronze bust of a grinning baby, 8½in. high, on a gray marble base. (Hobbs Parker) $95

52

Bronze figure of a woman about to throw a javelin, by M. Bouraine, circa 1920, 37cm. high. (Sotheby, King & Chasemore)$1,095

A pair of ormolu chenets, with a lion and a winged gryphon, 48cm. high. (Christie's) $1,380

19th century European bronze model of a French cannon, mounted on slate, 16cm. long.(Robert W. Skinner Inc.) $175

Bronze study of the gelding cob 'Darkie', by W. Wasdell Trickett, 21cm. high. (Sotheby, King & Chasemore) $330

Bronzed metal figure of a negro boy on a bamboo stool with a basket on his knee, 32in. high.(John H. Raby & Son)
$2,240

Bronze figure of a wolfhound by Jules Moigniez, 19th century, 25cm. high. (C. G. Sloan & Co. Inc.) $650

One of a pair of ormolu wall lights with scrolled back plates, 24in. high. (Christie's) $1,000

Gilded bronze figure by Pierre Jules Mene, signed, 'Moorish Hunter', 55cm. high. (C. G. Sloan & Co. Inc.) $1,800

19th century bronze ship's signal cannon. (Phillips)$760

One of a pair of bronze ewers, the handles each with a putti seated on a phoenix, circa 1880, 58.5cm. high. (Sotheby's Belgravia)
$825

Second Empire bronze jardiniere with circular rim, circa 1860, 61cm. diam. (Sotheby's Belgravia) $2,305

1930's bronze and alabaster figure of a dancing girl, signed Blacz, 35cm. high. (Smith-Woolley & Perry)
$245

Bronze group of three figures by Albert Ernest Carrier-Belleuse, signed, 50cm. high. (C. G. Sloan & Co. Inc.) $1,700

Pair of gilt bronze figures of a man and woman, 11in. high. (Bradley & Vaughan) $1,115

One of a pair of gilt bronze mounted marble lamps, circa 1900, 39.6cm. high. (Sotheby's Belgravia) $685

One of a pair of Regency bronze and ormolu candelabra, 80cm. high overall. (Graves, Son & Pilcher) $2,860

Silvered bronze nude dancer by Lorenzl, 1930's, 30.5cm. high. (Sotheby's Belgravia) $470

Preiss painted bronze and ivory figure of 'The Archer', 47cm. high. (Hy. Duke & Son) $9,125

One of a pair of Louis XV ormolu candlesticks with fluted nozzles, circa 1760, 25.5cm. high. (Sotheby's) $1,415

One of a pair of six-light candelabra, 1870's. (Sotheby's Belgravia) $400

Gilt and patinated bronze candelabrum, circa 1860, 114cm. high. (Sotheby's Belgravia)$2,585

Bronze and ivory figure of a dancing girl by L. Sosson, signed, 14in. high. (Morphets) $905

One of a pair of bronze and ormolu candelabra, circa 1820, 21½in. high. (Christie's) $1,420

Bronze and ivory figure of Boehm-Hennes. (Christie's S. Kensington) $2,620

Pair of French bronze figures by H. Dumaige, 65cm. high. (Graves, Son & Pilcher) $3,720

Art Nouveau bronze bust of a young woman, signed Nelson, 1889. (Robert W. Skinner Inc.) $1,050

19th century Italian bronze statue of Venus on black marble base, 42.5cm. high. (Taylor Lane & Creber) $350

One of a pair of 19th century Japanese bronze models of Manchurian cranes. (Christie's S. Kensington) $4,410

Bronze and ivory figure of a dancing girl with castonets by Henry Fugere, signed, 17in. high. (Morphets) $1,215

Lorenzl patinated bronze figure of a young girl, 1920's, 22.5cm. high. (Sotheby's Belgravia) $235

One of a pair of early 19th century gilt and patinated bronze candelabra, signed Clodion. (Sotheby's Belgravia) $1,365

Tiffany bronze two-light chamberstick with blown-out green glass holders, 15cm. high. (C. G. Sloan & Co. Inc.) $700

One of a pair of gilt bronze and marble urns, circa 1910, 42cm. high.(Sotheby's Belgravia) $685

Bronze and ivory dancer 'The Flame Leaper' by F. Preiss. (Phillips) $8,495

BRONZE

Art Deco spelter figure, signed B. Cipriani, on marble base. (Alfie's Antique Market)
$365

Chinese bronze jackdaw, 30cm. high. (V. & V.)
$375

19th century South African Imperial gallon standard bronze measure with ebony handles, 20cm. diam. (Boardman)
$560

One of a pair of late 19th century bronze Marley horses, after Coustou 50cm. high. (Sotheby's Belgravia)
$1,215

Early 16th century North German bronze laver, 35cm. wide. (Sotheby's)
$3,745

Late 19th century Shosei bronze koro and cover, surmounted by a shi-shi, 32cm. high. (Sotheby's Belgravia)
$1,215

One of a pair of early 19th century George III gilt bronze cassolettes, 25.5cm. high. (Sotheby's)
$1,545

A pair of bronze figures, each holding a book, 55cm. high. (Warner, Shepherd & Wade)
$1,980

Preiss ivory and bronze figure 'Ada May—Lighter than Air', dated 1936. (Phillips)
$2,070

Bronze and ivory figure of a Dutch girl, unsigned, 6in. high. (Morphets)
$215

Set of three late 19th century bronze carp, 35 and 21.5cm. high. (Sotheby's Belgravia)
$680

One of a pair of gilt bronze, champleve and alabaster urns, circa 1870, 47.5cm. high. (Sotheby's Belgravia)
$1,150

Japanese bronze bowl and cover, 21cm. high. (Parsons, Welch & Cowell) $660

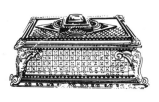

Late 19th century bronze and champleve enamel jewel box, Austrian, 11.5cm. wide. (Robert W. Skinner Inc.) $250

Rare Italian bronze oil lamp in the form of a satyr, circa 1500. (Sotheby's)$70,000

German bronze figure of an eagle, circa 1900, 58in. high. (Robert W. Skinner Inc.) $3,000

Bronze figure of St. Francis, signed P. Fosca, Naples, 61cm. high, circa 1900. (Sotheby's Belgravia) $315

Bronze equestrian group of a young Queen Victoria riding side saddle, by John Henry Foley. (Sotheby's Belgravia) $4,635

One of a pair of parcel gilt bronze models of Samurai, signed Miyao, 39cm. high. (Phillips) $29,900

Bronze group of Diana the Huntress with stag, signed F. Barbedienne, 80cm. high. (Burtenshaw Walker) $995

Small bronze bust of King George V, signed Sydney Marsh. (Butler & Hatch Waterman) $95

One of a pair of Barbedienne bronze ewers, signed, circa 1870, 62.5cm. high.(Sotheby's Belgravia) $385

Seiya bronze model of a lion striding forward, 51cm. long. (Sotheby, King & Chasemore) $375

Rare Renaissance bronze candlestick, 30cm. high, drilled for electricity. (Sotheby's) $935

BRONZE

One of a pair of bronze vases and covers surmounted with mythical beasts, circa 1900, 40cm. high. (Sotheby's Belgravia) $490

One of a pair of ormolu models of sphinxes on square Porta Santa Rara marble bases, 11¾in. high. (Sotheby's Belgravia) $1,810

Bronze fawn by Rembrandt Bugatti, 30.5cm. high. (Lambert & Symes) $4,115

One of a set of four 19th century gilt metal wall lights, 1ft. 10in. high. (Sotheby's) $1,510

One of a pair of gilt bronze candelabra, circa 1870, 60cm. high. (Sotheby's Belgravia) $1,100

19th century bronze figure of a knight on his charger, signed E. Fremiet, 48cm. high. (May Whetter & Grose) $900

One of a pair of English gilt bronze mounted porcelain lamps, fitted for electricity, 71cm. high. (Sotheby's Belgravia) $2,105

Verdigris patinated metal figure of a woman archer on black marble base, 55cm. high. (Sotheby's Belgravia) $445

Japanese bronze hawk perched on a tree trunk, 36cm. high. (Lawrence Fine Art) $375

Art Deco bronze and ivory group of dancing figures. (Harrods) $5,080

One of two similar Giyoko bronze archers, circa 1900, on wood stands, 44 and 41.5cm. high. (Sotheby's Belgravia) $1,405

Spelter figure of a boy standing beneath a palm tree, circa 1900, 42.5cm. high. (Sotheby's Belgravia) $170

One of a pair of mid 19th century wall lights, 15in. high. (Sotheby's) $1,465

Late 19th century Masayoshi bronze incense burner and cover, 20.5cm. (Sotheby's Belgravia) $445

Bronze fountain representing a youth sitting on a turtle, circa 1918, (Alfie's Antique Market) $300

One of a pair of Qing dynasty bronze figures of Buddhistic lions, 29.5cm. long (Christie's) $1,410

19th century bronze wine vessel of trumpet form, 68.5cm. high. (Sotheby's Belgravia) $560

Bronze figure of a hoop dancer on bronze and marble base, marked 'Morin', circa 1920, 17.75cm. high. (Sotheby's Belgravia) $280

Art Deco cold-painted bronze statuette on green onyx base, slightly damaged. (Raymond Inman) $720

Poertzel bronze and ivory group 'The Butterfly Girls', 1930's, 42.5cm. high. (Sotheby's Belgravia) $6,085

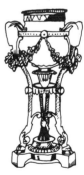

Bronze statuette of Aphrodite with a dolphin at foot, 75cm. high. (Lambert & Symes) $4,960

One of a pair of late 19th century Japanese cast and chased bronze vases, 30cm. high. (Taylor Lane & Creber) $310

Decorative Art Deco bronze ashtray. (Alfie's Antique Market). $75

Gilt bronze and porcelain vase with pierced rim, 47cm. high, circa 1870. (Sotheby's Belgravia) $415

BRONZE

Amusing E. David bronze mask pendant, circa 1925, 5cm. wide. (Sotheby's Belgravia) $440

Bronze lion, circa 1900, on hardwood stand, 59cm. long. (Sotheby's Belgravia) $315

Good Gurschner bronze vase, 18cm. high, circa 1910. (Sotheby's Belgravia) $395

One of a pair of Directoire style ormolu and dyed agate cassolettes, 55cm. high. (Sotheby, King & Chasemore) $735

Theodore Riviere bronze group of a man and woman, circa 1900, 32cm. high. (Sotheby's Belgravia) $1,530

Art Nouveau bronze candelabra, designed by Georges de Feure, circa 1900, 33cm. high. (Sotheby's Belgravia) $1,380

One of a pair of bronze faun candlesticks. (Nicholas) $880

Pair of bronze figures of Centaurs, 49cm. high. (Sotheby King & Chasemore) $4,060

4th/3rd century B.C. Etruscan figure in bronze of Herakles, 2¾in. high. (Christie's) $330

Early 16th century Venetian bronze processional cross, 48.5cm. high. (Christie's) $600

Late 19th century bronze group of toads, 8.5cm. wide. (Sotheby's Belgravia) $825

L. Kann gilt bronze mug with cylindrical body, 10cm. high, circa 1900. (Sotheby's Belgravia) $240

Large pair of bronze Venetian door knockers. (Gray's Antique Mews) $420

Pair of early 20th century bronze rats, each holding a nut. (Sotheby's Belgravia) $390

Gurschner bronze vase, circa 1910, of oval section and flared rim. (Sotheby's Belgravia) $920

Japanese bronze eagle. (Stride's) $5,310

Art Deco French spelter figure on tri-colored marble base. (Alfie's Antique Market) $295

One of a pair of patinated bronze Hagenauer bookends, 20th century, 16.5cm. high. (Sotheby's Belgravia) $615

Benin bronze figure of a temple guard, 19cm. high. (Phillips) $150

Late 19th century Seiya bronze figure of an elephant, 28cm. wide. (Sotheby's Belgravia) $535

Roman bronze from the 1st or 2nd century A.D. 18½in. high. (Christie's) $30,400

One of a pair of Qing dynasty bronze censers cast as standing geese, 14in. high. (Christie's) $1,440

Art Nouveau gilt bronze dish by A. Vibert, circa 1900, 15.5cm. high. (Sotheby's Belgravia) $480

19th century Russian bronze group, inscribed and stamped 1878, 16in. high. (Phillips) $2,360

Chinese black and gold lacquer brush box with serpentine sides, 11in. long. (C. G. Sloan & Co. Inc.) $300

Chinese black and gold lacquer lift-top octagonal tea caddy with two-compartment pewter box, 10in. long. (C. G. Sloan & Co. Inc.) $250

Victorian burr walnut writing slope with brass mounts, 1ft.2in. wide, circa 1880. (Sotheby, King & Chasemore) $1,039

Early 20th century French rectangular ivory veneered jewel casket, 29.5cm. long. (Sotheby's Belgravia) $1,420

Coachbuilder's tool chest and contents, tools bearing the stamp of John Hartley, circa 1839. (Christie's S. Kensington) $3,164

Bavarian brass and amboyna jewel coffer, circa 1900, 34cm. wide. (Sotheby's Belgravia) $1,201

Victorian coromandelwood and brass tantalus with three bottles, 12in. wide.(Gray's Antique Mews) $620

Victorian walnut liqueur box, crossbanded in satinwood. (Biddle & Webb) $540

Mahogany apothecary's chest, circa 1830, five bottles missing, 28cm. wide. (Sotheby's Belgravia) $1,070

Unusual fruitwood tea caddy, circa 1830, 10½in. wide, with rosewood lidded tea containers. (Christopher Sykes) $192

19th century Japanese lacquer cigar case, 5in. wide. (Christopher Sykes) $192

Sheraton period tea caddy, circa 1800, 7in. wide, in mahogany with ebony stringing. (Christopher Sykes) $146

Qianlong cinnabar lacquer box and cover of ruyi head section, 5in. wide. (Sotheby's) $95

Brass-bound Circassian walnut tea chest with lift top, 14½in. wide. (C. G. Sloan & Co. Inc.) $1,350

Chinese black and gold lacquer lift-top tea caddy, fitted with original pewter caddy, 8½in. long. (C. G. Sloan & Co. Inc.) $275

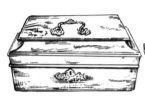

Chippendale period mahogany tea caddy, circa 1770, with brass handle, 11in. long. (Christopher Sykes) $192

Rioro nuri two-tier jubako, upper fitted as a suzuribako and lower part as a kowasibako. (Christie's S. Kensington) $293

Sheraton mahogany tea caddy, circa 1800, 12in. long. (Christopher Sykes) $149

Model of a terrestrial globe in the form of a string box, 4¼in. high, circa 1890. (Christopher Sykes) $192

Edwardian optometrist's outfit with lenses, rules, test cards and ophthalmo-scope. (Alfie's Antique Market) $226

Snuff box in the form of an Oriental slipper, circa 1780, 3½in. long. (Christopher Sykes) $63

John Paul Cooper galuchat box and cover, circa 1900, 9.3cm. wide. (Sotheby's Belgravia) $240

Mid 18th century English etui of tapering form with tortoiseshell body, 10cm. high. (Sotheby Beresford Adams) $260

Regency tea caddy, inlaid with brass and mother-of-pearl floral design. (Gray's Antique Mews) $370

Austrian necessaire box by Nicolaus Rozet, circa 1800, 11½in. wide.. (Sotheby's) $1,140

One of a pair of George III satinwood tea caddies with crossbanded hexagonal lids, 12cm. wide. (Christie's) $985

Early Louis XVI marquetry box, veneered in harewood and tulipwood, circa 1775, 11¾in. wide. (Sotheby's) $855

19th century Florentine ebony and pietra dura casket, 17in. wide. (Christie's) $2,485

Mid 18th century English silver and hardstone etui, 10.5cm. long. (Sotheby's) $525

Late 17th century walnut and rosewood casket with hinged lid mounted with gilt brass bands, 14in. wide. (Christie's) $1,765

18th century tortoiseshell and silver pique tea caddy, silver mounted, 12.5cm. high. (Grays Antique Mews) $1,880

Antique iron-bound oak decanter set, fully fitted, 16¾in. wide. (C. G. Sloan & Co. Inc.) $675

Large Georgian crossbanded mahogany tea caddy with brass handle, 14½in. wide. (Moore, Allen & Innocent) $1,150

17th century French iron missal box with hinged lid and hidden locking mechanism. (Christie's) $1,295

Fine gilt etui with chatelaine hook embossed all over with a scroll decoration, fully fitted. (May Whetter & Grose) $485

Mid 18th century lacquered casket with serpentine lid decorated with a hunting scene, 11¾in. wide. (Christie's) $830

Late 17th century walnut and rosewood casket with cross-banded top, 15¼in. wide. (Christie's) $825

German lacquered papier mache snuff box by W. Stockmann & Co., circa 1800, 9.3cm. diam. (Sotheby's) $810

17th century Dutch East Indies tortoiseshell casket with silver gilt strapwork mounts, 8¾in. wide. (Sotheby's) $2,025

Late 17th century rosewood casket with crossbanded top and gilt brass borders, 15½in. wide. (Christie's) $940

'Fairy Tree' biscuit tin designed by Mabel Lucie Attwell, sold with jigsaw puzzle. (Phillips) $35

17th century needlework covered casket, with iron carrying handle, 20in. wide. (Christie's) $3,105

Early 19th century circular papier mache snuff box by W. Stockmann & Co., Germany, 9.2cm. diam. (Sotheby's) $450

Late 19th century European burl walnut lap desk with inlaid top, 13½in. wide. (Robert W. Skinner Inc.) $300

Early 19th century German circular papier mache snuff box, 9.5cm. diam. (Sotheby's) $810

Mid 19th century Continental amboyna wood and ebonised tantalus, interior fitted with four decanters and ten glasses. (Phillips) $790

Mid 18th century George III gold-mounted green jasper etui, 86mm. high.(Christie's) $1,560

Early 19th century silver mounted tortoiseshell casket with domed lid, 8¼in. wide. (Christie's) $1,550

Mid 19th century Japanese rectangular lacquer box, 12cm. wide,
with mother-of-pearl inlay.
(Robert W. Skinner Inc.)
$1,900

Victorian silver-mounted tortoiseshell box by George Fox, London,
1896, 10¼in. wide. (Hobbs Parker)
$805

Maori wood treasure box of rectangular
form, finely carved in high relief,
22 x 8½in. (Sotheby's)
$51,480

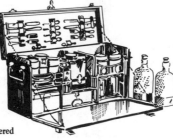

17th century English embroidered
casket depicting Charles and
Henrietta Maria, 10in. wide, in
glazed case. (Messenger, May &
Baverstock) $1,970

Motorist's picnic service, circa
1920, fully fitted. (Christie's S.
Kensington) $1,075

19th century coromandel wood
table bureau inlaid with ivory,
52cm. wide. (Pearsons)
$2,160

Gold-mounted ivory veneered
tea caddy. (Sotheby's)
$705

17th century needlework casket,
fitted as a dressing case, in glazed
case, 16in. wide. (Messenger,
May & Baverstock) $2,880

17th century embroidered casket
with Biblical scene, 11in. high,
on bun feet, in glazed case.
(Messenger, May & Baverstock)
$1,200

Antique mahogany brass-bound
lift-top box, 15in. wide. (C. G.
Sloan & Co. Inc.) $525

Japanese black and gold lacquer
sumi box with mother-of-pearl
inlay, 9in. long. (C. G. Sloan
& Co. Inc.) $1,100

Early 19th century tole decorated dome topped document
box, 6¾in. high, New York.
(Robert W. Skinner Inc.)
$825

Antimone enamelled Art Deco pierrot box. (Grays Antique Mews) $35

Louis XVI ebony and marquetry casket in the manner of Andre Charles Boulle, 16½in. wide. (Christie's) $4,505

Interesting Qianlong lacquer box and cover in the form of a bat, with fitted interior, 16¾in. wide. (Sotheby's) $700

One of a pair of tin tea storage bins by Henry Troemner, Philadelphia, circa 1870, 22½in. high. (Robert W. Skinner Inc.) $750

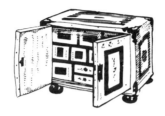

Late 18th century Indian carved ivory and tortoiseshell miniature cabinet, 24.7cm. high. (Buckell & Ballard) $2,185

Georgian mahogany knife box with brass fittings.(Smith-Woolley & Perry) $1,210

One of a pair of 'Victory V' urn tins in pre-Raphalite style, 1ft.0½in. high. (Sotheby's Belgravia) $70

Swan's stereoscopic treasury with burr-walnut casing, circa 1870, 23.5cm. wide. (Sotheby's Belgravia) $450

Huntley & Palmers 'Showman' biscuit tin of heart shape, circa 1893, 6¼in. high. (Sotheby's Belgravia) $85

Mid 19th century Tunbridgeware jewel casket. (Sotheby's Belgravia) $1,200

Rare Georgian tea caddy, circa 1770, chased and pierced to all sides. (Sotheby's)$9,100

Qianlong cinnabar lacquer box and cover of circular section, 7in. diam. (Sotheby's) $410

CADDIES & BOXES

George III tortoiseshell tea caddy with silver mountings, 18cm. wide. (Lawrence Fine Art) $170

Mahogany apothecary's chest, circa 1830, five bottles missing, 28cm. wide. (Sotheby's Belgravia) $1,070

Late 18th century rolled paperwork tea caddy, inset with picture of girl. (Hy. Duke & Son) $855

Mid 19th century mahogany writing slope with tambour superstructure, 46cm. wide. (Sotheby's Belgravia) $405

English apothecary's chest in mahogany case with brass handles, circa 1825, 29cm. wide. (Sotheby's Belgravia)$760

Late 19th century Chinese cloisonne dome top casket, 15cm. long. (Robert W. Skinner Inc.) $200

Early 19th century English apothecary's chest in mahogany, 23cm. wide, closed. (Sotheby's Belgravia) $950

George III satinwood cutlery box with serpentine hinged lid, 19cm. wide. (Christie's) $585

Large English apothecary's chest in stained wood, circa 1890, 18½in. wide. (Sotheby's Belgravia) $255

Louis XVI marquetry tea caddy with molded corners, circa 1775, 22cm. wide. (Sotheby's) $2,125

Victory 'cradle' tin, English, circa 1890. (Sotheby's Belgravia) $480

Mid 18th century lacquer and wood box by Mochizuki Hanzan. (Bonhams) $7,080

Late 18th century rolled paperwork tea caddy, inset with picture of a girl. (Hy. Duke & Son) $1,095

George III rectangular satinwood tea caddy banded in kingwood and box-wood, 23cm. wide. (Lawrence Fine Art) $135

Late 18th century rolled paperwork tea caddy. (Hy. Duke & Son) $835

Mid 19th century English double-sided apothecary's chest in mahogany case, 23cm. wide.(Sotheby's Belgravia) $1,055

Walnut dressing case in well figured wood with mirror and eleven glass containers, circa 1860, 30.5cm. wide. (Sotheby's Belgravia) $205

English rectangular gilt metal necessaire, circa 1770, 8.2cm. wide. (Sotheby's) $715

19th century mahogany apothecary's chest, fully fitted. (Phillips) $1,095

Inlaid mahogany Adams urn-shaped knife box on square base and four bun feet, 27¾in. high. (Butler & Hatch Waterman) $785

Mahogany apothecary's chest with recessed brass carrying handles, 21.5cm. wide, circa 1830. (Sotheby's Belgravia) $610

George III rolled paperwork tea caddy, circa 1790. (Sotheby's) $430

Mahogany and iron tea caddy in the shape of a pear. (Sotheby's) $1,215

One of a pair of Hepplewhite inlaid mahogany knife boxes with brass lock plates, 15in. high. (C. G. Sloan & Co. Inc.) $1,750

Japanese 19th century boxwood butterfly-shaped box with mother-of-pearl and ivory inlay, 8cm. wide. (Robert W. Skinner Inc.)$170

1930's 'Players Navy Cut' tobacco tin, 10 x 7.5cm.(Grays Antique Market) $20

Neapolitan tortoiseshell pique toilet box, 14.5cm. wide, circa 1740. (Sotheby's) $2,645

Inlaid case with four decanters and nine glasses. (Laurence & Martin Taylor) $455

Rare marquetry casket attributed to David Roentgen, circa 1775. (Sotheby's) $7,490

Transfer and hand-painted sycamore jewelry box by G. Meekison, Montrose, circa 1830, 28cm. wide. (Sotheby's) $435

Late 19th century French silver-mounted singing bird in an enamel box, 10.2cm. wide. (Sotheby's) $1,310

Late Victorian office desk piece, 13in. high, with stationery compartment. (Butler & Hatch Waterman) $145

Early 18th century style Italian walnut and ebonised casket of architectural design, 10¾in. wide.(Drewatt, Watson & Barton) $660

Staunton ivory chess set, stamped Asprey, London, circa 1900. (Sotheby's Belgravia) $800

Louis XIV boulle casket with paneled domed lid inlaid in marquetry, 20¾in. wide. (Christie's) $5,640

19th century tiered box and flask in the form of a double gourd vase, 27.6cm. high.(Sotheby's) $730

Late 19th century inlaid wood games box with view of a castle, 26cm. wide. (Robert W. Skinner Inc.) **$100**

William and Mary marquetry lace box with inlaid lid, 21½in. wide. (Boardman) **$1,560**

17th century Spanish embossed leather deed box with hinged lid and wrought-iron lockplate, 53cm. wide. (Christie's) **$995**

Early 19th century coromandel-wood tantalus fitted with four bottles. (Cooper Hirst) **$705**

17th century Prague Imperial Court workshop table cabinet, 38cm. wide. (Sotheby's) **$8,890**

Tartan tea caddy by Charles Stiven, Laurencekirk, circa 1830, 20cm. wide. (Sotheby's) **$625**

Tortoiseshell and silver tea caddy, 1896, 11cm. wide. (Alfie's Antique Market) **$595**

Japanese lacquer picnic box of octagonal form with gilt decoration, 35cm. diam. (C. G. Sloan & Co. Inc.) **$550**

French or Flemish brass-bound oyster-kingwood veneered strong box, 1ft.2¼in. wide. (Sotheby's) **$1,055**

Sheraton mahogany knife-box of square tapering form with ebony and boxwood stringing, 55cm. high. (Jackson-Stops & Staff) **$630**

Late 19th century European walnut veneer tea caddy, brass and ivory-bound, 30cm. wide. (Robert W. Skinner Inc.) **$85**

George III satinwood cutlery urn with stepped lid, circa 1790, 2ft.4in. high. (Sotheby's) **$965**

Mid 19th century sliding box camera with Imbert et Maunory 'Vallantin' lens. (Sotheby's Belgravia) $1,025

Brin's patent spy-glass camera. (Christie's S. Kensington) $5,500

Mid 19th century French sliding box camera, 41.5cm. long. (Sotheby's Belgravia) $1,025

Rare black Leica IIIF 'red dial' camera, 36mm. long, circa 1956. (Sotheby's Belgravia) $2,675

Fine Ica Sirene 105 folding plate camera, 6.5 x 9cm., circa 1925, with instruction booklet, all in original box. (Sotheby's Belgravia) $130

Fine Ernemann Liliput plate camera, circa 1925, in original box.(Sotheby's Belgravia) $70

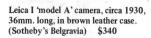

Bellieni stereo jumelle camera, French, 1900, with twin Zeiss Protar lenses. (Sotheby's Belgravia) $350

Leica I 'model A' camera, circa 1930, 36mm. long, in brown leather case. (Sotheby's Belgravia) $340

Sanderson tropical hand-and-stand camera with Goerz Dagor shutter, circa 1920. (Sotheby's Belgravia) $585

Ernemann Ernoflex folding reflex camera, circa 1923, 19cm. high. (Sotheby's Belgravia) $455

Rare German Kodak Duo 620 Series II camera, circa 1939. (Sotheby's Belgravia) $245

German Goerz folding reflex Ango camera, circa 1908, 23.5cm. high. (Sotheby's Belgravia) $215

Palmos Jena focal-plane roll-film camera, 1902. (Christie's S. Kensington)$2,640

French Sangor-Shepherd 'The Myrioscope' stereoscopic camera by Gaumont, circa 1900. (Sotheby's Belgravia) $230

Sinclair Una Traveller hand-and-stand camera. (Christie's S. Kensington) $2,735

Fine Sanderson teak wood field camera, 22cm. high, circa 1910, in leather case. (Sotheby's Belgravia) $365

Ernemann Rolf II folding roll-film camera in original box, circa 1925. (Sotheby's Belgravia) $85

German Ernemann Liliput plate camera, circa 1925, with single plate holder. (Sotheby's Belgravia) $85

Rare Fallowfield facile 'detective' camera by Miall, circa 1890, 24.7cm. high. (Sotheby's Belgravia) $465

Austrian Goerz minicord twin lens reflex camera, circa 1951. (Sotheby's Belgravia)$360

German Kamera-Werkstatten patent etui 'de luxe' folding camera, circa 1927, 9cm. high. (Sotheby's Belgravia) $265

English wet-plate camera, 4 x 5in., circa 1860, with single element lens. (Sotheby's Belgravia) $1,520

Fine Ica Sirene 135 folding plate camera, 9 x 12cm.(Sotheby's Belgravia) $35

German Leica camera, 36cm. long, circa 1950, in Leitz ever-ready case. (Sotheby's Belgravia) $460

CANE HANDLES

19th century jeweled gold parasol handle converted to a table seal, 9.2cm. long. (Christie's N. York) $1,800

Malacca walking stick with carved ivory handle, circa 1880, 85cm. long.(Sotheby's Belgravia) $630

Faberge two-color gold and nephrite parasol handle, St. Petersburg, circa 1900, 5.5cm. high. (Sotheby's)$2,795

Late 18th century three color gold combined handle and snuff box. (Bonham's) $2,420

Late 19th century Faberge gold, enamel and smokey quartz parasol handle, 8.3cm. high. (Sotheby's) $5,475

French Art Nouveau gold-mounted parasol handle embossed with flowers. (Christie's) $720

Perfume dispensing walking stick inscribed F. A., 1884, 36in high. (Sotheby's Belgravia) $330

Unusual early 19th century boxwood and bamboo walking cane, handle 15cm. high, possibly German. (Sotheby's) $645

George II gold-topped malacca walking cane, London, 1744. (Christie's)$1,140

Mid 18th century gentleman's gold topped walking cane. (Phillips) $255

18th century ivory and Narwhal walking stick, 96.5cm. long. (Sotheby's) $475

19th century parasol handle with turtle shell stem, green hardstone knob and gold bands. (Ronald J. Garwood's) $770

Gentleman's malacca, Wedgwood and silver walking stick with ivory handle, 34¾in. long. (Christopher Sykes) $170

Rare Chelsea cane handle in the form of a girl's head, 2¾in. high. (Olivers) $2,375

Victorian walking stick with snuff box handle, maker's initials E.N. 1887. (Christie's S. Kensington) $540

18th century malacca staff with ivory pommel and tapering shaft, 56in. high. (Christie's) $675

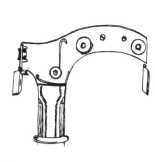

Early 20th century French walking cane, gold-colored rose diamond and sapphire set handle on bamboo shaft. (Sotheby's Belgravia) $645

Carved ivory handle with silver screw attachment by Cooper Brothers & Sons, Sheffield, 1901, 15cm. high. (Sotheby's Belgravia) $225

Ben Akiba miniature walking stick camera. (Christie's S. Kensington) $7,685

Brigg lady's umbrella, bamboo shaft with gold mounted tortoiseshell handle, 1905, 93.5cm. long. (Sotheby's Belgravia) $320

William IV silver topped walking cane by John Linnit, London, 1831, 40in. long. (Sotheby's) $2,485

Bent cane walking stick handle, 9in. long. (Christopher Sykes) $25

Unusual walking stick handle of naturally formed blackthorn, 12in. long. (Christopher Sykes) $25

French green silk parasol with frosted quartz fox mask knop. (Heathcote Ball & Co.) $495

CAR MASCOTS

Nickel plated 'Minerva' car mascot. (Christie's) $300

Stylish falcon car mascot with Art Deco style wings, 4in. high, circa 1930. (Sotheby's Belgravia) $95

Standing figure of the Esso man, 5½in. high, on a radiator cap. (Christie's)$250

Rolls-Royce kneeling lady car mascot, 3½in. high, circa 1940. (Sotheby's Belgravia) $105

Scottish Infantryman car mascot, circa 1930, 6¼in. high. (Sotheby's Belgravia) $135

Farman car mascot by Colin George, figure standing with wings outstretched, French, 7½in. wide. (Sotheby's Belgravia) $725

Charlie Chaplin car mascot, figure with cane and 'Little Tramp' costume, circa 1925, 4¼in. high. (Sotheby's Belgravia) $225

Star car mascot, with dancing nymph at the centre, 3¾in. high, circa 1925. (Sotheby's Belgravia) $125

Mercury type car mascot in winged helmet and sandals, circa 1930, 7in. high. (Sotheby's Belgravia) $105

Triumph Dolomite style car mascot with winged nymph standing on a globe, circa 1940, 5in. high. (Sotheby's Belgravia) $40

Speed nymph car mascot in the form of a naked woman, circa 1935, 6¼in. high. (Sotheby's Belgravia) $60

One of two speed nymph car mascots, circa 1935, 6¾in. high. (Sotheby's Belgravia) $125

Decorative 'winged head' car mascot, circa 1930, 16.5cm. high. (Sotheby's Belgravia) $120

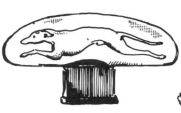

Lalique glass greyhound car mascot in original metal mount, 1920's, 19.75cm. wide. (Sotheby's Belgravia) $1,640

Lalique glass dragonfly mascot, 1920's, 21cm. high.(Sotheby's Belgravia) $1,870

Laligue glass car mascot 'The Spirit of the Wind', circa 1925, 26cm. wide. (Sotheby's Belgravia) $3,745

Lalique glass swallow mascot, 1930's, 15cm. high. (Sotheby's Belgravia) $1,520

Lalique glass car mascot 'Chevaux', circa 1925, 10cm. high. (Sotheby's Belgravia) $1,675

'Coq', a lalique brown glass mascot modelled as a cockerel, 1920's 24cm. high. (Sotheby's Belgravia) $1,755

Unusual Bentley car mascot, signed Gordon Crosby, circa 1927, 14.5cm. high. (Sotheby's Belgravia) $1,895

Etling frosted glass figure of a naked woman with chrome metal stand fitted for electric light, 1930's, 20.5cm. high. (Sotheby's Belgravia) $700

Lalique glass hawk mascot, 1930's, 15cm. high.(Sotheby's Belgravia) $890

Silver plated motoring mascot modeled as the 'Bristol Bulldog' fighter plane. (Christie's S. Kensington) $730

Decorative 'angel' car mascot in cast bronze, circa 1930, 18.5cm. high.(Sotheby's Belgravia) $155

Carved wooden decoy mallard duck, 13½in. long. (Christopher Sykes) $150

Sycamore wood butter marker, circa 1830, 5in. diam. (Christopher Sykes) $85

Carved wood and gilded eagle, circa 1810, 18½in. wide. (Christopher Sykes)$108

17th century Italian carved, painted and giltwood angel, slightly damaged, 25in. high. (Robert W. Skinner Inc.) $500

Jacques Staunton tournament chess set in box-wood and ebony, in original box, circa 1880. (Sotheby's Belgravia) $540

One of a pair of 19th century carved wood models of stags, 8in. high. (Christopher Sykes) $198

Good Toleware polished chamberstick, circa 1840, 2½in. high, by H. F. & Co. (Christopher Sykes) $63

Chemist's boxwood bottle holder with screw-on domed lid, circa 1860, 6in. high. (Christopher Sykes)$40

Olivewood Scandinavian carved jug, with carved pattern, 4¼in. high, circa 1860. (Christopher Sykes) $63

Military ship's figurehead in dark green uniform, 124.5cm. high. (Sotheby's Belgravia)$1,895

Rare mask from the South Eastern Congo of the Jokwe tribe, sold with tight fitting costume, 55in. high. (Christopher Sykes) $847

Early 19th century pinewood bowl, possibly American, 15in. diam. (Christopher Sykes) $146

German Regency giltwood wall bracket with lobed shelf, 22in. wide. (Christie's)$1,205

Beechwood butter marker, circa 1840, 4½in. diam. (Christopher Sykes) $80

Carved wood decoy teal duck, 12in. long, with glass eyes. (Christopher Sykes) $150

Fine mid 19th century Italian ship's figurehead from The Benvolio. (Alfie's Antique Market) $2,147

Japanese portrait sculpture, late Kamakura period, lacquered in red, brown and cream. (Ader, Picard, Tajan) $54,360

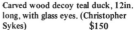

Early 16th century South German boxwood carving of St. Christopher, 22in. high. (Phillips) $9,900

18th century Japanese carved Noh mask of a demon, 6¼in. high. (Robert W. Skinner Inc.) $300

One of a pair of George III mahogany and brass candlesticks, circa 1790, 13½in. high. (Sotheby's)$775

Shield-shaped family horse coach panel, circa 1840, 17½in. wide. (Christopher Sykes) $192

19th century human face mask of the Senufo tribe, 13½in. high. (Christopher Sykes) $644

16th century Spanish polychrome oak processional head, 34cm. high. (Christie's) $1,800

19th century Chinese export black and gold lacquer hanging lantern, 56cm. high. (Christie's) $1,510

A Solomon Islands wood bowl of deep oval form, the handles carved as the front half of fishes, 21in. wide. (Christie's) $430

Huon Gulf wood mask of almost rectangular form, 13¼in. high. (Sotheby's) $1,755

Early 18th century carved wood panel showing the infant Christ and John the Baptist, 34in. long. (Sotheby, King & Chasemore) $1,440

Nootka carved wood figure squatting on his haunches with the hands resting on the knees, 22.5cm. high. (Sotheby's) $2,575

Tyrolean limewood bust of a female jester wearing a tall hat and tightly laced bodice, 19in. wide, 17th century. (Sotheby's) $1,755

A Kongo wood female figure seated with the straight legs apart, 12in. high.(Sotheby's) $260

Bavarian limewood figure of the angel from an Annunciation scene, by Erasmus Grasser, 32in. high, late 15th century. (Sotheby's) $23,400

Pair of South German Netherlandish limewood figures of the Virgin and St. John, 33in. high, circa 1680. (Sotheby's) $4,265

Franconian limewood figure of St. Leonard with padlock and chain in his right hand, circa 1510, 20in. high. (Sotheby's)$7,490

A Yoruba circular wood bowl and cover probably by a member of the Falade family, 15in. diam. (Christie's) $390

Mid 19th century English mariner ship's figurehead, 140cm. high. (Sotheby's Belgravia) $1,065

Late Qing dynasty inlaid wood panel inset with mother-of-pearl, 77.5cm. diam. (Christie's) $420

Swabian relief of the Dormition of the Virgin, surrounded by Apostles, 29in. wide, early 16th century. (Sotheby's) $5,615

A fine Shira Punu wood mask with pouting reddened lips, 10½in. high. (Christie's) $8,330

CARVED WOOD

18th-19th century carved wood figure of two putti and a book, 38in. wide, French. (C. G. Sloan & Co. Inc.) $375

A Bembe wood female standing with a knife held in an upraised right hand, 7in. high. (Sotheby's) $1,170

A Madri wood feast dish carved in relief with Tikis in spread eagled posture, 22in. wide. (Christie's) $1,815

Burgundian limewood figure of an Apostle, the bearded figure with thick hair, 35½in. high, circa 1440. (Sotheby's) $10,295

Late 15th century North French polychrome figure of St. Martha with long flowing hair, 36¼in. high. (Sotheby's) $10,765

A fine Mbala wood maternity group, the mother standing with a child on her hip, 17in. high. (Christie's) $10,165

Bavarian limewood figure of the Virgin attributed to the workshop of Erasmus Grasser, 33in. high, late 15th century. (Sotheby's) $14,040

A Lower Congo wood mask of helmet-like form, the prognathus jaw jutting forward, 14¼in. high. (Sotheby's)$19,980

A fine Yoruba large wood bowl by Arowogun, carved in high relief with five figures, 10½in. high. (Christie's) $1,330

Mid 19th century carved oak font cover, 42in. high. (Sotheby's Belgravia) $130

CARVED WOOD

Tongan wood pole club, the entire surface covered with finely engraved geometric decoration, 38¼in. long. (Sotheby's) $350

20th century American woodcock carving on weatherbeaten log, 20cm. long. (Robert W. Skinner Inc.) $200

Fine American Indian Eastern Woodlands club of slender curving gunstock type, 28½in. long. (Sotheby's) $7,490

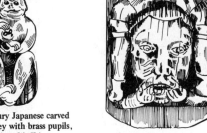

Mid 19th century Japanese carved wooden monkey with brass pupils, 6cm. high. (Robert W. Skinner Inc.) $100

15th century carved wood Roffboss on wooden shield, 46cm. high. (Lawrence Fine Art) $1,685

19th century Oriental carved root-wood figure of a demon god, set with semi-precious stones. (Edgar Horn) $355

South German polychrome wood figure of the Virgin and Child, possibly Nuremberg, 42½in. high, early 16th century.(Sotheby's) $14,510

A Jokwe wood chair, the rectangular back support carved with a head, 24½in. high. (Christie's) $1,430

17th/18th century Italian carved and polychromed figure 'Christ Blessing', 43in. high. (C. G. Sloan & Co. Inc.) $1,100

Early 20th century German carved walnut shelf bracket decorated with birds, 10½in. high. (Robert W. Skinner Inc.) $100

Antique Chinese bamboo carving 'Two Immortals in Boat', 7cm. high. (C. G. Sloan & Co. Inc.) $175

19th century German carved wood Pieta, 24cm. high. (Robert W. Skinner Inc.) $775

Fiji wood missile club, the striking section with a bulbous projection, 18in. long.(Sotheby's) $235

Olivewood souvenir watch stand, circa 1900, 150mm. long. (Sotheby's) $150

Northern Plains Indian wood club with a gunstock-like terminal inset with traces of horsehair, 32in. long. (Sotheby's) $3,040

Trobriand Island wood canoe prow ornament carved in an intricate series of curvilinear motifs. (Sotheby's) $980

Early 19th century Norwegian sycamore peg tankard, 22cm. high. (Christie's) $885

15th century carved figure of an enthroned bishop, Cologne. (Phillips) $6,085

16th century German boxwood carving of Saint Sebastian, 47.5cm. high. (C. G. Sloan & Co. Inc.) $4,500

A Chokwe wood chair with a well carved female figure beneath the seat. (Sotheby's) $3,040

Carved oak figure of an angel, wings missing 137cm. high. (Mat Whetter & Grose) $480

A Dan wood passport mask, the heart-shaped face with a painted chin, 3½in. high. (Sotheby's) $230

One of a pair of George III giltwood pelmets, 76in. wide. (Christie's) $1,210

American coconut shell carved with male and female portrait busts. (Christie's) $130

83

CARVED WOOD

Fine Tahitian wood bowl with a pouring lip in the tapering section at one end, 30½in. long, 18th century. (Sotheby's) $30,420

A Fiji priest's wood oil dish, the shallow leaf-shaped bowl on two short legs. (Christie's) $1,160

Samoan Kava bowl, supported by twelve circular legs, 18½in. wide. (Sotheby's) $540

Fine Styrian polychrome limewood figure of the seated Virgin, attributed to the Master of Judenburg, 26½in. high, circa 1420. (Sotheby's) $28,080

A fine Ibo wood mask, the triangular face with small pierced eyes, 18in. high. (Christie's) $3,145

South German or Austrian polychrome bust of a male saint wearing a crown, 14in. high, late 15th century. (Sotheby's) $13,570

A Yoruba wood maternity presentation bowl, the kneeling female figure with a child at her back, 9¾in. high. (Christie's)$775

Swabian limewood relief of the Beheading of St. James, 24¾ x 24in., circa 1520.(Sotheby's) $8,060

Fine Utrecht oak group of The Deposition, the Virgin lowers the dead body of Christ, 20in. wide, mid 15th century. (Sotheby's) $39,780

A fine Ibo wood helmet mask, the eyes slit within circular depressions, 14in. high.(Christie's) $1,015

French pinewood relief of the Pieta, the Virgin supporting the dead body of Christ across her lap, circa 1500, 34in. wide. (Sotheby's) $11,230

A Mambila wood antelope mask of helmet like form, 20½in. high. (Sotheby's) $270

Hawaiian Ko'u wood food bowl of shallow circular form, 11in. wide. (Sotheby's) $935

East Caroline Islands wood bowl on four short cylindrical legs, 8½in. diam. (Sotheby's) $540

An Ibo wood relief dish and cover of circular form with sharply tapering sides, 15in. diam. (Christie's) $435

A Kuba helmet mask, the mouth and nose protruding and covered with polychrome bead decoration, 14¾in. high.(Sotheby's) $680

A Yoruba wood presentation bowl in the form of a kneeling female figure, 15in. high. (Christie's) $905

An Ogoni wood mask with articulated lower jaw, 8in. high. (Christie's) $390

Flemish gilt and polychrome panel, carved with two soldiers in front of a city wall, 16in. high, early 16th century. (Sotheby's)$4,915

A Hemba wood stool supported by two standing figures, 18½in. high. (Sotheby's) $980

Lower Rhine oak relief of Christ on the road to Calvary, 22½in. high, circa 1500. (Sotheby's) $3,910

A Baule wood mask, the triangular face with pierced slit eyes, 11in. high. (Sotheby's) $1,640

Victorian carved oak wine rack with brass handles. (Alfie's Antique Market)$140

A Bassa wood family mask with a pointed chin and domed forehead, 7in. high. (Sotheby's) $120

85

CARVED WOOD

17th century Spanish polychrome wood bust of St. John, 67cm. high. (Sotheby's) $935

'Gladstone' carved wood nutcrackers, 8in. high, in satin-wood. (Smith-Woolley & Perry) $30

One of a pair of Tyrolean polychrome and giltwood angels, 17in. high, early 15th century.(Sotheby's) $21,060

Papuan Gulf wood figure pendant, the female figure of flattened form, 15in. high. (Sotheby's) $585

North Italian polychrome wood figure of St. John the Baptist, 28in. high, mid 16th century. (Sotheby's)$4,680

A Haida wood bear dance mask with a large circular handle, 20in. tall. (Sotheby's)$1,215

North Italian pine figure of a female saint, crowned and holding a book in her left hand, 40in. high, circa 1300. (Sotheby's) $4,680

Large South German wood figure of St. Florian in armour, with a visor raised, 5ft.8½in. high, early 16th century.(Sotheby's)$19,190

French carved oak bust of Louis XIV, attributed to the circle of Desjardins, 30in. high, circa 1700. (Sotheby's) $7,020

Samoan wooden club, the handle of diamond-shaped section, 49in. long. (Sotheby's) $515

Carinthian limewood relief of St. John the Baptist, holding a book, on which a lamb is seated, 38½in. high. circa 1510.(Sotheby's) $11,700

Fiji wood paddle club with a dark glossy patina, 49¾in. long. (Sotheby's)$630

Tyrolean polychrome figure of Christ as Man of Sorrows, 36¾in. high, circa 1520. (Sotheby's) $7,020

Lower Sepik wood mask of convex oval form, the small pierced eyes contained in raised oval surrounds, 17½in. high. (Sotheby's)$1,215

Leti wood ancestor figure on a tiered base, 28¼in. high. (Sotheby's) $820

British Guiana wood macana of typical hour-glass form, 14¾in. high. (Sotheby's) $585

Tyrolean Gothic limewood figure of a male saint, 37½in. high, late 15th century. (Sotheby's) $6,085

Fine Bavarian polychrome limewood figure of St. George with long hair and a tall hat, 3ft.11in. high, early 16th century. (Sotheby's)$23,400

A Chokwe wood figure of a Sovereign standing in a flat circular base, the legs slightly flexed. (Sotheby's) $163,800

Lower Rhenish polychrome wood group of St. Roch, wearing a broad-rimmed hat, 23½in. high, mid 16th century. (Sotheby's) $5,150

New Caledonian wood bird-headed club with a circular boss representing the eye on either side, 28in. long. (Sotheby's) $585

South German polychrome figure of a bishop saint, some original color, 32in. high, circa 1400. (Sotheby's) $6,550

Ojibway wood ball-headed club, the striking section held in a beak-like device, 24¼in. long. (Sotheby's) $3,980

New Caledonian wood gable figure representing a male figure standing atop a short staff, 25in. high. (Sotheby's)$1,405

87

CHANDELIERS

Late 17th/early 18th century Dutch brass chandelier, 2ft.7in. high. (Sotheby's) $3,860

George III style Irish hexagonal-shaped ormolu lantern with serpentine-shaped panels, 90cm. high. (Jackson-Stops and Staff) $2,675

Late 17th century Dutch brass chadelier, 4ft.6in. wide. (Sotheby's) $10,530

Rare William IV gilt brass kolza oil lantern, circa 1830, 2ft.1in. diam. (Sotheby's) $2,055

Silvered and gilt metal Wiener Werkstatte chandelier, 1920's, 80cm. wide. (Sotheby's Belgravia) $1,995

Gilt-bronze chandelier, circa 1840-60, 42in. wide, fitted for electricity. (Sotheby's Belgravia) $610

Tiffany Studios leaded glass inverted basket-form shade, 52.5cm. diam. (C. G. Sloan & Co. Inc.)$2,500

Italian Empire ormolu twelve-light chadelier, 91.5cm. diam. (Christie's) $2,050

Mid 20th century glass chandelier with sixteen scrolling arms, 147cm. high. (Sotheby's Belgravia) $1,530

19th century Venetian eight-branch chandelier, 4ft.3in. high. (Sotheby's) $1,120

Mid 19th century gilt-bronze chandelier, 84cm. high. (Sotheby's Belgravia) $985

19th century pierced brass and silver chadelier from the Middle East, 48in. long. (Robert W. Skinner Inc.) $700

18th century Arita 'sander' with pierced top, painted with peonies and foliage, 9.7cm. wide. (Sotheby's) $585

Early 18th century Arita wine cup of conical form, 8.1cm. high.(Sotheby's) $195

Early 18th century Arita 'sander' top pierced with twenty-one holes, 10cm. wide. (Sotheby's) $780

Late 17th century large Arita vase of octagonal ovoid form, 53.4cm. high. (Sotheby's) $3,415

Early 19th century Arita bowl in the form of Mount Fuji, 21.5cm. wide. (Sotheby's) $585

Late 17th century Arita vase of octagonal form decorated with horses and foals, 39.5cm. high. (Sotheby's)$1,830

Late 17th century Arita jar of square section with slightly flared neck, 28.2cm. high. (Sotheby's) $4,390

Late 17th/early 18th century Arita bowl painted in iron-red enamel, 19.5cm. diam. (Sotheby's) $390

Late 17th century Arita vase of double gourd form with flared neck, 38.5cm. high. (Sotheby's) $1,270

Unusual mid 18th century Arita dish of deep rounded form with petal-lobed rim, 32cm. diam. (Sotheby's) $730

One of a pair of early 18th century Arita beakers, covers and stands, decorated in iron-red enamels. (Sotheby's) $635

Late 17th century attractive Arita saucer of quatre-lobed form, 14.4cm. diam. (Sotheby's) $1,025

89

ATTIC

An Attic black figure Siana cup from the circle of the 'C' painter, circa 550 B.C. (Christie's)$5,195

An Attic black figure pottery Kylix, the interior with a central Gorgon's mask, 6th century B.C. (Sotheby's) $2,605

An Attic black figure Skyphos with incised detail, 10¾in. wide, late 6th century B.C. (Christie's) $1,300

BAYREUTH

Bayreuth blue and white cylindrical tankard with pewter foot rim and cover, circa 1740, 28.5cm. high. (Christie's) $670

Mid 18th century Bayreuth faience tankard with pewter cover and foot, 14.5cm. high. (Sotheby's) $1,125

Bayreuth red stoneware tea caddy and cover with gilt decoration, 10.5cm. high, circa 1730-40. (Sotheby's) $7,745

BELLEEK

Belleek basket of oval form, circa 1880, pierced overall with lattice-work, 12¾in. wide. (Sotheby's Belgravia) $570

Rare Belleek 'Chinese tea ware' tray, molded with a dragon, circa 1879, 15¼in. diam. (Sotheby's Belgravia) $405

Belleek basket of oval shape in criss-cross lattice, circa 1900, 27cm. wide. (Sotheby's Belgravia) $575

Fine Belleek matt and glazed parian ice pail and cover by Robert Williams Armstrong, 47cm. high. (Sotheby, King & Chasemore) $3,600

Belleek ice pail with decorative lid. (Stride & Son) $1,100

Late 19th century Belleek kettle on stand in the form of a dragon, 14in. high. (Robert W. Skinner Inc.) $3,300

Late 19th century Berlin figure of a fruit seller, 21.8cm. high. (Sotheby's Belgravia)$185

Berlin cabinet cup and saucer, dated 1829, cup with portrait of young man. (Sotheby's Belgravia) $435

One of a pair of Berlin japanned faience vases and covers, circa 1720, 63cm. high. (Sotheby's) $3,510

Berlin dinner plate, 26.5cm. diam., circa 1767. (Sotheby's)$940

Late 19th century Berlin religious plaque of a young woman at a shrine, 33cm. high. (Sotheby, King & Chasemore) $1,950

Berlin Royal presentation armorial pierced two-handled basket, painted with the Russian eagle, 21cm. wide, circa 1775. (Christie's) $2,400

Berlin plaque painted with a young woman in prayer, 23.5cm. high, mid 19th century. (Sotheby's Belgravia) $3,555

Berlin part teaset, mid 19th century, each piece gilt decorated. (Sotheby's Belgravia) $790

Berlin rectangular porcelain plaque painted by L. Eckarith, 39 x 30cm.(Christie's) $9,320

One of a pair of late 19th century Berlin vases and covers with blue-ground bodies, 34.7cm. high. (Sotheby's Belgravia) $1,445

One of a pair of Berlin ornithological plates with shaped borders, circa 1790, 25cm. diam. (Christie's) $3,120

Berlin armorial two-handled baluster vase, circa 1775, 10cm. high. (Christie's)$1,800

BERLIN

One of a pair of Berlin pastille burners and covers with urn-shaped bodies, 17cm. high, circa 1870. (Sotheby's Belgravia) $360

Late 19th century oval Berlin fruit bowl with pierced handles, 38cm. wide. (Sotheby's Belgravia) $320

One of a pair of Berlin two-handled ice buckets, cover and liners, circa 1795, 23.5cm. high. (Christie's) $910

One of a set of nine Berlin plates, circa 1900, 20.8cm. diam. (Sotheby's Belgravia) $615

Berlin porcelain vase with double scrolling serpent handles, 46cm. high. (C. G. Sloan & Co. Inc.) $1,200

One of twelve Berlin plates with pierced basketwork borders, circa 1795, 24.5cm. diam. (Christie's) $4,800

Late 19th century Berlin plaque painted by Grison, 31.5cm. high. (Sotheby's Belgravia) $2,370

Part of a Berlin part service for dinner and dessert. (Christie's) $4,200

Late 19th century Berlin plaque, 23.8 x 16cm. (Sotheby's Belgravia) $1,735

One of a pair of Berlin armorial miniature ewers, circa 1775, 89.5cm. high. (Christie's) $4,320

Berlin group emblematic of Arithmetic, circa 1765, 30.5cm. high. (Christie's) $1,200

Berlin vase and cover, circa 1900, painted with sprays of garden flowers, 44.5cm. high. (Sotheby's Belgravia) $775

One of a pair of 18th century ormolu mounted blanc-de-chine globular vases, 24cm. high. (Christie's) $1,480

Late 17th/early 18th century blanc-de-chine figure of a lady bathing, 9cm. wide. (Christie's) $445

Late 17th century blanc-de-chine group of Guanyin above small standing acolytes, 23cm. high. (Christie's) $330

Oriental blanc-de-chine of goddess holding a lotus flower, 18in. high. (Lowery & Partners) $270

Chinese blanc-de-chine seated figure of Guanyin on a lotus throne, 43.5cm. high, mark of Wanli on base. (Sotheby's) $4,390

One of a pair of blanc-de-chine figures of boy acolytes, 28cm. high. (Sotheby's) $2,320

BLUE & WHITE

Transitional blue and white pear-shaped bottle vase, circa 1640, 34.5cm. high. (Christie's) $2,585

Transitional blue and white oviform jar, circa 1650, 25.5cm. high. (Christie's) $940

Transitional blue and white sleeve vase, circa 1650, 38.5cm. high. (Christie's)$2,350

Transitional blue and white sleeve vase, circa 1640, 46.5cm. high. (Christie's) $1,880

Transitional blue and white sleeve vase, circa 1640, 43.5cm. high. (Christie's)$2,235

Transitional blue and white beaker vase, circa 1640, 44.5cm. high. (Christie's) $2,235

One of a pair of Bow blue and white plates painted with the 'Golfer and Caddy' pattern, circa 1760, 17.5cm. diam. (Christie's) $700

Bow blue and white flattened hexagonal sauceboat, slightly chipped, circa 1752, 18cm. wide. (Christie's) $280

Bow blue and white octagonal plate, circa 1752, 22cm. diam. (Christie's) $560

Bow figure of a bagpiper in black tricorn hat, circa 1758, 25.5cm. high. (Christie's) $820

Pair of Bow candlestick groups emblematic of Summer and Autumn, circa 1765, 26cm. high. (Christie's) $1,685

Rare Bow figure of June in flower-sprigged robe, circa 1755-60, 16.5cm. high. (Sotheby's) $525

Bow figure of a dancer, repaired, circa 1755, 17cm. high. (Christie's) $470

Set of Bow white figures of the seated seasons, circa 1755, 13.5cm. high. (Christie's) $2,105

Bow figure of a Turkish lady in pale yellow headdress, circa 1755, 18cm. high.(Christie's) $935

One of a pair of Bow famille rose oblong octagonal dishes, circa 1753, 27.5cm. wide. (Christie's) $610

Rare Bow white figure of Liberty, circa 1750-55, 25.5cm. high. (Sotheby's)$855

Bow bell-shaped mug with loop handle, circa 1760, 14.5cm. high. (Christie's) $940

One of a pair of Bow blue and white octagonal plates painted with the 'Jumping Boy' pattern, circa 1760, 17cm. diam. (Christie's) $1,125

Bow blue and white fluted oval sauceboat with loop handle, circa 1760, 15cm. wide. (Christie's) $280

Early Bow shell bowl painted in underglaze blue, circa 1752, 13cm. diam. (Sotheby's) $620

Brightly colored Bow candlestick group, circa 1760, 10cm. high. (Sotheby's) $1,115

Pair of Bow figures of Summer and Winter, circa 1760, 15cm. high. (Sotheby's) $950

Bow figure of Winter from a set of The Seasons, circa 1758, 12.5cm. high. (Sotheby's) $430

Bow figure of Earth, circa 1760, 27cm. high. (Christie's) $515

Pair of Bow white figures of Kitty Clive and Henry Woodward, circa 1750, 25.5 and 26.5cm. high. (Christie's) $2,640

Bow figure of a shepherdess with a lamb at her feet, circa 1765, 17.5cm. high. (Sotheby's) $450

Bow figure of Fame as a winged nymph, circa 1760, 17cm. high. (Christie's) $660

One of a pair of Bow 'Birds in Branches' chambersticks, circa 1765, 24cm. high. (Christie's) $1,145

Bow figure of a young vintner carrying a hod of grapes, circa 1758, 15.5cm. high. (Sotheby's) $715

Bristol delft polychrome charger, cracked and riveted, circa 1710, 34cm. diam. (Christie's) $1,030

Documentary Bristol blue and white hexagonal creamboat, circa 1750, Benjamin Lund's factory, 11cm. wide. (Christie's) $28,800

Bristol delft polychrome plate painted with a cockerel, circa 1750, 20cm. diam. (Christie's) $1,170

Bristol delft polychrome salt of cylindrical form, 8cm. wide, circa 1730. (Christie's) $610

Bristol fluted teacup, coffee cup and saucer painted in green, circa 1775-78. (Sotheby's) $320

Bristol delft blue and white campana vase with scroll handles, circa 1750, 19cm. high. (Christie's)$700

Bristol delft blue and white dish, piece missing from rim, circa 1730, 35cm. diam. (Christie's) $420

Rare Bristol yellow-ground tureen and cover, circa 1775, 30cm. wide. (Sotheby's) $1,650

Bristol delft blue and white inscribed and dated plate, 1727, 21cm. diam. (Christie's) $5,150

One of a pair of Bristol coffee cups and saucers painted with flowers, circa 1770, 12cm. high.(Sotheby's) $565

Blue and white delft plate, probably Bristol, circa 1710, 22.5cm. diam. (Christie's) $2,060

Bristol coffee cup and saucer painted on a white ground with sprigs of flowers, circa 1770-80. (Sotheby's) $225

One of a pair of ironstone china soup tureens, part of a dinner service, circa 1820. (Sotheby Bearne) $2,645

Redware teapot and cover of globular shape, circa 1750-60, 14cm. high. (Sotheby's) $450

Maw & Co. earthenware vase designed by Walter Crane, 21.6cm. high, 1880's. (Sotheby's Belgravia) $1,950

Part-glazed parian centrepiece, circa 1860, 21½in. high. (Sotheby's) $665

Part of a thirty-two-piece John Bevington dessert set, dated for 1874. (Sotheby's Belgravia) $1,235

English porcelain baluster vase, probably Spode, circa 1820, 16.5cm. high. (Christie's) $310

One of a pair of English porcelain campana vases with rope twist handles, circa 1820, 38.6cm. high. (Christie's) $6,580

Part of an eighteen-piece Thomas Ford and Charles Ford dessert set, circa 1872. (Sotheby's Belgravia) $715

Early 19th century Adams blue jasperware jug. (H. Spencer & Sons) $290

English parian group of 'The Wounded Scout', circa 1870, 48cm. high. (Phillips) $780

Aynsley & Co. inscribed and dated jug with cerise-ground body, 1861, 22.5cm. high. (Sotheby's Belgravia) $225

Linthorpe pottery claret jug with electroplated mount, circa 1885, 24.5cm. high. (Sotheby's Belgravia) $635

Flared cylindrical vase painted by John Randall, circa 1830, 20cm. high. (Christie's) $455

Amusing Burmantofts faience wall plaque, circa 1895, 61.8cm. diam., circa 1895. (Sotheby's Belgravia) $315

A mid 18th century Pecten-shell teapot and cover of pear-shape, 6in. high. (Sotheby's)$965

One of two brown glazed pottery flasks, larger 25cm. high. (C. G. Sloan & Co. Inc.) $150

Part of a good John Ridgway tea service, each piece painted with flowers, circa 1840.(Sotheby's Belgravia) $715

Rye pottery bulbous vase and cover applied with grapes and hops, 47.5cm. high. (Burrows & Day) $415

Late 18th century 'Hearty-goodfellow' Toby jug, 29cm. high, hat restored. (Sotheby's) $660

Unusual small polychrome 'blue dash' saucer dish, early 18th century, 10cm. diam. (Sotheby's) $9,910

Rye pottery vase and cover with cylindrical neck and rope pattern handles, 31cm. high. (Burrows & Day) $150

One of a pair of Yabu Meizan earthenware vases, circa 1900, 30.5cm. high. (Sotheby's Belgravia) $2,060

Part of a Mason's ironstone part dinner and dessert service printed in underglaze blue. (Christie's) $5,130

A mid 18th century white salt-glazed jug of hexagonal pear-shape with flared foot, 4½in. high. (Sotheby's) $135

20th century Wemyss-ware cat with green glass eyes, 31.5cm. high. (Sotheby's) $1,930

A Cockpit Hill sauceboat, the saltglazed body molded with the 'pineapple' pattern, 6in. wide, circa 1760.(Sotheby's)$180

A Nottingham stoneware jug with globular double walled body, circa 1700, 3½in. high (damaged). (Sotheby's) $925

A 'Rodney's Sailor' Toby jug, the figure seated on the chair inscribed 'Dollars', 12in. high, late 18th century.(Sotheby's) $1,155

A Carter, Stabler & Adams, Poole pottery dish after the original design by Truda S. Adams, 31cm. diam., circa 1924. (Sotheby's Belgravia)$240

Sailor Toby jug in black hat, blue jacket and white breeches, circa 1800, 30cm. high. (Christie's) $1,115

A massive Burmantofts faience vase decorated in the De Morgan taste with galleons at sea, 97cm. high, circa 1885. (Sotheby's Belgravia) $2,835

Pair of late 18th century English creamware figures with polychrome decoration, 9¼in. high. (Robert W. Skinner Inc.)$225

One of a pair of Branham Barum-ware vases with dragon handles, 53.5cm. high, dated 1897. (Sotheby's Belgravia) $180

Early 17th century English stone-ware jug, the globular body with tall cylindrical neck, 6¼in. high. (Sotheby's) $1,000

Daniel green-ground crested shaped oval dish, circa 1827, 42cm. wide. (Christie's) $1,010

Royal Lancastrian globular lustre vase, dated 1924, 10.5cm. high. (Christie's) $175

18th century famille rose Canton enamel bowl with pale blue interior, 11cm. diam. (Christie's) $705

19th century Chinese Canton water pitcher, 13¾in. high. (Robert W. Skinner Inc.) $500

Mid 19th century Canton famille rose punchbowl, chipped, 37cm. diam. (Christie's) $395

One of a pair of Canton bulbous vases with Dog of Fo handles, 42.5cm. high. (Burrows & Day) $830

One of a pair of mid 19th century Canton famille rose yellow-ground baluster vases and domed covers, 64cm. high. (Christie's) $3,525

Daoguang Canton vase, brightly enamelled with Buddhist lions, 60.5cm. high. (Sotheby's Belgravia) $795

One of a pair of mid 19th century porcelain Cantonese vases. (Sotheby Beresford Adams) $6,440

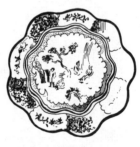

Famille rose Canton enamel octafoil dish, border with alternate panels, 30cm. diam. (Christie's) $350

One of a pair of blue-ground Canton vases, mid 19th century, one repaired. (Sotheby, King & Chasemore) $895

19th century Cantonese ovoid vase with everted rim, neck molded with dragons and lions, 60cm. high. (H. Spencer & Sons) $1,170

Mid 19th century Canton vase painted in vivid famille rose enamels, 62cm. high. (Sotheby, King & Chasemore) $755

Large Tongzhi Canton vase, neck with lion handles, 86.5cm. high. (Sotheby's Belgravia) $1,355

19th century Canton punch pot with fitted dome cover, 21cm. high. (Robert W. Skinner Inc.) $800

Large Quangxu Canton bowl painted with birds and butterflies amongst flowers, 47.5cm. diam. (Sotheby's Belgravia) $725

Large Canton famille rose punch-bowl with wood stand, 58.5cm. diam. (Christie's) $3,055

One of a pair of Tongzhi Canton vases, each painted with landscapes, applied with dragon handles. (Sotheby's Belgravia) $1,215

Large Canton famille rose baluster vase and domed cover, 63.5cm. high. (Christie's) $1,080

One of two Cantonese baluster vases. (Christie's S. Kensington) $1,830

One of a pair of late 19th century Canton vases decorated in enamels, 50.8cm. high. (Vincent & Vander-pump) $1,055

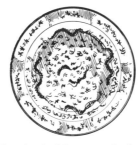

One of a pair of Canton enamel yellow-ground dishes with borders of birds, bats and butterflies, 45cm. diam. (Christie's) $1,365

One of a pair of Guangxu Canton vases, 33cm. high. (Sotheby's Belgravia) $935

One of a large pair of Canton porcelain vases, painted in famille rose enamels, mid 19th century, 88cm. high. (Sotheby, King & Chasemore) $9,515

Guangxu Canton vase of square section with pierced and enamelled decoration, 44cm. high. (Sotheby's Belgravia) $1,030

Early 19th century Canton famille rose baluster vase with wood stand, 89.5cm. high. (Christie's) $3,290

CAPODIMONTE

Capodimonte white group of La Dichia-razione, circa 1750, 14cm. high. (Christie's) $1,200

Capodimonte teacup and saucer with gilt rims, circa 1760. (Christie's) $3,840

One of a pair of Capodimonte bas-relief plaques with gilt metal frames, 36cm. high, (C. G. Sloan & Co. Inc.) $550

CARDEW

A Michael Cardew Winchcombe pottery slipware coffee pot and cover, 20cm. high, circa 1926-39. (Sotheby's Belgravia)$250

A Michael Cardew Abuja stoneware wine jar and cover, 31.5cm. high, circa 1959. (Sotheby's Belgravia) $525

A Michael Cardew Winchcombe pottery vase, the ovoid body with pronounced potting lines, 32cm. high. (Sotheby's)Belgravia) $565

CASTEL DURANTE

Castel Durante dated two-handled oviform pharmacy jar, 1575, 32cm. high. (Christie's) $1,315

One of a pair of Deruta drug jars, 1661, 32cm. high. (Sotheby's) $3,040

Castel Durante dated two-handled oviform pharmacy jar, slightly cracked, 1574, 32cm. high. (Christie's) $4,540

CASTELLI

Early Castelli oval dish painted with horsemen hunting deer, 1660-1680, 46.5cm. wide. (Christie's) $1,795

17th century Castelli drug jar with tapering neck, 20.5cm. high. (Sotheby's) $655

Castelli armorial dish painted by Liborio Grue, circa 1740, 28.8cm. diam. (Christie's) $2,630

Rare Caughley eye bath with shell-mounted oval cup and pedestal foot, circa 1785, 5cm. high. (Sotheby's) $1,045

Caughley cress dish and stand with scalloped and barbed rim, circa 1775-80. (Sotheby's) $330

A Caughley barrel-shaped cream jug with sparrow beak spout, 2¾in. high, circa 1780.(Sotheby's) $355

CHALKWARE

Mid 19th century chalkware sitting cat, Pensylvania, 13½in. high. (Robert W. Skinner Inc.)$550

Mid 19th century chalkware rooster, Pennsylvania, 11in. high. (Robert W. Skinner Inc.) $850

Mid 19th century chalkware sitting dog, Pennsylvania, 13¼in. high. (Robert W. Skinner Inc.)
$800

CHELSEA

A Chelsea scent bottle of flattened oval shape decorated with gilt butterflies, 3¼in. high, circa 1760. (Christie's)$210

A rare Chelsea octagonal bowl, finely decorated in the manner of J. H. O'Neale, 6½in. wide, 1752-56. (Christie's) $15,750

A miniature Chelsea figure of a gardener with a rake, 2¼in. high, 1755-60. (Christie's)$440

An attractive Chelsea-Derby Arbour group of lovers, 8in. high, about 1770-80. (Sotheby's) $715

A boldly modelled Chelsea group of a wolf being savaged by two dogs, 12¼in. high, 1756-69. (Christie's) $965

Chelsea hexagonal vase and cover painted in the Kakiemon style, circa 1752, 26.5cm. high. (Christie's) $10,575

Chelsea bonbonniere of a reclining shepherd and shepherdess, circa 1760-65, 6.5cm. high. (Sotheby's) $1,650

Rare Chelsea octagonal cup and saucer painted in Kakiemon enamels, circa 1749-52. (Sotheby's) $2,620

Chelsea scent bottle in the form of a young boy, circa 1760, 7cm. high. (Sotheby's) $1,265

Chelsea 'Girl-in-a-Swing' scent bottle showing a sleeping girl with a dog, 1755, 9cm. high. (Sotheby's) $970

Pair of Chelsea figures of a gallant and companion, circa 1770, 28cm. high. (Christie's) $2,810

Chelsea figure of a monk reading a book, circa 1755-60, 12cm. high. (Sotheby's) $1,360

'Girl-in-a-Swing' triple scent bottle modelled as a hen and her chicks, circa 1751, 7.5cm. high. (Christie's) $2,230

Rare Chelsea figure of Ceres in the white, circa 1749-50, 30.5cm. high. (Sotheby's) $4,375

One of a pair of Chelsea plates painted in colored enamels, circa 1755-58, 20.5cm. diam. (Sotheby's)$1,190

One of a pair of Chelsea octagonal dishes, circa 1752, 25cm. diam. (Sotheby's) $2,350

Early Chelsea 'acanthus leaf' teapot and cover in white, circa 1745-49, 11cm. high. (Sotheby's) $2,025

Rare early Chelsea pedestal, circa 1751-52, 10.5cm. high. (Sotheby's) $945

Chelsea chicken box and cover, circa 1755, 9.5cm. wide. (Christie's) $3,840

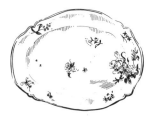

Chelsea shaped oval dish painted with flowers, circa 1755, 34.5cm. wide, red anchor mark. (Christie's) $610

Chelsea thimble in hinged silver filigree case, circa 1700, 2cm. high. (Christie's) $2,880

One of a pair of Chelsea plates with shaped gilt rims, circa 1763, 22cm. diam. (Christie's) $1,295

A pair of rare Chelsea busts of The Seasons, circa 1756-58, 10cm. high. (Sotheby's) $570

Rare Chelsea white 'acanthus leaf' cream jug, circa 1745-50, 10cm. high. (Sotheby's) $3,775

Chelsea 'Girl-in-a-Swing' scent bottle and stopper formed as a hawk, 6cm. high, circa 1751-54. (Christie's) $7,680

Pair of Chelsea candlestick figures each of a gallant and his companion, circa 1765, 27.5cm. high. (Christie's) $2,280

Chelsea figure of a shepherdess with a lamb, gold anchor mark, circa 1760, 18.5cm. high. (Christie's) $935

Rare Chelsea Kakiemon style beaker, circa 1751-52, 5.5cm. high. (Sotheby's) $825

Chelsea flared bowl and domed cover with green twig handles, circa 1756, 27.5cm. wide. (Christie's) $2,120

Chelsea baluster vase, slightly chipped, circa 1758, 20.5cm. high. (Christie's) $1,285

Qianlong famille rose 'tobacco-leaf' shaped oval tureen and cover, 18.5cm. wide. (Christie's) $880

Rare Kuan polychrome jar, mark of the Chia Ching period, 35.5cm. high. (Phillips) $523,600

Armorially decorated Chinese export oval platter, circa 1800, 42.5cm. long. (C. G. Sloan & Co. Inc.) $475

Late Kangxi Doucai saucer dish, 20cm. diam. (Christie's) $705

One of a pair of Qing dynasty blanc-de-chine models of plum trees, 19.5cm. high.(Christie's) $310

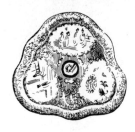

19th century Chinese trefoil rose medallion tray with shaped rim, 27.5cm. diam. (Robert W. Skinner Inc.) $400

Chinese transitional blue and white jar and cover, 32cm. high. (Sotheby's) $2,930

One of a pair of late 19th century Continental garden seats sold with carved wooden stands. (Manchester Auction Mart) $2,345

One of two late 18th/early 19th century Chinese turquoise glazed models of hawks, 34cm. high. (Christie's) $810

One of a pair of early 19th century Chinese porcelain ormolu mounted vases, 105cm. high. (Bonhams) $34,160

Dish from a set of three pairs of Chinese export porcelain blue and white meat dishes of the Fitzhugh pattern. (Christie's S. Kensington) $3,060

One of a pair of 19th century Chinese rose medallion vases, 25cm. high. (Robert W. Skinner Inc.) $350

Chinese export salad bowl with notched corners and dark blue borders, 23cm. diam. (C. G. Sloan & Co. Inc.) $650

Late 19th century Chinese covered tureen with fruit finial, 26cm. wide. (Robert W. Skinner Inc.)$400

Chinese export Marquise-shaped covered vegetable dish, circa 1800, with reeded handles, 33cm. long. (C. G. Sloan & Co. Inc.)$750

Chinese porcelain vase, sold with carved hardwood stand. (Locke & England) $1,275

16th/early 17th century Swatow saucer-dish painted in blue enamel, 35cm. diam. (Christie's) $165

Chinese yellow glazed Buddhistic lion, paw resting on a pierced ball, 28cm. high. (Geering & Colyer) $180

Tongzhi celadon-ground umbrella stand modelled with two bronze dragons, 63cm. high. (Sotheby's Belgravia) $235

One of a pair of Chinese figures of standing cockerels, 38cm. high. (Christie's) $1,645

Straw-glazed buff pottery figure of a standing soldier, early Tang dynasty, 37cm. high.(Christie's) $1,545

Red glazed teabowl of the Yongzheng period with plain white interior, 7cm. diam. (Christie's) $855

Blue and white moonflask dating from Tao Kuang period. (Christie's S. Kensington) $1,855

Transitional blue and white jardiniere with deep rounded sides, 23.5cm. wide. (Sotheby's) $1,095

CLARICE CLIFF

One of two Clarice Cliff plates designed by Laura Knight, 1934, 25.25cm. diam. (Sotheby's Belgravia) $585

Part of a fifty-piece dinner service, 'The Biarritz Bizarre', designed by Clarice Cliff, 1930's. (Sotheby's Belgravia) $1,800

Clarice Cliff tureen and cover, 1934, 19.5cm. high.(Sotheby's Belgravia) $560

Clarice Cliff 'bizarre' vase, 21cm. high, 1930's.(Sotheby's Belgravia) $95

Clarice Cliff two-person breakfast set of eight pieces, 1930's, teapot 12cm. high.(Sotheby's Belgravia) $400

Large Clarice Cliff vase with baluster body, 1930's, 41cm. high. (Sotheby's Belgravia) $335

COALPORT

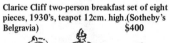

Coalport pastille burner and cover, encrusted with flowers, with detachable roof, circa 1830, 11.5cm. high. (Sotheby's Belgravia) $924

Part of a Coalport part tea and coffee service of thirty-one pieces, circa 1825. (Christie's) $1,895

Coalport pastille burner and cover, with gilt flecks, circa 1830, 11.5cm. high. (Sotheby's Belgravia) $685

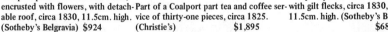

Coalport globular two-handled vase and cover, encrusted with flowers, 29.5cm. high. (Christie's) $740

Coalport pale yellow-ground botanical part dessert service, circa 1820. (Christie's) $3,525

One of a pair of Coalport candlesticks, heavily encrusted with flowers, 23cm. high. (Christie's) $640

Coalport bombe flower-pot and pierced cover, circa 1810, 29cm. wide. (Christie's) $840

Coalport parian figure of the Duke of Wellington, circa 1852, 10¼in. high. (Sotheby's Belgravia) $425

Part of a Coalport orange-ground part tea and coffee service, circa 1810. (Christie's) $980

Part of a Coalport John Rose blue-ground part tea and coffee service, circa 1810. (Christie's) $960

One of a pair of Coalport vases and covers, circa 1910, 13½in. high. (Sotheby's Belgravia) $1,665

Coalport part dessert service, circa 1820, painted with bouquets of flowers. (Christie's)$2,585

Coalport jardiniere and stand by John Rose, circa 1800-1810, 22.5cm. high. (Sotheby's) $215

Coalport gold-ground two-handled cup, cover and stand, circa 1805.(Christie's) $425

Coalport claret-ground racing trophy and cover with gilt twig handles, circa 1853, 29cm. high. (Christie's) $2,160

Part of a Coalport part dessert service, circa 1805. (Christie's) $1,010

Coalport or Minton flower-encrusted vase, 10½in. high, circa 1830. (Sotheby's) $355

Part of a Coalport matt green-ground dessert service decorated with flowers, circa 1820.(Christie's)$6,110

109

COMMEMORATIVE

'Victoria Regina' commemorative mug, 1837, 3in. high. (Sotheby's Belgravia) $1,000

Good and rare Sunderland 'coal trade' jug, circa 1820, 17.2cm. high. (Sotheby's Belgravia) $245

'Caroline' mug, body printed in black, circa 1820, 2¾in. high. (Sotheby's Belgravia) $570

Commemorative creamware mug with portrait of George IV, circa 1800, 14.5cm. high. (Christie's) $980

A rare Coronation Day teapot and cover, transfer-printed in black with two portraits of Queen Victoria and Windsor Castle, 1838, 24.8cm. (cracked). (Sotheby's Belgravia) $476

Very rare 'Queen Victoria' child's mug, circa 1837-38, 3in. high. (Sotheby's Belgravia) $405

COPELAND

Copeland and Garrett moulded jug depicting a Gretna Green marriage, circa 1840. (Alfie's Antique Market) $115

Part of a fifteen-piece Copeland dessert service each painted with colorful sprays of flowers, 1852. (Sotheby's Belgravia) $715

Copeland parian jug of ovoid form, circa 1872, 26.1cm. high. (Sotheby's Belgravia) $490

'The Bride', a Copeland unglazed bust of a young girl, inscribed R. Mont, 1861, 37.5cm. high. (Smith-Woolley & Perry)$180

Copeland commemorative tyg, 6in. high, 1900. (Sotheby's Belgravia) $450

Large Copeland parian figure of 'Go to Sleep', circa 1865, 17½in. high. (Sotheby's Belgravia) $570

110

Part of a Copenhagen porcelain botanical fruit set. (Taylor Lane & Creber) $480

COPER, HANS

One of a pair of Copenhagen vases, circa 1870, 38cm. high. (Sotheby's Belgravia)$475

Copenhagen snuff box and cover modelled as the head of a dog, circa 1793, 6.5cm. wide. (Christie's) $840

Good Hans Coper black stoneware vase with teardrop body, circa 1970, 15cm. high. (Sotheby's Belgravia) $4,680

Hans Coper stoneware vase, 3¾in. diam., 1960. (Sotheby's Belgravia) $1,260

Hans Coper stoneware vase with onion body and narrow neck, circa 1970, 18cm. high. (Sotheby's Belgravia) $1,640

Hans Coper stoneware vase with globular body, circa 1967, 19.5cm. high. (Sotheby's Belgravia) $7,255

DAOGUANG

A good Hans Coper stoneware 'Funnel' pot with a semi-opaque buff glaze, 31cm. high.(Sotheby's Belgravia) $2,310

A Hans Coper stoneware vase the cylindrical body with wasp waist and cylindrical mouth, 20.5cm. high. (Sotheby's Belgravia) $1,365

Yellow glazed bowl incised on the interior, of the Daoguang period, in fitted box, 12cm. diam. (Christie's) $1,545

One of a pair of Daoguang sang-de-boeuf bottle-vases, 29cm. high. (Sotheby's Belgravia) $610

One of a pair of Daoguang period famille rose graviata pale-blue-ground bowls, 14.5cm. diam. (Christie's) $4,285

A rare mid 18th century Dutch Delft barber's shaving bowl. (Vernon's) $575

Early 18th century Delft blue and white posset pot and cover. (Parsons, Welch & Cowell) $1,070

Early 18th century Dutch Delft dish in Wanli style, slightly chipped. (Sotheby's) $700

One of a pair of Dutch Delft tobacco jars, 18th century, with brass covers, 21cm. high. (Sotheby's) $1,310

One of a pair of Dutch Delft melon tureens, covers and stands, circa 1759-64, 19cm. wide. (Sotheby's) $4,700

18th century Dutch Delft tobacco jar with brass cover, 29.5cm. high. (Sotheby's) $700

One of a pair of Dutch Delft blue and white peacock pattern dishes, circa 1720, 35cm. diam.(Christie's) $835

One of a set of six mid 17th century Dutch Delft tiles painted with birds, 13cm. square. (Sotheby's) $610

One of a pair of Dutch Delft blue and white dishes, circa 1720, 35cm. diam.(Christie's) $955

Early 18th century Dutch Delft plaque of quatrefoil shape, 46cm. high. (Sotheby's) $350

Mid 18th century Dutch Delft dish painted in shades of blue, 34.2cm. diam.(Sotheby's) $420

Dutch Delft tobacco jar bearing the title 'Havana', circa 1790, 28cm. high. (Sotheby, King & Chasemore) $440

Dutch Delft peacock pattern dish painted in blue, 35cm. diam. (Lawrence Fine Art) $330

Dutch Delft polychrome figure of a parrot, circa 1725, 21cm. high. (Christie's) $1,075

Mid 17th century Dutch Delft tile, one of a set of four, slightly damaged. (Sotheby's) $325

DE MORGAN

De Morgan ruby lustre saucer-dish painted by Fred Passenger, 37cm. diam. (Christie's) $1,640

De Morgan lustre bowl painted with fabulous fish amongst swirling waves, 33.5cm. diameter. (Sotheby's Belgravia) $440

De Morgan lustre charger painted in shades of copper, 41.5cm. diam. (Christie's) $1,080

A large William de Morgan lustre charger with two comical fish on the depressed centre roudel, 52cm. diam., circa 1888-1907. (Sotheby's Belgravia) $1,010

Large De Morgan bottle-vase painted by Fred Passenger, circa 1882-88, 58.7cm. high. (Sotheby's Belgravia) $4,880

De Morgan lustre charger painted by Charles Passenger in ruby and ochre, 34cm. diam. (Christie's) $670

De Morgan lustre deep charger decorated by Charles Passenger, 46.5cm. diam. (Christie's) $7,020

A De Morgan vase painted by Fred Passenger in Isnik taste, 25cm. high, circa 1888-97. (Sotheby's Belgravia) $965

De Morgan lustre charger painted in pink and copper lustre, 36cm. diam., slightly cracked. (Christie's) $310

Derby yellow-ground d-shaped bough pot with ram's head handles, 1796-1800, 24.5cm. wide. (Christie's) $985

One of a pair of chambersticks by Wm. Duesbury & Co., circa 1765, 13cm. wide. (Christie's) $565

Derby blue and white oval sauceboat painted with pagodas and flowers, circa 1768, slightly cracked. (Christie's) $325

One of a pair of Royal Crown Derby 'jewelled' vases, date code 1908, 10¼in. high. (Sotheby's Belgravia) $3,925

Royal Crown Derby earthenware dinner service, dated for 1898. (Sotheby's Belgravia) $855

One of a pair of Derby lime-ground bucket-shaped ice-pails, covers and liners, circa 1795-1800, 25cm. high. (Christie's) $2,040

One of a pair of landscape plaques possibly Derby, circa 1830, 8½in. wide. (Sotheby's Belgravia) $665

Two late 19th century Samson 'Derby' figures, 6¾in. and 6½in. high. (Sotheby's) $335

Derby circular plaque painted by Jockey Hill, in giltwood frame, 14.5cm. diam., circa 1795-1800. (Christie's) $2,075

One of a pair of Derby yellow-ground flared flower-pots with fixed gilt handles, 13cm. high, circa 1800. (Christie's) $1,440

Pair of Derby figures of a monk and nun, circa 1770, 14.5cm. and 13.5cm. high. (Christie's) $890

One of a pair of Derby flared flower-pots and two handled stands, circa 1815, 19cm. high. (Christie's) $1,465

Derby blue and white shell-moulded sauceboat, circa 1770, 14.5cm. wide. (Christie's) $395

Derby yellow-ground bucket-shaped chocolate cup, cover, and trembleuse saucer, circa 1795. (Christie's) $4,800

Derby d-shaped bough pot with gilt ram's head handles, 1796-1800, 24.5cm. wide.(Christie's) $470

Derby flared flower vase and pierced cover, circa 1795-1800, 11cm. high. (Christie's) $1,095

A pair of Derby botanical oval dishes, circa 1795-1800, 27cm. high. (Sotheby's) $2,240

One of a pair of Derby figures of a recumbent stag and hind, circa 1765, about 17cm. wide. (Christie's) $1,170

Derby yellow-ground oval milk jug with angular handle, by Duesbury & Co., circa 1800, 13.5cm. wide. (Christie's) $1,175

Derby inkwell of waisted cylindrical form, circa 1820, 10cm. high. (Christie's) $490

One of a pair of Derby plates by Wm. Duesbury & Co., circa 1758, 20.5cm. diam. (Christie's) $940

Derby pale yellow-ground two-handled cache pot by Wm. Duesbury & Co. , circa 1790, 7.5cm. high. (Christie's) $1,175

A pair of Derby candlestick figures, circa 1760, 23cm. high.(Christie's) $1,450

Derby powdered-purple ground octagonal coffee cup and saucer, circa 1780. (Christie's) $3,275

One of a pair of Derby figures of rams. (Phillips) $340

Tureen from a Derby part dinner service by Robert Bloor & Co., circa 1825. (Christie's) $4,460

19th century Derby white glazed porcelain group of three pug dogs, on ebonised plinth.(Lowery & Partners) $185

Derby figure of a girl in flowered skirt, circa 1760, 23.5cm. high. (Christie's) $490

One of a pair of Derby crested green-ground campana vases painted by Thomas Steel, circa 1830, 29cm. high. (Christie's) $5,875

Derby figure of a pedlar girl, by William Duesbury & Co., circa 1765, 19cm. high. (Christie's) $670

Rare Derby figure of Joseph Grimaldi as 'Clown', 14cm. high, circa 1830. (Sotheby's) $145

Derby baluster jug with scroll handle and fluted lip, circa 1762, 23cm. high. (Christie's) $1,145

Derby figure of Falstaff, by Robert Bloor & Co., circa 1825.(Christie's) $355

Derby bough-pot and pierced cover of bombe form, 19cm. wide, circa 1795-1800. (Christie's)$465

Part of a Derby blue-ground part dinner and dessert service with gilt decoration, circa 1820. (Christie's) $2,630

Bloor Derby tureen, cover and stand, circa 1820-30, 5¼in. wide.(Sotheby's) $760

An interesting early Derby writing set supported on five scroll feet, 10¼in. long, circa 1758-60. (Christie's) $1,175

Part of a Derby blue-ground topographical part dessert service, circa 1820. (Christie's) $5,405

A fine Derby plate painted by William Billingsley, circa 1785. (Sotheby's) $800

A rare and brightly coloured Derby group of Isabella, Gallant and a Jester, 11¼in. high, circa 1765. (Sotheby's) $1,575

A Derby plate vigorously painted by Moses Webster, early 19th century. (Sotheby's) $380

DOCCIA

Rare Doccia enamel snuff box with gilt metal mounts, circa 1740, 10.1cm. wide. (Sotheby's) $1,365

Doccia white mythological group of Venus and Adonis with Cupid, circa 1748, 23cm. high. (Christie's) $1,560

Doccia rectangular plaque modelled as portrait busts, circa 1745-50, 12.5cm. high. (Christie's) $2,160

DOUCAI

Early 18th century Doucai Yan-yan vase painted with an audience scene, 45cm. high. (Christie's) $1,320

Early 18th century Doucai dish painted with flower sprays, 35.5cm. diam. (Christie's) $835

Doucai pear-shaped vase with globular neck, 39cm. high, 18th century. (Christie's) $1,905

117

DOULTON

Large and rare Doulton stoneware jardiniere, dated 1880, 39.4cm. wide, with hair crack. (Sotheby's Belgravia)$425

Doulton saltglaze stoneware figure of a Boer War soldier, circa 1900, 30.5cm. high. (Sotheby's Belgravia) $525

One of eight Royal Doulton service plates, 11cm. diam., with etched borders. (C. G. Sloan & Co. Inc.) $400

Large Royal Doulton oviform vase, lightly molded , 47cm. high. (Christie's) $285

Doulton earthenware mouse part chess set of twenty-three pieces, circa 1885, 5.5 to 11cm. high. (Sotheby's Belgravia) $260

Large Doulton baluster vase decorated by William Parker, 44.5cm. high. (Christie's) $310

One of two Doulton stoneware circular two-handled candlesticks, circa 1872, 28cm. high. (Sotheby's Belgravia) $305

Doulton stoneware vase decorated by Frank Butler, 23.2cm. high, dated 1876.(Sotheby's Belgravia) $280

Royal Doulton figure of Guy Fawkes. (Christie's S. Kensington) $505

One of a pair of Royal Doulton vases, painted by J. Hancock, 22.5cm. high, circa 1910. (Sotheby's Belgravia) $455

Doulton stoneware 'Toby' moonflask, circa 1920, 20.4cm. high. (Sotheby's Belgravia) $330

Doulton stoneware baluster jug with hinged silver cover, 1877, 21.5cm. high. (Sotheby's Belgravia) $265

Rare Royal Doulton flambe guinea-fowl decorated by Fred Moore, 13.7cm. long, 1930's. (Sotheby's Belgravia) $305

Royal Doulton pottery vase by Hannah Barlow. (Sotheby Bearne) $960

Rare Doulton group of Europa and The Bull. (Phillips) $2,560

Doulton oviform vase with incised body with flared neck, 46cm. high. (Christie's) $215

Royal Doulton vase and cover painted by J. H. Plant, circa 1900, 21cm. high. (Sotheby's Belgravia) $955

Silver mounted Doulton stoneware lemonade jug decorated by Hannah Barlow, dated 1883, 23.5cm. high. (Sotheby's Belgravia) $235

Rare Doulton George Tinworth saltglazed stoneware boy jester, 12.5cm. high, circa 1886. (Sotheby's Belgravia)$425

Royal Doulton bronzed pottery group after Noke, designed by Stanley Thorogood. (Taylor Lane & Creber)$420

One of a pair of Royal Doulton stoneware vases decorated by Florence Barlow, 1903, 28cm. high. (Sotheby's Belgravia) $590

One of a pair of Doulton stoneware vases with flared cylindrical bodies, circa 1891-1902, 31.8cm. high. (Sotheby's Belgravia) $870

One of a pair of Doulton style wall plates, 16½in. diam. (Clive Emson & Co.) $200

One of a pair of Royal Doulton vases, painted by J. Hancock, 22.5cm. high, circa 1910. (Sotheby's Belgravia)$455

119

DOULTON

A Royal Doulton stoneware circular bowl by Mark V. Marshall, 18cm. diam., circa 1910. (Christie's) $230

A Royal Doulton 'Chang' bowl by Harry Nixon, the lobed body beneath a petal rim, 29cm. diam., circa 1925.(Sotheby's Belgravia) $505

Doulton stoneware mouse modelled by George Tinworth, 7cm. high, dated 1884. (Sotheby's Belgravia) $315

A Doulton stoneware circular candlestick on square base, modelled by Emily E. Stormer, 22cm. high, 1878. (Christie's) $295

An early silver mounted Doulton stoneware carafe decorated by George Tinworth, 26cm. high, 1874. (Sotheby's Belgravia) $290

An early Doulton earthenware jug freely painted with grotesque birds and dogs, 28.5cm. high, circa 1869-72.(Sotheby's Belgravia) $355

A good electroplated mounted Doulton stoneware covered jug decorated by Mary Mitchell, 20.5cm. high, dated 1880. (Sotheby's Belgravia)$630

Pair of Doulton stoneware vases each incised by Hannah Barlow, 24.5cm. high, dated 1885. (Sotheby's Belgravia) $545

A large good Doulton stoneware vase incised by Hannah Barlow, 35.5cm. high, circa 1891.(Sotheby's Belgravia) $1,220

One of a pair of Doulton stoneware circular squat candlesticks by Eliza Simmance, 17cm. high, 1875. (Christie's) $505

A Doulton stoneware menu-holder modelled by George Tinworth, 12cm. high, circa 1885. (Christie's) $400

Doulton faience clockcase in the form of a longcase clock, 35cm. high.(Christie's)$355

A Doulton stoneware jardiniere, the cylindrical body incised by Florence Barlow, 18.5cm. high, dated 1877. (Sotheby's Belgravia) $295

A Doulton stoneware beaker by George Tinworth with contemporary silver rim, 13.5cm. high, circa 1880. (Christie's) $160

A large late 19th century Doulton Impasto vase, signed J. Kelsall, 15½in. high. (Robert W. Skinner Inc.) $750

A Doulton Lambeth stoneware vase by Mark V. Marshall, 23.5cm. high, circa 1905. (Sotheby's Belgravia) $670

Doulton earthenware jardiniere and stand, 122cm. high, circa 1880. (Sotheby's Belgravia) $730

An unusual Doulton stoneware bottle-vase decorated by Mark V. Marshall, 24cm. high. (Sotheby's Belgravia)$200

A rare Doulton Crown Lambeth-ware faience vase, the shouldered ovoid body painted by Hannah Barlow, 30.5cm. high, circa 1891-1903. (Sotheby's Belgravia) $650

A good silver mounted Doulton stoneware lemonade set, each piece incised by Hannah Barlow, dated 1878. (Sotheby's Belgravia) $1,365

An unusual Doulton 'Sung' vase molded in the Chinese taste, 1927. (Sotheby's Belgravia) $590

Royal Doulton 'Captain Cook' loving cup, circa 1930, 9½in. high.(Sotheby's Belgravia) $500

A good Doulton stoneware jardiniere painted by Florence Barlow, in pate-sur-pate, 23cm. high. circa 1885. (Sotheby's Belgravia) $545

An interesting and early silver mounted Doulton stoneware jug, incised by Hannah Barlow, 21cm. high, 1872. (Sotheby's Belgravia) $590

DRESDEN

Gilt bronze and Dresden ewer with curved handles, circa 1860, 25.5cm. high. (Sotheby's Belgravia) $240

Late 19th century Dresden yellow-ground cruet, fitted with two ewers and covers, 23cm. high. (Sotheby's Belgravia) $495

Mid 19th century Dresden topographical cup and saucer with gilt borders. (Sotheby's Belgravia) $435

One of a pair of late 19th century schneeballen vases and covers, 57.7cm. high. (Sotheby's Belgravia) $1,775

Late 19th century framed Dresden oval plaque, 19.5cm. long. (Sotheby's Belgravia) $590

Late 19th century Dresden centrepiece with shallow pierced bowl, 40cm. diam. (Sotheby's Belgravia) $675

Late 19th century Dresden plaque painted by H. Wrigel, signed, 14 x 10cm. framed and glazed. (Sotheby's Belgravia) $820

Mid 19th century Dresden porcelain mantel clock, with eight-day movement. (Locke & England) $2,660

Late 19th century framed Dresden plaque painted with 'Good Night', 25.3 x 17.5cm. (Sotheby's Belgravia) $1,985

One of a pair of Dresden parakeets on tree stump bases, 41cm. high. (Lambert & Symes) $1,935

Pair of late 19th century Dresden figures of a gallant and a lady, 49 x 50.5cm. high. (Sotheby's Belgravia) $1,695

One of a pair of late 19th century Dresden bottle vases and covers, 47cm. high. (Sotheby's Belgravia) $900

Late 19th century Dresden schnee-ballen bowl and cover, 42cm. wide, painted with hunting scenes. (Sotheby's Belgravia) $855

Plate from a fourteen-piece Dresden dinner service, circa 1910, painted with game birds. (Sotheby's Belgravia) $805

Late 19th century Dresden tureen, cover and stand, 23cm. diam. (Sotheby's Belgravia) $240

One of a pair of late 19th century Dresden yellow-ground cassolettes, 27.5cm. high.(Sotheby's Belgravia) $675

Twelve-piece Dresden potschappel monkey band, circa 1900. (Sotheby's Belgravia) $865

Dresden four-light candel-abra, circa 1900, 50cm. high, minor chips. (Sotheby's Belgravia) $560

Late 19th century Dresden plaque, 19.5 x 14.4cm. (Sotheby's Belgravia) $1,210

Late 19th century Dresden clock case with enamelled dial, 46cm. high. (Sotheby's Belgravia) $875

Late 19th century framed Dresden plaque, 26 x 21.5cm. (Sotheby's Belgravia) $1,645

One of a pair of late 19th century Dresden vases and covers, 53cm. high. (Sotheby's Belgravia) $875

Late 19th century pair of Dresden figures inspired by Gainsborough, 27.5 and 30cm. high. (Sotheby's Belgravia) $485.

One of a pair of Dresden bottle vases and covers, 48.5cm. high, circa 1900. (Sotheby's Belgravia) $1,445

Early 17th century Netherlands majolica blue dash charger, 32cm. diam. (Christie's) $11,950

Large Continental colored earthenware half-length figure of a negro minstrel, circa 1900, 75cm. high. (Sotheby's Belgravia) $2,180

One of a set of eleven late 19th century Beehive porcelain dessert plates with painted mythical scenes, 7in. diam. (Robert W. Skinner Inc.) $425

A late Apulian red figure bell-krater by the Como Painter, 10½in. high, late 4th century B.C. (Christie's) $1,890

One of a pair of late 19th century Continental glazed earthenware pedestals, 98cm. high. (Sotheby's Belgravia) $970

An Apulian red figure column-krater by the Schiller painter, 7¾in. high. (Christie's) $3,775

Late 19th century pair of large Continental colored biscuit figures, damaged, 60cm. high. (Sotheby's Belgravia) $575

A Continental porcelain plaque finely painted by Victor Hennequin, dated 1831. (Christie's) $8,400

Pair of Continental colored biscuit figures, slightly chipped, circa 1900, 52cm. high. (Sotheby's Belgravia) $460

Late 19th century Austrian covered urn with domed lid, 40cm. high. (Robert W. Skinner Inc.) $850

One of a set of six Continental silver teacups and saucers with porcelain liners and ivory handles, 51oz. (Phillips) $1,000

19th century Continental table centrepiece with pierced bowl. (Taylor Lane & Creber) $390

One of a pair of 18th century famille rose libation cups molded with lingzhi, 12.5cm. wide. (Christie's) $825

Hongxian famille rosebowl painted with peach branches, 17cm. diam. (Sotheby's Belgravia) $865

Qianlong famille rose cache-pot with hexafoil rim, 25cm. wide. (Christie's) $1,290

Triangular famille rose vegetable dish and cover, 33.5cm. high. (Sotheby's) $880

Famille rose tureen and cover modelled as a tortoise, 36cm. wide, repaired. (Christie's) $1,525

One of a pair of famille rose armorial plates, circa 1745, 22.5cm. diam. (Christie's) $565

Famille rose armorial oblong octagonal dish, circa 1775, 41cm. wide. (Christie's) $2,230

One of a pair of mid 19th century famille rose baluster vases with wood covers and stands, 35cm. high. (Christie's) $1,320

One of a pair of famille rose armorial oval dishes, Qianlong, circa 1750, 39.5cm. wide. (Christie's) $2,935

One of a pair of Tongzhi famille rose vases with baluster bodies, 46cm. high. (Sotheby's Belgravia) $1,055

One of a pair of famille rose rectangular plaques with floral borders, 38cm. wide. (Christie's) $1,410

One of a pair of late 19th century famille rose figures of phoenix, 47.5cm. high. (Sotheby's Belgravia) $1,310

FAMILLE VERTE

Large famille verte baluster vase of Meiping proportions, 44cm. high. (Christie's) $1,130

18th century Chinese famille verte roundel on carved rosewood stand, 24cm. diam. (C. G. Sloan & Co. Inc.) $350

Tongzhi period famille verte vase, fitted for electricity, 45.5cm. high. (Sotheby's Belgravia) $445

Early 18th century famille verte dish, 34.5cm. diam. (Christie's) $615

One of a pair of famille verte Oriental figures. (Christie's S. Kensington) $1,190

One of a pair of early 18th century famille verte dishes, 32.5cm. diam. (Christie's) $2,230

FRANKENTHAL

Mid 18th century Frankenthal figure of a man, 16.2cm. high. (Phillips) $1,265

Frankenthal dish with pierced border, 30cm. diam. (Christie's) $1,440

Frankenthal group of Meleager and Atalanta, 42cm. high, circa 1780. (Sotheby's) $840

Frankenthal figure of a lady playing a harp, circa 1765, 15.5cm. high. (Sotheby's) $1,160

Frankenthal group, circa 1770, of a countrywoman milking a goat. (Christie's & Edmiston's)$1,430

Frankenthal group of Komodianten modelled by J. P. Melchior, 1787, 26cm. high. (Christie's) $2,880

Frankfurt two-handled shaving bowl with pierced drainer, circa 1720, 30.5cm. wide. (Christie's) $625

German faience plate, probably Frankfurt, circa 1700, 35.5cm. diam. (Sotheby's) $655

Late 17th century Frankfurt circular spice box of tin-glazed earthenware, 28.5cm. diam. (Lawrence Fine Art) $440

Early 18th century Frankfurt miniature baluster vase of octagonal section, 15.5cm. high. (Sotheby's) $840

Late 17th century Frankfurt faience dish of lobed silver shape, 30.5cm. diam. (Sotheby's) $525

Late 17th century Frankfurt jug with spirally fluted body, cracked, 23.5cm. high. (Sotheby's) $727

FRENCH

One of a pair of Mennecy silver-mounted cylindrical pomade-pots and covers, circa 1750, 16cm. high. (Christie's) $2,160

Early 19th century French Art pottery vase depicting Labourers performing various tasks, 14½in. high. (Robert W. Skinner Inc.) $400

Late 19th century Clement Massier Art pottery vase with cut away chinoiserie decoration, signed Golfe-Juan, 8¼in. high. (Robert W. Skinner Inc.) $130

One of a pair of late 19th century French snuff boxes, 8cm. wide. (Sotheby's) $1,330

Late 19th century French colored biscuit figures of rustic lovers, 39cm. high. (Sotheby's Belgravia) $335

19th century French rose medallion covered tureen with bracket handles, 12.5cm. wide. (Robert W. Skinner Inc.) $125

One of a pair of unusual French gilt metal mounted vases, circa 1870, 25.3cm. wide.(Sotheby's Belgravia) $435

Late 19th century French tobacco box with reeded metal mounts, 13cm. wide. (Sotheby's) $450

Late 19th century French bleu-celeste-ground bowl, 28cm. diam. (Sotheby's Belgravia)$385

Rare Chantilly figure of a gardener holding a basket of fruit, circa 1740, 16cm. high. (Christie's) $2,250

Late 19th century pair of French colored biscuit figures, 57cm. high. (Sotheby's Belgravia) $1,395

Late 19th century French group of figures, 42cm. high. (Sotheby's Belgravia) $625

Slightly chipped china cat by Emile Galle with picture of creeping mouse painted on back. (W. H. Lane & Son) $1,135

Large French earthenware figure of a water carrier, circa 1910, 106cm. high. (Sotheby's Belgravia) $1,470

Late 19th century French gilt bronze mounted earthenware jardiniere, 48cm. wide. (Sotheby's Belgravia) $710

One of a pair of French porcelain market stall groups, 29.5cm. high, circa 1850-60. (Sotheby, King & Chasemore) $895

Pair of late 19th century French models of terriers, 17 and 18cm. high. (Sotheby's Belgravia) $345

Blue-ground French enamel caddy, circa 1900, 10cm. high. (Sotheby's) $425

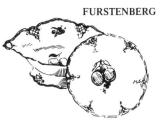

Furstenberg shaped oblong gold mounted etui, circa 1760, 11cm. long. (Christie's) $240

Late 18th century Furstenberg figure of a fisherman, 12.5cm. high. (Sotheby's) $1,520

Part of a ten-piece Furstenberg dessert service, circa 1900, each piece painted with fruit. (Sotheby's Belgravia) $625

Furstenberg figure of 'Hope', 20cm. high, circa 1760, leg restored. (Sotheby's) $2,905

Rare Furstenberg group of a lady and gentleman embracing, 10cm. high, circa 1775. (Sotheby's) $5,325

Furstenberg figure of Leda modelled by C. G. Schubert, 16.3cm. high, circa 1784. (Sotheby's) $920

GERMAN

Early 18th century German fluted plate with everted rim, 33cm. diam. (Sotheby's) $490

19th century German porcelain centrepiece, by Helena Wolfson, 48cm. high. (May Whetter & Grose) $325

One of a pair of late 18th century German cachepots, 10.7cm. high. (Sotheby's) $655

Hutschenreuter, Selb model of a snowy owl, 1930's, 24cm. high. (Sotheby's Belgravia) $235

18th/19th century Rhenish stoneware inkstand in the form of a lion, 22cm. long. (Sotheby's) $2,575

Late 17th century German Creussen stoneware apostle tankard with pewter rim and cover, 13cm. high. (Christie's) $4,780

Rare Ansbach dish of fluted oval form, 26.5cm. diam., circa 1765-70. (Sotheby's) $610

Large German earthenware figure of an Arab, circa 1880, 86cm. high. (Sotheby's Belgravia) $770

German commemorative snuff box, circa 1757, 8.3cm. wide.(Sotheby's) $3,095

Crailsheim faience cylindrical tankard, circa 1790, 17.5cm. high. (Christie's) $525

Rare Ansbach plate decorated with the Berliner Muster, 27cm. diam., circa 1767. (Sotheby's) $985

German cylindrical tankard, circa 1740, 20cm. high. (Christie's) $910

An Annaberg pear-shaped tankard with pewter foot rim and hinged cover, 17th century, 23.5cm. high. (Christie's) $3,780

Set of four Bing & Grondahl biscuit porcelain roundels, 14.5cm. diam., late 19th century. (Sotheby, King & Chasemore) $355

Hanau blue and white baluster vase, circa 1700, 29cm. high. (Christie's) $525

German faience double-gourd vase painted in harlequin pattern, circa 1730, 23.5cm. high. (Christie's) $1,195

Large late 19th century Sitzendorf centrepiece with pierced flared bowl, 54.5cm. high. (Sotheby's Belgravia) $1,260

An Erfurt cylindrical tankard painted with single flowers within quatrefoil panels, circa 1760, 26.5cm. high. (Christie's)$590

A Goldscheider terracotta wall mask of a young girl with flowers in her hair, 1930's. (Sotheby's Belgravia) $180

A Goldscheider terracotta wall mask of a young woman holding a Scottie dog, 1930's. (Sotheby's Belgravia) $190

A Goldscheider terracotta wall mask, the young woman with bright orange hair and lips, 1930's. (Sotheby's Belgravia) $190

GOSS

19th century cherub wall pocket impressed W. H. Goss. (Vernon's) $265

Goss porcelain model of St. Nicholas Chapel, Ilfracombe. (Christie's S. Kensington) $185

Round Tower, Windsor, by Goss, circa 1900, 5½in. diam., uncolored. (Sotheby's Belgravia) $475

Rare Goss model of 'The Hop Kiln, Headcorn, Kent'. (Sotheby's Belgravia) $2,095

Early 20th century Goss model of the Old Smithy, Gullane, 7.2cm. high. (Sotheby's Belgravia) $340

19th century Staffordshire tyg, by Goss. (Vernon's) $125

Model of Portman Lodge, Bournemouth, by Goss. (Christie's S. Kensington) $610

19th century Bideford mortar by Goss. (Vernon's) $16

Goss model of Isaac Walton's Cottage. (Christie's S. Kensington)$1,285

GUANGXU

Guangxu figure of Shou Lao in famille rose, 58cm. high. (Sotheby's Belgravia)$560

Guangxu period saucer dish in iron-red with two dragons, 34cm. diam. (Christie's) $3,095

One of a pair of Guangxu sang-de-boeuf flambe vases, 57cm. high. (Sotheby's Belgravia)$700

One of a pair of Guangxu famille verte cranes, 45cm. high. (Sotheby's Belgravia)　$1,310

Large Guangxu blue and white vase painted with mythological creatures, 88cm. high. (Sotheby's Belgravia) $6,320

Guangxu famille verte vase with flared cylindrical body, 45.5cm. high. (Sotheby's Belgravia) $725

HAN

Han dynasty censer in a shallow dish, chipped, 16cm. diam. (Christie's) $310

Large unglazed grey pottery tomb brick of the Han dynasty, 124cm. long. (Christie's) $4,045

Han/early Six Dynasties unglazed grey pottery oviform vase with short neck, •27.5cm. high. (Christie's) $170

Green glazed pottery well-head of the Han dynasty, 26cm. high. (Christie's)　$2,025

Unglazed grey pottery figure with banded headdress, Han dynasty, 11.5cm. high. (Christie's)　$620

Green glazed pottery baluster vase of the Han dynasty with fixed ring handles, 35.5cm. high. (Christie's) $950

A good Shoji Hamada stoneware bottle vase of rectangular section, 19.5cm. high, 1963. (Sotheby's Belgravia) $4,830

A good Shoji Hamada square dish, the press molded body covered overall in a thick Nuka glaze, 29.7cm. wide, circa 1963. (Sotheby's Belgravia) $2,520

A Shoji Hamada stoneware tea-bowl, the body covered in a pale green glaze, 13.5cm. diam., circa 1958. (Sotheby's Belgravia) $1,365

HOCHST

Hochst faience teapot with chinoiserie decoration. (Phillips) $4,390

One of a pair of Hochst teacups and saucers with landscape vignettes, circa 1765. (Christie's) $1,730

Hochst circular slop bowl, interior painted with flower sprays, circa 1765, 17.5cm. diam. (Christie's) $1,010

Hochst tureen and cover with pine cone knop, circa 1763-66, 20cm. wide. (Sotheby's) $3,860

A Hochst globular teapot and cover with pine cone finial, circa 1755, 18cm. wide. (Christie's) $1,300

Hochst group of three children, circa 1900, 18.5cm. high. (Sotheby's Belgravia)$530

Hochst jug and cover with ovoid body, circa 1770. (Sotheby's) $1,575

Rare Hochst barber's bowl with deep oval center, 29cm. wide, circa 1760. (Sotheby's) $1,695

Hochst coffee pot and cover with branch handle, 24cm. high, circa 1755-65. (Sotheby's) $1,175

133

IMARI

Early 18th century Chinese Imari circular barber's bowl with everted rim, 27.5cm. diam. (Christie's) $705

Rare late 17th century Imari incense burner in the shape of a beehive, 10.7cm. high.(Sotheby's) $730

One of a set of six Imari rice bowls with lids. (Clive Emson & Co.) $165

Imari vase and cover in deep underglaze blue, 42cm. high, circa 1700. (Sotheby, King & Chasemore) $1,770

One of a pair of Chinese plates, circa 1740, 23.5cm. diam.(Christie's) $1,880

One of a pair of late 19th century Imari vases and covers painted in underglaze blue, 41cm. high. (Sotheby's Belgravia) $935

Large late 19th century Japanese Imari vase painted and gilt, 81cm. high.(Sotheby's Belgravia) $2,340

Part of a sixty-one piece Japanese Imari porcelain service.(Sotheby's Belgravia) $1,030

Late 19th century Imari tokuri of square section with canted corners, 24.2cm. high. (Sotheby's) $780

Large 18th century Imari bowl and cover painted in underglaze blue, enamels and gold, 50.8cm. high. (Lawrence Fine Art) $1,760

Large 19th century Imari circular dish decorated in enamels, 61cm. diam. (Lawrence Fine Art) $530

Late 18th/early 19th century large Imari vase of double gourd form, 49cm. high. (Sotheby's) $1,950

Imari saucer dish painted with eagles devouring a crane, 71cm. wide. (Phillips) $4,830

17th century Imari baluster vase, 42cm. high.(Phillips) $4,370

Early 18th century Chinese Imari circular barber's bowl, 27.5cm. wide. (Christie's) $985

Large 19th century Imari bottle and stopper with short cylindrical neck, 36.8cm. high. (Sotheby's) $1,220

One of a pair of late 17th century Imari dishes with wide everted rims, 32.3cm. diam.(Sotheby's) $1,950

Early 18th century Chinese Imari oviform jar and cover, 23.5cm. high. (Christie's) $790

One of a pair of unusual Japanese Imari vases, circa 1900, 29.3cm. high. (Sotheby's Belgravia) $470

Unusual 18th century Imari garniture decorated in iron-red and green enamels. (Sotheby's) $855

Large late 19th century Imari baluster form vase with everted rim, 75cm. high. (Locke & England) $1,805

One of a pair of 18th century Imari ovoid jars and covers in underglaze blue, 53.3cm. high. (Lawrence Fine Art) $1,760

Large 19th century Imari circular dish decorated with a lady playing a flute, 61cm. diam.(Lawrence Fine Art) $395

One of a pair of Imari bottle vases, 15¾in. high. (Clive Emson & Co.) $770

135

Large Japanese Imari circular charger in underglaze blue, iron-red and gilt, 46cm. diam. (Henry Spencer & Sons) $515

One of a pair of Imari models of carp leaping above swirling waves, early 18th century, 24.5cm. high. (Christie's) $1,155

Mid 19th century Japanese Imari bowl with floral decorations in shaped cartouches, 8¾in. diam. (Robert W. Skinner Inc.) $1,700

One of a pair of early 18th century Imari pear-shaped urns, 40.7cm. high. (Christie's) $1,155

19th century Japanese Imari footed bowl, 19in. diam. (Robert W. Skinner Inc.) $800

One of a pair of Imari vases in excellent condition, 76cm. high. (Lalonde Bros. & Parham) $5,370

Early 18th century Imari baluster jar painted in typical colors, 30.8cm. high. (Christie's) $1,155

Fine pair of Japanese Imari ovoid vases and covers in underglaze blue, iron-red and gilt, 56cm. high. (Henry Spencer & Sons) $1,355

One of a pair of rare small late 17th century Imari figures of men wearing kimonos, 10.7cm. high. (Sotheby's) $585

19th century Japanese Imari charger decorated with five Oriental pheasants, 24¼in. diam. (Robert W. Skinner Inc.) $1,350

19th century Imari club-shaped dish with central design of floral arrangements, 11¾in. wide. (Robert W. Skinner Inc.) $175

Late 19th century Japanese Imari charger with exotic bird centre motif, 14¾in. diam. (Robert W. Skinner Inc.) $375

Mid 18th century Italian Faenza tureen and cover of ribbed oval form, 19cm. wide. (Sotheby's) $1,520

Milan shaped circular plate with chocolate rim, circa 1760, 27.5cm. diam.(Christie's) $1,795

Italian Pesaro creamware documentary dated oval two-handled tureen and cover, 1786, 29.5cm. wide. (Christie's) $3,585

Late 19th century Cantagalli majolica ewer, 71.5cm. high, on ebonised wood stand. (Sotheby's Belgravia) $550

Castelli wet-drug jar, damaged, circa 1680, 22.5cm. high. (Christie's) $620

A Gindri white figure of a nymph emblematic of summer, holding a sheaf of corn, circa 1760. (Christie's) $95

Late 15th century Florentine albarello decorated with blue and yellow, 29.5cm. high. (Sotheby's) $6,050

Faenza albarello decorated in ochre, green and blue, circa 1500, 15cm. high.(Sotheby's) $3,630

Florentine oak leaf jar with double strap handles, circa 1430-40, 21.5cm. high. (Sotheby's) $3,630

South Italian majolica dish, cracked and chipped, circa 1650, 41cm. diam. (Christie's) $2,150

Italian 18th century faience Commedia Dellarte figure, 16.5cm. high.(Sotheby's) $935

Italian Bassano oval tureen stand with molded shell border, circa 1760, 37cm. wide. (Christie's) $670

137

JAPANESE

Early 20th century Nippon porcelain blown out plaque of five horses heads. (Robert W. Skinner Inc.) $625

Japanese Kizan earthenware figure of a cat, mid 19th century, 12cm. wide. (Sotheby's Belgravia) $540

Fukagawa bowl with incurved rim, 15½in. high, circa 1900. (Sotheby's Belgravia) $1,020

Hexagonal baluster vase and domed cover, circa 1826-30, 48.5cm. high. (Christie's) $1,440

Late 19th century Fukagawa yellow-ground vase, 18in. high. (Sotheby's Belgravia) $1,500

One of a pair of Japanese earthenware vases with hexagonal bodies, 1870's, 25cm. high. (Sotheby's Belgravia) $1,495

Japanese porcelain figure of a geisha, 11in. high, in famille noire and polychrome enamels. (Lowery & Partners) $30

18th century Arita vase of pear shape, 30cm. high. (Sotheby's) $1,830

Mid 19th century Japanese earthenware vase, 36cm. high. (Sotheby's Belgravia) $375

Japanese porcelain plate decorated by Mortimer Menpes, circa 1876, 25cm. diam. (Sotheby's Belgravia) $195

19th century Japanese china, ginger jar and cover, 12¼in. high. (Vernon's) $65

Japanese porcelain plate decorated by Mortimer Menpes, circa 1876, 24.8cm. diam. (Sotheby's Belgravia) $120

Early 18th century Kakiemon hexa-foil dish painted with flowers, 10.8cm. wide. (Christie's) $1,000

Late 17th/early 18th century Kakiemon jardiniere, one of a pair, 31.5cm. diam. (Sotheby's) $6,100

18th century Kakiemon bowl of deep octagonal form with everted brown edged rim, 18.1cm. diam. (Sotheby's) $635

One of a pair of attractive late 17th/early 18th century Kakiemon dishes, restored, 18.3cm. diam. (Sotheby's) $585

Early 18th century Kakiemon small bowl painted in iron-red, 13.6cm. diam. (Christie's) $1,000

Late 17th century Kakiemon dish of shallow lobed form, 19cm. diam. (Sothey's) $1,585

Late 17th/early 18th century Kakiemon deep bowl with narrow rim, 15.7cm. diam. (Christie's) $2,380

Early 18th century Kakiemon bowl of octagonal form with everted rim, 11.8cm. diam. (Sotheby's) $535

Rare mid 17th century Kakiemon round dish with wide rim, 30cm. diam. (Sotheby's) $685

Mid 17th century attractive Kakiemon plate with wide everted rim, 31cm. diam. (Sotheby's) $4,880

Late 17th/early 18th century Kakiemon octagonal shallow bowl, 15.1cm. wide. (Christie's) $1,905

Rare late 17th/early 18th century Kakiemon bowl pierced with wide band of interlocking circles, 13.8cm. diam. (Sotheby's) $635

19th century Kangxi beehive-shaped brushpot, decorated in pale blue glaze, 8 cm. diam.(Sotheby's Belgravia) $235

Early Kangxi blue and white bowl painted with the eight Daoist Immortals, slightly chipped. (Christie's) $1,995

Kangxi blue and white bowl painted with scholars and ladies, 21cm. diam. (Christie's) $1,055

One of a pair of Kangxi blue and white baluster vases and domed covers, 46cm. high. (Christie's) $2,350

Kangxi green dragon dish colored in green enamel, 17.6cm. diam.(Sotheby's) $1,830

Blue and white baluster bottle vase, Kangxi, painted with four cranes in flight, 24.5cm. high. (Christie's) $445

Kangxi doucai vase painted with an audience scene, 36cm. high. (Christie's) $705

One of a pair of Kangxi ginger jars and domed covers, with ormolu mounts. (Lawrence Fine Art) $3,410

Kangxi famille verte tapering square vase, 47cm. high. (Christie's) $2,350

One of a pair of Kangxi famille verte saucer dishes, slightly chipped, 31cm. diam. (Christie's) $1,525

Kangxi mounted blue and white pear-shaped vase with silvered metal neck top, 30cm. high. (Christie's) $330

One of two Kangxi famille verte dishes painted with a cockerel and a pheasant, 23.5cm. diam. (Christie's) $895

140

Kangxi blue and white Monteith bowl with eight-toothed rim, 32.5cm. diam. (Christie's) $2,585

Large Kangxi blue and white fishbowl of deep 'U' form, 49cm. deep.(Sotheby, King & Chasemore) $6,345

Kangxi blue and white deep globular censer with flaring neck, 24cm. diam. (Christie's) $660

Kangxi famille verte tapering square vase, 48cm. high. (Christie's) $1,175

One of a pair of Kangxi famille verte teabowls and saucers with wood stands. (Sotheby's) $390

Kangxi famille verte figure of an immortal, 10cm. high. (Christie's) $800

Early Kangxi blue and white oviform jar, 26.5cm. high.(Christie's) $1,055

Late Kangxi pencilled blue and white jardiniere of barrel shape, 16.5cm. high. (Sotheby's) $1,170

Kangxi famille rose jardiniere painted with panels of fishermen and children playing, 24cm. wide. (Sotheby's Belgravia) $470

One of a pair of Kangxi blue and white vases with wood stands, 34cm. high. (Sotheby, King & Chasemore) $1,050

One of a pair of large blue and white Kangxi dishes, 47.5cm. diam. (Christie's) $3,290

Kangxi blue and white brush pot painted in bright cobalt blue, 15cm. high. (Grays Antique Mews)$2,025

141

KINKOZAN

Unusual Kinkozan earthenware vase with gourd body, circa 1900, 28.5cm. high. (Sotheby's Belgravia) $1,335

Kinkozan earthenware teapot and cover, painted and gilt, circa 1900, 12.5cm. high. (Sotheby's Belgravia) $205

Kinkozan earthenware vase with discus body and tall flared neck, circa 1900, 28.5cm. high. (Sotheby's Belgravia) $1,605

KOREAN

Korean black pottery broad globular jar of the Silla dynasty, 17.5cm. diam. (Christie's) $950

Korean grey pottery baluster jar of the Silla dynasty, in fitted box, 16.5cm. wide. (Christie's) $625

13th/14th century Korean inlaid celadon bowl inset in black and white, 20cm. diam. (Christie's) $880

KUTANI

One of a pair of Kutani plates with foliate borders, circa 1900, 36.5cm. diam. (Sotheby's Belgravia) $280

Unusual 19th century Kutani style cricket box and cover, 14.4cm. wide.(Sotheby's) $535

Late 17th century Ko-Kutani style saucer of multi-lobed form, 15.2cm. diam. (Sotheby's) $855

Late 17th/early 18th century rare Ko-Kutani style Tokuri with tapering neck, 20.4cm. high. (Sotheby's) $5,850

Rare late 17th century Ko-Kutani bottle, neck slightly damaged, 15.8cm. high. (Sotheby's) $780

Kutani figure of an exotic bird on a tree stump, circa 1900, 28.5cm. high. (Sotheby's Belgravia) $155

Lambeth delft blue and white ovi-form drug jar, named, circa 1720, 17.5cm. high. (Christie's) $375

Lambeth delft polychrome Royalist plate, circa 1714, chipped, 21.5cm. diam. (Christie's) $3,395

Lambeth delft blue and white wet-drug jar, named, circa 1720, 18cm. high. (Christie's) $470

LEACH

Early Bernard Leach stoneware vase with spherical body and swollen rim, circa 1930, 25.5cm. high.(Sotheby's Belgravia) $1,755

Important Bernard Leach cut-sided stoneware bowl, covered in olive celadon glaze, circa 1960, 31.5cm. diam. (Sotehby's Belgravia) $5,615

Bernard Leach stoneware bottle-vase of square section, circa 1963, 37cm. high. (Sotheby's Belgravia) $3,745

Bernard Leach stoneware teapot and cover, 1960's, 19.3cm. high, slightly chipped. (Sotheby's Belgravia) $350

Unusual Bernard Leach earthenware tile of circular section, 14cm. diam., circa 1920-30. (Sotheby's Belgravia) $185

Bernard Leach stoneware teapot and cover with cane handle, 19cm. wide. (Christie's) $320

Bernard Leach stoneware bottle vase of rectangular section, circa 1965, 20.3cm. high. (Sotheby's Belgravia) $1,175

Late Bernard Leach stoneware jug with thick black glaze, 27.4cm. high. (Christie's) $360

Bernard Leach vase decorated in wax-resist, 7cm. high, circa 1960. (Sotheby's Belgravia) $260

LEEDS

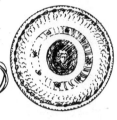

A Leeds creamware ship decorated plate, circa 1800-1820, 9¾in. diam. (Christie's) $305

Partial Leeds Pottery teaset, circa 1790. (Robert W. Skinner Inc.) $175

A Leeds plate painted in sepia with a portrait of the Duke of Marlborough, 9¾in. diam., circa 1780. (Sotheby's) $755

LIVERPOOL

Liverpool blue and white bowl with indented rim, circa 1755, 16.5cm. diam. (Christie's) $280

Liverpool blue and white flared teabowl and saucer, circa 1760. (Christie's) $470

Liverpool blue and white bowl, William Ball's factory, circa 1760, 14.5cm. diam. (Christie's) $305

Liverpool blue and white baluster mask-jug printed with flowers, circa 1780, 14cm. high. (Christie's) $185

Liverpool figure of La Nourrice, restored, circa 1755-60, 15cm. high. (Christie's) $1,215

One of a pair of rare Liverpool delft wall pockets, circa 1760, 21cm. long. (Sotheby's) $710

Liverpool blue and white fluted sauceboat, William Ball's factory, circa 1760. (Christie's) $515

Late 18th century Liverpool creamware bowl, printed with a ship, 33cm. diam. (Phillips) $2,300

Liverpool blue and white bowl, Philip Christian's factory, circa 1765, 19.5cm. diam. (Christie's) $200

144

Late 17th century rare 'oak-leaf' charger, probably London, 13½in. wide. (Sotheby's) $475

London delftware white fuddling cup, circa 1690, 8cm. high. (Christie's) $1,195

Rare London Royal portrait 'blue-dash' charger, late 17th century, 33cm. diam. (Sotheby's) $7,290

LONGTON HALL

Longton Hall oval leaf-molded dish painted with an insect and a flower-spray, circa 1755, 30.5cm. wide. (Christie's) $700

Longton Hall cabbage-leaf molded bowl with painted centre, 21.5cm. diam., circa 1755. (Christie's) $2,040

Longton Hall teabowl and saucer painted with flowers and branch, circa 1755. (Christie's)$515

LOWESTOFT

Lowestoft blue and white spirally molded butterboat, circa 1785, 10cm. wide. (Christie's)$420

Jumbo punch-pot made by the Lowestoft factory, about 1770-75, 21cm. high. (Sotheby's) $900

Lowestoft oval blue and white butterboat, circa 1775, 11cm. wide. (Christie's) $515

Lowestoft creamboat of ewer shape, painted in underglaze blue, circa 1775, 10cm. wide. (Sotheby's) $375

Lowestoft blue and white baluster jug and cover, finial restored, circa 1775, 23.5cm. high. (Christie's) $395

Lowestoft creamboat of Chelsea ewer type, circa 1775, 10cm. wide. (Sotheby's) $425

LUDWIGSBURG

Ludwigsburg plate with gilt border to rim, circa 1770, 26.5cm. diam. (Sotheby's) $1,975

Rare Ludwigsburg teapot and cover supported on three twig feet, 13cm. high, circa 1770. (Sotheby's) $3,870

Ludwigsburg circular shallow dish painted with two finches, 20.5cm. diam. (Christie's) $625

LUSTRE

Pilkington's lustre jar and cover designed by Gordon Forsyth, 14.5cm. high. (Christie's) $375

Moore & Co. Sunderland lustre bowl, circa 1850, 12¾in. diam. (Sotheby's Belgravia) $260

Royal Lancastrian globular lustre vase, dated 1925, 18.5cm. high. (Christie's) $305

A Pilkington's Royal Lancastrian vase painted by Gordon M. Forsyth, in gold lustre, 22.3cm. high, circa 1914. (Sotheby's Belgravia) $420

A Pilkington's Royal Lancastrian loving cup decorated by William S. Mycock, 27cm. high, circa 1914. (Sotheby's Belgravia) $800

Large late 18th century lustre jug with polychrome decoration, 27cm. high. (May Whetter & Grose) $250

MARSEILLES

Marseilles plate, probably Robert, circa 1765, 25cm. diam.(Christie's) $765

One of a pair of Marseilles bouquetiers and covers, circa 1760-70, 28.5cm. high. (Sotheby's) $2,350

One of a pair of Marseilles plates, circa 1770, 24cm. diam. (Christie's) $1,195

146

One of a pair of amusing Martin Brothers jardinieres, each incised with mischievous monkeys, 27.5cm. high, dated 7-1894.(Sotheby's Belgravia) $1,050

An unusual Martin Brothers gourd vase with sharply defined ribbing, 44cm. high, dated 1910. (Sotheby's Belgravia) $355

Martin Brothers chamber candlestick incised with comical fish and sea creatures, 11cm. high, dated 6-1899. (Sotheby's Belgravia) $460

One of a pair of unusual Martinware vases, 26.5cm. high, 6-1904. (Sotheby's Belgravia) $585

A Martin Brothers spoon warmer modelled as an endearing grotesque, squatting on all fours, 13cm. high, dated 1878. (Sotheby's Belgravia) $1,365

Martin Brothers stoneware vase with elongated ovoid body, 35.5cm. high, dated 4–1887. (Sotheby's Belgravia)$665

A Martin Brothers miniature vase incised in low relief with fish and eels, 8cm. high, circa 1900. (Sotheby's Belgravia)$380

Rare electroplate-mounted Martin Brothers ewer, 29.2cm. high, dated 14.10.79. (Sotheby's Belgravia) $470

A Martin Brothers stoneware vase incised with ferocious winged grotesques, 21.4cm. high, dated 3-1903. (Sotheby's Belgravia) $1,430

A Martin Brothers bird standing with his head endearingly cocked to one side, 28.5cm. high, dated 20-7-1905. (Sotheby's Belgravia) $2,100

An unusual Martin Brothers vase incised with fantastic birds, 23.5cm. high, dated 9-1892. (Sotheby's Belgravia) $1,470

A large and rare Martin Brothers bird with detachable head, 47cm. high, dated 11-1895.(Sotheby's Belgravia) $12,600

MARTINWARE

Martin Brothers face jug modelled on both sides, 17.6cm. high. (Christie's) $595

Late Martin Brothers stoneware 'Grotesque' toothpick-holder, 14cm. wide, dated '13-37. (Sotheby's Belgravia) $380

Martinware vase with painted incised design of birds and flowers, dated 1889, 22.5cm. high. (Geering & Colyer) $525

Martin Brothers stoneware jug with ribbed rim, 20.7cm. high, dated 19.6.85. (Sotheby's Belgravia) $190

Martin Brothers two-handled globular vase with everted rim, 29.2cm. high, dated 10-1911. (Christie's) $1,270

Martin Brothers stoneware tankard with tapering body, 21.8cm. high, dated 31.11.79. (Sotheby's Belgravia) $140

Martin Brothers stoneware vase with ovoid body, dated 1-1896, 34cm. high. (Sotheby's Belgravia) $705

Martin Brothers stoneware imp musician playing a banjo, 10.2cm. high, dated 1-1910, on wooden base. (Sotheby's Belgravia) $350

Martinware oviform vase decorated with scrolling foliage, 24.5cm. high, 6-1898. (Christie's) $380

Martinware jug with incised design of birds, signed and dated 1885, 22.5cm. high. (Geering & Colyer) $395

Martin Brothers saltglazed stoneware double-handled loving cup, circa 1890, 15cm. high. (Sotheby, King & Chasemore) $575

Martinware slender vase with incised designs of dragons, signed and dated 1901, 28cm. high. (Geering & Colyer) $310

Bottger Meissen red stone-ware coffee pot, circa 1715, 14.5cm. high. (Phillips) $6,900

Pair of late 19th century Meissen candelabra, 22.5cm. high. (Sotheby's Belgravia) $1,445

Mid 18th century Meissen bowl, cover and stand, 17.5cm. diam. stand. (Sotheby's) $1,355

One of a pair of mid 18th century Meissen groups of two putti, 18cm. high. (Sotheby's) $1,640

One of a pair of Meissen Marcolini plates with pierced borders, circa 1790, 24cm. diam. (Christie's) $2,160

One of a pair of late Meissen groups of elephants, 38cm. high, damaged. (Christie's) $2,455

Meissen figure of a thrush with incised plumage, circa 1745, 16cm. high. (Christie's) $2,280

Pair of late 19th century Meissen porcelain groups of children, 17.7cm. high. (Parsons, Welch & Cowell) $1,520

One of a pair of 20th century Meissen figures of magpies, 44.5cm. high. (Sotheby's Belgravia) $615

Meissen blue and white plate from the Kinder a la Raphael series, circa 1765, 23.5cm. diam. (Christie's) $575

One of a pair of late Meissen vases and covers applied with cherubs and flowers, 61cm. high. (Phillips) $4,190

One of a pair of 19th century Meissen pierced border plates, 25cm. diam. (Grays Antique Market) $835

149

Late Meissen circular ecuelle, cover and stand encrusted with flowers, 23.5cm. diam. (Christie's) $840

Part of a Meissen decorated dessert service, plates 23.8cm. diam. (Sotheby's Belgravia) $950

Late 19th century Meissen outside-decorated oval tray, 44cm. wide. (Sotheby's Belgravia) $345

One of a pair of mid 19th century Meissen pot-pourri vases and covers, 29cm. high. (Sotheby's Belgravia) $2,875

Late 19th century Meissen group of rustic children, 18cm. high.(Sotheby's Belgravia) $1,090

One of a pair of Meissen red dragon decorated baluster vases with silvered mounts, 36cm. high. (C. G. Sloan & Co. Inc.) $600

Meissen figure of 'Te Les Accouple modelled as a Cupid, circa 1900, 12.8cm. high. (Sotheby's Belgravia) $400

Late 19th century Meissen rectangular plaque, framed, 35 x 41cm. (Sotheby's Belgravia) $415

Mid 19th century Meissen chocolate pot and cover, 13.4cm. high. (Sotheby's Belgravia) $590

Meissen chinoiserie group modelled as an Oriental gentleman and child, 17cm. high, 1910. (Sotheby's Belgravia) $665

Late 19th century Meissen group of a proposal, 25.5cm. high. (Sotheby's Belgravia) $1,210

Late 19th century Meissen table bell, 10cm. high, with pierced angular handle. (Sotheby's Belgravia) $780

Meissen figure of a seated cat, slightly chipped, circa 1750, 4cm. high. (Christie's) $385

Meissen Kakiemon two-handled, double-lipped sauceboat with scroll handles, circa 1735, 25cm. wide. (Christie's) $525

One of a set of twelve Meissen 'onion pattern' cream jugs, circa 1900, 6.2cm. high. (Sotheby's Belgravia) $460

One of two Meissen vases with gilt fluted circular foot, circa 1907, 26.5cm. high.(Sotheby's Belgravia) $1,260

Part of a seventeen-piece Meissen coffee service painted with flowers. (Sotheby's Belgravia) $1,815

One of a pair of late 19th century Meissen vases each applied with foliate handles, 25.5cm. high. (Sotheby's Belgravia) $1,135

Unusual Meissen 'Bottger Steineug' candlestick in Art Deco taste, 25.5cm. wide, circa 1930.(Sotheby's Belgravia) $390

Meissen oval two-handled soup tureen and cover, circa 1740, 34cm. wide, slightly repaired. (Christie's) $2,160

Meissen clock case with enamelled dial, circa 1880, 28.5cm. wide. (Sotheby's Belgravia)$2,055

Late 19th century Meissen outside decorated musical group, 37cm. high. (Sotheby's Belgravia) $1,380

Mid 19th century Meissen group of 'Lessons in Love', 29cm. high. (Sotheby's Belgravia) $2,115

Late 19th century Meissen group of lovers. (Sotheby's Belgravia) $505

Late 19th century Meissen basket of oval shape, sides pierced with basket weave, 33cm. wide. (Sotheby's Belgravia)$675

Part of a twenty-four piece Meissen 'butterfly pattern' service, circa 1900. (Sotheby's Belgravia) $2,770

Mid 19th century Meissen yellow-ground gilt bronze mounted ink-stand, 31cm. wide. (Sotheby's Belgravia) $675

Late 19th century Meissen figure of a parrot, 32cm. high. (Sotheby's Belgravia) $725

Late 19th century garniture of three Meissen fruit stands, 41.5 and 30cm. high. (Sotheby's Belgravia) $3,975

One of a pair of Meissen figures of hares, circa 1750, 16cm. high. (Christie's) $6,720

One of a pair of late 19th century Meissen candle-sticks, 13.5cm. high. (Sotheby's Belgravia) $390

Late 19th century pair of Meissen groups of Peace and War, 21cm. and 19cm. high. (Sotheby, King & Chasemore) $945

Meissen cylindrical needle case painted with Watteau figures, circa 1760, 10cm. high. (Christie's) $1,800

Early 20th century Meissen group of lovers at a spinet, 15.5cm. wide. (Sotheby's Belgravia)$770

Large early 20th century Meissen out-side-decorated group of a shepherd and his sheep, 40cm. high.(Sotheby's Belgravia) $580

Late 19th century Meissen group of three dogs, 14cm. high, slightly chipped. (Sotheby's Belgravia) $1,060

One from a set of six late 19th century Meissen 'onion pattern' plates, 23.5 and 20cm. diam. (Sotheby's Belgravia)$770

Two late 19th century Meissen putti groups, 12 and 12.7cm. high. (Sotheby's Belgravia) $1,885

Meissen hot water jug and cover with pear-shaped body, 18cm. high, circa 1900. (Sotheby's Belgravia) $435

Late 19th century blue and white Meissen centrepiece, 57cm. high. (Sotheby's Belgravia) $3,615

Rare mid 19th century Meissen solitaire of nine pieces. (Sotheby's Belgravia) $1,010

Mid 19th century Meissen ewer emblematic of Air, 66cm. high. (Sotheby's Belgravia) $1,085

Mid 19th century Meissen ewer, 62.5cm. high. (Sotheby's Belgravia) $1,205

Pair of late 19th century Meissen groups of studious putti, 18.5 and 21cm. high. (Sotheby's Belgravia) $965

Late 19th century Meissen candelabra clockcase and stand, 56cm. high.(Sotheby's Belgravia) $2,170

Late 19th century Meissen group emblematic of 'The Arts', 20.3cm. high. (Sotheby's Belgravia) $580

Late 19th century Meissen ten-piece tete-a-tete set. (Sotheby's Belgravia) $965

One from a set of five early 20th century Meissen dessert plates, 23.8cm. diam. (Sotheby's Belgravia) $1,735

MEISSEN

Large Meissen campana-shaped vase with classical scene, late 19th century. (Henry Spencer & Sons) $1,380

Mid late 19th century Meissen paperweight modelled as a dog, 19.2cm. long.(Sotheby's Belgravia) $290

Early Meissen dish of deep hexa-foil form, 15cm. diam., circa 1730-35. (Sotheby's) $1,520

Late Meissen tureen and cover modelled as a swan, 38cm. wide. (Christie's) $2,565

Meissen sweetmeat dish on tall stand, modelled by J. J. Kandler, circa 1745, 29.5cm. high. (Christie's)$3,360

Late 19th century Meissen figure group, 15in. high. (Vernon's) $1,250

One of two late Meissen baluster vases molded with fruit and flowers, 36.5 and 34.5cm. high.(Christie's) $1,630

A pair of Meissen midnight-blue-ground jars and covers, circa 1875, 24.8cm. high. (Sotheby's Belgravia) $1,305

Meissen figure of a maiden, circa 1900, 44.5cm. high.(Sotheby's Belgravia) $900

Meissen blue and white plate from the Kinder a la Raphael series, circa 1765, 23.5cm. diam. (Christie's) $910

Two Meissen figures of a shoemaker and his companion, 21cm. high, circa 1745. (Phillips) $5,520

One of a pair of Meissen Marcolini plates with pierced borders, circa 1790, 24cm. diam. (Christie's) $2,400

Mettlach pottery wall plaque enamelled and incised, 42.5cm. diam. (Burrows & Day) $100

One of a pair of Mettlach vases decorated with scenes of the four seasons, signed C. Warth, 35cm. high. (Alfie's Antique Market) $1,070

A Mettlach plate depicting a girl with long hair, 9¼in. diam., circa 1900. (Robert W. Skinner Inc.) $275

Mettlach pottery stein, engraved and polychrome glazed scene of 'King Hops on Parade', 9in. high, circa 1900. (Robert W. Skinner Inc.) $500

Mettlach plaque decorated after J. Stahl, circa 1900, 46.8cm. diam. (Sotheby's Belgravia) $820

Late 19th century Mettlach stein, signed H. Schlitt, 30cm. high. (Robert W. Skinner Inc.) $625

Late 19th century Mettlach stein with molded foot, 19.5cm. high. (Robert W. Skinner Inc.) $700

Two Mettlach steins of tapering cylindrical form, circa 1910, 21 and 25cm. high. (Sotheby's Belgravia) $755

Large Mettlach stoneware vase with ovoid body, circa 1900, 45cm. high. (Sotheby's Belgravia) $865

One of a pair of Mettlach ewers decorated with hunting scenes, circa 1910, 43cm. high.(Sotheby's Belgravia) $1,375

Mettlach stein decorated with William Tell and his son, circa 1910, 26.5cm. high. (Sotheby's Belgravia) $805

Large silver-mounted Mettlach stoneware jug, 47.5cm. high. (Sotheby's Belgravia)$855

Late Ming dynasty copper gilt censer, 13.3cm. wide, incised mark Hu Wen-ming Zhi. (Sotheby's) $415

16th/early 17th century Ming celadon censer and cover, modelled as a seated duck, 20cm. high. (Christie's) $1,880

16th/17th century Ming celadon tripod jardiniere, cracked, 28.5cm. diam. (Christie's) $940

Unusual late Ming jar, Wanli, with shouldered body, 12.6cm. high. (Sotheby's) $195

Late Ming blue and white saucer dish, late 16th/early 17th century, 17in. diam. (Christie's) $895

Rare late Ming dynasty enamelled Fujian vase of baluster shape, 15cm. high. (Sotheby's) $465

Late Ming blue and white baluster vase and shallow domed cover, circa 1630, 47cm. high. (Christie's) $2,585

Late Ming blue and white oviform jar, repaired, Wanli, 40.5cm. high. (Christie's) $750

Large late Ming blue and white oviform jar, slightly damaged, Wanli, 55cm. high. (Christie's) $4,230

Chia Ching period Ming blue and white bottle of pear shape, 30.2cm. high. (Sotheby's) $5,125

Provincial Ming stoneware pot with four lugs, 10in. high. (Vernon's) $315

Late 16th/early 17th century blue and white Ming square bottle, 26cm. high. (Christie's) $1,055

One of a pair of Minton 'cloisonne' moonflasks, dated for 1870, 19.7cm. high.(Sotheby's Belgravia) $610

Good Minton solitaire set, date code for 1862. (Sotheby's Belgravia) $380

Unusual Minton 'cloisonne' inkstand with central penholder, 1868, 17cm. high. (Sotheby's Belgravia) $490

One of two Minton 'cloisonne' vases, 16cm. high, dated for 1868. (Sotheby's Belgravia) $635

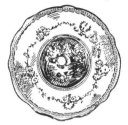

One of two Minton apple-green-ground dessert plates, circa 1910, 9in. diam. (Sotheby's Belgravia) $500

One of a pair of Minton majolica garden seats, dated for 1861, 46.2cm. high.(Sotheby's Belgravia) $1,585

Impressive Minton pate-sur-pate vase decorated by Alboine Birks, 1891, 65cm. high. (Sotheby's Belgravia) $4,635

One of a pair of Minton candlestick figures of a gardener and his companion, 23cm. high. (Christie's) $1,340

Minton Oriental vase on stepped brown and gilt base, 31cm. high, dated 1869. (Sotheby's Belgravia) $465

Minton 'cloisonne' vase, body of intersecting rings, 20.5cm. high, dated for 1869. (Sotheby's Belgravia) $220

One of a set of five Minton art pottery studio plaques, dated for 1872-74, 50.8cm. wide. (Sotheby's Belgravia) $5,610

Part of a fifty-one-piece Minton 'Japonaise' porcelain tea service, circa 1870-80. (Sotheby, King & Chasemore) $520

157

MOORCROFT

Large Moorcroft saltglaze vase, circa 1925, 35.8cm. high. (Sotheby's Belgravia)$800

Moorcroft bowl with interior decorated with 'Moonlit Blue' palette, circa 1925, 26øm. diam. (Sotheby's Belgravia) $305

Moorcroft 'Hazeldene' vase decorated in Eventide palette, circa 1925, 21cm. high. (Sotheby's Belgravia) $905

Moorcroft Macintyre Florianware vase, circa 1903, 20.3cm. high. (Sotheby's Belgravia)$590

Moorcroft vase with flared body, dated 1914, 20.3cm. high. (Sotheby's Belgravia) $305

One of a pair of unusual Moorcroft Macintyre Florianware vases, 27.5cm. high, circa 1900. (Sotheby's Belgravia) $475

Unusual and early Moorcroft Florian vase, circa 1898, 30.5cm. high. (Sotheby's Belgravia) $925

One of a pair of large Moorcroft vases, dated 1918, 38cm. high. (Sotheby's Belgravia) $905

Moorcroft Macintyre Florian vase, circa 1903, 23cm. high. (Sotheby's Belgravia) $290

Moorcroft Macintyre 'Hesperian-ware' vase with pear-shaped body, circa 1902, 43cm. high. (Sotheby's Belgravia) $950

Moorcroft vase with flared cylindrical body, 13cm. high, circa 1921-30. (Sotheby's Belgravia) $350

Moorcroft Macintyre Florianware bottle-vase, circa 1898, 23cm. high. (Sotheby's Belgravia) $715

MOORCROFT

One of a pair of Moorcroft Macintyre Florianware bonbonnieres, each slip trailed with stylised dahlias, 19cm. high, circa 1903. (Sotheby's Belgravia) $630

A good Moorcroft Macintyre Florianware tyg, slip trailed with spiralling freesia sprays, 25.3cm. high, circa 1898. (Sotheby's Belgravia) $715

Moorcroft Macintyre Florianware bottle-vase, circa 1898, 26cm. high. (Sotheby's Belgravia) $570

MORTLAKE

A Mortlake saltglazed stoneware tankard with a panel showing Hogarth's 'Midnight Modern Conversation', late 18th century, 8¼in. tall. (Sotheby's) $165

A Mortlake stoneware goblet applied on either side with a rectangular panel, circa 1800, 7in. high. (Sotheby's) $240

A Mortlake stoneware jug with hinged silver cover by Wm. Key, London, circa 1790, 9in. high. (Sotheby's) $400

NANTGARW

Nantgarw London-decorated plate with lobed rim, circa 1820, 25cm. diam. (Christie's) $1,440

Nantgarw slop bowl of flared circular shape, circa 1817-22, 15cm. wide. (Sotheby's) $215

Nantgarw London-decorated plate painted with a flower spray, circa 1817-22, 22.5cm. diam. (Sotheby's) $910

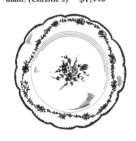

Nantgarw plate painted with flowers, circa 1820, 23.5cm. diam.(Christie's) $960

Nantgarw lobed oval dish from the Macintosh service, circa 1820, 29.5cm. wide. (Christie's) $2,400

One of a pair of Nantgarw London-decorated plates with shaped gilt dentil rims, circa 1820, 25cm. diam. (Christie's)$2,760

159

NAPLES

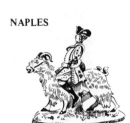

Naples figure of Count Bruhl's tailor, circa 1900, 24cm. high. (Sotheby's Belgravia) $380

Part of a late 19th century Naples coffee set of seventeen pieces, pot 20.3cm. high. (Sotheby's Belgravia) $435

19th century Naples white figure of a cherub riding on a dolphin, 10¾in. high. (Vernon's) $135

Naples white glazed group of Leda, the Swan and three Graces, 42.5cm. high. (Burrows and Day) $110

Documentary Naples figure of a young man in the white, 16cm. high, 1786-1815. (Sotheby's) $750

Late 19th century Schwarza Naples tankard and cover, 30cm. high. (Sotheby's Belgravia) $290

NEWHALL

Newhall jug decorated with sprigs of flowers, 4½in. high. (Vernon's) $105

Part of a Newhall pale blue part dessert service printed with fruit, circa 1815. (Christie's) $1,340

Teapot from a Newhall bone china part tea and coffee service, circa 1815. (Christie's) $535

NYMPHENBURG

Nymphenburg figure of a parrot, circa 1765, 15.5cm. high, slightly chipped. (Christie's) $4,080

Nymphenburg porcelain chinoiserie group, after Bustelli, circa 1765. (Christie's) $1,840

A Nymphenburg figure of a condor modelled by Dominicus Auliczek, circa 1765, 16.5cm. high. (Christie's) $5,460

160

One of two early 19th century tureens and covers, 32.5cm. long. (Christie's) $3,525

19th century Oriental teapot decorated in blue, rust and gilt, 15.5cm. wide. (Vernon's) $135

One of a pair of mid 19th century deep green-glazed figures of seated mythical beasts, 16.5cm. long. (Christie's) $895

Blue and white pear-shaped jug with loop handle, early 18th century, with silver mounts and hinged cover, 22cm. high. (Christie's) $1,645

Small late 17th/early century bowl of quatre-lobed shape, 13.8cm. diam. (Sotheby's) $685

One of two 17th/18th century gilt-metal-mounted deep blue-glazed pear-shaped ewers, 22cm. high. (Christie's) $985

Large Oriental baluster vase, slightly damaged. (Raymond Inman) $1,005

One of a pair of unusual 19th century porcelain stands, 24cm. high. (Sotheby's) $975

Kangxi blue and white ginger jar. (Grays Antique Mews) $405

Kangxi blue and white double baluster vase and domed cover painted with peony heads, 50.5cm. high. (Christie's) $1,650

Late 18th century turquoise-green-glazed tureen and cover modelled as a crab, 27cm. wide, slightly chipped. (Christie's) $2,820

18th/19th century blue and white vase of Ming design, 19in. high. (Bracketts) $1,260

One of a pair of unusual Paris vases, circa 1850, 33.8cm. high. (Sotheby's Belgravia) $575

Pair of Paris biscuit porcelain groups, colored and gilt decorated, 24cm. high, circa 1870. (Sotheby's Belgravia) $625

Late 19th century gilt metal mounted Paris rose pompadour-ground dish, 31cm. wide. (Sotheby's Belgravia) $215

One of a pair of Paris pot pourri jars and covers of square section, circa 1830, 22.3cm. high. (Sotheby's Belgravia) $1,375

Part of a Paris 'Angouleme sprig' pattern composite part service, circa 1800, dish 37.8cm. wide. (Sotheby's Belgravia) $1,045

Paris 'mermaid' salt with small chip, circa 1840, 19cm. high. (Sotheby's Belgravia) $170

One of a pair of Paris 19th century porcelain jardinieres, 37.5cm. diam. (Woolley & Wallis) $1,275

A pair of Paris white biscuit groups, circa 1800, 30cm. high. (Christie's) $840

One of a pair of Paris cornucopia vases of octagonal section, early 19th century, 31.7cm. high. (Lawrence Fine Art) $640

One of a pair of mid 19th century Paris vases with gilt feet and rims, 43cm. high. (Sotheby's Belgravia) $725

Paris porcelain tea service in Empire style. (Christie's) $3,260

One of a pair of late 19th century Paris vases and stands, 82.5cm. high. (Sotheby's Belgravia) $1,425

Early 19th century Paris saucer dish decorated with a map, 18cm. diam. (Sotheby's) $470

Part of a Paris pale yellow-ground part coffee service painted with scenes of the Seasons. (Christie's) $3,570

One of a pair of late 18th/early 19th century Paris vases, 19cm. high. (Sotheby's) $470

DU PAQUIER

Du Paquier trembleuse cup, cover and stand, circa 1720-25, 11cm. high. (Sotheby's) $4,110

Rare Du Paquier jug of ovoid shape and with scroll handle, circa 1825-35, 27.5cm. high. (Sotheby's) $7,260

Rare Du Paquier trembleuse saucer with pierced scrolled gallery, circa 1725. (Christie's) $2,880

PETIT, JACOB

One of a pair of Jacob Petit scent flasks and stoppers, circa 1840, 27cm. high. (Sotheby's Belgravia) $945

Pair of Jacob Petit vases, circa 1840, 21.6cm. high. (Sotheby's Belgravia) $580

One of a pair of Jacob Petit vases, circa 1840, 26.5cm. high. (Sotheby's Belgravia)$600

PLAUE

Late 17th century Plaue centre-piece with pierced flared bowl, 30.5cm. high. (Sotheby's Belgravia) $670

Pair of late 19th century Plaue fruit stands, 35cm. high. (Sotheby's Belgravia)$830

Late 19th century Plaue centre-piece with pierced bowl, 40.5cm. high. (Sotheby's Belgravia) $645

163

Plymouth porcelain sauceboat of silver shape decorated in the Chinese manner, 7in. long. (Taylor Lane & Creber)$900

Rare Plymouth figure of Autumn with shell and scroll molded base, circa 1770, 14cm. high. (Sotheby's) $775

Plymouth mug with waisted bell-shaped body and ribbed handle, circa 1770, 16cm. high. (Sotheby's) $1,505

POT LIDS

The Rose Garden, a rare small lid with manufacturer's inscription for G. T. Jerram. (Sotheby's Belgravia) $685

The Garden Terrace, a medium-small lid with raised floral and beehive border. (Sotheby's Belgravia) $635

A False Move, an unusual large pot lid in good condition. (Sotheby's Belgravia) $390

Bear Hunting, a small pot lid with retailer's inscription for Ross & Sons, in good condition.(Sotheby's Belgravia) $830

Polar Bears, a small lid with additional gilt line border. (Sotheby's Belgravia) $685

Arctic Expedition, small lid with double line border, rim grazed. (Sotheby's Belgravia)$1,220

Rare large lid with a clear print of Belle Vue Tavern (with Tatnell's cart). (Sotheby's Belgravia) $1,510

Pegwell Bay, for S. Banger, Shrimp Sauce Manufacturer, rare large pot lid with clear print. (Sotheby's Belgravia)$1,415

Pot lid by Mayer Bros., circa 1850, 12.7cm. diam. (Sotheby's) $6,480

One of a pair of late 19th century Potschappel pot pourri vases and covers, 15cm. high. (Sotheby's Belgravia) $240

One of a pair of late 19th century Potschappel wall brackets, 30cm. high. (Sotheby's Belgravia) $435

One of a pair of late 19th century Carl Thieme Potschappel vases and covers, 35cm. high. (Sotheby's Belgravia) $455

Part of a set of twelve members of a late 19th century Potschappel monkey band, 13 to 16.5cm. high. (Sotheby's Belgravia) $875

PRATTWARE

A Prattware flask with a portrait of Admiral Howe, 5½in. high, circa 1795. (Sotheby's)$275

Late 18th/early 19th century Pratt type cow creamer and cover, 14cm. high. (Sotheby's) $380

Unusual small Prattware Toby jug, late 18th/early 19th century, 17cm. high. (Sotheby's) $910

Prattware figure of 'The Lost Sheep', circa 1780-90, 21cm. high. (Sotheby's) $335

Late 18th century Prattware group of 'The Babes in the Wood'. (Sotheby, King & Chasemore) $165

Prattware Toby jug with blue coat and yellow breeches, circa 1780-90, 24.5cm. high. (Sotheby's) $480

Early Qianlong famille rose punchbowl slightly chipped, 39cm. diam. (Christie's) $2,820

Qianlong famille rose violin-shaped bidet painted with exotic butterflies, 53cm. wide. (Christie's) $2,802

Qianlong blue and white tureen and cover, 34cm. wide. (Sotheby, King & Chasemore) $805

Early Qianlong famille rose globular bottle vase with slender neck, 28cm. high. (Christie's) $880

One of a pair of Qianlong famille rose armorial tureens, covers and stands with paw feet, 40cm. wide. (Christie's) $23,500

Qianlong blue and white double gourd vase with wood stand, 28.8cm. high. (Sotheby's) $4,150

Qianlong famille rose armorial pear-shaped jug and cover, circa 1765, 14cm. high. (Christie's) $470

Part of a late Qianlong Masonic part tea and coffee service. (Christie's) $2,465

Qianlong baluster form porcelain vase with carved hardwood stand. (Locke & England) $1,275

Early Qianlong famille rose deep dish with a phoenix in flight, 34.5cm. diam. (Christie's) $1,175

A pair of Qianlong famille rose fan-shaped dishes, 25.5cm. wide. (Christie's) $800

Qianlong armorial plate painted in famille rose enamels, 23cm. diam. (Sotheby, King & Chasemore) $440

Mid 18th century Qianlong teapot decorated with coats-of-arms, 5½in. high.(Dacre, Son & Hartley) $320

Unusual Qianlong pierced white brush-pot with two flattened sections, 16.5cm. long. (Sotheby's) $535

One of pair of early Qianlong famille rose cylindrical jardinieres, 26.5cm. wide. (Christie's) $3,760

Qianlong blue and white fishbowl with deep rounded sides, 65cm. wide. (Sotheby's) $17,080

Early Qianlong famille rose oval barber's bowl, 31.5cm. wide. (Christie's) $1,220

Qianlong famille rose cafe-au-lait ground slender conical coffee-pot and shallow domed cover, 27.5cm. high. (Christie's) $750

One of a pair of Qianlong famille verte standing figures of boys.(Christie's S. Kensington) $1,190

Eight late Qianlong famille rose figures of Daoist immortals, 22cm. high. (Christie's) $3,760

One of a pair of Qian-long blue and white octagonal barrel-shaped garden seats, 48.5cm. high.(Christie's) $3,290

Early Qianlong famille rose bell-shaped mug painted with five fish, 15.5cm. high. (Christie's) $1,410

Early Qianlong famille rose globular bottle vase with high slender neck, 28cm. high. (Christie's) $925

One of a pair of Qianlong famille rose ginger jars with wood covers, 18.5cm. high.(Sotheby, King & Chasemore) $660

167

Qing dynasty celadon tripod globular censer with rope-twist handles, 24cm. wide. (Christie's) $1,295

Unusual early Qing dynasty white marble brick, 27.5cm. long, with indented groove handle. (Sotheby's) $780

Late Qing dynasty famille rose bottle vase with cylindrical neck, 52cm. high. (Christie's) $3,525

Mid-late Qing dynasty biscuit group of three scholars in front of a pagoda, 21cm. high. (Christie's) $200

Mid-late Qing dynasty mustard-yellow-ground pear-shaped vase painted with a dragon, 33.5cm. high. (Christie's) $835

White glazed pear-shaped bowl of the Qing dynasty, applied with dragons, 7cm. wide. (Christie's) $355

ROCKINGHAM

One of a pair of Rockingham scent bottles of depressed square shape, circa 1830-35, 7.5cm. high. (Sotheby's) $1,235

Rockingham porcelain milk jug and egg cup, circa 1835, 11cm. high and wide respectively. (Christie's) $845

Rockingham white scent bottle and stopper, circa 1835, 8cm. high. (Christie's) $315

Rockingham rectangular desk set painted with flowers and foliage, circa 1835, 23.5cm. wide. (Christie's) $1,080

Rockingham oblong octagonal basket, circa 1831-40, 22cm. wide. (Sotheby's) $1,505

Rockingham white and gilt miniature inkstand in the form of a shoe, 1826-30, 12.5cm. wide. (Christie's) $560

Green-ground leaf-shaped chamber candlestick by Rockingham, 12.5cm. wide, circa 1835. (Christie's) $580

Rockingham baluster pot pourri jar and pierced cover, circa 1835, 27.5cm. wide. (Christie's) $1,295

Rockingham miniature basket with twig over-handle, circa 1837, 10cm. wide. (Christie's) $1,150

Rockingham white biscuit figure of a Swiss girl, 19.5cm. high, 1826-30. (Christie's) $490

Pair of Rockingham biscuit figures of a Swiss boy and girl, 20 and 21cm. high, circa 1826-30. (Christie's) $1,800

Rockingham figure of Napoleon in black hat and green coat, 20cm. high, circa 1826-30. (Christie's) $625

Rockingham miniature periwinkle blue-ground octagonal ewer and basin, 1826-30. (Christie's) $760

Rockingham primrose-leaf-molded part tea and coffee service, circa 1826-30. (Christie's) $865

Rockingham flared cylindrical pot pourri basket and pierced cover, circa 1835, 8.5cm. diam. (Christie's) $560

Rockingham crested toast rack with three pierced gilt racks, circa 1835, 21cm. wide. (Christie's) $890

Rockingham figure of a Russian pilgrim, circa 1826-30, 16.5cm. high. (Christie's) $670

Miniature Rockingham inkstand in the form of an elephant and castle, 1826-30, 11.5cm. wide. (Christie's) $1,005

ROOKWOOD

Rookwood pottery vellum vase, signed A. R. Valentien, 1905, 12in. high. (Robert W. Skinner Inc.) $5,100

Rookwood pottery standard glaze cornucopia vase with swirl rim, Cincinnati, Ohio, 1892, 6in. high. (Robert W. Skinner Inc.) $400

Rookwood pottery matt glaze vase decorated with fish, 12¾in. high, Cincinnati, Ohio, circa 1901. (Robert W. Skinner Inc.) $4,000

ROYAL DUX

Royal Dux figure of a maiden in a gold robe, seated on a conch shell, 33cm. high. (Cooper Hirst) $485

Early 20th century Royal Dux group of two game dogs and pheasant, 45cm. wide. (Sotheby's Belgravia) $320

Pair of Royal Dux busts of a maiden and her companion, 29cm. high, circa 1910. (Sotheby's Belgravia) $460

Royal Dux group of lovers, after Hampel, inscribed, circa 1910, 47cm. high. (Sotheby's Belgravia) $410

Royal Dux centrepiece of a bowl in the form of a shell with two nymphs at one end, 43cm. high, circa 1910. (Sotheby's Belgravia) $920

One of a pair of Royal Dux figures of Mediterranean watercarriers, circa 1910, 50cm. high. (Sotheby's Belgravia)$775

Large Royal Dux camel group, 59.5cm. high, circa 1910, in green, pink and brown. (Sotheby's Belgravia) $1,010

Royal Dux figure of Diana, forming a vase, 32cm. high, circa 1910. (Sotheby's Belgravia) $370

Large pair of Royal Dux figures of water carriers. (Henry Spencer & Sons) $1,430

170

Ruskin high-fired vase with trumpet-shaped body covered in lavender and mauve glaze, 24.5cm. high, dated 1906. (Sotheby's Belgravia) $355

Ruskin high-fired vase with shouldered globular body, dated 1925, 17.5cm. high. (Sotheby's Belgravia) $350

A Ruskin high-fired vase with finely mottled plum, lavender and mauve glaze, 23.5cm. high, dated 1912. (Sotheby's Belgravia) $230

Ruskin high-fired cylindrical vase in mottled purple and blue glaze, 19cm. high, 1907. (Christie's) $355

Ruskin high-fired shouldered pear-shaped vase with tapering neck, 39.5cm. high. (Christie's) $720

Ruskin high-fired vase with shouldered globular body, dated 1925, 17.5cm. high. (Sotheby's Belgravia) $350

RUSSIAN

Porcelain group of 'The Barrister's Judgement' by Gardner, Moscow, circa 1860-70, 13.1cm. wide, on octagonal base. (Sotheby's) $810

One of a pair of Russian armorial plates with pierced borders, circa 1870, 25.5cm. diam. (Christie's) $960

Part of a late 19th century seventy-nine-piece dinner service by M C. Kuznetsov, with dark blue borders. (Sotheby's) $2,190

SAMSON

Late 19th century Samson 'Meissen' figures of a cook and a maiden, 21cm. high. (Sotheby's Belgravia) $310

Late 19th century Samson famille rose vase, 45cm. high. (Sotheby's Belgravia) $250

Pair of late 19th century Samson 'Hochst' figures of blackamoors, 13 and 14cm. high. (Sotheby's Belgravia) $385

Rectangular French snuff box, circa 1900, probably Samson, 8.5cm. wide. (Sotheby's) $475

Large Samson figure of a seated hound, the snout with bared teeth, 57cm. high. (Christie's) $1,460

Late 19th century Samson famille verte dish, 45.8cm. diam. (Sotheby's Belgravia) $385

Set of late 19th century Samson 'Derby' street vendors and entertainers 15 to 18cm. high. (Sotheby's Belgravia) $820

Pair of late 19th century Samson 'Derby' groups, 26 and 30.5cm. high. (Sotheby's Belgravia) $475

One of a pair of late 19th century Samson 'Meissen' swans, 17 and 18.5cm. high. (Sotheby's Belgravia) $485

Late 19th century pair of Samson figures of Continents 'Europe' and 'Asia' 27cm. high. (Sotheby's Belgravia) $435

Late 19th century set of four Samson figures of The Continents, 27 to 28cm. high. (Sotheby's Belgravia) $920

One of a pair of late 19th century Japanese Satsuma vases of baluster form, 22cm. high. (Robert W. Skinner Inc.) $450

Mid 19th century Meigyoku Satsuma vase of hexagonal section, 25cm. high. (Sotheby's Belgravia) $1,920

Mid 19th century Takuzan Satsuma vase with flared neck, 30cm. high. (Sotheby's Belgravia) $490

One of a pair of Satsuma vases of square section with formal borders, 30.5cm. high. (Lawrence fine Art) $705

Small mid 19th century Bizan Satsuma beaker vase of lozenge section 16cm. high. (Sotheby, King & Chasemore) $465

19th century Satsuma signed Imperial vase, 16in. high. (Grays Antique News) $2,975

One of a pair of fine small Satsuma bottles, 10cm. high. (Christie's S. Kensington) $1,665

Mid 19th century Satsuma earthenware koro and silver-plated cover, 10.5cm. diam. (Sotheby's Belgravia) $535

Early 19th century Japanese Satsuma vase with stand, neck damaged, 18.5cm. high. (Robert W. Skinner Inc.) $225

Mid 19th century Shozan Satsuma vase painted and gilt with flowers. (Sotheby's Belgravia) $610

One of a pair of Hododa Satsuma vases painted with warriors and courtesans, circa 1900, 37cm. high. (Sotheby's Belgravia) $1,030

Mid 19th century Baigyokuzan early Satsuma vase with pierced handles, 24.5cm. high. (Sotheby's Belgravia) $470

173

SEVRES

Late 19th century Sevres box by Delys, signed, 14.5cm. wide. (Sotheby's Belgravia)$780

Late 19th century Sevres gilt metal mounted rose pompadour ground box and cover, 14.5cm. wide. (Sotheby's Belgravia) $475

Sevres pink-ground ewer and basin dated for 1768, basin 25cm. wide. (Christie's) $1,440

One of a pair of early 19th century gilt bronze mounted Sevres vases, 28cm. high. (Sotheby's Belgravia) $475

One of a pair of Sevres plates, dated for 1786 and 1787, 24cm. diam. (Christie's) $840

Good gilt bronze mounted Sevres pot pourri vase and cover, circa 1835, 14cm. high. (Sotheby's Belgravia) $665

One of a pair of mid 19th century Sevres gilt bronze mounted vases with painted necks, 28.8cm. high. (Sotheby's Belgravia)$710

Outside-decorated Sevres chocolate set, dated for 1840-42, tray 45cm. wide. (Sotheby's Belgravia) $1,380

Late 19th century champleve enamel Sevres vase, painted and signed by Armand, 46.5cm. high. (Sotheby's Belgravia) $665

One of a pair of Sevres pate-sur-pate vases, 35cm. high, dated for 1865. (Sotheby's Belgravia) $1,380

One of a pair of Sevres pattern bleu-celeste ground cylindrical jardinieres, 26.5cm. diam. (Christie's)$930

One of a pair of Sevres bleu-de-roi ground vases and covers, 54cm. high. (Sotheby's Belgravia) $1,470

Sevres cushion-shaped dish with gilt dentil rim, 20.5cm. wide, dated for 1792. (Christie's) $455

Part of a Sevres dessert service decorated with flowers, dated for 1770. (Christie's) $1,320

Sevres bleu nouveau double trencher salt, dated for 1787, 12.5cm. wide. (Christie's) $265

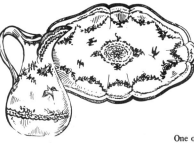

One of a pair of gilt bronze mounted Sevres vases, painted and signed by Hazel, circa 1880, 40cm. high.(Sotheby's Belgravia) $1,010

Sevres pear-shaped ewer and basin decorated in blue enamel and gold, dated for 1769, basin 26cm. wide. (Christie's)$1,440

One of a pair of Sevres bleu nouveau vases of baluster form, 18cm. high, dated for 1764. (Christie's) $960

Sevres pattern bleu-celeste ground vase and cover, body with portraits of Louis XVI, 49cm. high. (Christie's) $630

Mid to late 19th century Sevres gilt bronze mounted table garniture, slightly damaged. (Sotheby's Belgravia) $3,025

One of a pair of Sevres pattern bleu-celeste ground jewelled two-handled vases and covers, restored, 40cm. high. (Christie's) $1,305

One of a pair of Sevres oval plaques, late 19th century, 24.8cm. high. (Sotheby's Belgravia) $590

Sevres pear-shaped jug and cover, dated for 1764, 13.5cm. high. (Christie's) $385

Sevres biscuit group of 'L'education de l'amour', circa 1765, 30cm. high. (Christie's) $1,080

One of a pair of Sevres porcelain and ormolu cache pots.(Bradley & Vaughan) $2,420

Sevres pattern bleu-nouveau-ground ormolu mounted casket of quatrefoil form, 31.5cm. wide. (Christie's) $1,185

Early 19th century Sevres porcelain punchbowl, 38cm. high. (Harrods Auctions) $770

One of a pair of Sevres pattern pink-ground ormolu mounted two-handled cylindrical vases and covers, 56cm. high. (Christie's)$1,450

Sevres pattern pink-ground jardiniere with shell molded handles, 22cm. wide. (Christie's) $690

One of a pair of ormolu Sevres candelabra, 1870's, 81cm. high. (Sotheby's Belgravia) $5,405

Bulbous Sevres vase and cover with brass mounts, 76cm. high. (Rowland Gorringe) $2,440

Part of a mid 19th century 'Sevres' bleu-celeste-ground chocolate service of seventeen pieces. (Sotheby's Belgravia) $4,335

One of a pair of champleve-mounted Sevres vases and covers, painted by P. Rocha, signed, circa 1900.(Sotheby's Belgravia) $1,185

One of a pair of Sevres pattern bleu-nouveau-ground two-handled vases and covers, 46cm. high.(Christie's) $1,185

Sevres pattern bleu-celeste-ground two-handled oviform vase, handle restored, 53cm. high. (Christie's) $840

Large 'Sevres' gilt-bronze-mounted vase and cover painted by H. Desprez, 79cm. high.(Sotheby's Belgravia) $3,615

A Spode blue and white meat dish depicting a sporting scene. (Christie's) $440

Spode pastille burner and cover, circa 1830, 4in. high. (Sotheby's Belgravia) $505

Teapot from a Spode part tea service, circa 1825. (Christie's) $780

One of a pair of Spode blue-ground waisted chocolate cups, covers and stands, circa 1820, 13cm. wide. (Christie's) $895

Copeland Spode two-handled mug with a design of golfers. (Sotheby's) $1,560

Rare Spode pearlware pot pourri with pierced outer cover, circa 1820, 23.5cm. high. (Sotheby, King & Chasemore) $365

One of a pair of Spode blue-ground spill vases, circa 1820, 11cm. high. (Christie's) $375

Part of a Spode part tea and coffee service painted in Imari style, circa 1820. (Christie's) $1,560

Spode blue and white tower pattern jardiniere on stand. (John Francis, Thomas Jones & Sons) $930

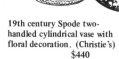

Part of a Spode part dessert service in a famille rose palette, circa 1820. (Christie's) $4,905

19th century Spode two-handled cylindrical vase with floral decoration. (Christie's) $440

Part of a Spode pearlware part dinner and dessert service painted with flowers. (Christie's) $1,895

STAFFORDSHIRE

Staffordshire serpentine fronted writing case, 7cm. wide, circa 1770. (Sotheby's)$1,430

Staffordshire saltglaze polychrome teapot and cover with crabstock spout and handle, circa 1750, 15.5cm. wide. (Christie's) $515

Staffordshire snuff box with gilt metal mounts, circa 1765, 6.3cm. wide. (Sotheby's) $856

One of two Staffordshire bonbonnieres, screw tops lacking, circa 1800, 8cm. high. (Christie's) $335

Staffordshire figure of Princess, circa 1853, 10in. high. (Sotheby's Belgravia)$130

Staffordshire Wesleyan Chapel money box. (Phillips) $610

Staffordshire Toby jug with a warty face, circa 1820, 24cm. high.   (Christie's) $335

Brightly coloured Staffordshire 'Alliance' group, circa 1854, 12in. high. (Sotheby's Belgravia) $235

Large Staffordshire vase of Coalport type, damaged, circa 1830, 23¼in. high. (Sotheby's Belgravia) $500

Staffordshire saltglaze blueground oviform vase with trellis-pattern border, circa 1755, 11cm. high.(Christie's) $935

Staffordshire figure of Elijah, in excellent condition. (Alfie's Antique Market) $300

Staffordshire saltglaze bottle with garlic neck and pearshaped body, circa 1750, 22.5cm. high.(Christie's) $655

178

Staffordshire saltglaze polychrome teapot and cover, circa 1755, 15.5cm. wide. (Christie's) $750

Staffordshire serpentine fronted writing case, circa 1770, 7cm. wide.(Sotheby's) $2,125

Miniature Staffordshire globular teapot and cover with faceted spout, circa 1750, 12.5cm. wide. (Christie's) $890

Staffordshire figure 'A Winter's Tale', circa 1852, 11¼in. high. (Sotheby's Belgravia)$100

Staffordshire pearlware cow-creamer group with brown hide, circa 1780, 16.5cm. wide. (Christie's) $350

Rare Staffordshire figure of Henry V trying on the crown, circa 1847, 14½in. high. (Sotheby's Belgravia) $3,095

Staffordshire vase and cover, circa 1820, 13¼in. high. (Sotheby's Belgravia) $260

Staffordshire figure of 'The Allied Powers', circa 1854, 11¾in. high. (Sotheby's Belgravia) $855

Staffordshire glazed redware conical miniature coffee pot and cover, circa 1755, 16.5cm. high. (Christie's) $470

Staffordshire saltglaze agateware figure of a seated cat, circa 1755, 8.5cm. high. (Christie's) $470

One from a set of six Staffordshire plates, circa 1890, 8½in. diam. (Sotheby's Belgravia) $810

Staffordshire saltglaze polychrome Jacobite teapot and cover, circa 1745, 12.5cm. high. (Christie's) $700

179

Staffordshire porcellaneous figure of a poodle and pups, circa 1840, 9.7cm. long. (Sotheby's Belgravia) $195

Staffordshire saltglaze teapot and cover applied with stags above fleur de lys, 4in. high, circa 1735. (Sotheby's) $440

Unusual Staffordshire porcellaneous pen-holder group of a spaniel and pups, circa 1840, 12.2cm. long. (Sotheby's Belgravia) $270

Unusual Staffordshire pastille burner and cover, circa 1840, 12cm. high.(Sotheby's Belgravia) $415

Late 17th/early 18th century Staffordshire slipware dish, pierced for suspension, 32.5cm. diam. (Sotheby's) $30,375

A Staffordshire pottery 'Showman' group with a Savoyard wearing a tall orange and yellow hat, 8in. high, about 1800-20. (Sotheby's) $1,050

One of two Staffordshire pearlware figures, circa 1800, 16cm. high. (Christie's) $380

A pair of early 19th century Staffordshire busts of Nelson and The Duke of York, 15cm. high. (Sotheby's) $825

A Staffordshire redware jug, the body applied with four figures of ladies, circa 1750, 8¾in. high. (Sotheby's) $505

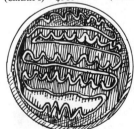

A Staffordshire slipware baking dish of circular form, 11¼in. diam., late 18th century. (Sotheby's) $1,010

An Obadiah Sherratt bull baiting group with the showman wearing a green jacket, 9½in. high, early 19th century. (Sotheby's) $1,260

Rare Staffordshire slipware strainer with piecrust edge, late 18th century, 27.5cm. diam. (Sotheby's) $2,675

Mid 18th century Staffordshire salt-glaze sauceboat in white, 6½in. wide. (Sotheby's) $250

One of a pair of Staffordshire porcelain dogs lying at rest, circa 1830, 9cm. wide. (Sotheby's Belgravia) $230

One of a pair of Staffordshire saltglaze pierced oval two-handled baskets, circa 1750, 22.5cm. wide. (Christie's) $480

Well modelled Staffordshire figure of a poodle holding a basket, 12cm. long, circa 1830. (Sotheby's Belgravia) $195

A rare pair of Staffordshire porcelaneous models of leopards, circa 1830. (Sotheby's Belgravia) $560

Rare Staffordshire group of fighting dogs, circa 1830, 11cm. wide. (Sotheby's Belgravia) $340

A Staffordshire Toby jug and cover, the red-faced toper seated and holding a jug of foaming ale, 10¼in. high, late 18th century. (Sotheby's) $460

A rare Staffordshire model of a stallion standing in front of an oak tree, 12in. high, circa 1800. (Sotheby's) $2,730

Staffordshire equestrian figure of Queen Victoria, untitled, 21cm. high, circa 1840. (Sotheby's Belgravia) $315

STRASBURG

One of three Strasburg shaped circular soup plates, circa 1765, 24.5cm. diam. (Christie's) $1,145

Strasburg faience white figure of Gilles, after Watteau, circa 1765, 30.5cm. high. (Christie's) $4,560

One of three Strasburg shaped circular soup plates, circa 1765, 24.5cm. diam. (Christie's) $1,075

181

SWANSEA

Swansea milk jug of unusual shape, design heightened with gilding, 15.5cm. wide, circa 1814-22. (Sotheby's) $335

Oval Swansea dish with lobed rim, circa 1817-22, 29cm. long. (Sotheby's) $355

Swansea porcelain cup and saucer with red, green and gilt motifs. (Geering & Colyer) $360

Swansea plate, slightly repaired, circa 1815, 21.5cm. diam. (Christie's) $335

Swansea cabaret, painted with garden flowers, circa 1817. (Christie's) $1,440

One of a pair of Swansea cushion-shaped dishes painted by Wm. Pollard, circa 1820, 20.5cm. diam. (Christie's) $2,640

TANG

Buff pottery figure of a recumbent ram, probably Tang dynasty, 13cm. long. (Christie's) $215

Unglazed red pottery figure of a mounted Western Asiatic, Tang dynasty, 33cm. high. (Christie's) $1,000

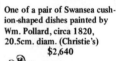

One of a pair of unglazed buff pottery figures of mounted ladies, Tang dynasty, 31.5cm. high. (Christie's) $9,045

Yue type broad pear-shaped vase with dish-shaped lip, Tang dynasty, 14.5cm. diam. (Christie's) $960

Glazed pottery tripod dish of the Tang dynasty, painted with a flying goose, 29cm. diam. (Christie's) $26,180

Tang dynasty figure of a seated Buddhistic lion in grey stone, 15cm. high. (Christie's) $1,190

Tournai barrel-shaped mustard pot with scroll handle, circa 1770, 6.5cm. high. (Christie's) $615

Tournai plate with spirally molded rim, circa 1775, 27.8cm. diam. (Sotheby's) $1,450

Tournai 'Drageoire' or sweetmeat bowl, circa 1760, 15cm. high. (Christie's) $430

Tournai plate with shaped rim molded with spiral ribs, 24.5cm. diam., circa 1760-70. (Sotheby's) $970

A rare pair of Tournai figures of gardeners, 17cm. high, circa 1765. (Sotheby's) $6,700

One of a pair of Tournai armorial shaped circular plates, circa 1770, 24cm. diam. (Christie's) $1,660

URBINO

Urbino Istoriato crespina, slightly damaged, circa 1540, 16cm. diam. (Christie's) $3,345

An Urbino Istoriato circular tazza painted with a nymph, circa 1550, 23.5cm. diam. (Christie's) $2,100

Urbino Istoriato crespina painted with Apollo, circa 1550, 22.5cm. diam. (Christie's) $1,435

Urbino Istoriato dish painted with Pan and Apollo, circa 1560, 44.5cm. diam.(Christie's) $4,065

One of a pair of Urbino waisted pharmacy jugs, painted with Bishop's mitres, circa 1590, 19cm. high. (Christie's) $2,940

Urbino Istoriato plate painted with Hercules, circa 1550, 24cm. diam. (Christie's) $1,435

Mid 19th century Vienna decorated vase with flared body, 19.3cm. high. (Sotheby's Belgravia) $380

Late 19th century Vienna rectangular tray painted with an oval panel, with raised and pierced rim, 39.5cm. wide. (Sotheby's Belgravia) $1,155

Late 19th century Vienna centre-piece with flared everted rim, 31cm. high. (Sotheby's Belgravia) $315

A late Vienna circular plaque depicting a bust of Beethoven, painted by Richter, 28.5cm. diam. (Christie's) $755

Late 19th century circular Vienna tray showing a maiden and a Cupid, 36cm. diam. (Sotheby's Belgravia) $1,090

A late Vienna plate, painted with a scene from classical mythology, 24.5cm. diam. (Christie's) $380

One of a pair of late 19th century Vienna vases and covers, signed, 36.8cm. high. (Sotheby's Belgravia) $1,230

Late Vienna royal-blue-ground garniture de cheminee painted by Hans Stadler and E. Latter. (Christie's) $5,590

One of a pair of good Vienna vases and covers painted by Wagner, signed, circa 1900, 20cm. high. (Sotheby's Belgravia) $1,395

Vienna plate painted by Wagner, signed, 22.5cm. diam., circa 1900. (Sotheby's Belgravia) $625

Pair of mid 19th century Vienna figures of Harlequins, 19 and 16.5cm. high. (Sotheby, King & Chasemore) $685

Vienna plate painted by Wagner, signed, 24.3cm. diam., circa 1900. (Sotheby's Belgravia) $725

One of eleven Vincennes plates painted with flowers, dated for 1754, 26cm. diam. (Christie's) $1,150

Vincennes cup and saucer decorated with landscapes, 1754, hair crack. (Sotheby's) $445

Vincennes circular chamber pot with gilt rim, 1750-53, 20cm. wide. (Christie's) $235

Vincennes biscuit figure of a boy playing bagpipes, circa 1752, 19.5cm. high. (Sotheby's) $795

Vincennes dish of lobed quatrefoil shape painted with two birds in a landscape, 1753, 28cm. wide. (Sotheby's) $2,350

One of a pair of Vincennes small bleu lapis campana vases, dated for 1755, 9cm. high. (Christie's) $2,640

VOLKSTEDT

Volkstedt figure of a fruit seller, circa 1900, 23cm. high.(Sotheby's Belgravia) $150

Pair of late 19th century Volkstedt groups of lovers, 21.5cm. and 22cm. high. (Sotheby's Belgravia) $480

Volkstedt coffee pot and cover with pear-shaped body, circa 1760-65, 20cm. high. (Sotheby's) $1,790

VYSE

Pottery cat by Charles Vyse in mottled brown and olive-green glaze, 24cm. high. (Christie's) $620

Large oviform vase by Charles Vyse, decorated with swimming fish, 24.5cm. high.(Christie's) $525

'The Bonbon Seller' by Charles Vyse, 22cm. high, dated 1922. (Sotheby's Belgravia)$460

Wedgwood black basalt encaustic-decorated Krater vase with arched loop handles, circa 1810, 33cm. wide. (Christie's) $890

Wedgwood Fairyland lustre 'Malfrey' pot and cover, 1920's, 7in. diam. (Sotheby's Belgravia) $3,585

Wedgwood Fairyland lustre bowl, exterior decorated with 'Poplar Trees' pattern, 22.5cm. diam., 1920's. (Sotheby's Belgravia) $835

One of a pair of Wedgwood black basalt oval plaques of Augustus and Nero, circa 1780-90, 14.5cm. high. (Sotheby's) $285

Part of a twenty-six-piece Wedgwood cream-ware part service, early 19th century. (Sotheby's) $1,245

Late 19th century Wedgwood three-color jasper-dip vase, 5½in. high. (Sotheby's Belgravia) $855

Late 19th century Wedgwood black basalt bust of Mercury, 47cm. high. (Sotheby's Belgravia) $715

Wedgwood Fairyland lustre plaque with a midnight-blue-ground, 1920's, 18.5cm. wide. (Sotheby's Belgravia)$2,605

Wedgwood Fairyland lustre 'Florentine' vase decorated with goblins, 17.5cm. high, 1924-29. (Sotheby's Belgravia) $2,140

Wedgwood Fairyland lustre bowl gilt with fairies, circa 1925, 20cm. diam. (Christie's) $820

Large Wedgwood Fairyland lustre vase, gilt on a dark-blue-ground, 60cm. high, circa 1920. (Phillips) $6,440

Teapot from a Wedgwood pearlware part tea and coffee service, circa 1815. (Christie's) $1,910

Wedgwood Fairyland lustre footed flared bowl, circa 1925, 22.5cm. diam. (Christie's) $1,520

Wedgwood Fairyland lustre bowl, 6½in. diam., circa 1920. (Sotheby's Belgravia) $955

Wedgwood Fairyland lustre bowl interior decorated with elves, 1920's, 27.5cm. diam. (Sotheby's Belgravia) $455

Wedgwood Fairyland 'Malfrey' pot and cover decorated with the 'Bubbles II' pattern, 1920's, 18cm. diam. (Sotheby's Belgravia) $2,750

Wedgwood and Bentley teapot and cover in black basalt, 13cm. high. (Sotheby's) $860

Wedgwood and Bentley basalt plaque with portrait of Benjamin Franklin, circa 1760-70, 7.5cm. diam. (C. G. Sloan & Co. Inc.) $300

Wedgwood Fairyland lustre vase with ovoid body, 23cm. high, 1920's. (Sotheby's Belgravia) $1,435

Late 18th century Wedgwood blue jasper 'Leda' vase and cover, 27cm. high. (Sotheby's) $1,460

Wedgwood lustred tapering oviform vase decorated in blue, Portland Vase mark, 20cm. high, circa 1925. (Christie's)$700

Wedgwood black basalt encaustic-decorated globular two-handled vase, circa 1800, 28.5cm. high. (Christie's) $2,225

Wedgewood candelmas lustre cylindrical vase with flared neck, circa 1925, 28.5cm. high. (Christie's) $1,075

Wedgwood black basalt plaque showing Hercules and the Lion, 19cm. high, circa 1780-90. (Sotheby's) $260

187

WEDGWOOD

Wedgwood Fairyland lustre bowl decorated with river landscapes. (Henry Spencer & Sons) $1,655

Rare Wedgwood-Greatbach redware teapot and cover. (Phillips) $5,200

One of a pair of finely modelled Wedgwood medallions within ormolu borders, 12cm. wide. (Sotheby's) $630

A rare Wedgwood caneware triple bamboo flower vase, 8¼in. high, late 18th century. (Sotheby's) $840

Part of a rare forty-piece Wedgwood bone china dessert service. (Phillips)$1,475

Wedgwood black basalt two-handled oviform vase painted in red, circa 1815, 30cm. high. (Christie's) $1,825

Wedgwood black basalt vase with raised polychrome enamelled floral motif, late 19th century, 6in. high.(Robert W. Skinner Inc.) $110

Pair of Wedgwood wall plates, painted by J. Wiiliams, circa 1870, 12in. diam. (Sotheby's Belgravia) $475

A Wedgwood 'Dice' pattern vase of campana-shape, 7in. high, early 19th century. (Sotheby's) $840

19th century Wedgwood basalt bust of Shakespeare, 12¼in. tall. (Robert W. Skinner Inc.) $425

Late 19th century Wedgwood three-colour jasper-dip vase and cover, 8¾in. high. (Sotheby's Belgravia) $545

A Wedgwood black basalt bust of Rousseau, 21¼in. high, late 19th century. (Sotheby's) $670

Wemyss-ware 'Stuart' jardiniere, restored, circa 1900, 23cm. high. (Sotheby's) $240

Unusual Wemyss-ware sponge bowl and liner, circa 1910, 24.5cm. wide. (Sotheby's) $385

Wemyss-ware cauldron by Robert Heron & Sons, circa 1900, 25cm. high.(Sotheby's) $455

Wemyss pottery cat painted with roses, 30.5cm. high. (Phillips) $965

Large Wemyss-ware Bovey pottery nursery pig, circa 1930, 44cm. long. (Sotheby's) $1,325

Early 20th century Wemyss-ware 'sailor' jug, 27.5cm. high. (Sotheby's) $315

Wemyss-ware 'Elgin' vase by Robert Heron & Sons, circa 1900, 44.5cm. high. (Sotheby's) $625

Large Wemyss-ware slop bucket and cover, circa 1900, 29.4cm. high. (Sotheby's) $265

Wemyss-ware vase of tear form, circa 1920, 29cm. high. (Sotheby's) $480

Large Wemyss-ware tyg painted with cockerels and hens, circa 1900, 28cm. high. (Sotheby's) $290

Wemyss-ware plate by Robert Heron & Sons, circa 1900, 21.5cm. diam. (Sotheby's) $335

Rare Wemyss-ware loving cup painted with rooks and rabbits, circa 1900, 13.4cm. high. (Sotheby's) $770

189

WESTERWALD

A Westerwald grey stoneware baluster jug incised with the head and shoulders of Queen Mary II, 1689-93. Christie's) $800

Westerwald stoneware globular jug with scrolling flowering foliage, circa 1700, 21cm. high. (Christie's) $810

Westerwald pale brown stoneware cylindrical tankard, early 17th century, 18.5cm. high. (Christie's) $835

18th century Westerwald stoneware jug, 20.4cm. high. (Sotheby's) $800

Westerwald stoneware square flask with pewter mount and screw cover, circa 1680, 25cm. high. (Christie's) $1,675

Westerwald stoneware globular jug molded with the initials RAR, circa 1710, 18cm. high. (Christie's) $810

Westerwald dated globular stoneware jug, dated 1691, 18cm. high. (Christie's) $1,910

Westerwald globular jug with silvered metal cover, circa 1740, 23cm. high. (Christie's) $910

Westerwald globular jug, dated 1691, 29cm. high. (Christie's) $1,910

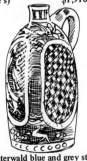

A Westerwald blue and grey stoneware flask, incised with panels of storks, circa 1720. (Christie's) $420

18th century Westerwald stoneware globular jug, 26cm. high. (Christie's) $430

Westerwald stoneware square flask with pewter mounts, screw cover and swing handle, circa 1650, 18cm. high. (Christie's) $4,300

Miniature Whieldon teapot and cover with crabstock spout and handle, circa 1750, 14cm. wide. (Christie's) $700

Whieldon cow-creamer group, circa 1755, 18cm. wide. (Christie's) $610

Whieldon cabbage-leaf molded cream-boat, circa 1765, 12cm. wide. (Christie's) $1,355

Rare and interesting Whieldon transfer printed wall vase, circa 1750-60, 23cm. high. (Sotheby's) $2,185

Very rare Astbury-Whieldon tea party group with negro servant, circa 1740, 17cm. high. (Sotheby's) $65,610

Whieldon bust of a man with gray-green skull cup, circa 1750, 13.5cm. high. (Christie's) $1,145

WOLFSOHN

Late 19th century set of Helena Wolfsohn monkey bandsmen, 12.5 to 17.5cm. high. (Sotheby's Belgravia) $915

Late 19th century pair of Helena Wolfsohn bottle and covers, 33cm. high. (Sotheby's Belgravia) $335

Late 19th century Helena Wolfsohn liqueur set, stand 28cm. wide. (Sotheby's Belgravia) $775

Late 19th century pair of Helena Wolfsohn vases of double-gourd form, 17.5cm. high. (Sotheby's Belgravia) $290

191

Ralph Wood model of a goat on a rocky base, circa 1770-80, horns restored, 16cm. high. (Sotheby's)$1,460

Ralph Wood figure of a squirrel seated on his haunches, circa 1775, 18.5cm. high. (Christie's) $2,340

Ralph Wood glazed figure of a cockerel, circa 1770-80, 22cm. high. (Sotheby's) $2,310

Ralph Wood Toby jug of conventional type, circa 1780, 24.5cm. high. (Christie's) $550

Large oval plaque by Ralph Wood of 'Patricia and her Lover', circa 1770, 35cm. high, slightly cracked. (Sotheby's) $6,320

Rare Ralph Wood figure of Bacchus, circa 1770, 22cm. high. (Sotheby's) $970

Ralph Wood group of the Vicar and Moses, circa 1770, 24cm. high, slightly cracked. (Sotheby's) $1,115

A pair of Ralph Wood figures of a gardener and his companion, circa 1770-80, 19cm. high. (Sotheby's) $6,320

A rare Ralph Wood figure of a sailor holding his hat at his side, 5¾in. high, circa 1775. (Christie's) $1,300

Ralph Wood figure of Charity, circa 1770, 21cm. high. (Sotheby's) $585

Rare Ralph Wood plaque of a child riding a lion, circa 1770, 21cm. diam.(Sotheby's) $3,160

Ralph Wood figure of a gardener, circa 1770-80, 20cm. high, slightly chipped. (Sotheby's) $925

Ralph Wood figure of a recumbent goat, horns and ears restored, circa 1780, 18cm. wide. (Christie's) $890

Ralph Wood Staffordshire shepherd boy with lamb. (Phillips) $160

Ralph Wood fox-mask sauceboat with swan's neck handle, circa 1780, 18.5cm. wide. (Christie's) $540

Rare Ralph Wood figure of King David playing a lyre, circa 1770, 30cm. high. (Sotheby's) $1,410

A Ralph Wood plaque of 'Three Grooms Carousing', molded in relief, 8½in. high, circa 1775. (Christie's) $3,570

Ralph Wood Toby jug, circa 1780, 24.5cm. high. (Christie's) $480

A brightly coloured Ralph Wood 'Bacchus' jug, the god wearing a lion skin across his shoulder, 12¾in. high, circa 1775. (Christie's) $590

Rare Ralph Wood group of St. George and the Dragon, tail of horse restored, 27.5cm. high. (Sotheby's) $2,310

Ralph Wood white figure of Benjamin Franklin, circa 1775, 34cm. high. (Sotheby's) $875

Ralph Wood figure of Diana the Huntress, circa 1770, 21cm. high. (Sotheby's) $970

An interesting marked Ralph Wood mask-jug with a satyr's smiling face, 8½in. high, circa 1770. (Christie's) $1,010

One of a pair of Ralph Wood figures of haymakers, circa 1770-80, 7¾in. high. (Sotheby's) $1,215

193

Tureen from a Chamberlain's Worcester lime green-ground crested part dinner service, circa 1835. (Christie's) $2,350

Worcester puce-ground coffee cup and saucer painted in the manner of James Giles, circa 1775.(Christie's)$2,810

Royal Worcester jardiniere painted with poppies.(Samuel Rains & Son) $425

Royal Worcester pierced vase, 20cm. high, circa 1880. (Sotheby's Belgravia) $610

Rare Flight, Barr & Barr yellow-ground garniture of three vases and covers, circa 1790-95, restored. (Sotheby, King & Chasemore) $635

Worcester blue and white herringbone-molded coffee pot and domed cover, circa 1765, 21.5cm. high. (Christie's) $890

Royal Worcester Turk, 1891, 6¾in. high. (Sotheby's Belgravia) $425

One of a pair of Worcester Flight, Barr & Barr sauce tureens and covers. (Phillips) $5,615

Royal Worcester Art Deco vase and cover, date code for 1919, 20cm. high. (Sotheby, King & Chasemore) $310

One of two Chamberlain's Worcester pot pourri vases and covers, circa 1810, 13cm. high. (Christie's) $375

Worcester blue-ground part dessert service, centres painted with flowers, circa 1825. (Christie's) $5,615

One of a pair of Royal Worcester vases painted by J. Stinton. (H. Spencer & Sons) $1,450

One of six Worcester orange-ground crested side plates, circa 1805, 18.5cm. wide. (Christie's) $895

Worcester armorial cushion-shaped dish, circa 1805, 22cm. wide. (Christie's) $495

Worcester blue and white barrel-shaped cream jug, circa 1775, 7.5cm. high. (Christie's) $325

Large Royal Worcester pierced vase and cover, 1890, 21½in. high. (Sotheby's Belgravia) $1,190

Fine Worcester porcelain tea and coffee service of twenty-two pieces, circa 1760. (Sotheby, King & Chasemore) $6,100

Large Royal Worcester figure of 'The Bather Surprised', 1893, 25¼in. high. (Sotheby's Belgravia) $835

Royal Worcester vase decorated with a view of Arundel Castle, 38cm. high. (Sotheby, King & Chasemore) $425

A pair of Royal Worcester three-light 'double-figure' candelabra, 1886, 19in. high. (Sotheby's Belgravia) $1,620

Royal Worcester vase decorated with relief gilding, date code for 1878, 22.5cm. high. (Sotheby, King & Chasemore) $335

Grainger's Worcester pierced vase and cover, 1870's, 13in. high. (Sotheby's Belgravia) $1,310

Part of a twenty-six-piece Barr Worcester tea and coffee service, circa 1792-1804. (Sotheby's) $1,770

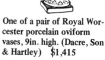

One of a pair of Royal Worcester porcelain oviform vases, 9in. high. (Dacre, Son & Hartley) $1,415

195

Royal Worcester teapot and cover, dated for 1882, 15.8cm. high. (Sotheby's Belgravia) $1,090

Worcester blue and white teabowl and saucer, circa 1758. (Christie's) $980

Worcester spirally-mounted milk jug with double scroll handle, circa 1770, 8.5cm. high. (Christie's) $820

Early Worcester cream jug of pear shape, circa 1752-55, with sparrow-beak spout, 7.5cm. high. (Sotheby's) $235

Worcester chocolate cup and stand with wavy rim, circa 1770-75. (Sotheby's) $190

Unusual Royal Worcester 'flower-holder', painted by H. Stinton, dated for 1904, 7¾in. high. (Sotheby's Belgravia) $665

One of a pair of Worcester baskets, circa 1765-1770, 20cm. diam. (Sotheby's) $2,125

Rare Royal Worcester 'Limoges enamel' ewer and stand, dated for 1865, 12¾in. high. (Sotheby's Belgravia)$1,785

One of a pair of Flight, Barr & Barr shell-shaped dishes, circa 1820-30, 21cm. high.(Sotheby's) $495

Part of a Royal Worcester coffee set of nineteen pieces with six silver gilt spoons, 1953.(Sotheby's Belgravia) $1,235

Pair of Royal Worcester earthenware figures of 'Joy' and 'Sorrow', circa 1880, 10½in. high. (Sotheby's Belgravia) $475

Chamberlain's Worcester cache-pot and stand of bucket shape, circa 1790-1810, 18cm. diam. (Sotheby's) $330

Well documented Worcester miniature sugar bowl, cover and stand, 1758. (Laidlaws) $4,515

One of two Worcester quatrefoil two-handled baskets, pierced covers and stands, circa 1770, stands 25cm. wide. (Christie's) $6,550

One of a pair of Worcester Barr, Flight & Barr cushion-shaped dishes, circa 1805, 25.5cm. wide. (Christie's) $1,010

Unusual Royal Worcester figure of a gnome in the white, 1870's 7¾in. high. (Sotheby's Belgravia) $225

Worcester coffee cup and saucer, painted with Budai, circa 1760-65. (Sotheby's) $520

Royal Worcester figure of 'The Bather Surprised', dated for 1918, 15½in. high.(Sotheby's Belgravia) $405

Worcester Barr, Flight & Barr square salad bowl from the Stowe service, circa 1813, 27.5cm. wide.(Christie's) $3,600

Part of a one hundred and five-piece Chamberlain's Worcester turquoise-ground dinner service, dated for 1846. (Sotheby's Belgravia) $855

Worcester blue and white pear-shaped milk jug, circa 1768, 10cm. high. (Christie's) $1,495

Worcester blue and white pear-shaped bottle, circa 1758, 26cm. high. (Christie's) $980

Worcester blue and white stand for a finger-bowl, with lobed rim, circa 1755, 14.5cm. diam. (Christie's) $610

Royal Worcester pierced and double-walled goblet, 1875, 19cm. high. (Sotheby's Belgravia) $730

Worcester lobed oval sauceboat painted with a stag hunt, circa 1754, 18cm. wide. (Christie's) $625

Chamberlain's Worcester muffin warmer and domed cover, 1802-05, 26cm. wide. (Christie's) $1,055

Royal Worcester equestrian figure of a Welsh mountain pony, 26cm. wide. (Christie's) $670

One of a pair of Worcester orange-ground urn-shaped ice pails, covers and liners, circa 1800, 36cm. high. (Christie's) $12,220

One of a pair of Worcester cushion-shaped dishes painted with named views, circa 1820, 23cm. wide. (Christie's) $355

Large Royal Worcester vase and pierced cover, painted by Harry Stinton, 1938, 43cm. high. (Phillips) $2,990

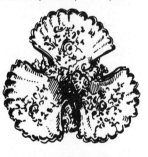

Grainger's Worcester pierced centrepiece, 77cm. high. (Christie's) $2,215

Worcester three-shell centrepiece with fluted edges, circa 1768, 16.5cm. wide. (Christie's) $935

Large porcelain Royal Worcester figure 'The Bather Surprised', by Sir Thomas Brock, 61cm. high. (Phillips) $2,070

Worcester bell-shaped mug printed in black with a portrait of George II, circa 1760, 15cm. high. (Christie's) $980

One of a pair of Royal Worcester reticulated vases, dated 1904, 12in. high. (Sotheby's Belgravia) $2,855

One of a pair of Worcester flared flower pots and stands, circa 1805, 17.5cm. high. (Christie's) $935

Fine Chinese Yongzheng ruby back saucer dish, 21cm. diam. (H. Spencer & Sons) $610

Yellow glazed saucer dish of the Yongzheng period, 13.5cm. diam. (Christie's) $1,010

One of a pair of Yongzheng famille rose egg-shell soup plates, 21.5cm. diam. (Christie's) $1,645

Yongzheng famille rose deep plate with minor chips, 19cm. diam. (Christie's) $375

One of a pair of Yongzheng doucai saucer dishes painted with stags, 16.3cm. diam. (Sotheby's) $1,510

One of a pair of Yongzheng doucai saucer dishes, 16cm. diam. (Sotheby's) $1,710

YORKSHIRE

Bearded Toby jug, possibly Yorkshire, on a yellow base, circa 1810, 24cm. high. (Christie's) $445

Late 18th century Yorkshire pottery money box in the form of an elephant, 11.5cm. high. (Sotheby Beresford Adams) $240

Yorkshire pottery Bacchus jug, circa 1800, 30.5cm. high. (Christie's) $595

ZURICH

Zurich saucer painted with a riverscape, 13.8cm. diam., circa 1765-70. (Sotheby's) $275

Zurich jug with scroll molded spout, circa 1765, 12.5cm. high. (Sotheby's) $235

Zurich sugar bowl and cover with gilt fruit knop, circa 1765, 10cm. high. (Sotheby's) $1,645

George III ebonised bracket clock by George Morison, Aberdeen, 18½in. high. (Sotheby's) $3,745

Early 18th century striking bracket clock with repousse basket top, signed Edward Speakman, London, 37cm. high. (Christie's) $5,260

George III mahogany striking bracket clock signed Robert Leumes, London, 56cm. high. (Christie's) $3,345

Early 18th century ebonised striking bracket clock with inverted bell top, 39cm. high. (Christie's) $1,965

Ebonised quarter striking bracket clock by Isaac Goddard, London, 39.5cm. high. (Christie's) $5,260

George III ebonised striking bracket clock, dial signed Geo. Lee, Coventry, 45.5cm. high. (Christie's) $2,270

George I ebony quarter repeating bracket clock signed Jasper Taylor, London, 38cm. high. (Christie's) $3,585

Ebony striking bracket clock by Daniel Quare, London, with gilt metal basket top, 51cm. high. (Christie's) $13,145

Ebony quarter striking bracket clock by Fromanteel and Clarke, 47cm. high. (Christie's) $6,690

Georgian musical bracket clock by J. Thwaites which plays eight tunes. (James & Lister Lea) $5,880

Oak quarter repeating bracket clock in domed case, circa 1880, 57cm. high. (Sotheby's Belgravia) $940

Ebony striking bracket clock by George Graham, London, 15cm. high. (Phillips) $25,300

18th century bracket clock inscribed Moore, London, 42cm. high. (Phillips) $3,565

Early 18th century ebonised striking bracket clock, signed on a plaque Isaac Papavoine, London, 35cm. high. (Christie's) $6,000

Early George III ebonised quarter-striking bracket clock, dial signed Cha. Cabrier, London, 49cm. high. (Christie's) $4,800

Early 18th century ebonised striking bracket clock by Daniel le Count, London, 35.5cm. high. (Christie's) $5,020

George III mahogany musical bracket clock, dial signed Jas. Berry, Pontefract, 22in. high. (Sotheby's) $7,485

Ebonised timepiece bracket clock with gilt metal repousse basket top, signed Christopher Maynard, London, 30.5cm. high. (Christie's) $4,300

A late George III ebonised miniature bracket clock by Dwerrihouse and Carter, London 20cm. high. (Phillips) $2,520

Profusely carved oak bracket clock with both Westminster and eight bell chimes. (Andrew Grant) $1,465

George III period mahogany domed bracket clock dial inscribed Geo. Yonge, London, 46cm. high. (Geering & Colyer) $1,485

An early 19th century mahogany bracket clock by James McCabe, Royal Exchange, 23.5cm. high. (Phillips) $1,430

Georgian mahogany ormolu mounted bracket clock by Edward Tutet, London, 56cm. high. (C. G. Sloan & Co. Inc.) $2,400

Late George III mahogany bracket clock of small size by Henry Pace, London, 24cm. high. (Phillips) $1,430

BRACKET CLOCKS

Unusual George II ebonised quarter repeating bracket clock by Francis Raynsford, London, 51cm. high. (Sotheby's) $4,265

Ebonised quarter repeating bracket clock by John Clowes, London, in molded domed case, 39cm. high. (Sotheby's) $4,140

George III mahogany bracket clock by Saml. Leak, London, 43cm. high. (Sotheby's) $2,135

George III ebonised striking bracket clock by Richard Holmes, London, 46cm. high. (Christie's) $3,510

George III mahogany bracket clock, dial signed Jams. Chater, London, 46cm. high. (Sotheby's) $2,185

Early 18th century ebony striking bracket clock, backplate signed Robert Williamson, London, 32cm. high. (Christie's) $5,615

Ebonised bracket clock, circa 1900, 53cm. high. (Sotheby's Belgravia) $1,215

18th century mahogany quarter repeating bracket timepiece, dial signed Cawley Chester, 42cm. high. (Sotheby's) $2,530

Rare late 18th century mahogany alarm bracket clock, dial signed Eardley Norton, London, 30.5cm. high. (Christie's) $8,425

Mid Georgian ebonised striking bracket clock by Edward Faulkner, London, 52cm. high. (Christie's) $2,880

Vernis Martin musical bracket clock by Markwick Markham Borrell, London, 64cm. high. (Christie's) $5,260

Quarter repeating mahogany bracket clock by Reid & Sons, Newcastle, circa 1890, 43cm. high. (Sotheby's Belgravia) $630

George II ebonised quarter repeating bracket clock, signed Yates, London, 48cm. high. (Sotheby's) $3,790

Victorian oak cased bracket clock of Gothic design, 19th century. (Butler & Hatch Waterman) $1,340

Rare late 17th century ebony veneered quarter repeating bracket timepiece, by Edmund Massey, London, 34cm. high. (Sotheby's) $11,140

Ebony and gilt bronze bracket clock by E. H. Bell, Leicester, 66cm. high, circa 1870. (Sotheby's Belgravia) $1,520

George III mahogany hooded bracket clock by John Ellicott, London, 84cm. high. (Christie's) $7,955

Early 18th century ebony striking bracket clock with embossed basket top and frets, signed John Barnett, London, 33cm. high. (Christie's) $8,190

Quarter striking oak bracket clock, circa 1900, 50cm. high, with Westminster chimes. (Sotheby's Belgravia) $840

Late Victorian mahogany bracket clock in domed case, with ormolu surmounts. (Morphets) $1,795

Late 18th century ebonised quarter repeating bracket clock by William Harrison, London, 33cm. high. (Christie's) $2,810

George III fruitwood striking bracket clock, signed John Fladgate, London, 30.5cm. high. (Christie's) $10,515

Louis XIII ebonised striking bracket clock, plaque signed Duhamel, Paris, 42cm. high. (Christie's) $5,150

Late 19th century German mahogany bracket clock in arched inlaid case, 44.5cm. high. (Sotheby's Belgravia) $910

BRACKET CLOCKS

Queen Anne ebonised striking bracket clock with repousse basket top, signed Isaac Papavoine, London, 37cm. high. (Christie's) $6,690

George II walnut quarter repeating bracket clock, signed Jno. Ellicott, London, 48cm. high. (Sotheby's) $4,030

An ebonised bracket clock with ormolu embellishments, 16¾in. high, circa 1890. (Sotheby's Belgravia) $840

Dutch bracket clock, dial signed Ellicott, London, case with gilt metal urn finials, 79cm. high. (Christie's) $4,780

Mid 19th century mahogany bracket clock in the style of Nathaniel Delander, 47cm. high. (Sotheby's Belgravia) $3,275

Small ebonised bracket clock by William Harrison, London, circa 1760, 30cm. high, with brass molding and frets. (Sotheby's) $4,140

Small bracket clock, mid 19th century, case and dial plate Austrian or Swiss. (Henry Spencer & Sons) $725

Mahogany chiming bracket clock, in case with gilt bronze flambeau, circa 1880, 80cm. high. (Sotheby's Belgravia) $2,105

Late 17th century ebony veneered quarter repeating bracket clock by Edward Speakman, London, 14½in. high. (Sotheby's) $8,425

English ormolu mounted quarter chiming mahogany bracket clock, by Evans, Royal Exchange, London, 75cm. high. (Lawrence Fine Art) $3,745

Ebony veneered quarter repeating bracket clock by Samuel Davy, Norwich, 50.8cm. high. (Lawrence Fine Art) $3,040

Ebonised chiming bracket clock with inverted basket top, circa 1880, 75cm. high. (Sotheby's Belgravia) $2,105

Quarter striking Dutch kingwood bracket clock, signed Clarke and Dunster, 59cm. high. (Christie's) $4,780

Early 19th century ebonised bracket clock by Grant, Fleet Street, London, 37.5cm. high. (Parsons, Welch & Cowell) $1,525

Small ebony veneered bracket clock by John Ellicott, London, 39cm. high. (Sotheby's) $5,690

Late 17th century olivewood basket top bracket clock, 33cm. high. (Sotheby's) $7,110

Mahogany bracket clock with painted circular dial, 1840's, 49cm. high, on lobed bun feet. (Sotheby's Belgravia) $655

Ebony veneered quarter repeating bracket clock by Thos. Martin, London, 37cm. high.(Sotheby's) $3,555

Ebonised quarter repeating bracket timepiece by William Hill, Walsingham, 48.5cm. high. (Sotheby's) $2,645

George III bracket clock by William Pike. (Sotheby Bearne)$2,540

George III mahogany bracket clock, dial signed Webster, London, 45cm. high, sold with bracket. (Sotheby's) $2,605

Rosewood chiming bracket clock inlaid with cut-brass foliage, 79cm. high, 1890's. (Sotheby's Belgravia) $2,225

Repeating ebonised mahogany and gilt bronze bracket clock by P. Caron, London, 1880's, 66cm. high. (Sotheby's Belgravia) $3,465

Early George III mahogany bracket clock, dial signed Richard Style, London, 19in. high. (Sotheby's) $4,915

CARRIAGE CLOCKS

Rare ormolu musical and automaton carriage clock by Japy Freres, 30cm. high. (Christie's) $10,765

Lacquered brass miniature carriage clock in Empire style case, 10cm. high. (Christie's) $700

A Liberty & Co. 'Cymric' silver rectangular carriage clock, Birmingham, 1904. (Christie's) $1,050

French brass capucine alarm clock by A. Newall, Bordeaux, 30.5cm. high. (Lawrence Fine Art) $1,055

Unusual gilt metal porcelain panelled striking carriage clock, 16cm. high. (Christie's)$1,755

French carriage clock, by H. Jacot, circa 1875. (Grays Antique Mews) $1,195

A porcelain mounted carriage timepiece, the dial signed Shreve, Crump & Law, Boston, 3¼in. high. (Sotheby's) $2,100

Rare ormolu miniature carriage clock, case with chased decoration, 7cm. high. (Christie's) $1,640

French champleve enamel repeater carriage clock, 8in. high. (C. G. Sloan & Co. Inc.) $3,100

French repeating gilt brass carriage clock with enamel dial, circa 1900, 19cm. high. (Robert W. Skinner Inc.)$850

English bronze carriage clock by Jas. McCabe, London, in original mahogany travelling case, 18cm. high.(Christie's) $4,445

A rare gilt, brass and enamel carriage timepiece, signed L. Leroy & Co. (Bonhams)$2,520

Very rare minute-repeating grande sonnerie alarm carriage clock, 6¾in. high. (Sotheby's)$5,150

Late 19th century French ormolu cased carriage clock by Goldsmith's Co., 16cm. high.(Langlois)$1,450

Unusual English carriage clock by R. & S. Garrard, London, 6½in. high, with red leather case. (Sotheby's)$6,550

Hour repeating alarm clock by Leroy et Fils, Paris, circa 1880, 17cm. high. (Sotheby's Belgravia) $1,195

French brass carriage clock by Henri Jacot, with lever movement and push repeat, 16cm. high. (Phillips) $1,220

French brass carriage clock by H. Jacot, 15.5cm. high, with leather case. (Phillips) $1,355

French brass carriage clock with lever movement inscribed Rapassee Par Leroy Fils, 13cm. high.(Phillips) $1,175

English duplex three-train bronzed carriage clock by Dent, with shaped handle, 23cm. high. (Christie's) $13,145

Brass carriage clock by E. W. Smith, London, with fusee movement, 12.5cm. high. (Phillips) $1,170

Lacquered brass miniature carriage clock in Empire style case, 9cm. high. (Christie's) $795

A French brass miniature carriage timepiece with lever movement, 7.5cm. high. (Phillips) $355

A small mosaic and enamel carriage timepiece, the lever movement signed Klaftenberger, Paris, 3¾in. high. (Sotheby's) $3,400

French brass carriage clock with lever movement, push repeat and alarm, 16.5cm. high. (Phillips)$1,050

An unusual early 19th century French travelling alarm timepiece and lighter inscribed Brevet D'Invention, 3¾in. high. (Sotheby's) $945

19th century brass carriage clock with lever movement and push repeat, 12.5cm. high. (Phillips) $1,010

Porcelain mounted carriage clock, dial signed Alexander & Son, Paris, 14cm. high. (Sotheby's) $1,725

Carriage clock with enamel dial in moulded rectangular case, 17.5cm. high, with leather travelling case. (Sotheby's) $1,185

Late 19th century French carriage clock, with cylinder movement, 4½in. high. (Vernon's) $230

Grande sonnerie carriage clock by Jas. Muirhead & Sons, Glasgow, 18cm. high, with Corinthian columns. (Sotheby's) $2,115

Quarter repeating enamel mounted alarm carriage clock, circa 1880. (Sotheby's Belgravia) $8,570

CARRIAGE CLOCKS

Lacquered brass oval carriage clock with enamel dial, circa 1880, 18.5cm. high. (Sotheby's Belgravia) $835

Porcelain mounted gilt metal striking carriage clock in travelling case, 13.5cm. high. (Christie's) $2,210

Gilt metal grande sonnerie calendar carriage clock by Leroy & Cie, Paris, 17cm. high. (Christie's) $5,615

Satinwood mantel chronometer by Joyce Murray, London, 22cm. high. (Sotheby's) $4,030

Miniature enamel striking carriage clock with Arabic chaptered enamel dial, 11.5cm. high. (Christie's) $4,915

Swiss carriage clock, enamel dial signed Dimier Geneve, with centre seconds, 14.5cm. high. (Sotheby's)$1,265

Lacquered brass miniature alarm carriage clock in corniche case, 8cm. high. (Christie's) $585

Brass oval striking carriage clock with travelling case, 14cm. high. (Christie's) $1,295

Very small lacquered brass and enamel carriage clock, 5.75cm. high. (Christie's) $980

Lacquered brass and porcelain striking carriage clock with stepped base and cornice, 16.5cm. high.(Christie's) $1,990

Hour repeating gilt brass carriage clock by J. R. Losada, London, 19cm. high, circa 1860. (Sotheby's Belgravia) $7,050

English engraved ormolu and malachite miniature carriage clock, case set with green agate panels, 7cm. high. (Christie's) $1,755

Mid 19th century gilt bronze quarter repeating calendar alarm carriage clock by Brequet, Paris, 19cm. high. (Sotheby's Belgravia) $1,195

Engraved gilt bronze oval cased hour repeating carriage clock, 15cm. high. (Sotheby's Belgravia) $1,030

English carriage clock in ormolu case with entwined foliage corner columns, 12.5cm. high. (Christie's) $3,345

Grande sonnerie alarm carriage clock with enamel dial, 14.5cm. high. (Sotheby's) $2,070

Porcelain mounted oval striking clock with repeat alarm on gong, 15cm. high. (Christie's) $3,040

Late 19th century miniature brass carriage lever timepiece, 8cm. high, with leather case. (Sotheby's Belgravia) $480

Gilt metal and enamel miniature carriage clock with domed base and cornice, 8.5cm. high. (Christie's) $1,170

Miniature gilt metal carriage clock with ivorine dial and twist Corinthian columns, 9.5cm. high. (Christie's) $1,405

Alarm carriage clock with enamel dial and centre seconds, 16cm. high. (Sotheby's) $1,010

Brass quarter repeating carriage clock in gorge case, circa 1880, 18cm. high. (Sotheby's Belgravia) $1,315

Rare French three-train chiming carriage clock by Richard & Co., 18cm. high.(Christie's) $4,560

Gilt metal oval miniature porcelain carriage clock by Drocourt, 8.25cm. high. (Christie's) $1,990

Large gilt metal chronometer carriage clock, enamel dial signed Sewill, 23.5cm. high. (Christie's) $8,890

Rare French quarter striking carriage clock by Berthoud, Paris, 25cm. high. (Christie's) $2,870

Gilt metal and porcelain striking carriage clock with enamel dial, 18cm. high. (Christie's) $1,755

Lacquered brass striking carriage clock by Gay, Lamaille & Co., 15cm. high. (Christie's) $1,920

Gilt metal quarter striking carriage clock by Jacot, 14.7cm. high. (Christie's) $1,870

Brass oval striking carriage clock with lever platform, lacking carrying handle, 14cm. high. (Christie's) $815

Fine lacquered brass striking carriage clock, case with Corinthian pillars, 17.5cm. high. (Christie's) $1,075

Fine gilt metal grande sonnerie calendar carriage clock with travelling case, 23cm. high. (Christie's) $12,480

209

Composed gilt bronze and white marble clock garniture, circa 1880. (Sotheby's Belgravia) $680

An ormolu bronze and white marble clock garniture, the enamel dial signed 'Raingo Freres Paris'. (C. G. Sloan & Co. Inc.) $3,300

Galle blue and white faience clock garniture, clock 60.5cm. high. (Christie's) $2,640

19th century three-piece Sevres biscuit clock garniture, the clock surmounted by a maiden teasing a winged cupid. (C. G. Sloan & Co. Inc.) $1,200

Three-piece Renaissance style bronze and Dore bronze clock garniture by J. E. Caldwell, clock 74cm. high. (C. G. Sloan & Co. Inc.) $5,500

Bronze, onyx and marble garniture, 3.87m. high. (Sotheby's Belgravia) $207,400

Victorian porcelain clock garniture. (Biddle & Webb) $2,055

An ormolu and white marble clock garniture, the dial signed Tiffany & Co., New York, France. (Sotheby's) $2,600

Late 19th century French ormolu and marble clock garniture, 16½in. high. (Robert W. Skinner Inc.) $500

French gilt spelter porcelain mounted clock garniture by Japy Freres, clock 33cm. high. (Lawrence Fine Art) $375

Gilt spelter and porcelain clock garniture, circa 1880's, clock 17¾in. high. (Sotheby's Belgravia) $705

White marble and gilt bronze clock garniture, signed R. W. Lomax, Manchester, circa 1880. (Sotheby's Belgravia) $395

Silvered bronze timepiece garniture, circa 1870, clock 42cm. high. (Sotheby's Belgravia) $620

Gilt bronze and electrotype clock garniture, circa 1880, clock 46cm. high. (Sotheby's Belgravia) $660

Three-piece Tiffany & Co. champleve enamel clock garniture, the vase flanked by two seated putti. (C. G. Sloan & Co. Inc.) $3,600

19th century clock garniture with gilt metal mounts, clock 17¼in. high. (Taylor Lane & Creber) $195

GRANDFATHER CLOCKS

Large Edwardian mahogany chiming longcase clock, door with glazed panels, 275cm. high. (Christie's) $8,640

18th century mahogany longcase clock by Francis Perigal, London, 94in. high. (Graves, Son & Pilcher) $4,840

Early 18th century wall alarm timepiece in burr-walnut and inlaid case, 6ft.6in. high. (Messenger May & Baverstock) $2,925

Mid 19th century mahogany longcase clock, dial signed indistinctly, 241cm. high.(Sotheby's Belgravia) $890

Early 19th century month-going seaweed marquetry longcase clock by Tho. Carter, London. (Phillips) $10,120

Early month longcase clock by Tho. Tompion, London, slightly restored, 6ft.6in. high. (Sotheby's) $21,330

Walnut longcase clock by George Graham, London, 7ft.5in. high. (Christie's) $31,070

Early Georgian green lacquer longcase clock by Tho. Reynolds, Oxford, 8ft. high. (Messenger May & Baverstock) $2,925

18th century burr-walnut longcase clock. (Plaza, New York) $5,750

Early 18th century walnut marquetry longcase clock with eight-day striking movement.(Locke & England) $6,540

Early George III green lacquered longcase clock by Benj, Smith, Canterbury. (Phillips) $4,140

18th century longcase clock by Tho. Richardson, Weaveram, in mahogany case with fluted pilaster corners. (Taylor, Lane & Creber) $1,185

Mid 18th century Dutch burr-walnut longcase clock by Tho. Thomsen, Amsterdam. (Phillips) $7,360

Mid 19th century George III style mahogany longcase clock by J. Scott, Paisley, 7ft. 4in. high. (Sotheby's) $1,445

Regency mahogany regulator timepiece by James McCabe, London. (Phillips) $8,740

George III mahogany longcase clock, dial signed John Gale, London,(Christie's) $5,520

Early 18th century walnut and marquetry longcase clock by John Aylward, Guildford. (Phillips) $13,800

Edwardian mahogany striking and chiming clock with glazed door. (Bradley & Vaughan) $3,630

Walnut and seaweed marquetry longcase clock, dial signed Wm. Camden, London. (Christie's) $4,080

Small walnut marquetry longcase clock, dial signed Joseph Windmills, London, 6ft.6in. high.(Sotheby's) $15,210

GRANDFATHER CLOCKS

   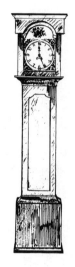 

Inlaid mahogany North Welsh longcase clock by Jones, Bethseda, 7ft.8in. high. (Lowery & Partners) $795

Chippendale style mahogany Westminster chimes longcase clock by Daniel Pratt's Son, Mass., 97in. high. (C. G. Sloan & Co. Inc.)$1,100

Gothic revival longcase clock by J. C. Jennens & Son, London, 107in. high. (C. G. Sloan & Co. Inc.) $10,400

American cherrywood longcase clock, 84in. high. (C. G. Sloan & Co. Inc.) $1,350

Late 19th century dark mahogany chiming longcase clock. (Andrew Grant)$840

 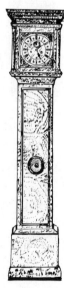 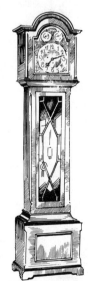 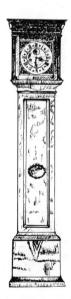 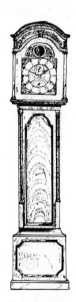

Late 18th century oak and mahogany longcase clock by Samuel Ashton, Bredbury. (Locke & England) $1,145

Walnut longcase clock, dial signed Jos. Windmills, London, 6ft.10in. high. (Sotheby's) $4,680

Edwardian longcase clock with brass dial and Westminster chimes, mechanism by Reid & Son, Newcastle. (Worsfolds) $2,410

Dutch quarter striking walnut longcase clock by Fromanteel & Clarke, 6ft.11in. high. (Christie's) $10,755

George III mahogany longcase clock by Charles Massey, Lambeth, 7ft.1in. high. (Sotheby's) $3,510

Dutch longcase clock by D. K. Schooman, Arnhem, 98in. high. (C. G. Sloan & Co. Inc.) $4,250

19th century oak longcase clock by Jasper Harman, London, with brass face. (Locke & England) $1,375

Regency period longcase regulator by Thos. Richardson, Manchester, in mahogany case. (Irelands) $2,830

Late 18th century oak longcase clock with scrolled pediment, by Thomas Knight, Birmingham. (Locke & England) $1,080

Late 17th century walnut and marquetry inlaid longcase clock by Ed. Norton, Warwick, 7ft.4in. high. (Geering & Colyer) $8,360

Seaweed marquetry longcase clock by Joseph Jackeman, London, 212cm. high. (Christie's) $4,064

Mahogany cased eight-day longcase clock with brass face, by Henry Rigby, Liverpool, circa 1790.(Frank B. Marshall) $4,975

18th century walnut cased longcase clock by Richard Peckover, London. (Phillips) $4,080

Walnut and marquetry longcase clock, 6ft.9in. high. (Christie's) $3,585

Early 18th century marquetry longcase clock by Thos. Wightman, London. (Phillips) $7,850

GRANDFATHER CLOCKS

George IV mahogany longcase regulator with domed top, 188cm. high. (Christie's) $5,150

George III Scottish oak longcase clock by Mathew Lyon, Lanark, 7ft.7in. high. (Sotheby's) $1,265

Grandfather clock by E. Barker, Framlingham, in mahogany case with inlay to the door. (Bracketts) $1,745

Marquetry longcase clock by Samuel Barrow, London, 7ft.1in. high. (Sotheby's) $6,320

Edwardian musical longcase clock in elaborately carved oak case, by Harrison & Son, Darlington, 8ft.6in. high. (Morphets) $4,405

Dutch ebonised longcase clock by Joseph Norris, Amsterdam, 6ft. 2in. high. (Christie's) $6,690

George III mahogany musical longcase clock, dial signed Robt. Beets Lynn, 259cm. high. (Christie's) $6,000

Mid 18th century oak longcase clock by Jn. Swinbourne, Dilston. (Locke & England) $1,405

George III mahogany longcase clock by Ellicott, London, 8ft.2in. high. (Sotheby's) $5,382

Georgian black and gold laquer longcase clock signed Adamson Tadcaster, 93½in. high. (C. G. Sloan & Co. Inc.) $2,200

George III mahogany longcase clock by Thomason Fitter, London, 7ft. 11in. high. (Sotheby's) $3,450

William and Mary marquetry longcase clock, dial signed Chr. Gould, London, 206cm. high. (Christie's) $15,210

George III quarter-striking, chiming, calendar mahogany longcase clock, by Shakeshaft, Preston, 250cm. high. (Christie's) $6,550

Rare George II astronomical longcase clock by Wm. Webster, London, in walnut veneered case, 221cm. high. (Christie's) $11,230

Mahogany longcase clock inlaid with boxwood and ebonised stringing, signed Smith, Putney. (Sotheby, King & Chasemore) $1,345

Late 17th century marquetry longcase clock by John Martin, London, 6ft. 10in. high. (Christie's) $7,650

George III mahogany longcase clock, dial signed Percival Mann, London, 247cm. high. (Christie's) $3,600

Walnut marquetry longcase clock by Joseph Windmills, circa 1700, with brass dial.(Stride & Son) $17,850

Late 17th century seaweed marquetry longcase clock by Cha. Gretton, London, 7ft.7in. high. (Christie's) $6,000

Early 18th century walnut longcase clock with oyster-work and marquetry. (Locke & England) $7,260

217

GRANDFATHER CLOCKS

Rare marquetry quarter repeating month longcase clock by Claude Du Chesne, 8ft. 2in. high. (Sotheby's) $15,210

George II burr-yew musical longcase clock by Robt. Henderson, London, 244cm. high. (Christie's) $15,210

18th century walnut longcase clock by J. Windmills, London, 82in. high. (Edwards, Bigwood & Bewlay) $14,950

Georgian mahogany chiming longcase clock, signed John Brice, 240cm. high. (Christie's) $3,360

Marquetry longcase clock by Tompion. (Sotheby's) $21,960

Early 18th century walnut Dutch striking longcase clock, dial signed J. van Ceule Le Jeune Hagae, 7ft.2in. high. (Sotheby's) $5,850

George II walnut chiming longcase clock, dial signed John Ellicott, London, 7ft.10in. high. (Sotheby's) $12,170

Boulle and ormolu cased Comptoise clock, 7ft.8½in. high. (Graves, Son & Pilcher) $8,570

Thomas Tompion walnut month going longcase clock, 6ft.8½in. high. (Christie's) $35,850

George III mahogany chiming musical longcase clock by Daniel De St. Leu, 8ft.5in. high. (Sotheby's) $7,360

218

Walnut longcase clock, dial signed Willm. Charles, Chepstow, 7ft.3in. high. (Sotheby's) $3,680

Walnut longcase clock by Richard Peckover. (Phillips) $4,010

Mahogany longcase clock by John Laurence of Lancaster, 8ft.3in. high. (Vernon's) $3,000

George III mahogany longcase clock, dial signed Ellicott, London, 247cm. high. (Christie's) $6,320

George III lacquered musical longcase clock with chinoiserie decoration, 252cm. high. (Christie's) $5,615

Month duration walnut longcase clock by Thos. Tompion, London, unnumbered, 198cm. high. (Christie's) $63,180

19th century Dutch walnut and marquetry longcase clock, 8ft.5in. high. (Christie's) $2,390

18th century walnut cased longcase clock by Justin Vulliamy. (V. & V.) $7,810

Mahogany longcase clock by Joseph Knibb, London, 6ft.4in. high. (Christie's) $12,430

18th century month going seaweed marquetry longcase clock by Thomas Carter, London. (Phillips) $10,470

Early 19th century mahogany longcase clock by W. Rutherford, Hawick, 90½in. high. (Sotheby's Belgravia) $1,050

Early 18th century Dutch marquetry longcase clock, dial signed Preter Klock, Amsterdam, 224cm. high. (Christie's) $11,230

Carved oak pedestal clock by C. Lupton, Cornhill, London, 190.5cm. high, 1870-90.(Sotheby's Belgravia) $1,920

Early 19th century mahogany longcase clock by Jno. Telford, Wigton, 89in. high.(Sotheby's Belgravia) $1,145

George I seaweed marquetry month duration longcase clock by Peter Garon, London, 285cm. high. (Christie's) $10,530

Flame mahogany longcase clock with Gothic type cresting, 7ft.2in. high. (Lawrence Fine Art)$1,450

Eight-day longcase clock by Joseph Knibb. (Burtenshaw Walker) $8,435

18th century mahogany longcase clock, disc inscribed Joshua Allsop, East Smith Field, 6ft11in. high. (Parsons, Welch & Cowell) $5,060

George I green lacquer longcase clock signed Samuel Harris, London, 9ft. high. (Sotheby's) $3,320

Oak longcase clock by J. Balling, Shepton Mallet, 7ft.6in. high (Lawrence Fine Art) $610

George III Scottish mahogany longcase clock signed T. Barclay, Montrose, 7ft.1in. high. (Sotheby's) $1,945

Oak longcase clock by John Miller, London, with square brass dial, 6ft.6in. high. (Lawrence Fine Art) $1,755

Mahogany longcase clock, dial signed Thos. Clare, Warrington, 8ft.8in. high, circa 1790. (Sotheby's) $2,370

Early 18th century walnut cased longcase clock by John Archambo. (Woolley & Wallis) $4,115

Eight-day longcase clock in mahogany and satinwood case with marquetry decoration, by Maple & Co., London. (Burtenshaw Walker) $4,440

Marquetry longcase clock, circa 1700, 6ft.10in. high. (Sotheby's) $5,925

George III mahogany longcase clock by Jno. Shelton, London, in molded case, 213cm. high. (Christie's) $7,020

Mahogany regulator with silvered dial, signed W. H. Davis, London, 6ft.3in. high. (Sotheby's) $5,450

Figured mahogany longcase clock by Wm. Garrat, Wapping, 7ft.3½in. high. (Lawrence Fine Art) $1,170

Month duration walnut longcase clock by Joseph Knibb, London, 196cm. high. (Christie's) $39,780

221

LANTERN CLOCKS

Early Georgian lantern clock by George Horsnail, (Graves, Son & Pilcher) $2,380

17th century wing lantern clock with posted frame with pierced and engraved cresting pieces, 41cm. high. (Phillips)$2,690

Rare chiming lantern clock by W. Monk, 17in. high. (Sotheby's) $3,975

Early English brass lantern clock by James Gray, Shaftesbury, 36.2cm. high. (Lawrence Fine Art) $4,680

17th century English brass lantern clock by Isaac Papanoine, 12in. high. (Robert W. Skinner Inc.) $1,500

Late 17th century brass lantern clock by Thomas Dyde, London, 34cm. high. (Phillips) $2,415

German lantern clock in iron posted frame with shaped corner posts, 33cm. high. (Sotheby's) $2,070

Mid 19th century brass lantern clock, 15½in. high. (Sotheby's Belgravia) $505

Brass lantern clock by C. E. Price, London, 40cm. high. (C. G. Sloan & Co. Inc.) $500

Rare lantern clock, 16in. high, frame with armorial cresting pieces. (Sotheby's) $2,105

18th century French brass lantern clock, slightly damaged, 21cm. high. (Robert W. Skinner Inc.) $900

17th century brass lantern clock by John Pennock, 38cm. high. (Phillips) $1,920

Mid 19th century mantel clock with plain arched top, by Thos. Sherwood, Leeds, 42.5cm. high. (Butler & Hatch Waterman) $490

Unusual bronze mantel clock contained in vase case supported by two shi-shi, circa 1900, 73.5cm. high. (Sotheby's Belgravia) $1,215

Edwardian mahogany cased mantel clock by Elkington. (Vernon's) $90

Louis XV style Buhl bracket clock by Payne & Co., London, 60cm. high, with eagle pediment. (Lowery & Partners) $1,125

French ormolu and black marble mantel clock, 42.5cm. high. (C. G. Sloan & Co. Inc.) $750

Mid 19th century Continental timepiece with Meissen porcelain decoration. (Locke & England) $2,685

A good French 19th century ormolu and marble lyre clock. (Parsons, Welch & Cowell) $840

An Art Deco bronze, black onyx and marble mantel clock on a rectangular marble base, 57.2cm. wide. (Christie's) $1,150

Late 18th century musical automaton by John Mottram. (Bonhams) $47,200

Late 19th century gilt brass mantel clock with inset porcelain panels. (Locke & England) $715

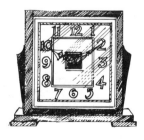

An Art Deco lapis lazuli and Aventurine mantel clock with Swiss lever movement, 28.5cm. wide. (Christie's) $2,310

Unusual Oriental style gilded French clock, ebonised with ivory insets, circa 1870. (Grays Antique Mews) $2,140

223

Marquetry inlaid
mantel clock with
Roman numerals,
10in. high. (Clive
Emson & Co.)
$175

Second Empire gilt bronze
mantel clock with Roman
numerals, circa 1860, 64cm.
high. (Sotheby's Belgravia)
$940

Large Louis Philippe
ormolu and Sevres
porcelain urn clock,
63.5cm. high.
(Christie's)
$4,760

Empire ormolu chariot mantel
clock, circa 1810, 40.5cm. high.
(Sotheby's) $2,360

19th century brass striking
mantel clock in glazed bronze
case, signed Smith & Sons,
32cm. high. (Christie's)
$1,005

Red boulle mantel clock
with gilt dial, circa 1900,
42cm. high. (Sotheby's
Belgravia) $870

17th century ebonised
clock with alarm, back-
plate signed Edward
East, London, 42cm.
high. (Christie's)
$9,560

Gilt bronze perpetual
calendar mantel clock
by Gibson, Belfast, circa
1880, 53.5cm. high.
(Sotheby's Belgravia)
$2,340

Ormolu and white
marble calendar lyre
mantel clock, 56.6cm.
high, circa 1860.
(Sotheby's Belgravia)
$4,500

Walnut mantel timepiece,
dial signed H. Taute, King-
ston, 26cm. high.
(Sotheby's) $1,705

Unusual early 19th century
French musical mantel timepiece by Alibert, Paris, 13in.
high. (Sotheby's)$655

Italian night clock, case
of altar form with floral
marquetry, 84cm. high.
(Christie's)$4,780

Brass-inlaid ebonised chiming mantel clock, dial signed Brockhouse & Tunnicliff, Derby, 22in. high. (Sotheby's) $2,105

Early 19th century French bronze and ormolu mantel timepiece, dial signed De Cann, Versailles, 29cm. high. (Sotheby's) $3,775

Ormolu mounted malachite vase clock of Louis XVI design, 28cm. high.(Christie's) $2,005

Unusual George IV brass-inlaid mahogany clock and bracket, dial signed B. Edwards, London, 46cm. high. (Sotheby's) $1,425

Boulle clock and bracket, circa 1870, 28cm. high. (Sotheby's Belgravia) $2,775

Fine carved oak three train mantel clock with arched brass faced dial, 70cm. high. (Andrew Grant)$1,680

Gilt bronze and tortoise-shell mantel clock with enamel dial, circa 1880, 39.6cm. high.(Sotheby's Belgravia) $540

Late 19th century gilt metal and enamel boudoir clock, probably Viennese, 7.5cm. high. (Sotheby's Belgravia) $355

French gilt metal four glass calendar mantel clock, stamped C. R., 38cm. high.(Christie's) $3,600

Ormolu and porcelain perpetual calendar mantel clock by Leroy et Fils, Paris, 43cm. high. (Lawrence Fine Art) $3,980

Lalique Art Deco style mantel clock, 30cm. high, on silvered metal illuminated base. (Renton & Renton) $3,780

Small gilt metal German table clock surmounted by a bell, 173mm. high, circa 1600.(Sotheby's) $3,450

225

Gilt brass strut clock, signed French, Royal Exchange, London, 14.5cm. high. (Lawrence Fine Art) $840

Louis XVI ormolu-mounted marble mantel clock, enamel dial signed Gavelle l'aine a Paris, circa 1785, 51cm. high. (Sotheby's) $1,180

Late 19th century Swiss musical mantel clock in fruitwood case, 38cm. high. (Sotheby's Belgravia) $390

Regency boulle clock and bracket, circa 1720, dial signed Mynuel a Paris, 84cm. high. (Sotheby's) $3,160

Ormolu and jewelled Sevres porcelain mantel clock, circa 1880, 51cm. high. (Sotheby's Belgravia) $3,760

Regency polychrome boulle clock, movement signed De Forges a Dijon, 89cm. high. (Christie's) $4,520

French gilt brass mantel clock with galleried top, 44.5cm. high. (Lawrence Fine Art) $560

Louis XV Vernis Martin bracket timepiece and bracket, dial signed Dubois a Paris, 67cm. high. (Sotheby's) $2,925

Louis XV boulle clock and bracket, dial signed Burgeat a Versailles, circa 1745, 89cm. high. (Sotheby's)$3,275

Ormolu- mounted Sevres mantel clock, signed Bourdin, 80cm. high, 1870's. (Sotheby's Belgravia)$10,105

Rosewood mantel clock, dial signed Breese, London, in flat topped case, 23.5cm. high. (Lawrence Fine Art) $2,105

Mid 19th century 'Sevres' gilt bronze-mounted clock case, 38cm. high. (Sotheby's Belgravia) $725

Gilt bronze and porcelain mantel clock, circa 1860, 33cm. high, dial signed by Jre. Eglese. (Sotheby's Belgravia) $495

Unusual gilt metal travelling or desk clock by S. F. Hancock, London, 6¼in. high. (Sotheby's) $2,575

French porcelain mounted ormolu mantel clock, by S. Marti, 39.4cm. high. (Lawrence Fine Art) $655

Regency boulle clock and bracket, circa 1720, 97cm. high, signed Terrier a Paris. (Sotheby's) $2,575

Empire ormolu mantel clock, dial signed Laborie a Paris, circa 1810, 53.5cm. high. (Sotheby's) $6,610

Louis XV boulle quarter repeating timepiece and bracket, signed Leroy a Paris, circa 1750, 56cm. high. (Sotheby's) $2,925

Early 20th century Swiss musical apostle clock by D. Allard & Cie, 102cm. high. (Sotheby's Belgravia) $1,105

Boulle clock and bracket, by Francois Doyen a Paris, circa 1730, 102cm. high. (Sotheby's) $3,040

George III Vernis Martin organ clock by Spencer & Perkins, London, 140cm. high.(Christie's) $28,680

Early 19th century repeating mantel clock, dial signed Arnold and Dent, London. (Sotheby, King & Chasemore) $4,400

German Empire amboyna wood mantel clock with enamel dial, 42cm. high. (Christie's) $950

Louis XV ormolu mantel clock, dial signed Jn. Baptiste Baillon, circa 1760, 43cm. high. (Sotheby's) $6,085

Liberty & Co. pewter clock designed by Archibald Knox, 20.25cm. high, circa 1905. (Sotheby's Belgravia) $1,790

19th century French ormolu mantel clock, gilt dial with floral border, 43.5cm. high. (Burrows & Day) $585

Late 19th century French bronze, cartel clock signed E. de Labroue Fbt. a Paris, 40.5cm. diam. (Sotheby's Belgravia) $845

17th century gilt metal striking table clock, silver dial with Roman numerals. (Sotheby's) $6,900

Large eight-day mahogany boulle mantel clock, by Tritschler & Miller, London, 75cm. high.(Andrew Grant) $3,120

Gilt bronze and porcelain mantel timepiece, by Edward & Sons, 22cm. high, circa 1900.(Sotheby's Belgravia) $380

Second Empire gilt bronze mantel clock with fluted columns, circa 1850, 34cm. high. (Sotheby's Belgravia) $620

Gilt bronze mantel timepiece by Payne, London, circa 1850, 20.5cm. high. (Sotheby's Belgravia) $740

Large bronze and marble mantel clock, 75cm. high, 1880's.(Sotheby's Belgravia) $660

Willaim IV rosewood mantel clock, dial signed Thomas, 444 Kingsland Road, 43cm. high, circa 1835.(Sotheby's Belgravia) $1,005

Clock in the form of a tower surmounted by a revolving vane, by James Cox, London. (Phillips) $18,565

Bronze and champleve enamel mantel clock, late 19th century, 36cm. high. (Sotheby's Belgravia) $820

19th century French lyre clock, by A. D. Mougin, in gilt brass mounted onyx case, 37.5cm. high.(Burrows & Day) $840

Regency brass inlaid mahogany mantel clock by Yonge & Son, Strand, 52cm. high, sold with bracket.(Sotheby's) $2,300

19th century French ormolu mantel clock with white enamel dial, 43.5cm. high. (Burrows & Day) $5,030

Louis XVI ormolu and alabaster mantel clock, dial signed D. F. Dubois, Paris, 43cm. high. (Christie's)$4,800

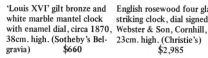

George III brass inlaid ebonised chiming mantel clock, dial signed Jackson, Merton, 63cm. high.(Sotheby's) $1,725

'Louis XVI' gilt bronze and white marble mantel clock with enamel dial, circa 1870, 38cm. high. (Sotheby's Belgravia) $660

English rosewood four glass striking clock, dial signed Webster & Son, Cornhill, 23cm. high. (Christie's) $2,985

Bronze and white marble mantel clock by Leroy of Paris, circa 1870, 58cm. high.(Sotheby's Belgravia) $595

Late 19th century French porcelain mounted ormolu mantel clock. (Parsons, Welch & Cowell)$630

Late 19th century American 'John Bull' cast iron clock by Bradley & Hubbard, 42cm. high. (Sotheby's Belgravia) $725

Gilt metal mantel timepiece, backplate signed Payne, 163 New Bond St., 25.5cm. high, on velvet covered stand. (Sotheby's) $505

Liberty & Co. pewter clock designed by Archibald Knox, circa 1903, 20.5cm. high. (Sotheby's Belgravia) $2,105

Ormolu mantel clock, dial signed Raingo Freres a Paris, circa 1870, 56cm. wide.(Sotheby's Belgravia) $2,305

Liberty & Co. 'cymric' silver and enamel clock, Birmingham 1904, 12.25cm. high.(Sotheby's Belgravia) $1,170

Gilt bronze and verde antico mantel clock, 1870's, 62cm. wide. (Sotheby's Belgravia) $1,130

Gilt bronze mantel clock in drum case, circa 1870, 46cm. high. (Sotheby's Belgravia) $210

Early 19th century pendule d'officier, 8in. high, with enamel dial.(Sotheby's) $2,810

Boulle mantel clock, dial with enamel numerals, circa 1880, 48cm. high. (Sotheby's Belgravia) $420

Early 19th century Viennese mahogany automaton mantel clock surmounted by an eagle, 78.5cm. high. (Sotheby's Belgravia) $610

Louis XIV pendule religieuse with circular dial signed I. Thuret, Paris, 58cm. high. (Christie's) $2,810

Early 17th century gilt metal crucifix clock, possibly by Nicolaus Siebenhaer, 305mm. high. (Sotheby's) $8,740

Lacquered brass and porcelain mantel clock, signed Japy Freres, circa 1900, 32cm. high. (Sotheby's Belgravia) $305

Unusual clock set of Australian design fitted with German movement. (Taylor, Lane & Creber) $585

Gilt bronze mantel clock with open Brocot movement, 34cm. high, circa 1900. (Taylor, Lane & Creber). $670

Early 20th century French gilt bronze mounted clock, signed by Dumas, 26cm. high. (Sotheby's Belgravia) $400

Small late 19th century French ormolu striking timepiece on stand. (Hexton & Cheney) $155

Black marble and green onyx desk strut clock, signed Cartier, 17cm. high. (Christie's) $3,980

'Louis XV' gilt bronze mantel clock on stand, 51cm. high, circa 1850. (Sotheby's Belgravia) $1,130

French Empire burr-maple table regulator clock with enamel dial, 44cm. high.(Christie's) $3,960

French bronze mantel clock signed Pre. Leurtier a Paris, 56cm. high. (Sotheby's Belgravia) $2,045

Liberty & Co. 'Tudric' pewter clock designed by Archibald Knox, circa 1903, 14cm. high. (Sotheby's Belgravia) $1,215

Unusual hall clock in oak, quarter striking on nine tubular bells, circa 1891, 236cm. high. (Sotheby's Belgravia) $2,810

Unusual French striking clock, dated 1835, 57cm. high. (Christie's) $910

Gilt bronze and marble mantel clock, circa 1850, 47.5cm. high. (Sotheby's Belgravia) $930

Gilt bronze combined timepiece and aneroid barometer, 1880's, 17cm. high, in leather case.(Sotheby's Belgravia) $910

Gilt bronze mantel clock on stand, circa 1850, 28cm. high. (Sotheby's Belgravia)$610

231

An early Louis XVI ormolu mantel clock flanked by figures of cherubs, circa 1775. (Sotheby's)
$3,150

Louis XVI marble and ormolu mantel timepiece, the drum-shaped movement surmounted by an eagle, 36cm. high. (Phillips) $670

Mid 20th century French enamel and gilt-metal mantel clock in the form of a screen, 11.5cm. high. (Sotheby's Belgravia) $630

19th century ormolu mounted ebonised Arc de Triomphe clock, 24in. high. (C. G. Sloan & Co. Inc.) $400

An Empire ormolu mantel clock with outside anchor escapement, 13½in. high, 1815. (Sotheby's) $840

A Liberty & Co. Tudric pewter and enamel clock, 18cm. high, circa 1905. (Sotheby's Belgravia) $505

An Austrian Zappler timepiece, the dial with Roman chapters, 5in. high. (Sotheby's) $575

Late 19th century French glass and brass mantel clock sold by Shreve, Crump and Law, Boston, 12in. high. (Robert W. Skinner Inc.) $325

19th century Louis XVI style ormolu mantel clock with inset Sevres plaques, 19½in. high. (Robert W. Skinner Inc.) $1,200

A Restoration ormolu Temple clock, the circular white enamel dial signed Kinable, 15½in. high, circa 1825. (Sotheby's) $1,680

An Empire ormolu mantel clock with circular white enamel dial signed D'Arthois Fila A Paria, 15½in. high, 1815. (Sotheby's) $1,260

17th century German gilt metal bronze table timepiece, surmounted by an Eastern figure, 23cm. high. (Phillips) $4,200

Brass skeleton timepiece by W. Slater, Holloway, on marble base, circa 1870, 38.8cm. high. (Sotheby's Belgravia)$955

Irish brass striking skeleton clock by Law & Son, Dublin, 46cm. high. (Christie's) $1,960

Unusual and interesting skeleton clock by Wm. Strutt, Derby, 23.5cm. high. (Christie's) $2,225

Mid 19th century brass skeleton clock. (Edgar Horn) $1,190

A good mid 19th century brass skeleton clock representing the Royal Pavilion, Brighton. (Phillips) $3,255

A Victorian brass skeleton timepiece, the movement with anchor escapement, 33cm. high. (Phillips) $630

19th century brass skeleton timepiece on ebonised stand, 32cm. high. (Phillips) $795

19th century brass skeleton clock with striking movement. (Moore, Allen & Innocent) $590

19th century skeleton clock with open silvered dial, 40cm. high. (Taylor Lane & Creber) $770

Skeleton clock by Smith & Sons of Clerkenwell, London, 1ft. 4½in. high. (Sotheby's) $2,100

A 19th century brass skeleton clock with a silvered chapter ring inscribed William Grace Clerrenwell, 21¾in. high.(Geering & Colyer) $1,200

Brass cathedral skeleton clock by Vaughan, Newport, 52cm. high. (Sotheby, King & Chasemore) $1,135

233

WALL CLOCKS

Late Louis XV cartel clock, dial signed Le comte a Paris, 81cm. high, circa 1770. (Sotheby's) $4,720

George III mahogany wall timepiece, silvered dial signed Jabez Smith, London, 15½in. high. (Sotheby's)$1,640

18th century Friesian stoelklok with repousse gilt mounts, 2ft.4in. high. (Sotheby's) $1,755

Early 19th century wall clock in octagonal walnut, mahogany and brass inlaid case, by B. Mosser & Co., 13in. high. (Taylor Lane & Creber) $180

Early electric wall clock in mahogany case, 5ft.2in. high, circa 1860, possibly by Henry Kerr.(Christie's) $8,125

Willard type presentation banjo clock with acorn finial, 41in. high. (C. G. Sloan & Co. Inc.) $950

Grandfather movement brass face and single hand, signed James Smyth, Saxmundham, circa 1735. (Clive Emson)$375

Mid 18th century black lacquered and chinoiserie Act of Parliament clock by J. Ireland, 1.17m. high. (Phillips) $2,225

Early 20th century Waltham mahogany banjo clock, 40in. high. (Robert W. Skinner Inc.) $1,250

Tavern or coaching inn clock by Thomas Field, Bath, circa 1780, in black lacquered case. (Locke & England) $5,245

Mahogany wall regulator, dial signed Brock, London, with triangular base and pediment, 5ft.4in. high. (Sotheby's)$3,450

Mid Georgian giltwood cartel clock, dial signed Stepn. Thorogood, London, 88cm. high. (Christie's) $2,660

234

Louis XVI ormolu cartel clock, dial signed Cronier, Paris, circa 1780, 77cm. high. (Sotheby's) $2,596

Unusual and very small 18th century alarm wall timepiece, dial signed C. Bucourt a Neelle, 4½in. high. (Sotheby's) $1,755

Mid 18th century Louis XV ormolu cartel clock, dial signed Le Grand a Paris, 51cm. high. (Sotheby's) $4,210

Gilt bronze mounted ebonised wood wall clock, circa 1880, 87.5cm. high. (Sotheby's Belgravia) $845

Black and gold lacquered Act of Parliament timepiece, dial 29½in. diam. (Lawrence Fine Art) $1,640

Louis XVI parquetry cartel clock by Cronier, Paris, 110cm. high. (C. G. Sloan & Co. Inc.) $5,750

Mid 19th century French eagle and swag wall clock, 32in. high. (Robert W. Skinner Inc.) $1,100

Victorian wall clock with glass front showing brass pendulum and weights and horse surmounts. (Allen & May) $305

Empire ormolu cartel clock of small size, signed Breguet et Fils, 33cm. high. (Sotheby's Belgravia) $3,855

18th century English lacquered Act of Parliament wall clock, signed Benj. Booth, 165cm. high. (Christie's) $1,920

19th century walnut and marquetry wall clock by Lond of Uffculme, 32in. high. (Taylor Lane & Creber) $335

19th century Vienna regulator wall clock in walnut case, 120cm. high. (Sotheby, King & Chasemore) $720

WALL CLOCKS

Victorian mahogany framed wall clock with brass pendulum. (Vernon's) $380

E. Ingraham & Co., mahogany Ionic wall clock with reverse painted lower door 21½in. high, circa 1880. (Robert W. Skinner Inc.) $250

Victorian walnut framed wall clock with floral inlay, 75cm. high. (Vernon's) $210

An unusual ormolu quarter repeating Cartel timepiece with a 6 inch enamel dial late 18th century. (Sotheby's) $2,415

Regulator wall timepiece by D. Pratt & Sons, Boston, 34in. high, circa 1850. (Robert W. Skinner Inc.) $1,250

Vienna regulator clock in walnut case, 5ft.10in. high, with white enamel dial. (John Francis, Thomas Jones & Sons) $2,400

Oak regulator wall timepiece inscribed, E. Howard & Co., Boston, 31½in. high. (Robert W. Skinner Inc.) $1,400

Late 19th century Gilbert calendar wall regulator timepiece, 45in. high, Winstead, Connecticut. (Robert W. Skinner Inc.) $475

L. F. & W. W. Carter weight driven double dial calendar clock, 32in. high, late 19th century, Bristol, Connecticut. (Robert W. Skinner Inc.) $875

E. Howard gallery clock in walnut and burr veneered frame, 52½in. high, Boston, Massachusetts. (Robert W. Skinner Inc.) $3,250

Mahogany banjo regulator with 8 day weight driven movement by Joshua Seward, Boston 1831, 64in. high. (Robert W. Skinner Inc.) $3,250

Late Louis XV ormolu quarter repeating Cartel timepiece by Juhel A Paris, 20in. high, circa 1770. (Sotheby's) $4,830

236

American gold open-face watch by
E. Howard & Co., Boston, 53mm.
diam. (Christie's N. York)
$500

18ct. gold hunting cased centre seconds
keyless lever watch by J. Hargreaves,
1892, 57mm. diam. (Sotheby's
Belgravia) $795

Old chronometer by Margetts,
London, No. 85. (Laurence &
Martin Taylor) $500

19th century gold fob watch,
gem-set. (Phillips)$1,895

Gold hunter-cased minute-repeating
lever watch, London, 1912, 55mm.
diam. (Christie's) $6,240

19th century oval rock crystal cased
verge watch by Frederic Duval, Paris,
88mm. long. (Sotheby's)
                    $2,300

Swiss gold hunter cased lever
watch by Henry Bequelin,
Locle, 43mm. diam.(Christie's)
          $350

Gold repousse pair-cased verge watch and
gilt metal chatelaine by Allen Walker,
London, 1784, 54mm. diam. (Christie's)
                    $5,735

Half quarter-repeating lever watch
by Charles Frodsham, London,
51mm. diam. (Phillips)
                    $7,130

Gold open-face lever watch by
Robert Brandt, Geneva, 45mm.
diam. (Sotheby's Belgravia)
          $305

Swedish silver cased stopwatch signed And.
Lundstedt, Stockholm, 58mm. diam.
(Christie's) $1,920

Victorian 18ct. gold gentleman's
open-face pocket watch, Chester
hallmarked. (Sotheby, King &
Chasemore) $485

Gold hunting cased fusee keyless watch by Thomas Lancaster Whipp, Rochdale, 1874, 44mm. diam. (Sotheby's) $1,660

Gold and enamel bracelet watch by Moricand & Degrange, Geneva, circa 1830, movement 30mm. diam. (Sotheby's)$3,335

18-carat gold hunting cased lever watch by Thomas Russell & Son, Liverpool, 1855, 53mm. diam. (Sotheby's Belgravia) $955

18-carat gold open-faced lever watch by Barrauds & Lund, London, 1842, 41mm. diam., with a key. (Sotheby's Belgravia) $500

Silver pair-cased six-hour dialled verge watch by Tho. Tompion and Geo. Graham, London, 56mm. diam. (Sotheby's) $8,530

Continental gold dual time lever watch with thermometer, 52mm. diam., in engine-turned case. (Christie's)$1,910

18-carat gold half hunting cased keyless lever chronograph by Douglas & Son, Greenock, 1851, 51cm. diam. (Sotheby's Belgravia) $695

Swiss gold half hunter-cased minute repeating keyless lever watch, 53mm. diam. (Christie's) $2,760

French gold quarter repeating and musical watch, 57mm. diam. (Christie's) $3,360

Mid 18th century repousse gold pair-cased quarter repeating verge watch by Joseph Martineau Senr., London, 51mm. diam.(Sotheby's) $4,030

Mid 19th century gold and enamel cylinder watch by Vaucher Freres of Fleurier, 26mm. diam. (Sotheby's) $1,045

18-carat gold open-faced lever watch by Henry Frodsham, Liverpool, 1836, 44mm. diam., with floral key. (Sotheby's Belgravia) $955

Swiss gold hunter-cased tourbillon keyless lever watch, dial signed A. Ecalle, Paris, 53mm. diam. (Christie's) $29,875

Oval gilt metal Turkish verge watch, circa 1700, 53mm. diam. (Sotheby's) $2,300

Silver hunting cased crab-tooth duplex watch with double dial, 49mm. diam. (Sotheby's Belgravia) $1,040

18-carat gold half-hunting cased keyless lever watch by Waltham Watch Co., 1908, 49mm. diam. (Sotheby's Belgravia) $595

Swiss gold hunter-cased quarter repeating keyless lever watch with enamel dial, 57mm. diam. (Christie's) $8,160

Late 18th century enamelled gold pair-cased repeating pocket watch. (Sotheby, King & Chasemore) $2,300

Gold and enamel open-faced cylinder watch in engine-turned case, 46mm. diam. (Sotheby's Belgravia) $550

Silver hunter-cased pocket chronometer by Grimalde and Johnson, London, 1810, 58mm. diam. (Christie's) $3,110

Gold repousse pair-cased verge watch, movement signed Jno. Markham, London, 56mm. diam. (Christie's) $2,455

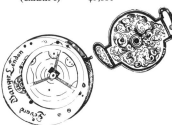

Gold duplex watch by John Blaylock, Carlisle, 1841, 51mm. diam. (Sotheby's) $1,565

Very rare silver verge watch, backplate signed Edward Banger, London, 59mm. diam. (Christie's) $7,490

Rare American silver open-faced chronometer watch by Hamilton Watch Co., 68mm. diam. (Christie's N. York)$1,200

Repousse gold pair-cased verge
clockwatch by T. Eastland,
London, mid 18th century,
53mm. diam. (Sotheby's)
$12,325

Swiss gold minute repeating keyless lever
watch, enamel dial, 53mm. diam.
(Christie's) $2,880

Repousse gold pair-cased half
quarter repeating verge watch
by Miroir, London, 46mm.
diam., mid 18th century.
(Sotheby's) $5,380

Gilt metal pair-cased verge watch,
movement signed Delahoyde,
Dublin, 54mm. diam. (Christie's)
$325

Early 18th century silver pair-cased
verge watch by James Walker, London,
with crank key, 57mm. diam.
(Sotheby's) $1,185

Gold open-faced universal time
keyless lever watch in engine-
turned case, 50mm. diam.
(Sotheby's Belgravia)$910

Gold and enamel verge watch by
Larpent & Jurgensen, Copenhagen,
circa 1790, 39mm. diam.
(Sotheby's) $1,870

Gold hunting cased keyless lever watch by
Arnold & Frodsham, 1857, 55mm. diam.
(Sotheby's) $2,490

Small silver pair-cased verge
watch by D. Quare, London,
45mm. diam. (Christie's)
$3,345

Late Victorian gentleman's
silver pocket watch in working order. (Vernon's)S90

Silver pocket chronometer by John R.
Arnold, London, 1805, 61mm. diam.
(Christie's) $5,495

Silver pair-cased calendar verge
watch, movement signed Markwick, London, circa 1680, 51mm.
diam. (Christie's) $6,085

Swiss gold Jacquemart verge watch, 57mm. diam. (Christie's) $6,000

18-carat gold hunting cased keyless lever watch by J. Harris & Sons, London, 1890, 52mm. diam. (Sotheby's Belgravia) $810

Small early 19th century gold watch by Molier, Geneva, 29.5mm. diam. (Sotheby's) $1,955

Gold and enamel verge watch by L'Epine, Paris, 39mm. diam., circa 1790. (Sotheby's) $2,690

Gold open-faced half quarter repeating pocket chronometer by George Moore, London, 1840, 53mm. diam. (Sotheby's) $6,635

18-carat gold open-faced lever watch by J. W. Benson, London, 1885, 49mm. diam. (Sotheby's Belgravia) $525

French gold quarter repeating musical cylinder watch, signed Prevost Freres a Toulouse, 59mm. diam. (Christie's) $6,000

Gold hunter-cased minute repeating free-sprung lever keyless watch, London, 1886, 53mm. diam. (Christie's) $7,200

Gold and enamel pair-cased verge watch by Jacques Coulin and Amy Bry, circa 1790, 41mm. diam. (Sotheby's) $3,510

Gold and enamel verge watch by Jacques Broche & Co., Berlin, circa 1770, 43mm. diam. (Sotheby's) $4,680

Continental silver Jacquemart verge watch with quarter repeating movement, 55mm. diam. (Christie's) $1,680

Gold pair-cased verge watch by George Graham, London, 1726, 50mm. diam. (Christie's) $3,110

241

French gold quarter repeating cylinder watch by Leroy et Fils, 46mm. diam. (Christie's) $1,145

French gold quarter repeating and musical cylinder watch, 58mm. diam. (Christie's) $4,800

French gold quarter repeating cylinder watch in engine-turned case, 52mm. diam. (Christie's) $1,440

Gold half hunting cased five-minute repeating keyless lever watch, 1886, 42mm. diam. (Sotheby's) $3,320

Continental gold musical and quarter repeating cylinder watch, 59mm. diam. (Christie's) $4,540

Fine French quarter repeating watch in slim engine-turned case, 47mm. diam. (Christie's) $1,910

Gilt metal pair-cased verge watch by Jas. Green, London, 58mm. diam. (Christie's) $765

Swiss gold musical keyless lever watch, 56mm. diam. (Christie's) $3,585

18th century gilt metal cased pocket chronometer by Charles Haley, 51mm. diam. (Sotheby's) $5,215

Early 18th century silver verge watch by Morin, Marchinville, with polychrome enamel miniature, 50mm. diam. (Sotheby's) $2,185

Swiss gold open-faced watch by Vacheron and Constantin, Geneva, 47mm. diam. (Christie's N. York) $650

Silver sun and moon verge watch by James Cobb, London, circa 1700, 48mm. diam. (Sotheby's) $2,990

Rare gold and gem-set hunter-cased minute-repeating keyless lever watch, London, 1894, 40mm. diam. (Christie's) $18,720

Gold open-faced duplex watch by Ganthony of London, 1818, 50mm. diam. (Sotheby's) $935

Silver pair-cased verge watch by Johan Bushman, London, circa 1700, 58mm. diam. (Sotheby's) $1,380

Gold quarter repeating Jaquemart verge watch in engine-turned case, 58mm. diam. (Christie's) $9,830

Swiss gold musical cylinder watch in engine-turned case, 38mm. diam. (Christie's) $4,540

Gold quarter repeating cylinder watch by Breguet, with enamel dial, 57mm. diam. (Christie's) $14,040

Gold half hunting cased keyless lever Karrusel by Johnson Walker & Tolhurst, London, 1899, 52mm. diam. (Sotheby's) $9,955

Silver triangular cased keyless lever watch, dial painted with masonic emblems, 60.5mm. high.(Sotheby's) $1,420

Georgian gold and enamel repeating verge watch by Robert Fleetwood. (Phillips) $7,140

Early 18th century gilt metal verge Oignon by Gaudin, Versailles, 58mm. diam. (Sotheby's) $2,415

Early 18th century silver verge watch by Paul Lullin with oval polychrome enamel miniature, 47mm. diam. (Sotheby's) $1,150

Silver pair-cased verge watch by John Moncrief, London, circa 1700, 55mm. diam. (Sotheby's) $1,495

243

WATCHES

18ct. gold hunting cased keyless lever watch, hallmarked 1928, 51mm. diam. (Sotheby's Belgravia) $795

18ct. gold half hunting cased keyless lever watch by J. W. Benson, 1912, 51mm. diam. (Sotheby's Belgravia) $585

Late 19th century Swiss minute-repeating perpetual calendar lever chronograph by Le Coultre & Co., 58mm. diam. (Phillips)
$20,700

18th century silver pair-cased watch by Jas. Woodgate, London, 52mm. diam. (Phillips)$380

Gold and enamel cylinder watch by James McCabe, London, 54mm. diam.(Christie's) $3,585

Late 18th century gold pair-cased verge watch signed Dowson, 48mm. diam. (Phillips)$945

Gold repousse pair-cased verge watch signed Jno. Berry, Manchester, 60mm. diam. (Christie's) $6,240

A lever watch by Barraud's, London, converted from duplex, 18ct. gold, 1828. (Phillips)
$1,050

Mid 18th century gilt metal and shagreen cased verge watch by Anthony Marsh, London, circa 1760. (Christie's) $565

A table roller lever watch by Lautier, Bath, 18ct. goldcase, 1819. (Phillips)
$840

English gold open-face cylinder watch by Matthew Hick, York, 40mm. diam. (Christie's N. York) $300

An early 18th century silver pair-cased verge watch by Joseph Ledgard, London. (Phillips)
$965

CLOISONNE

One of a pair of cloisonne koros and covers, circa 1900, 11.5cm. high. (Sotheby's Belgravia) $290

Cloisonne plate decorated with a crab beneath a plant, 30.5cm. diam., circa 1900. (Sotheby's Belgravia) $290

17th/18th century cloisonne enamel straight-sided hexagonal jar, 14cm. high. (Christie's) $1,190

Cloisonne plate decorated with a butterfly and flowers, 24.5cm. diam., circa 1900. (Sotheby's Belgravia) $245

Large cloisonne vase with lobed body decorated with hanging panels, circa 1900, 91cm. high. (Sotheby's Belgravia) $3,035

One of a pair of cloisonne plaques decorated with pheasants amongst peony, 30.5cm. diam., circa 1900.(Sotheby's Belgravia) $415

One of a large pair of cloisonne vases with lobed bulbous bodies, 91cm. high, circa 1900. (Sotheby's Belgravia) $1,505

19th century Chinese eight lobed cloisonne tray depicting two five-toed dragons, 16½in. diam. (Robert W. Skinner Inc.) $225

One of a pair of cloisonne vases of square section and on blueground, circa 1900, 47cm. high. (Sotheby's Belgravia)$875

Sato cloisonne vase decorated with panels of waves, flowers and foliage, circa 1900, 9.5cm. high.(Sotheby's Belgravia) $290

Cloisonne vase with bulbous body and waisted neck with silver wire decoration, circa 1900, 46cm. high. (Sotheby's Belgravia) $655

Gin Bari cloisonne vase decorated with three panels, circa 1900, 22.5cm. high, with wood stand and box. (Sotheby's Belgravia) $1,265

CLOISONNE

Pair of Xianfeng cloisonne enamel birds, 18cm. high. (Sotheby's Belgravia) $890

One of a pair of cloisonne enamel cockerel tureens and covers, 26.5cm. high. (Christie's)$2,350

One of a pair of Chinese blue-ground cloisonne enamel terrapins, 13.5cm. (Lawrence Fine Art) $860

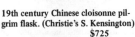

19th century Chinese cloisonne pilgrim flask. (Christie's S. Kensington) $725

One of a pair of Oto Tameseiro cloisonne vases, circa 1900, 24cm. high. (Sotheby's Belgravia)$700

One of a pair of Guangxu cloisonne vases decorated with flowers and foliage, 37cm. high. (Sotheby's Belgravia) $980

Late 18th century cloisonne urn and cover, Qianlong, 27in. high. (Dacre, Son & Hartley) $11,830

16th/17th century Ming cloisonne enamel shallow bowl mounted in bronze, 14.5cm. wide. (Christie's) $1,000

Late 19th century Chinese cloisonne tobacco jar with pierced finial, 14cm. high. (Robert W. Skinner Inc.) $150

Japanese cloisonne vase on green and flecked ground, 40cm. high. (C. G. Sloan & Co. Inc.) $500

One of a pair of cloisonne vases, circa 1900, 31cm. high.(Sotheby's Belgravia) $585

Large 19th century cloisonne enamel oviform vase with flaring neck, 67cm. high. (Christie's) $5,875

Cloisonne koro and cover with lobed body, circa 1900, 9cm. high, with wood stand. (Sotheby's Belgravia) $700

One of a pair of cloisonne enamel ewers and covers modelled as ducks, 29cm. long. (Christie's) $1,995

One of a pair of Qianlong cloisonne enamel figures of standing mythical bovines, 21cm. long. (Christie's) $3,290

Russian kovsh, cloisonne enamelled with flowers and foliage, 27oz., 1899-1908, 33cm. wide. (Neales) $7,320

Late 19th century Chinese cloisonne opaque enamel on copper charger, 31cm. diam. (Robert W. Skinner Inc.) $175

One of a pair of cloisonne vases with narrow necks, circa 1900, 6.5cm. high. (Sotheby's Belgravia) $350

Chinese hexagonal cloisonne vase with multi-color floral and fan motifs, 31cm. high. (C. G. Sloan & Co. Inc.) $275

18th century cloisonne enamel vase modelled as a tree trunk, 22cm. high. (Christie's) $2,585

Cloisonne enamel beaker vase of the Qianlong period, 16.5cm. high. (Christie's) $9,995

16th century Ming cloisonne enamel tripod cylindrical censer with wood cover, 10cm. diam. (Christie's) $475

One of a pair of 18th century ormolu mounted cloisonne enamel censers and covers, 23cm. high. (Christie's)$3,760

Cloisonne koro and cover with bulbous body, circa 1900, 9.5cm. high. (Sotheby's Belgravia) $245

247

CLOISONNE

Late Ming dynasty cloisonne enamel hot water bowl, 6¼in. diam. (Sotheby's)$1,060

Early 20th century Norwegian cloisonne enamel vesta case, oblong, by Marius Hammer, 4.8cm. high. (Sotheby's Belgravia) $190

Large Jiaqing cloisonne enamel bowl painted with butterflies and flowers, 14¼in. diam. (Sotheby's) $1,150

One of an unusual pair of cloisonne enamel ewers in the form of Buddhist lions, 6¼in. high, on wood stands. (Sotheby's) $965

16th century Ming cloisonne enamel compressed globular censer and pierced stepped domed cover with loose loop handles, 9in. diam. (Christie's) $5,590

18th century cloisonne enamel jar of compressed baluster form, 4in. high. (Sotheby's) $1,290

Qianlong cloisonne enamel beaker of gu form, 9¾in. high. (Sotheby's) $830

Japanese cloisonne enamel altar garniture of octagonal section. (Messenger May & Baverstock) $1,390

16th century cloisonne enamel vase of hu form, sides set with loose rings, 10¼in. high. (Sotheby's) $1,240

Large Qianlong cloisonne enamel pilgrim bottle with knopped neck, 16in. high.(Christie's) $2,215

Early 17th century cloisonne enamel dish of shallow form, 9½in. diam. (Sotheby's) $875

18th/19th century cloisonne enamel censer with copper liner, 13¼in. high. (Christie's) $2,565

Burmese brass cooking vessel, 60cm. diam. (V. & V.'s) $475

Part of a collection of fifteen mid 19th century tin-lined copper saucepans and skillets, by Temple & Crook. (Sotheby's Belgravia) $715

Early 19th century brass tea urn. (J. M. Welch & Son) $185

16th century brass box bearing portraits of Calvin & Luther, 14cm. long. (Robert W. Skinner Inc.) $400

Mahogany plate bucket with brass carrying handle. (Hall, Wateridge & Owen) $315

Art Nouveau copper and brass vase, circa 1900. (Alfie's Antique Market) $85

Renaissance style brass andirons on curved legs, 82cm. high. (C. G. Sloan & Co. Inc.) $525

Rare fire grate and dogs, part of the Pluto and Prosperine scheme, 1855. (Sotheby's Belgravia) $3,850

Large brass lectern in the form of an eagle, 180cm. high, 1897. (Sotheby's Belgravia) $1,290

Fine brass shell-shaped coal receptacle with scoop, 20in. wide. (Locke & England) $315

Large brass samovar and six fitted brass tea glass holders and tray, circa 1900, by V. S. Batacheva, 53.2cm. high. (Sotheby's) $450

Early 19th century Regency brass bound pail with brass liner and handle, 35.5cm. high. (Plaza, New York) $1,400

249

COPPER & BRASS

Late 19th century Flemish brass candlestick, 10.8cm. high. (Sotheby's) $820

German brass tobacco box by Iohann Heinrich Giese, circa 1760, 15.5cm. long. (Sotheby's) $1,195

Late 19th century cast brass deity, Nepal, with three heads and eight arms, 12cm. high. (Robert W. Skinner Inc.) $340

Large brass lantern of hexagonal form, 106cm. wide, Guangxu period. (Sotheby's Belgravia) $120

Mid 19th century Spanish chestnut warmer with brass charger, 39½in. diam. (Sotheby's Belgravia) $680

16th century Italian gilt copper ciborium with vase stem, 20cm. high. (Sotheby's) $470

Nepalese copper gilt figure of Bodhisattva, 33cm. high, decorated with turquoise inlay. (Henry Spencer & Sons) $1,030

Pair of copper-coated figures of Diana and Actaeon, 1890's, 106cm. high.(Sotheby's Belgravia) $1,755

16th century German copper beaker with engraved body, 17cm. high. (Robert W. Skinner Inc.) $1,500

19th century copper preserving pan with two loop handles, 38.5cm. diam. (Jackson-Stops & Staff) $230

Victorian brass coal helmet with embossed decoration. (Biddle & Webb) $445

19th century copper tea urn with domed cover, 47.5cm. high. (Jackson-Stops & Staff) $155

250

Chinese copper dragon, 1.07m. high. (Raymond Inman) $560

19th century Dutch brass tobacco box, lid etched with two figures in a landscape, 15cm. long. (Taylor Lane & Creber) $170

16th century brass candlestick with large conical base, 12.5cm. high. (Sotheby's) $655

Early 19th century copper peat bucket on ball feet.(Phillips) $440

Victorian brass coal scuttle in the form of a shell, sold with a brass coal shovel. (Taylor Lane & Creber) $470

Near Eastern copper charcoal burner of circular form with pierced domed cover and brass loop handles, 47cm. diam. (Jackson-Stops & Staff) $170

18th century Dutch brass milk churn. (Phillips) $180

Early 19th century fire grate with brass mounts, 2ft.6in. wide. (Taylor Lane & Creber)$385

Double-lidded copper hot milk container. (Phillips)$220

Copper figure of a Bodhisattva, dated 1770, 18.5cm. high. (Christie's) $350

19th century brass equestrian model of the Duke of Wellington, on marble plinth, 62.5cm. high. (Capes, Dunn & Co.) $780

Early 16th century Nuremberg brass alms dish, broad-rim stamped with shell pattern, 38.7cm. diam. (Sotheby's) $1,215

15th century tinned copper basin with convex base, 10¼in. diam. (Sotheby's) $325

George III mahogany plate pail with brass handle. (Phillips) $2,760

14th century Italian Fars brass bowl with convex base, 9¾in. diam. $1,340

Tiffany sterling silver and copper teapot, circa 1890, 12.5cm. high. (Robert W. Skinner Inc.) $600

Iserlohn brass tobacco box by Iohann Heinrich Hamer, circa 1762, 6in. long. (Sotheby's) $1,735

Spanish brass candlestick of squat form with pierced hexagonal nozzle, circa 1600, 4½in. high. (Christie's) $585

Benin brass bell of conical form with horse head on one side, 13cm. high. (Sotheby's) $1,870

Early 17th century brass warming pan, pierced and punched, on steel handle. (Christie's S. Kensington) $505

One of a pair of 17th century Dutch brass candlesticks with pierced nozzles, 7½in. high. (Christie's) $690

17th century Safavid copper basin with sharply rounded sides and upright rim, 8in. diam. (Sotheby's) $325

One of a set of three Dewsbury brass conical measures by D. Grave & Co., London, 1893. (Christie's) $1,545

14th/15th century Mamluk brass candlestick base of truncated conical form, 11¾in. diam. (Sotheby's) $1,125

Brass standard yard measure inscribed City of Bradford, with turned lignum vitae handles. (Christie's) $620

George III mahogany plate bucket with brass handle and rim, circa 1780, 33cm. high. (Sotheby's) $1,555

18th century Safavid copper bowl of hemisperical form on a shallow splayed foot, 9½in. diam. (Sotheby's) $475

One of a set of seven Leeds brass bound copper conical measures inscribed City of Leeds, in fitted pine case. (Christie's) $1,430

Iserlohn brass tobacco box by Iohann Heinrich Hamer, circa 1757, 6¼in. long. (Sotheby's) $1,475

19th century brass chalice with curved sides, 11in. high.(Christie's) $355

Rare 13th century Limoges copper and champleve enamel pricket candlestick, 11½in. high. (Sotheby's) $17,775

James I brass warming pan with steel handle, dated 1620.(Christie's) $865

Large modern Indian brass figure of Padmapani, 130cm. high. (Sotheby's) $925

One of a set of eleven brass conical measures inscribed Corpn. of Halifax, 1893. (Christie's)$3,215

Early 16th century Flemish brass candlestick with incurved base and drip pan, 9¾in. high. (Sotheby's) $1,775

One of a set of eight Huddersfield brass conical measures by D. Grave & Co., London. (Christie's) $2,360

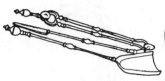

Dutch brass tobacco box engraved with pastoral scenes, 6½in. long. (Lawrence Fine Art) $440

Victorian set of brass fire implements. (Vernon's) $190

18th century Dutch brass and copper tobacco box, 15cm. long. (Robert W. Skinner Inc.) $350

Late 19th century American gilded stagecoach weather vane on modern tripod base, 34½in. long. (Robert W. Skinner Inc.) $500

Benin brass belt mask in the form of a face, 16.5cm. high. (Sotheby's) $470

Barnard, Bishop and Barnard cast brass fireplace surround, 1873, 45.2cm. wide.(Sotheby's Belgravia) $390

Set of thirty Halifax decimal bell-metal weights in fitted mahogany case. (Christie's) $2,380

Late Victorian brass spirit kettle on stand, 87cm. high. (Sotheby, King & Chasemore) $145

Art Nouveau pewter smoking companion with brass match box stand, 32cm. long. (Geering & Colyer) $310

One of a pair of mid 18th century brass candlesticks on single knop stems. (Sotheby, King & Chasemore) $200

Florentine Renaissance copper gilt reliquary casket from the circle of Brunelleschi, dated 1446. (Christie's) $88,200

One of a pair of Georgian brass candlesticks with fitted candle ejectors. (Sotheby, King & Chasemore) $265

17th century Dutch copper and brass tobacco box, 6¼in. wide. (Robert W. Skinner Inc.) $400

Copper running horse weather vane with hollow body, 23½in. high. (C. G. Sloan & Co. Inc.) $475

Rare Iserlohn 'Battle of Martinique' brass tobacco box, circa 1762, by Iohann Heinrich Hamer, 6in. wide. (Sotheby's) $1,430

One of a pair of German copper and brass torcheres with later frosted glass shades, dated 1847. (Christie's) $1,125

Set of sixteen Leeds bell-metal weights, 1883, smaller weights in fitted mahogany case. (Christie's) $2,620

Iranian silver and copper inlaid brass ewer, circa 1200, made in Khurasan, decorated with signs of the zodiac. (Sotheby's) $227,050

Victorian copper and brass kettle. (Vernon's) $150

17th century English brass warming pan, pierced and decorated with a star motif. (Phillips) $1,245

Four gallon copper measure. (Vernon's) $200

George III brass and steel spit jack, stamped P. Pearson, 11in. high. (Christie's) $1,190

George III brass and steel serpentine front grate, 2ft.2in. wide. (Vernon's) $700

West African brass covered reliquary figure. (Bonhams) $220

COSTUMES

18th century Dutch engraved brass and leather purse. (Robert W. Skinner Inc.) $85

Commemorative silk handkerchief printed with the opening of the Liverpool and Manchester Railway. (Phillips) $165

William and Mary gentleman's jacket in dun coloured felt, 1690's. (Sotheby's Belgravia) $6,960

Beaded dress of white, yellow and silver beads and sequins on muslin ground, 1920's. (Sotheby's Belgravia) $625

Long brilliant blue sequinned evening dress with narrow belt and feather fan. (Sotheby's Belgravia) $960

Jacques Fath long evening dress, Paris, early 1950's, with strapless top. (Sotheby's Belgravia) $410

Balenciaga blue satin dress, Paris, late 1930's. (Sotheby's Belgravia) $625

Late 19th century Hungarian apron from the Mezokovesd region. (Sotheby's Belgravia) $145

Hand made Spanish shawl with turquoise flowers on a cream background. (Coles, Knapp & Kennedy) $305

Indian beadwork pouch with floral decoration. (C. G. Sloan & Co. Inc.) $375

19th century Chinese embroidered silk ch'ao-kua with brocade silk lining, 48in. long. (Robert W. Skinner Inc.) $475

Late 19th century lady's robe, finely embroidered on a purple damask ground. (Sotheby's Belgravia) $600

One of two mid 19th century sporrans of the Atholl Highlanders, 45cm. long. (Sotheby's) $180

Black chiffon and beaded evening dress with side-dipping hem, 1928. (Sotheby's Belgravia) $265

Blue georgette beaded dress with simulated buckle, 1920's. (Sotheby's Belgravia) $480

Cream striped organdie two-piece gown trimmed with emerald green velvet, circa 1900. (Sotheby's Belgravia) $95

Black georgette beaded dress worked with clear beads, 1922-24. (Sotheby's Belgravia) $310

Late 19th century dragon robe in maroon silk embroidered with polychrome silks. (Sotheby's Belgravia) $720

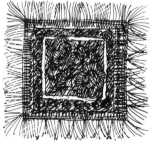

Hand made Spanish shawl with purple flowers on a orange background, 5ft. 3in. square. (Coles, Knapp & Kennedy) $325

Black two-tiered cloak, circa 1900's, by G. Worth.(Phillips) $590

257

19th century American Plains Indian buckskin jacket, circa 1880. (Phillips)　$1,055

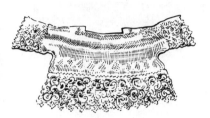

Rare late 17th century alb of crimped linen and lace, circa 1690. (Phillips)　$4,330

Pair of men's kid gloves said to have belonged to Edward VII. (Harrods)　$95

Black, salmon-pink, green and blue beaded dress and jacket, 1920's. (Sotheby's Belgravia)　$1,195

Fortuny 'Delphos' dress of champagne pleated silk, signed, circa 1914. (Sotheby's Belgravia)　$2,025

Apricot and ecru lace-trimmed chiffon nightdress sold with other items of underwear. (Sotheby's Belgravia)　$425

Pale torquoise crepe and lace nightdress and matching jacket, labelled Bradleys, sold with two petticoats. (Sotheby's Belgravia) $270

19th century Chinese embroidered silk ch'ao-kua with brocade silk lining, 48in. long. (Robert W. Skinner Inc.)　$475

One of a pair of bordered and framed Chinese sleevebands, circa 1850. (Alfie's Antique Market)　$155

Mid 19th century Indian Kutch Aba or dress from the Banni region. (Sotheby's Belgravia)　$575

Plains Indian beadwork on doeskin leggings and moccasins. (C. G. Sloan & Co. Inc.) $300

A Sioux Indian hide jacket decorated with geometric motif beadwork. (Sotheby's) $1,580

Victorian silver mounted sporran of white horsehair, Edinburgh, 1900. (Sotheby's) $360

Unusual black and red panne velvet and pleated georgette dress and jacket, 1940's. (Sotheby's Belgravia) $165

Diagonally pleated cream chiffon evening dress, 1960's, belonged to Marilyn Monroe. (Sotheby's Belgravia) $1,835

Bright red georgette beaded dress, French, 1920's. (Sotheby's Belgravia)$385

Black sequinned and net dress and belt, with flaring hem, circa 1930. (Sotheby's Belgravia) $465

Rare early 18th century damask banyan in red silk lined in gold. (Sotheby's Belgravia) $1,440

19th century German textile fragment, 5ft.6in. x 3ft.11in. (Robert W. Skinner Inc.) $100

Full length racoon fur coat with high collar. (Coles, Knapp & Kennedy) $700

259

COSTUME

Pair of American Plains Indian hide and quill-work moccasins, 9½in. long. (Sotheby's) $3,040

Chilkat wool blanket woven in mountain goat wool, 68in. wide. (Sotheby's) $11,700

Marilyn Monroe's pink-mesh bra. (Sotheby's Belgravia) $1,015

Black chiffon evening dress embroidered in the Art Deco style, circa 1925. (Sotheby, King & Chasemore) $155

Early 19th century finely embroidered pale blue silk kimono with furisode sleeves. (Sotheby's Belgravia) $2,510

Cream silk brocade evening dress with flaring sleeves, circa 1840. (Sotheby's Belgravia) $240

Shawl of Paisley design, predominantly mauve, circa 1860, 65 x 139in. (Sotheby's Belgravia) $330

17th century embroidered stomacher, mounted on linen and frame, 10 x 13 x 13in. (Robert W. Skinner Inc.) $400

Embroidery panel of silk threads on cotton fabric, 36 x 25in. (Robert W. Skinner Inc.) $425

Blue brocade dress with V neckline, braid applied to waistline, circa 1850. (Sotheby's Belgravia) $130

Chinese lady's informal robe, circa 1880, with ivory satin ground. (Sotheby's Belgravia) $310

Two-piece green and cream silk jacket and skirt, 1867, sold with belt and bag. (Sotheby's Belgravia) $135

Simon & Halbig 'Indian' doll in scarlet satin sari and red veil, 17½in. high. (Sotheby's Belgravia) $495

Steiner 'walking, talking' bisque-headed doll with blue glass eyes, 17½in. high. (Sotheby's Belgravia) $830

Early 20th century German bisque-head character boy doll, 13in. long. (Robert W. Skinner Inc.)$200

Shoulder papier-mache 'split-head' doll, 15in. high, with extra clothes. (Sotheby's Belgravia) $660

Armand Marseille bisque doll with weighted brown eyes, in stiffened net dress and lace bonnet, 13in. high. (Sotheby's Belgravia) $455

Good Simonne shoulder-bisque doll with kid body, circa 1860, 18½in. high. (Sotheby's Belgravia) $2,070

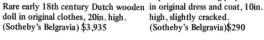

Mid 19th century porcelain shoulder-headed doll with wooden lower limbs, sold with clothes and a book. (Sotheby, King & Chasemore) $1,695

Rare early 18th century Dutch wooden doll in original clothes, 20in. high. (Sotheby's Belgravia) $3,935

Papier-mache 'Googly-eyed' doll in original dress and coat, 10in. high, slightly cracked. (Sotheby's Belgravia)$290

Bru Jeune bisque doll, Paris, marked number 7, with original dress and shoes.(Sotheby's Belgravia)$455

DOLLS

Jumeau bisque doll with later clothes, 22in. high, with glass eyes and fair wig. (Sotheby's Belgravia) $2,030

French bisque-headed poupard doll. (Harrods) $315

Bisque-headed Bebe doll. (Christie's S. Kensington) $2,190

Large bisque-headed doll with blonde wig, marked on the head 191 17, 81cm. high. (Sotheby, King & Chasemore) $820

Lehmann tinplate dancing sailor, circa 1920, German, 7¾in. high. (Sotheby's Belgravia) $260

Late 19th century German bisque-head character girl doll by Simon & Halbig, 19in. long. (Robert W. Skinner Inc.) $150

Composition portrait doll modelled as Shirley Temple. (Christie's S. Kensington) $350

Wax over composition-headed doll with wardrobe and accessories.(Christie's S. Kensington) $1,785

Armand Marseille bisque-headed doll with blonde wig, 48cm. high. (Sotheby, King & Chasemore) $530

Jumeau doll, 21in. high, in original dress. (Bradley & Vaughan) $2,420

Mid 19th century German shoulder papier-mache doll, circa 1840, 13½in. high. (Sotheby's Belgravia) $2,030

French bisque-headed Bebe doll, circa 1878. (Christie's S. Kensington) $1,340

Early 19th century Grodnertal wooden doll, feet repaired, 19½in. high. (Sotheby's Belgravia) $860

Armand Marseille bisque socket head baby doll, circa 1920, with composition body and limbs. (Thomas Watson) $245

Simonne bisque doll, 1860's, with contemporary clothes, 18in. tall. (Sotheby's Belgravia)$1,910

Bisque-headed Jumeau doll. (Christie's S. Kensington) $2,040

Lehmann walking sailor, German, circa 1905, 7½in. long, one hand missing. (Sotheby's Belgravia) $145

Bisque swivel-headed Bebe doll, 10in. high. (Christie's S. Kensington) $3,650

Fine quality Parisienne doll by Fernand Gaultier. (Phillips) $2,760

Mid 19th century doll in display case, circa 1860, 40in. high x 26½in. wide. (Sotheby's Belgravia) $670

Baby girl doll with composition body, German, 20in. long. (Andrew Grant) $150

George III painted wood doll, circa 1780, 12in. high, left arm missing. (Sotheby's Belgravia) $1,555

Girl doll with jointed composition body, by Armand Marseille, Germany, 17in. long. (Andrew Grant) $225

Late 19th century bisque-headed doll by Jumeau in original dress and coat, 42cm. high. (Sotheby, King & Chasemore) $2,375

263

Circular Birmingham snuff box, circa 1750, 6.2cm. diam. (Sotheby's) $425

White-ground 'honeysuckle group' snuff box, circa 1760, 8.5cm. wide. (Sotheby's) $620

Circular Birmingham patch box, circa 1760, 4.7cm. diam. (Sotheby's)$215

Rare Bilston enamel snuff box formed as a woman's head, circa 1765, 7.5cm. high.   (Christie's) $1,630

Bilston boar's head bonbonniere, circa 1765-1770, 7.8cm. long. (Sotheby's) $945

Late 19th century Viennese enamel pedestal bon-bon dish, 10.5cm. high. (Sotheby's Belgravia) $685

One of a pair of Viennese enamel vases in French style, circa 1925, 13cm. high. (Sotheby's Belgravia)$805

Rare Battersea bottle ticket of vine leaf form, by James Gwin and Simon-Francois Ravenet, circa 1755, 7cm. wide. (Sotheby's) $2,950

One of a pair of late 19th century silvered enamel candlesticks, 15cm. high. (Sotheby's) $715

Embossed Bilston snuff box with domed lid, circa 1780, 5.7cm. wide. (Sotheby's) $155

Late 18th century Bilston pink linen-ground snuff box, 9.1cm. wide. (Sotheby's) $310

Mid 18th century enamel snuff box, by Christian Friedrich Herold, 7.5cm. wide.(Sotheby's) $2,855

Interesting yellow-ground snuff box, circa 1755-60, 6.2cm. wide. (Sotheby's) $595

Late 19th century Viennese enamel boat-shaped sweetmeat dish, unmarked, 14cm. long. (Sotheby's Belgravia) $830

Bilston oval enamel bonbonniere formed as a resting bull, circa 1800, 3.8cm. long. (Christie's) $1,150

Staffordshire enamel sander, 18th century, with gilt metal mounts, 4.5cm. high. (Christie's) $410

Early 20th century champleve enamel figure of a Lohan seated on a mule, 47.5cm. high. (Sotheby's Belgravia) $980

Circular Bilston patch box, circa 1765, 4.5cm. diam. (Sotheby's) $905

One of a pair of English enamel table candlesticks, probably Staffordshire, circa 1770, 12in. high. (Christie's) $425

Bilston bird bonbonniere painted as an eagle, circa 1770. (Sotheby's) $1,555

One of a pair of late 19th century enamelled vases with linenfold necks, 43cm. high. (Sotheby's Belgravia)$980

Embossed Bilston spaniel bonbonniere, circa 1770, 5.8cm. wide. (Sotheby's)$1,380

Late 18th century Bilston enamel bird bonbonniere, 3.5cm. long. (Christie's) $2,160

Late 19th century small Viennese enamel coffee can and saucer. (Sotheby's Belgravia) $310

ENAMEL

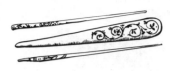

Good pair of late 19th century French enamel and gilt metal opera glasses, 10cm. wide. (Sotheby's Belgravia)$425

Champleve enamel and silver gilt desk set, St. Petersburg, circa 1890, 18.5cm. long, in red leather case. (Sotheby's)$405

19th century Limoges enamel casket with engraved gilt metal mounts. (Phillips) $4,600

Early 20th century Austro-Hungarian enamel, hardstone and gem-set bonbon dish, 12.5cm. long. (Sotheby's Belgravia) $1,010

Late 19th century Viennese enamel and rock crystal oval vase and cover, 12cm. long, by Hermann Ratzersdorfer. (Sotheby's Belgravia) $3,040

Silver gilt, rock crystal and enamel dish, 50cm. diam. (Phillips) $13,800

Late 19th century Viennese silver gilt and enamel jug, 8.7cm. high. (Sotheby's Belgravia) $305

Three mid 12th century Cologne copper gilt and enamel plaques of saints. (Sotheby's) $187,000

Faberge circular silver and enamel bowl with lobed body, Moscow, 1899-1900, 13.2cm. diam. (Christie's)$4,105

German enamelled rectangular cigarette case, circa 1900, 10.1cm. long. (Sotheby's Belgravia) $935

French parcel gilt and enamelled silver pendant brooch, circa 1850, 6cm. high. (Sotheby's Belgravia) $305

Attractive Russian enamel box by Pavel Ovchinnikov, circa 1900. (Phillips) $1,950

266

French enamel and gilt metal jewel casket, circa 1885, 15.5cm. long. (Sotheby's Belgravia) $565

Circular silver gilt and shaded enamel pill box, Moscow, 1908-1917, 5.3cm. diam. (Sotheby's) $1,190

German enamel snuff box, after Boucher, circa 1760, 8.2cm. wide. (Sotheby's) $2,990

Limoges enamel oval dish, after Pierre Reymond, 19in. long. (Sotheby's) $6,160

One of a set of six George III enamel candlesticks, circa 1770, 31cm. high. (Christie's) $2,600

Late 19th century Viennese painted enamel hexagonal box, 5.5cm. long. (Sotheby's Belgravia) $760

One of a pair of early 20th century Tiffany bronze and enamel bookends, 13cm. high. (Robert W. Skinner Inc.) $250

Part of a six-piece miniature Viennese enamel suite of a table, settee and four chairs. (C. G. Sloan & Co. Inc.) $700

Heart-shaped silver and enamel snuff box, 6.8cm. high, 1722-1726. (Sotheby's) $1,495

Enamel and gilt metal casket, circa 1885, 19.5cm. long. (Sotheby's Belgravia) $395

Mid 20th century Hungarian gilt metal and enamel model of a ceremonial coach, 17cm. long. (Sotheby's Belgravia) $855

Late 19th/early 20th century Viennese enamel oval box with silver gilt metal borders, 9.7cm. long. (Sotheby's Belgravia) $755

267

Chapel fan, inscribed with hymns and psalms, 25.3cm. long, with wooden sticks, 1796. (Sotheby's Belgravia) $490

Dutch ivory brise fan, circa 1730, 20.3cm. long. (Sotheby's Belgravia) $635

French foiled ivory fan with mother-of-pearl guards, circa 1760, 27cm. long. (Sotheby's Belgravia) $290

English ivory fan with pierced sticks, circa 1770, 29cm. long, with paper case. (Sotheby's Belgravia) $470

Unmounted Northern European fan leaf, circa 1740, 53cm. wide. (Christie's S. Kensington) $1,200

Painted fan, possibly Spanish, circa 1760.(Christie's) $1,055

Mother-of-pearl fan, Spanish, circa 1870, 27.2cm. long. (Sotheby's Belgravia) $235

George III commemorative fan with ivory sticks and guards, 1789, 25.8cm. long. (Sotheby's Belgravia) $590

French pierced and gilt mother-of-pearl fan, signed E. Parmentier, circa 1850, 28.2cm. long.(Sotheby's Belgravia) $475

Japanese ivory fan with lacquered guards, circa 1900, 27cm. long. (Sotheby's Belgravia) $1,010

Dutch pierced ivory fan, painted with Biblical scenes, 1790, 29cm. long, with paper case. (Sotheby's Belgravia) $495

Dutch pierced and foiled ivory fan with chicken-skin mount, circa 1760, 28cm. long. (Sotheby's Belgravia) $495

Late 19th century Japanese shibayama ivory brise fan, 27.5cm. long. (Sotheby's Belgravia) $715

French fan with mother-of-pearl sticks, restored, 1755, 26.3cm. long. (Sotheby's Belgravia) $475

Mid 19th century 'Mandarin' fan with ivory guards, 28cm. long. (Sotheby's Belgravia) $565

Early 19th century Chinese lacquer brise fan with foliate flower borders, 22cm. long. (Sotheby's Belgravia) $670

Pierced ivory fan with case, circa 1770, 29.5cm. long. (Sotheby's Belgravia) $315

Mid 18th century ivory fan with silvered paper mount, 27.8cm. long. (Sotheby's Belgravia) $130

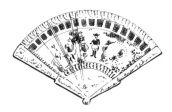

Chinese ivory brise fan, circa 1710, 20.5cm. long. (Sotheby's Belgravia) $505

Dutch ivory brise fan, re-ribboned, circa 1730, 21.8cm. long. (Sotheby's Belgravia) $450

BEDS & CRADLES

American painted country bed in red and black, 50in. wide, circa 1800. (Robert W. Skinner Inc.) $2,100

Pel B3 chromed tubular steel single bed, 1930's, 92cm. wide.(Sotheby's Belgravia) $680

Ormolu mounted kingwood and marquetry bed on cabriole legs, 68in. wide. (Christie's) $4,465

French or Italian late 18th century grey-painted lit a La Polonnaise with ribbon tied crestings, 78in. wide. (Christie's) $1,325

Ormolu mounted mahogany and satinwood half-tester bed, circa 1900, 70in. wide. (Sotheby's Belgravia) $7,285

George III satinwood painted four-post bed with arched, molded canopy, circa 1790, 5ft.7in. wide. (Sotheby's) $41,650

Parcel gilt Regency mahogany four-poster bedstead with pineapple finials. (Hy. Duke & Son) $7,140

19th century Florentine carved walnut bedstead, 54¼in. wide. (Phillips) $5,280

Louis XVI painted lit a baldequin with bow-fronted tester, 4ft.9in. wide, circa 1780. (Sotheby's) $945

19th century American Victorian walnut cradle on stand with shaped and pierced splats, 36in. high. (Robert W. Skinner Inc.) $200

17th century Dutch or German oak cradle with paneled tapering body, 38½in. wide. (Christie's) $1,710

Early 18th century English oak cradle of coffin form, 18in. wide.(Robert W. Skinner Inc.) $500

270

Antique American tiger maple high-post bed, circa 1840, 60in. wide. (C. G. Sloan & Co. Inc.)$750

Rare walnut and parcel gilt day bed by Austin Osman Spare, 1920's, 74½in. long. (Sotheby's Belgravia) $5,520

Late 19th century American Victorian brass bed of tube construction, 56in. wide. (Robert W. Skinner inc.) $900

Partly 17th century oak four-post bed, carved with strapwork and masks, 64½in. wide. (Christie's) $6,345

Elizabethan oak full-tester bed, paneled canopy and headboard heavily carved, circa 1600, 55in. wide. (Boardman) $4,580

Antique oak four-poster bed with paneled canopy and headboard and gadrooned posts. (Locke & England) $3,430

17th century German baroque walnut bed with relief carving, 66in. wide. (Robert W. Skinner Inc.) $600

Large Guangxu hardwood canopy bed. (Sotheby's Belgravia) $950

Late 18th/early 19th century Chinese carved wood and lacquer bed with paneled canopy, 8ft.3in. wide. (Sotheby's) $3,905

Early 19th century Swiss bedstead with paneled ends. (Phillips) $5,930

Mid 17th century oak cradle with turned acorn finials at the corners, 3ft. wide. (Sotheby's)$1,555

'Louis XVI' giltwood bed with arched headboard, circa 1900, 70in. wide. (Sotheby's Belgravia) $1,550

BOOKCASES

Fine Georgian bookcase with three open shelves, on bun feet, 36½in. wide. (Locke & England) $3,345

One of a pair of Regency rosewood and parcel gilt dwarf bookcases, 54in. wide. (Christie's) $4,115

Regency mahogany double-sided library bookstand on trestle ends, joined by a turned stretcher, 36in. wide. (Christie's) $2,785

George III satinwood and mahogany open bookcase with five stepped shelves, 48in. wide. (Christie's) $1,950

Early Victorian breakfront bookcase with molded cornice. (Locke & England) $1,980

Mahogany standing bookcase, circa 1805, 2ft.5in. wide. (Sotheby's) $1,795

Mid 20th century mahogany bookcase with glazed doors, 72in. wide. (Sotheby's Belgravia) $1,480

Late 19th century mahogany inlaid bookcase with two astragal glazed doors, 3ft.1in. wide. (Lawrence Fine Art) $1,355

One of a pair of late 19th century 'George III' mahogany bookcases with glazed doors, 80¼in. wide. (Sotheby's Belgravia) $6,635

19th century mahogany bookcase with two arched astragal glazed doors, 4ft.9in. wide. (Lawrence Fine Art) $1,755

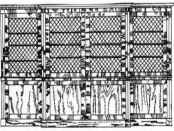

William IV breakfront bookcase with overhanging cornice, circa 1835, 134in. wide. (Sotheby's Belgravia) $5,125

Georgian mahogany bookcase, 5ft.8in. wide, with double glazed doors. (Raymond Inman) $3,840

Edwardian mahogany two-tier revolving bookstand with decoration in 'Adam' taste.(Russell, Baldwin & Bright) $1,870

One of a pair of Regency dwarf bookcases in rosewood with brass rails, 2ft.10in. wide. (Messenger May & Baverstock) $4,360

Edwardian revolving bookcase with Art Nouveau inlay. (Locke & England) $1,140

Galle fruitwood marquetry revolving bookcase with fretwork panels, circa 1900, 45cm. square. (Sotheby's Belgravia) $1,870

Regency mahogany breakfront bookcase with paneled and arched cornice, 86in. wide. (Christie's) $7,260

Regency rosewood revolving three-tier booktable, circa 1810, 2ft.4½in. high. (Sotheby, King & Chasemore) $7,920

Early 20th century oak bookcase with molded cornice, 45½in. wide. (Christie's) $4,320

Regency mahogany open bookcase with four graduated shelves, 42½in. wide. (Drewatt, Watson & Barton) $1,540

19th century mahogany breakfront bookcase, 8ft.8in. wide. (Drewatt, Watson & Barton) $8,360

Early 20th century sectional oak bookcase with glazed partitions, 3ft.2in. wide. (Vernon's) $150

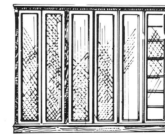

19th century rosewood bookcase, 9ft.2in. wide. (Drewatt, Watson & Barton) $1,805

George III mahogany breakfront bookcase made in the style of William Vile. (Christie's) $40,460

BOOKCASES

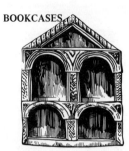

Early 17th century three-tier oak wall shelf of nailed construction. (Boardman) $2,905

William IV rosewood book rack with baluster gallery, circa 1835, 16in. wide. (Sotheby's Belgravia) $780

Mahogany bookstand with serpentine top and spindle supports on a turned column. (May Whetter & Grose) $310

Early 19th century whale-end shelf, 37in. wide. (Robert W. Skinner Inc.) $900

Late George II mahogany double breakfront library bookcase with repaired cornice, circa 1815, 10ft. wide. (Sotheby's) $6,832

Georgian mahogany apse bookcase, 3ft.1in. wide. (Capes, Dunn & Co.) $550

Hepplewhite revival satinwood breakfront bookcase, late 19th century. (Christie's S. Kensington) $21,470

William IV mahogany and parcel gilt standing bookshelf with scrolled cresting, 51in. wide. (Christie's) $1,755

Regency mahogany breakfront bookcase with molded cornice, 93in. wide. (Christie's) $10,710

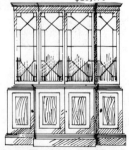

George III mahogany breakfront bookcase, circa 1770, 7ft.2½in. wide. (Sotheby's) $8,425

Georgian mahogany bookcase with figured paneled doors, 3ft.4½in. wide.(Lawrence Fine Art) $1,450

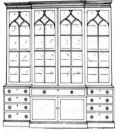

Early 19th century mahogany breakfront bookcase with glazed doors. (Biddle & Webb) $6,050

Edwardian mahogany and inlaid revolving bookcase with three small drawers, 1ft.6½in. square. (Taylor Lane & Creber) $540

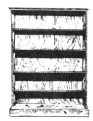

Late Victorian stripped pine bookshelves with beaded decoration, 3ft. wide. (Vernon's) $175

Victorian walnut open bookshelves with a shaped white marble top. (Vernon's) $450

19th century carved walnut Italian library bookcase, 8ft. wide. (Alonzo Dawes & Hoddell) $4,840

Regency mahogany bookcase in two parts with scrolled pediment, 98in. wide. (Christie's) $4,520

Unusual 19th century mahogany bookcase with brass galleried top, 4ft.2½in. wide. (Taylor Lane & Creber) $655

Sheraton glazed bookcase with astragal doors, 3ft.11½in. wide. (Honiton Galleries) $595

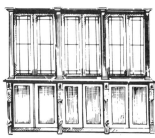

Fine 19th century mahogany bookcase with three double glazed doors, 9ft.7in. wide. (W. H. Lane & Son) $3,840

Victorian oak bookcase in Gothic style with machiciolated cornice, 71in. wide. (Christie's) $6,580

Mid Victorian walnut bookcase or display cabinet with concave frieze, 118cm. wide. (H. Spencer & Sons) $1,395

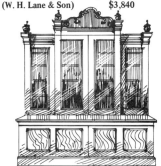

Mid Victorian mahogany bookcase, almost 10ft. high, in excellent condition. (Peter Wilson & Co.) $6,610

Mid Georgian mahogany bookcase with broken pediment and two glazed cupboard doors, 51½in. wide. (Christie's) $3,525

BUREAUX

George I walnut bureau, cross-banded and inlaid, on bracket feet, 3ft. wide. (Messenger May & Baverstock) $7,630

Mid 19th century walnut and marquetry bureau de dame with shaped apron, 39½in. wide. (Sotheby's Belgravia) $2,465

Mid 18th century Sicilian or Maltese walnut and parquetry bureau, 4ft.5in. wide. (Sotheby's) $5,150

Mid 20th century 'transitional' mahogany quarter veneered bureau a cylindre, 48in. wide. (Sotheby's Belgravia) $1,285

Dutch marquetry bureau with floral inlay and ornate brass handles, 3ft.3in. wide. (Messenger May & Baverstock) $6,105

Continental walnut bureau on square cut cabriole legs, 3ft. wide. (Allen & May) $455

18th century South German walnut bureau with brass handles. (Bradley & Vaughan) $9,680

Mid 19th century German rosewood and boulle cylinder bureau with raised superstructure, 48in. wide. (Christie's) $3,615

18th century American mahogany bureau, lid carved with a shell, 41in. wide. (Christie's) $3,290

Late 19th century Scandinavian oak bureau, inlaid with ebony and boxwood stringing, 43in. wide.(Sotheby's Belgravia) $560

Walnut bombe escritoire in Louis XV style, with ormolu mounts, 30in. wide. (Lambert & Symes) $4,840

Ormolu mounted mahogany bureau a cylindre, 19th century, 35½in. wide. (Christie's) $2,165

276

Early 18th century burr-walnut bureau, re-veneered, 3ft.2½in. wide. (Sotheby's)$1,685

19th century bonheur du jour in mahogany with pierced brass gallery, 2ft.6in. wide. (Taylor Lane & Creber) $1,185

18th century walnut and chevron-banded bureau, 2ft.9in. wide, circa 1720. (Sotheby, King & Chasemore) $6,830

Queen Anne walnut bureau, cross-banded in satinwood with brass drop handles, 32in. wide.(Morphets) $2,360

19th century French ebonised and ormolu mounted bureau de dame with Sevres plaques, 2ft.1in. wide. (Sotheby, King & Chasemore) $1,585

American mahogany and oak bureau with sloping hinged lid, 40in. wide. (Christie's) $2,350

George I walnut bureau with brass handles and escutcheons. (Phillips) $5,060

18th century Dutch mahogany bureau in two parts, circa 1780, 3ft.8½in. wide. (Sotheby, King & Chasemore) $4,320

Early Georgian fall-front bureau in walnut with inlaid crossbanding. (Clive Emson) $4,445

Early 19th century carved oak bureau in the Abbotsford manner.(Vernon's) $700

French writing bureau, flap with floral marquetry, 24in. wide. (Honiton Galleries) $845

George II walnut bureau, 3ft. wide, circa 1755, with later bracket feet. (Sotheby's) $6,190

Early George III provincial walnut standing bureau, circa 1770, 3ft. 1in. wide. (Sotheby's) $1,015

Good quality late 19th century French design rosewood and floral marquetry bureau de dame with ormolu mounts. (Locke & England) $1,065

18th century oak bureau on bracket feet, 2ft.6in. wide. (Honiton Galleries) $1,860

Rare William and Mary black-japanned bureau, circa 1690, 2ft. 11in. wide. (Sotheby's) $3,905

George I walnut bureau, circa 1720, 3ft.1in. wide. (Sotheby's) $5,545

Georgian oak bureau, fitted interior with sunken well, 3ft. 3in. wide. (Lawrence Fine Art) $935

William and Mary pollard elm bureau in two parts, 30½in. wide. (Christie's)$2,855

18th century South German walnut bureau with line and butterfly inlay, 2ft.3in. wide. (Bracketts) $1,815

Late 18th century Dutch satin-wood cylinder bureau with raised upper section, 46in. wide. (Christie's) $4,285

Queen Anne style oak desk on stand with slant top, 32in. wide. (C. G. Sloan & Co. Inc.) $1,400

Mahogany cylinder bureau of Louis XVI style with three quarter galleried top, 64½in. wide. (Christie's) $3,810

William and Mary style walnut and featherbanded bureau, circa 1800. (Sotheby, King & Chasemore) $1,805

Early Georgian bureau in straight-grain walnut, 2ft.2in. wide. (Strides) $2,835

Edwardian satinwood bureau, painted in the style of Angelica Kauffmann, 2ft.9in. wide. (Sotheby's) $1,890

18th century Dutch walnut and marquetry bombe bureau, 43in. wide. (Christie's) $2,855

Early 18th century Georgian oak bureau on shaped plinth base, 36in. wide. (Lawrence Fine Art) $1,005

18th century Dutch marquetry bombe bureau on ball and claw feet, 48in. wide. (Burtenshaw Walker) $7,260

18th century walnut fall-front bureau with fitted interior. (Worsfolds) $4,340

William and Mary walnut bureau in two parts with oyster veneered top, 40in. wide. (Christie's) $4,840

Louis XVI style mahogany cylinder bureau with white marble top, 48in. wide. (C. G. Sloan & Co. Inc.) $1,400

18th century Dutch marquetry bombe bureau veneered in mahogany. (Woolley & Wallis) $6,600

George I walnut bureau with brass handles, on bracket feet.(Messenger May & Baverstock) $7,630

Late Georgian oak bureau with brass handles and escutcheons. (Biddle & Webb) $1,330

Walnut bureau with bombe base, 46in. wide. (John H. Raby) $7,070

279

Georgian oak bureau on shaped bracket feet. (Lawrence Fine Art) $770

Mid 18th century American Chippendale tiger maple and maple slant top desk, 39in. wide. (Robert W. Skinner Inc.) $6,000

Georgian mahogany bureau with rococo brass handles and escutcheons, 3ft.5in. wide. (Lawrence Fine Art) $2,340

Mahogany and marquetry bureau, circa 1890, 36in. wide. (Sotheby's Belgravia) $1,705

Rare George III mahogany estate bureau cabinet, crossbanded in tulipwood, 47in. wide.(Lawrence Fine Art) $2,165

18th century Continental figured walnut fall-front bureau with shaped apron. (Bradley & Vaughan) $9,760

Queen Anne walnut and featherbanded bureau, circa 1710, 3ft. wide.(Sotheby, King & Chasemore) $3,905

Bamboo and lacquer cylinder bureau. circa 1880, with tambour front, 42in. wide. (Sotheby's Belgravia) $330

Painted Georgian fall-front mahogany bureau. (Raymond Inman) $3,600

George I walnut bureau with brass ring handles, oval escutcheons and bracket feet, 29in. wide. (Dacre, Son & Hartley) $4,785

Georgian oak bureau on bracket feet, drawers with brass loop handles, 36in. wide.(Burtenshaw Walker) $1,420

Mid 18th century George II walnut bureau on bracket feet, 3ft. wide. (Sotheby's) $5,000

George I walnut bureau on bracket feet, with brass handles. (Sotheby Bearne) $10,470

Early 18th century Dutch marquetry bureau with double bombe front. (Boardman) $9,760

Queen Anne figured walnut bureau with brass handles, 36in. wide. (Graves, Son & Pilcher) $3,534

Inlaid Georgian mahogany bureau on bracket feet, with knob handles and ivory escutcheons, 40in. wide. (Burtenshaw Walker) $1,605

Lady's 19th century French kingwood and brass mounted bureau, circa 1865. (Sotheby, King & Chasemore) $1,640

18th century South German walnut bureau with boxwood inlay and original brass handles, 45in. wide. (Boardman) $4,880

George III oak and elm bureau with walnut lined fall flap, circa 1770, 30in. wide. (Sotheby, King & Chasemore) $1,180

Mahogany cylinder bureau with brass gallery, by Edwards & Roberts. (Parsons, Welch & Cowell) $3,420

18th century South German walnut bureau with serpentine front and brass handles. (Bradley & Vaughan) $9,120

Late George III mahogany bureau with brass fittings, on ogee bracket feet, 42in. wide. (Thomas Watson & Son) $6,085

18th century North European kingwood bureau. (Drewatt, Watson & Barton) $14,520

Georgian mahogany bureau on splay feet, with inlaid stringing, 36in. wide. (Burtenshaw Walker) $1,345

American Chippendale maple slant front desk, circa 1755, 37½in. wide. (Robert W. Skinner Inc.) $3,000

Early George III mahogany merchant's desk with galleried top, circa 1765, 3ft. 4in. wide. (Sotheby's) $1,950

19th century French rosewood bombe shaped cylinder bureau. (Bradley & Vaughan) $2,095

19th century stripped pine bureau with brass handles and bracket feet, 3ft. wide. (Vernon's) $505

Walnut and Dutch marquetry bureau. (Christie's S. Kensington) $8,050

Mid 18th century oak bureau on bracket feet, original brass handles and escutcheons. (Honiton Galleries) $1,475

George I walnut bureau, circa 1720, 2ft.7½in. wide.(Sotheby's) $4,680

Walnut Queen Anne style secretary desk with molded cornice and fretwork carved doors, 36in. wide. (C. G. Sloan & Co. Inc.) $1,250

18th century walnut veneered slope front bureau, 36¾in. wide. (Taylor Lane & Creber) $3,270

American mahogany ox-box slant top desk, Massachusetts, circa 1760, 41½in. wide. (C. G. Sloan & Co. Inc.) $4,600

Late 19th century Louis XV style gilt and painted bureau de dame by R. J. Horner & Co., New York, 28in. wide. (Robert W. Skinner Inc.) $800

Antique American mahogany ox-box desk, Massachusetts, circa 1760, 42in. wide. (C. G. Sloan & Co. Inc.) $3,500

George III mahogany bureau bookcase with molded and dentil cornice, circa 1770, 3ft.9in. wide. (Sotheby's) $3,905

Antique walnut bureau bookcase in early Georgian style. (Russell, Baldwin & Bright) $10,765

Mahogany bureau cabinet with glazed doors, 3ft.7in. wide. (Sotheby's) $1,660

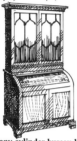

Mahogany cylinder bureau bookcase, crossbanded in rosewood, early 19th century, 3ft.10in. wide. (Lawrence Fine Art) $2,105

Early 20th century Georgian style mahogany bureau bookcase. (Bradley & Vaughan) $2,300

Plain George III mahogany bureau bookcase with open pediment and wooden handles. (Worsfolds) $4,360

Queen Anne walnut bureau cabinet with double arched molded cornice and two glazed doors, 40½in. wide. (Christie's) $15,730

Walnut bureau bookcase with candle slides and shaped top, 3ft.5in. wide. (Russell, Baldwin & Bright) $10,765

18th century Dutch or North German palisander bureau cabinet with arched molded cornice, 48in. wide. (Christie's) $8,675

Queen Anne walnut bureau, restored. (Manchester Auction Mart) $10,890

Walnut secretaire cabinet with molded cornice and mirror door, 24½in. wide. (Christie's) $4,760

Late 19th century mahogany and satinwood inlaid glazed top bureau bookcase, 35in. wide. (Locke & England) $1,915

BUREAU BOOKCASES

Dutch colonial padoukwood bureau cabinet, circa 1740, 3ft. 4½in. wide. (Sotheby's) $8,890

South German walnut bureau cabinet with serpentine upper top, 41in. wide.(Christie's) $9,520

Queen Anne burr-walnut bureau cabinet with fitted interior, 3ft. 3½in. wide. (Sotheby's) $11,900

Fretted pedimented bureau bookcase in mahogany with double glazed doors. (Raymond Inman) $1,950

Early 18th century North German or Dutch walnut and parcel gilt bureau cabinet, circa 1720, 4ft. wide. (Sotheby's)$9,515

Mid 18th century South German or Swiss amaranth and parquetry bureau cabinet, 47½in. wide. (Christie's) $33,740

Queen Anne burr-walnut bureau cabinet. (Sotheby Bearne) $19,515

Mulberry veneered bureau cabinet of Queen Anne design, 41in. wide, with double arched top. (Morphets) $16,185

Edwardian mahogany and satinwood chevron-banded bureau bookcase, 3ft.4in. wide, circa 1910. (Sotheby, King & Chasemore) $1,945

George III mahogany bureau bookcase, circa 1775, 3ft.6in. wide. (Sotheby, King & Chasemore) $1,575

Chippendale mahogany bureau cabinet, circa 1760, 3ft.4½in. wide. (Lawrence Fine Art) $4,095

Small George III provincial walnut and elm bureau cabinet, circa 1770, 2ft.1½in. wide.(Sotheby's) $1,910

284

Georgian mahogany bureau bookcase with scroll pediment, 43in. wide. (Boardman)$6,590

Edwardian mahogany and inlaid bureau bookcase with pierced cornice and double glazed doors, 2ft.5in. wide. (Taylor Lane & Creber) $630

Late Victorian satinwood bureau cabinet with molded cornice, 97cm. wide.(H. Spencer & Sons) $3,480

George II walnut bureau bookcase with mirror glazed doors. (Biddle & Webb) $6,775

Late 18th century Chippendale cherry-wood serpentine secretaire bookcase, Central Massachusetts, 39¾in. wide. (Robert W. Skinner Inc.)
$19,000

George III 18th century oak and mahogany banded bureau bookcase, 3ft.7in. wide, with pierced swan neck pediment. (Coles, Knapp & Kennedy) $1,685

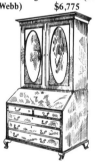

Georgian mahogany bureau cabinet with molded cornice, doors with mahogany ovals banded with rosewood, 4ft.2in. wide. (Lawrence Fine Art) $2,810

South German walnut and olivewood bureau cabinet, circa 1740. (Bonhams)
$13,420

Edwardian mahogany bureau bookcase, crossbanded with satinwood, circa 1910, 3ft.2½in. wide. (Sotheby, King & Chasemore)
$1,465

Small George I figured walnut bureau cabinet, 2ft.1½in. wide. (Boardman) $7,075

18th century mahogany bureau bookcase with fluted frieze and dentil cornice, 3ft.6in. wide. (Moore, Allen & Innocent) $4,200

Mid Georgian mahogany bureau bookcase with dentil cornice, on bracket feet.(Locke & England)$2,785

285

CABINETS

Chinese teak cabinet of the Ming dynasty, with brass mounts, 38in. wide. (C. G. Sloan & Co. Inc.)$2,100

Late 18th century country maple canted wall cabinet, probably New Hampshire, 49½in. high. (Robert W. Skinner Inc.) $2,100

Victorian ebonised pier cabinet with bow-shaped top, on inlaid plinth base, circa 1870, 62in. wide. (Lawrence Fine Art) $730

Carved oak cabinet on stand with carved frieze, 55in. wide. (C. G. Sloan & Co. Inc.) $750

Chinese hardwood curio cabinet with eight-shelf frame, 35in. wide. (C. G. Sloan & Co. Inc.) $750

Late 18th century Dutch oak cabinet on stand with arched fielded panel doors, 37in. wide. (Lawrence Fine Art) $410

Rare George II small mahogany spice or filing cabinet on stand, circa 1735, 1ft.8in. wide. (Sotheby's)$1,635

Gilt bronze mounted satinwood side cabinet, 31in. wide, circa 1880-1900. (Sotheby's Belgravia) $2,305

Unusual 19th century Japanese cabinet and matching stand, front inset with cloisonne plaques, 5ft. high. (Grays Antique Mews) $3,925

Chinese hardwood cabinet, cupboard and shelves joined by fretwork panels, 36in. wide. (Christie's)$3,130

Mid 19th century Victorian Renaissance revival buffet cabinet, American, 59in. wide. (Robert W. Skinner Inc.) $750

Mid 18th century Liege oak bureau cabinet with molded gadrooned cornice, 55in. wide. (Christie's) $35,700

Small 19th century collector's cabinet, 19in. wide, interior with one shelf. (Butler & Hatch Waterman) $145

Burr-walnut side cabinet with gilt bronze leaf-cast mounts, 59½in. wide, 1860's. (Sotheby's Belgravia) $3,465

19th century marquetry pedestal cabinet with inset marble top, 33in. wide. (Christie's) $3,855

Victorian Renaissance revival ebonised wood cabinet, 19in. wide, circa 1865. (Robert W. Skinner Inc.) $350

Mid 19th century ormolu mounted boulle meuble d'appui, 52in. wide. (Christie's) $1,310

One of a pair of American mahogany Egyptian revival cabinets, circa 1830, 24in. wide. (C. G. Sloan & Co. Inc.) $6,000

19th century Continental ebonised cabinet on stand, 18½in. wide. (Taylor Lane & Creber) $180

19th century boulle bonheur du jour on cabriole legs. (Taylor Lane & Creber) $3,320

One of a pair of Victorian side cabinets with glazed top doors. (Bradley & Vaughan) $5,325

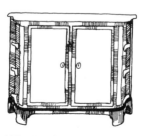

Venetian burr-walnut cabinet of bombe shape with bronze handles, 44in. wide. (Christie's) $9,640

French First Consulate mahogany side cabinet, circa 1805, 4ft. wide. (Woolley & Wallis) $2,340

Early 19th century George III two-section gun cabinet in mahogany, 27¾in. wide. (Robert W. Skinner Inc.) $1,800

CABINETS

Victorian walnut side cabinet by Seddon & Co., London, 73½in. wide. (Christie's) $1,995

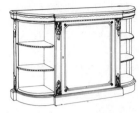

Walnut side cabinet in well-figured wood, circa 1870, with mirrored centre cupboard, 65in. wide. (Sotheby's Belgravia) $1,495

George III green-painted and gilded side cabinet with eared bowed top, 74in. wide. (Christie's)$1,475

Mid Victorian figured walnut folio cabinet with leather lined top, stamped Gillow, 45in. wide. (Christie's) $9,680

One of a pair of walnut side cabinets, doors with velvet-lined trellis, circa 1860, 33in. wide. (Sotheby's Belgravia) $1,685

Ebonised and marquetry side cabinet by Henry Ogden, Manchester, 1865-70, 70in. wide. (Sotheby's Belgravia) $1,450

Scarlet and gold lacquer cabinet on stand of Charles II design, 46in. wide. (Christie's) $7,260

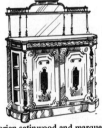

Victorian satinwood and marquetry side cabinet with mirror panel back, 63in. wide. (Christie's) $1,620

Italian pietra dura breakfront cabinet, circa 1860. (Bonhams) $8,425

Late 17th century Spanish ebony and tortoiseshell cabinet on stand, 48½in. wide. (Christie's) $5,235

One of a pair of 19th century ebonised and boulle ormolu mounted cabinets, 2ft.10¾in. wide, circa 1860.(Sotheby, King & Chasemore) $1,220

One of a pair of William IV rosewood veneered cabinets, circa 1830, 3ft.2½in. wide.(Sotheby's) $4,390

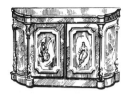

Walnut side cabinet in well-figured wood and with two painted doors, 1860's, 65in. wide. (Sotheby's Belgravia) $960

Victorian figured walnut, crossbanded and marquetry inlaid credenza, 6ft.1in. wide. (Geering & Colyer)$2,640

Satinwood side cabinet by James Lamb, Manchester, with marble top, 74in. wide. (Sotheby's Belgravia) $2,105

William and Mary walnut cabinet, circa 1700, 3ft.1½in. wide, with later bracket feet.(Sotheby's) $3,275

Serpentine boulle side cabinet, circa 1870, 42½in. wide. (Sotheby's Belgravia) $965

18th century Japanese black and gold lacquer cabinet on stand, 29½in. wide. (Christie's) $4,405

William and Mary mulberry cabinet in the manner of Coxed & Woster, circa 1690, 3ft.4in. wide. (Sotheby's) $11,230

18th century Goanese cabinet in two sections, on later stand, 2ft.10in. wide. (Allen & May) $5,015

One of a pair of stained beechwood cabinets on stands, stamped H. Fourdinois, 43½in. wide.(Christie's) $3,600

Regency rosewood dwarf cabinet with rectangular top crossbanded with tulipwood, 37½in. wide. (Christie's) $2,500

Flemish 17th century ebony cabinet on stand, drawers and doors with painted panels, 2ft.8in. wide. (Andrew Grant) $15,575

Ornate mid 19th century French ebonised and ormolu cabinet, 3ft.4in. wide. (Andrew Grant) $2,160

CABINETS

One of a pair of red boulle side cabinets with gilt bronze friezes, 32in. wide. (Sotheby's Belgravia) $1,175

Walnut side cabinet with acanthus carved cornice, 1840's, 4ft.6in. wide. (Sotheby's) $625

Walnut music cabinet inlaid with boxwood stringing and foliage, 1850's, 24in. wide. (Sotheby's Belgravia) $885

Mid 19th century boulle side cabinet with 18th century top, with brass molding, 48in. wide. (Sotheby's Belgravia) $1,285

Boulle side cabinet with breakfront frieze, circa 1870, 80in. wide. (Sotheby's Belgravia) $1,995

Rare Regency lacquer side cabinet with marble top, circa 1805, 3ft.3in. wide. (Sotheby's) $4,390

Boulle side cabinet with rectangular top, 1860's, 41½in. wide. (Sotheby's Belgravia) $1,080

William IV side cabinet of breakfront form with gray marble top, 6ft.6in. wide, circa 1830. (Sotheby's) $2,735

George III fiddle-back mahogany cabinet on chest. (Woolley & Wallis) $4,620

Early 17th century Spanish walnut vargueno with pierced iron lockplates, 41¾in. wide. (Christie's) $5,470

Early 18th century Italian ebonised table cabinet with rising top, 2ft.11in. wide, on later stand. (Messenger May & Baverstock) $5,850

George I double domed black lacquer cabinet on giltwood stand. (Messenger May & Baverstock) $9,595

Early 18th century white-painted parcel gilt and marblised reliquary cabinet, circa 1730, 2ft.6½in. wide. (Sotheby's) $975

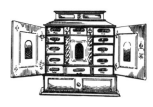

Mid 17th century German walnut cabinet, circa 1650, formerly on a stand, 2ft.5½in. wide. (Sotheby's) $2,685

Mid 19th century kingwood cabinet with brass mounts and gallery, 1ft.5in. wide. (Sotheby's) $625

Charles II walnut cabinet on stand with stepped cornice, 91cm. wide. (H. Spencer & Sons) $2,640

Late 17th century olivewood parquetry cabinet on stand with oyster-veneered design, 5ft. 9in. wide. (Sotheby's) $2,340

Chinese red lacquer cabinet on chest with pierced giltwood panels, 41in. wide. (Locke & England) $1,125

One of a pair of George IV rosewood cabinets, circa 1820, 2ft. 1in. wide. (Sotheby's) $4,285

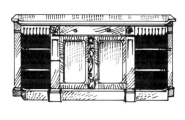

Late William IV rosewood side cabinet, 1830's, 81½in. wide. (Sotheby's Belgravia) $1,170

Mahogany and marquetry side cabinet with dentil cornice, circa 1880, 46¼in. wide. (Sotheby's Belgravia) $2,760

Mid 18th century Japanese lacquer cabinet, 65cm. wide. (Bonhams) $2,000

Walnut and ivory inlaid cabinet, circa 1880, inscribed F. del Seldarto, 35½in. wide. (Sotheby's Belgravia) $4,230

James I black-japanned cabinet on stand with arcaded top, 25½in. wide. (Christie's) $2,400

291

CABINETS

Mahogany side cabinet with pierced gallery above two glazed doors, 1880's, 37in. wide. (Sotheby's Belgravia) $410

Ebony and amboyna porcelain mounted side cabinet, circa 1870, 72in. wide. (Sotheby's Belgravia) $1,660

19th century Moorish hardwood and inlaid breakfront table cabinet, 2ft.4in. wide. (Sotheby's) $465

George IV mahogany side cabinet with reeded top, circa 1825, 3ft.6½in. wide. (Sotheby's) $1,590

George III satinwood side cabinet crossbanded in kingwood, 3ft.9in. wide, circa 1795. (Sotheby's) $7,615

19th century Japanese lacquer cabinet inset with cloisonne panels, 36in. high. (Messenger May & Baverstock) $3,720

18th century Goanese rosewood cabinet with sixteen drawers inlaid with bone, 31½in. wide. (Christie's) $3,450

Oak and rosewood bookcase/cabinet with glazed upper section, circa 1910, 184cm. wide. (Sotheby's Belgravia) $1,285

Gregory & Co. ebonised music cabinet, doors with pottery panels, mid 1870's, 20in. wide. (Sotheby's Belgravia) $290

Majorelle Art Nouveau mahogany cabinet, circa 1900, frieze carved with floral decoration. (Sotheby's Belgravia) $1,170

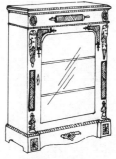

Ebonised side cabinet with single glazed door, corners with porcelain plaques, 1880's, 35in. wide. (Sotheby's Belgravia) $730

Gregory & Co. ebonised mahogany music cabinet with painted doors, 1870's, 18¼in. wide. (Sotheby's Belgravia) $340

Mid Victorian walnut cabinet with spiral twist columns and two glazed doors. (Outhwaite & Litherland) $1,695

Chippendale period mahogany library cabinet with rising top section, 3ft.8in. wide. (Locke & England)$2,300

Early 18th century Dutch japanned hanging wall cabinet with arched molded cornice, 4ft.9in. wide.(Sotheby's) $4,390

Rosewood cabinet on stand, doors inlaid with mother-of-pearl, stamped Graham & Biddle, London, 22½in. wide. (Christie's) $1,320

One of a pair of ebonised and pietra dura inlaid side cabinets with black marble tops, circa 1870, 32½in. wide.(Sotheby's Belgravia) $1,690

17th century Spanish oak vargueno with hinged fall-flap mounted with gilt iron plaques, 43½in. wide. (Christie's) $4,045

George II mahogany architectural cabinet by William Hallet, circa 1765, 3ft. 8in. wide. (Sotheby's) $20,700

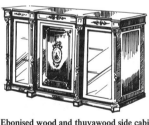

Ebonised wood and thuyawood side cabinet, circa 1870, 72in. wide, door with porcelain panel. (Sotheby's Belgravia) $995

Late 17th century black lacquered cabinet on stand, 40in. wide. (Phillips) $5,060

Mid 18th century Spanish Colonial oak and walnut tabernacle cabinet on stand, 3ft.1in. wide. (Sotheby's) $1,465

Walnut side cabinet with mirrored superstructure and white marble top, circa 1870, 59½in. wide. (Sotheby's Belgravia) $740

Late 19th century Italian pietra dura and ebony cabinet on stand, 67cm. wide. (H. Spencer & Sons) $2,640

Regency rosewood canterbury with pierced sides and four divisions, on turned feet. (Locke & England) $625

William IV mahogany canterbury with three scrolled divisions, circa 1830, 2ft. 7½in. wide. (Sotheby's) $1,465

Regency rosewood canterbury with stylised lyre uprights. (Locke & England) $705

Rosewood canterbury with serpentine dividing rails and pierced sides, circa 1850, 24in. wide. (Sotheby's Belgravia) $880

Victorian brass canterbury in four sections and on tripod supports. (Taylor Lane & Creber) $335

Victorian walnut supper canterbury with revolving tiers and turned spindle galleries. (Hall, Wateridge & Owen) $890

Victorian bamboo magazine holder. (Alfie's Antique Market) $180

Unusual early Victorian burr-walnut music cabinet, 51cm. wide. (Sotheby, King & Chasemore) $1,355

19th century rosewood canterbury/whatnot, 21in. wide. (R. H. Ellis & Sons) $590

Early Victorian burr-walnut canterbury with brass gallery, base with glazed paneled door. (Butler & Hatch Waterman) $1,415

Victorian carved rosewood canterbury, American, circa 1860, 23½in. wide. (Robert W. Skinner Inc.) $325

Sheraton mahogany music canterbury. (Christie's & Edmiston's) $1,330

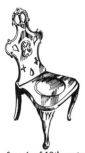

One of a pair of 19th century yew-wood hall chairs with pierced and carved backs, solid dish seats.(Hall, Wateridge & Owen)$2,340

Two of a set of eight carved dining chairs with cane seats. (Clive Emson & Co.) $685

Heavily carved oak hall chair. (Andrew Grant) $70

One of a set of six mahogany framed balloon back dining chairs. (Clive Emson & Co.) $770

Two of a set of seven Victorian mahogany dining chairs with tapestry upholstered seats. (D. M. Nesbit & Co.) $1,425

One of a set of four Dutch walnut and marquetry dining chairs with cabriole legs and claw and ball feet. (Christie's) $2,975

One of a matched set of eight elm spindleback rush seat dining chairs. (Burtenshaw Walker) $2,640

Two of a set of eight late 19th century Chippendale style dining chairs. (Bradley & Vaughan) $3,870

One of a set of eight Regency mahogany dining chairs with drop-in seats. (Christie's) $5,475

One of a set of six 19th century carved oak dining chairs including two carvers. (Russell, Baldwin & Bright) $2,340

Two of a set of six single and two carver mahogany Hepplewhite style chairs with Prince of Wales Feather decoration. (Honiton Galleries) $1,310

One of a set of five 18th century Dutch walnut and marquetry dining chairs with arched curved backs. (Christie's)$11,425

One of a set of six mid 19th century mahogany dining chairs with waisted backs and stuffed seats. (Sotheby's Belgravia) $960

One of a set of four 'George III' mahogany dining chairs, circa 1870, on square chamfered legs. (Sotheby's Belgravia) $470

One of a set of twelve mahogany 'Empire' dining chairs, circa 1900. (Sotheby's Belgravia) $1,455

One of a set of six Austrian mahogany dining chairs with rectangular backs. (Christie's) $7,615

One of a set of six oak dining chairs with button upholstered backs and seats, circa 1860. (Sotheby's Belgravia) $540

One of a set of six George IV dining chairs with curved toprails, circa 1825. (Sotheby's) $2,025

One of a set of twelve mahogany dining chairs with arched padded backs, circa 1910. (Sotheby's Belgravia) $955

One of a set of six mid 19th century New England ladderback dining chairs. (Robert W. Skinner Inc.) $3,000

One of a set of four early 20th century 'George III' dining chairs with oval backs. (Sotheby's Belgravia) $525

One of a set of ten late 17th century 'Harlequin' Derbyshire chairs.(Sotheby's) $7,650

One of a set of ten mahogany dining chairs, circa 1870, with padded back. (Sotheby's Belgravia) $1,895

One of a pair of Hepplewhite carved mahogany shield-back chairs, circa 1790.(Sotheby, King & Chasemore)$2,205

One of a set of six Victorian single chairs in mahogany. (Bradley & Vaughan) $1,935

One of a set of six William and Mary walnut chairs with caned back and seats, circa 1690. (Sotheby's) $3,345

One of a pair of mid Georgian mahogany chairs with Gothic splats, circa 1760. (Sotheby's) $1,495

One of a set of four Victorian mahogany hall chairs. (J. M. Welch & Son) $515

One of a set of five Federal cherrywood side chairs, circa 1795, 37in. high. (Robert W. Skinner Inc.) $2,600

One of a set of six oak dining chairs, American, 20th century, with leather seats. (Robert W. Skinner Inc.) $900

One of a set of six late George III mahogany rail back chairs with nailed hide seats, circa 1795. (Sotheby, King & Chasemore) $1,855

One of a set of six hardwood chairs with waved toprails, 19th century. (Christie's) $3,875

One of a set of six rosewood salon chairs, 19th century. (Bradley & Vaughan) $2,420

One of a set of six George I style carved walnut caned back dining chairs, circa 1910. (Sotheby, King & Chasemore) $4,175

One of a set of six Irish Georgian fruitwood dining chairs with waved ladder backs. (Christie's) $1,950

One of a set of eight William IV mahogany dining chairs. (Stride's) $3,295

One of a set of four Hepplewhite style dining chairs with shield-shaped backs. (Butler & Hatch Waterman) $520

One of a set of six early Georgian oak dining chairs with curved solid baluster splats. (Christie's) $4,265

One of a pair of four slat maple and ash side chairs, mid 18th century, New Hampshire, 43in. high. (Robert W. Skinner Inc.) $550

One of a set of six George II mahogany chairs with arched rectangular backs, lacking upholstery. (Christie's) $8,295

One of a set of seven yew back chairs with elm seats. (Bradley & Vaughan. $3,800

One of a set of six 'Harlequin' George III mahogany hall chairs, circa 1800. (Sotheby, King & Chasemore) $730

One of a set of six oak dining chairs, circa 1870, with button upholstered seats. (Sotheby's Belgravia) $615

One of a set of five George I walnut chairs, circa 1725. (Sotheby, King & Chasemore) $9,510

297

DINING CHAIRS

One of a set of eight mahogany dining chairs, seat rail stamped Jack, circa 1850. (Sotheby's Belgravia) $1,970

Two of a set of twelve fine Regency mahogany dining chairs on sabre legs.(Christie's) $13,310

One of a pair of George II red walnut chairs, circa 1730, with a solid vase splat. (Sotheby's) $1,685

One of a set of six early Victorian dining chairs with carved backs. (Dacre, Son & Hartley) $345

Two of a set of six Chippendale style mahogany chairs. (C. G. Sloan & Co. Inc.) $1,750

One of a set of eight Sheraton black and gilt painted chairs with cane seats and splats, circa 1800. (Sotheby, King & Chasemore) $2,205

One of a pair of fine 19th century Continental ebony and ebonised Jacobean hall chairs, inlaid with ivory. (Locke & England) $470

Two of a set of ten unusual early 19th century salamander elbow chairs with caned seats. (Phillips & Jolly) $12,205

Oak dining chair with tall ladder back, 1903, by Chas. Rennie Mackintosh, with rush seat . (Christie's & Edmiston's)$4,080

One of a set of six 19th century Chippendale style carved mahogany chairs. (Sotheby, King & Chasemore) $1,800

Two from a set of eight Hepplewhite style mahogany dining chairs with shield backs. (C. G. Sloan & Co. Inc.) $1,000

One of a set of eight George III mahogany dining chairs with shield-shaped backs. (Christie's) $5,475

One of a set of four early Victorian walnut balloon back standard chairs with original velvet. (Locke & England) $1,195

Two from a set of seven Chippendale style mahogany dining chairs. (C. G. Sloan & Co. Inc.) $1,900

One of four carved ebony chairs. (Parsons, Welch & Cowell) $2,280

One of a set of six George III mahogany dining chairs with curved top rails. (Christie's) $3,570

Two from a set of three Hepplewhite mahogany shield-back chairs, with floral seats. (C. G. Sloan & Co. Inc.) $500

One of a set of six early 19th century rosewood dining chairs with caned seats. (Honiton Galleries.) $1,860

One of ten Regency rosewood dining chairs on sabre legs, with cane seats. (Burtenshaw Walker) $6,160

Two from a set of six Hepplewhite period mahogany fluted-frame dining chairs, circa 1785. (Neales) $2,485

One of six Sheraton design mahogany dining chairs on turned fluted legs. (Burtenshaw Walker) $2,970

One of a set of six 'Hepplewhite' fluted shield-back chairs with pierced splats, 20th century. (Neales) $1,615

Two chairs from a nine-piece diningroom suite including table. (Dacre, Son & Hartley) $3,695

One of a set of twelve William IV faded mahogany dining chairs, circa 1835, with faults. (Lawrence Fine Art) $5,150

DINING CHAIRS

One of a set of four 18th century Chippendale style mahogany dining chairs. (Phillips) $3,795

One of a set of eight mahogany dining chairs with vase-shaped splats. (Taylor Lane & Creber) $2,510

One from a set of six 19th century walnut framed salon chairs with tapestry panels and seats. (Taylor Lane & Creber)$870

One of a set of four Scottish elm chairs by George Walton, circa 1890. (Sotheby's) $820

One from a 19th century Dutch set of six dining chairs. (Phillips & Jolly)$2,880

One of a set of six walnut side chairs with arched shield backs, circa 1860.(Sotheby's Belgravia) $1,105

One of a set of six Carolean style carved dark oak chairs with stuffed seats. (Smith-Woolley & Perry) $850

One of a set of six mahogany dining chairs, mid 19th century. (Sotheby's Belgravia) $895

One of a set of eight mahogany dining chairs, each with concave toprail, 1840's. (Sotheby's Belgravia) $1,450

Two from a set of eight Chippendale style mahogany dining chairs with ball and claw feet. (Messenger May & Baverstock) $5,670

One of a pair of walnut dining chairs with pierced baluster splats, early 18th century. (Christie's) $940

One of a set of six 19th century walnut framed balloon back dining chairs, on cabriole legs. (Taylor Lane & Creber) $2,052

One of a set of eight marquetry dining chairs, Dutch, mid 19th century, each with arched tops. (Sotheby's Belgravia) $5,170

One of a set of six walnut balloon back dining chairs on molded cabriole legs, circa 1860. (Sotheby's) $1,325

One of a set of four Chippendale carved mahogany chairs with brocade covered seats, circa 1765. (Sotheby, King & Chasemore) $9,760

One of a pair of mid 18th century Dutch walnut and marquetry dining chairs. (H. Spencer & Sons) $1,825

One of a pair of standard satinwood dining chairs with cane seats. (Phillips) $810

One of a set of four mid Victorian carved walnut dining chairs with shaped balloon backs. (Dacre, Son & Hartley) $920

One of a set of five George I walnut dining chairs, circa 1725. (Sotheby, King & Chasemore) $9,020

One of a set of six Sheraton single dining chairs. (Graves, Son & Pilcher) $8,880

One of a set of twelve old rail and wheel back cottage dining chairs. (Butler & Hatch Waterman) $1,220

One of a pair of mid 18th century walnut dining chairs. (Drewatt, Watson & Barton)$1,320

Late William and Mary beechwood side chair on octagonal turned legs, circa 1695. (Sotheby's) $315

One of a pair of Continental painted and decorated dining chairs with cane seats. (Allen & May) $910

Two from a set of seven 'Harlequin' Hepplewhite period mahogany framed dining chairs. (Moore, Allen & Innocent) $1,560

One of a set of six carved mahogany single chairs by Marsh, Jones, Cribb & Co., circa 1900. (Dacre, Son & Hartley) $1,940

One of a set of eight George III mahogany dining chairs with vase-shaped splats. (Christie's)$8,930

One of a set of ten oak dining chairs in 17th century style with twist turned stretchers. (H. Spencer & Sons) $5,905

One of a pair of early 18th century Dutch walnut dining chairs with carved and pierced backs. (Graves, Son & Pilcher) $660

One of a pair of Georgian mahogany single dining chairs with oval backs. (Allen & May)$160

DINING CHAIRS

One of a set of six Victorian rosewood balloon back dining chairs. (Cooper Hirst) $1,410

Two from a set of ten early George III mahogany chairs.   (Phillips) $50,820

One of a set of four Victorian walnut chairs with shaped crest rails. (Burrows and Day) $655

One of a set of six 20th century Hepplewhite style fluted shield back dining chairs. (Neales) $1,585

Two from a very fine set of ten 19th century Chippendale design mahogany chairs with pierced splats. (Locke & England) $4,400

One of a set of twelve giltwood drawingroom chairs, 1840's.(Sotheby's Belgravia) $1,020

One of a set of seven step down Windsor side chairs, circa 1800, 35in. high. (Robert W. Skinner Inc.) $3,000

Two from a set of eight 19th century Chippendale style mahogany dining chairs, with pierced back splats. (Burtenshaw Walker)$2,015

One of a set of six early George II red walnut dining chairs, circa 1735. (Neales) $5,735

One of a set of eight Victorian rosewood balloon back chairs.(Christie's S. Kensington) $4,840

Two from a set of twelve Chippendale design mahogany framed dining chairs on cabriole legs and ball and claw feet. (Biddle & Webb) $4,840

One of a pair of North European walnut armchairs each with Art Nouveau leaves, circa 1890. (Sotheby's Belgravia) $755

302

One of a set of six Regency mahogany dining chairs with canework seats. (Capes, Dunn & Co.) $1,760

Two from a set of twelve Portuguese dining chairs with carved cresting rails. (Lawrence Fine Art) $3,510

One of a set of seven Regency mahogany dining chairs with rope twist backs. (Raymond Inman) $5,040

One of a set of eight late 19th century walnut dining chairs with barley-twist supports. (Sotheby's Belgravia) $1,560

Two from a set of seven William IV dining chairs on chamfered taper legs. (Burtenshaw Walker) $1,420

One of a set of eight William IV mahogany chairs.(Stride's) $3,265

One of a set of six early 19th century rosewood dining chairs, stamped G. Hill, circa 1830. (Sotheby's) $3,625

Two from a set of seven George III mahogany dining chairs, circa 1800. (Sotheby's) $5,370

One of a set of six Victorian walnut rococo design balloon back dining chairs, circa 1860. (Neales) $1,410

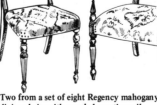

George III mahogany side chair with shaped and molded toprail, circa 1760. (Sotheby's) $635

Two from a set of eight Regency mahogany dining chairs with paneled cresting rail. (Lawrence Fine Art) $4,680

George III mahogany side chair with pierced interlaced splat, circa 1760. (Sotheby's) $585

303

DINING CHAIRS

One of a set of six Regency style dining chairs, 19th century. (Lawrence Fine Art) $2,105

Two from an unusual set of six 19th century oak frame dining chairs, stamped W. Priest. (W. H. Lane & Son) $1,200

One of a set of six Sheraton tiger maple fancy chairs, circa 1820, with balloon seats. (Robert W. Skinner Inc.) $3,000

One of a set of six walnut chairs on cabriole legs, circa 1855. (Sotheby's Belgravia)$1,590

Two from a set of eighteen William IV mahogany dining chairs, with slip-in seats, circa 1835. (Lawrence Fine Art) $7,490

One of a set of six Victorian mahogany drawingroom chairs with cameo-shaped backs. (Morphets) $1,680

One of a set of six painted arrow back side chairs, Massachusetts, circa 1820. (Robert W. Skinner Inc.) $3,000

Two from a set of six Victorian 'Hepplewhite' mahogany dining chairs and matching carvers. (Taylor Lane & Creber) $1,805

One of a pair of late 19th century Eastern United States Victorian ebonised wood side chairs, 39in. high. (Robert W. Skinner Inc.) $875

One of six Charles II style oak side chairs on turned and blocked legs. (C. G. Sloan & Co. Inc.) $1,150

Two from a set of eight Chippendale style mahogany dining chairs with tapestry covered seats. (Frank R. Marshall) $5,150

One of a set of six Dutch walnut and marquetry dining chairs on cabriole legs. (Christie's) $4,285

Late 19th century wicker platform rocker, American, height of back, 46in. (Robert W. Skinner Inc.) $175

One chair from a French walnut suite in rose brocade. (Lambert & Symes) $3,025

One of a pair of George II Library armchairs. (Phillips)$9,810

Mahogany, leather upholstered jockey's scales with an Avery balance, circa 1900. (Nock Deighton) $660

Mid 19th century American Victorian laminated and carved rosewood armchair, 42½in. high. (Robert W. Skinner Inc.) $2,100

Louis XVI carved beechwood fauteuil on reeded and tapered legs. (C. G. Sloan & Co. Inc.) $850

Victorian walnut sewing chair with front cabriole legs. (Andrew Grant) $160

Anglo-Indian hardwood side chair with pierced and carved arched back, circa 1870. (Sotheby's Belgravia) $375

19th century occasional chair with rosewood frame and upholstered back and seat, on short cabriole legs. (Butler & Hatch Waterman) $230

Large walnut armchair with pierced back, circa 1870. (Sotheby's Belgravia) $940

One of a pair of 18th century French Louis XV fauteuils en cabriolet, 35in. high. (Robert W. Skinner Inc.) $1,300

French Empire mahogany bergere with carved giltwood accents, on short sabre legs. (C. G. Sloan & Co. Inc.) $1,400

EASY CHAIRS

George II carved mahogany and upholstered occasional chair, circa 1755. (Sotheby, King & Chasemore) $1,005

One of a pair of French carved armchairs in rococo style, in need of restoration. (Scott & Muirhead) $1,745

George III walnut Gainsborough armchair with padded arms. (Lawrence Fine Art) $935

Antique mahogany bergere chair upholstered in tapestry. (Lambert & Symes) $870

Carved walnut X-framed open armed chair, upholstered in gold brocade. (Lambert & Symes) $820

Late 17th century walnut armchair with molded and carved front stretcher, circa 1680. (Sotheby's) $925

Chippendale mahogany library chair, upholstered in gros point and petit point tapestry. (Lambert & Symes) $9,195

18th century Gainsborough chair with mahogany legs and arms. (Graves, Son & Pilcher) $3,080

George I open armchair with arched padded back on cabriole legs and pad feet. (Christie's) $3,930

George III mahogany and upholstered tub-shaped armchair, circa 1800. (Sotheby, King & Chasemore) $1,150

Unusual lacquered wood rocking chair, 1960's, 76cm. deep. (Sotheby's Belgravia) $235

Part of a 'Louis XVI' beechwood drawingroom suite, circa 1880. (Sotheby's Belgravia) $1,525

306

One of a pair of early 18th century Liege grained bergeres a oreilles. (Christie's)$6,665

Late Victorian carved walnut nursing chair with buttoned back and castored feet. (Dacre, Son & Hartley) $295

Chippendale mahogany Gainsborough armchair with cabriole legs, upholstered in gros point and petit point tapestry. (Lambert & Symes) $6,290

One of a pair of Italian white-painted and parcel gilt armchairs. (Sotheby's) $9,045

One of a set of four George III beechwood armchairs with stuffed backs, circa 1785. (Sotheby's) $5,300

Mid Victorian carved mahogany balloon back easy chair with scroll carved arm supports. (Dacre, Son & Hartley)$525

George III carved mahogany Gainsborough armchair, circa 1760. (Sotheby, King & Chasemore) $1,465

One of a set of eight George III giltwood armchairs with oval-shaped backs, circa 1780. (Sotheby, King & Chasemore) $28,350

One of a pair of George II giltwood saloon chairs with slightly arched backs. (Christie's) $16,455

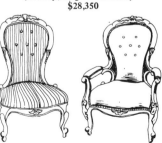

Regency mahogany metamorphic library steps formed as an open armchair. (Christie's) $1,190

Matching pair of walnut framed Victorian chairs. (Bradley & Vaughan) $1,160

George III giltwood open armchair with oval padded back on paneled square tapering legs. (Christie's) $855

307

Button backed upholstered armchair, late 1850's.(Sotheby's Belgravia) $745

Walnut wing armchair with stuffed arched back, on short cabriole legs, 1930's. (Sotheby's Belgravia) $265

Armchair from a seven-piece suite of rosewood drawingroom furniture, 1890's.(Sotheby's Belgravia) $1,250

Walnut upholstered armchair with buttoned back, circa 1860, on cabriole legs and scroll feet.(Sotheby's Belgravia) $610

Mahogany armchair with arched top with overhanging canopy, circa 1870.(Sotheby's Belgravia) $835

George III mahogany open armchair with cartouche-shaped padded back. (Christie's) $1,510

Fruitwood armchair, stamped Gillows, 1830-40, on cabriole legs. (Sotheby's Belgravia) $790

Two chairs from a suite of 'Louis XV' giltwood furniture of seven pieces, circa 1880.(Sotheby's Belgravia) $13,665

William and Mary ebonised beechwood wing armchair, circa 1685, re-railed. (Sotheby's)$2,420

One of a set of four 'Louis XVI' giltwood armchairs, circa 1880.(Sotheby's Belgravia) $1,270

George III painted fauteuil by Thomas Chippendale with cartouche-shaped back, circa 1765. (Sotheby's) $8,090

Chair from a three-piece suite of drawingroom furniture, circa 1880. (Sotheby's Belgravia) $1,025

One of a pair of Continental Louis XV style walnut fauteuils, 19th century, on cabriole legs.(Lawrence Fine Art) $655

Mid Victorian carved walnut nursing chair with leaf carved apron.(Dacre, Son & Hartley) $760

Rosewood button-upholstered armchair with padded back and arms, circa 1860, sold with a nursing chair. (Sotheby's Belgravia) $1,230

George III mahogany library chair of Gainsborough type.(Phillips) $5,520

19th century American rosewood nursing chair with curved and scrolled padded back.(Christie's) $390

George III open armchair. (Drewatt, Watson & Barton) $1,230

'Louis XV' giltwood armchair with serpentine seat, circa 1880. (Sotheby's Belgravia) $375

Laminated and plywood chaise longue by Heal's, 1930's, 140cm. high. (Sotheby's Belgravia) $1,355

Victorian mahogany lady's chair with button back. (Jacobs & Hunt) $1,160

George III mahogany bergere given to Lord Nelson by Lady Hamilton. (Christie's) $2,930

One of a pair of Louis XVI painted fauteuils stamped St. Georges, circa 1780.(Sotheby's) $2,005

Early Georgian walnut wing armchair on cabriole legs and ball and claw feet.(Christie's) $2,075

309

ELBOW CHAIRS

George III ash and almond Windsor chair with hoop back, circa 1760. (Sotheby's) $895

One of a pair of George III mahogany armchairs with stuffed oval backs, circa 1780. (Sotheby's) $2,320

English oak wheel-backed Windsor armchair. (C. G. Sloan & Co. Inc.) $700

One of a pair of Antique Spanish walnut armchairs with trestle feet. (C. G. Sloan & Co. Inc.) $1,600

One of a pair of George II walnut chairs with interlaced loop splats, circa 1730. (Sotheby's) $1,365

Antique oak armchair with carved paneled back. (Honiton Galleries) $1,115

One of a pair of American 20th century Gothic revival oak hall chairs, 72in. high. (Robert W. Skinner Inc.) $400

Charles II oak armchair with carved back, dated 1682. (Sotheby's) $1,650

17th century carved oak panel back armchair with pierced scrolling cresting rail. (Lawrence Fine Art) $385

Early 20th century Damascus walnut corner armchair, inlaid with mother-of-pearl. (Sotheby's Belgravia) $330

Red lacquered folding mandarin's chair decorated with bronze plaques. (D. M. Nesbit & Co.) $2,660

Charles II caned walnut armchair with carved toprail and spiral-twist supports, circa 1670. (Sotheby's) $1,010

Chippendale mahogany corner chair, Boston, Massachusetts, circa 1755, restored. (Robert W. Skinner Inc.) $2,100

Late 18th century American brace back Windsor armchair, 38½in. high.(Robert W. Skinner Inc.) $2,000

One of a set of twelve 'Empire' mahogany dining chairs, circa 1900. (Sotheby's Belgravia) $1,645

One of a set of six Carolean style carved oak dining chairs. (Sotheby Bearne) $1,380

One of a 'Harlequin' set of six elm and yew Windsor chairs, early 19th century. (Sotheby's) $2,125

Lady's armchair with tapestry seat and matching oval padded back. (Clive Emson & Co.) $85

Child's 18th century oak wing rocking chair with shaped back and box seat, 28in. high.(Dacre, Son & Hartley) $295

Mid 18th century bow back Windsor armchair, New England, 35¼in. high. (Robert W. Skinner Inc.) $2,700

American William and Mary maple and ash banister armchair, circa 1700. (Robert W. Skinner Inc.) $2,600

Early 18th century yew and elm Windsor chair in original condition. (Davis & Son) $1,170

Venetian lacquered gondola chair. (C. G. Sloan & Co. Inc.)$400

18th century Windsor elbow chair with yew-wood spindle and pierced vase splat back. (Russell, Baldwin & Bright) $935

311

ELBOW CHAIRS

One of a pair of George III mahogany armchairs with shield-shaped backs, circa 1790, restored. (Sotheby's) $2,805

One of a set of eight George III mahogany chairs with double lyre crossbars, circa 1800. (Sotheby's) $6,100

One of a set of twelve late George III elm dining chairs, circa 1810. (Sotheby's) $3,295

One of a set of seven George III mahogany chairs with reeded rectangular frames, circa 1780. (Sotheby's) $2,530

One of a pair of Edwardian mahogany elbow chairs with broken swan's neck cresting rails. (Smith-Woolley & Perry) $460

One of a set of twelve mid 19th century mahogany dining chairs by F. Fell, with brass stringing.(Sotheby's Belgravia) $4,445

One of a set of nine early 20th century 'George III' mahogany dining chairs. (Sotheby's Belgravia) $1,405

One of a pair of ebonised armchairs with padded backs and arms, 1870's.(Sotheby's Belgravia) $895

George III beechwood open armchair with shield-shaped back and paneled frame. (Christie's) $1,330

One of a set of six George III painted armchairs, circa 1800.(Sotheby's) $2,575

One of a set of eight George III mahogany chairs of Hepplewhite design, circa 1795, restored. (Sotheby, King & Chasemore) $3,830

One of a set of eight George III mahogany ladderback chairs, including one armchair, circa 1800. (Sotheby's) $4,445

17th/18th century child's oak high chair with bobbin back, arms and legs. (Christie's) $1,485

One of a pair of George III mahogany open armchairs with paneled oval backs. (Christie's) $8,230

Early 17th century oak X-framed folding chair with double paneled back. (Christie's) $3,840

One of a set of four 18th century Windsor chairs. (Graves, Son & Pilcher) $2,880

One of a pair of 17th century French pearwood elbow chairs with loose leather covered seats. (Lowery & Partners) $700

One of a set of ten reproduction dining chairs with pierced splats. (Gribble, Booth & Taylor) $1,870

Mid 19th century Battle Abbey Abbot's throne in oak. (Christie's) $975

Unusually well-carved 17th century oak wainscot chair in excellent condition. (James & Lister Lea) $1,800

One of a pair of late 17th century Venetian walnut open armchairs with pierced and carved stretchers. (Drewatt, Watson & Barton) $1,450

One of a pair of Regency mahogany bergeres with scrolled caned backs. (Christie's) $3,290

One of a set of five George III ebonised and parcel gilt open armchairs. (Christie's) $4,465

Early George III mahogany open armchair with pierced Gothic pattern splat. (Christie's) $2,300

313

ELBOW CHAIRS

Ebonised mahogany 'Jacobean' armchair designed by E. W. Godwin, circa 1880, with cane seat. (Sotheby's Belgravia) $585

Late 19th century Renaissance revival walnut Dante-style chair, American, 48in. high. (Robert W. Skinner Inc.) $500

One of a set of twelve Edwardian carved walnut dining chairs in Chippendale style, circa 1910. (Sotheby, King & Chasemore) $4,030

One of a set of eight Regency brass-inlaid rosewood dining chairs, circa 1820. (Sotheby's) $11,085

George II walnut armchair by Giles Grendy with pierced splat, circa 1735, restored. (Sotheby's) $5,000

Black-painted chair designed by Charles Rennie Mackintosh, 1906, 75cm. high. (Sotheby's Belgravia) $1,640

One of a set of four Louis XV painted fauteuils, stamped Dargagny, circa 1760. (Sotheby's) $7,020

William and Mary walnut armchair with arched cane splat, circa 1690. (Sotheby's) $430

One of a pair of George III mahogany armchairs with shield-shaped backs, circa 1780. (Sotheby's) $2,855

One from a set of eight Regency mahogany diners. (Sotheby's) $4,045

One of a pair of mid 18th century Italian white and parcel gilt armchairs, circa 1770. (Sotheby's) $9,270

Late 18th century American maple, ash and pine brace back armchair, 44in. high. (Robert W. Skinner Inc.) $1,150

One of a set of eight mahogany dining chairs, circa 1890, banded with satinwood. (Sotheby's Belgravia) $1,090

Late Victorian elm smoker's chair on turned legs with a double 'H' stretcher. (Vernon's) $150

19th century French beechwood lady's chair. (Alfie's Antique Market) $215

Chippendale period mahogany elbow chair. (Drewatt, Watson & Barton). $1,760

19th century mahogany armchair in Chippendale style, upholstered in floral tapestry. (H. C. Chapman & Sons) $445

One of a pair of Edwardian inlaid mahogany elbow chairs. (Smith-Woolley & Perry) $460

One of a set of eight mahogany open armchairs of George III design. (Christie's) $9,760

Louis XV beechwood fauteuil with molded shaped back, circa 1765, formerly painted white. (Sotheby's) $880

One of a pair of mahogany armchairs with carved serpentine toprails, circa 1765. (Sotheby's) $6,425

One of a pair of late 18th century Italian giltwood armchairs, circa 1790. (Sotheby's) $1,415

One of a pair of Chinese hardwood armchairs, circa 1880, 125cm. high. (H. Spencer & Sons) $1,290

One of a pair of late 17th century Venetian walnut open armchairs, (Drewatt, Watson & Barton) $1,365

ELBOW CHAIRS

Late 17th century Flemish walnut armchair with arched padded back, circa 1690. (Sotheby's) $830

One of a set of eight oak, ash and elm 'Mendlesham' chairs, 1880-1900, with rush seats. (Sotheby's Belgravia) $960

Early 19th century painted and gilded armchair in the manner of George Smith, circa 1820. (Sotheby's) $3,050

One of a pair of mid 19th century steel rocking chairs, probably North European. (Sotheby's Belgravia) $1,270

One of a set of six Austrian or German walnut armchairs, circa 1820. (Sotheby's) $4,445

One of a set of six mid 19th century 'George III' mahogany dining chairs.(Sotheby's Belgravia) $1,440

Mid 19th century French walnut 'Renaissance' armchair with carved back. (Sotheby's Belgravia) $655

One of a set of four late 19th century painted metal chairs with latticework seats.(Sotheby's Belgravia) $1,050

18th century elm, beech and yew framed Windsor armchair with curiole stretcher.(Taylor Lane & Creber) $590

One of a set of eight 'Charles II' beechwood dining chairs with cane seats and splats, circa 1880. (Sotheby's Belgravia) $2,110

One of a set of ten late 19th century carved mahogany chairs in the Chippendale manner. (Sotheby, King & Chasemore) $1,770

One of a pair of joined oak panel back armchairs. (Lawrence Fine Art) $305

19th century mahogany serpentine chest of drawers with pierced brass plates, 3ft.1in. wide. (Lawrence Fine Art)$1,755

Early 19th century oak chest of drawers, flanked by spirally fluted columns, 23in. wide. (Sotheby Bearne) $325

Inlaid and banded mahogany chest of four drawers. (R. H. Ellis & Sons) $2,755

Sheraton figured mahogany bowfront chest of drawers, lined in boxwood, 2ft.11in. wide. (Lawrence Fine Art)$725

19th century shaped walnut veneered chest with gilt mountings, 2ft. wide. (W. H. Lane & Son) $385

Late 17th century Genoese walnut chest of drawers, 4ft.8½in. wide. (Sotheby's) $5,850

Small Georgian oak chest, top with cavetto molded edge, 2ft.8½in. wide. (Lawrence Fine Art) $750

19th century French Provincial Louis XVI walnut six drawer chest with marble top, 145cm. high. (Plaza, New York) $3,600

Early Georgian walnut batchelor chest of four drawers, on bracket feet, 30in. wide. (Burtenshaw Walker) $8,495

George II mahogany chest of drawers with moulded top and brushing slide, 3ft.10in. wide, circa 1750. (Sotheby's) $4,390

Georgian figured mahogany bow-front chest of drawers with brass loop handles, 2ft.9in. wide. (Lawrence Fine Art) $1,170

American Chippendale cherrywood tall chest of drawers with molded cornice, 36in. wide. (Robert W. Skinner Inc.) $2,750

CHEST OF DRAWERS

19th century serpentine figured mahogany chest of four drawers, 3ft.7in. wide. (Lawrence Fine Art) $1,405

Small Georgian mahogany chest of drawers with brass drop handles, 33in. wide. (Parsons, Welch & Cowell) $925

Mid 19th century elm brass-bound military chest in two parts, 37½in. wide.(Sotheby's Belgravia) $1,125

Georgian mahogany chest of drawers with boxwood line, 4ft. wide. (Lawrence Fine Art) $420

Late 18th century boulle Wellington chest of seven drawers. (Vernon's)$1,250

Georgian mahogany chest of four drawers with brass bail handles, 2ft.7in. wide. (Geering & Colyer) $970

Early English dark oak country made carved chest of four drawers, 41in. wide. (Andrew Grant) $300

Jacobean oak chest of three long drawers with molded fronts. (Olivers) $1,090

George III mahogany serpentine chest with crossbanded top, on bracket feet, 41in. wide. (Christie's) $4,230

Queen Anne walnut chest of drawers on bun feet, circa 1710, 3ft.1in. wide. (Sotheby's) $770

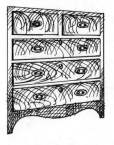

20th century mahogany straight front chest of five drawers, 4ft. wide.(Clive Emson & Co.) $95

Walnut and marquetry chest of drawers, 97cm. wide. (Christie's) $6,775

Mid 18th century South German stained burr-maple and marquetry chest of three drawers, 42in. wide. (Christie's)
$20,485

18th century Dutch burr-walnut serpentine chest with molded top, 35½in. wide.(Christie's)
$4,720

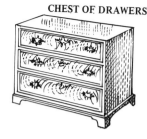

Antique walnut chest of three drawers with brass handles. (Allen & May)
$220

19th century mahogany military chest of six drawers with brass mounts and handles, 45in. wide. (Moore, Allen & Innocent)
$670

Georgian serpentine fronted inlaid and banded mahogany chest of four drawers with brass handles, 3ft.7in. wide. (R. H. Ellis & Sons)
$2,665

Mid 19th century Continental walnut chest of three long drawers, 3ft. wide. (Vernon's)
$650

William and Mary walnut and oyster veneered chest of six drawers, 102cm. wide. (Jackson-Stops & Staff)
$1,825

Early 18th century Austrian walnut chest of drawers with four crossbanded drawers, 26in. wide, sides inlaid with the Imperial Eagle. (Christie's)
$2,735

19th century Dutch marquetry and mahogany tall chest, inlaid with satinwood, circa 1835, 3ft. 3¾in. wide. (Sotheby, King & Chasemore) $2,435

Charles II walnut chest of drawers. with planked rectangular top, 95cm. wide. (H. Spencer & Sons)
$2,400

Antique oak paneled chest of three drawers with brass handles, 39in. wide. (Allen & May) $585

19th century serpentine front chest of drawers with brass handles, 3ft.6in. wide.(Taylor Lane & Creber) $1,390

CHEST OF DRAWERS

George III mahogany small chest with molded top, circa 1775, 2ft.10½in. wide. (Sotheby's) $5,615

Late 17th century oak upright chest with molded cornice, 52in. wide. (Christie's) $600

17th century Carolean walnut chest of drawers, molded in geometric panels. (H. Spencer & Sons) $2,440

Charles II oak chest of drawers, circa 1670, 3ft.1in. wide, with molded rectangular top. (Sotheby's) $815

George I walnut chest of five drawers, 2ft.7in. wide, circa 1725. (Sotheby's) $7,810

Anglo-Dutch walnut and seaweed marquetry chest of drawers, circa 1690, 3ft.4in. wide. (Sotheby's) $7,255

Georgian mahogany chest of four drawers with rosewood banding, 30in. wide. (Worsfolds) $1,325

Federal grain painted blanket chest, Vermont, circa 1800, 39½in. wide, with two drawers.(Robert W. Skinner Inc.) $1,200

American Chippendale mahogany bow-front chest of four drawers, 44in. wide. (C. G. Sloan & Co. Inc.) $1,200

Mid 18th century American country Chippendale birch tall chest with applied cornice, 36in. wide. (Robert W. Skinner Inc.) $3,400

George II burr-elm chest of five drawers, 81cm. wide. (Bonham's) $1,855

Continental carved and inlaid chest of five drawers, 23in. wide. (Lawrence Fine Art)$1,185

Floral marquetry chest of four drawers with shaped top, 2ft.10in. wide. (Honiton Galleries) $2,380

American Victorian walnut chest of six drawers, circa 1860, 24½in. wide. (Robert W. Skinner Inc.) $1,000

19th century straight front chest of five drawers on splayed legs, 49in. wide. (W. H. Lane & Son) $190

Mid 18th century New England Chippendale pine chest of drawers, 33¾in. wide. (Robert W. Skinner Inc.) $1,600

Victorian bow-fronted mahogany chest of drawers with turned wooden knobs, 3ft.7in. wide. (Vernon's) $275

Georgian mahogany set of five drawers with brass drop handles. (Warren & Wignall) $500

18th century Continental inlaid walnut chest of three drawers. (R. H. Ellis & Sons) $3,520

Late 19th century print chest of two parts, in mahogany. (Phillips) $6,760

Charles II oak chest of drawers, circa 1680, 3ft.1½in. wide. (Sotheby's) $710

Chippendale cherrywood tall blanket chest, New England, circa 1760, 36in. wide, with lift top. (Robert W. Skinner Inc.) $3,500

Chippendale cherrywood chest of drawers, New England, circa 1780, 42in. wide. (Robert W. Skinner Inc.) $2,600

19th century rosewood veneered Wellington chest, 2ft. wide. (Edgar Horn) $570

CHEST ON CHESTS

Chippendale cherrywood chest on chest, Pennsylvania, circa 1770, 38in. wide. (Robert W. Skinner Inc.) $2,500

Early 18th century Queen Anne style walnut chest on chest with fitted pierced plate and loop handles. (Langlois) $3,160

Mid Georgian amaranth tallboy with molded cornice with ivory and ebony border, 43in. wide. (Christie's) $3,290

Georgian mahogany inlaid tallboy on ogee feet with fluted canted corners and carved cornice, 42in. wide. (Burtenshaw Walker) $1,420

Late 19th century American custom Chippendale mahogany and mahogany veneer block front chest on chest, 40in. wide. (Robert W. Skinner Inc.) $3,100

Early George I walnut tallboy, circa 1720, 41½in. wide. (Lawrence Fine Art) $11,400

George I walnut secretaire tallboy, circa 1720, 107cm. wide. (Sotheby, King & Chasemore) $7,955

Georgian mahogany chest on chest with original handles. (Biddle & Webb) $1,575

George III mahogany tallboy with molded beaded and dentil cornice, on bracket feet, 48in. wide. (Christie's) $1,585

George III mahogany tallboy with molded cornice, circa 1780, 3ft.7in. wide. (Sotheby's) $2,050

18th century Chippendale style mahogany tallboy on bracket feet, 32in. wide. (Burtenshaw Walker) $1,420

George II walnut tallboy in two parts, 3ft.7¾in. wide, circa 1740. (Sotheby's) $7,170

George II walnut chest on chest with nine drawers, 103cm. wide. (H. Spencer & Sons) $3,480

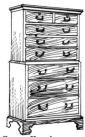

Late George II mahogany secretaire tallboy, circa 1760, 3ft.6½in. wide. (Sotheby's) $1,825

Late 18th century mahogany veneered tallboy in two parts, 3ft.9in. wide. (Taylor, Lane & Creber) $815

Georgian mahogany chest on chest with brass drop handles, 39in. wide. (Moore, Allen & Innocent) $6,000

Chippendale style mahogany chest on chest with broken arch top, on ogee bracket feet, 42in. wide. (C. G. Sloan & Co. Inc.) $1,200

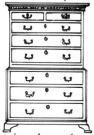

Georgian mahogany chest on chest with molded cornice and blind fret carving on frieze. (Biddle & Webb) $1,200

George I walnut tallboy with eight drawers, on bracket feet, 42½in. wide. (Christie's) $6,775

Georgian figured walnut chest on chest with reeded canted corners, 43in. wide. (Moore, Allen & Innocent) $16,800

George I burr-walnut tallboy with molded cornice, on bracket feet, 42in. wide. (Christie's) $9,870

Late Georgian mahogany tallboy chest with reeded brass handles, 45in. wide, on bracket feet. (Thomas Watson & Son) $1,520

George III mahogany tallboy, circa 1770, 3ft.7½in. wide. (Sotheby, King & Chasemore) $2,040

Antique walnut tallboy/secretaire with brass drop handles, on bracket feet, 41in. wide. (Butler & Hatch Waterman) $11,120

CHEST ON STANDS

Charles II oak chest on stand with molded top and waved stretchers, 37in. wide. (Christie's) $3,890

18th century oak chest on stand with molded cornice, on ball feet. (Lawrence Fine Art) $750

17th century oak chest on stand with dentil cornice, drawers with geometric paneled fronts, 45in. wide.(Lawrence Fine Art) $865

Walnut chest on stand in Queen Anne manner, with brass peardrop handles, 2ft.8in. wide. (Lawrence Fine Art)$1,355

Late 17th century oak coffer-on-chest with paneled lid and front, 55in. wide. (Christie's) $720

Early 17th century crossbanded walnut chest on stand with brass handles and escutcheons, 3ft.4in. wide. (Geering & Colyer) $1,375

American Queen Anne mahogany highboy, New England, circa 1740, on cabriole legs, 34½in. wide. (C. G. Sloan & Co. Inc.)$9,000

Early 18th century oak chest on stand with brass steel locks, 41in. wide. (Lawrence Fine Art) $2,280

American cherrywood Queen Anne highboy on cabriole legs, 36in. wide. (C. G. Sloan & Co. Inc.) $2,200

Early Georgian black and gold lacquer chest on stand, 39in. wide. (Christie's) $3,995

Early 18th century oyster veneered chest on later stand. (Drewatt, Watson & Barton) $5,940

Queen Anne cherrywood and maple highboy, New England, circa 1770, 37in. wide. (Robert W. Skinner Inc.) $4,250

19th century American custom William and Mary walnut and burr veneer inlaid flat-top highboy, 39¾in. wide. (Robert W. Skinner Inc.) $800

Guangxu lacquered cupboard on stand, 84cm. wide. (Sotheby's Belgravia) $585

Early 18th century burr-elm chest on stand, circa 1720, 97cm. wide. (Sotheby, King & Chasemore) $2,200

William and Mary walnut chest on stand, circa 1695, 3ft.2in. wide. (Sotheby's) $2,410

Walnut bow-fronted tallboy with cross-banded borders, 3ft.2in. wide. (Capes, Dunn & Co.) $1,560

Antique walnut chest of six drawers with brass drop handles, 40in. wide. (Lambert & Symes) $2,180

William and Mary oak chest on stand, circa 1690, 3ft.0½in. wide. (Sotheby's) $2,390

American Chippendale maple highboy with molded cornice and dentil carving, 76in. high, circa 1760. (Robert W. Skinner Inc.) $8,500

Queen Anne walnut chest on stand of nine drawers, 3ft.3in. wide. (Sotheby, King & Chasemore) $1,415

Early 18th century Queen Anne walnut chest on stand with molded cornice, 3ft.11½in. wide. (Sotheby's) $9,520

Mid 20th century inlaid mahogany reproduction chest on stand. (Lowery & Partners) $470

18th century Dutch banded walnut chest on stand, 43½in. wide. (Graves, Son & Pilcher) $1,730

CHIFFONIERS

Regency rosewood chiffonier with brass inlay, circa 1810, 3ft.9½in. wide. (Sotheby's) $2,170

William IV mahogany chiffonier with gallery back, 36in. wide. (Locke & England) $1,695

Mid 19th century mahogany chiffonier with paneled cupboard doors, 3ft.6in. wide. (Vernon's)$400

Early 19th century rosewood chiffonier with galleried top, 33in. wide. (Lawrence Fine Art) $615

Small Victorian mahogany chiffonier with shaped back panel, 3ft.11in. wide. (Butler & Hatch Waterman) $340

Regency calamanderwood chiffonier with raised superstructure, 39in. wide. (Christie's) $2,195

Mid Victorian ebony and amboyna chiffonier with tripartite mirror-glazed back, 72in. wide.(Christie's) $2,180

Early 20th century French Empire style chiffonier in fruitwood veneers, with marble top, 38in. wide. (Robert W. Skinner Inc.)$1,600

Late Louis XV kingwood chiffonier stamped Caumont with marble top, 3ft.3in. wide, circa 1775.(Sotheby's) $11,230

Regency rosewood chiffonier of simple style with paneled doors. (Stride's) $750

American Victorian walnut sideboard with carved and molded top crest, circa 1870, 50in. wide. (Robert W. Skinner Inc.) $900

William IV mahogany chiffonier with gallery back on scrolled brackets, 36in. wide. (Locke & England) $1,695

Small mahogany pot cupboard by Emile Galle, on fluted feet, 21in. wide. (Christie's) $1,610

American Federal mahogany bidet stand with kidney-shaped cutout, 19in. high. (Robert W. Skinner Inc.) $100

Mid Georgian mahogany tray-top night table, 21in. wide. (Locke & England) $660

French parquetry table de nuit, on square tapering legs, 21in. wide. (Christie's) $3,615

COMMODE CHESTS

Late George III mahogany tray-top commode with serpentine three-quarter gallery, 64cm. wide. (H. Spencer & Sons) $790

American Sheraton inlaid mahogany night table, circa 1800, with square top, 32½in. high. (C. G. Sloan & Co. Inc.) $325

Ormolu mounted mahogany commode with Carrara marble top, 54¼in. wide. (Christie's) $6,190

Attractive 19th century side cabinet crossbanded with mahogany and satinwood, 62in. wide, circa 1890. (Sotheby Bearne) $3,780

Franco-Flemish transitional and marquetry commode with marble top, 51in. wide. (Christie's) $3,215

Early 20th century French Empire style commode in fruit wood veneers, 44in. wide. (Robert W. Skinner Inc.) $1,600

One of two matching walnut commodes, New England, circa 1870, one double and one single. (Robert W. Skinner Inc.) $800

Ormolu mounted breakfront commode with marble top and marquetry panels to doors, 50in. wide. (Renton & Renton) $11,710

COMMODE CHESTS

One of a pair of 19th century demi-lune commodes with porcelain medallions. (Edgar Horn) $2,380

18th century North Italian walnut and kingwood strung commode, 1.4m. wide. (Phillips) $6,670

Late 18th century Milanese walnut commode with crossbanded top, circa 1790, 3ft. wide. (Sotheby's) $4,950

18th century French bombe walnut commode on splayed hoof feet, with bronze handles. (Fox & Sons) $10,235

Late 18th century Italian rosewood and marquetry commode with marble top, 49in. wide. (Christie's) $7,230

Sycamore and marquetry commode in the style of John Cobb. (Christie's) $7,480

Louis XV provincial oak commode with serpentine top, 43in. wide. (Christie's) $3,540

Late 19th/early 20th century French Louis XV style petite commode in mahogany, 20in. wide. (Robert W. Skinner Inc.) $1,500

German fruitwood commode with serpentine top, 42in. wide. (Christie's) $2,855

Late 19th century bow fronted commode with marble top, 29in. wide. (Sotheby's Belgravia) $1,010

Transitional mahogany and marquetry commode with gray marble top, Dutch, 50in. wide. (Christie's) $4,330

Louis XV parquetry petite commode, 18th century, with brown marble top, 23in. wide. (C. G. Sloan & Co. Inc.) $5,750

Mid 19th century rosewood and ormolu commode. (Hall, Wateridge & Owen) $10,025

Sheraton design satinwood bow-shaped side commode by Gillows, circa 1780, 4ft.6in. wide. (Locke & England) $10,755

Louis XV style marquetry commode with marble top, 50½in. wide. (Geering & Colyer) $6,480

18th century French Hugenot cape commode of stinkwood, yellow wood and beefwood, 46½in. wide. (Christie's) $8,330

Mid 18th century Louis XV provincial walnut commode with parquetry side panels, 4ft.0½in. wide. (Sotheby's) $4,210

George III satinwood commode crossbanded with rosewood and purpleheart, 44in. wide. (Christie's) $5,950

Dutch ironwood bombe commode with shaped top, on hairy paw feet, 39½in. wide. (Christie's) $1,710

Late 18th century Dutch marquetry commode with hinged top crossbanded with maplewood, 46in. wide. (Christie's) $6,190

Mid 18th century Liege oak commode with molded serpentine top, 56in. wide. (Christie's) $8,090

One of a pair of inlaid Neopolitan commodes on shaped brass toed legs, 1ft.10in. wide. (Allen & May) $6,385

French inlaid mahogany petite commode, circa 1900. (Bradley & Vaughan) $8,470

Mid 18th century German oak serpentine commode inlaid with plumwood lines, 43in. wide. (Christie's) $2,380

Mid 18th century Louis XV provincial painted walnut commode with serpentine front, 4ft.2½in. wide. (Sotheby's) $2,810

Late 18th century Milanese rosewood and kingwood crossbanded commode, 49½in. wide. (Sotheby Bearne) $9,195

18th century French Louis XV three-drawer commode in fruitwood with crossbanded inlay, 36in. wide. (Robert W. Skinner Inc.) $1,200

American rosewood commode with molded marble top, 43in. wide. (Christie's) $730

Late 18th century Dutch mahogany and marquetry commode with gilt brass handles and keyhole plates, 52in. wide. (Parsons, Welch & Cowell) $1,670

George III mahogany commode, top and sides inlaid with satinwood ovals, 45¼in. wide. (Christie's) $13,310

Continental walnut commode inlaid with panels of marquetry foliage, 32in. wide. (Heathcote Ball & Co.) $1,780

Mid 18th century Italian rosewood commode with crossbanded top, 53in. wide. (Christie's) $8,675

Louis XV petite commode by J. C. Ellaume, with bombe sides and front, 31¼in. wide. (C. G. Sloan & Co. Inc.) $6,250

Louis XV kingwood and tuiipwood small commode, stamped Chevallier, circa 1755, 2ft.7in. wide.(Sotheby's) $5,850

Mid 18th century French provincial walnut bombe commode, 4ft.1½in. wide, with white marble top. (Fox & Sons) $10,235

Louis XV ormolu mounted kingwood parquetry small commode with marble top, circa 1735, 1ft.11½in. wide. (Sotheby's) $3,745

Late 18th century Dutch mahogany commode with rectangular top, 54in. wide. (Christie's)$2,290

Mid 18th century Italian walnut commode with serpentine crossbanded top, 58½in. wide. (Christie's)$11,750

Early 18th century Regency kingwood parquetry commode, top with molded brass border, 4ft.3in. wide. (Sotheby's) $11,700

Late 18th century North Italian rosewood and marquetry commode, 43in. wide. (Christie's) $10,575

CORNER CUPBOARDS

Late 18th century German or Swedish fruitwood commode with chamfered breakfront top, 49in. wide. (Christie's) $3,405

Louis XV provincial walnut commode with serpentine top, 46in. wide. (Christie's)$6,190

American pine corner cupboard with dentil frieze and bracket feet, 52in. wide. (C. G. Sloan & Co. Inc.) $1,150

Late George III mahogany and marquetry bow-front corner cupboard with ogee molded cornice, 79cm. wide.(H. Spencer & Sons)$975

19th century French Empire bowfront encoignure in mahogany, 71in. high. (Robert W. Skinner Inc.) $1,800

Late 18th century American country Chippendale corner cupboard with open shelves, 43in. wide. (Robert W. Skinner Inc.) $3,600

Georgian mahogany corner cabinet of honey color , on shaped bracket feet, 40in. wide. (Lawrence Fine Art) $2,280

American pine corner cupboard with molded cornice, 41in. wide. (C. G. Sloan & Co. Inc.)$850

331

CORNER CUPBOARDS

George III black and gold lacquer encoignure veneered in Chinese lacquer panel, 25½in. wide. (Christie's)$4,635

18th century South German walnut floor standing corner cupboard with bow centre, 2ft.4in. wide. (Bracketts) $1,355

Venetian painted standing corner cupboard with canted corners, 2ft.5in. wide, reconstructed. (Sotheby's) $1,530

Flemish design heavily carved oak corner cupboard. (Edwards, Bigwood & Bewlay) $655

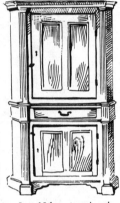

Dutch floral marquetry standing corner cupboard with arched molded cornice, 46in. wide. (Christie's) $8,675

Late 18th century Dutch walnut and marquetry standing corner cupboard with arched cresting, 82.5cm. wide. (H. Spencer & Sons) $4,160

Late 18th century American pine grain painted corner cupboard with molded cornice, 46in. wide. (Robert W. Skinner Inc.) $2,000

Mid 18th century George II mahogany standing corner cupboard with swan-neck pediment, 3ft. 5½in. wide. (Sotheby's) $7,140

18th century Dutch marquetry corner cupboard, 3ft.10in. wide, with two tall arched doors.(Woolley & Wallis) $8,360

Ebonised corner cupboard with bevel-glazed superstructure, circa 1880, 35½in. wide. (Sotheby's Belgravia) $230

Painted satinwood Sheraton revival standing corner cabinet, outlined with rosewood, late 19th century, 26in. wide. (Neales) $2,110

George III white-painted and parcel gilt corner cupboard, circa 1765, 4ft. 1½in. wide. (Sotheby's) $1,025

332

Queen Anne walnut corner cupboard with domed top and reeded side columns. (Moore, Allen & Innocent) $6,000

Late 19th century Sheraton painted satinwood revival standing corner cabinet, 26in. wide. (Neales) $2,150

Bow-fronted hanging corner cupboard with inlaid and crossbanded doors. (Honiton Galleries) $480

Early 18th century walnut hanging corner cupboard, circa 1710, 112cm. high. (Sotheby, King & Chasemore)$2,060

George III japanned standing corner cabinet, circa 1765, 4ft.1in. wide. (Sotheby's) $975

Satinwood d-shaped corner cabinet, inlaid with marquetry, circa 1910, 33in. wide. (Sotheby's Belgravia)$2,390

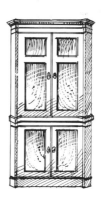

18th century oak double corner cupboard with panelled doors. (Walker, Barnett & Hill) $1,320

Late 19th century mahogany bow-fronted corner standing cupboard. (Bradley & Vaughan) $1,210

Sheraton period mahogany two-stage corner cabinet with swan-neck pediment, circa 1790, 33in. wide. (Neales) $2,205

19th century inlaid mahogany two-part corner cupboard with glazed top. (Honiton Galleries) $870

George II mahogany corner cabinet with dentil molded cornice, circa 1760, 4ft.1in. wide. (Sotheby's) $3,540

George III standing corner cabinet, with astragal glazed doors, circa 1765, 3ft.8in. wide. (Sotheby's) $975

COURT CUPBOARDS

Welsh oak press cupboard with six paneled doors, 4ft.9in. wide, late 18th century. (Lawrence Fine Art) $1,755

17th century oak court cupboard with rectangular top and coffered frieze, 41½in. wide. (Christie's) $4,780

17th century carved oak court cupboard with scroll carved cornice, 4ft.8in. wide. (Butler & Hatch Waterman) $1,525

George II oak tridarn with open top section, circa 1740, 4ft.7in. wide, handles replaced. (Sotheby's) $3,960

17th century oak press with fluted cornice on baluster supports, 75½in. wide. (Christie's) $1,830

Mid 17th century oak court cupboard with carved frieze, butterfly hinge handles, 52in. high. (Locke & England) $2,420

Charles II oak court cupboard with molded cornice and carved frieze, 5ft.5in. wide, circa 1680. (Sotheby's) £1,885

William and Mary oak court cupboard, circa 1690, 5ft.4½in. wide.(Sotheby's) $2,105

Charles II oak court cupboard, upper section with fluted frieze, circa 1665, 5ft.6½in. wide. (Sotheby's)$3,305

Modern stained beechwood court cupboard in 17th century style, 44½in. wide. (Sotheby's Belgravia) $660

19th century oak court cupboard with carved cornice, 60in. wide. (Smith-Woolley & Perry)$850

Welsh oak tridarn with molded breakfront cornice, 56½in. wide. (Christie's) $7,320

Walnut, burr-walnut and tulipwood side cabinet, circa 1870, 72in. wide. (Sotheby's Belgravia) $1,555

Late 16th century Tuscan walnut credenza with deep molded edge, 7ft.7in. wide. (Sotheby's) $12,170

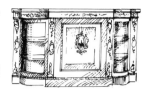

Louis XVI design ebony credenza with gilt brass mounts, 59¾in. wide. (Locke & England) $1,664

Ebonised and porcelain mounted side cabinet, 1860's, 74½in. wide. (Sotheby's Belgravia) $1,145

Tulipwood serpentine credenza, top inset with glazed panel, circa 1870, 57in wide.(Sotheby's Belgravia) $1,590

Victorian ebonised and amboyna wood banded credenza with ormolu mounts, circa 1870, 6ft. 6in. wide. (Sotheby, King & Chasemore) $1,150

Boulle side cabinet, top with four out-set panels, circa 1870, 79in. wide. (Sotheby's Belgravia) $1,835

Well-figured and burr-walnut serpentine side cabinet, labeled O. L. Dalzell, circa 1860, 73in. wide. (Sotheby's Belgravia) $2,510

Serpentine boulle side cabinet, circa 1870, 82½in. wide, with two glazed cupboard doors. (Sotheby's Belgravia) $2,700

Walnut side cabinet in well-figured wood with gilt bronze mounts, 1850's, 79in. wide. (Sotheby's Belgravia) $2,750

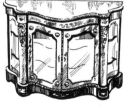

Mid 19th century red boulle credenza with marble top.(Ernest R. de Rome) $1,760

19th century figured walnut and ormolu credenza inlaid with satinwood, centre doors with Sevres plaques, 78in. wide. (Morphets) $4,485

CUPBOARDS

George II mahogany clothes press with molded dentil cornice, 49in. wide. (Christie's) $2,585

Mid 18th century Welsh oak cupboard with fielded panelled doors. (Phillips & Jolly) $1,680

17th century German oak schrank with angled corners and carved frieze, 54in. wide. (Boardman) $7,320

19th century mahogany linen press with dentil cornice, 4ft. wide. (Lawrence Fine Art) $890

Charles II oak parlour cupboard with lozenge and strapwork carving, circa 1660. (Neales) $3,740

17th century Dutch oak Beeldenkast cupboard with wide cornice, 65in. wide. (Boardman) $8,295

17th century North German oak cupboard with fret carved panels, 62in. wide. (Boardman) $4,025

17th century Flemish oak and ebony press with overhanging cornice, 71½in. wide. (Christie's) $5,520

18th century Catalon walnut and fruitwood cupboard. (Phillips) $4,150

Edwardian Art Nouveau linen press by Shapland and Petter, circa 1900, 56½in. wide. (Sotheby's Belgravia) $650

17th century Dutch oak cupboard with carved frieze, 65in. wide. (Boardman) $4,150

Antique Flemish oak side cupboard. (Phillips) $4,045

336

17th century Dutch ebony cupboard or Utrechtkast.(Boardman) $5,520

17th century Italian walnut cupboard with two paneled doors, 38in. wide. (Drewatt, Watson & Barton) $5,150

Flemish oak cupboard, heavily carved, circa 1660, 4ft.5in. wide. (Sotheby's) $4,680

George III mahogany linen press with three drawers, on bracket feet. (Cooper Hirst) $715

Charles II oak and walnut veneered dole cupboard with dentilled cornice, 46½in. wide. (Christie's) $3,480

18th century Dutch fruitwood linen press with shaped apron. (Osmond Tricks)$3,220

German oak four door cupboard, 1661. (Boardman) $5,500

Mid 18th century American palladian pine built-in wall cupboard, 42in. wide. (Robert W. Skinner Inc.) $1,700

Georgian oak hanging cupboard with molded cornice and two paneled and fielded doors, 70in. wide. (Christie's) $1,800

Small 17th century North German oak and parquetry cupboard, 62in. wide. (Boardman) $4,270

19th century pine painted cupboard with bombe chest, 4ft.11in. wide. (Coles, Knapp & Kennedy) $965

17th century Dutch oak and ebony cupboard with overhanging cornice, 59in. wide. (Boardman) $3,660

CUPBOARDS

James I standing cupboard in oak, circa 1620, 4ft.2in. wide. (Sotheby's) $2,150

American country pine grain painted cupboard, circa 1800, 73in. high. (Robert W. Skinner Inc.) $2,900

Charles II oak hutch, circa 1670, 2ft. 7½in. wide. (Sotheby's) $3,420

Regency mahogany linen press with sliding shelves, circa 1820, 4ft.1in. wide. (Lawrence Fine Art) $910

17th century oak hanging cupboard with molded cornice and two paneled doors, 60in. wide. (Christie's) $1,680

George III mahogany linen press, doors with satinwood oval inlays, 52in. wide. (Lawrence Fine Art) $935

French Gothic oak standing cupboard with canted top, 3ft.8½in. wide. (Sotheby's) $3,895

Late 17th century Breton oak lit clos decorated with brass studs, 6ft.1½in. wide. (Geering & Colyer) $865

18th century Italian marquetry inlaid linen press in mahogany, 43in. wide. (Robert W. Skinner Inc.) $1,800

Early George III mahogany clothes press with broken pediment and molded cornice, 50½in. wide. (Christie's) $4,840

Mid 17th century oak cupboard with molded cornice and dentil frieze, 3ft.10in. wide, restored.(Sotheby's) $1,650

Georgian mahogany linen press, on ogee feet, 4ft.7in. wide. (Lawrence Fine Art) $980

338

American country Federal grain painted pine cupboard, circa 1800, 49½in. wide. (Robert W. Skinner Inc.) $900

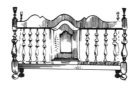

18th century walnut dole cupboard with central arched door, 34in. wide. (Boardman) $830

American Federal cherrywood pie safe with double doors, circa 1795, 40in. wide. (Robert W. Skinner Inc.) $2,000

Late 18th century New England pine cupboard with open top, 32½in. wide. (Robert W. Skinner Inc.) $1,300

19th century linen press with arcaded cornice, 50in. wide. (W. H. Lane & Son) $480

French rosewood and marquetry inlaid and ormolu mounted cupboard with marble top, 35cm. square. (Lambert & Symes) $1,935

Unusual mid 18th century oak cupboard on stand. (Neal Sons & Fletcher) $3,510

Oak press with molded overhanging cornice above carved doors. (Christie's) $1,440

Flemish oak cupboard with molded cornice and tapering frieze drawers, 57in. wide. (Christie's) $2,030

Charles II oak cupboard with paneled frieze drawer, partly inlaid with bone and mother-of-pearl, 105cm. wide. (Christie's) $3,240

American painted kas, New England, circa 1800, with molded cornice, 55in. wide. (C. G. Sloan & Co. Inc.) $1,200

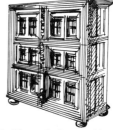

Flemish carved oak press with molded cornice above paneled cupboard doors, 64in. wide. (Lawrence Fine Art) $7,070

DAVENPORTS

Mid 19th century Indian Vizagapatam teak wood Davenport, 35in. wide. (Christie's S. Kensington) $1,340

Unusual Regency rosewood lady's Davenport work table, circa 1815, 1ft.2½in. wide. (Sotheby, King & Chasemore) $1,220

Walnut Davenport with serpentine flap, 32½in. wide, circa 1870. (Sotheby's Belgravia) $685

Very rare mid 19th century Irish yew-wood Davenport inlaid with marquetry. (Parsons, Welch & Cowell) $7,700

Walnut Davenport with hinged super-structure, circa 1860, 32½in. wide. (Sotheby's Belgravia) $615

Walnut Davenport with fitted interior, circa 1870, 32¼in. wide. (Sotheby's Belgravia) $745

Very good Victorian walnut Davenport with 'piano' slope top and fretted gallery. (Morphets) $1,960

Late 19th century American Victorian mahogany slant top desk with gallery top, 25in. wide. (Robert W. Skinner Inc.) $375

Walnut Davenport with leather lined top, 1ft.7¼in. wide, circa 1840. (Sotheby's) $1,110

19th century rosewood Davenport with satinwood inlay and gilt gallery, 1ft.9in. wide. (W. H. Lane & Son) $625

19th century Burmese carved teak Davenport on bird and animal supports. (Vernon's) $650

Walnut Davenport with a stationery compartment, 21in. wide, 1860's. (Sotheby's Belgravia) $565

340

Oak and pollard oak Davenport with green leather slope, circa 1850, 24½in. wide. (Sotheby's Belgravia) $865

Heavily carved mid Victorian oak Davenport with canted sliding front, 28in. wide. (Dacre, Son & Hartley) $1,020

Walnut Davenport with lidded and fitted superstructure, 21in. wide, circa 1870. (Sotheby's Belgravia) $715

Rosewood Davenport, front with twist-turn supports, formerly with a super-structure, circa 1850, 24in. wide. (Sotheby's Belgravia) $980

Pollard-elm Davenport with mir-rored superstructure, front with barley-twist supports, circa 1860, 24in. wide. (Sotheby's Belgravia) $1,030

Georgian small mahogany Davenport with revolving sliding top, 14in. wide. (Parsons, Welch & Cowell) $3,300

Early 20th century Damascus walnut marquetry Davenport, 22½in. wide. (Sotheby's Belgravia) $870

Victorian walnut Davenport with bowed front, circa 1860, 23in. wide. (Sotheby Bearne) $2,200

Victorian walnut Davenport with pier-ced gallery. (Russell, Baldwin & Bright) $2,015

Victorian walnut Davenport with hinged leather writing slope. (Pearsons) $1,320

Late Regency period Davenport in rose-wood with tray top, 2ft. wide. (Geering & Colyer) $1,240

Walnut Davenport with hinged super-structure, 31½in. wide, circa 1870. (Sotheby's Belgravia) $565

DISPLAY CABINETS

Victorian glazed display cabinet.
(Outhwaite & Litherland)
$4,595

Late George III mahogany table display
cabinet with single shelf, circa 1815, 2ft.
10¾in. wide. (Sotheby's) $440

Mahogany and marquetry display
cabinet with glazed top, circa
1910, 26in. wide. (Sotheby's Belgravia) $720

Early 18th century Dutch parcel ebony
and satin hardwood vitrine, 57in. wide.
(Boardman) $6,710

19th century kingwood veneered
bombe vitrine. (Woolley & Wallis)
$2,760

Early 20th century Art Nouveau
oak display cabinet, 60in. high.
(Christie's & Edmiston's)$1,010

Mahogany display cabinet with two
glazed cupboard doors, 1880's,
45in. wide. (Sotheby's Belgravia)
$910

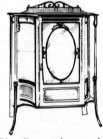

Edwardian carved rosewood and
inlaid display cabinet with molded and pierced top, 45in. wide.
(Dacre, Son & Hartley)
$1,060

Early 20th century 'William and
Mary' walnut display cabinet on
stand with molded frieze, 46½in.
wide. (Sotheby's Belgravia)
$1,075

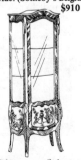

Early 20th century gilt brass mahogany Vernis Martin vitrine with serpentine glazed doors, 23in. wide.
(Sotheby's Belgravia) $1,490

Mid 18th century Dutch walnut and marquetry vitrine with shaped top and double
paneled doors, 6ft.8in. wide.(Messenger
May & Baverstock) $7,490

Fine Chinese Chippendale style
mahogany display cabinet with
shaped pagoda top, 3ft.10in. wide.
(Messenger May & Baverstock)
$2,925

Mahogany serpentine display cabinet with glazed cupboard door, 27in. wide, circa 1910. (Sotheby's Belgravia)$670

Walnut side cabinet in well-figured wood, inlaid with boxwood stringing, 30in. wide, circa 1840. (Sotheby's Belgravia) $740

Flemish oak hanging display cabinet with acanthus cresting and molded cornice, 26in. wide. (Christie's) $1,375

Mahogany vitrine with glazed door and sides and with gilt bronze mounts, circa 1900, 28in. wide. (Sotheby's Belgravia) $1,870

18th century Dutch marquetry vitrine with serpentine fronted drawers, 61in. wide. (Boardman) $8,050

Crossbanded and herringbone inlaid walnut display cabinet on bracket feet, 3ft.7½in. wide. (Geering & Colyer) $4,250

Ormolu mounted mahogany vitrine cabinet of Louis XVI style with marble top, 28½in. wide. (Christie's) $2,095

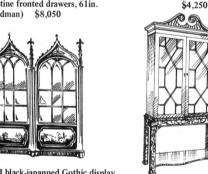

George III black-japanned Gothic display cabinet by Ince and Mayhew, circa 1765, 6ft.5in. wide. (Sotheby's) $18,790

Elaborate display cabinet with fretwork cornice. (Raymond Inman) $2,105

Satinwood and Sevres mounted display cabinet with mirror-lined top part, circa 1870, 31½in. wide. (Sotheby's Belgravia)$2,040

19th century French walnut ormolu mounted vitrine with Vernis Martin panels, 51in. high.(Christie's S. Kensington) $3,095

Mahogany display cabinet with glazed doors, 36in. wide, circa 1910. (Sotheby's Belgravia) $1,610

343

DISPLAY CABINETS

20th century American custom Renaissance revival giltwood curio cabinet, 27in. wide. (Robert W. Skinner Inc.) $1,300

18th century Dutch marquetry vitrine of shallow depth. (Swetenham's) $12,320

Shaped front walnut marquetry display cabinet, 5ft. high, on paneled cupboard base. (Woolley & Wallis) $7,260

German inlaid display cabinet, top section with pillars and mirror back, circa 1900-05. (Sotheby's Belgravia) $610

20th century Edwardian satinwood escritoire-vitrine with bow-front and broken arch pediment. (Graves, Son & Pilcher) $4,620

Kingwood and gilt bronze mounted vitrine by F. Linke, circa 1910, 26in. wide. (Sotheby's Belgravia) $3,640

Mahogany 'Vernis Martin' vitrine with bow-front, 27in. wide, circa 1900. (Sotheby's Belgravia) $1,130

19th century French kingwood and ormolu vitrine with marble top, 32in. wide. (Morphets) $2,535

French kingwood and ormolu mounted vitrine with Vernis Martin panels, circa 1890, 4ft.1½in. wide.(Sotheby, King & Chasemore) $3,250

One of a pair of mid Georgian mahogany display cabinets, 51in. wide. (Christie's) $7,260

Mahogany display cabinet with carved top panel, 3ft.6in. wide. (Clive Emson & Co.) $280

Victorian walnut music cabinet with brass gallery and satinwood inlaid top. (Biddle & Webb), $485

20th century European gessoed, painted and gilt vitrine cabinet, 66in. high. (Robert W. Skinner Inc.) $325

Regency rosewood display cabinet, upper part of Gothic pattern, 43in. wide. (Christie's) $4,600

Early 20th century American Victorian oak china cabinet with molded top, 46in. wide. (Robert W. Skinner Inc.) $600

Late 19th century German Renaissance revival walnut curio cabinet with mirrored gallery, 69in. high. (Robert W. Skinner Inc.)$625

Art Nouveau display cabinet in mahogany, with paneled legs, 123cm. wide. (H. Spencer & Sons) $830

Late 19th century French Louis XV style walnut veneer vitrine, 25½in. wide. (Robert W. Skinner Inc.) $550

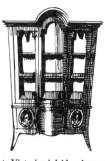

Kingwood and Vernis Martin vitrine with arched cresting, circa 1900, 55in. wide. (Sotheby's Belgravia) $6,580

Late Victorian inlaid mahogany bow-fronted display cabinet. (Edgar Horn) $1,095

Early 20th century Louis XV style serpentine fronted vitrine with Vernis Martin panels and brass feet, 43in. wide. (Sotheby Bearne) $3,160

18th century Dutch marquetry and walnut display cabinet, circa 1770, 4ft.3in. wide. (Sotheby, King & Chasemore) $4,440

George III mahogany bookcase display cabinet with fluted frieze, circa 1775, 4ft.10in. wide. (Sotheby's) $12,690

Kingwood and marquetry vitrine with glazed doors. (Bradley & Vaughan) $3,800

DRESSERS & BUFFETS

George III oak dresser, circa 1770, 5ft.2½in. wide. (Sotheby's) $2,030

Charles II oak dresser with narrow rectangular planked top, 174cm. wide. (H. Spencer & Sons) $2,350

17th century oak buffet or court cupboard with carved frieze and platform base, 4ft.3½in. wide. (Coles, Knapp & Kennedy) $480

Late 16th century Henry II carved walnut buffet with leaf-carved cornice, 4ft.9in. wide. (Sotheby's) $9,360

18th century oak enclosed dresser. (Parsons, Welch & Cowell) $2,690

Mid 18th century oak dresser with brass swan neck handles, 67in. wide. (Locke & England) $2,910

Late 18th century dresser with multi-shelf rack and brass handles. (Locke & England)$1,870

Late Georgian dresser with molded cornice, lower part with hexagonally paneled doors, 63½in. wide. (Christie's) $3,170

18th century oak dresser with geometrically molded fronts. (Walker, Walton & Hanson) $2,440

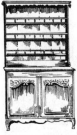

Small early 18th century North Wales oak dresser, 4ft.2in. wide. (Frank R. Marshall)$9,195

18th century French provincial oak dresser with brass barrel hinges, 50in. wide. (Parsons, Welch & Cowell) $1,475

Fine German walnut buffet with arched molded cornice, circa 1740, 8ft.6in. wide. (Sotheby's) $10,295

Early George III oak dresser, 72in. wide. (Sotheby, King & Chasemore) $1,605

16th century North European oak buffet, top of inverted breakfront form, 54in. wide. (Boardman) $7,565

George II oak backless dresser with pierced brass handles, circa 1730, 77½in. wide. (Neales) $4,880

18th century oak dresser with cupboards and drawers. (Sotheby Bearne) $2,420

18th century oak dresser with molded cornice and brass handles, 194cm. wide. (Jackson-Stops & Staff) $4,010

Late 17th century oak dresser with molded cornice, base with three drawers, 77in. wide. (Christie's) $2,400

George III oak dresser with shelves, cupboards and drawers, 57in. wide, restored. (Sotheby, King & Chasemore) $2,240

Small 18th century oak Welsh dresser with three-shelf open plate rack, 5ft. wide. (Dickinson, Davy & Markham) $3,120

18th century elm dresser with three shelves. (Drewatt, Watson & Barton) $4,290

George III oak dresser and delft rack with molded cornice, drawers with brass drop handles, 183cm. wide. (H. Spencer & Sons) $5,040

18th century oak and inlaid dresser with plain molded cornice, brass handles and ivory escutcheons, 5ft.4in. wide. (Butler & Hatch Waterman) $2,615

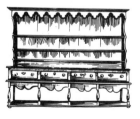

Large 18th century Montgomeryshire oak dresser with three shelves, 8ft. wide. (Boardman) $7,810

347

Georgian oak dresser base with brass drop handles, 79in. wide. (Hall, Wateridge & Owen) $2,340

Unusual mid 18th century George II walnut dresser, 5ft. wide. (Sotheby's) $6,240

Charles II oak dresser base, drawers applied with geometric molding, 6ft.9½in. wide, circa 1670. (Sotheby's) $2,715

Early 19th century oak cottage dresser, 57in. long. (Lawrence Fine Art) $2,620

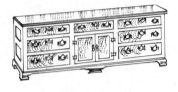

Georgian oak dresser base with mahogany crossbanding, circa 1800, 78in. long. (Lawrence Fine Art) $6,385

Queen Anne dresser, rack with molded cornice, circa 1705, 4ft. 7in. wide. (Sotheby's) $4,320

Fine Georgian oak dresser, top crossbanded with mahogany, 87in. wide. (Christie's) $4,080

George III oak dresser, circa 1780, 6ft.10in. wide, later handles. (Sotheby's) $2,300

George II oak dresser base with six drawers, circa 1750, 6ft.2½in. wide. (Sotheby's) $2,300

Mid 18th century oak dresser with low two-shelf rack, 4ft.9in. wide. (Sotheby's) $1,250

Charles II oak dresser base with two plank molded top circa 1685, 5ft. 10½in. wide. (Sotheby's) $4,250

George III oak dresser with molded cornice, circa 1770, 6ft.1in. wide. (Sotheby's)$3,540

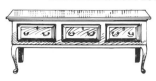

Early Georgian oak dresser base with shaped underfrieze, 83in. wide. (Locke & England) $1,755

18th century American country pine pewter dresser with molded cornice, 81in. wide. (Robert W. Skinner Inc.) $4,500

Early Georgian oak backless dresser base on cabriole legs. (Walker, Barnett, & Hill) $1,320

George II Welsh dresser, rack with molded cornice, 6ft.4in. wide, circa 1750. (Sotheby's) $2,830

18th century oak dresser, 37½in. tall, 19in. deep, 6ft.6in. long. (Vernon's) $2,100

George III oak dresser with molded and shaped pediment, 6ft.1in. wide, circa 1760. (Sotheby's) $4,955

Jacobean oak dresser on turned legs, with geometric molded design, 74in. long. (Burtenshaw Walker) $3,300

Henri II carved walnut buffet, mid 16th century. (Sotheby's) $9,440

Early 18th century oak dresser base with three drawers in frieze and pot board, 5ft.3in. wide. (Worsfolds) $4,070

French provincial oak buffet with food cupboard above, 51½in. wide. (Irelands) $1,770

Late 17th century oak dresser base in poor condition. (Cubitt & West) $2,740

Late 17th/early 18th century oak dresser with six drawers and pot board. (Biddle & Webb) $2,970

DRESSERS

Georgian oak dresser with molded cornice and a solid pot board, 79in. wide. (Christie's) $3,670

18th century oak low dresser with molded rounded rectangular top, 72in. wide. (Christie's) $2,510

Early 18th century walnut dresser with later top, crossbanded in mahogany and with ball and claw feet, 88in. wide. (Christie's) $2,375

18th century oak dresser with enclosed base and three open shelves. (Locke & England) $4,150

18th century oak dresser with eared molded cornice and three tiers of shelves, 74½in. wide. (Christie's) $2,375

18th century open dresser with lower pot shelf, raised on square section legs, 4ft.11in. wide. (Taylor Lane & Creber) $2,045

DUMB WAITERS

Georgian mahogany three-tier circular dumb waiter. (Russell, Baldwin & Bright) $1,640

Late George III revolving dumb waiter, circa 1805, 1ft.11in. diam. (Sotheby's) $1,355

Regency mahogany dumb waiter on tripod stand. (Vernon's) $1,750

George III mahogany three-tier dumb waiter. (Bradley & Vaughan) $1,090

Queen Anne mahogany dumb waiter with three shelves, diam. 24in. (C. G. Sloan & Co. Inc.) $900

Georgian three-tier mahogany dumb waiter with tripod base, 44in. high.(Moore, Allen & Innocent) $670

350

18th century oak lowboy with brass handles. (Russell, Baldwin & Bright) $1,870

American Queen Anne cherrywood lowboy, circa 1760, 32½in. wide, restored. (Robert W. Skinner Inc.) $2,750

George I walnut lowboy, 33in. wide. (Sotheby, King & Chasemore) $2,360

Early Georgian oak lowboy with crossbanded top, 31in. wide. (Lawrence Fine Art)$1,505

Late 18th century walnut lowboy with three drawers. (Biddle & Webb) $1,150

Queen Anne style chinoiserie lacquered lowboy, 36in. wide. (C. G. Sloan & Co. Inc.) $850

18th century Continental oak lowboy with ovolo molded edge, 29in. wide. (Lawrence Fine Art) $500

Early Georgian mahogany lowboy with pierced brass handles and slender club supports. (Lawrence Fine Art) $1,140

18th century walnut and line inlaid lowboy with brass handles, 2ft.6in. wide. (Geering & Colyer) $3,380

Georgian oak lowboy with line inlay, 30in. wide. (Lawrence Fine Art) $1,095

Dutch floral marquetry lowboy on cabriole legs, 30in. wide. (Hall, Wateridge & Owen) $700m

American Chippendale walnut lowboy with shell carvings, 39in. wide. (C. G. Sloan & Co. Inc.)$1,600

351

'George II' japanned and parcel gilt desk with leather inset top, 1900-1920, 55½in. wide. (Sotheby's Belgravia) $1,390

Elegant rosewood and sycamore desk, circa 1930, 127cm. wide. (Sotheby's Belgravia) $680

Mahogany pedestal desk with leather lined top, circa 1900, 59½in. wide. (Sotheby's Belgravia) $840

18th century mahogany kneehole dressing table with brass handles. (Russell, Baldwin & Bright) $9,360

Walnut pedestal desk by Edwards & Roberts, London, circa 1870, 42in. wide. (Sotheby's Belgravia) $1,230

Victorian mahogany cylinder front pedestal desk with fitted interior, 4ft.9in. wide. (Andrew Grant) $1,555

George I walnut kneehole writing table, circa 1725, 2ft.6in. wide, on bracket feet. (Sotheby's) $7,615

George I walnut finish kneehole desk with brass handles. (Clarke Gammon) $6,370

Unusual early George II oak kneehole secretaire writing table, circa 1730, 2ft.7½in. wide. (Sotheby's) $1,370

William IV rosewood pedestal desk with tooled leather top, 3ft.3in. wide, circa 1835. (Sotheby, King & Chasemore) $1,680

Victorian mahogany pedestal desk, with fitted superstructure, 4ft. wide. (Woolley & Wallis) $1,365

Chippendale period mahogany kneehole desk, top restored, 44in. wide. (Drewatt, Watson & Barton) $1,540

19th century mahogany pedestal desk with leather top, 3ft.8½in. wide. (Lawrence Fine Art) $1,125

George I walnut small kneehole desk with herringbone banding, 81cm. wide. (H. Spencer & Sons) $2,110

Mid 19th century mahogany partner's desk, with leather top, 60in. wide. (Sotheby's Belgravia) $3,315

Edwardian mahogany partner's desk with leather top. (Clarke Gammon) $5,380

Georgian mahogany partner's desk with red leather inset, 56in. wide. (Lawrence Fine Art) $5,015

George III style mahogany partner's desk, modern, 60in. wide. (Sotheby's Belgravia) $1,660

Early 18th century walnut kneehole desk with herringbone inlay, 33in. wide. (Burtenshaw Walker) $5,280

Queen Anne style walnut kneehole desk with crossbanded top, 51in. wide. (C. G. Sloan & Co. Inc.) $825

Mid Georgian mahogany kneehole desk on bracket feet, 40½in. wide. (Christie's) $1,950

Queen Anne burr-walnut kneehole desk on later bracket feet, 32in. wide. (Christie's) $3,335

Victorian mahogany cylinder desk with adjustable well, 53½in. wide. (Coles, Knapp & Kennedy) $1,025

Mid Georgian mahogany kneehole writing desk with brass locks and handles. (Walker, Barnett & Hill) $3,740

PEDESTAL & KNEEHOLE DESKS

George III mahogany partner's desk with molded leather-lined top, circa 1770, 5ft.5½in. wide. (Sotheby's) $15,470

George III mahogany kneehole desk with crossbanded rectangular top, 34½in. wide. (Christie's) $1,800

Early 19th century architect's kneehole desk in mahogany, 5ft. wide. (Boardman) $4,685

18th century mahogany kneehole dressing table. (Russell, Baldwin & Bright) $8,800

Art Deco desk by Waring & Gillow, circa 1930. (Sotheby's Belgravia) $3,045

George II red walnut kneehole desk with molded rectangular hinged top, 39½in. wide. (Christie's) $2,240

George III mahogany partners' desk with leather top, 65½in. wide. (Christie's) $10,375

Late 19th century 'George I' yellow lacquered kneehole desk painted in chinoiserie, 33½in. wide.(Sotheby's Belgravia) $585

George III mahogany library desk with leather-lined top, 55½in. wide. (Christie's) $7,650

Queen Anne walnut kneehole desk of fine color , on turned feet, 36½in. wide. (Christie's) $7,525

Victorian rosewood and marquetry desk in the style of Holland & Sons, crossbanded in satinwood, 66in. wide.(Christie's) $3,760

18th century walnut veneered kneehole desk with crossbanded and herringbone stringing, 32in. wide. (Taylor Lane & Creber) $3,270

One of a pair of Chinese mother-of-pearl inlaid hardwood screens, 60cm. high. (Sotheby, King & Chasemore) $450

Early 19th century Chinese hardwood screen. (Phillips)
$1,550

Late 19th century lacquer, ivory and mother-of-pearl three-fold screen, 183cm. wide open. (Sotheby's Belgravia) $280

Louis XVI giltwood fire screen with oval panel of Aubusson tapestry, circa 1770, 2ft.3in. wide.(Sotheby's)$1,880

18th century painted leather six-leaf screen, 80in. high. (Christie's) $2,420

Regency rosewood fire screen with woolwork and tapestry floral panel, 48in. high.(Smith-Woolley & Perry) $330

Rectangular four-leaf wood table screen with pale green bowenite panels, 48.5cm. high.(Christie's)
$750

Regency satinwood and rosewood inlaid pole fire screen with embroidered panel, on splay support, 4ft.4in. high. (Hobbs Parker) $210

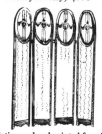

Satinwood and painted four-fold screen with oval glazed panels, circa 1900, 70¼in. high. (Sotheby's Belgravia) $980

Tongzhi giltwood screen with carved panel and cresting, 112cm. high. (Sotheby's Belgravia)
$980

Four-fold applique screen with continuous scene and brocade floral border.(Lawrence Fine Art) $395

Chinese rosewood circular table screen inset with marble panel, 76cm. high.(Burrows & Day)
$325

SCREENS

18th century Dutch painted leather six-fold screen decorated in reds, blues and greens, 95½in. high. (Christie's) $8,820

Chinese embroidered silk fire-screen, circa 1900, 72cm. wide. (Sotheby's Belgravia) $585

Early 18th century painted four-leaf screen after J. B. Lanscroon, 94in. high. (Christie's) $2,080

Late 19th century American stained glass fire-screen with brass frame, 24in. wide. (Robert W. Skinner Inc.) $425

Fine early 19th century Chinese export black and gold lacquer eight-leaf screen, 78½in. high. (Christie's) $14,925

Fine three-fold Victorian scrap screen. (Locke & England) $160

Ivory applied four-fold low screen carved with flowers, circa 1900, 117.5cm. high. (Sotheby's Belgravia) $315

Mid Georgian mahogany pole screen with arched adjustable banner panel, 73¼in. high. (Christie's) $4,165

Early 19th century Chinese scarlet and gold lacquer four-leaf screen, 45in. high. (Christie's) $1,760

Embroidered silk four-fold screen decorated with cranes, circa 1900, 200cm. high. (Sotheby's Belgravia) $1,265

Carved giltwood three-fold boudoir screen, lower sections covered in green satin. (Butler & Hatch Waterman) $320

Victorian oak four-fold dressing screen with four stained glass panels, 66in. high. (Lawrence Fine Art) $600

356

18th century Dutch painted leather four-leaf screen, 78in. high. (Christie's) $3,270

Oak and stained glass fire-screen with two leaded glass doors, circa 1870, 112cm. wide. (Sotheby's Belgravia) $740

19th century Japanese lacquered five-panel screen, 63in. high. (Robert W. Skinner Inc.) $800

Three-fold French gilt screen. (Ball & Percival) $350

18th century Chinese coromandel lacquer eight-fold low screen, 46¼in. high. (Christie's) $3,525

Early 19th century Chinese export black and gold lacquer four-leaf screen, 79in. high. (Christie's)$1,585

Blue lacquer two-fold screen, circa 1900, 194cm. high. (Sotheby's Belgravia) $2,480

Inlaid miniature four-fold soft metal screen, 14cm. high. (Sotheby, King & Chasemore) $825

Mother-of-pearl and ivory inlaid two-fold screen, circa 1900, 192cm. high. (Sotheby's Belgravia) $1,265

One of a pair of William IV pole screens on hexagonal stems and carved circular bases. (Taylor Lane & Creber) $455

Late 19th century four-fold lacquer and ivory screen applied with flowers and birds, 252cm. high. (Sotheby's Belgravia) $1,165

Early 20th century rosewood four-fold screen inset with brass panels, 229cm. high. (Sotheby's Belgravia) $820

Mahogany secretaire chest, circa 1840, 50in. wide. (Sotheby's Belgravia) $600

Mid 19th century American shaker pine bureau with tambour top, 39½in. wide. (Robert W. Skinner Inc.)$2,100

George III mahogany secretaire, inlaid with satinwood and ebony, 4ft. 1in. wide. (Lawrence Fine Art) $890

American Federal mahogany inlaid bow-front secretaire chest, circa 1795, 42in. wide. (Robert W. Skinner Inc.) $2,800

Ormolu mounted kingwood and marquetry secretaire a abattant, fitted as a cocktail cabinet, circa 1860, 43½in. wide. (Sotheby's Belgravia) $2,455

Edwardian inlaid mahogany breakfront escritoire. (Phillips) $2,200

Red boulle secretaire with dummy serpentine front and white marble top, 1860's, 24in. wide.(Sotheby's Belgravia) $1,050

Unusual mother-of-pearl inlaid polychrome lacquer secretaire on stand, 49½in. wide. (Christie's) $4,105

19th century Sheraton style inlaid escritoire with satinwood crossbanding. (Edgar Horn)$970

19th century French floral marquetry and walnut secretaire a abattant, 54cm. wide.(Sotheby, King & Chasemore)$1,980

Fine Regency satinwood secretaire cabinet, crossbanded in ebony, 34in. wide. (Burtenshaw Walker) $8,800

George IV Gothic revival mahogany secretaire cabinet, circa 1820, 2ft. 5½in. wide.(Sotheby's)$1,405

George II walnut secretaire chest with quartered crossbanded top, 30½in. wide. (Christie's) $4,520

Rosewood secretaire with stepped superstructure, circa 1850, 52½in. wide. (Sotheby's Belgravia) $550

Regency rosewood secretaire with gray marble top, 64in. wide. (Christie's) $5,475

William IV mahogany secretaire with gallery shelf, 42in. wide. (Thomas Watson & Son) $1,215

George I walnut secretaire tallboy, circa 1720, 107cm. wide. (Sotheby, King & Chasemore) $7,750

Dutch walnut and marquetry secretaire a abattant, 37in. wide. (Sotheby's Belgravia) $1,125

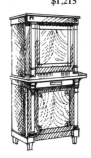

Regency rosewood secretaire by S. Jamar, inlaid with brass, 31in. wide. (Christie's) $2,370

Small French style escritoire in harewood with gilt metal mounts, by Robert Strahan, Dublin, 35in. wide. (Butler & Hatch Waterman) $3,490

Fine William IV rosewood and gilt mounted escritoire, 42in. wide. (Locke & England)$3,536

William and Mary walnut secretaire chest, 3ft.8in. wide, circa 1690. (Sotheby's) $4,445

American Renaissance revival walnut and burl veneer roll-top secretaire. circa 1865, 53in. wide. (Robert W. Skinner Inc.) $3,000

George III satinwood secretaire cabinet with molded cornice crossbanded with rosewood, 44½in. wide. (Christie's) $4,760

SECRETAIRE BOOKCASES

Late George III mahogany secretaire cabinet with two geometrically glazed doors, 47in. wide. (Christie's) $3,760

American mahogany secretaire bookcase with Gothic glazed doors, 38in. wide. (C. G. Sloan & Co. Inc.) $1,400

Regency mahogany secretaire with molded cornice above two Gothic pattern glazed doors, 45¼in. wide. (Christie's) $5,125

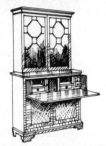

Georgian mahogany secretaire bookcase, 4ft.2in. wide. (Lawrence Fine Art) $3,160

George III mahogany secretaire bookcase, circa 1780, 4ft.1in. wide. (Sotheby, King & Chasemore) $3,660

Late George III satinwood secretaire cabinet with three-quarter galleried top, 37½in. wide. (Christie's) $3,465

Georgian mahogany Sheraton-style secretaire bookcase. (Burtenshaw & Walker) $8,210

Early 19th century mahogany secretaire cabinet with brass ring handles, 113cm. wide. (H. Spencer & Sons) $2,455

American Empire mahogany secretary desk with glazed doors, 42in. wide. (C. G. Sloan & Co. Inc.) $600

Early 19th century George III mahogany secretaire bookcase, 3ft.4in. wide. (Sotheby's) $4,405

George III mahogany breakfront secretaire bookcase, circa 1780, 84in. wide. (J. Francis; T. Jones & Son) $13,920

19th century mahogany secretaire bookcase with glazed doors. (Parsons, Welch & Cowell) $2,180

20th century Custom mahogany and mahogany veneer Federal style secretary, Brookline, Massachusetts, 38in. wide. (Robert W. Skinner Inc.) $1,150

Hepplewhite style lady's desk with tapered legs, 31¼in. wide. (C. G. Sloan & Co. Inc.) $950

Late George III mahogany secretaire cabinet, circa 1800, 3ft.6½in. wide. (Sotheby's) $3,170

George III Chippendale style secretaire bookcase. (Phillips) $13,100

Georgian mahogany secretaire with later bookcase top, 39½in. wide. (Thomas Watson & Son) $1,755

Marquetry inlaid mahogany secretaire bureau bookcase, 48½in. wide.(Clive Emson & Co.) $1,905

George III mahogany secretaire bookcase, 133cm. wide. (Bonhams) $8,785

Victorian walnut bookcase with cylinder fall-front revealing a fitted writing interior. (Biddle & Webb)$4,475

George III secretaire bookcase with pierced swan neck pediment, drawers inlaid with boxwood and ivory.(Phillips & Jolly) $13,910

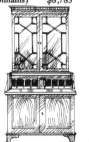

Sheraton design mahogany and satinwood inlaid secretaire bookcase, 48in. wide. (Locke & England) $3,120

Late 18th century Sheraton period mahogany secretaire bookcase, 63in. wide. (Woolley & Wallis) $8,280

Mid Georgian mahogany secretaire bookcase with glazed doors and brass handles. (Walker, Barnett & Hill) $4,400

SETTEES & COUCHES

Walnut button-upholstered chair-back settee on scrolled legs, restored, 72in. wide. (Sotheby's Belgravia) $1,290

Early 'George II' walnut and burr-walnut chair-back settee, 56in. wide, circa 1900-20. (Sotheby's Belgravia) $2,605

Mid 19th century American mahogany sofa with curved triple arched back, 61in. wide. (Christie's) $830

Mid 19th century 'George III' mahogany triple-back settee, carved with scrolling leaves. (Sotheby's Belgravia) $1,055

One of a pair of mid 19th century carved rosewood meridiennes by John Henry Belter. (Morton's Auction Exchange) $19,000

One of a pair of early George II giltwood and gesso sofas by Wm. Kent, circa 1730, 6ft.5in. wide. (Sotheby's) $8,090

Mid 19th century cast-iron garden seat with slatted bench seat, 60½in. wide. (Sotheby's Belgravia) $715

Early 18th century walnut settee with stuffed, serpentine back, 3ft. 11in. wide. (Sotheby's) $1,075

Joined oak settle with four fielded panel back carved with geometric shapes, 6ft. wide. (Lawrence Fine Art) $305

North German button-upholstered walnut settee with arched carved back, 72½in. wide, circa 1850. (Sotheby's Belgravia)$1,005

Mid Georgian red walnut sofa with arched padded back, possibly Irish, 78in. wide. (Christie's) $3,415

18th century German carved oak settle with iron box seat, 6ft.1in. wide. (Lawrence Fine Art) $1,030

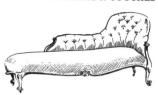

Louis XVI style Duchess brise in three sections, on turned and fluted tapering legs. (Lawrence Fine Art) $1,030

Oak settle with tall back and sides, circa 1900, 58½in. wide.(Sotheby's Belgravia) $715

Rosewood framed chaise longue with spoon-back and extended scroll arm supports. (Locke & England) $1,760

Settee from a suite of drawing-room furniture with bowed toprails, circa 1880.(Sotheby's Belgravia) $975

Rare early George III mahogany chaise longue with arched buttoned-back, circa 1765, 6ft. wide. (Sotheby's) $1,905

Late 17th century oak settle with carved and paneled back, 68in. wide. (Dacre, Son & Hartley) $460

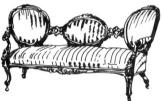

Late 18th century Italian painted and parcel gilt settee, 7ft. wide, circa 1770. (Sotheby's) $1,950

Victorian walnut framed settee. (Sotheby Bearne) $2,310

Early 20th century Edwardian inlaid mahogany settee, 54in. wide. (Sotheby Bearne) $505

Guangxu rosewood settle with pierced back, 138.5cm. wide, on heavy cabriole legs. (Sotheby's Belgravia) $610

Walnut chaise longue with button-upholstered back, late 1850's. (Sotheby's Belgravia) $935

Victorian oak settle, carved in the Gothic style, 72in. wide. (Christie's & Edmiston's) $575

Small mahogany settee with shell and leaf carved toprail, on cabriole legs and scroll feet, circa 1870. (Sotheby's Belgravia) $370

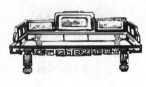

Late 18th century Chinese hardwood day bed with pierced and carved frieze, 6ft.5in. wide. (Sotheby's) $1,200

Walnut settee with button upholstered back and arms, 77½in. wide, late 1850's. (Sotheby's Belgravia) $1,250

Settee from a suite of transitional giltwood drawing room furniture, circa 1880.(Sotheby's Belgravia) $6,350

George I oak settle with four shaped panels on back, 4ft. 10in. wide, circa 1720. (Sotheby's) $675

Mid 19th century 'Louis XV' small giltwood canape with cane frame, 45in. wide. (Sotheby's Belgravia) $1,355

Late 19th century inlaid mahogany three-chair back settee. (Honiton Galleries) $545

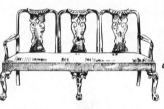

Mahogany Chippendale three-backed settee with vase-shaped splats, 69in. wide. (C. G. Sloan & Co. Inc.) $1,900

Unusual early 17th century curved and hooded oak settle, 5ft.1in. high. (Coles, Knapp & Kennedy) $3,980

17th century carved oak paneled settle with arcaded panels, 57in. wide. (Lawrence Fine Art) $320

19th century Regency mahogany tete-a-tete with S-form back, 46in. long. (Robert W. Skinner Inc.) $850

Mid 18th century needlework covered mahogany settee, 7ft. 7in. wide. (Sotheby's) $6,345

Regency brass-inlaid mahogany chaise longue, circa 1810, 5ft. 8in. long. (Sotheby's) $1,125

Hepplewhite mahogany sofa with molded scrolling armrests, 79in. long. (C. G. Sloan & Co. Inc.) $1,900

One of a pair of Regency ebonised and gilded sofas of Grecian form, 83in. wide. (Christie's) $4,345

Late 19th century American walnut sofa with floral and acanthus carved framework, 7ft. wide. (Robt. W. Skinner Inc.) $500

Jacobean carved oak settle, with animal-form hand rests, 76in. long. (C. G. Sloan & Co. Inc.) $850

George III giltwood sofa with arched padded back, 72in. wide. (Christie's) $2,260

18th century country beech settle with paneled and curved back, 72in. long. (Robert W. Skinner Inc.) $1,400

Late 19th century Chinese relief carved teak settee, 53in. long. (Robert W. Skinner Inc.) $2,100

Mid 18th century English mahogany settee with shaped wing back. (May Whetter & Grose) $1,065

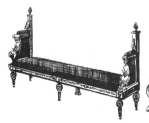

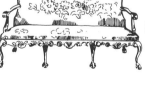

One of a pair of giltwood banquettes with padded arms, circa 1830, 103½in. wide. (Christie's) $4,580

Mahogany Chippendale style settee with camel back, on six curved legs, 77in. wide. (C. G. Sloan & Co. Inc.)$1,500

George III giltwood sofa with curved and waved back, 69in. wide. (Christie's)$2,380

SETTEES & COUCHES

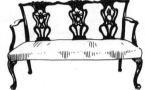

One of a pair of Victorian walnut love seats, New England, circa 1870, 56in. wide. (Robert W. Skinner Inc.) **$900**

20th century American custom mahogany Chippendale settee with straight open back, 60in. wide. (Robert W. Skinner Inc.) **$625**

20th century European vis-a-vis with carved toprail and back, 50½in. wide. (Robert W. Skinner Inc.) **$650**

Walnut revolving Duchesse, 1860's, with padded seat backs. (Sotheby's Belgravia) **$2,120**

Rare 18th century English conversation settee in Adam style, with beech frame, 10ft.6in. long. (Taylor Lane & Creber) **$5,460**

Sofa from a mid 19th century American Victorian walnut and burr-veneer Renaissance revival parlour set. (Robert W. Skinner Inc.) **$1,150**

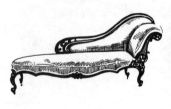

Part of a Victorian walnut framed parlour suite, circa 1860, nine pieces in all. (Sotheby Bearne) **$5,125**

Charles II oak settle, back with three fielded panels, circa 1680, 4ft.7½in. wide. (Sotheby's) **$1,675**

Victorian mahogany framed, dralon upholstered chaise longue on turned legs. (R. K. Lucas & Son) **$625**

Part of a thirteen-piece drawingroom suite, including four stools. (Sotheby's Belgravia) **$7,585**

19th century giltwood Duchesse brise in Louis XV style. (Capes, Dunn & Co.) **$580**

Adam style painted satinwood sofa, 75in. long. (Lawrence Fine Art) **$955**

Georgian mahogany serpentine side-board, edged in boxwood, with brass ring handles, 5ft.5in. wide. (Lawrence Fine Art) $1,355

Late 18th century mahogany sideboard of outset bow-front form, urn pedestals veneered with oval satinwood.(Sotheby Beresford Adams) $12,540

Federal mahogany inlaid side-board, Middle Atlantic States, circa 1800, 67in. wide. (Robert W. Skinner Inc.) $2,500

Late 18th century George III serpentine front sideboard in mahogany, 72in. long. (Robert W. Skinner Inc.) $2,600

American oak sideboard, top with two leaded glass doors, circa 1900, 43in. wide. (Robert W. Skinner Inc.) $400

Georgian breakfront mahogany side-board with bowed ends, 5ft.6in. wide. (Moore, Allen & Innocent) $1,800

Regency mahogany breakfront side-board. (Turner, Rudge & Turner) $1,365

American Sheraton mahogany bow-front serving board, circa 1810, 45in. wide. (C. G. Sloan & Co. Inc.) $7,250

Late 19th century satinwood Shera-ton revival semi-elliptical kneehole sideboard, 54in. wide. (Neales) $2,575

Small Georgian mahogany sideboard with tray top and brass knob handles, 49in. wide. (Butler & Hatch Waterman) $630

Pedestal sideboard with mirror back and wine cellarette, 7ft. wide. (David Symonds) $505

19th century bow-fronted sideboard of Sheraton design veneered in figured mahogany, 7ft. long. (W. H. Lane & Son) $900

Regency mahogany breakfront sideboard with inlaid front, ring handles, 6ft.2in. wide. (Lawrence Fine Art) $3,160

Mahogany and satinwood sideboard by William Morris and Co., 1900-1910, 63¼in. wide. (Sotheby Belgravia) $575

Georgian mahogany serpentine sideboard edged in boxwood with brass ring handles, 5ft.5in. wide (Lawrence Fine Art) $1,355

George III serpentine mahogany sideboard crossbanded in tulipwood, 4ft.6in. wide, circa 1780. (Sotheby's) $5,370

One of a pair of mahogany sideboards, 48in. wide, circa 1910. (Sotheby's Belgravia) $910

George III bow-front mahogany sideboard, circa 1780, 5ft. wide, top crossbanded in tulipwood. (Sotheby's) $3,395

George III bow-fronted mahogany sideboard, circa 1790, 4ft. wide. (Sotheby's) $1,145

George III bow-front sideboard, circa 1785, 4ft.10½in. wide. (Sotheby's) $2,690

George III mahogany breakfront sideboard with brass gallery, circa 1790, 6ft.2¼in. wide. (Sotheby's) $2,380

George III mahogany bow-fronted sideboard with banded and inlaid edge, 6ft. long. (Messenger, May & Baverstock) $4,360

Small late 19th century satinwood revival semi-elliptical kneehole sideboard, 54in. wide. (Neales) $2,530

American mahogany sideboard with bowed three-quarter galleried top, 66½in. wide. (Christie's) $680

Small George III mahogany sideboard with reeded edge, 3ft.5in. long. (Messenger, May & Baverstock) $4,580

20th century mahogany breakfront sideboard on tapered legs with spade feet, 5ft. wide. (Vernon's) $150

George III mahogany and inlaid sideboard with brass rail back and handles, 85in. wide. (Dacre, Son & Hartley) $1,705

Regency mahogany sideboard with bowed rectangular top, 50½in. wide. (Christie's) $4,230

Regency mahogany pedestal sideboard with inlaid ebonised and boxwood stringing, 207.7cm. wide. (Jackson-Stops and Staff) $1,215

Early Victorian mahogany sideboard on turned legs, 5ft. wide. (Cooper Hirst) $1,265

Sheraton style Edwardian mahogany sideboard inlaid with oak, fruitwood, satinwood and boxwood by Solomon Baxter. (West London Auctions) $3,120

Large carved sideboard in pollard oak by Thomas Turner, circa 1870. (Capes, Dunn & Co.) $3,305

George III mahogany bow-fronted sideboard, crossbanded with rosewood, 71¾in. wide. (Christie's) $3,630

Late 18th century broken serpentine front mahogany sideboard with ebony and boxwood banding, 72in. long. (Moore, Allen & Innocent) $1,500

A small 20th century Jacobean style oak sideboard. (Vernon's)$100

George III mahogany and crossbanded sideboard with bowfront. (Phillips) $8,320

369

STANDS

Late George III mahogany adjustable duet stand with brass candle holders, circa 1810, 4ft. high. (Sotheby's) $1,510

Guangxu stained hardwood urn stand with inset marble top, 80cm. high. (Sotheby's Belgravia) $655

Italian stained beech hall stand, heavily carved, circa 1860, 45in. wide. (Sotheby's Belgravia) $585

Late 19th century parquetry occasional table with trefoil top and pierced gallery, 14in. wide. (Sotheby's Belgravia) $375

One of a pair of 19th century Italian gilt torcheres, 4ft.6in. high. (Alfie's Antique Market)$1,605

One of a pair of mahogany diningroom pedestals and urns, circa 1780, 5ft.6in. high. (Sotheby's) $4,910

One of a pair of parcel gilt ebonised wood torcheres, circa 1870, fitted for electricity, 69in. high. (Sotheby's Belgravia) $705

One of a pair of Italian painted and giltwood torchere stands, 6ft.3in. high. (Lawrence Fine Art) $1,170

One of a pair of Regency mahogany diningroom pedestals with marble tops, circa 1820, 2ft.2in. wide. (Sotheby's) $5,125

One of a rare pair of George II mahogany table stands, circa 1750, 8¼in. diam. (Sotheby's)$925

Walnut jardiniere on cabriole legs, with marquetry inlay and ormolu mounts, 26in. wide. (Lambert & Symes) $4,115

Late 19th/early 20th century giltwood and plaster torchere with circular top, 21in. diam. (Sotheby's Belgravia) $540

370

William IV adjustable rosewood duet stand, 3ft.8in. high, circa 1830, on bun feet. (Sotheby's) $1,510

19th century kingwood lidded plant stand with gilt metal scrollwork and gallery rail. (Russell, Baldwin & Bright) $1,170

Square mahogany urn stand on tapering legs, ormolu mounted and with marble top, 30cm. square. (Lambert & Symes) $630

Zograscope, mounted on turned mahogany frame with ivory finials, 2ft. high. (Simmons & Lawrence) $160

One of a 20th century pair of blackamoor candelabra, 82cm. high. (Sotheby's Belgravia) $2,350

Rosewood folio rack with adjustable lattice rests on trestle supports, 44½in. high, 1840's. (Sotheby's Belgravia) $1,215

18th century oak rushlight' with wrought-iron snuffer,' 87.5cm. high.(Christie's) $710

Late George II carved wood and white-painted house letter box, circa 1755, 4ft.1½in. high. (Sotheby's)$1,170

American Federal mahogany candle stand, circa 1795, 23½in. high, with tilt-top. (Robert W. Skinner Inc.) $1,300

Italian walnut center stand with two graduated square tiers, 1870's, 21¼in. wide. (Sotheby's Belgravia) $340

Antique cluster column kettle stand. (Allen & May) $365

Edwardian mahogany and inlaid serpentine shaped plant stand, 15in. wide. (Dacre, Son & Hartley) $415

STANDS

19th century walnut stand with circular top, pierced triple pedestal and carved feet, 13½in. diam. (W. H. Lane & Son) $225

Early 19th century decanting cradle. (Christie's) $1,364

Georgian mahogany wig stand with undershelf, on tripod base. (Hall, Wateridge & Owen) $680

19th century solid mahogany torchere. (Alfie's Antique Market) $215

Solid rosewood embroidery frame with trestle supports, circa 1850, 48in. wide. (Sotheby's Belgravia) $400

Late 19th century satinwood spinning wheel with detachable top, 1.16m. high.(Phillips)$1,170

Mahogany music stand, circa 1840, on quadruple foot. (Bradley & Vaughan) $1,015

American Victorian walnut hall tree, signed T. Brooks & Co., New York, 36in. wide. (C. G. Sloan & Co. Inc.) $800

Unusual Regency mahogany duet table with quadruple flap, 23½in. diam. (Christie's) $1,380

Early 18th century German kingwood and purpleheart meuble d'entre deux, 29½in. wide.(Christie's) $1,785

Rare late 18th century brass spinning wheel on mahogany stand, 35in. high. (Hy. Duke & Son) $3,510

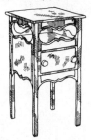

Early 19th century American Federal grain painted stand, 15in. wide. (Robert W. Skinner Inc.)$550

372

Late 19th century American Renaissance revival marble top stand, 16in. wide. (Robert W. Skinner Inc.) $425

Kalliope musical Christmas tree stand, 59cm. wide, circa 1900. (Sotheby's Belgravia) $875

Mid 19th century American Pennsylvania Federal painted pine waterbench, 63in. wide. (Robert W. Skinner Inc.) $700

19th century French kingwood and ormolu stand with square marble top, 4ft. high. (Andrew Grant) $1,640

One of a pair of Biedermeier mahogany jardiniere stands with galleried tops, 32in. wide. (Christie's) $1,430

One of a pair of late 18th century Italian giltwood torcheres, 49¼in. high. (Christie's) $1,190

Rare twin spindle spinning wheel, 4ft.4in. high. (Clive Emson & Co.) $330

One of a pair of gilt metal mounted kingwood jardiniere stands with famille rose jardinieres, 43½in. high. (Christie's) $1,665

19th century beechwood spinning wheel on three bobbin-turned supports, 2ft.8in. high. (Sotheby's) $715

19th century lignum vitae reel stand. (Sotheby's) $1,470

Louis XV style marquetry inlaid three-drawer stand on cabriole legs, 18½in. wide. (C. G. Sloan & Co. Inc.) $850

Late 19th century American walnut pedestal with caryatid supports. (Robert W. Skinner Inc.) $650

373

Queen Anne walnut stool with drop-in seat and cabriole legs joined by a baluster H-stretcher, 19¼in. wide. (Christie's) $4,285

Georgian mahogany gout stool with leather upholstery end and seat, 22in. wide.(Christie's) $310

One of a pair of Louis XV giltwood stools attributed to J. B. Tilliard, 26in. wide. (Christie's) $18,800

Guangxu rosewood and marble stool with rectangular top, 48cm. wide. (Sotheby's Belgravia) $425

Mid Georgian walnut fender stool with padded seat, 49½in. wide. (Christie's) $13,035

Rare late 16th century Italian iron and brass faldistorio with padded seat, 25in. wide. (Christie's) $1,555

Victorian carved walnut rectangular stool, circa 1850, 2ft. wide.(Sotheby, King & Chasemore) $845

Regency rosewood and cut brass inlaid harpist's seat, circa 1815, 2ft.4½in. high. (Sotheby, King & Chasemore) $7,920

18th century English Charles II walnut bench with upholstered seat, 21in. long. (Robert W. Skinner Inc.) $400

Adam style painted satinwood dressing stool, with kick-out feet. (Lawrence Fine Art) $160

Pel chromed tubular steel bathroom stool with cork top, 1930's, 44.5cm. square. (Sotheby's Belgravia) $115

Charles I oak joint stool with molded rectangular top, 46cm. wide. (Christie's) $2,280

One of a pair of Victorian walnut serpentine-shaped foot stools, 14in. wide. (Dacre, Son & Hartley) $400

Queen Anne walnut stool on cabriole legs edged with C-scrolls, 22½in. wide. (Christie's) $6,190

One of a pair of late 18th century mahogany framed stools on molded tapering legs. (Locke & England) $1,170

Joined oak stool with shaped frieze, 1ft.6in. wide. (Lawrence Fine Art) $305

Regency green-painted X-frame stool carved with lion masks, 34½in. wide. (Christie's) $1,100

Mid 18th century gesso and gilt mahogany framed stool on four carved cabriole legs with shell mounts. (Locke & England) $1,950

One of a pair of Louis XV beechwood stools with nailed serpentine seats, 17½in. wide. (Christie's) $5,875

One of a pair of George I walnut stools with needlework drop-in seats, 21in. wide. (Christie's) $3,660

Queen Anne walnut stool, seat covered in gros and petit-point needlework, 19in. diam. (Christie's) $4,285

Joined oak box stool with carved sides and front. (Lawrence Fine Art) $560

Late 19th century European walnut piano bench supported by two bears, 36in. long. (Robert W. Skinner Inc.) $850

17th century oak joint stool, 18in. wide. (Sotheby, King & Chasemore) $755

American Victorian incised walnut and burl veneer parlor set of a sofa and two chairs, circa 1870. (Robert W. Skinner Inc.) $850

Two-piece Art Nouveau carved mahogany suite with carved backs and arms, settee 49in. long. (C. G. Sloan & Co. Inc.) $1,000

American 20th century walnut parlor set of two pieces. (Robert W. Skinner Inc.) $600

A three-piece Renaissance revival parlor set, Eastern United States. (Robert W. Skinner Inc.) $800

Part of a six-piece 'Louis XV' parcel-gilt walnut drawingroom suite, each piece with molded frame. (Sotheby's Belgravia) $1,920

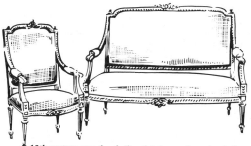

19th century carved and gilt painted gesso framed upholstered suite, in rose-pink dralon.
(Sotheby, King & Chasemore) $825

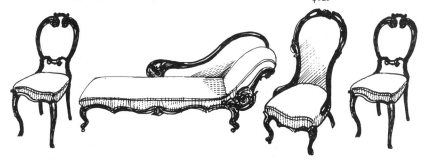

Part of a Victorian walnut nine-piece drawingroom suite on cabriole legs. (Burtenshaw Walker)
$4,320

Part of an eight-piece 19th century salon
suite framed in walnut'with stringing inlay.
(Taylor, Lane & Creber) $2,050

Part of an American six-piece Victorian
Renaissance revival rosewood parlor set,
circa 1860. (Robert W. Skinner Inc.)
$2,300

Late 19th/early 20th century Art Nouveau design bedroom suite by J. Groschkos, Berlin.
(Locke & England) $1,375

One of a pair of George III mahogany card tables with baize lined serpentine tops, 36in. wide. (Christie's) $15,730

Late 18th century mahogany fold-over tea table, crossbanded with satinwood. (T. Bannister & Co.) $800

19th century Sheraton mahogany tea table, folding top with boxwood lines, restored, 3ft. wide. (Lawrence Fine Art) $490

Victorian walnut card table, serpentine folding top with baize lined interior, circa 1850, 3ft. wide. (Lawrence Fine Art) $980

William IV carved rosewood card table with beaded edge, fold-over top, 36in. wide. (Dacre, Son & Hartley) $715

One of a pair of Regency rosewood card tables with crossbanded tops, 35½in. wide. (Christie's) $4,520

George IV brass inlaid rosewood card table with swivelling top, circa 1825, 2ft.11in. wide. (Sotheby's) $1,170

19th century mahogany boxwood and brass inlaid tea table with fold-over top, 36in. wide. (Dacre, Son & Hartley) $1,680

George II walnut card table with folding top, 35in. wide. (Christie's) $3,335

Mid 18th century mahogany tea table, possibly Irish, 36¼in. wide.(Christie's) $3,215

George III fold-over top card table in rosewood. (Taylor, Lane & Creber) $1,090

Red boulle folding card table on cabriole legs. (Ernest R. de Rome) $1,650

One of a pair of George III mahogany tea and card tables with folding tops, 36in. wide. (Christie's) $5,170

Antique mahogany serpentine folding tea table on triangular fluted legs, 36in. wide. (Lambert & Symes) $2,660

Sheraton mahogany semi-circular tea table with folding top and square tapering legs with thimble feet, 3ft. 2in. diam. (Butler & Hatch Waterman) $1,155

One of a pair of William IV rosewood fold top tea tables on bulbous pedestals, 3ft. wide. (Taylor Lane & Creber) $1,165

American Queen Anne maple tea table with tapering round legs on pad feet, 34in. wide. (C. G. Sloan & Co. Inc.) $1,000

Early 18th century tea table with lobed baize lined folding top, 35in. wide. (Christie's) $2,023

George II red walnut games table with traingular triple-flap top, 36½in. wide. (Christie's) $5,565

Walnut Queen Anne style card table with folding top, on cabriole legs and ball and claw feet, 33in. wide. (Lambert & Symes) $3,390

Rosewood and marquetry inlaid folding semi-circular card table, 38in. wide. (Lambert & Symes) $3,390

Walnut card table with rectangular top and cabriole legs, 36in. wide.(Christie's) $4,165

Mahogany Queen Anne period folding card table with shell carved decoration, 34in. wide. (Butler & Hatch Waterman) $980

George III satinwood card table with d-shaped baize lined top crossbanded with rosewood, 36in. wide.(Christie's) $4,115

379

Walnut porcelain mounted card table with swivel top inlaid with kingwood, 37in. wide, circa 1860. (Sotheby's Belgravia) $2,295

Rosewood and marquetry envelope card table inlaid with boxwood, circa 1900, 2ft.5in. wide. (Sotheby's) $725

Georgian mahogany semi-lunar card table, edged in boxwood. (Lawrence Fine Art) $585

George III rosewood card table with folding top and tapering sabre legs, 3ft.2in. wide. (Lawrence Fine Art) $1,265

Serpentine rosewood card table on a baluster stem and four cabriole legs, 26in. wide, circa 1855. (Sotheby's Belgravia) $750

Georgian mahogany card table with inlaid d-shaped top, 3ft. wide. (Lawrence Fine Art) $980

Late George II mahogany tea or card table with serpentine top, circa 1760, 3ft. wide. (Sotheby's) $1,665

One of a pair of good mid 19th century walnut and marquetry card tables, 34½in. wide. (Sotheby's Belgravia) $3,980

Kingwood and marquetry card table with swivelling top, circa 1860, 34in. wide. (Sotheby's Belgravia) $2,700

Mother-of-pearl and brass inlaid ebony card table, circa 1870, 36in. wide. (Sotheby's Belgravia) $1,080

William IV mahogany tea table on baluster column, circa 1835, 123cm. wide. (Sotheby's Belgravia) $325

American Queen Anne cherrywood tea table with applied molded edge, 29½in. wide. (Robert W. Skinner Inc.) $1,700

Edwardian inlaid card table on square tapering legs. (Cooper Hirst) $835

19th century marquetry card table with fold-over top, 34in. wide. (Smith-Woolley & Perry) $945

One of a pair of 'George III' painted satinwood card tables with canted rectangular tops, 1880's, 35½in. wide. (Sotheby's Belgravia) $2,575

One of a pair of early 19th century rosewood and mahogany card tables. (Mallams) $3,415

Regency fold top pedestal table veneered in rosewood and with brass inlay, 3ft. wide. (Taylor Lane & Creber)$470

One of a pair of 19th century Sheraton style mahogany card tables, 36in. wide. (Woolley & Wallis) $16,185

'George III' mahogany and marquetry card table, circa 1860. (Sotheby's Belgravia)$1,115

Early George II oak tea or games table of triangular shape, circa 1735, 2ft.5¾in. wide. (Sotheby's)$575

George II walnut tea table with semi-circular folding top, 32¼in. wide. (Christie's) $1,830

George III marquetry card table, cross-banded in tulipwood and inlaid with satinwood, circa 1785, 3ft.3¾in. wide. (Sotheby's) $2,855

18th century folding mahogany tea table. (Flick & Son) $775

Sheraton period mahogany card table on tapering legs with spade feet. (Parsons, Welch & Cowell) $1,045

381

19th century Sheraton design card table, top inlaid with satinwood, 30in. wide. (Morphets) $1,085

Early Victorian rosewood card table, 36in. wide. (Sotheby Bearne) $595

Walnut fold-over card table/writing desk inlaid with brass. (Andrew Grant) $1,225

George III marquetry tea or games table, circa 1780, 2ft.9in. wide. (Sotheby's) $1,660

American Federal mahogany card table with swell front, circa 1795, 36½in. square. (Robert W. Skinner Inc.) $3,600

George I red walnut circular fold-over card table with concealed fold-out gateleg, 2ft.6in. diam. (Andrew Grant) $1,860

Sheraton period mahogany semi-elliptical folding tea table, circa 1790, 36in. wide. (Neales) $1,165

18th century Irish carved mahogany tea table of Chippendale design, 3ft. wide. circa 1770. (Sotheby, King & Chasemore) $4,150

George I red walnut folding card table on cabriole legs, circa 1725, 34½in. wide. (Neales) $1,510

Red walnut folding-top card table with original green baize lining. (M. Phillip H. Scott) $4,620

Rare Federal mahogany inlaid card table, Massachusetts, circa 1790, 36in. wide. (Robert W. Skinner Inc.) $2,600

Mid 19th century pollard oak fold-over top tea table. (Christie's S. Kensington) $1,100

Semi-circular folding card table, top in burred veneer, with square tapering legs. (Butler & Hatch Waterman) $2,440

Burr-walnut card table with baize-lined interior, circa 1860, 38in. wide. (Sotheby's Belgravia) $755

Late 18th century George III games table in mahogany, 38¾in. wide. (Robert W. Skinner Inc.)$650

American Victorian Renaissance revival walnut games table, 36½in. wide, circa 1865. (Robert W. Skinner Inc.) $350

CENTER TABLES

Edwardian mahogany folding card table with swivel top with boxwood and ebonised stringing, 21in. wide closed. (Butler & Hatch Waterman) $220

Federal mahogany card table by John and Thomas Seymour, Massachusetts, circa 1795, 35½in. square. (Robert W. Skinner Inc.) $3,100

Rosewood center table with serpentine octagonal top, inlaid with foliage and boxwood stringing, circa 1900, 32½in. wide. (Sotheby's Belgravia) $350

Late 19th century boulle center table with serpentine top, 52in. wide. (Sotheby's Belgravia) $2,070

Louis XV style mahogany center table with shaped round top, 30in. diam. (C. G. Sloan & Co. Inc.) $550

Regency mahogany and parcel gilt center table by Thomas Hope, circa 1810, 4ft.6in. diam. (Sotheby's) $3,295

Dutch walnut and marquetry center table with serpentine top, 32in. wide. (Christie's) $5,235

Empire bronze and ormolu center table with marble top, 34½in. diam. (Christie's) $9,640

Late 19th century Chinese hardwood and marble table, inlaid
with mother-of-pearl, 34in. wide.
(Christie's & Edmiston's)
$1,955

Mid 19th century Italian walnut Renaissance center table, 53in. wide.(Sotheby's
Belgravia) $1,755

Mid 18th century Chinese lacquer
table with pierced carved frieze,
3ft.3½in. wide, distressed.
(Sotheby's) $1,170

Late 19th century boulle serpentine
center table on cabriole legs, 51in.
wide. (Sotheby's Belgravia)
$2,070

William IV marble and stained oak
center table, circa 1835, 34in. wide.
(Sotheby's Belgravia) $655

Red boulle center table of rectangular
serpentine outline, circa 1870, 58¼in.
wide. (Sotheby's Belgravia)
$1,220

Mid 19th century center table with crossbanded top, 72in. wide. (Christie's)
$6,100

Early 18th century Dutch red
walnut center table with shaped
top, 1ft.7½in. wide.(Sotheby's)
$3,660

Early 18th century oak table a gibier
with red and gray marble top, 40½in.
wide. (Christie's) $4,285

Walnut and marquetry center table
with square veneered top, circa 1860,
47½in. wide. (Sotheby's Belgravia)
$1,990

Serpentine marquetry center table
with inlaid top, circa 1880, 39in.
wide. (Sotheby's Belgravia)
$685

Boulle serpentine center table, circa
1870, 40½in. wide. (Sotheby's Belgravia) $1,175

George IV mahogany library table on scrolled supports with foliate carving, 72in. diam. (Christie's) $2,820

17th century Dutch floral marquetry center table joined with a serpentine stretcher. (Mallams) $3,415

Victorian oak library table with octagonal top, 58in. wide. (Christie's) $1,525

Inlaid marble center table with octagonal top, 1850's, 73.5cm. wide. (Sotheby's Belgravia) $860

Louis XV style ebonised boulle and ormolu mounted table, 139.5cm. wide. (Jackson-Stops & Staff) $1,215

George III mahogany and satinwood center table, crossbanded in rosewood, circa 1790, 2ft. wide. (Sotheby's) $1,365

Victorian marquetry center table, 32in. diam. (Christie's S. Kensington) $1,140

'Louis XV' kingwood and parquetry center table, circa 1860, 39in. wide. (Sotheby's Belgravia) $1,760

Unusual chinoiserie rosewood table, English, circa 1890. (Sotheby's Belgravia) $880

Octagonal rosewood center table on four spirally reeded supports, circa 1880, 38½in. wide. (Sotheby's Belgravia) $470

Boulle center table inset with leather writing surface, circa 1870, 30in. wide. (Sotheby's Belgravia) $1,755

Collinson & Lock mahogany center table with oval top, 1870's, 46½in. diam. (Sotheby's Belgravia) $465

CONSOLE TABLES

North German or Swedish giltwood console d'applique with marble top, circa 1750, 2ft.8in.wide.(Sotheby's) $1,520

One of a pair of mid 18th century North Italian carved giltwood corner consoles with marble tops, 1ft.11in. wide. (Sotheby's) $1,080

George III console table with kingwood veneered top and giltwood frame, circa 1770. (Sotheby's) $1,585

Regency painted and giltwood console table with simulated marble top, circa 1815, 3ft. 9¾in. wide. (Sotheby's) $830

Mid 19th century Danish or Swedish oak console table with white marble top. (Sotheby's Belgravia) $655

George III carved and giltwood console table with marble top, circa 1765, 4ft. wide. (Sotheby's) $5,295

William IV parcel gilt rosewood console table with white marble top, circa 1830, 3ft.10in. wide. (Sotheby's) $1,075

One of a pair of carved walnut corner console tables, South German or North Italian, late 1870's, 26 x 33in. (Sotheby's Belgravia) $733

One of a pair of console tables, top inlaid with satinwood, 3ft. 11in. wide. (Lawrence Fine Art) $655

Late 18th century Dutch or German pollard elm console desserte with gray and white marble top, 38¼in. wide. (Christie's) $2,735

18th/19th century giltwood console table with white marble top, 2ft. 9in. wide. (Sotheby's)$2,320

Mid 19th century walnut serpentine console table, Italian, 51in. wide. (Sotheby's Belgravia) $1,245

William IV mahogany breakfast or dining table with oval top, circa 1830, 4ft.11in. wide. (Sotheby's) $4,635

Rosewood oval breakfast table with tip top, 64in. wide, late 1830's. (Sotheby's Belgravia)$1,215

Marquetry table top, without base. (Bradley & Vaughan) $3,390

Regency rosewood center table with tip-up top crossbanded with oak, 46½in. diam. (Christie's) $2,380

Regency rosewood breakfast table on a platform base with paw feet. (Stride & Son) $1,625

Circular mahogany dining table on carved center pillar.(Honiton Galleries) $480

Regency rosewood circular breakfast table, inlaid with brass arabesques, on a square pillar with splayed legs. (Christie's & Edmiston's) $7,550

Breakfast table in rosewood banded flame mahogany. (Bradley & Vaughan) $2,080

Victorian walnut veneer and marquetry tip-top center table on carved and turned base, 51in. diam. (Andrew Grant) $5,290

Regency mahogany drum table with leather lined top, on quadripartite base and scrolled feet, 48in. diam. (Christie's) $3,450

Victorian walnut dining table and set of four chairs.(Biddle & Webb) $2,975

Biedermeier mahogany center table with circular top and four drawers, 46¾in. diam. (Christie's) $1,430

387

DINING TABLES

Mid Victorian mahogany center table, inlaid with boxwood, rosewood, walnut and other woods, 46½in. diam. (Phillips) $1,490

Walnut and marquetry breakfast table with octagonal tip-top, circa 1840, 58in. wide. (Sotheby's Belgravia) $2,750

Victorian oak center table, stamped A. Stranks, circa 1860, 52in. wide. (Christie's) $1,220

Regency calamanderwood table, 4ft. 5in. wide, circa 1820, hexagonal top inlaid with brass band. (Sotheby's) $1,205

Regency rosewood center table with tip-up top on turned beechwood shaft, 51½in. diam. (Christie's) $2,320

Brass inlaid circular rosewood breakfast table, 50in. diam. (Sotheby's Belgravia) $1,680

19th century mahogany loo table with circular tip-top on turned pillar support, 3ft.5½in. diam. (Taylor Lane & Creber)$515

Regency mahogany extending dining table with d-shaped ends, 9ft.6in. long extended. (Sotheby's) $6,190

George IV brass inlaid rosewood drum topped library table, 3ft. 11in. diam., circa 1825. (Sotheby's) $3,625

Victorian rosewood marquetry table by John Howard & Sons, London, 132cm. diam. (Phillips) $2,300

Georgian circular mahogany tilt-top breakfast table on turned pedestal, 52in. diam. (Moore, Allen & Innocent) $2,640

Early 19th century circular rosewood breakfast table, 101.6cm. diam. (Churchman's) $1,405

Modern 'George III' circular mahogany dining table on quadruple legs, 66in. diam., by Redman & Hales Ltd. (Sotheby's Belgravia) $810

Walnut marquetry breakfast table with circular lobed top, 53in. diam., 1860's. (Sotheby's Belgravia) $4,385

Rosewood circular dining table with tip-up top, 1840's, 48¼in. diam. (Sotheby's Belgravia) $670

Victorian circular mahogany tripod tip-top table, 31in. diam. (Allen & May)$280

Parquetry and marquetry mahogany center table on tripod base with gilt bronze mounts, 35in. diam., circa 1880. (Sotheby's Belgravia) $925

Walnut loo table with scalloped edge. (Outhwaite & Litherland) $3,025

19th century mahogany breakfast table, 43in. wide on a tripod base. (Sotheby Bearne) $350

Early Victorian mahogany pedestal extending dining table with four leg pedestal, 55in. wide. (Allen & May) $935

Oval walnut loo table in well-figured wood with turned column, late 1850's, 50in. wide.(Sotheby's Belgravia) $480

William IV rosewood circular tilt-top table on lion's paw feet, 57in. diam. (Smith-Woolley & Perry) $775

Walnut and marquetry circular breakfast table with inlaid top, 57¼in. diam. (Sotheby's Belgravia) $5,380

19th century walnut inlaid loo table. (Bradley & Vaughan) $1,450

19th cenfury American Greco-Roman revival walnut marble top table, 41in. long. (Robert W. Skinner Inc.) $350

Regency irónwood dining table with molded circular tip-up top, 74in. diam. (Christie's) $7,260

Rosewood breakfast table, molded rim above a tapering stem with lotus carved base, circa 1840, 48in. diam. (Sotheby's Belgravia) $725

George IV brass inlaid rosewood breakfast table, circa 1825, 4ft.6in. wide. (Sotheby's) $4,340

19th century circular rosewood breakfast table with tip-up top, 123cm. diam. (May Whetter & Grose) $820

Late 18th century Chippendale mahogany tea table, New England, 44in. square. (Robert W. Skinner Inc.) $1,000

19th century circular rosewood dining table. (Taylor Lane & Creber) $900

George III mahogany snap-top table with piecrust edge, on tripod support. (Biddle & Webb) $1,065

Mahogany breakfast table with segmentally veneered top, 47½in. diam., circa 1840. (Sotheby's Belgravia) $830

Late George III mahogany breakfast or dining table, circa 1800, 3ft.1½in. wide. (Sotheby's) $2,225

Mahogany breakfast table with veneered circular top, 48in. diam., 1840's. (Sotheby's Belgravia) $590

Regency rosewood circular library drum table, top inlaid with double brass line, circa 1820, 3ft.6in. diam. (Sotheby's) $2,650

Mahogany and marquetry dressing table with adjustable mirror, late 1890's, 48¼in. wide. (Sotheby's Belgravia) $670

Early Victorian bird's-eye maple and marquetry kneehole dressing table and matching mirror. (Christie's S. Kensington) $4,165

Regency birchwood and rosewood dressing table with three-quarter galleried top, 46in. wide. (Christie's) $1,645

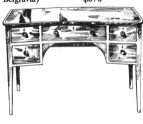

George III faded mahogany dressing table with concave-fronted top and arched kneehole, 46¼in. wide.(Christie's) $2,930

American rosewood chest of drawers with octagonal mirror, 37in. wide. (Christie's) $730

Queen Anne walnut dressing table with inlaid top and cabriole legs, 38in. wide. (C. G. Sloan & Co. Inc.) $950

Antique rosewood marble top dresser with oval mirror, stretcher with urn finial, 43½in. wide. (C. G. Sloan & Co. Inc.) $1,300

Part of a late 19th century American bamboo turned maple and maple veneer bedroom set. (Robert W. Skinner Inc.) $5,000

19th century French Empire serpentine-fronted dressing table with six drawers, 36in. wide. (Burtenshaw Walker) $1,285

Hepplewhite inlaid mahogany Beau Brummel dressing table, with satinwood line inlay, 32½in. wide. (C. G. Sloan & Co. Inc.) $1,400

Heal's sycamore dressing table and stool, 1930's, with circular mirror, 189cm. wide. (Sotheby's Belgravia) $655

George III satinwood dressing table with divided twin-flap top, 28in. wide. (Christie's) $3,510

DROP-LEAF TABLES

English walnut occasional gateleg table with two raised stands on top, circa 1900, 46½in. wide. (Sotheby's Belgravia) $575

Antique mahogany drop-leaf pedestal dining table with two drawers, 41in. wide. (Allen & May) $360

19th century mahogany oval drop-leaf dining table, 66in. long. (Sotheby Bearne) $950

Mid 18th century mahogany dining table of oval form, with turned legs and pad feet, 3ft.7in. wide. (Taylor Lane & Creber) $685

Queen Anne cherrywood dining table, Connecticut, circa 1760, 42½in. wide. (Robert W. Skinner Inc.) $2,100

Charles II oak gateleg table with opposing frieze drawers, circa 1660, 6ft.8in. wide. (Sotheby's) $8,295

Georgian mahogany corner table with fold-down flap on tapering legs, 3ft. 6in. wide. (Hobbs Parker) $340

American Chippendale walnut drop-leaf table on cabriole legs, 48in. wide, open. (C. G. Sloan & Co. Inc.) $950

Mid 18th century New England country Queen Anne cherry and hickory butterfly table, 40in. wide. (Robert W. Skinner Inc.) $1,200

George III mahogany oval drop-leaf dining table on pad feet, circa 1770, 4ft. 3in. wide. (Sotheby, King & Chasemore) $720

American custom oak gateleg table, circa 1920, 43 x 40in. (Robert W. Skinner Inc.) $375

Walnut Sutherland table on trestle legs joined by a turned stretcher. (Bradley & Vaughan) $530

Jacobean style oak gateleg table on turned and blocked legs and stretchers, 60in. wide, open. (C. G. Sloan & Co. Inc.) $1,200

Charles II oak and walnut gateleg table with oval top, circa 1680, 3ft.9in. wide. (Sotheby's) $1,935

17th century walnut gateleg table with oval twin-flap top, 75½in. wide, open. (Christie's) $3,960

17th century oval oak gateleg table on turned legs and underframe, 32in. wide. (D. M. Nesbit & Co.) $555

Early 18th century oak oval gateleg table on turned underframe, 66in. wide. (Burtenshaw Walker) $3,740

Oak gateleg table with oval top and spiral twist legs, 5ft.5in. wide, open. (Sotheby's) $2,905

17th century oak gateleg table with oval twin-flap top, 68in. wide, open. (Christie's) $3,840

17th century double gateleg table with oval top and baluster turned legs. (Stanilands) $1,215

Oval oak gateleg table on baluster turned legs, 5ft.6in. wide, open. (Butler & Hatch Waterman) $980

William and Mary oak gateleg table with oval top, circa 1690, 3ft.7½in. long. (Sotheby's) $1,100

17th century oak gateleg table, circa 1660, 91.5cm. wide. (Sotheby, King & Chasemore) $700

Antique oak gateleg table with drawer at one end, 4ft. wide. (Allen & May) $200

17th century joined oak center table with two plank top, 4ft.9in. wide. (Lawrence Fine Art) $840

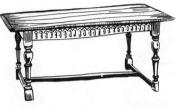

Partly 17th century joined oak dining table with four plank top and molded frieze, 6ft.0½in. long. (Lawrence Fine Art) $890

17th century oak refectory table with quadruple plank top, 110in. wide. (Christie's) $6,160

Late 17th century oak draw leaf dining table, 72in. long. (Drewatt, Watson & Barton) $3,850

Oak refectory table made from 17th century wood, with three plank top, 7ft.10in. long. (Sotheby's) $3,945

Oak refectory table with bulbous carved legs and central stretcher, 7ft.4in. long.(Worsfolds) $1,205

17th century oak draw-leaf dining table with plank top, 84in. wide, extended. (Christie's) $2,520

William IV mahogany extending dining table, circa 1835. (Sotheby, King & Chasemore) $3,535

Charles X oak draw-leaf table with ringed baluster legs, circa 1640, 6ft.7in. long, closed.(Sotheby's) $3,480

Late Regency mahogany twin pillar dining table, 1830's, 10ft. long, open. (Lawrence Fine Art) $3,875

Fine mid Victorian carved oak dining table, 67in. wide. (Locke & England) $915

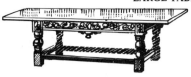

Late 17th century oak dining table with plank top, 99in. wide. (Christie's) $5,760

George III mahogany two pedestal dining table, circa 1800, 4ft.2in. wide.(Sotheby's) $7,200

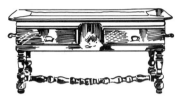

French provincial walnut refectory table with two sliding panels in front, 67in. long. (C. G. Sloan & Co. Inc.) $1,500

Burr-oak extending dining table with molded border, circa 1840. (Sotheby's Belgravia) $2,040

Regency mahogany dining table with telescopic underframe, 158in. long, open. (Lawrence Fine Art) $3,190

Early 19th century mahogany banqueting table on six turned wrythen legs, 37in. wide. (Laurence & Martin Taylor) $3,535

17th century German or Swiss cherrywood refectory table with plank top, 102in. wide. (Christie's) $6,345

Early oak refectory table with pegged joints and iron handle to single drawer, 6ft.8in. long. (Worsfolds) $1,980

19th century oval extending dining table with mahogany frame and satinwood inlay, 9ft.9in. wide. extended. (W. H. Lane & Son) $1,920

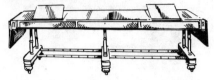

Unusual William IV mahogany library table with six hinged reading supports, circa 1835, 8ft.6in. wide. (Sotheby's) $6,100

Victorian oak telescopic table on bulbous carved legs, 14ft.6in. long fully extended. (Vernon's) $800

Early 18th century William and Mary maple and pine tavern table, 40in. wide, New England. (Robert W. Skinner Inc.) $1,800

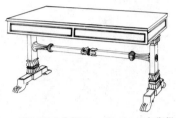

Unusual late Regency kingwood and parcel gilt library table, circa 1825, 54in. wide. (Sotheby Bearne) $9,025

Late 17th century Spanish walnut center table with scrolling trestle supports, 6ft.10in. wide.(Sotheby's) $1,650

17th century German oak serving table with two-plank top, 58in. long. (Boardman) $2,180

Early 18th century William and Mary tavern table in walnut, Pennsylvania, 40in. wide. (Robert W. Skinner Inc.) $1,000

Early 18th century South German solid walnut refectory table on shaped trestle-end supports, 4ft.6½in. wide. (Bracketts) $1,695

Mid 17th century Flemish oak draw-leaf table on four baluster bulbous legs, 4ft.8in. long. (Sotheby's) $5,850

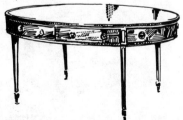

George III mahogany oval library table, 66in. wide. (Drewatt, Watson & Barton) $7,040

Victorian walnut shaped top occasional table on carved column and splayed feet supports. (Biddle & Webb) $510

Burr-walnut occasional table, 1850's, top inlaid with satinwood bandings, 42in. wide, 1850's. (Sotheby's Belgravia) $640

19th century mahogany veneered night table with twin flaps, 1ft. 7in. wide. (W. H. Lane & Son) $550

Late 19th century Chinese teak carved occasional table on cabriole legs. (Robert W. Skinner Inc.) $500

Late 19th century American Victorian rosewood tilt-top tea table, 19in. diam.(Robert W. Skinner Inc.) $450

One from a set of three Victorian papier mache tables, hand-painted with roses. (Butler & Hatch Waterman) $120

George III mahogany architect's table. (Biddle & Webb) $2,095

Chippendale mahogany tilt-top tea table with circular top, circa 1755, 33½in. diam. (Robert W. Skinner Inc.) $950

George III mahogany table, circa 1765, 2ft. wide. (Sotheby's) $4,445

Pietra Dura top table on central column, 30½in. high. (Robert W. Skinner Inc.) $600

Walnut poudreuse with panel carved top enclosing a mirror, 32¼in. wide, circa 1880. (Sotheby's Belgravia) $660

19th century French gilt metal circular occasional table, top set with Sevres plate. (D. M. Nesbit & Co.) $3,630

397

OCCASIONAL TABLES

'George III' mahogany supper table, 29¼in. diam., circa 1870-90. (Sotheby's Belgravia) $830

One of a pair of ormolu mounted mahogany display tables by Henry Dasson, dated 1886, 20½in. wide. (Sotheby's Belgravia) $9,400

19th century English Victorian fruit-wood pedestal table, 30in. high. (Plaza New York) $1,200

Mid 19th century ebonised papier mache snap-top table, inlaid with mother-of-pearl, 28in. wide. (Dacre, Son & Hartley) $370

English walnut marquetry and parquetry kidney-shaped table inlaid with tulipwood, circa 1860, 49in. wide. (Sotheby's Belgravia) $1,870

Round tripod table with painted decoration. (Laurence & Martin Taylor) $364

'Louis XVI' ormolu and marble table with circular top, circa 1880, 20½in. diam. (Sotheby's Belgravia) $5,875

Nest of three parquetry inlaid rosewood occasional tables by Emile Galle, largest 2ft. wide. (Lawrence Fine Art) $1,640

Tulipwood table a rognon, cross-banded top inlaid with a basket of flowers, circa 1890, 24in. wide. (Sotheby's Belgravia) $1,125

Verre eglomise and painted octagonal table, mid 1850's, 22in. wide. (Sotheby's Belgravia) $190

Late Victorian oval mahogany occasional table inlaid with satinwood and hollywood, 30½in. wide. (Taylor Lane & Creber) $795

One of a pair of ebonised and porcelain mounted occasional tables, 1880's, 16in. diam. (Sotheby's Belgravia) $985

398

George II mahogany tripod table with plain top, circa 1750, 2ft.3in. diam. (Sotheby's) $1,585

Gothic oak and parquetry occasional table, feet joined by a molded 'X' stretcher, circa 1840, 28½in. wide. (Sotheby's Belgravia) $625

Oak and marquetry occasional table, top inset with lift out panel, 1850-60, 30in. diam. (Sotheby's Belgravia) $385

Chippendale mahogany tilt-top tea table with square top, circa 1760, 44in. (Robert W. Skinner Inc.) $850

Late 19th century japanned display table with glazed top and sides, 35½in. wide. (Sotheby's Belgravia) $855

George II circular red walnut tea table on gun barrel column, 2ft.5in. diam. (Lawrence Fine Art) $655

Majorelle two-tiered tea table, circa 1900, 76cm. high, with floral inlaid decoration. (Sotheby's Belgravia) $820

Mid 19th century specimen marble table, base carved with scrolls, 70½in. wide. (Sotheby's Belgravia) $3,040

George III mahogany kettle stand, top with spindle gallery, inlaid with brass line, circa 1765, 10½in. diam. (Sotheby's)$4,285

Late 17th century Gloucestershire oak table chair with solid seat, 70.5cm. wide.(Christie's) $3,840

Late Louis XV marquetry table en chiffoniere with serpentine front, circa 1760, 1ft.5in. wide. (Sotheby's) $5,150

Venetian Lacca Povera occasional table, top with raised border, 29in. wide. (Christie's) $1,005

18th century red lacquer table with square top, 41in. wide. (Christie's) $8,195

Regency style rectangular occasional rosewood table inlaid with brass, 34in. wide. (Hobbs Parker)$145

Late 17th century oak communion table with carved frieze and drawer. (Lowery & Partners) $350

Early George III red walnut tripod table with tip-up top, 25in. wide. (Christie's) $6,535

Early 20th century 'William and Mary walnut and seaweed marquetry occasional table, 32½in. wide. (Sotheby's Belgravia) $740

Unusual Charles II pearwood gateleg table, circa 1685, 1ft. 11½in. square. (Sotheby's) $1,675

Small French etagere with brass gallery and marble top, 20in. wide. (Butler & Hatch Waterman) $695

Late 19th century French marquetry and parquetry tricoteuse with deep gallery, 76cm. long. (H. Spencer & Sons) $2,185

Painted and inlaid mahogany Edwardian oval occasional table with undershelf, 23in. wide. (Lambert & Symes) $895

Chippendale design mahogany snap-top table with dished top, 24in. diam. with tripod support. (Morphets) $1,130

George III burr-yew wood reading table outlined in boxwood and ebony stringing with candle slides at side. (Phillips) $4,870

19th century gilt-metal mounted mahogany gueridon with white marble top, 22½in. diam. (Christie's) $1,930

Regency mahogany circular tea table with reeded edge, 37in. diam. (Lawrence Fine Art) $820

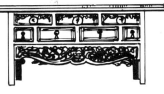

Late 17th century Chinese Huanf hua li altar table in hardwood. (Sotheby Beresford Adams) $8,295

Louis XVI ebony table de milieu, attributed to Adam Weisweiler. (Christie's) $26,180

George II mahogany tripod stand, gallery with turned ivory balusters, circa 1740, 11in. diam. (Sotheby's) $4,045

Walnut reading table with hinged velvet-lined top 31in. wide. (Christie's) $2,585

Louis XVI style mahogany etagere with gilt-metal mounts, 71in. wide. (Sotheby Bearne) $890

Oval kingwood occasional table, ormolu mounted, with brass gallery. (Lambert & Symes) $970

Dutch marquetry semi-circular occasional table, frieze enclosed by two doors, 2ft.4½in. wide. (Geering & Colyer) $865

American walnut tilt-top bird-cage table, 18½in. diam. (C. G. Sloan & Co. Inc.) $325

Giltwood Louis XVI style Sevres table, 25½in. diam. (C. G. Sloan & Co. Inc.) $2,500

Nest of four 19th century Chinese padoukwood tables inlaid with mother-of-pearl. (Phillips) $560

Mahogany and marquetry occasional table on slender cabriole legs, circa 1890, 18in. diam. (Sotheby's Belgravia) $755

American Sheraton inlaid mahogany night table, circa 1800, with square top, 32½in. high. (C. G. Sloan & Co. Inc.) $325

George III Sheraton mahogany pedestal Pembroke table, top with canted corners, 2ft.8in. long. (Lawrence Fine Art)$1,170

Dutch marquetry Pembroke table on square tapering legs. (Ekins, Dilley & Handley)$2,135

George II mahogany Pembroke table with twin-flap top, crossbanded with satinwood, 41in. wide, open. (Christie's) $1,880

One of a pair of Custom Hepplewhite tiger maple and mahogany veneer Pembroke tables, American, 20th century, 36in. wide. (Robert W. Skinner Inc.) $450

19th century serpentine mahogany Pembroke table, square legs with fan inlays, 30in. wide. (Lawrence Fine Art) $1,050

George III satinwood Pembroke table with oval top crossbanded in tulipwood, circa 1780, 3ft.2in. wide. (Sotheby's) $1,445

Chippendale mahogany Pembroke dining table on cabriole legs and ball and claw feet, 5ft.2in. wide. (Morphets) $5,665

Victorian mahogany Pembroke table on reeded legs with brass castors, 103cm. wide. (Vernon's) $225

19th century Pembroke table on square tapering legs. (Bradley & Vaughan) $1,160

Small oval Pembroke table on tapered legs, 37½in. wide. (Butler & Hatch Waterman) $305

Late 18th century mahogany Pembroke table. (Sotheby, King & Chasemore) $615

Late 18th century cherrywood inlaid Pembroke table, American, 36in. wide. (Robert W. Skinner Inc.) $900

Late 19th century Federal mahogany Pembroke table on square tapering legs, 39½in. wide. (Robert W. Skinner Inc.) $1,400

Early George III mahogany Pembroke table on square blind and open fret carved legs, 3ft.1in. wide, circa 1765. (Sotheby's) $3,295

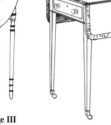

One of a pair of late George III mahogany Pembroke tables with oval tops, circa 1780, 2ft.9½in. wide. (Sotheby's)$7,320

Rare George III kingwood Pembroke table, circa 1790, 2ft.1in. wide. (Sotheby's) $3,170

American walnut Pembroke table, Pennsylvania, circa 1790, 39in. wide, open. (C. G. Sloan & Co. Inc.) $1,300

American Federal mahogany Pembroke table, top with rounded corners, circa 1795, 39in. wide. (Robert W. Skinner Inc.) $950

George III mahogany 'spider-leg' Pembroke table, circa 1770, 2ft. 4½in. wide. (Sotheby's) $1,100

George III mahogany oval Pembroke table, circa 1770, 2ft.11in. open. (Sotheby's) $3,627

George III mahogany Pembroke table with top crossbanded in rosewood, circa 1790, 3ft. wide. (Sotheby's) $1,880

George III kingwood Pembroke table with oval top inlaid with satinwood, 37¾in. wide.(Christie's) $11,130

George III harewood table, circa 1790, 2ft.8in. wide. (Sotheby's) $3,980

403

George III mahogany side table, circa 1765, 5ft.6½in. wide. (Sotheby's) $1,845

George III painted side table with d-shaped top, 47in. wide. (Christie's) $1,935

Charles II oak side table, top with molded border, 59in. wide. (Christie's) $960

William and Mary walnut side table with crossbanded quartered top, 37½in. wide. (Christie's) $2,560

One of a pair of late 18th century satinwood and marquetry pier tables, one of which was inscribed 'Belonged to Sir Walter Scott'. (Sotheby Beresford Adams) $14,630

Unusual mid Georgian red walnut side table, possibly Irish, 69½ wide. (Christie's) $5,325

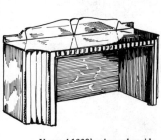

'George III' mahogany table with well figured rectangular top, circa 1880, 34in. wide. (Sotheby's Belgravia) $700

Italian white-painted and silvered pier glass and table, 48in. wide. (Christie's) $8,195

Unusual 1930's mirror glass side table in shades of peach and pink, 157cm. wide. (Sotheby's Belgravia) $470

Bugatti side table, square top and shelf covered with vellum and applied with beaten copper, 64cm. square, circa 1900. (Sotheby's Belgravia) $1,825

18th century elm side table, French, circa 1750. (Sotheby, King & Chasemore)$1,125

George III satinwood side table with three-quarters gallery and crossbanded in rosewood, 1ft. 8½in. wide, circa 1770. (Sotheby's) $5,000

One of a pair of George II painted and parcel gilt side tables, circa 1740, 6ft.long. (Sotheby's) $16,590

Early 19th century mahogany side table with one flap, on turned legs. (Allen & May) $770

Mahogany side table with triple-bowed top crossbanded with ebony, 63in. wide. (Christie's) $14,100

George II walnut and marquetry side table with cabriole legs, circa 1730, 2ft.7in. wide. (Sotheby's) $5,235

18th century mahogany side table with serpentine top and oval brass handles, 3ft. 4in. wide. (Butler & Hatch Waterman) $3,380

Early 18th century elm side table, circa 1720, 79cm. wide. (Sotheby, King & Chasemore) $2,455

Italian painted side table, top painted to imitate marble, circa 1820, 4ft.5in. wide. (Sotheby's) $1,755

George II walnut side table with molded quarter-veneered top, circa 1730, 2ft.7½in. wide. (Sotheby's) $3,810

George III giltwood side table, 122cm. wide. (Bonhams) $6,590

George II blue-painted and parcel gilt side table with breche violette marble top, 53in. wide.(Christie's) $8,785

One of a pair of Regency mahogany side tables with narrow tops, 72in. wide. (Christie's) $4,700

18th century South German inlaid walnut side table. (Phillips) $3,335

405

Early George II walnut two-drawer side table, circa 1735, 41½in. wide. (Neales) $995

One of a pair of Italian walnut side tables, circa 1815, 2ft.8in. wide. (Sotheby's) $1,755

18th century English Adam influence server in mahogany with bow-front, 44in. wide. (Robert W. Skinner Inc.) $400

17th century Swiss fruitwood side table on chamfered square legs, 64in. wide. (Christie's) $5,185

George II giltwood side table with Portor marble top on cabriole legs and hoof feet, 46½in. wide. (Christie's) $2,685

Late 17th century Swiss walnut side table with rectangular top, 41½in. wide. (Christie's) $4,105

George II giltwood side table, circa 1735. (Sotheby's) $14,520

New England Victorian walnut turtle top table, circa 1870, 37in. wide. (Robert W. Skinner Inc.)$850

Onyx and ormolu three-tiered table, circa 1891, 31in. high. (Robert W. Skinner Inc.) $1,400

Late 17th century giltwood side table, 5ft. wide. (Sotheby's) $2,410

George III mahogany serpentine fronted side table, 3ft.6in. wide, circa 1770. (Sotheby, King & Chasemore) $7,655

20th century American Chippendale style mahogany marble top table, 60in. wide. (Robert W. Skinner Inc.) $1,200

Regency rosewood sofa table, top
crossbanded with pollard-yew,
60in. wide, open. (Christie's)
$15,470

Regency rosewood sofa table, top
crossbanded with burr-maple, 59½in.
wide. (Christie's) $1,910

Georgian inlaid mahogany sofa
table on twin supports, oval inlaid
pattern to top, 44in. wide.
(Burtenshaw Walker)$1,090

Regency calamanderwood sofa
table with reeded borders, 40in.
wide, open. (Christie's)
$1,585

Georgian mahogany and parcel gilt sofa
table with splay feet and brass castors.
(Sotheby's) $1,400

Regency rosewood sofa table, twin-
flap top crossbanded with maplewood, on sabre legs, 57in. wide,
open. (Christie's)$4,760

Sheraton design satinwood sofa
table, crossbanded top lined with
ebony, 61in. wide, open. (Lawrence Fine Art) $1,085

Regency mahogany sofa table, crossbanded and inlaid, 58in. wide. (Morphets)
$1,300

George III faded rosewood sofa
table, crossbanded with satinwood,
66in. wide.(Christie's)$6,100

Regency mahogany sofa table
with twin-flap top crossbanded
with rosewood, 56½in. wide,
open. (Christie's) $2,585

Regency mahogany sofa table with
rounded ends, top crossbanded
with rosewood, 64½in. wide, open.
(Christie's) $3,185

Late George III rosewood sofa table
with rounded twin-flap top, on baluster-shaped trestle ends, 54¾in. wide,
open. (Christie's) $3,185

Small Regency rosewood sofa
table on trestle supports.
(Sotheby's) $10,950

Late George III mahogany sofa table
with rosewood crossbanding, 4ft.
11in. wide, circa 1800. (Sotheby's)
$6,830

Georgian inlaid mahogany sofa
table on twin supports, 36in. wide.
(Burtenshaw Walker) $2,960

Good Regency burr-elm sofa
table with canted sabre legs,
4ft.11in. wide, circa 1810.
(Sotheby's) $4,390

Fine Regency rosewood sofa and
games table with rich brass inlay,
3ft. wide. (Messenger May &
Baverstock) $7,850

Regency pollard oak sofa table
with twin-flap top, 57½in. wide.
(Christie's) $7,075

Fine small Regency rosewood
sofa table with black painted
border, 4ft.8½in. open.
(Sotheby's) $10,765

Regency sofa table with twin-flap
top crossbanded with rosewood,
63½in. wide. (Christie's)
$3,570

Regency rosewood sofa table,
inlaid with satinwood marquetry.
(Graves, Son & Pilcher)
$3,600

Regency mahogany sofa table,
top inlaid with brass and
ebony, 5ft.5in. wide.
(Sotheby's) $4,760

Regency rosewood sofa table with
all-over brass inlay, supported on
vase-shaped column, 4ft.8in. wide.
(Messenger May & Baverstock)
$2,810

Late George III satinwood and
mahogany sofa table, circa
1820, 4ft.11in. wide. (Sotheby's)
$5,060

William IV rosewood sofa table with two drawers and two dummy drawers. (H. C. Chapman & Son) $1,430

Regency rosewood sofa table crossbanded with satinwood, circa 1810, 4ft.10in. wide. (Sotheby's) $3,130

Regency rosewood sofa table, top crossbanded in maplewood outlined with ebony and boxwood lines, 65in. wide, open. (Christie's) $6,535

George III mahogany and satinwood sofa table with chamfered corners, circa 1800, 5ft.1in. wide. (Sotheby's) $5,235

Early 19th century rosewood and parcel gilt sofa table, 53½in. wide when open. (Christie's) $1,350

Fine quality antique walnut sofa with reeded legs on brass castors. (Lambert & Symes) $3,510

Late George III rosewood-veneered games and sofa table, circa 1800, with ivory handles, 5ft.0½in. wide. (Sotheby's) $15,470

Unusual Regency kingwood sofa table inlaid with boxwood, circa 1810, 5ft.3in. wide. (Sotheby's) $5,235

Georgian mahogany sofa table with crossbanded top and two drawers. (Christie's & Edmiston's) $2,380

Good Regency mahogany sofa table, possibly Scottish, circa 1810, 5ft.5½in. wide, open. (Sotheby's) $4,095

Early 19th century dining rosewood sofa table on central turned pillar with platform base. (Honiton Galleries) $1,010

Regency mahogany sofa table with rosewood crossbands, circa 1815, 44½in. wide. (Neales) $2,050

409

WORKBOXES & GAMES TABLES

Walnut chess and work table with quarter-veneered top on pierced lyre supports, 75cm. wide, circa 1860. (Sotheby's Belgravia) $945

19th century Oriental lacquered work table decorated with chinoiserie, 25in. wide. (Hobbs Parker) $975

Victorian games and work table, circa 1855, with hinged and swivel top, 1ft.10in. wide. (Sotheby, King & Chasemore) $760

Sheraton rosewood work table, inlaid with satinwood stringing, circa 1790, 1ft.10in. wide. (Sotheby, King & Chasemore) $1,080

Figured and inlaid walnut work table on turned legs. (Edwards, Bigwood & Bewlay) $1,005

Unusual early Regency amboyna work table crossbanded in rosewood, circa 1810, 2ft.5½in. wide. (Sotheby's) $2,810

Rosewood games table, top inlaid for chess, circa 1840, 34in. wide. (Sotheby's Belgravia) $900

Regency larchwood games table, top crossbanded with rosewood, on trestle ends, 38in. wide. (Christie's) $5,080

'William IV' grained rosewood work table, circa 1830, 15in. wide. (Sotheby's Belgravia) $1,050

Burr-walnut work table with hinged oval top, late 1850's, 24½in. wide. (Sotheby's Belgravia) $960

Mid Victorian walnut games and sewing table with fold-over top, 67cm. wide. (H. Spencer & Sons) $1,040

George III mahogany work table with concave fronted top, 2ft. 2in. wide. (Lawrence Fine Art) $840

German walnut parquetry games table, top with a central star medallion,circa 1730, 3ft. 5in. wide. (Sotheby's) $2,575

George IV mahogany rectangular work table, flaps inlaid with ebony stringings, 23in. wide. (Burrows & Day) $350

Late 19th century rosewood inlaid work table on square tapering legs. (T. Bannister & Co.) $470

Viennese cherrywood work table with hinged circular lid, circa 1825, 1ft.6in. diam. (Sotheby's) $3,745

Regency mahogany lady's work table on four fluted and turned legs. (Aldridges) $760

Edwardian mahogany inlaid work table with drawer and splayed legs. (Alfie's Antique Market) $700

One of a pair of burr-elm and mahogany sewing tables, circa 1795, 1ft. 6in. wide. (Sotheby's) $3,095

German walnut work table of globe form with domed cover, 21in. wide. (Christie's) $2,965

George III mahogany and kingwood-banded oval-shaped work table, circa 1790, 1ft.6in. wide. (Sotheby, King & Chasemore) $1,320

Victorian rosewood and cross-banded and inlaid sewing table with ormolu mounts, 29in. high. (Smith-Woolley & Perry) $510

American Greco-Roman revival mahogany games table, circa 1820, 36in. wide. (Robert W. Skinner Inc.) $500

19th century rosewood sewing table, decorated with inlay work. (W. H. Lane & Son) $505

Unusual Louis XV kingwood and tulipwood work table on lyre-shaped trestle ends, 10¼in. wide. (Christie's) $6,580

Fine Victorian burr-walnut veneer sewing and card table on turned trestle supports, 30in. wide. (Andrew Grant) $780

George III satinwood games table with square tapering legs and slender cross stretchers. (Sotheby's) $2,805

Early Victorian mahogany sewing table with drop flaps and U-shaped center support. (Vernon's) $565

Xianfeng mother-of-pearl inlaid papier-mache games table, 68.5cm. high. (Sotheby's Belgravia) $365

Mid 19th century papier-mache and mother-of-pearl sewing table with domed top, 20½in. wide.(Sotheby's Belgravia) $2,170

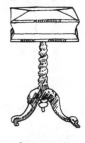

Victorian mahogany sewing and games table with chessboard top, on carved tripod base. (Andrew Grant) $485

Lady's walnut writing and sewing table. (Outhwaite & Litherland) $1,075

Rosewood teapoy on tapered twisted stem and three shaped splay feet. (Andrew Grant) $350

Biedermeier walnut work table on trestle supports and one stretcher, 25in. wide. (Bracketts)$365

Late 19th century decorated mahogany workbox with sewing well and hand-painted decoration. (Edgar Horn) $855

Charles X mahogany work and writing table with hinged mirror-lined top, circa 1820, 1ft.8in. wide. (Sotheby's) $1,555

American Federal mahogany work table, Boston, circa 1810, 27½in. wide, drawers with ivory knobs. (C. G. Sloan & Co. Inc.) $1,900

Chippendale mahogany games table, Boston, circa 1760, 33½in. wide. (Robert W. Skinner Inc.) $21,000

Victorian walnut scalloped-edge work table. (Edgar Horn) $545

19th century sewing table with rising top and wool well, 1ft.5in. high. (Taylor Lane & Creber) $490

Late 19th century Renaissance revival walnut and burl veneer sewing table, 21in. wide. (Robert W. Skinner Inc.) $600

Sheraton mahogany work table with ivory escutcheons, 19in. wide. (Morphets) $710

Victorian rosewood teapoy. (Russell, Baldwin & Bright) $655

Victorian walnut games table with lift-up top, on carved support. (Biddle & Webb) $850

Early Victorian satinwood sewing table with lift top. (Langlois) $980

Regency rosewood games table, top with bowed spindle-galleried elm end sections, 34in. wide. (Christie's) $2,905

Federal mahogany work table, American, circa 1800, 36¼in. high, on four turned and rope carved legs. (Robert W. Skinner Inc.) $500

Irish mid Georgian mahogany games table with reversible top, 31½in. wide. (Christie's) $3,465

413

Walnut serpentine writing desk with leather top, 1850's, 53½in. wide. (Sotheby's Belgravia)$2,810

Early Victorian mahogany library table with inlaid top, on stretcher base, 52½in. by 19in. (Vernon's) $1,000

Damascus parquetry writing desk, top inlaid with various bandings, circa 1900, 118cm. wide. (Sotheby's Belgravia) $610

Lady's mahogany bonheur du jour with painted panels, signed L. Lebrum. (Swetenhams) $4,870

George III mahogany tambour writing desk, top crossbanded and inlaid with stringing, circa 1790, 3ft.9½in. wide. (Sotheby's) $5,710

Early 20th century stained hardwood bonheur du jour with ivory panels of flowers, 106cm. wide. (Sotheby's Belgravia)$865

One of a pair of William IV mahogany writing tables, tops edged with reel ornament, 48in. wide. (Christie's) $2,350

Boulle bureau de dame, circa 1860, 33in. wide. (Sotheby's Belgravia) $1,590

George III octagonal mahogany library table with leather-lined top, circa 1800, 3ft.11½in. wide. (Sotheby's) $3,570

George III satinwood bonheur du jour, circa 1790, 2ft.1¼in. wide. (Sotheby's) $2,320

Regency mahogany library table with leather lined top and splayed quadripartite base, 46½in. wide. (Christie's) $4,390

Mahogany writing rostrum, circa 1860, 26¼in. wide. (Sotheby's Belgravia) $980

Regency pollard elm writing table with ebonised border and stepped bar feet, 40in. wide. (Christie's) $1,695

Late 18th century Federal mahogany inlaid desk, Pennsylvania, 42in. wide. (Robert W. Skinner Inc.) $5,000

Early 19th century Louis XV style amboyna, kingwood and marquetry brass mounted writing table, 4ft.2in. wide. (Andrew Grant) $6,050

18th century lady's mahogany writing desk with tambour top, 39in. wide. (Moore, Allen & Innocent) $3,240

Victorian mahogany writing table on turned supports with leather lined top. (Vernon's) $200

Mahogany Carlton House desk of Regency design with pierced three quarter gallery, 48in. wide. (Christie's) $3,055

'Louis XV' kingwood bureau de dame with shaped superstructure, circa 1860, 39in. wide.(Sotheby's Belgravia) $6,580

Unusual Regency mahogany writing table in the manner of George Smith, 42½in. wide. (Christie's) $7,320

19th century walnut bonheur du jour with glass fronted doors and pierced gallery. (Worsfolds) $1,916

Walnut and inlaid shaped bonheur du jour with ormolu mounts, 24in. wide. (Lambert & Symes) $725

George III library table with leather-lined top, circa 1800, 3ft. wide. (Sotheby's) $2,870

20th century walnut and ormolu mounted bonheur du jour, 32in. wide. (Smith-Woolley & Perry) $1,870

WRITING TABLES & DESKS

Victorian electroplated inkstand with writing slope.(Christie's S. Kensington) $1,100

Carlton House desk on square tapering legs.(Lalonde Bros. & Parham) $3,995

Late 17th/early 18th century joined oak inlaid writing table, 2ft.7½in. wide.(Lawrence Fine Art) $515

Walnut writing table, top of serpentine outline, circa 1870, 39¾in. wide. (Sotheby's Belgravia) $755

Mahogany writing desk with hinged top, on trestle base joined by a leather covered stretcher, circa 1890, 23in. wide. (Sotheby's Belgravia) $335

Late 19th century Second Empire mahogany bureau plat with quarter veneered top, 57in wide.(Sotheby's Belgravia) $880

George III satinwood bonheur du jour with galleried super-structure, 2ft. wide, circa 1790. (Sotheby's) $5,710

Kingwood and parquetry writing table with leather top, circa 1870, 47in. wide.(Sotheby's Belgravia) $4,390

Kingwood bonheur du jour, cupboard doors applied with book backs, circa 1900, 27½in. wide. (Sotheby's Belgravia) $1,365

George IV rosewood library table with brass bound top, circa 1815, 3ft. wide. (Sotheby's) $5,400

Fine 18th century mahogany architect's table.(Phillips) $2,990

Bertram & Sons 'Louis XVI' mahogany bureau plat with leather-lined top, 44½in. wide, circa 1880. (Sotheby's Belgravia)$1,450

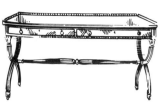

Writing table in the style of Henry Holland. (Christie's S. Kensington) $2,095

Unusual early 20th century red lacquer writing table, 116cm. wide.(Sotheby's Belgravia) $2,105

Early 19th century French writing table on tapered legs with spade feet. (Neales) $7,260

Early 19th century French bow-end writing table with leather inset, 58½in. wide. (Neales) $7,260

William and Mary adjustable mahogany reading table, circa 1830, 2ft. 2¾in. wide.(Sotheby's) $1,660

George IV brass inlaid rosewood library or writing table, 3ft.8in. wide, circa 1820. (Sotheby's) $4,580

George III style red-japanned small Carlton House writing table, 2ft. 7in. wide.(Sotheby's) $2,320

Late 18th century brass-inlaid mahogany bonheur du jour, 1ft.3in. wide, stamped C. Topino.(Sotheby's) $2,360

Victorian satinwood and marquetry bonheur du jour by Holland & Sons, 53½in. wide.(Christie's) $4,515

Edwards and Roberts rosewood writing desk, inlaid with boxwood and ivory cherubs, circa 1890, 44in. wide. (Sotheby's Belgravia) $3,860

Early Victorian writing table with leather lined top, on reeded legs. (Vernon's) $300

Late 18th century English rosewood bonheur du jour in excellent condition.(Lacy Scott) $19,510

Regency rosewood writing table, top inlaid with brass lines, with pierced lyre-shaped end supports, 60in. wide. (Christie's) $4,635

19th century American Hepple-white mahogany tambour desk, 32¾in. wide. (Robert W. Skinner Inc.) $900

George III mahogany tambour fronted writing table, circa 1800, 42in. wide. (Neales) $1,730

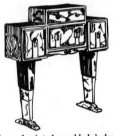

Unusual painted wood lady's desk, 1920's central section with fall-front, 117cm. wide. (Sotheby's Belgravia) $700

French boulle and ormolu writing table with inset leather top. (Andrew Grant) $1,130

American Victorian rosewood and walnut desk on frame, 22in. wide, circa 1870. (Robert W. Skinner Inc.) $450

Louis XV kingwood bureau plat with leather-lined top and three drawers, 45in. wide. (Christie's) $7,710

Oak Wootton desk with maple-lined interior, 1874, 55in. wide.(Sotheby's Belgravia) $4,740

Contre-partie boulle writing table of Louis XV design, 34in. wide. (Christie's) $2,890

George IV satinwood writing table with gilt metal gallery, circa 1825, 1ft.11in. wide. (Sotheby's) $1,910

Early 20th century Art Nouveau lady's writing table in walnut, 34in. wide, Italian. (Robert W. Skinner Inc.) $2,300

Bamboo writing desk, inset with Chinese black and cinnamon lacquer panels, 20¼in. wide, circa 1900. (Sotheby's Belgravia) $495

Edwardian inlaid mahogany Carlton House desk with brass galleried back. (R. H. Ellis & Sons) $6,225

Tulipwood and purpleheart table a ecrire, 30in. wide. (Christie's) $2,620

19th century mahogany twin pedestal writing table, 3ft.4in. wide. (Taylor Lane & Creber) $470

19th century mahogany framed writing desk with locking paneled double door, 3ft.6in. wide. (W. H. Lane & Son) $625

19th century Carlton House desk, 5ft. wide, on square tapered legs with spade feet. (Anderson & Garland) $5,950

Louis XV style ormolu mounted mahogany parquetry Harlequin bonheur du jour, 26in. wide. (C. G. Sloan & Co. Inc.) $800

George III bonheur du jour, made in West Indian satinwood by Gillows. (Sotheby Bearne) $10,890

George III satinwood and marquetry cylinder writing table, 99cm. high. (Bonham's) $8,295

Mahogany bonheur du jour with cupboard superstructure, inset with a print. (Christie's S. Kensington) $1,760

Sheraton mahogany writer's table with inclining top and side drawer, 24in. wide. (Hall, Wateridge & Owen) $2,690

Regency mahogany writing table, crossbanded with rosewood and with boxwood line inlay. (Drewatt, Watson & Barton) $3,410

Satinwood cheveret with adjustable writing slope, 20½in. wide. (Phillips & Jolly) $4,400

419

Charles II oak linen chest with plank top, dated 1649, 164cm. wide. (H. Spencer & Sons) $770

17th century Spanish embossed leather trunk with hinged domed lid and wrought-iron lockplate, 39in. wide. (Christie's) $1,140

Small Tuscan walnut cassone with raised molded edge, circa 1650, 2ft.3in. wide. (Sotheby's) $1,640

18th century Italian miniature cassone on paw feet with inlaid pattern to lid and front, 29in. wide. (Burtenshaw Walker) $1,340

Early 19th century Chinese export black and gold lacquer decorated spice chest, 35½in. wide. (Woolley & Wallis)$1,055

Continental oak chest with rising top, on raised bun feet, 3ft.9in. wide. (Geering & Colyer) $1,000

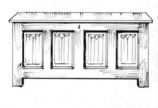

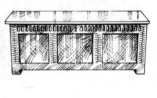

17th century oak coffer with paneled front and ends with linen fold carving, 4ft.3½in. wide. (Taylor Lane & Creber) $1,870

Mid 19th century oak and pine blanket chest or coffer with domed top, 37in. wide. (Sotheby's Belgravia)$165

Oak coffer with plain lid and thumb carved front panels, 52in. wide.(Butler & Hatch Waterman) $335

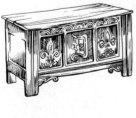

17th century oak coffer with plank top, carved frieze and paneled front, 45in. wide.(Dacre, Son & Hartley) $750

Dutch Colonial padoukwood chest with brass lockplates, 17th century, 55in. wide. (Christie's) $2,510

Early 18th century cupboard chest with original brass handles, 4ft.7in. wide. (Butler & Hatch Waterman) $1,220

16th century oak coffer with plain hinged lid and carved front, 41½in. wide. (Christie's) $1,560

15th/16th century oak coffer with carved front panel, 72in. wide. (Christie's) $1,675

Mid 18th century oak and elm dresser base on bracket feet. (Sotheby Bearne)$1,825

Small heavily carved oak coffer with paneled front.(Harrods) $920

George I walnut rug chest with herringbone inlay and brass escutcheons, and handles, 4ft.2in. wide. (Moore, Allen & Innocent) $4,320

Early 17th century Spanish walnut cassone, heavily carved and on lion paw feet, 4ft.7½in. wide. (Sotheby's) $2,685

17th century style carved oak coffer on four baluster supports with stretcher base, 30in. wide. (Smith-Woolley & Perry) $460

Early 18th century oak coffer with paneled front and sides, 5ft.2in. long. (Vernon's) $500

17th century oak paneled blanket chest with plain top, 4ft.4in. wide. (Lowery & Partners) $470

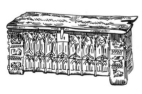  

Carved oak clamped chest with iron locks, 5ft.1in. wide. (Lawrence Fine Art) $1,590

Late 15th/early 16th century oak ark of peg construction with chamfered domed lid, 53in. wide. (Christie's) $1,230

17th century Flemish brass and leather covered coffer with domed lid, 140cm. wide. (Christie's) $1,065

Unusual early 16th century oak chest of plank construction, 3ft. 11½in. wide. (Sotheby's) $1,085

Charles II oak coffer with two-plank lid, circa 1660, 4ft.3in. wide. (Sotheby's) $710

17th century carved oak coffer with three-plank top, and marquetry inlaid front panels, 66½in. wide. (Lawrence Fine Art) $1,185

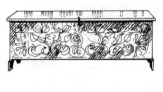

17th century oak dower chest with steel locks and brass handles, 38in. wide. (Lawrence Fine Art) $775

Oak coffer with original hasp and hinges in iron, 3ft.11½in. wide. (Butler & Hatch Waterman) $465

Late 17th century walnut storage chest with paneled front, 40in. long. (Robert W. Skinner Inc.) $350

Mid Georgian black and gold lacquer coffer on stand, 52in. wide. (Christie's)$4,285

American country pine grain bin with slant lid, circa 1810, 45in. wide. (Robert W. Skinner Inc.) $475

16th century oak chest with paneled top and sides, 3ft.8½in. wide. (Sotheby's) $1,650

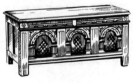

Gothic oak chest of solid plank form with iron hinges and clasps, circa 1500, 5ft.9in. wide.(Sotheby's) $12,980

Charles I oak and marquetry linen press, 152cm. wide. (H. Spencer & Sons) $1,248

17th century inlaid oak coffer with three arcaded panels, 48in. wide. (D. M. Nesbit & Co.) $970

Marquetry inlaid mahogany lift-top chest, 61½in. long, with brass banding. (C. G. Sloan & Co. Inc.) $850

German marquetry chest with arched flower-filled panels, circa 1620, 5ft. 5in. wide. (Sotheby's) $3,275

Portuguese walnut coffer with carved front panels, 5ft.8in. long. (Worsfolds) $1,430

American painted blanket chest with lift top, 42½in. wide. (C. G. Sloan & Co. Inc.) $1,000

Late 17th century oak paneled coffer with lozenge carving. (Vernon's) $600

18th century oak mule chest with paneled front, on block feet, 4ft. 4¾in. wide. (Geering & Colyer) $415

Georgian chinoiserie black lacquer chest on stand, 42in. wide. (C. G. Sloan & Co. Inc.) $5,250

Old oak strong box with three steel hinges, 2ft.3in. wide. (Allen & May) $955

Mid 18th century oak dower chest, 79cm. wide, circa 1740. (Sotheby, King & Chasemore) $935

18th century Canadian country birch and pine storage box with lift top, 43in. wide. (Robert W. Skinner Inc.) $1,200

Early 17th century plank built coffer with plain lid, 3ft.4in wide. (Butler & Hatch Waterman) $565

Oak side cupboard enclosed by two Gothic style engraved doors with brass fittings. (Clive Emson & Co.) $385

WARDROBES & ARMOIRES

North German rosewood and ebony armoire with molded cornice, late 17th/early 18th century, 77in. wide. (Christie's) $5,665

Light oak wardrobe, designed by Peter Waals, 54in. wide, circa 1930-1935. (Sotheby's Belgravia) $3,360

17th century Flemish or North German oak armoire, doors inlaid with ebony panels, 73½in. wide. (Christie's) $6,480

Late 17th century Dutch Colonial ebony and amaranth armoire with molded cornice, 44in. wide. (Christie's) $1.480

Georgian mahogany breakfront wardrobe with molded cornice, 8ft.1in. wide. (Parsons, Welch & Cowell)$1,870

Louis XVI Norman Nuptual oak armoire, circa 1770, 6ft.7½in. high. (Sotheby's)$3,775

Dutch walnut armoire with arched molded cornice and bombe base, 68in. wide. (Christie's)
          $7,520

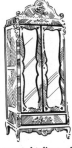

Gilt metal mounted tulipwood armoire with two mirror-glazed doors, 37in. wide. (Christie's) $2,045

Flemish carved oak armoire with carved cornice and panels, 5ft. 6in. wide. (Sotheby's)
          $4,010

Biedermeier mahogany armoire of pylon shape with stepped pedimented cornice, 36in. wide.(Christie's)
          $1,595

George III mahogany breakfront wardrobe with broken arched cornice, 84in. wide. (Lawrence Fine Art)
          $2,965

Fine ormolu mounted mahogany and satinwood armoire, circa 1900, 57in. wide. (Sotheby's Belgravia)
          $4,935

Early 18th century German stained pine armoire with molded cornice, 55in. wide.(Christie's)$1,730

French provincial chestnut armoire with double domed cornice, 18th century, 5ft. wide. (Lawrence Fine Art) $1,870

Late 18th century Dutch mahogany armoire with triangular pediment, 70½in. wide. (Christie's) $2,510

Late 17th/early 18th century Flemish walnut armoire with over-hanging cornice, 73in. wide. (Christie's) $3,110

17th century 'Aumbrey' with carved panels, standing on turned feet, 6ft. wide. (Laurence & Martin Taylor) $3,080

Dutch padoukwood armoire with molded dentil cornice, late 18th century, 76½in. wide. (Christie's) $3,190

Early 18th century Normandy armoire with carved frieze, 6ft. wide. (W. H. Lane & Son) $2,040

Three-piece bamboo bedroom suite with lacquered panels. (Biddle & Webb)$1,210

Dutch mahogany wardrobe with shaped domed pediment and three bombe-shaped drawers, 5ft.5¼in. wide.(Geering & Colyer) $3,105

Mid 18th century South German walnut armoire inlaid with various other woods, 5ft.5in. wide. (Bracketts) $2,660

Louis XV kingwood bas d'armoire with two glazed doors, 44¾in. wide. (Christie's) $2,290

Continental oak armoire, 57in. wide. (John H. Raby) $1,030

WASHSTANDS

Early 19th century American Country Federal washstand, 18in. wide. (Robert W. Skinner Inc.) $1,400

Antique Dutch mahogany marquetry inlaid washstand, circa 1790, with olivewood and satinwood urn and pewter basin. (C. G. Sloan & Co. Inc.) $3,750

American Hepplewhite mahogany washstand, circa 1800, on square tapering legs, 14½in. square. (C. G. Sloan & Co. Inc.) $850

Early 19th century mahogany corner washstand with under-shelf. (Vernon's) $450

Victorian marble top washstand on a walnut stretcher base. (Vernon's) $170

Early 19th century inlaid mahogany basin stand with hinged cover. (Vernon's) $360

WHATNOTS

Rosewood etagere with three open shelves and two drawers, circa 1840, 24in. wide. (Sotheby's Belgravia) $1,050

Walnut whatnot in well-figured and burr-wood circa 1860, 28in. wide.(Sotheby's Belgravia) $770

One of a pair of Regency rosewood four-tier whatnots, 20in. wide. (Christie's) $5,085

Victorian three-tier etagere with floral marquetry and rosewood crossbanding, 1ft.6in. wide. (Taylor Lane & Creber)$360

Attractive Victorian walnut whatnot with two drawers. (Andrew Sharpe & Partners) $695

George IV rosewood etagere supported on brass columns joined by brass lattice grilles, 1ft.3in. wide, circa 1825. (Sotheby's) $4,045

Early 19th century sarcophagus-shaped wine cooler in mahogany, hinged cover with carved finial. (Locke & England) $660

Antique American Greek revival painted cellarette, Baltimore, circa 1800, with tapering sides. (C. G. Sloan & Co. Inc.) $550

Early 19th century mahogany wine cooler of sarcophagus shape with paw feet. (Vernon's) $675

Fine Regency mahogany oval wine cooler in the manner of Gillows, 27in. wide. (Christie's) $5,970

Late George III satinwood cellarette, lid crossbanded in mahogany, on square tapering legs, 18½in. wide. (Christie's) $1,495

George III mahogany oval jardiniere with brass bands and ring handles, circa 1775, 1ft.11½in. wide. (Sotheby's) $1,400

Georgian mahogany brass bound wine cooler with two-handled liner, 16in. diam. (Lawrence Fine Art) $750

George III mahogany wine cooler with crossbanded octagonal lid and satinwood banded body, 21in. wide. (Christie's) $2,975

Mahogany brass bound cellarette on stand with bail handles, 26½in. high. (C. G. Sloan & Co. Inc.) $1,100

Marquetry and satinwood cellarette on stand with domed top, inlaid in late 19th century, 25in. wide. (Christie's) $660

Late 18th century Sheraton style mahogany wine cooler on turned legs. (Vernon's) $700

George III mahogany cellarette with oval inlaid lifting top cross-banded in rosewood, 20in. wide. (Christie's) $1,470

WINE COOLERS

Walnut cellarette of sarcophagus form with domed lid, circa 1840, 33in. wide.(Sotheby's Belgravia)$620

William IV mahogany sarcophagus wine cooler with lead lining and four paw supports.(Dickinson, Davy & Markham)$1,380

Oval Georgian mahogany brass bound wine cooler with lion mask handles. (Buckell & Ballard) $2,370

Octagonal mahogany wine cooler, lead lined and bound with brass, on square splay legs. (Boulton & Cooper) $2,195

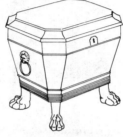

Regency mahogany cellarette of sarcophagus shape on lion paw feet, circa 1815, 1ft. 11in. wide. (Sotheby's) $1,415

George III period mahogany cellarette with rosewood crossbanded domed cover, 18in. wide. (Geering & Colyer) $1,035

Late 18th century George III mahogany and satinwood cellarette, 19½in. wide. (Christie's) $1,400

Rare Regency mahogany pedestal cellarette with bowed front and dipped top, 3ft.4in. wide, circa 1800. (Sotheby's)$2,320

18th century mahogany oval cellarette with hinged top inlaid with brass and with brass handles, 55cm. wide. (Phillips) $1,940

Early George III mahogany octagonal wine cooler, top veneered in segments, 1ft.6in. wide, circa 1765. (Sotheby's)$2,170

Mahogany sarcophagus-shaped cellarette, lead lined and supported on four claw feet. (Lacy Scott) $1,795

18th century Dutch marquetry wine cooler in square form with four inset Delft tiled panels, 21in. high. (Smith-Woolley & Perry) $390

Silesian engraved flared beaker with fluted sides, circa 1735, 14.5cm. high. (Christie's) $665

Saxon-engraved glass beaker of bell shape, circa 1745, 10.5cm. high. (Christie's) $275

German glass beaker engraved with hunting scenes. (Christie's S. Kensington) $540

Mid 19th century Bohemian amber flash transparentemail beaker with waisted bowl, 13cm. high. (Christie's) $1,595

18th century German enamelled glass beaker of tapered cylindrical form, 3¼in. high. (Robert W. Skinner Inc.)$200

Silesian engraved beaker with ogee bowl, circa 1760, 11.5cm. high. (Christie's) $910

19th century German marriage humpen with shaped base, 23.5cm. high. (Sotheby's Belgravia) $285

Bohemian Royal Portrait armorial beaker and cover, early 18th century, 19.5cm. high. (Christie's) $4,290

Bohemian overlay beaker enamelled with hunting scenes, circa 1850, 14.8cm. high. (Sotheby's Belgravia) $805

Newcastle purple and white slag glass beaker. (Vernon's)$35

Small German beaker, enamelled with a flower, dated 1721, 7cm. high. (Lawrence Fine Art) $420

Thuringian dated armorial beaker with bell bowl, 1733, 12cm. high.(Christie's) $875

One of a pair of Bohemian ruby glass bottles and stoppers, circa 1850, 24.5cm. high. (Sotheby's Belgravia) $170

Rare sealed wine bottle with flattened ovoid body, 1723, 6¾in. high. (Sotheby's) $905

Green blown glass bottle with etched decoration and dated 1829, 30cm. high. (C. G. Sloan & Co. Inc.) $125

Early 20th century one pint brown glass beer bottle with screw-in stopper. (Vernon's) $10

Red glass Barrel Bitters bottle, American, circa 1860-80, 9¼in. high. (Robert W. Skinner Inc.) $40

Early 19th century American blown three-mold aqua bottle, 21cm. high. (Robert W. Skinner Inc.) $350

Codd's glass mineral bottle with amber stopper. (Vernon's) $40

Blown-in mold bottle in green color , New England, circa 1825, 6¼in. high. (Robert W. Skinner Inc.)$900

Rare overlay oviform bottle and stopper, signed, 8¾in. high. (Christie's) $5,795

One of a pair of pressed glass bar bottles with flared bases, Sandwich, Massachusetts, 10in. high, circa 1850. (Robert W. Skinner Inc.) $425

French blown-in mold Pocahontas bottle, circa 1830, 2 x 2¼in. (Robert W. Skinner Inc.) $500

Heavily swirled glass brandy bar bottle in emerald green, 27.5cm. high, circa 1840-60. (Robert W. Skinner Inc.) $290

Rare early tavern bottle of strong green metal, 1684, 6in. high. (Sotheby's) $3,330

Birdcage ink bottle on square base, in pale green glass, 3¼in. high, circa 1860-90. (Robert W. Skinner Inc.) $50

Green glass wine bottle, 1707. (Christie's S. Kensington) $1,935

American blown three-mold bottle in olive green glass, circa 1830, 17cm. high. (Robert W. Skinner Inc.) $275

Iridescent cobalt blue bottle by Loetz with tall tapering neck, 28.5cm. high. (Christie's) $1,560

Late 19th century English carboy, one of a pair, on wooden base, 107cm. high. (Sotheby's Belgravia) $715

Serving bottle with globular body and slender tapering neck, circa 1730, 19.5cm. high.(Christie's)$820

Amber glass Indian Queen Bitters bottle, circa 1870-80, 12¼in. high. (Robert W. Skinner Inc.)$50

Quezal iridescent glass and silver overlay bottle, inscribed Quezal, 22.5cm. high.(Christie's) $1,320

Mid 19th century pressed amber glass Bitters bottle by A. M. Bininger & Co., 32cm. high. (Robert W. Skinner Inc.) $180

Early sealed wine bottle, 1729, 8¼in. high. (Sotheby's) $665

Late 19th century clear glass ammonia bottle by Clarke. (Vernon's) $20

431

BOWLS

19th century Eastern United States three-color cut-glass bowl, 5in. diam. (Robert W. Skinner Inc.) $225

Tiffany Favrile glass bowl, 26cm. diam., slightly cracked. (Sotheby, King & Chasemore) $120

Early 19th century American expanding dip mold amber glass bowl, 20cm. diam. (Robert W. Skinner Inc.) $1,900

Findlay onyx opalescent covered sugar bowl, circa 1890, Ohio, 5¾in. high. (Robert W. Skinner Inc.) $175

Bronze mounted iridescent glass bowl, by Loetz, circa 1900, 23.5cm. high. (Sotheby's Belgravia) $585

Early 20th century Irish brilliant cut glass punchbowl, sold with matching stand, 14¼in. high. (Robert W. Skinner Inc.) $1,600

19th century Webb two-color cameo glass bowl, signed, 9½in. diam. (Robert W. Skinner Inc.)$1,350

Daum iron mounted glass bowl in red glass, signed, 10¼in. diam. (Christie's) $695

Cameo glass bowl in frosted glass overlaid in pink and white, 1880's, 7.3cm.(Sotheby's Belgravia) $675

Part of a late 19th century set of eighteen Venetian bowls and stands, 15.8cm. diam. (Sotheby's Belgravia) $355

16th century Venetian 'chalcedony' bowl with everted rim, 12.5cm. diam. (Christie's) $625

Orrefors engraved glass bowl and plate, 1927, 38cm. long. (Sotheby's Belgravia) $1,125

Antique American brilliant-cut punchbowl, 34.6cm. diam. (C. G. Sloan & Co. Inc.) $530

Lalique glass bowl with star-shaped fern design, signed, 35cm. diam. (Andrew Grant) $250

Large early 20th century Sinclaire & Co. intaglio cut fruit bowl, Corning, New York. (Robert W. Skinner Inc.) $500

Late 19th century Eastern United States cut glass two-part punch-bowl, 14in. diam. (Robert W. Skinner Inc.) $1,000

Opaque blue bowl and stand, circa 1850, 27.5cm. high. (Sotheby's Belgravia) $285

Portrait overlay footed bowl in ruby glass, circa 1850, 28cm. high. (Sotheby's Belgravia) $365

Lalique opalescent glass 'sirens' bowl, circa 1930, 20.75cm. diam. (Sotheby's Belgravia) $350

Early 20th century iridescent glass bowl, marked Quezal, New York, 13cm. diam. (Robert W. Skinner Inc.) $400

Hawkes cut glass fruit bowl, Corning, New York, circa 1900, 12in. diam. (Robert W. Skinner Inc.) $450

Galle etched and enamelled glass bowl and cover, circa 1900, 19cm. high. (Sotheby's Belgravia) $1,520

Galle cameo glass bowl, marked, circa 1900, in milky gray glass, 18.8cm. diam. (Sotheby's Belgravia) $1,075

Overlay footed bowl in ruby and white, on tall pedestal base, circa 1850, 34.8cm. high. (Sotheby's Belgravia) $605

CANDLESTICKS

Glass candlestick, cylindrical nozzle set on a domed and folded foot, 2¾in. high, circa 1720. (Sotheby's) $95

Silesian stemmed taperstick on octagonally molded stem, circa 1740, 13.5cm. high. (Christie's) $305

One of a pair of powder blue glass candlesticks, circa 1835, 17.5cm. high.(Robert W. Skinner Inc.) $400

Small baluster taperstick on high terraced foot, circa 1745, 13cm. high. (Christie's) $320

Freeblown glass candlestick, Massachusetts, circa 1860, 8½in. high. (Robert W. Skinner Inc.) $220

Pressed glass candlestick, Sandwich, Massachusetts, 1830-35, 6in. high. (Robert W. Skinner Inc.) $825

Airtwist glass candlestick with fluted cylindrical nozzle, circa 1750, 20cm. high. (Christie's)$500

One of a pair of Regency ormolu and cut-glass candlesticks, 39cm. high. (Christie's)$2,140

One of a pair of Canary dolphin glass candlesticks, with petal rim cup, circa 1845, 25cm. high. (Robert W. Skinner Inc.) $300

Pressed glass candlestick in cobalt blue, Sandwich, Massachusetts, 1830-35, 5½in. high. (Robert W. Skinner Inc.) $850

One of a pair of pressed glass candlesticks, Sandwich, Massachusetts, 1835-45, 7½in. high. (Robert W. Skinner Inc.) $725

Composite stemmed candlestick on radially ribbed domed foot, circa 1770, 26cm. high. (Christie's) $640

18ct. gold mounted clear glass powder box by Alfred Clark, 11.5cm. long, London, 1901. (Sotheby's Belgravia) $1,585

Bohemian ruby-stained casket with metal mounts, circa 1860, 16cm. wide. (Sotheby's Belgravia) $545

'Bulle de Savon' opaline ormolu mounted casket with canted angles, circa 1830, 15cm. high.(Christie's) $820

CUPS & MUGS

Late 19th century Viennese enamel and rock crystal cup by Hermann Ratzersdorfer, 22.5cm. high. (Sotheby's Belgravia)$7,020

Agata peachblow punch cup by the New England Glass Co., circa 1887, 2½in. high. (Robert W. Skinner Inc.) $600

Late 19th century Viennese enamel and rock crystal cup by Hermann Ratzersdorfer, 22.5cm. high. (Sotheby's Belgravia)$7,020

Bell-shaped glass mug with reeded scroll handle, circa 1760, 11.5cm. high. (Christie's) $265

Glass mug with bulbous lower part molded with diamonds, circa 1730, 9.5cm. high. (Christie's) $290

Glass mug of bell shape with gadrooned lower part on circular foot, circa 1760, 11.5cm. high. (Christie's) $145

Two-handled jelly glass, circa 1750, 10cm. high. (Christie's)$295

Late 19th century Viennese enamel and rock crystal peacock cup, 25.7cm. high, by Hermann Ratzersdorfer. (Sotheby's Belgravia) $7,720

Northwood purple carnival glass punchbowl and stand with cups, Ohio, circa 1910, 10in. high. (Robert W. Skinner Inc.) $400

DECANTERS

Engraved decanter and stopper of Jacobite significance, decorated with flowers, circa 1760, 27cm. high. (Christie's) $310

Barrel-shaped decanter by the Waterloo Glass Co., Cork, circa 1820, 27cm. high. (May Whetter & Grose) $370

Engraved bottle decanter and stopper, 1731, with globular body inscribed with the initials RL, 26cm. high. (Christie's) $310

Engraved decanter and stopper of mallet shape, 'Madeira' in a floral cartouche, circa 1760, 29.5cm. high. (Christie's) $425

Lynn bottle-decanter, globular body with horizontal ribbing, circa 1770, 18.5cm. high. (Christie's) $385

Walnut decanter box in well-figured and burr-wood, 28cm. wide, circa 1870. (Sotheby's Belgravia) $695

Engraved glass decanter and stopper, circa 1800, 20.5cm. high. (Christie's) $545

Glass serving-bottle with square body and slender tapering neck, circa 1740, 18cm. high. (Christie's) $865

Mid 19th century green Mary Gregory decanter depicting a boy in white. (Vernon's) $150

One of a pair of engraved glass decanters, circa 1780, 25cm. high. (Sotheby's) $525

Electroplated three-bottle frame and three wine labels, circa 1850, 45.3cm. high. (Sotheby's Belgravia) $610

Blown three-mold miniature decanter, Sandwich, Massachusetts, circa 1828, 3½in. high. (Robert W. Skinner Inc.) $450

Engraved decanter and stopper of mallet shape, circa 1765, 29cm. high. (Christie's) $425

Miniature freeblown glass decanter and stopper, circa 1830, Sandwich, Massachusetts, 3½in. high. (Robert W. Skinner Inc.) $275

Engraved decanter and stopper of club shape, for 'Whiteport', circa 1760, 24cm. high. (Christie's) $310

Bottle decanter and stopper, globular body molded with 'nipt diamond waies', circa 1740, 26cm. high. (Christie's)$230

19th century glass decanter, Bristol red, with plated stopper. (Alfie's Antique Market) $165

Engraved decanter and stopper of mallet shape, with Cyder inscription, circa 1765, 28cm. high. (Sotheby's) $545

English silver-on-copper cut crystal decanter set by Betjemann's, 30cm. high. (C. G. Sloan & Co. Inc.)$700

Blown Masonic clear glass decanter with fluted bottom border, 28cm. high. (Robert W. Skinner Inc.) $175

Rectangular two-bottle decanter stand by Reily & Storer, London, 1836, 26cm. long, 28.6oz. (Sotheby's Belgravia)$980

Rare bottle-decanter with square body, circa 1730, 35cm. high. (Christie's) $685

Silver plated wine cruet of trefoil shape, 16½in. high, fitted with three bottles. (Burrows & Day) $310

One of four glass Horn of Plenty decanters, American, circa 1850. (Robert W. Skinner Inc.) $350

DISHES

Mary Gregory enamelled dish with everted rim, circa 1880, 13½in. diam. (Vernon's) $300

Boat-shaped dish signed R. Lalique, France, in frosted glass with pierced handles, 52cm. long. (C. G. Sloan & Co. Inc.)$1,200

Late 19th century two-color glass compote, European, 9¾in. diam. (Robert W. Skinner Inc.) $300

Pedestal stemmed sweetmeat glass with double ogee bowl and domed and ribbed foot, circa 1745, 14.5cm. high. (Christie's) $215

Early 20th century Libbey Glass salesman sample cut-glass plate, Toledo, Ohio, 6in. diam. (Robert W. Skinner Inc.) $1,200

Sweetmeat dish with ribbed double ogee bowl, circa 1730, 6¼in. high. (Sotheby's) $200

Early 20th century fluted oval rock crystal dish, probably Austrian, 16.2cm. long. (Sotheby's Belgravia) $1,870

'Opale' opaline ormolu mounted oval sweetmeat dish with marble striations in the glass, circa 1830, 15cm. wide. (Christie's) $505

Daum cameo glass dish and cover, circa 1900, 8.7cm. wide. (Sotheby's Belgravia) $1,170

Sweetmeat dish, shallow double ogee bowl with a band of lozenge cutting, circa 1770, 15.5cm. high. (Christie's) $50

Late 19th century Tuthill cut-glass dish, signed, Middletown, New York, 8¾in. long. (Robert W. Skinner Inc.) $350

Small baluster sweetmeat glass with double ogee bowl, circa 1725, 10cm. high. (Christie's) $865

Late 19th century Eastern United States two-colored cut-glass compote, 6in. diam. (Robert W. Skinner Inc.) $175

Lalique frosted glass dish, boat-shaped body with flat scroll handles, 1920's, 47.5cm. long. (Sotheby's Belgravia) $515

Smoked glass dish with everted rim molded with three sea nymphs, 1930's, marked 'A. Verlys, France', 38.75cm. diam. (Sotheby's Belgravia) $375

Rare sweetmeat glass with flared ribbed bowl, circa 1730, 7in. high. (Sotheby's) $285

Viennese enamel and rock crystal dish with hardstone medallion, late 19th century, 17cm. diam.(Sotheby's Belgravia) $1,870

Cut-glass sweetmeat dish, the double ogee bowl with a band of oval within lozenge cutting, circa 1770, 15cm. high. (Christie's) $85

Small late 19th century Viennese enamel and rock crystal covered vase and circular dish by Hermann Ratzersdorfer. (Sotheby's Belgravia) $1,405

Late 17th century sweetmeat glass, bowl with gadrooned lower part and folded rim, 9.5cm. high. (Christie's)$265

Sweetmeat glass with double ogee bowl, on domed and folded foot, circa 1740, 8cm. high.(Christie's) $290

Late 17th century sweetmeat glass with gadrooned bowl, 9cm. high. (Christie's) $190

Late 19th century Eastern United States cut-glass dish in cornucopia and cross-hatch patterns.(Robert W. Skinner Inc.) $225

Late 19th/early 20th century gilt metal mounted rock crystal pedestal dish, 11cm. high. (Sotheby's Belgravia) $610

FLASKS

Unusual engraved glass pilgrim flask with flattened ovoid body, circa 1860, 29cm. high, set on wood base. (Sotheby's Belgravia) $340

One of a pair of Lalique scent flasks and stoppers of tapering square form, signed, 20.5cm. high. (Christie's) $380

Galle purple flask with everted rim, circa 1900, 13cm. high.(Sotheby's Belgravia) $1,125

Bohemian Lithyalin flask and stopper of marbled glass, circa 1840, 33cm. high. (Christie's) $525

Silver mounted cut-glass fish scent flask by Sampson Mordan, 1884, 17cm. long. (Sotheby's Belgravia) $375

Bohemian enamelled glass flask, circa 1661. (Sotheby's) $12,375

Frosted glass scent flask and stopper of tapering cylindrical form, by R. Lalique, 5in. high. (Christie's)$525

Set of three Bohemian 'Schwarzlot' and gilt flasks with pear-shaped bodies,16.5cm. high, 18th/19th century.(Sotheby's) $1,430

Rare scent flask and stopper by Maurice Marinot, on spreading foot, 7½in. high. (Christie's) $2,320

Central European enamelled glass flask with pewter screw cap, circa 1750, 21cm. high. (Sotheby's) $950

Late 17th century South German ruby glass baluster flask with applied rim foot, 15cm. high. (Christie's) $2,510

French gold mounted clear glass scent flask with interior stopper, circa 1840, 10.1cm. high. (Sotheby's Belgravia) $255

440

Dutch armorial goblet, funnel bowl engraved with the arms of the Seven Provinces, circa 1750, 32cm. high. (Christie's) $820

Dutch engraved friendship goblet with slightly waisted bowl inscribed 'De Goede Vrindschap', circa 1765, 28cm. high. (Christie's) $390

Dutch armorial goblet, funnel bowl engraved with the arms of the Province of Transylvania, circa 1765, 20.5cm. high. (Christie's) $585

Saxon engraved goblet and cover with thistle-shaped bowl and facet-cut knopped finial, circa 1735, 44.5cm. high. (Christie's) $2,535

Dutch engraved goblet with thistle-shaped bowl having facet-cut lower part, circa 1760, 22cm. high. (Christie's) $875

Silesian engraved goblet with fluted oval quatrefoil ogee bowl, circa 1750, 17.5cm. high. (Christie's) $1,015

Massive Bohemian blue overlay goblet engraved with a hunting scene, circa 1860, 37cm. high. (Christie's) $865

Arnsdorf blue overlay goblet engraved by G. J. Ostritz, circa 1860, 19cm. high. (Christie's) $4,330

Large baluster goblet with flared funnel bowl, circa 1725, 24cm. high. (Christie's) $1,785

Opaque twist goblet, ogee bowl with honey-comb molded lower part, circa 1765, 19cm. high. (Christie's) $380

Bohemian pink-flash goblet and cover engraved in the manner of Pfohl, circa 1870, 32cm. high. (Christie's) $625

Plain stemmed Jacobite goblet with bucket bowl engraved with a rose, circa 1740, 17cm. high. (Christie's) $1,140

GOBLETS

Commemorative baluster goblet with engraved flared bowl, circa 1712, 18cm. high. (Christie's) $1,800

German dated two-color goblet with thick-walled flared bowl, circa 1692, 20cm. high. (Christie's) $2,510

Very large glass goblet, circa 1700, bowl with gadrooned lower part, 22cm. high.(Christie's) $1,545

Dutch-engraved Newcastle marriage goblet with funnel bowl, circa 1760, 19cm. high. (Christie's) $5,235

Pedestal stemmed goblet with panel molded waisted ogee bowl, circa 1745, 19cm. high. (Christie's) $570

Airtwist goblet, ogee with honey-comb molded lower part, circa 1750, 17cm. high. (Christie's) $155

Heavy baluster goblet with funnel bowl supported on a cyst above a ball knop, circa 1700, 17cm. high. (Christie's) $665

One of a pair of engraved glass goblets from the Imperial Glass Factory, 21cm. high, dated for 1911 and 1912. (Sotheby's) $2,025

Bohemian ruby stained goblet and cover with bell bowl, circa 1850, 51cm. high. (Sotheby's Belgravia) $1,160

Baluster goblet, the bucket bowl with everted rim, 17.5cm. high, circa 1724. (Christie's) $905

Baluster goblet with slender bell bowl supported on an annulated knop, circa 1715, 21cm. high. (Christie's) $665

Bohemian ruby-flashed goblet and cover with double ogee bowl, circa 1840, 34.5cm. high. (Sotheby's Belgravia) $755

Lauenstein goblet with waisted bowl, circa 1745, engraved with scenes of the seasons, 23cm. high. (Sotheby's) $430

Bohemian engraved and transparentemail goblet with hexagonal bowl, circa 1845, 12.5cm. high. (Christie's) $4,800

Baluster goblet with flared funnel bowl, circa 1710, 19cm. high. (Christie's) $2,140

Bohemian ruby-flash goblet, bowl engraved with a jockey astride a galloping horse, circa 1845, 12.5cm. high. (Christie's) $1,680

442

Pedestal stemmed glass goblet with flared trumpet bowl, circa 1745, 18cm. high. (Christie's) $480

Heavy baluster glass goblet with flared funnel bowl, circa 1705, 18cm. high. (Christie's) $480

Baluster goblet with tulip-shaped bowl having solid lower part, circa 1725, 17cm. high. (Christie's) $525

Mammoth cut-glass goblet with large bucket bowl, circa 1840, 35.2cm. high. (Sotheby's Belgravia) $125

Bohemian engraved color twist goblet and cover, circa 1760, 24cm. high. (Christie's) $840

Goblet of dark emerald green tint, circa 1760, 13.5cm. high. (Christie's) $335

Large ruby tinted goblet with gilt flecking and Griffon pattern stem, 37.5cm. high. (Burrows & Day) $45

Large ruby tinted and gilt decorated goblet with applied moldings, on knopped stem, 26cm. high. (Burrows & Day) $70

Baluster wine goblet with funnel bowl, 5¾in. high, circa 1700. (Sotheby's) $310

Bohemian semi-translucent Lithyalin fluted goblet, circa 1840, 11cm. high. (Christie's) $2,880

Pedestal stemmed glass goblet with hexagonally molded stem on folded foot, circa 1730, 16.5cm. high. (Christie's) $265

German armorial goblet and cover, engraved with a coat of arms, circa 1770, 26cm. high. (Christie's) $1,440

Potsdam/Zechlin engraved mythological goblet, possibly by Johann Christian Bode, circa 1735, 21cm. high. (Sotheby's) $5,950

Thuringian marriage goblet by G. E. Kenckel, circa 1730, 20.5cm. high. (Christie's) $6,720

Dutch engraved goblet with waisted bowl, circa 1745, 18.8cm. high. (Sotheby's) $855

Jacobite goblet with bucket bowl decorated with rose and single bud, circa 1750, 8½in. high. (Sotheby's) $620

443

American three-mold cobalt blue cream jug, circa 1830, 11.5cm. high. (Robert W. Skinner Inc.) $475

Late 19th century cut-glass water pitcher, Eastern United States, 6½in. high, with saw-tooth rim. (Robert W. Skinner Inc.) $700

19th century American amberina conical water pitcher, 8½in. high. (Robert W. Skinner Inc.) $175

Late 17th century glass cream jug with clipped scroll handle, 9cm. high. (Christie's) $290

Blown glass water pitcher by Thomas Caines, South Boston Glass Co., circa 1815, 6¾in. high. (Robert W. Skinner Inc.) $350

Pressed glass water pitcher with applied handle, 9¼in. high. (Robert W. Skinner Inc.) $150

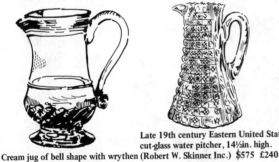

Cream jug of bell shape with wrythen molded lower part, circa 1720, 10cm. high. (Christie's) $335

Late 19th century Eastern United States cut-glass water pitcher, 14½in. high. (Robert W. Skinner Inc.) $575 £240

Cut-glass Irish jug with applied loop handle, circa 1820, 7¾in. high. (Sotheby's) $310

Early 18th century pear-shaped cream jug with clipped scroll handle, 9cm. high. (Christie's) $290

Daum mounted cameo glass jug, neck with silver-colored metal mount, circa 1900, 23cm. high. (Sotheby's Belgravia) $980

Lynn glass pear-shaped cream jug with everted rim and scroll handle, circa 1770, 9cm. high. (Christie's) $240

Silver mounted clear glass claret jug by Hunt & Roskell, London, 1857, 34.5cm. high. (Sotheby's Belgravia) $1,755

One of a pair of French champagne jugs with silver colored metal mounts, circa 1900, 27.4cm. high. (Sotheby's Belgravia) $2,340

French Empire style silver and cut crystal ewer, 25cm. high. (C. G. Sloan & Co. Inc.) $450

Clear glass jug attributed to Koloman Moser, in crackled and marble-veined glass, 18.7cm. high. (Christie's) $360

Late 19th century German electro-plated glass claret jug, 33.5cm. high. (Sotheby's Belgravia)$255

Early 18th century baluster-shaped glass jug with loop handle, 14cm. high. (Christie's) $1,000

LIQUEUR & WATER SETS

Part of a liqueur set of a clear and frosted glass jug and ten glasses by T. Laloque. (Christie's)$380

An Art Deco Bristol glass and metal decanter set, Eastern United States, circa 1927. (Robert W. Skinner Inc.) $100

Part of a liqueur set of a clear and frosted glass carafe and twelve glasses, by R. Lalique. (Christie's) $400

Brass inlaid ebony decanter box with hinged top, 26.7cm. high, circa 1870. (Sotheby's Belgravia) $685

Black lacquer cocktail set. (Alfie's Antique Market) $104

American black wooden butler holding a rack with glasses, circa 1900, 48cm. high. (Robert W. Skinner Inc.) $1,100

Albertine covered jar, New Bedford, Massachusetts, circa 1885. (Robert W. Skinner Inc.) $525

Lalique 'Druids' opalescent glass jar, 10cm. diam. (Sotheby, King & Chasemore) $670

Late 19th century American hanging leaded glass shade, 26¼in. diam. (Robert W. Skinner Inc.)$750

Rare glass globular teapot and cover, circa 1725, 15cm. wide. (Christie's) $770

Pair of Lalique glass bookends, engraved 'R. Lalique', 1920's, 19.25cm. high. (Sotheby's Belgravia) $1,640

One of a pair of Regency table lights with ormolu and glass bases, 30in. high. (Moore, Allen & Innocent) $7,200

Molded glass pomade jar in the form of a bear, Sandwich, Massachusetts, circa 1845, 3¾in. high. (Robert W. Skinner Inc.)$200

One of a pair of overlay lustres in green and white, cut and enamelled with flowers, circa 1850, 37cm. high. (Sotheby's Belgravia) $775

Engraved miniature glass urn and cover, 18th/19th century, 15cm. high. (Sotheby's) $715

Lalique frosted and enamelled glass incense burner with chromed metal fitment, 1930's, 13.5cm. high.(Sotheby's Belgravia) $305

Late 18th century architectural lunette window, 94in. long. (Robert W. Skinner Inc.) $850

Early 20th century Tiffany gold iridescent pepper shaker, New York, 2¾in. high. (Robert W. Skinner Inc.) $150

Clichy inkwell of hexagonal shape, with opaque turquoise ground, cover with gilt metal mount, 11.4cm. high. (Sotheby's) $4,165

Late 19th century amberina glass overshot basket with looped handle, 12.5cm. high. (Robert W. Skinner Inc.)$325

Lalique glass inkwell with domed body, 1920's, 16cm. diam. (Sotheby's Belgravia) $140

One of a pair of cut-glass two-light candelabra, circa 1780, 71cm. high. (Christie's) $3,360

Large Scottish school leaded stained glass window, circa 1900, 290cm. high. (Sotheby's Belgravia) $3,585

Portrait overlay lustre in green, circa 1850, 30cm. high. (Sotheby's Belgravia) $355

Galle faience cat, enamelled mark E. Galle Nancy, 1880's, 34cm. high. (Sotheby's Belgravia) $1,125

American amberina castor set, circa 1890, in plated silver frame. (Robert W. Skinner Inc.) $350

German polychrome leaded glass panel in oval mahogany frame, circa 1880, 165cm. high.(Sotheby's Belgravia) $935

Early 20th century Handel leaded slag glass hanging shade, 22½in. diam., Meriden, Connecticut. (Robert W. Skinner Inc.) $800

Late 19th century stained glass panel, Boston, signed W. J. McPherson-Boston, 15¼in. high. (Robert W. Skinner Inc.) $425

Pressed glass miniature covered tureen, Sandwich, Massachusetts, circa 1828, 3in. long. (Robert W. Skinner Inc.) $600

447

PAPERWEIGHTS

Signed St. Louis concentric mille-fiori paperweight with central dancing devil cane, 7.8cm. diam. (Sotheby's) $2,760

St. Louis clematis and jasper-ground weight, 6.5cm. diam. (Sotheby's) $530

Cut St. Louis concentric mushroom paperweight, in tones of white and blue, 7.3cm. diam. (Sotheby's) $2,070

Rare Baccarat peach weight in tones of orange and green, on star-cut base, 7.3cm. diam. (Sotheby's) $5,710

St. Louis crown paperweight with alternate, white, translucent green and translucent red threads, 6.5cm. diam. (Sotheby's) $665

St. Louis mushroom paperweight, top and sides cut with printies, 7.5cm. diam. (Sotheby's) $1,235

Baccarat mushroom weight with star-cut base, 7.8cm. diam.(Sotheby's) $570

Baccarat patterned millefiori weight set with white and coral pink canes, on star-cut base, 8.3cm. diam. (Sotheby's) $620

Clichy close-millefiori weight with tightly packed ground of canes, 7.8cm. diam. (Sotheby's)$355

Clichy turquoise 'barber's pole' concentric millefiori weight, 7.2cm. diam. (Christie's) $1,255

Clichy swirl weight with alternate lime green and white staves, 7.5cm. diam. (Christie's) $800

Clichy flat bouquet weight with shaded pink rose and white convolvus. (Sotheby's) $23,000

Rare patterned millefiori paperweight with seven clusters of
canes, probably Clichy, 7.4cm.
diam.(Sotheby's) $1,380

Scattered moss-ground paperweight, 6.7cm.
diam. (Sotheby's) $6,425

Baccarat dog-rose weight, flower
with white petals, 6.6cm. diam.
(Sotheby's) $875

Baccarat translucent green overlay
weight with four concentric rows of
canes, 6.7cm. diam. (Sotheby's)
          $1,190

Clichy green color-ground weight set
with four concentric rows of canes,
7.5cm. diam. (Sotheby's) $545

Baccarat strawberry weight, clear
glass enclosing a green leafy spray
and two strawberries, 7cm. diam.
(Sotheby's) $1,070

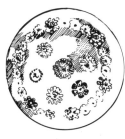

Baccarat patterned millefiori weight
in clear glass, 7.7cm. diam.
(Sotheby's) $525

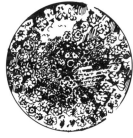

Clichy concentric millefiori weight with
outer red and white staves, 7.5cm.
diam. (Sotheby's) $430

St. Louis crown paperweight with
alternate twisted ribbons of
white filigree, 6.8cm. diam.
(Sotheby's) $1,190

Clichy color-ground paperweight,
opaque turquoise-ground set with
green canes, 8cm. diam.(Sotheby's)
          $950

Clichy color-ground sulphide
paperweight, set with a crystallo-
ceramic portrait bust, 7.3cm. diam.
(Sotheby's) $1,665

St. Louis pom-pom weight on star-
cut base, 7.5cm. diam.(Sotheby's)
          $1,665

449

PAPERWEIGHTS

Baccarat 'shamrock and butterfly' paperweight, 8cm. diam. (Sotheby's) $1,265

St. Louis dahlia weight with dark purple flower, on star-cut base, 8.1cm. diam. (Sotheby's) $1,610

Rare pansy pedestal paperweight, 5.5cm. high. (Sotheby's) $1,010

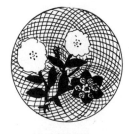

Clichy flat bouquet weight with central pink clematis.(Sotheby's) $11,000

Baccarat faceted double overlay paperweight with colored garlands. (Sotheby's) $7,800

Baccarat dated close millefiori weight, 1849, 6.5cm. diam. (Christie's) $595

Clichy faceted scattered millefiori weight with pink central rose, 7.2cm. diam. (Christie's) $960

St. Louis pear weight, naturalistically modelled, 8.5cm. wide. (Christie's) $275

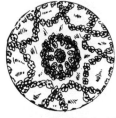

Clichy patterned millefiori weight in turquoise and white surrounded with pink, 6.5cm. diam.(Christie's) $1,025

Baccarat faceted turquoise-overlay patterned millefiori weight on star cut base, 8cm. diam.(Christie's) $1,595

St. Louis signed and and dated mushroom weight, 1848, 7.3cm. diam. (Christie's) $1,825

Baccarat faceted pansy weight in puple and yellow, 7.3cm. diam. (Christie's) $910

Clichy barber's pole paperweight, 7.2cm. diam. (Sotheby's) $1,380

Rare St. Louis butterfly paperweight, diamond-cut base, 7.5cm. diam. (Sotheby's) $920

Rare fruit pedestal weight, clear glass set with a life-like peach, 6cm. high. (Sotheby's) $1,840

Baccarat pink double clematis paperweight with star-cut base, 8cm. diam. (Sotheby's) $735

St. Louis carpet-ground paperweight in salmon pink and blue with central bust of the Empress Josephine. (Sotheby's) $9,250

Baccarat mushroom weight on star cut base, 8cm. diam. (Christie's) $640

St. Louis concentric millefiori mushroom weight on star cut base, 7.5cm. diam. (Christie's) $865

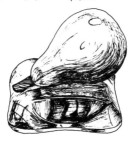

Rare St. Louis blown pear weight, 6.5cm. square at base, slightly chipped. (Sotheby's) $950

Clichy swirl weight with alternate mauve and white staves, 7.5cm. diam. (Christie's) $1,025

St. Louis crown weight with spiral twisted ribbons. (Sotheby's) $7,000

Clichy garlanded posy weight, 6.7cm. diam. (Christie's) $1,825

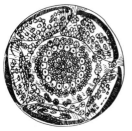

Clichy faceted patterned millefiori weight with central turquoise and white cane, 8cm. diam. (Christie's) $1,025

451

SCENT BOTTLES

Early 20th century two-color cameo glass perfume bottle by Thomas Webb, 5¼in. high. (Robert W. Skinner Inc.) $1,450

Webb cameo scent-flask with hinged silver cover, Birmingham, 1884, circa 1884, 23cm. long. (Christie's) $1,080

Burmese glass scent bottle with silver screw cap, circa 1885, 13cm. high. (Sotheby's Belgravia) $300

Bohemian transparentemail hexagonal scent bottle and stopper, circa 1840, 16cm. high. (Christie's) $295

Mid 19th century Continental lithyalin cologne bottle on pedestal base, 6in. high. (Robert W. Skinner Inc.) $300

Lalique glass bottle and stopper of ovoid form, 1920's, 28.8cm. high. (Sotheby's Belgravia) $375

Early Lalique glass perfume bottle with quatrefoil stopper, 1920's, 15.5cm. high. (Sotheby's Belgravia) $700

Lalique glass scent bottle and stopper, 1930's, 11.7cm. high. (Sotheby's Belgravia) $255

Clichy scent bottle and stopper, opaque turquoise base set with central pink and green rose, 13.5cm. high. (Sotheby's) $1,380

Turquoise opaline ormolu mounted scent bottle and stopper of compressed spherical form, circa 1830, 11cm. high. (Christie's) $585

Decorated clear glass perfume bottle and stopper, 13.75cm. high. (Sotheby's Belgravia) $200

Tiffany iridescent glass perfume bottle and stopper, circa 1900, 11.5cm. high. (Sotheby's Belgravia) $700

Unsigned Webb two-color cameo glass perfume flask, 7in. long, circa 1900. (Robert W. Skinner Inc.)$2,000

One of a pair of Bohemian overlay scent bottles and stoppers of bell shape, circa 1860, 11.5cm. high. (Sotheby's Belgravia) $285

Webb 'ivory' silver mounted scent bottle of tear drop form, circa 1885, 13cm. long. (Christie's) $735

'Bleu ciel' opaline scent bottle and stopper decorated in silver and gilt, circa 1830, 11.5cm. high. (Christie's) $820

Double overlay cameo glass scent bottle by Thomas Webb & Sons, with silver top, 26cm. high. (Sotheby's Belgravia)$830

Unusual St. Louis scent bottle in the form of a pear, 11cm. high. (Sotheby's) $855

Pressed glass cologne bottle, Sandwich, Massachusetts, circa 1840, 6½in. high. (Robert W. Skinner Inc.) $200

One of a pair of Lalique glass scent bottles, of square section, 1920's, 14cm. high. (Sotheby's Belgravia) $630

Clichy scent bottle and stopper with depressed globular body, 19cm. high. (Sotheby's) $3,570

Lalique glass perfume bottle and stopper for Cyclamen by Coty, 1920's, 13.5cm. high. (Sotheby's Belgravia) $1,030

Ruby cameo glass scent bottle with silver hinged lid by Horton & Allday, Birmingham, 1887, 11.8cm. high. (Sotheby's Belgravia) $1,330

Clichy scent bottle and stopper with opaque turquoise ground set with red and white cane, 13.5cm. high. (Sotheby's) $1,310

TANKARDS

Gilt amethyst-tinted tankard, cylindrical body inscribed in gilt, circa 1800, 5½in. high. (Sotheby's) $335

Viennese enamel and rock crystal flagon, 19.1cm. high, circa 1890. (Sotheby's Belgravia) $3,745

Early 18th century glass tankard with ribbed everted rim and applied scroll handle, 13.5cm. high. (Christie's) $155

TAZZAS

'Opale' opaline ormolu mounted two-handled tazza, bowl surmounted by two eagles, circa 1830, 23cm. wide. (Christie's) $525

Small 'bleu lavande' opaline tazza, shallow bowl with border of gilt foliage, circa 1830, 9.5cm. diam. (Christie's) $310

Opaque opaline ormolu mounted two-handled tazza, painted in the atelier of Desvigne, circa 1830, 21cm. wide. (Christie's) $740

'Opale' opaline gilt metal mounted two-handled tazza with widely flared bowl on a tapering stem, circa 1835, 14.5cm. wide. (Christie's) $370

One of a pair of turquoise opaline ormolu mounted two-handled tazzas, circa 1830, 19cm. wide. (Christie's) $2,535

Small baluster tazza, with vertical gallery supported on two cushion knops, circa 1730, 11cm. diam. (Christie's) $215

'Gorge de Pigeon' opaline ormolu mounted two-handled tazza, compressed bowl with flared rim, circa 1830, 19cm. wide.(Christie's)$2,925

Bohemian glass tazza the shallow dish decorated with white threads, 9.5cm. high.(Sotheby's) $260

'Opale' opaline ormolu mounted two-handled tazza, foot chased with a pin cushion pattern, 20.5cm. wide, circa 1830. (Christie's) $700

Baccarat tumbler, body with molded panels around an oval cartouche with flower and butterfly, 8.8cm. high. (Sotheby's) $690

Turquoise opaline flared tumbler on circular foot, circa 1830, 8.5cm. high. (Christie's) $585

Baccarat tumbler, oval cartouche enclosing an enamelled spray of flowers, 9.2cm. high.(Sotheby's) $690

North Bohemian armorial cylindrical tumbler on star cut base, circa 1810, 11.5cm. high. (Christie's) $640

Blue flared tumbler, gilt by William Absalon, circa 1790, 11.5cm. high. (Christie's) $195

Bohemian tumbler of almost thistle shape with engraved oval panel, circa 1850, 16.4cm. high.(Sotheby's Belgravia) $110

Georgian glass pint tumbler engraved with a coach and four, 10.2cm. high. (Lawrence Fine Art) $815

18th century German enamelled glass tumbler, 12cm. high. (Sotheby's) $1,380

Baccarat tumbler, cylindrical body with molded panels and central oval cartouche enclosing a pink rose, 9.8cm. high. (Sotheby's)$430

18th century engraved Central European tumbler with flared sides. (Sotheby's) $1,545

Glass tumbler of bell shape with everted rim, circa 1760, 11.5cm. high.(Christie's) $215

Anton Kothgasser transparentemail ranftbecher, Vienna, circa 1820, 11.5cm. high. (Christie's) $9,120

VASES

Rare Mount Washington peachblow vase with scalloped rim, New England, circa 1890, 4¼in. high. (Robert W. Skinner Inc.) $2,500

Iridescent glass vase with squat lobed body, circa 1900, 7.5cm. high. (Sotheby's Belgravia) $200

Tiffany iridescent glass vase, 18cm. high, 1914. (Sotheby, King & Chasemore) $2,310

19th century English deep yellow blown vase by Webb, 8½in. high. (Robert W. Skinner Inc.)$150

Satin glass mother-of-pearl vase, America, circa 1880, 7in. high. (Robert W. Skinner $175

Blue aurene decorated vase by Steuben Glass Works, Corning, New York, circa 1905, 6¾in. high. (Robert W. Skinner Inc.) $1,700

Late 19th century Burmese glass vase, New Bedford, Massachusetts, 11¾in. high. (Sotheby's Belgravia) $750

Late 19th century Eastern United States cut glass flower center in Harvard pattern, 7½in. diam. (Robert W. Skinner $375

Wheeling peachblow vase, West Virginia, circa 1890, 8¾in. high. (Robert W. Skinner Inc.)$275

Tiffany trumpet-shaped glass vase on domed foot, 37.5cm. high. (C. G. Sloan & Co. Inc.) $650

Late 19th century Eastern United States cut glass vase, 10in. high. (Robert W. Skinner Inc.) $155

Early 20th century Tiffany Favrile glass floriform vase, New York, 10¾in. high. (Robert W. Skinner Inc.) $1,000

Large early 20th century Daum Nancy mottled glass vase, France, 12in. diam. (Robert W. Skinner Inc.) $225

Free-form Art glass vase, by Tiffany, on dome foot, 26cm. high. (C. G. Sloan & Co. Inc.) $500

Early 20th century Wave Crest opalene glass vase by C. F. Monroe Co., Meriden, Connecticut. (Robert W. Skinner Inc.) $90

Loetz type sterling overlay vase with blue iridescent glass, circa 1900, 7in. high. (Robert W. Skinner Inc.) $650

Very rare Thomas Webb cameo glass vase and cover in amethyst overlaid in white, circa 1885, 29.5cm. high. (Sotheby's Belgravia) $10,650

Amberina glass vase with bulbous body, circa 1890, 18cm. high. (Robert W. Skinner Inc.) $300

19th century American amberina vase of baluster shape, 9¾in. high. (Robert W. Skinner Inc.) $100

Lalique frosted glass vase depicting two doves, signed, 1930's, 24cm. high. (Neales) $350

St. Louis shot vase with funnel bowl, millefiori base, 16cm. high. (Sotheby's) $2,260

Early 20th century Tiffany blue/purple iridescent Favrile glass vase, 30cm. high. (Robert W. Skinner Inc.) $550

Late 19th century cut glass flower vase, American, 20cm. high. (Robert W. Skinner Inc.)$300

One of a pair of St. Louis overlay Macedoine vases, bowl with waved rims, 14cm. high. (Christie's) $365

Very rare Webb 'gem cameo' vase in mid-blue overlaid with white, 1889, 25.4cm. high.(Sotheby's Belgravia) $6,290

French engraved glass vase, base marked Escalier de Cristal Paris, 28cm. high, 1870's.(Sotheby's Belgravia) $255

Small Galle carved cameo glass vase, 9.5cm. high, circa 1900. (Sotheby's Belgravia) $935

Late 19th century peach-bloom vase of slender pear shape, 32cm high. (Sotheby's Belgravia) $510

One of a pair of Egermann Lithyalin ormolu mounted oviform vases with slender flared necks, circa 1834, 43cm. high. (Christie's) $2,880

One of an unusual pair of glass bottle vases, each with an interior painting, 34cm. high, with wood stands. (Sotheby's Belgravia) $795

Double-handled glass vase, by W. Northwood, 1883, 33cm. high.(Sotheby's Belgravia) $1,035

Legras cameo glass vase, circa 1900, 24.5cm. high. (Sotheby's Belgravia) $700

Enamelled opaque-white vase painted with flowers, possibly Tyneside or London, circa 1770, 6¾in. high. (Sotheby's) $2,140

Clutha vase designed by Christopher Dresser, of flat shape, 39.4cm. high. (Lawrence Fine Art) $530

Stevens and Williams 'silveria' oviform vase with everted ogee rim, circa 1890, 23.5cm. high. (Christie's) $1,440

Portrait overlay vase in ruby glass with enamel decoration, circa 1850, 42.5cm. high. (Sotheby's Belgravia). $615

18th century Peking translucent deep red glass bottle vase, 24cm. high. (Christie's) $305

Webb ruby cameo glass vase, dated 1895, overlaid in white, 13.2cm. high. (Sotheby's Belgravia) $1,210

Tiffany iridescent glass spill vase with gilt bronze foot, circa 1900, 34.25cm. high. (Sotheby's Belgravia) $820

Galle etched and enamelled cameo glass vase, circa 1900, 9cm. high. (Sotheby's Belgravia) $560

Clutha glass vase attributed to Christopher Dresser, circa 1885, 51.7cm. high. (Sotheby's Belgravia) $1,025

Overlay glass vase of pear shape, circa 1850, 30cm. high.(Sotheby's Belgravia) $355

One of a pair of Bohemian glass overlay vases, 19.7cm. high. (Lawrence Fine Art) $570

Enamelled opaline glass vase with flared neck, circa 1850, 44.4cm. high. (Sotheby's Belgravia) $870

Ruby overlay vase with flared rim, panels enamelled with flowers, circa 1850, 29cm. high. (Sotheby's Belgravia) $310

Stevens and Williams 'silveria' two-handled vase with flared neck, 34cm. high, circa 1890, (Christie's) $840

One of a pair of cut glass vases, circa 1850, 59.2cm. high. (Sotheby's Belgravia) $400

Bohemian amber vase with hexagonal bowl engraved with deer and hounds, 20.3cm. high. (Lawrence Fine Art) $220

VASES

Cameo glass vase by Galle in blue and red overlaid on amber, circa 1900, 25cm. high. (Grays Antique Mews)$1,785

Tiffany gold/blue iridescent Favrile glass vase with flaring neck, early 20th century, 22cm. high. (Robert W. Skinner Inc.)　$475

Unsigned Webb two-color cameo glass vase, circa 1900, 7¾in. high. (Robert W. Skinner Inc.)　$2,800

Late 19th century peach-bloom bottle vase with tall cylindrical neck, 23.5cm. high. (Sotheby's Belgravia)　$315

Galle enamelled and applied glass vase on octagonal red marble base, 1890's, 28cm. high. (Sotheby's Belgravia)　$585

Unusual Galle cameo glass vase with trumpet base, circa 1900, 26cm. high. (Sotheby's Belgravia)　$655

Late 19th century Mount Washington Burmese stick vase, 29cm. high. (Robert W. Skinner Inc.)　$1,350

Galle cameo glass vase, circa 1910, 18in. high, decorated with grapes and leaves. (Robert W. Skinner Inc.)　$1,100

Royal Flemish vase in mustard yellow with ruffled rim, circa 1889. (Robert W. Skinner Inc.)　$1,400

Royal Flemish glass modified stick vase, circa 1889, 33cm. high. (Robert W. Skinner Inc.)　$1,500

French cameo glass vase, signed De Vez, circa 1905, 7¾in. high. (Robert W. Skinner Inc.) $550

Pressed glass vase in emerald green, Sandwich, Massachusetts, 1835-45, 10in. high. (Robert W. Skinner Inc.)　$600

Durand flared-form Art glass vase, signed, with gold feather decoration, 30cm. high. (C. G. Sloan & Co. Inc.) $425

Daum Nancy cameo glass vase, signed, circa 1900, 11¼in. high.(Robert W. Skinner Inc.) $900

Lalique vase decorated with pairs of budgerigars, 24cm. high. (Harrods Auctions) $505

Coralene and Rubina glass vase with flared neck, late 19th century, America, 7¾in. high. (Robert W. Skinner Inc.)$200

One of a pair of green overlay glass vases with flared mouths, circa 1860, 45cm. high. (Sotheby's Belgravia) $1,330

Daum Nancy cameo glass vase with tapering and bulbous body, signed, circa 1905, 9in. high. (Robert W. Skinner Inc.) $1,000

Stevens and Williams two-color cameo glass vase, circa 1900, labelled, 14in. high. (Robert W. Skinner Inc.) $3,800

One of a pair of pressed glass vases, Sandwich, Massachusetts, circa 1840, 10in. high. (Robert W. Skinner Inc.)$650

Pressed glass vase in canary yellow, Sandwich, Massachusetts, circa 1840, 5¾in. high. (Robert W. Skinner Inc.)$425

Burmese glass vase, labeled Mount Washington Glass Co., circa 1890, 11¾in. high. (Robert W. Skinner Inc.) $1,150

Early 19th century American footed Hawkes cut glass vase, 20in. high. (Robert W. Skinner Inc.) $900

St. Louis ruby-flashed vase, body cut with petal flutes, 18cm. high. (Sotheby's) $620

461

VASES

Blue baluster vase, gilt in the atelier of James Giles, circa 1765, 21cm. high. (Christie's) $1,650

Late 19th century Tiffany Favrile gold iridescent vase, New York, with rolled neck, 6¾in. high. (Robert W. Skinner Inc.) $1,150

One of a pair of amethyst giant thumbprint vases, Sandwich, Massachusetts, circa 1850, 10½in. high. (Robert W. Skinner Inc.) $775

Opaque opaline ormolu mounted two-handled vase on square ormolu base, circa 1830, 37cm. high. (Christie's) $585

Opaline campana vase of lemon-yellow tint with gilt rims, circa 1860, 43cm. high. (Christie's) $740

One of a pair of turquoise opaline ormolu mounted two-handled oviform vases, necks with everted rims, 34cm. high. (Christie's) $2,730

Late 19th century Eastern United States three-branch cranberry glass epergne, 20½in. high. (Robert W. Skinner Inc.) $175

Late 19th century Tiffany Favrile paper-weight vase, New York, 6in. high. (Robert W. Skinner Inc.) $3,700

Late 19th century Mount Washington decorated Jack-in-the-Pulpit vase, New Bedford. (Robert W. Skinner Inc.) $200

One of a pair of American Libbey amberina Art glass vases, circa 1900, 9in. high. (Robert W. Skinner Inc.) $950

American gold iridescent Art glass vase, signed Aurene 729, circa 1900. (Robert W. Skinner Inc.) $300

'Bulie de Savon' opaline ormolu mounted two-handled vase with waisted neck, circa 1830, 16.5cm. high. (Christie's) $935

462

Opaque twist cordial glass with funnel bowl, circa 1770, 15.5cm. high. (Christie's) $205

Color twist firing glass with ovoid bowl, circa 1770, 10cm. high. (Christie's) $1,255

Dutch engraved pedestal stemmed wine glass, circa 1750, 18.5cm. high. (Christie's) $570

Color twist wine glass with waisted bucket bowl, circa 1770, 17.5cm. high. (Christie's) $615

Late 19th century Eastern United States two-color cut-glass wine glass, 4½in. high. (Robert W. Skinner Inc.)$325

Engraved opaque twist wine glass of Jacobite significance, circa 1770, 15.5cm. high. (Christie's) $295

Tartan twist wine glass with bell bowl, circa 1770, 17.5cm. high. (Christie's) $890

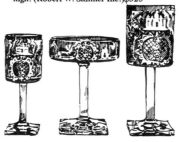

Part of a thirty-two-piece Bohemian glass drinking set, late 19th century. (Sotheby's Belgravia) $605

Engraved color twist wine glass with bell bowl, circa 1770, 18cm. high.(Christie's) $1,370

Rare mixed twist Jacobite wine glass with bell bowl, circa 1760, 17.5cm. high. (Christie's) $545

Rare late 19th century unsigned Dorflinger two-color cut-glass wine glass, Eastern United States, 4½in. high. (Robert W. Skinner Inc.) $150

Engraved plain stemmed ale glass with funnel bowl, circa 1745, 18cm. high. (Christie's)$170

463

WINE GLASSES

Opaque twist wine glass with inscribed bowl, circa 1765, 18cm. high. (Christie's) $960

Sporting opaque twist wine glass with ogee bowl, circa 1770, 15cm. high. (Christie's) $480

17th century Facon de Venise wine glass with conical bowl, 15.5cm. high. (Sotheby's) $880

Air twist wine glass of Jacobite significance, circa 1750, 15cm. high. (Christie's)$240

Irish engraved cordial glass with funnel bowl, probably Dublin, circa 1740, 16.5cm. high. (Christie's) $525

Custard glass with strongly ribbed funnel bowl with everted rim, circa 1750, 4½in. high. (Sotheby's) $115

Engraved water glass of drawn trumpet shape, circa 1758, 15.5cm. high. (Christie's) $840

17th century Venetian wine glass with waisted bowl on a hollow cigar-shaped stem, 20.5cm. high. (Sotheby's) $1,070

Toasting glass of slender drawn trumpet shape, circa 1750, 21.5cm. high. (Christie's) $430

Stipple-engraved wine glass, by David Wolff, circa 1770, 6¼in. high. (Sotheby's) $5,950

17th century roemer of green-tinted metal with cup-shaped bowl, 15.3cm. high. (Sotheby's) $1,095

Air twist Jacobite wine glass with bell bowl engraved with a rose and a bud, circa 1750, 16.5cm. high.(Christie's)$530

Jacobite air twist wine glass, funnel bowl, engraved with a sunflower, circa 1750, 15cm. high. (Christie's) $310

Wine glass with pan-topped bowl on a multi-spiral air twist stem, circa 1750, 6¾in. high. (Sotheby's) $190

Facet-stemmed Jacobite wine glass with funnel bowl, circa 1780, 15cm. high. (Christie's) $480

Engraved wine glass with ogee bowl and opaque twist stem, circa 1760, 5¾in. high. (Sotheby's) $165

Ale glass with round funnel bowl finely engraved with hops and barley, circa 1750, 8¼in. high. (Sotheby's) $405

Short Wrythen ale glass with funnel bowl, circa 1730, 5½in. high. (Sotheby's) $525

Early liqueur glass with bell bowl on folded conical foot, 5in. high, circa 1730. (Sotheby's) $235

Wine glass of drawn trumpet shape, on folded foot, circa 1740, 17.5cm. high. (Christie's) $290

Composite stemmed wine glass with bell bowl, circa 1750, 17cm. high. (Christie's) $240

Wine glass with flared bucket bowl on double-knopped multi-spiral air twist stem, circa 1750, 6in. high. (Sotheby's) $165

Mead glass, bowl with honeycomb design molding, circa 1730, 11cm. high.(Christie's) $215

One of a set of seven gilt wine glasses, circa 1770, 6in. high. (Sotheby's)$1,475

Cordial glass with small ogee bowl, circa 1760, 7½in. high.(Sotheby's) $335

Fine early ale glass with conical bowl, circa 1700, 5½in. high.(Sotheby's) $950

17th century Facon de Venise wine glass with round bowl on a ribbed knob stem, 12.5cm. high. (Sotheby's)$1,070

Facet-stemmed ale glass with slender funnel bowl, circa 1780, 16cm. high. (Christie's) $170

Baluster wine glass with round funnel bowl, circa 1720, 7in. high.(Sotheby's) $715

Dutch Royal engraved wine glass with flared bowl, 17.5cm. high, circa 1740. (Sotheby's) $855

Cordial glass, ogee bowl set on a double series opaque-twist stem, circa 1760, 6¾in. high. (Sotheby's) $190

Dutch engraved glass with thistle bowl on a knopped stem, circa 1750, 18.5cm. high. (Sotheby's) $500

465

Opaque twist cordial glass with funnel bowl, circa 1770, 15cm. high. (Christie's) $215

Color twist wine glass with ogee bowl, circa 1770, 14.5cm. high. (Christie's) $205

Engraved airtwist cordial glass of drawn trumpet shape, circa 1750, 17cm. high. (Christie's) $730

Color twist wine glass with bell bowl, circa 1770, 16.5cm. high. (Christie's) $425

Balustroid wine glass, bowl of drawn trumpet shape, circa 1740, 18cm. high. (Christie's) $215

Airtwist wine glass with bell bowl, stem with an applied vermicular collar, circa 1750, 16cm. high. (Christie's) $270

Incised twist toasting glass of drawn trumpet shape, circa 1755, 16.5cm. high. (Christie's)$425

Composite stemmed wine glass, bowl set on a double-stem, circa 1750, 17cm. high. (Christie's) $230

Baluster wine glass with bell bowl supported on a cushion knop, circa 1720, 15.5cm. high. (Christie's) $390

Lynn opaque twist wine glass, funnel bowl with horizontal ribs and stem with a gauze core, circa 1765, 16.5cm. high. (Christie's) $290

Newcastle Dutch engraved wine glass, inscribed 'Hansie in de Kelder', circa 1750, 19cm. high. (Christie's) $930

Jacobite opaque twist wine glass bucket bowl engraved with a rose and a bud, circa 1770, 16cm. high.(Christie's) $310

Baluster wine glass with a bell bowl, stem with a triple annulated knop, circa 1715, 16.5cm. high. (Christie's) $390

One of two 18th century freeblown airtwist wine glasses, 7in. high. (Robert W. Skinner Inc.) $250

Engraved balustroid wine glass, bell bowl with a border of fruiting vine, circa 1735, 17cm. high. (Christie's) $195

Plain stemmed cordial glass with pan-topped bucket bowl, circa 1745, 16.5cm. high.(Christie's)$425

Baluster wine glass with funnel bowl, inverted baluster stem with base knop, circa 1700, 12cm. high. (Christie's) $290

Engraved airtwist ale glass with two ears of barley, circa 1750, 19cm. high. (Christie's)$390

Engraved water glass with flared bowl, engraved with a border of arabesques, circa 1750, 13cm. high. (Christie's) $290

Rare engraved opaque twist wine glass with octagonal ogee bowl, circa 1765, 15cm. high. (Christie's) $570

Composite stemmed wine glass of drawn trumpet shape, stem with beaded baluster knop, circa 1750, 18cm. high. (Christie's) $350

Heavy baluster wine glass, bell bowl supported on a knop above a slender drop knop, circa 1710, 17cm. high.(Christie's)$580

Baluster wine glass, generous bell bowl set on a drop knop, circa 1720, 19cm. high. (Christie's) $270

Color twist wine glass with pan-topped bowl, circa 1770, 14.5cm. high. (Christie's) $1,550

Airtwist wine glass of slender waisted bucket bowl, circa 1750, 18.5cm. high. (Christie's) $135

Anglo-Venetian wine glass, funnel bowl with gadrooned lower part, circa 1690, 14cm. high. (Christie's) $465

Rare opaque twist engraved cider glass, inscribed 'Cyder', circa 1765, 20.4cm. high. (Christie's) $1,745

Dutch engraved wine glass with thistle-shaped bowl, lower part cut with arched and faceted flutes, circa 1760, 19.5cm. high. (Christie's) $545

Jacobite airtwist wine glass of drawn trumpet shape engraved with a rose, circa 1750, 15cm. high. (Christie's) $505

Baluster ale glass with straight-sided funnel bowl, circa 1700, 18cm. high. (Christie's) $800

Balustroid wine glass with bell bowl supported on a short plain section, circa 1730, 16.5cm. high. (Christie's) $215

Tartan twist wine glass with a bell bowl, stem with an opaque corkscrew core, circa 1770, 16cm. high. (Christie's) $370

Pedestal stemmed champagne glass with cup topped bowl on a hexagonal stem, circa 1745, 17cm. high. (Christie's) $835

Airtwist wine glass, funnel bowl on a double-knopped stem filled with spirals, circa 1750, 17.5cm. high. (Christie's) $335

Toasting glass of slender drawn trumpet shape on conical foot, circa 1750, 19.5cm. high.(Christie's) $475

Balustroid ale-flute with slender bell bowl, 1730, 18.5cm. high.(Christie's) $1,310

Engraved plain stemmed cordial glass of drawn trumpet shape, Irish, circa 1745, 18cm. high. (Christie's) $475

Four-sided pedestal stemmed wine glass with thistle-shaped bowl, circa 1715, 15.5cm. high.(Christie's) $1,905

Mixed-twist wine flute of trumpet shape, circa 1760, 19cm. high. (Christie's) $410

Baluster wine glass with funnel bowl on inverted baluster stem, circa 1705, 16cm. high. (Christie's) $570

Baluster cordial glass with bell bowl, circa 1720, 16.5cm. high. (Christie's) $715

Airtwist toasting glass of drawn trumpet shape, circa 1750, 19cm. high. (Christie's) $430

Baluster wine glass with bell bowl on triple annulated knop, circa 1730, 16.5cm. high.(Christie's) $590

Baluster wine glass supported on triple annulated knop terminating on a domed foot, circa 1715, 15cm. high. (Christie's) $760

Toasting glass of slender drawn trumpet shape, circa 1750, 21.5cm. high. (Christie's) $340

Engraved water-glass with triple ogee bowl, Newcastle, circa 1750, 12cm. high. (Christie's) $170

Rare Beilby color twist cordial glass with small funnel bowl, circa 1770, 17.5cm. high. (Christie's) $7,200

Kit-Kat wine glass of drawn trumpet shape, circa 1745, 17.5cm. high. (Christie's) $285

Rare canary yellow color twist ale glass. (Phillips) $1,950

Small baluster wine glass with funnel bowl, circa 1715, 12cm. high. (Christie's) $215

Ale flute with slender trumpet bowl, circa 1750, (Sotheby's) $525

Baluster toastmaster's glass, thick conical bowl, supported on a quadruple annulated knop, circa 1725, 13.5cm. high. (Christie's) $430

Dutch engraved Newcastle wine glass showing a hen and her chicks, circa 1750, 18cm. high. (Christie's) $1,905

Airtwist wine glass with bell bowl, stem with central coil collar, circa 1750, 18.5cm. high. (Christie's) $1,905

16th century Venetian goblet, bowl with everted rim, 14.5cm. high. (Christie's) $2,040

Mercury-twist wine glass of drawn trumpet shape, circa 1750, 17cm. high. (Christie's) $260

Engraved plain stemmed ale glass of Jacobite significance, circa 1750, 18cm. high. (Christie's) $140

Pedestal stemmed champagne glass, rounded bowl with shallow pan-topped rim, circa 1745, 14.5cm. high. (Christie's) $155

Rare Beilby color twist cordial glass engraved with leaves, circa 1770, 17.5cm. high. (Christie's) $4,800

Baluster cordial glass with flared bowl, circa 1720, 7in. high. (Sotheby's) $905

Mercury-twist wine glass with pan-topped bowl, stem with two entwined spirals, circa 1750, 16.5cm. high. (Christie's) $120

Baluster wine glass with waisted bowl set on a wide collar above a plain stem, circa 1725, 16cm. high. (Christie's) $240

Engraved light baluster wine glass with trumpet-shaped bowl, Newcastle, circa 1750, 18.5cm. high. (Christie's) $760

Engraved facet-stemmed wine glass with funnel bowl, circa 1780, 16cm. high. (Christie's) $430

Rare George III 22ct. gold fox mask snuff box by John Allen, London, 1804, 3¼in. long, 4oz.1dwt. (Sotheby's) $10,945

English gold and mother-of-pearl snuff box, circa 1730, 8.5cm. wide. (Sotheby's) $1,475

18ct. gold rectangular cigarette case, engraved 'Cartier London', 4.1oz., 7.7cm. long.(Sotheby's Belgravia) $1,705

French gold and enamel scent flask, centered with enamel plaques and set with pearls, circa 1860, 12.4cm. high. (Sotheby's Belgravia) $1,590

Victorian 18ct. gold christening mug decorated with flower sprays by Hunt & Roskell. (Hobbs Parker) $6,220

French clear glass scent bottle with parcel gilt mounts, circa 1850, 13.3cm. high. (Sotheby's Belgravia) $560

Circular gold mounted Vernis Martin box, circa 1780, 6.6cm. diam. (Sotheby's) $380

Fine gold and enamelled circular desk clock by Faberge, St. Petersburg, 1899-1908, 12.2cm. diam.(Sotheby's) $19,040

French circular engine-turned gold snuff box by Pierre-Lucien Joittot, Paris, 1785. (Christie's) $3,600

14ct. yellow gold and cut crystal flask by Tiffany & Co., 12.5cm. high. (C. G. Sloan & Co. Inc.) $800

Austrian enamelled gold figure of a beerdrinker, 120mm. high. (Christie's) $2,520

Louis XV vari-colored gold fruit knife by Mathieu Coiny, Paris, 1761, 117mm. long. (Christie's) $4,080

Early 19th century Swiss gold and enamel snuff box, 8.6cm. wide.(Sotheby's $2,025

Austrian enamelled gold caricature of a grape harvester, 80mm. high. (Christie's) $3,360

Small early 19th century rectangular gold musical snuff box, French or Swiss, 57mm. long. (Christie's) $6,000

English gold and coral teether, circa 1735, 11.5cm. high. (Sotheby's) $1,840

Rolled gold watch key, oval swivel key set with a panel of chalcedony, 61.5mm. long. (Sotheby's Belgravia) $370

French gold sealing wax case with red enamel, Paris, circa 1783, 120mm. long. (Christie's) $1,200

George II gold and lapis lazuli snuff box, circa 1750, 60mm. long.(Christie's) $5,760

Narrow rectangular gold snuff box, possibly Prague, 1796, 90mm. long. (Christie's) $2,280

Rare George III 22ct. gold Irish provincial freedom box, 3in., circa 1795, 5oz.2dwt. (Sotheby's) $17,850

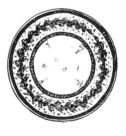

Indian gold presentation goblet with leaf-chased stem, 10.4oz., circa 1850, 12.5cm. high.(Sotheby's Belgravia) $5,450

18th century gold mounted cut-glass scent bottle, 83mm. high.(Christie's) $790

Gold and enamel circular miniature frame by Faberge, St. Petersburg, 1899-1908, 8.2cm. diam. (Sotheby's) $7,615

Silver gilt mounted carved pink hardstone desk seal by A. Fourrier, 1928, 7.4cm. long. (Sotheby's Belgravia) $375

Early 20th century gold mounted hardstone casket, lid inset with a small timepiece. (Sotheby's Belgravia) $6,160

Mottled pink and black agate rectangular etui. (Christie's S. Kensington) $350

Late 19th century enamelled and gemset silver gilt mounted oval agate dish, 15.6cm. long. (Sotheby's Belgravia) $610

Large pink coral group of a lady leaning back against a tree, surrounded by five climbing boys, 46.3cm. wide. (Christie's) $7,050

Solid agate butter boat of silver shape, circa 1740, 10cm. high. (Sotheby's) $2,430

Early 20th century Austrian-Hungarian enamel, hardstone and gemset bon bon dish, 10.7cm. long. (Sotheby's Belgravia) $1,640

Hardstone jug and six small cups and saucers, mid 19th century. (Sotheby's Belgravia) $780

Large coral group of three girls, slightly damaged, on wood stand, 23cm. high. (Christie's) $4,230

19th century gold mounted bloodstone desk seal, 83mm. long. (Christie's) $1,010

Late 19th century Chinese carved soapstone figure, graduated colour from gray to rust. (Robert W. Skinner Inc.) $600

Saltglaze agateware figure of a seated cat, restored, circa 1755, 12cm. high. (Christie's) $185

472

17th/18th century rhinoceros horn libation cup of flared octagonal section, 5¼in. high. (Sotheby's) $890

Late 17th century French oval horn snuff box, lid pressed with view of Rouen, 13.2cm. wide. (Sotheby's) $570

One of two interesting rhinoceros horn libation cups, 11cm. and 9cm. high. (H. Spencer & Sons) $705

Rare early 19th century rhinoceros horn ryton carved with flowers, 32cm. long. (Christie's)$710

Silver mounted tapering cylindrical horn jug and two beakers by Chawner & Co., London, 1875. (Sotheby's Belgravia) $750

Victorian silver mounted ceremonial horn, Edinburgh, 1885, 38cm. long. (Sotheby's)$725

Hornbill flattened rounded square bottle carved on both sides and with matching stopper. (Christie's) $285

Cow-horn armchair, back and sides made from three pairs of cow horns, circa 1900. (Sotheby's Belgravia) $350

Early 19th century shaped powder horn inset with mother-of-pearl and ebony, 20.5cm. long. (Robert W. Skinner Inc.) $90

Volunteer Baker Rifle powder flask, circa 1798, 13½in. long. (Wallis & Wallis) $545

Large 18th century rhinoceros horn libation cup, 10cm. high. (Sotheby's) $1,135

18th century military powder horn with brass nozzle cap, 15in. long. (Wallis & Wallis) $80

INROS

Late 18th/early 19th century inro in gold and silver hiramakie, signed Kaji-kawa saku. (Christie's) $1,300

19th century Japanese five-drawer inro in inlaid wooden case, 7.5cm. long. (Robert W. Skinner Inc.) $275

Late 18th/early 19th century four-case inro decorated in gold, black and red hiramakie, signed Chikahide.(Christie's) $1,140

Unusual late 18th/early 19th century five-case red lacquer inro, signed Koma Yasutada. (Christie's) $4,010

Unusual 19th century four-case inro, slightly worn, un-signed. (Sotheby's) $635

Mid 19th century Japan-ese four-case inro inlaid with mother-of-pearl, 7.5cm. high. (Robert W. Skinner Inc.)$175

18th century small four-case inro decorated with five workers, the reverse with two fans, unsigned. (Sotheby's) $205

18th century single-case inro of wide rounded form, unsigned. (Sotheby's) $430

Four-case Kinji inro, signed Jokasai, with attached cor-nelian bead ojime. (Christie's) $2,165

Late 18th/early 19th cen-tury four-case inro deco-rated in gold, silver and red hiramakie, unsigned. (Christie's) $990

Rare perfume container in the form of a sheath inro, in polished wood with staghorn runners, by the Asakusa school. (Sotheby's) $215

Unusual 19th century circu-lar three-case red lacquer inro, unsigned, with wood and ivory bead ojime. (Christie's) $1,480

Five-case inro decorated in gold and gray hiramakie and takamakie, signed Yoyusai. (Christie's) $1,060

19th century slender six-case inro decorated in gold hiramakie, signed Kajikawa. (Christie's) $1,005

19th century unsigned five-case cylindrical inro decorated in gold, silver and red hiramakie and okibirame. (Christie's) $1,300

Early 19th century Japanese four-case black lacquer inro with yellow and orange ojime bead, 7cm. long. (Robert W. Skinner Inc.) $700

Early 19th century two-case inro, unsigned, decorated in different layers of colored lacquer. (Christie's) $730

Four-case gold lacquer inro and carved netsuke and ojime, signed. (C. G. Sloan & Co. Inc.)$1,850

Early 17th century four-case inro decorated with a tsuitate and byobu, unsigned. (Sotheby's) $240

Early 19th century Japanese four-case dull brown lacquer inro, signed, 9cm. long. (Robert W. Skinner Inc.) $525

Three-case inro decorated with coiled dragons, signed Koma Yasuaki saku, early 19th century. (Christie's) $850

Fine five-case lacquer inro with square netsuke attached, signed Harumasa saku. (Lawrence Fine Art) $440

Early 19th century four-case inro, signed Shozan saku and kao.(Christie's) $685

19th century four-case inro, signed Shokasai, inlaid in ivory.(Christie's) $820

INSTRUMENTS

Early James Watt duplicating machine in mahogany box with brass rollers, circa 1825, 44.5cm. wide. (Sotheby's Belgravia) $475

Pair of 17th century brass tongs, 13.5cm. long. (Christie's) $455

18th century German cased engraved brass and steel equinoctial sundial, 6cm. square. (Robert W. Skinner Inc.) $850

Early 19th century ebony octant by Richardson, London, with ivory scale, 29cm. radius, in oak-case. (Sotheby's Belgravia) $525

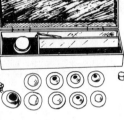

18th century ivory screw barrel pocket microscope, 185mm. long.(Sotheby's) $2,340

Brass telescope, stand and case by C. G. King, Boston, circa 1845. (Robert W. Skinner Inc.) $700

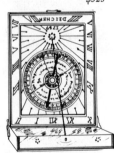

German fruitwood diptych dial, signed and dated Deicher 1789, 10.7cm. high. (Christie's) $1,555

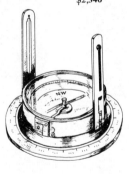

Late 19th century Scottish brass miner's dial by Fraser, London, 25.5cm. wide. (Sotheby's Belgravia) $905

Wakefield 56lb bell-shaped beam scale measure in fitted mahogany case. (Christie's) $595

Early 19th century Carpenter 'Cary type' pocket microscope and slides. (Sotheby's Belgravia) $525

Pivoted detent chronometer movement by Louis Berthoud, 70mm. diam. (Sotheby's) $11,700

Unusual Coombs Boynton 'instantaneous light' apparatus, circa 1835, 9cm. high. (Sotheby's Belgravia) $405

Early 18th century silver Butterfield dial by Macquart, Paris, 65mm. long, signed. (Sotheby's) $1,195

Early 18th century three-draw telescope with tooled board tubes, ebony mounts, 20.3cm. long. (Phillips) $760

American Columbia typewriter with circular letter index selection, circa 1895, 24.6cm. wide. ((Sotheby's Belgravia) $2,105

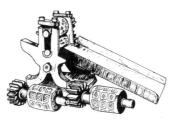

Bradford bell-metal and brass beam by W. & T. Avery Ltd., Birmingham. (Christie's) $420

English sweet-making machine in cast-iron, with brass scoop and copper pan, circa 1880's. (Sotheby's Belgravia) $420

Late 19th century Wheeler & Wilson type Britannia sewing machine. (Christie's) $1,495

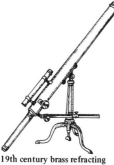

19th century brass refracting telescope with sighting tube and steadying bar, with mahogany case, 98cm. long.(Phillips) $905

English brass universal equinoctial ring dial, unsigned, 8.8cm. diam. (Christie's) $860

Late 19th century Ross brass monocular microscope, 28cm. high, in mahogany case. (Sotheby's Belgravia) $235

Bell-metal and brass beam, inscribed Morley, by W. & T. Avery Ltd., Birmingham. (Christie's) $335

Astronomical telescope by Newton & Co., London, with single pull and leather covered barrel. (W. H. Lane & Son) $600

Late 19th century Cary pocket sextant with silvered scale, 10cm. radius. (Sotheby's Belgravia) $1,310

INSTRUMENTS

Set of letter scales with brass weights, circa 1930. (Laurence & Martin Taylor) $80

Brass pocket microscope with racked pillar in mahogany box, 19cm. wide. (Lawrence Fine Art) $210

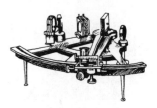

19th century brass sextant by Dolland, London in mahogany case. (Phillips) $950

Malby's terrestrial globe with steel support, dated Dublin, 1895, 18in. diam. (Sotheby's Belgravia) $310

Ship's brass telegraph, 45in. high. (Coles, Knapp & Kennedy) $240

Late George III mahogany terrestrial globe by Bardin, 1ft.1in. wide. (Sotheby's) $4,095

Fine brass refracting telescope with white enamelled barrel, inscribed T. Cooke & Sons, York. (Lawrence Fine Art) $1,755

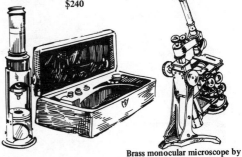

Early 19th century brass field microscope of cylindrical telescopic form, 30cm. high. (Taylor, Lane & Creber) $255

Brass monocular microscope by Ross, 50cm. high, in mahogany case. (Sotheby, King & Chasemore) $1,010

One of a pair of George IV mahogany table globes by Cary, one celestial and one terrestrial, circa 1820, 2ft.1in. high. (Sotheby's) $6,665

Late 19th century mahogany cased 48-hour chronometer by Arnold & Dent, London. (Locke & England) $2,420

English zoetrope with twelve printed strips, 1880's, 37cm. high. (Sotheby's Belgravia) $475

478

English Cary brass sextant, circa 1915, with silvered scale, 20cm. radius. (Sotheby's Belgravia) $475

18th century brass graphometer by Baradelle of Paris, 242mm. diam. (Sotheby's) $1,515

Early Sholes & Gliddon Remington typewriter. (Sotheby's Belgravia) $5,235

Brass theodolite, signed Cooke, Troughton & Simms, in fitted case, 29.8cm. high. (Lawrence Fine Art) $210

Late 19th century American double pan scales with knife blade balance, 75cm. high. (Robert W. Skinner Inc.) $240

George III mahogany zograscope with box viewer, circa 1795, 24in. wide. (Sotheby Bearne) $700

Eight-day marine chronometer by Webster, London. (Lalonde Bros. & Parham) $2,725

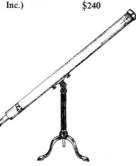

2¾in. Dolland brass refracting telescope on stand, signed, mid 19th century, length of tube 109cm. (Sotheby's Belgravia) $1,420

Frith's cosmoscope viewer in burr-walnut case inlaid with mother-of-pearl, circa 1870, 42.5cm. wide. (Sotheby's Belgravia) $525

18th century library globe by Loisel, Paris, dated 1787, 48cm. high. (Sotheby's) $980

Ship's brass telegraph, 42in. high. (Coles, Knapp & Kennedy) $240

Regency mahogany celestial globe by J. & W. Cary, London, 1816, 1ft.6in. diam. (Sotheby's) $4,095

George III enamelled gilt metal mounted mirror and magnifying glass, circa 1760, 26.6cm. long. (Christie's) $2,000

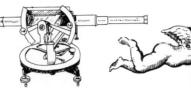

Early 20th century Troughton & Simms theodolite, 27cm. long, in mahogany case. (Sotheby's Belgravia) $655

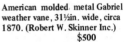

American molded metal Gabriel weather vane, 31½in. wide, circa 1870. (Robert W. Skinner Inc.) $500

Brass mounted Dobereiner lamp, circa 1830, 25cm. high. (Sotheby's) $610

Mid 19th century English brass miner's dial by Bate, London, 20cm. wide. (Sotheby's Belgravia) $240

19th century brass microscope by Ladd with chain adjustment. (Phillips) $380

W. Watson brass monocular microscope, circa 1920, 30.5cm. high. (Sotheby's Belgravia) $570

Good eight-day marine chronometer, diam. of bezel 13cm. (Sotheby's) $5,215

Late George III mahogany terrestrial globe by Bardin. (Sotheby's) $4,165

Circular brass sundial by John Rowley, circa 1720, 30.5cm. diam.(Sotheby's)$820

Terrestrial globe by W. & A. K. Johnston Ltd., on pine stand with turned legs, 1.22m. diam. overall. (Phillips)$1,545

Late 17th century brass ring dial, 5.3cm. diam., with chased suspension ring. (Phillips) $810

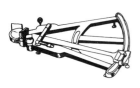

Large late 18th century ebony octant by Dring & Fage, London, radius 387mm. (Sotheby's) $2,575

Unusual early silver-cased pocket sundial, signed Butterfield, Paris. (Sotheby, King & Chasemore) $690

19th century brass six-draw telescope, mahogany outer tube and dust covers. (Phillips)$215

Mid 19th century Culper-type brass monocular microscope, 38cm. high. (Sotheby's Belgravia) $1,000

Good two-day marine chronometer by A. Johannsen, diam. of bezel 123mm. (Sotheby's) $1,685

English brass pocket microscope with racked column, circa 1825, 13cm. wide. (Sotheby's Belgravia) $355

Mid 19th century Edmund Wheeler brass monocular microscope, 35cm. high. (Sotheby's Belgravia) $280

Eight-day marine chronometer by Morris Tobias, diam. of bezel 135mm. (Sotheby's) $3,045

Brass monocular microscope, circa 1880, 43cm. high. (Sotheby's Belgravia) $355

Mid 18th century brass ring dial by Claude Langlois, 100mm. diam. (Sotheby's) $2,455

Early 19th century terrestrial globe by Cary, London, 61cm. high. (Churchman's) $2,880

Rare Sholes and Glidden typewriter. (Phillips) $3,170

INSTRUMENTS

Silver Butterfield dial, unsigned, in leather case, 6.7cm. greater dimension. (Christie's) $1,385

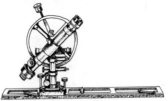

Early 20th century Swiss brass transit alidade by Kern & Co., 43cm. long. (Sotheby's Belgravia) $835

German silvered and gilt metal universal equinoctial dial by Johann Willebrend, with leather case. (Christie's) $2,985

Troughton & Simms brass Y-type theodolite, circa 1880, 28cm. high, in mahogany case. (Sotheby's Belgravia) $905

Early 18th century mahogany cased ship's compass by Thomas Wright, diam. of bezel 134mm. (Sotheby's) $690

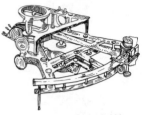

Early 19th century anodised brass double frame sextant by Worthington, London, 214mm. radius. (Sotheby's) $1,665

Mid 19th century English mahogany zograscope, 60cm. high, column with height adjustment. (Sotheby's Belgravia) $280

Britannia Wheeler & Wilson lockstitch type sewing machine with cast iron treadle table. (Christie's S. Kensington) $1,220

Chadburns brass ship's telegraph circa 1930, 115.5cm. high. (Sotheby's Belgravia) $855

Pratts ethyl gasolene lighter fuel dispenser. (Phillips) $180

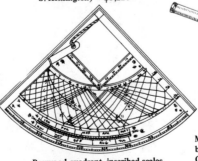

Boxwood quadrant, inscribed scales with punched figures, 11.4cm. radius. (Christie's) $1,340

Mid 19th century English 2½in. brass refracting telescope by Gilbert & Gilkerson, London, tube 29in. long. (Sotheby's Belgravia) $980

482

Ivory tablet dial by George
Reinmann, 1550, 68mm. x
52mm. (Sotheby's)
$3,745

19th century draughtman's brass
planometer by Sang, overall
length 380mm. (Sotheby's)
$840

French silver Butterfield dial,
signed Butterfield A Paris,
fitted shagreen case, 5.3cm.
greater dimension.(Christie's)
$1,195

Circular bronze sundial by T. Wright,
1746, 350mm. diam. (Sotheby's)
$1,330

Mid 19th century Casella brass
transit theodolite, 20cm. high,
in mahogany case. (Sotheby's
Belgravia) $835

Mid 19th century altitude instrument with hinged lignum vitae
members, 49.5cm. long.(Sotheby's
Belgravia) $260

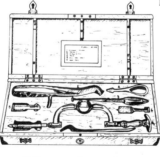

Early 19th century brass microscope by Dolland, London, in
mahogany case with ivory slides
and accessories. (Phillips)
$1,330

Italian surgeon's trepanning
instrument set by Cassetta,
1897, 36cm. wide. (Sotheby's
Belgravia) $310

18th century brass pillar dial,
inscribed Thomas Miller, Knowle,
9.5cm. high. (Phillips)
$1,000

French silver Butterfield type dial
by Chapotot, Paris, in leather
case, 7cm. greater dimension.
(Christie's) $3,110

American typewriter by The
American Typewriter Co., circa
1895, 25cm. wide. (Sotheby's
Belgravia) $525

German silvered and gilt metal
universal equinoctial dial by
And. Vogl, 7.2cm. greater
dimensions. (Christie's)
$1,195

IRON & STEEL

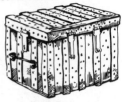

17th century German iron strong-box with nailed strapwork lid, 63.4cm. wide. (Christie's) $1,230

19th century New England tin Canada goose decoy, painted dark gray, 21½in. long. (Robert W. Skinner Inc.) $200

Early 16th century French late Gothic wrought iron casket on four buttress feet, 10in. long. (Sotheby's) $1,540

Belgian cast-iron stove 'Westminster', circa 1920, 27½in. high, finished in green enamel. (Sotheby's Belgravia) $655

Early 19th century American cast-iron tilting kettle, 14in. high. (Robert W. Skinner Inc.) $175

Cast-iron group of a Cossack kissing his sweetheart goodbye, 1880's, 38cm. high. (Sotheby's Belgravia) $170

One of a pair of cast-iron torchere stands, fitted for electricity, 4ft. 10in. high. (Lawrence Fine Art) $140

Mid 19th century cast-iron garden urn on two plinths, 104cm. high overall. (Sotheby's Belgravia) $575

One of a pair of early 18th century Austrian wrought iron candelabra, 26in. high. (Sotheby's) $1,215

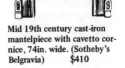

Mid 19th century cast-iron mantelpiece with cavetto cornice, 74in. wide. (Sotheby's Belgravia) $410

Wrought iron console table by Edgar Brandt, with black glass top, 112cm. wide, circa 1925. (Sotheby's Belgravia) $890

Belgian cast-iron stove in dusty-pink vitreous enamel, circa 1925, 19in. high. (Sotheby's Belgravia) $105

484

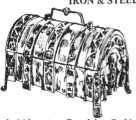

Mid 16th century Nuremberg steel casket etched on all sides, 11¾in. long. (Sotheby's) $4,265

One of a pair of 19th century cast-iron garden urns with fluted socles, 2ft.6in. diam. (Sotheby's) $1,415

Early 16th century French late Gothic iron casket with domed lid and swing handle, 10¼in. long. (Sotheby's) $4,265

Late 18th century American wrought iron skillet with rat-tail handle, 33¼in. long. (Robert W. Skinner Inc.)$125

Belgian cast-iron conservatory stove, 36in. high, circa 1910. (Sotheby's Belgravia)$375

Belgian cast-iron bow-fronted stove in blue/gray vitreous enamel, circa 1905, 29in. high. (Sotheby's Belgravia) $220

Cast-iron Scandinavian pot stove, marked Aadals Brug No. 77, circa 1890's, 72in. high. (Sotheby's Belgravia) $610

One of a set of twenty-two mid 19th century parcel gilt cast-iron panels, each cast with cherries and leaves. (Sotheby's Belgravia) $1,520

One of an unusual pair of tall six-light candelabra, circa 1900, 80in. high. (Sotheby's Belgravia) $1,055

18th century Spanish wrought iron well head with lily finial, 72in. high. (Robert W. Skinner Inc.) $800

Mid 19th century American metal rooster weathervane, 24in. high. (Robert W. Skinner Inc.) $1,500

Belgian cast-iron stove 'Derby', finished in dark green enamel, circa 1910, 43in. high. (Sotheby's Belgravia)$560

IVORY

Silver mounted tusk vesta box, Birmingham, 1909, 8.5cm. high. (Sotheby's Belgravia) $115

Late 19th century pair of whale's tooth scrimshaw, 10cm. high. (Sotheby's Belgravia) $265

Late 18th/early 19th century Dieppe ivory frame, centered by a thermometer, 22.2cm. high.(Sotheby's) $920

Late 19th century whale's tooth scrimshaw, 16.5cm. high. (Sotheby's Belgravia) $225

Late 18th century ivory figure of a Sennin, unsigned. (Sotheby's) $335

Priess carved ivory figure of a child, with a dove, 1920's, 18.6cm. high. (Sotheby's Belgravia) $700

Late 17th/early 18th century Dutch ivory-handled knife and fork, 18cm. and 15cm. long. (Sotheby's) $1,010

18th century Goanese ivory carving of the Virgin and Christ Child. (Phillips) $3,510

Chinese ivory carving of an old sage, Ming dynasty, 20cm. high. (C. G. Sloan & Co. Inc.) $1,500

Small late 19th century rectangular ivory cabinet, signed Hojitsusai Mitsuaki, 23.6cm. high. (Christie's)$1,450

Late 19th century whale's tooth scrimshaw, 16cm. high. (Sotheby's Belgravia) $365

Fine ivory carving of an old woman trying to trap four chicks, Meiji period, 34.3cm. high. (Christie's)$5,325

20th century American scrimshaw tusk, 33in. long. (Robert W. Skinner Inc.) $1,200

Unusual Balinese ivory shrine, circa 1900, 18cm. high, on wood stand. (Sotheby's Belgravia) $235

Large ivory Guanyin holding a lotus in a vase, circa 1900, 58.4cm. high. (Sotheby's Belgravia) $1,610

One of a pair of 19th century Chinese ivory carvings of standing saddled elephants, 23.2cm. high. (Christie's) $1,935

Well carved ivory figure of Kannon, signed Doko, 57.9cm. high. (Christie's) $3,870

Eskimo walnut ivory cribbage board. (Sotheby's) $575

Late ivory figure of a mother, signed Jushi(Toshiyuki) with kakihan. (Sotheby's) $285

19th century carved paper knife, 24cm. long. (Alfie's Antique Market) $475

Late 19th century pair of whale's tooth scrimshaw, one entitled 'Jane' the other 'Eliza', 12cm. high. (Sotheby's Belgravia) $485

Chinese carved Guanyin, 18.5cm. high. (C. G. Sloan & Co. Inc.) $1,200

Late 19th century ivory carving of an old woman and three children, signed Hozui, 14cm. high. (Christie's) $1,935

Well carved ivory group of a fisherman with two boys, signed Masakaze, 41.6cm. high. (Christie's) $3,995

Late 19th century French bone casket with domed hinged cover, 24.4cm. long. (Sotheby's Belgravia) $520

Mid 19th century ivory thermometer stand, English, 17.4cm. high. (Sotheby's Belgravia) $215

Ivory mirror case of circular form, Metropolitan France, circa 1330 A.D., 9.8cm. diam. (Phillips) $82,800

Late 19th century German ivory standing cup with cylindrical bowl, 33.5cm. high. (Sotheby's Belgravia) $1,890

Late 19th century German ivory plaque of curved panel form, 35.3cm. long. (Sotheby's Belgravia) $1,650

Ivory figure of a gnome on ivory plinth, 14.5cm. high overall. (Sotheby's Belgravia) $330

French ivory figure of Queen Elizabeth I, 20th century, 22.5cm. high. (Sotheby's Belgravia) $1,180

20th century tournament Staunton ivory chess set in ivory and natural, in fitted case. (Sotheby's Belgravia) $2,125

Late 19th century French ivory figure of a nymph holding a lyre, 25cm. high. (Sotheby's Belgravia) $1,225

Japanese ivory carving of an archer. (Phillips) $2,260

Ivory tankard of 16th century style, 4½in. high, with flat engined-turned lid. (Sotheby, King & Chasemore) $1,110

Carved ivory frame containing a miniature by Antonin Topart, circa 1880, 19.8cm. high overall. (Sotheby's Belgravia) $1,770

Unusual mid 19th century bone chess set, red and natural, each piece turned, 4.2 to 10.2cm. high. (Sotheby's Belgravia) $355

Mid 19th century French ivory figure of Cupid, on turned ivory base, 16.3cm. high. (Sotheby's Belgravia) $495

Mid 19th century English ivory chess set, each piece bobbin-turned, 4.8 to 11cm. high. (Sotheby's Belgravia) $520

17th century German ivory tazza, shallow dish centered by a figure of a putto, 24.5cm. high. (Sotheby's Belgravia) $2,360

Late 19th century ivory plaque, 20cm. long, in glazed ebonised wood frame. (Sotheby's Belgravia) $2,360

Late 19th century Continental ivory vase carved in high relief, 36.5cm. high. (Sotheby's Belgravia) $3,660

Turned ivory barometer stand, mid 19th century, engraved Smith, Beck & Beck, London, 21.5cm. high. (Sotheby's Belgravia) $305

Late 19th/early 20th century Belgian five-man wood and ivory beggar band, 15.5-17.5cm. high.(Sotheby's Belgravia) $850

Mid 19th century turned ivory thermometer stand in the form of a sundial, 12.7cm. high, engraved Brinton, Brighton. (Sotheby's Belgravia)$320

Large ivory tusk carving of a woman and child, 50cm. high. (Phillips & Jolly)$2,140

Finely carved Oriental ivory elephant decorated in Shibayama style, 28cm. high. (Phillips & Jolly) $2,740

Small carved ivory nude figure on faceted green marble base, 1930's, 18.5cm. high.(Sotheby's Belgravia) $445

Small late 19th century pan-bone scrimshaw, 8.3cm. wide. (Sotheby's Belgravia) $195

Silver-mounted whale's tooth scrimshaw, Birmingham, by Hilliard & Thomason, 16cm. long. (Sotheby's Belgravia) $775

French turned ivory miniature box, lid set with a miniature of a musician, circa 1785, 6.9cm. diam. (Sotheby's) $715

18th century carved ivory casket of almost square form, 14.5cm. high. (Sotheby's) $430

Late 19th century pair of whale's tooth scrimshaw, 11.5cm. high. (Sotheby's Belgravia) $290

Sri Lankan jeweled and gold-mounted ivory model of an elephant, 17.5cm. long. (Christie's) $2,050

Carved ivory figure of a pea-sant sowing seed. (Bradley & Vaughan) $3,145

Late 19th century carved ivory beggar band, probably Flemish, 12.5cm. high. (Sotheby's Belgravia) $1,315

18th century Bavarian ivory carving of Christ at the Column, by George Petel, 32cm. high. (Phillips) $14,260

Late 17th century Flemish oval ivory relief carved with a figure of Christ, 8cm. high. (Sotheby's) $370

Carved ivory Owo covered cup. (Christie's) $49,060

Late 19th century pair of deco-rated dolphin jaws, each 49cm. long. (Sotheby's Belgravia) $265

Mid 19th century whale's tooth scrimshaw, 11.5cm. high. (Sotheby's Belgravia) $175

Japanese lacquered wood and ivory figure of a Sarumawashi by Homin, circa 1900. (Sotheby, King & Chasemore) $1,270

Mid 19th century English decorated nautilus shell, 21.5cm. long. (Sotheby's Belgravia) $1,695

Carved ivory figure of a chicken keeper, signed Sei-shu O-kawa, 15cm. high. (Sotheby, King & Chasemore) $4,025

Mid 19th century American pair of whale's tooth scrimshaw, mounted on wooden plinths, 14.5cm. high. (Sotheby's Belgravia) $240

Tokyo school carved ivory figure of a sower, 23cm. high, circa 1910, Japanese. (Sotheby, King & Chasemore) $1,170

Large late 19th century carved whale's tooth, 20cm. long. (Sotheby's Belgravia) $410

Large Delhi carved ivory chess set, circa 1835, 6.5cm. to 12cm. high. (Sotheby, King & Chasemore) $1,025

Fine ivory carving of a short-eared owl, 18cm. high, signed Mitsuaki. (Phillips) $4,830

One of a pair of Chinese export ivory letter racks, 26cm. high. (H. Spencer & Sons) $750

Aeitsu carved ivory figure of 'The Basket Seller', Japanese, circa 1900, 11.5cm. high, signed. (Sotheby, King & Chasemore) $925

19th century prisoner-of-war bone miniature guillotine. (Christie's S. Kensington) $1,575

18th/19th century mottled pale gray and white jade shallow brush-washer, slightly damaged, 21.3cm. long. (Christie's) $1,195

Chinese white jade group of tortoise and crane, 7.5cm. high. (C. G. Sloan & Co. Inc.) $550

Mottled gray, pale and dark green jade carving of a water buffalo, repaired, 27.5cm. long. (Christie's)$445

17th century mottled celadon and brown jade carving of Shoulao squatting over a peach, 9cm. high. (Christie's) $2,390

White jade pendant of shaped rectangular form carved with a lotus spray, 2½in. high. (Sotheby's) $165

Olive green covered wine vessel with shield shaped body, 11.5cm. high. (Lawrence Fine Art) $1,320

18th century mottled pale spinach green jade rectangular gu-shaped vase, 21.7cm. high. (Christie's) $1,385

Pair of mottled pale and dark green jade carvings of ladies, with wooden stands, 22.9cm. high. (Christie's) $2,160

Fine Qianlong mottled gray jade cylindrical cricket cage fitted with dark green ends, 23.2cm. high. (Christie's) $2,630

17th/18th century mottled dark celadon jade flattened baluster vase with loose ring handles, 22.5cm. high. (Christie's) $1,790

Mottled beige, pale and apple-green jade rectangular table screen with wood stands, 16.1 x 14cm. (Christie's) $3,525

Qianlong spinach green jade pilgrim bottle and cover, 26cm. high, on stand. (Moore, Allen & Innocent) $1,800

Mottled gray and black jade carving of a water buffalo, 21.2cm. long.(Christie's)
$2,030

Mottled pale lavender and pale green jade circular bowl and cover with bud finial, 12.4cm. wide. (Christie's) $670

18th century celadon jade bucket-shaped bowl on four animal-mask feet, 14.9cm. diam. (Christie's)
$1,145

18th century spinach green jade incense burner and domed cover, 24.2cm. high. (Christie's)
$3,585

Pierced star-shaped jade pendant with central spiral florette, stone of pale celadon tone, 2¾in. diam.(Sotheby's) $120

18th/19th century pale gray jade flattened oviform vase and shallow domed cover, 10.8cm. high. (Christie's) $735

One of a pair of mottled spinach green jade oval plaques with wood stands, 26.6cm. high. (Christie's)
$1,455

Mottled gray jade rectangular table screen carved in relief with figures, probably Qianlong, 34.1cm. high. (Christie's) $5,260

Mottled white, russet, pale lavender, pale and dark green jade flattened baluster vase and domed cover, 28.3cm. high. (Christie's)
$2,350

Pale gray jade hexagonal gu-shaped vase with two pierced scrolling handles, 17.2cm. high. (Christie's)
$765

18th century mottled spinach green jade cylindrical brushpot, 17cm. high (Christie's) $20,315

Mottled pale and dark green jade carving of a female immortal with wood stand, 22.2cm. high. (Christie's)
$1,220

Attractive white jade pendant of rounded waisted form, 2in. high. (Sotheby's) $165

Attractively carved pale celadon jade button with scalloped petals, 2¼in. diam.(Sotheby's) $40

Jade pendant carved and pierced with a parrot amidst leafy boughs, 2in. high. (Sotheby's) $90

18th century mottled pale gray and beige jade two-handled circular incense burner and domed cover, 19cm. wide. (Christie's) $7,520

Pale green jade boulder carving, 6½in. high, on wood stand. (Sotheby's) $1,460

White jade urn of compressed spherical shape, 6.5cm. diam., with hardwood stand. (Lawrence Fine Art) $200

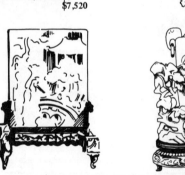

One of a pair of Chinese celadon jade table screens, circa 1800, 22.5cm. high. (Messenger May & Baverstock) $2,170

Mottled pale gray jade rounded rectangular vase and domed cover on wooden stand, 19.5cm. high. (Christie's) $1,075

One of a pair of mottled white and gray jade circular table screens, on wood stands, 16cm. diam. (Christie's) $2,150

Almost white 18th century jade carving of a recumbent water buffalo and qilin, 13.3cm. long. (Christie's)$7,170

Mottled, white, beige and apple-green jade snuff bottle carved as a toad, with coral stopper. (Christie's) $910

Large mottled celadon and russet jade boulder carved on both sides, probably 17th/18th century, 25.9cm. wide. (Christie's) $7,050

Pair of cabochon emerald and diamond scalloped cluster earrings. (Christie's) $2,955

Pair of gold and crystal Victorian 'fish bowl' pendant earrings. (Bonhams) $1,320

Diamond double-clip brooch, each designed as a ram's head scroll encircling a flowerhead. (Sotheby's) $2,930

Pair of diamond pendant earrings, cased by Mrs. Newman, circa 1900. (Sotheby's) $1,920

Pair of diamond collet and cluster pendant earrings in fitted case.(Christie's) $9,345

Pair of diamond two-stone pendant earrings. (Sotheby's) $4,600

Antique gold snake necklace with emerald and rose-diamond set head. (Christie's) $1,525

Art Nouveau white gold buckle form brooch set with three rows of baguette diamonds. (Taylor Lane & Creber) $1,520

White gold inverted staple link bracelet with five charms attached. (Christie's) $2,690

Gold, onyx, half-pearl and rose-diamond locket, circa 1865, in fitted case. (Sotheby's) $1,465

Diamond pendant designed as a Latin cross, pave-set with cushion-shaped stones. (Sotheby's) $1,660

Amethyst and diamond pendant, edged with diamond ribbons. (Sotheby's) $1,465

Victorian diamond and pearl collet and foliate scroll brooch pendant in fitted case. (Christie's) $1,720

Antique diamond, rose-diamond and opal collet, leaf and cluster festoon brooch, with triple drops. (Christie's) $2,005

Diamond, enamel and gold twin-flower spray brooch by Cartier, in fitted case. (Christie's) $845

Important diamond bracelet with pierced flexible band. (Christie's) $22,140

Victorian gold and blue enamel narrow bangle with diamond cluster center. (Christie's) $1,640

Art Deco pendant of diamond trellis form set with sixty-seven pearls and nine rubies. (W. H. Lane & Son)$720

Victorian diamond rose-diamond and pearl graduated collet and foliate scroll necklace. (Christie's) $3,445

Pair of Art Deco carved and pierced jade and onyx and diamond collet pendant earrings. (Christie's) $1,425

Brilliant and baguette diamond collet pierced double clip brooch by Cartier. (Christie's) $17,220

Antique diamond necklace forming tiara, brooches and a pair of earrings. (Christie's) $9,840

Victorian diamond brooch as a cat on gold fire-tongs. (Christie's) $1,355

Diamond flower-spray brooch by Cartier, in fitted case. (Sotheby's) $2,880

Diamond brooch designed as a scroll wound with ribbons. (Sotheby's) $5,760

Antique garnet, diamond and rose-diamond pendant cross. (Christie's) $2,830

Diamond-hinged bangle set with a triple row of stones, circa 1900. (Sotheby's) $5,280

Aquamarine and diamond bracelet designed as an oval cluster. (Sotheby's) $1,080

Navette diamond eternity ring.
(Christie's) $2,090

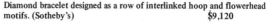

Diamond bracelet designed as a row of interlinked hoop and flowerhead
motifs. (Sotheby's) $9,120

Amethyst and diamond necklace
in fitted case. (Christie's)
$11,810

Art Nouveau hair comb with plique-a-jour
enamels, 13.5cm. long. (Phillips)
$1,010

Antique gold rosette and half-pearl
collet choker necklace.(Christie's)
$2,460

Late Victorian diamond-set butterfly
brooch. (Phillips) $3,520

Victorian gold and black enamel
bangle with turquoise star motifs.
(Christie's) $1,170

Moonstone, rose-diamond and gold
bangle, front designed as two hearts,
circa 1890.(Sotheby's) $1,010

Pair of pearl, brilliant and baguette diamond pendant earrings.
(Christie's) $4,445

Lalique glass pendant molded in intaglio,
1920's, 7.5cm. high. (Sotheby's Belgravia)
$680

Brilliant and baguette diamond
collet and ribbon fancy floral
spray brooch.(Christie's)
$2,705

Diamond bracelet set in three rows of stones, intersected by oval links.
(Sotheby's) $13,920

Diamond and onyx twin circle
bar brooch with diamond collet
centres. (Christie's)$4,915

Diamond brooch designed as a working model of a bicycle, circa 1900. (Sotheby's) $3,570

Gold and pearl pendant, by Carlo Giuliano, circa 1870. (Sotheby's) $950

Late 19th century gold, diamond and ruby brooch, 2.5cm. wide. (Sotheby's) $1,070

Diamond, dementoid garnet and gem set bird brooch. (Christie's S. Kensington) $4,760

Berlin iron brooch with ivory cameo, circa 1820. (Alfie's Antique Market) $230

Art and Craft opal pendant on silver, circa 1860. (Alfie's Antique Market) $590

Diamond fob watch, circular bezel mounted within a border of diamond ribbons. (Sotheby's) $1,755

Onyx and diamond brooch with initials A.L., circa 1880. (Sotheby's) $830

Ruby and diamond pendant designed as a trefoil cross, on a gold chain necklet. (Sotheby's) $1,035

19th century Italian gold mounted mosaic bracelet, stamped Carli, 65mm. long. (Christie's) $1,080

Diamond and ruby bangle set in 15ct. gold, circa 1900. (Alfie's Antique Market) $475

Gold and enamel brooch, unmarked, circa 1900, 3cm. wide, set with rose-cut diamonds. (Sotheby's) $425

Pair of diamond and black onyx earrings. (Sotheby Bearne) $2,380

Black onyx and diamond bracelet, (Sotheby Bearne) $970

Simulated jade and jet necklace, 1930's, 25cm. long. (Sotheby Belgravia) $305

498

Early 19th century Scottish oblong gold-mounted bloodstone vinaigrette, 29mm. long. (Christie's) $1,320

Early 19th century gold and enamel diamond ring. (Sotheby's) $3,320

Late 19th century moonstone and diamond crescent and star brooch, showing the man in the moon. (Sotheby's) $1,610

Late 19th century diamond brooch pendant in a ribbon bow and flower design. (Sotheby's) $1,230

Diamond set star-shaped bar brooch. (Geering & Colyer) $960

Opal and diamond brooch, circa 1900. (Sotheby's) $1,185

Late 19th century gold, half-pearl and turquoise necklet. (Sotheby's) $1,840

Black opal and diamond pendant on slender chain necklet, circa 1905. (Sotheby's) $5,685

Crystal and diamond brooch designed as a bow, circa 1925. (Sotheby's) $3,790

Black onyx and diamond ribbon bow brooch by Tiffany & Co. (Sotheby Bearne) $1,100

Diamond bracelet pave-set with circular and baguette-cut stones on expanding bracelet. (Sotheby's) $1,610

Gold enamel and diamond jarretiere bracelet, circa 1855. (Sotheby's) $2,380

Diamond set gold Maltese cross-shaped brooch/pendant. (Geering & Colyer) $1,690

Victorian diamond and half-pearl set floral gold festoon necklet. (Christie's S. Kensington) $2,560

Opal and diamond brooch/pendant of rosette design, circa 1900. (Sotheby's) $1,040

White gold and diamond circle pin, diamonds weighing 5.5ct. (C. G. Sloan & Co. Inc.) $1,100

Late 19th century French gold brooch. (McCartney, Morris & Barker) $325

Antique amethyst, diamond and rose-diamond heart-shaped brooch pendant. (Christie's) $1,905

Five-row black cultured pearl bracelet with large diamond collet. (Christie's) $3,415

Diamond bracelet, tonneau-shaped center with concealed watch. (Sotheby's) $2,845

Gold, carbuncle and rose diamond pendant designed as a Latin cross, circa 1850. (Sotheby's) $2,990

Victorian diamond and opal dragon-fly brooch. (H. Evans & Sons) $3,870

Gold and enamel necklet designed as a serpent, circa 1840, in fitted case. (Sotheby's) $1,305

Diamond double-clip brooch with lunette-shaped ends. (Sotheby's) $2,370

Diamond star-shaped brooch. (Biddle & Webb) $1,175

Diamond bracelet, circa 1925, in fitted case by Koch, Frankfurt and Baden-Baden.(Sotheby's) $4,740

Rare gold, pearl and turquoise Arts and Crafts pendant designed by Archibald Knox. (Phillips) $4,270

18ct. French gold, ruby and diamond brooch. (C. G. Sloan & Co. Inc.) $1,150

Gold harlequin opal, diamond and ruby brooch of three crested titmice on a branch, by Cartier, signed. (Geering & Colyer) $1,250

Diamond crescent-shaped brooch. (Biddle & Webb) $845

Mid 19th century gold brooch designed as a kestrel with platinum leaves and stem. (Sotheby's) $460

Gold, blue enamel, pearl and diamond necklet with heart-shaped pendant. (H. Spencer & Sons) $625

Attractive sapphire and diamond bracelet. (Sotheby's) $7,110

One of a pair of Art Nouveau style gold and turquoise earrings, circa 1900. (Alfie's Antique Market) $390

Russian gold brooch of two circular diamond set miniature portraits, 48mm. long. (Christie's) $3,600

English Art Nouveau gold and opal pendant and chain, circa 1900, 4.5cm. drop. (Sotheby's Belgravia) $375

Antique gold embossed mesh bracelet set with rubies, emeralds and diamonds.(Irelands) $15,575

Diamond and turquoise tiara on a ribbon and collet base, in fitted case. (Christie's) $9,270

Gold cross engraved with the Russian Orthodox cross, Moscow, 1908-1917, 4.5cm. high. (Sotheby's) $570

French gold-mounted diamond brooch in the shape of a bee with ruby eyes and double baroque pearl body. (W. H. Lane & Son) $890

18th century Spanish gold and emerald pendant, 6cm. long. (Sotheby's) $1,520

501

Handel table lamp with caramel slag glass paneled shade, Meriden, Connecticut, circa 1915, 23½in. high. (Robert W. Skinner Inc.) $750

Galle etched table lamp and shade, mounted in bronze, 40cm. high. (H. Spencer & Sons) $2,500

Late 17th century oil lamp of compressed form, 11cm. wide. (Christie's) $205

One of a pair of mid 19th century English white overlay lamps with marble bases, 47.5cm. high. (Robert W. Skinner Inc.) $800

Late 19th century English microscope lamp, adjustable brass stand holding oil lamp. (Sotheby's Belgravia) $305

Unusual silver gilt table lamp by Edward & Sons, Glasgow, 1937, 69oz.5dwt., 40cm. high. (Sotheby's)$2,217

American blown glass whale oil lamp, circa 1825, 9¼in. high. (Robert W. Skinner Inc.) $525

Tongzhi famille verte vase, fitted for electricity, 45.5cm. high. (Sotheby's Belgravia) $540

L. C. Tiffany 'orange poppy' lampshade on Art Nouveau base, 50cm. diam. (C. G. Sloan & Co. Inc.) $11,000

One of a pair of silver plated wall-lights, 66cm. high, 1880's. (Sotheby's Belgravia) $935

Handel reverse painted glass and bronzed metal table lamp, 18in. high, Meriden, Connecticut, circa 1922. (Robert W. Skinner Inc.) $2,100

Handel table lamp with open top, Meriden, Connecticut, circa 1910, 19½in. high. (Robert W. Skinner Inc.)$450

One of a pair of Powell & Hammer brass motor headlamps for the Morris Oxford, 24cm. long. (Sotheby, King & Chasemore) $285

Early 20th century Tiffany bronze and Favrile glass ten-light lily table lamp, 20½in. high. (Robert W. Skinner Inc.) $7,500

Etling frosted glass lamp on chromed metal base, 1920's, 26.5cm. wide. (Sotheby's Belgravia) $1,215

Art Nouveau table lamp in the form of a nude girl emerging from a flower, 36cm. high. (Burtenshaw Walker) $455

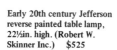

Early 20th century Jefferson reverse painted table lamp, 22½in. high. (Robert W. Skinner Inc.) $525

Signed Tiffany bronze floor lamp on slender shaft, shade with opalescent shaped beads. (C. G. Sloan & Co. Inc.) $2,800

Daum Nancy cameo boudoir lamp, the oval pierced nickel plated brass face with oval shaped glass vase. (Robert W. Skinner Inc.) $400

Papier mache masque lantern, 16½in. high. (Christie's S. Kensington) $430

Spelter lamp, stamped Rancoulet, 1890's, 94cm. high. (Sotheby's Belgravia) $470

Late 19th century American Gone-with-the-Wind lamp on cast brass base, 23½in. high.(Robert W. Skinner Inc.)$300

20th century American Jefferson bronzed metal and reverse painted table lamp, 21½in. high. (Robert W. Skinner Inc.) $550

One of a pair of Old Sheffield plate candlesticks with glass shades, circa 1800. (Phillips) $855

One of a pair of Georgian ceremonial coach lamps with silver plated interiors, 84cm. high. (J. M. Welch & Sons) $2,880

Tiffany 'Mandarin' leaded glass shade and flowering lotus bronze table lamp base. (Phillips) $26,000

One of a pair of earthenware and bronze oil lamps with opaque glass shades, circa 1880, 91cm. high. (Sotheby's Belgravia) $755

Bronze table lamp by Gorham & Co., circa 1900, 58cm. high. (Sotheby's Belgravia) $2,810

Handel bronze patinated metal table lamp with painted glass shade, circa 1910, 53cm. high. (Sotheby's Belgravia) $935

Brass and brown aurene floor lamp, 58in. high, circa 1910. (Robert W. Skinner Inc.) $1,100

Tiffany bronze and leaded glass table lamp, 23in. high, New York, circa 1900. (Robert W. Skinner Inc.) $10,000

Attractive coach lamp with plated interior. (J. M. Welch & Son) $220

Stephenson lead lock and shielded safety miner's lamp, circa 1826, 19.7cm. high. (H. C. Chapman & Sons) $650

Early 18th century oil lamp with globular body on up-turned foot, 15cm. wide. (Christie's) $395

One of a pair of brass and japanned metal coach lamps by Perry & Turner Ltd., Bristol. (May Whetter & Grose) $290

Bronze Art Nouveau lamp, circa 1900-1910, 52cm. high. (Sotheby, King & Chasemore) $840

Tiffany bronze and leaded glass table lamp, early 20th century, 24in. high. (Robert W. Skinner Inc.) $6,500

One of a pair of ormolu bras d'applique with leaf-cast candle arms, 25in. high, circa 1860. (Sotheby's Belgravia) $515

Art Deco lamp with flame shade and metal base. (Alfie's Antique Market) $60

Tiffany bronze three-light table lamp with green, white and gold glass shades, circa 1900. (Morton's Auction Exchange) $2,100

Elkington plate lamp with tiger, circa 1870, 77.5cm. high. (Grays Antique Market) $475

Decorative bronze lamp with beaten copper shade set with chips of clear glass and blue plastic, circa 1900, 58cm. high. (Sotheby's Belgravia) $890

Copper and brass ship's anchor lamp, complete, marked C. Gray, Arbroath. (J. M. Welch & Son) $395

Handel lamp of tree design, circa 1915, 22in. high. (Robert W. Skinner Inc.) $2,500

Large copper ship's search light, 18in. diam., on iron swivel base. (J. M. Welch & Son) $340

Galle cameo glass table lamp with shallow domed shade, circa 1900, 57cm. high. (Sotheby's Belgravia) $9,595

One of a pair of brass Lucas car oil head lamps. (J. M. Welch & Son) $305

Bronze lamp with basket weave caned and cotton shade above a pierced stand, circa 1900, 80cm. high. (Sotheby's Belgravia) $565

Double overlay and bronze mounted miniature lamp with tripod lily pad base, 16cm. high. (Christie's) $5,935

Double overlay glass table lamp with mush-room shade, 67cm. high. (Christie's) $11,025

19th century American three-colour oil lamp, on milk glass base, 14¾in. high. (Robert W. Skinner Inc.) $350

Daum glass table lamp and shade, signed on base, 14½in. high. (Christie's) $3,770

One of a pair of Lalique gilt metal mounted table lamps, 41cm. high. (Christie's) $665

Acorn leaded glass table lamp by Tiffany Studios, New York, 23in. high. (Christie's) $5,210

19th century Chinese hard-wood hanging lantern with glazed sides. (Christie's) $1,095

Silver table lamp by Hawksworth, Eyre & Co. Ltd., Sheffield, 1890, 54cm. high. (Sotheby's Belgravia) $840

Lalique gilt metal moun-ted table lamp with blue opalescent glass body, 33cm. high. (Christie's) $285

Daffodil leaded glass and gilt bronze table lamp by Tiffany Studios, New York. (Christie's) $12,720

19th century American two-colour oil lamp on double step down base, 14¼in. high. (Robert W. Skinner Inc.) $450

Mold blown cameo table lamp, signed Galle, circa 1900, 19½in. high. (H. C. Chapman & Son) $70,380

One of a pair of 17th century Italian lead garden ornaments, 57.5cm. high. (Robert W. Skinner Inc.) $950

George I lead cistern, dated 1727, 3ft.5in. high x 4ft.11½in. wide. (Sotheby's) $1,510

A fine lead cistern dated 1764, 39in. wide. (Vernon's) $1,200

18th century English lead figure of a naked youth holding cymbals, 135cm. high. (Christie's) $760

One of a pair of French white metal female figures with cupids, 48cm. high. (Vernon's) $250

18th century English lead figure of Christ, 124.5cm. high. (Christie's) $260

18th century English lead figure of a putto with one hand on his head, 81cm. high. (Christie's) $525

One of a set of four circular lead plaques of classical scenes, 70cm. diam. (Christie's) $1,310

One of a set of four oval lead plaques with scenes of putti, 61cm. high. (Christie's) $835

Late 19th century octagonal lead jardiniere cast with mice and other field animals, 21½in. diam. (Sotheby's Belgravia) $455

Large white statuary marble group of a young girl with a goat, 150cm. high, circa 1870. (Sotheby's Belgravia) $1,710

19th century Italian yellow marble model of the Lion of Lucerne, 39cm. long. (Christie's) $1,190

White marble group of two young lovers, signed L. Cigole, Roma, dated 1867, 69cm. high. (Sotheby's Belgravia) $5,370

Gray-veined white marble pedestal, circa 1900, stem with gilt bronze mounts, 109cm. high. (Sotheby's Belgravia) $1,270

American 20th century marble figure of a seated female nude, 53cm. high. (C. G. Sloan & Co. Inc.) $1,000

19th century marble figure of three amorini, 3ft.4in. high. (Hobbs Parker) $705

19th century German marble statue of Summer, signed Emile Wolff, 69.5cm. high. (Christie's) $1,665

20th century Italian marble figure of a servant girl by G. Gambogi, 60cm. high. (Christie's) $570

18th century Italian marble group of a boy and girl embracing, attributed to Maximilien Laboureur, 32cm. high. (Christie's) $905

White marble group of a young man and woman, circa 1880, 64cm. high. (Sotheby's Belgravia) $975

White statuary marble bust of a young girl, circa 1860, 68.5cm. high. (Sotheby's Belgravia) $270

White marble group of The Bathers, by Charles Leonard Hartwell, 1920's, 67cm. high. (Sotheby's Belgravia) $1,000

Mid 19th century marble and bronze Greco-Roman revival tazza, 12in. high. (Robert W. Skinner Inc.) $100

One of a set of four 19th century white marble urns of campana shape, 2ft.4½in. diam. (Sotheby's) $7,810

Italian white marble figure of a young woman dancing, 102cm. high, circa 1860. (Sotheby's Belgravia) $975

Two red marble supports from a fireplace, circa 1880, 94cm. high. (Sotheby's Belgravia) $1,525

Late 19th century Italian mosaic marble table top, 72cm. diam. (Sotheby's Belgravia) $1,560

19th century European marble statue of a woman wearing a toga, 24¼in. high. (Robert W. Skinner Inc.) $325

Pair of marble figures, signed Joes Claud de Cock, dated 1715, 85cm. high. (Aldridge's) $52,320

Black marble sculpture modelled as a polished scorpionfish, signed, 15½in. high. (Christie's) $10,430

Bronze and Porta Santa Rara marble fountain with molded circular dish top, 76cm. diam. (Christie's) $4,095

One of a pair of ormolu mounted marble urns, late 18th century, 36cm. high. (Sotheby's Belgravia) $770

Carrara marble figure by Cesare Lapini 'The Morning Star', 67.5cm. high. (C. G. Sloan & Co. Inc.) $1,500

Mid 19th century Italian marble figure La Penseuse, 30in. high. (Robert W. Skinner Inc.) $600

509

Kingwood and marquetry miniature writing table with shaped top, 54cm. wide. (Christie's) $1,325

American miniature walnut Renaissance revival bed, circa 1875, 21½in. long. (Robert W. Skinner Inc.) $275

Miniature Lombardy ivory inlaid walnut chest, circa 1700, 1ft. 7¾in. wide. (Sotheby's) $515

Mid 19th century American miniature Empire bureau, 9in. high. (Robert W. Skinner Inc.) $275

One of a pair of miniature corner chairs with bowed and carved crestings. (Sotheby Bearne) $445

Mid 18th century miniature walnut bureau, 8½in. wide. (Sotheby Bearne) $840

French provincial miniature stand with lifting top, legs joined by galleried stretcher, 9½in. wide.(C. G. Sloan & Co. Inc.) $700

Victorian miniature oak diningroom suite. (Woolley & Wallis) $145

George I walnut and crossbanded miniature chest of four drawers with side carrying handles, 16in. wide.(Smith-Woolley & Perry) $945

Mid 19th century American miniature Empire grained pine bureau, 21in. high. (Robert W. Skinner Inc.) $200

Queen Anne walnut miniature chest of drawers, circa 1710, 1ft.3in. wide. (Sotheby's) $1,055

Mid 19th century American miniature Empire pine bureau, two drawers with maple veneer, 10¼in. high. (Robert W. Skinner Inc.) $300

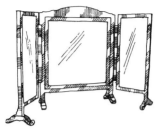

George III giltwood oval mirror, circa 1765, 3ft.6in. high. (Sotheby's) $2,105

Interesting Georgian mahogany triple concertina toilet mirror, 25¼in. high. (Coles, Knapp & Kennedy) $135

Queen Anne giltwood pier glass, circa 1710, 2ft.6½in. wide. (Sotheby's) $2,440

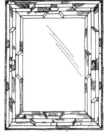

Queen Anne looking glass by Moore & Gumley, circa 1710, 4ft.1in. wide. (Sotheby's) $3,780

Mid 19th century French giltwood toilet mirror with oval swing plate, 79cm. wide. (Christie's) $1,445

Queen Anne gilt gesso mirror with leaf-covered frame, 1ft.5½in. wide. (Sotheby's) $270

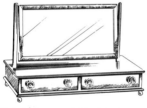

One of a pair of mid 18th century North European parcel gilt mahogany mirrors, 2ft.3in. wide. (Sotheby's) $3,510

Early 19th century Federal shaving mirror, Portland, Maine, 17in. high. (Robert W. Skinner Inc.) $225

Late George II giltwood wall mirror, circa 1760, 1ft.8½in. wide. (Sotheby's)$1,405

Late 19th century American Greco-Roman carved oak revival mirror. (Robert W. Skinner Inc.) $650

George III giltwood mirror with carved scrolled frame, circa 1760, 5ft.6½in. high. (Sotheby's) $14,430

George II rectangular mirror with giltwood frame.(Parsons, Welch & Cowell)$1,140

Silver-mounted toilet mirror, London, 1903. (Christie's S. Kensington) $1,985

Early 20th century Austrian shield-shaped dressing-table mirror with two columnar supports, 46cm. high. (Sotheby's Belgravia) $990

German carved giltwood and gesso looking glass with arched cresting, circa 1740, 1ft.11in. wide. (Sotheby's) $1,120

One of a pair of mid 19th century pier glasses with arched tops, circa 1840, 6ft. high. (Sotheby's) $1,075

Regency giltwood convex mirror with carved eagle above, circa 1815, 3ft.4in. high. (Sotheby's) $1,075

'George II' parcel gilt walnut wall mirror, late 19th century, 27in. wide. (Sotheby's Belgravia) $755

George III giltwood mirror in carved and pierced frame, 2ft.9½in. wide. (Sotheby's) $1,400

Anglo-Indian ivory veneered toilet mirror and two boxes, early 19th century. (Christie's) $3,265

Chippendale mahogany veneer and gilt mirror, frame bordered with gilt applied decoration, circa 1760, 60in. high. (Robert W. Skinner Inc.) $1,100

Late George II gilt looking glass, circa 1755, 4ft.2in. high. (Sotheby's) $4,620

Unusual George I black-painted and parcel gilt mirror, circa 1725, 2ft.7in. wide. (Sotheby's) $3,170

Early George II parcel gilt and walnut looking glass with divided plate, circa 1730, 2ft.4in. wide. (Sotheby's) $1,585

Easel mirror of shaped outline, silver mounts, London, 1901, 55cm. high. (Burrows & Day) $315

Early Georgian giltwood and gesso frame landscape overmantel mirror, 25¾ x 69in. (Geering & Colyer) $1,495

Early 19th century American mahogany shaving stand, drawers with turned ivory knobs, 19½in. wide. (Robert W. Skinner Inc.)$425

One of a pair of mid 18th century carved and giltwood girandoles, South German, 2ft.3½in. high. (Sotheby's) $2,685

18th century Dutch marquetry toilet mirror. (Sotheby, King & Chasemore) $865

Giltwood and plaster mirror with waisted rococo frame, circa 1840, 132cm. high. (Sotheby's Belgravia) $810

Early 18th century giltwood pier glass, 69in. high. (Christie's) $3,570

Neapolitan tortoiseshell pique mirror frame, 53cm. high, circa 1735-1745. (Sotheby's) $6,900

One of a pair of unusually small George III oval giltwood mirrors, circa 1765, 3ft. high. (Sotheby's) $7,140

'George II' parcel gilt walnut mirror, circa 1880, 120cm. high. (Sotheby's Belgravia)$490

Early 20th century Murano glass mirror with rococo cresting, 45in. wide. (Sotheby's Belgravia) $170

One of a pair of George III style oval giltwood wall mirrors, 4ft. 2in. high. (Sotheby's) $2,530

513

MIRRORS

Burr-walnut veneered dressing table mirror above two bull-nosed drawers. (Clive Emson) $60

Early George III giltwood overmantel with later shaped triple plates, 54in. wide. (Christie's) $2,440

Regency giltwood convex mirror, circa 1810, 2ft. wide. (Sotheby's) $1,025

George II inlaid wall mirror with carved gilding, 2ft.8in. wide. (Lowery & Partners) $655

Carved oak overmantel with molded frame, the sides with porcelain stands, 155.5cm. wide. (Sotheby's Belgravia) $820

Charles II carved wood mirror, English or Dutch, circa 1660, 3ft.6in. wide. (Sotheby's) $9,520

Early 18th century Dutch giltwood pier glass with divided beveled plate, 1ft. 6in. wide. (Sotheby's) $1,170

Late George II carved giltwood overmantel glass, circa 1760, 4ft.11in. wide. (Sotheby's) $6,345

German or French carved giltwood looking glass, circa 1725, 3ft.9in. wide. (Sotheby's) $3,745

Mid 19th century 'George I' giltwood wall mirror, border carved with leaves, 44½in. high. (Sotheby's Belgravia) $1,100

One of a pair of George II giltwood wall mirrors, circa 1755, 2ft.8in. wide. (Sotheby's) $4,880

Louis XV style carved giltwood pier mirror, 27in. wide. (C. G. Sloan & Co. Inc.) $1,200

514

Mid 19th century Italian giltwood and plaster mirror with inverted cornice, 174cm. high. (Sotheby's Belgravia) $865

George III giltwood overmantel mirror, circa 1760, 4ft.7in. wide. (Sotheby's) $2,455

20th century Japanese damascene and laquer frame, 29cm. high. (Robert W. Skinner Inc.) $275

Mid 19th century rococo revival giltwood mirror with divided mirror plate, 76in. wide. (Sotheby's Belgravia) $840

Royal Dux mirror frame in Art Nouveau style, in tones of creamy grey, circa 1910, 53cm. high. (Sotheby's Belgravia) $435

Queen Anne verre eglomise mirror with arched plate, 22½in. wide. (Christie's) $1,830

George II giltwood mirror with rope twist frame, 64in. high. (Christie's) $3,995

'George II' giltwood overmantel, circa 1840, 160cm. wide, flanked by two porcelain stands. (Sotheby's Belgravia) $770

Regency giltwood convex mirror with eagle cresting, circa 1815, 1ft.7in. wide. (Sotheby's) $975

George II carved and gilt gesso bevelled wall mirror, circa 1750, 1ft.10in. wide. (Sotheby, King & Chasemore) $880

Shagreen and ivory toilet mirror by Asprey, London, 30¾in. high. (Sotheby's Belgravia) $3,510

Early George III giltwood wall mirror, circa 1760, 2ft.3in. wide. (Sotheby's) $2,320

MISCELLANEOUS

Needlework sampler by Sally Oliver, 1801, of Upper Beverley, America, 19½ x 21in. (Robert W. Skinner Inc.) $5,500

A Jivard shrunken head, the lips sewn with twisted fibre suspending two long plaited tassels. (Christie's) $2,620

18th century needlework sampler by Mary Adamson, 1781, 31cm. high. (Robert W. Skinner Inc.) $150

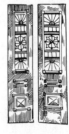

One of a pair of late 19th century American walnut and stained glass doors, 27in. wide. (Robert W. Skinner Inc.) $500

Needlework family record by Martha A. Chamberlain, Westmoreland, New Hampshire, 1833, 17 x 21in. (Robert W. Skinner Inc.) $550

Mid 17th century leather blackjack with baluster body, 50cm. high. (Christie's) $1,200

MODELS

Exhibition standard scale working model of Sir Goldsworthy Gurney's steam coach, circa 1827, 53.5cm. long. (Christie's) $9,560

Fine 1-inch scale model traction engine with Stephenson's link motion, 19½in. long.(Sotheby's Belgravia) $660

Live steam spirit-fired model paddle steamer marine steam plant, 80cm. long. (Sotheby's Belgravia) $615

Almost mint condition Carette stationary steam plant in original box, 6½in. wide. (Sotheby's Belgravia) $205

Exhibition standard 1 to 24 scale model of the Curtiss JN-4D 'Jenny', circa 1916, built by R. A. Burgess, 33cm. long. (Christie's) $1,790

Scale model of a pony trap wagonette with padded seats and brass carriage lamps, 28cm. long. (Sotheby's Belgravia) $235

2in. scale model of the Clayton Steam Wagon No. 45, with brazed copper firetube boiler, 84cm. long. (Christie's) $2,270

3in. scale Burrell showman's road locomotive and organ by P. H. Manning, Southport, 180in. long. (Christie's) $2,030

Finely detailed, coal-fired, live steam model of the Fowler fairground engine 'Lord Kitchener'. (Wm. H. Brown) $2,360

Fine European carved wooden model of a horse tram in mahogany, 53.4cm. long. (Sotheby's Belgravia) $190

Well-detailed 1in. to 1ft. scale model in wood and metal of the Bleriot Type XXVII single seater monoplane by P. Veale, 58.5cm. long.(Christie's) $1,790

Late 19th century unusual model of a Victorian horse-drawn dust-cart, 40.8cm. long. (Sotheby's Belgravia) $615

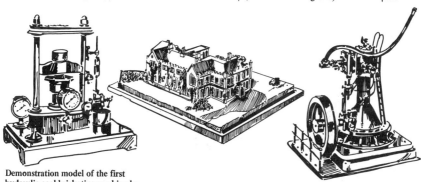

Demonstration model of the first hydraulic coal bricketing machine by Newton & Co., London, 40.5 x 35.5cm. (Sotheby's Belgravia) $260

Early 20th century architectural model of Flaxley Abbey, 46.5cm. wide. (Sotheby's Belgravia) $665

Good vertical stationary steam engine, 24.8cm. high.(Sotheby's Belgravia) $545

2in. scale model of the Burrell Special Scenic showman's road locomotive 'Thetford Town', 126cm. long. (Christie's) $3,107

Miniature oak model of a silk loom. (Phillips) $180

1in. scale model of the single cylinder two-speed, four-shaft traction engine, 'Minnie', 46cm. long. (Christie's) $1,435

517

MODEL SHIPS

Detailed ¼in. to 1ft. scale dockyard model of the U.S.S. 'Lexington' by R. Cartwright, 1978, 63cm. long. (Christie's) $1,315

Finely planked and rigged 1/32nd scale model of an ocean going dhow by D. A. Brogden, Skegness, 71cm. long. (Christie's) $1,315

Fully planked and rigged wood and metal model of the clipper 'Cutty Sark', by M. Gibb, 117cm. long. (Christie's) $1,315

Napoleonic prisoner-of-war bone ship model, 89cm. long. (Phillips) $32,200

Bing battleship, circa 1912, 29in. long. (Christie's S. Kensington) $1,640

Half-block dockyard model of a steam yacht, 94cm. long. (Sotheby's Belgravia) $485

Modern English model of a brig, 37cm. wide. (Sotheby's Belgravia) $605

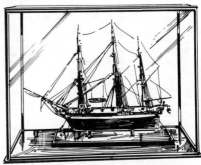

Late 19th century English model of a steam yacht with streamlined wooden hull. (Sotheby's Belgravia) $920

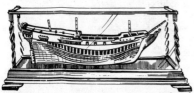

Planked and framed holly and mahogany dockyard model of a 32-gun frigate, 66cm. long. (Christie's) $1,145

Modern English well-detailed model of the Padstow lifeboat 'Joseph Hiram Chadwick', 107cm. long. (Sotheby's Belgravia) $970

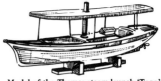

Model of the Thames steam launch 'Togo' by
P. Nunn, Sevenoaks, 135cm. long.(Christie's)
$835

Half-block model of the barque 'Aikshaw' with painted hull,
circa 1875, 142cm. long. (Sotheby's Belgravia)$1,695

Mid 19th century English model of the clipper 'John
Nicol Fleming', in glazed mahogany case, 76cm. long.
(Sotheby's Belgravia) $1,330

Fully rigged bone and horn model of an 88-gun man-of-
war, 46 x 69cm. (Christie's) $9,560

Builder's model of the steam launch 'Winifred', circa
1885, 68.5cm. long. (Christie's) $1,790

Modern English scale model of the clipper 'Piako' in
glazed case, 61cm. long. (Sotheby's Belgravia) $170

Detailed ¼in. to 1ft. scale fully planked and rigged
model of a Royal Navy Brig, by P. W. Kirby, Oxford,
86.5cm. wide. (Christie's) $1,005

Fully rigged French prisoner-of-war boxwood, bone,
horn and copper sheathed model of an English 80-gun
ship, 45.5cm. long. (Christie's) $7,170

Half-model of a fully square-rigged ship in a frame case.
(Banks & Silvers) $1,110

19th century American ivory ship model in mahogany case, 40cm. long. (Robert W. Skinner Inc.)
$1,075

MODEL TRAINS

One of two gauge '1' London, Midland and Scottish twin bogie corridor coaches by Bing. (Christie's) $405

3½in. gauge model of the Southern Railway 2-4-2 side tank locomotive No. 4, 66cm. long.(Christie's) $2,150

Gauge '1' spirit-fired live steam model of a London and North Eastern Railway 0-4-0 side tank locomotive, burner by Marklin. (Christie's) $1,555

Model of the Duchess of Buccleuch made in Sweden, 1961, 10ft. long. (Phillips) $19,040

Good 2½in. gauge model railway engine, the L.M.S. Railway Pacific Princess Royal, 63.5cm. long. (Fox & Sons) $2,440

Bassett-Lowke gauge '0' electric 4-4-2 tank locomotive by Bing, circa 1912, 29.2cm. long. (Sotheby's Belgravia)$665

Unusual early Bing gauge '3' live steam spirit-fired 4-4-0 engine, 35.5cm. long, circa 1902-06. (Sotheby's Belgravia) $1,420

Gauge '0' 2-rail electric model of the Pennsylvania Rail Road Class K4 'Pacific' locomotive and tender, 54.5cm. long. (Christie's) $955

Good 'coronation' gauge '0' electric 4-6-2 locomotive 'City of Bristol', 1ft.8½in. long.(Sotheby's Belgravia) $905

Rare gauge '1' spirit-fired live steam model of a Midland Railway 4-4-2 'Tilbury' side tank locomotive, burner by Bing.(Christie's) $3,585

Gauge '1' London, Midland and Scottish Railway 12-wheeled corridor dining car, by Bing for Bassett-Lowke. (Christie's) $165

Gauge '1' clockwork model of the London and North Eastern Railway 4-4-1 locomotive and tender, by Marklin for Bassett-Lowke. (Christie's) $835

Rare gauge '1' clockwork model of the London and North Eastern Railway Atlantic locomotive and tender by Marklin. (Christie's) $2,270

Early 20th century 2½in. gauge spirit-fired model of the Great Central Railway 4-6-0 locomotive and tender 'Sir Sam Fay', 82cm. long. (Christie's) $955

Special Marklin issue locomotive, tender and carriages, 1935. (Phillips) $5,950

Bing gauge '1' live steam spirit-fired 2-2-0 locomotive and tender, 39.5cm. long. (Sotheby's Belgravia)
$830

German spirit-fired 0-4-0 gauge '0' locomotive, circa 1915, 1ft.3¼in. wide. (Sotheby's Belgravia)
$520

Bassett-Lowke gauge '0' live steam spirit-fired 2-6-0 locomotive, 44.5cm. long, in original box. (Sotheby's Belgravia) $665

Gauge '1' spirit-fired live steam model of the Caledonian Railway 0-4-0 side tank locomotive with burner by Bing.(Christie's)
$1,145

MONEY BANKS

Victorian cast-iron mechanical money box in the form of two frogs, 1882, 20.5cm. long. (Bonham's)$385

Late 19th century American 'Leap Frog' money bank, 7½in. wide. (Sotheby's Belgravia) $550

Late 19th century American 'speaking dog' cast-iron money bank, 7¾in. long. (Sotheby's Belgravia) $240

Early 20th century English 'Hoopla' cast-iron money bank, 8½in. long, by John Harper & Co. (Sotheby's Belgravia)$225

Late 19th century American reclining Chinaman cast-iron mechanical bank, 8in. long. (Sotheby's Belgravia) $1,035

Unusual tinplate monkey mechanical bank, German, circa 1920, 6½in. high. (Sotheby's Belgravia) $115

MUSICAL BOXES & POLYPHONES

Bal-AMI 45-rpm. juke box, circa 1965, 133cm. high. (Sotheby's Belgravia) $120

19th century rosewood and inlaid musical cabinet with mirrored galleried top, 3ft.6½in. high. (Taylor Lane & Creber) $270

AMI Continental 45-rpm. juke box with curved display, circa 1961, 162cm. high. (Sotheby's Belgravia) $105

German disc musical photograph album by Unghans, circa 1910. (Sotheby's Belgravia) $620

Gem roller organ in stencil-decorated wooden case, circa 1890, 36cm. wide. (Sotheby's Belgravia) $950

Late 19th century American concert roller organ on oak case, 43cm. wide. (Sotheby's Belgravia) $950

522

German symphonium disc musical box with twenty-five metal discs, circa 1900, 46.7cm. wide. (Sotheby's Belgravia)$760

Late 19th century Swiss music box in inlaid walnut case, 25in. wide. (Robert W. Skinner Inc.) $675

English Melodia paper-roll organette, circa 1880-1890, 31cm. wide. (Sotheby's Belgravia) $260

Early 20th century French spring-wound mandoline barrel piano by Le Brestois, 108cm. wide. (Sotheby's Belgravia) $3,450

19th century Gloria mandoline zither music box in walnut and ebonised case, 22in. wide. (Boardman) $1,830

Bremond interchangeable cylinder musical box on stand, Swiss, circa 1880, 76cm. wide. (Sotheby's Belgravia) $3,330

Memod Freres Mira disc musical box, Swiss, circa 1908, sold with eleven metal discs, 107cm. high. (Sotheby's Belgravia) $3,810

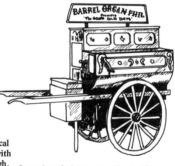

Street barrel piano on cart by A. Thomasso & Son.(Sotheby's Belgravia)$3,270

Early 19th century Astor & Co. chamber barrel organ in mahogany Gothic case, 178cm. high. (Sotheby's Belgravia) $1,430

American Edison Gem phonograph, model D, with original crane, 1912, sold with cylinders. (Sotheby's Belgravia) $760

Late 19th century Swiss musical box with eight tunes, in wooden marquetry case, 26in. long. (Robert W. Skinner Inc.) $1,900

German symphonium disc musical box in walnut veneered case, 36cm. wide, circa 1900.(Sotheby's Belgravia) $405

MUSICAL BOXES & POLYPHONES

Swiss cylinder musical box by
Lecoultre Freres, circa 1880,
53cm. wide. (Sotheby's
Belgravia) $645

19th century Swiss dancing doll
automata music box, 33in. wide.
(C. G. Sloan & Co. Inc.)
          $8,000

German disc organette by Amo-
rette, circa 1900, 43cm. wide,
sold with twenty-five zinc discs.
(Sotheby's Belgravia)$230

American Columbia AH disc
gramophone with large conical black horn and brass bell,
circa 1904. (Sotheby's
Belgravia) $690

Late 19th century peerless
pneumatic organ paper-roll
organette, 41cm. wide.
(Sotheby's Belgravia)$415

Good French Pathe Coquet phonograph in beechwood cabinet, circa
1904, with aluminum horn.
(Sotheby's Belgravia) $255

Late 19th century Swiss bells-
and-dolls-in-sight cylinder
musical box by Abrahams,
47cm. wide. (Sotheby's
Belgravia) $3,450

Craneophone horn gramophone
in inlaid wooden cabinet and
with eight petalled wooden horn.
(Sotheby's Belgravia) $560

Nicole Freres cylinder musical
box, 51cm. wide, circa 1860.
(Sotheby's Belgravia)$875

Late 19th century Swiss Bells-
and-drum-in-sight cylinder
musical box, 66cm. wide.
(Sotheby's Belgravia)$875

Late 19th century German 19in.
Symphonion disc musical box
in oak and walnut veneered case;
99cm. high. (Sotheby's Belgravia)
          $2,530

German polyphon disc musical
box lid inlaid in bone, circa
1900, 34cm. wide. (Sotheby's
Belgravia) $690

Nicole Freres mandoline cylinder musical box, circa 1885, 87cm. wide. (Sotheby's Belgravia) $2,645

Gramophone company style No. 5 trademark gramophone, in original leather carrying case, circa 1900.(Sotheby's Belgravia) $1,010

George IV silver rectangular musical box engraved with a cricketer, London 1824, 3½in. wide. (Geering & Colyer) $985

French Pathe Aiglon phonograph with handle-wound works, circa 1903. (Sotheby's Belgravia) $255

Mid 19th century Swiss Du Commun Girod Forte piano musical box, 41cm. wide. (Sotheby's Belgravia) $1,380

Early 19th century small barrel organ, 30.5cm. wide.(Sotheby's Belgravia) $690

Early 20th century German 10in. Symphonion bell disc musical box, 33cm. wide. (Sotheby's Belgravia) $965

Regina lift-top coin operated music box in carved oak case, sold with twenty discs, 21in. wide. (C. G. Sloan & Co. Inc.) $1,100

Late 19th century American Celestina paper-roll organette, 38cm. wide. (Sotheby's Belgravia) $875

Late 19th century German 12in. coin-operated Symphonium disc musical box, 147cm. high. (Sotheby's Belgravia)$1,725

E.M.G. mark XA gramophone in quartered oak case, with papier-mache horn, circa 1932. (Sotheby's Belgravia) $460

Edison diamond disc phonograph, circa 1915, in floor standing oak cabinet. (Sotheby's Belgravia) $345

Early 18th century horn in F by Daniel Kodisch, Nuremburg. (Sotheby's) $4,285

Violoncello by Santino Lauazza in Milan, 1718, 29in. length of back. (Sotheby's) $10,650

Pedal harp by I. & I. Erart, London, gilded and painted with vines, 170cm. high. (Parsons, Welch & Cowell) $1,150

English violin by Arthur Richardson, Crediton, 1924, length of back 14in. (Sotheby's) $1,905

Fine two-keyed boxwood oboe by George Goulding, London, circa 1800, length 57.3cm. (Sotheby's) $2,500

Mid 19th century simple-system rosewood flute by Louis Lot, Paris, sounding length 53.5cm. (Sotheby's) $975

Six-keyed boxwood clarinet in C by Goulding & Co., London, circa 1808, 59.8cm. long. (Sotheby's) $455

Seven-keyed boxwood oboe by Grenser and Wiesner, Dresden, circa 1800, 56.4cm. long. (Sotheby's) $1,905

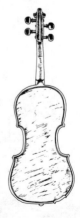

English violoncello by John Dixon, Cambridge, 1730, length of back 29¼in. (Sotheby's) $1,740

English violin by Alexander Hume, London, 1920, length of back 14¼in.(Sotheby's) $1,015

Violoncello by William Forster, London, length of back 28¾in.(Sotheby's) $1,905

Italian violin by Guiseppe Rossi, Rome, 1923, length of back, 14in., in shaped case. (Sotheby's) $770

Irish violin by John Delany, Dublin, in golden-brown color, length of back 14in. (Sotheby's) $2,260

Bell harp by John Simcock, Bath, circa 1740, 56.5cm. long. (Sotheby's) $1,905

English double-bass, length of back 43¾in., with canvas cover. (Sotheby's) $2,905

Early 19th century English serpent, body of leather-bound wood, total length 7ft.8in. (Sotheby's) $1,475

Moroccan nafir or trumpet with brass tube in three sections, 140.2cm. long. (Sotheby's) $190

Rosewood octavin, unstamped, circa 1900, 46cm. long. (Sotheby's) $1,070

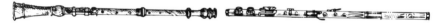
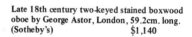

Early 19th century six-keyed pearwood bassoon by Christopher Gerock, London, 123cm. long. (Sotheby's) $1,045

Late 18th century two-keyed stained boxwood oboe by George Astor, London, 59.2cm. long. (Sotheby's) $1,140

Tyrolean violin by Matteus Goffriler, 1824, length of back 14in., sold with a bow. (Sotheby's) $1,985

Mandore by Christian Nonemacher, Genoa, 1732, total length 51.4cm. (Sotheby's) $2,500

Scottish violin by James W. Briggs, Glasgow, 1895, length of back, 14in. (Sotheby's) $3,145

French guitar by Thibout (fils), Caen, circa 1800, length 93.4cm. with wooden case. (Sotheby's) $665

MUSICAL INSTRUMENTS

Fine Italian violoncello by Antonio Gragnani, 1781, length of back 29¼in. (Christie's) $17,850

English copper serpent, mid 19th century, with brass mounts, 104in. long. (Sotheby's) $2,380

English viola by Walter H. Mayson, Manchester, 1890, length of back 16in. (Christie's) $950

Good French violin by H. C. Silvestre, Lyons, circa 1870, length of two-piece back 14in. (Christie's) $4,285

Fine eight-keyed ivory flute, stamped Drouet, London, circa 1820, sounding length 23in. (Christie's) $1,140

Eight-keyed boxwood flute, circa 1815, by D'Almaine & Co., London, sounding length 23in. (Christie's) $475

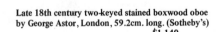

Late 18th century two-keyed stained boxwood oboe by George Astor, London, 59.2cm. long. (Sotheby's) $1,140

Four-keyed boxwood flute by V. Metzler, London, sounding length 21in. (Christie's) $380

Italianate violin by Nicolo Gagliano, 1736, with one-piece back, length of back 13¾in. (Christie's) $3,570

English violin by Emanuel Whitmarsh, London, 1888. (Buckell & Ballard) $1,800

Italian child's violin by Lorenzo and Tomaso Carcassi, length of back 13in. (Christie's) $3,215

Ivory thirteen-course German baroque lute, labeled Andreas Berr/Lauten und Geigenmacher in Wienn, 1699, 29½in. long. (Christie's) $9,495

Italian violin, attributed to Remo Solferino, 1912, with two-piece back, length of back 14in. (Christie's)$2,620

Good French violin by Louis Guersan, 1752, two-piece back varnished in golden-brown, length of back 14in. (Christie's) $7,140

Regency harp by Sebastian Evaros, London, with reeded support, 66¼in. high. (C. G. Sloan & Co. Inc.) $950

Mid 18th century Italian composite violin, unlabeled, length of back 14in. (Christie's) $1,545

Six-keyed boxwood clarinet, circa 1810, stamped Metzler, London, overall length 26in. (Christie's) $525

Mid 18th century two-keyed boxwood oboe, unstamped, overall length 23in. (Christie's) $1,545

Four-keyed boxwood flute stamped Paine & Hopkins/ No. 69 Cornhill/London, sounding length 21in. (Christie's) $240

Early 19th century six-keyed pearwood bassoon by Christopher Gerock, London, 123cm. long.(Sotheby's) $1,045

17th century Italian cello with English table. (Woolley & Wallis) $1,330

Italian violin by Romeo Antoniazzi, circa 1910, with two-piece back, length of back 14in. (Christie's) $2,380

Fine six-course ivory lute by Magno Tieffenbrucker, circa 1570. (Christie's) $9,495

French violin by Nicolas Mathieu, circa 1775, length of back 14in. (Christie's)$1,905

NETSUKE

19th century figure of a karako in Chinese costume, in stained ivory, unsigned. (Sotheby's) $335

Wooden netsuke of a large orange which opens to show two sages playing Go, cord attached. (Lawrence Fine Art) $240

Ivory figure of a basket maker, signed on a red lacquer tablet Gyokumin. (Sotheby's) $1,075

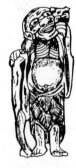

Early 19th century ivory netsuke figure of Gama Sennin, unsigned. (Sotheby's) $285

Lightly stained 19th century ivory study of a warrior on horseback, unsigned. (Sotheby's) $575

Bone netsuke of Chohi standing holding his beard, sword in his other hand. (Lawrence Fine Art) $200

Ivory netsuke of a moth resting on a lotus leaf. (Lawrence Fine Art) $130

19th century ivory manju of the Asakusa school, unsigned. (Sotheby's) $380

Late 19th century ivory figure of Fukusuke walking and carrying toys over one shoulder, unsigned. (Sotheby's) $955

Large group of nine masks clustered together, signed Tadachika. (Sotheby's) $450

Ivory netsuke of a horse with lowered head, signed Shuraku. (Sotheby's) $1,000

Unusual ivory netsuke study of a toad, half hidden in a lotus leaf, signed in seal form. (Sotheby's) $620

Small ivory netsuke of a model of a ferryboat and passengers, signed Ikkosai. (Sotheby's) $480

Small wood netsuke figure of a small boy seated and wearing a dancer's mask, signed Hokushu saku. (Sotheby's) $480

Ivory study of a seated crane, inscribed Mitsuhiro. (Sotheby's) $760

Late ivory netsuke of Confucius seated on the back of a two-horned kirin, signed. (Sotheby's) $355

Ivory study of a horse netsuke, signed Ryukosai. (Sotheby's) $545

Ivory figure of a Sambaso dancer, stained, signed Shogetsu. (Sotheby's) $215

Ivory model of a Shishimai mask, inscribed Tomotada. (Sotheby's) $380

Good wood netsuke model of the lantern ghost, signed Sansho with Kakihan. (Sotheby's) $1,005

Wood model of a Konoha Tengu mask, signed with a Kakihan. (Sotheby's) $455

Unusual ivory netsuke of a toy fish, signed Hidemasa, deeply stained. (Sotheby's) $430

Wood netsuke of a snail on a mushroom by Mitani Goho. (Sotheby's) $5,020

Late 18th century wood netsuke model of a wolf, unsigned, with inlaid ivory eyes. (Sotheby's) $430

Late 19th century ivory study of a Shishi, unsigned, style of Rensai. (Sotheby's) $620

Ivory netsuke of a fishing boat with six occupants, signed. (Lawrence Fine Art) $175

Wood netsuke figure of a warrior, signed Shuraku. (Sotheby's) $575

Well patinated late 18th/early 19th century ivory mask netsuke of Hannya. (Christie's) $590

Mid 19th century ivory Kagamibuta netsuke, signed Tenmin.(Christie's) $285

Unusual small ivory model of a ship, signed Ryumin.(Sotheby's) $240

Late 18th/early 19th century ivory netsuke of a fisherman and his nets, unsigned. (Christie's) $235

Fine 19th century large square ivory manju netsuke carved with two men wrestling, signed Dosho. (Christie's) $945

Late 19th century Japanese carved ivory netsuke of a man smoking a pipe, 3cm. high. (Robert W. Skinner Inc.) $130

Early 19th century ivory netsuke of Tobosaku dragging a branch from a peach tree, unsigned. (Christie's) $210

Late 19th century ivory figure of a boy on a recumbent ox, unsigned. (Sotheby's) $430

18th century patinated ivory seal netsuke of a priest, unsigned. (Christie's)$210

Early 19th century Kyoto school wood netsuke of a reclining tiger, signed Haru(Shun). (Sotheby's) $525

19th century ivory netsuke of a flying Buddhist angel, signed Mitsumasa. (Christie's) $400

Small ivory netsuke of a monkey by Masakazu of Osaka. (Sotheby's) $430

Small ivory group of Ashinaga and Tenaga, signed Romochika. (Sotheby's) $570

Early 19th century ivory Ryusa style netsuke carved with a Boddhisattva among lotus, unsigned. (Christie's) $565

Ivory group depicting the birth of Momotaro, signed Masanobu. (Sotheby's) $955

Early 19th century patinated ivory netsuke of a blind amma with a stick, unsigned. (Christie's) $825

Tokyo school carved ivory group of children on rocks, 20cm. high, signed Homei Hoson, slightly damaged. (Sotheby, King & Chasemore) $1,710

Late 19th century wood and ivory trick netsuke formed as a dancer's head, unsigned. (Christie's) $520

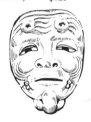

Late 19th century finely carved ivory mask netsuke of Okina, signed Homin. (Christie's) $475

Late 19th century ivory group of Daikoku and a Karako, unsigned. (Sotheby's) $355

Late 19th century ivory Kagami-buta netsuke with dark bronze disc, unsigned. (Christie's) $375

Late 17th/early 18th century
pewter 'ball' measure of half
pint capacity, 12.5cm. high.
(Sotheby's) $675

18th century European oval pewter serving
dish with wavy edges, 42.5cm. long.
(Robert W. Skinner Inc.) $160

18th century Northern French pewter flagon with d-shaped handle,
20cm. high. (Christie's)$330

17th century pewter 'wedge' baluster measure of quart capacity,
21.5cm. high. (Sotheby's)
          $1,575

Late 16th/early 17th century pewter
'Maidenhead' spoon with flattened hexagonal stem, 17cm. long. (Sotheby's)
          $605

Late 18th century German pew-
ter flagon dated for 1776,
Waiblingen, 26cm. high.
(Christie's) $1,270

One of a pair of Kayserzinn pewter
candlesticks, circa 1900, 42cm.
high. (Sotheby's Belgravia)
          $1,640

George II Norwich Wool Guild tankard, by
William Eddon, circa 1747, 17.5cm. high.
(Sotheby's) $2,260

Mid 18th century Swiss pewter
humpen, Zurich, engraved with
wriggle-work, 20cm. high.
(Christie's) $685

Early 18th century pewter 'ball'
measure of conventional form,
by Edward Quick, 9cm. high.
(Sotheby's) $540

19th century Dutch pewter commemorative wriggle engraved charger, 37cm.
diam. (Robert W. Skinner Inc.)
          $650

One of a pair of 19th century
Scottish pewter flagons, inscribed
Free Church Crailing, 1843, 30.5cm.
high. (Christie's) $415

17th century German square pewter water carrier, 23.5cm. high. (Geering & Colyer) $480

WMF silvered pewter dish, circa 1900, 22.5cm. high. (Sotheby's Belgravia) $585

Late 18th century pewter canteen with decoration at throat and base, 27.5cm. high. (Robert W. Skinner Inc.) $100

Fine and rare bell-based candlestick with plain socket, circa 1600, 21cm. high.(Sotheby's) $4,950

Mid 15th century pewter spoon with 'horned head-dress' knop and hexagonal stem, 17.5cm. long.(Sotheby's) $765

German silvered pewter Art Nouveau lamp with nautilus shell shade, circa 1900, 36.5cm. high. (Sotheby's Belgravia) $1,675

WMF silvered pewter mounted green glass decanter with pierced openwork stopper, circa 1900, 36.5cm. high. (Sotheby's Belgravia) $935

George III pewter flagon with double scroll handle, 31cm. high.(Christie's) $710

Charles I pewter flagon, handle stamped East Tuddenham, circa 1630-40, 28cm. high. (Sotheby's) $4,950

Late 17th century rare 'hammerhead' baluster measure in pewter, half pint capacity, 12cm. high. (Sotheby's) $1,015

Small late Stuart pewter flagon of plain tapering form, circa 1700, 19.5cm. high. (Sotheby's) $4,050

Mid 18th century Swiss pewter bauchkanne, dated for 1769, 21.5cm. high. (Christie's) $585

PEWTER

George III pewter ale jug, by Wm. Wright, London, 21cm. high. (Christie's) $1,420

Pewter strawberry dish, by George Beeston, circa 1750-60, 22cm. diam. (Sotheby's) $810

William and Mary 'capstan' salt in pewter decorated with gadrooned bands, 7cm. high. (Sotheby's) $1,015

Late 17th/early 18th century pewter 'ball' measure of gill capacity, engraved with initials, 10cm. high. (Sotheby's) $810

WMF silvered pewter tazza, circa 1900, 21.5cm. high. (Sotheby's Belgravia) $700

Lidless tavern pot in pewter, circa 1700, maker's mark IH, 14cm. high. (Sotheby's) $2,250

18th century German faience pewter mounted tankard with finial thumb lift, 18.5cm. high. (Robert W. Skinner Inc.) $275

18th century Dutch pewter one-handled hot water urn with domed lid, 37.5cm. high. (Robert W. Skinner Inc.) $425

Rare late 17th/early 18th century pewter 'ball' baluster measure of one pint capacity, 17.5cm. high. (Sotheby's) $1,395

One of a pair of alms or rosewater dishes, by Edward Leapidge, circa 1630, 41cm. diam. (Sotheby's) $5,000

Good William III or Queen Anne dome-lidded tankard, circa 1695-1705, 14cm. high. (Sotheby's) $1,665

One of six 18th century English pewter five-lobe wavy edge plates, by James Tisoe, London, 24cm. diam. (Robert W. Skinner Inc.) $700

18th century French pewter covered stew pail, 17.5cm. high. (Robert W. Skinner Inc.) $130

Rare 4th century A.D. pewter Romano-British dish, faults, 38cm. diam. (Sotheby's) $335

Late 17th century 'spool' salt in pewter with narrow everted rim, 4.5cm. high. (Sotheby's) $765

18th century Swiss pewter hexagonal wine canister with wriggle decoration, 22cm. high.(Robert W. Skinner Inc.) $225

Early Georgian pewter loving cup with two scrolled handles, 14.5cm. high. (Christie's) $465

18th century German pewter mounted ceremonial tankard with tapered oak body, 62.5cm. high.(Robert W. Skinner Inc.) $1,050

York 'acorn' flagon in pewter, by John Hardman or John Harrison, circa 1740-50, 31cm. high. (Sotheby's) $3,095

James I pewter flagon with scroll handle and shaped thumbpiece, hinge repaired, 35.5cm. high. (Christie's)$3,080

Boucheron stamped stoneware jug, signed, circa 1900, 27cm. high. (Sotheby's Belgravia)$1,125

Stuart pewter wriggled-work plate, by Moses West, circa 1680-85, 21.5cm. diam. (Sotheby's) $1,015

Late 18th century George III pewter ale flagon inscribed W. Hickford, Malden, 22cm. high. (Christie's) $590

Queen Anne plate with rare gadrooned border, circa 1700-10, 22.5cm. diam. (Sotheby's) $360

PEWTER

Rare mid 17th century wrigglework chalice in pewter, raised on baluster stem, 17cm. high. (Sotheby's) $1,595

18th century English double-flapped pewter inkstand with sand sprinkler, 15cm. long. (Robert W. Skinner Inc.) $180

18th century English pewter gallon baluster measure with shaped handle, 32cm. high. (Robert W. Skinner Inc.) $1,800

Late 18th century Dutch pewter flagon with flat circular cover, 23cm. high. (Christie's) $665

One of a pair of Kayserzinn pewter candlesticks designed by Hugo Leven, 42cm. high. (Christie's) $3,170

Early 18th century pewter flagon of tapering form by John Emes, London, 28cm. high. (Sotheby's) $1,825

16th century pewter spoon with seal top, 17cm. long, (Sotheby's) $360

One of a pair of pewter wrigglework plates by James Hitchman, London, circa 1720, 20cm. diam.(Sotheby's) $1,320

Early to mid 16th century pewter spoon with 'Lion Sejant' knop and hexagonal stem, 16cm. long. (Sotheby's) $585

18th century German pewter lidded tankard, 23cm. high. (Robert W. Skinner Inc.) $1,650

Rare small English pewter 'saucer' or spice plate, 16th century, 7in. diam. (Sotheby's) $1,145

Silvered pewter Art Nouveau clock, circa 1900, 62.5cm. high. (Sotheby's) Belgravia) $430

Early 17th century small pewter chalice with bucket-shaped bowl and ball-knopped stem, 7.5cm. high. (Sotheby's) $900

Octagonal trencher salt with slightly concave sides, 4.5cm. high, circa 1720. (Sotheby's) $675

Queen Anne pewter lidded tankard, circa 1710, 17.7cm. high. (Parsons, Welch & Cowell) $650

Early James I pear-shaped pewter spouted flagon, circa 1610, 9in. high. (Sotheby's)$11,855

17th century German relief-cast plate, 18.2cm. diam. (Sotheby's)$455

17th or early 18th century Dutch pewter flagon with shallow domed cover, 17.8cm. high. (Sotheby's) $3,190

Stuart pewter candlestick with banded cylindrical stem, circa 1680, 15cm. high. (Sotheby's) $1,685

16th century pewter spoon with 'melon' knop and hexagonal stem, 15cm. long. (Sotheby's) $405

One of a pair of early 18th century pewter pricket candlesticks with domed bases, 41cm. high. (Robert W. Skinner Inc.) $800

19th century pewter hot water jug with wood-mounted ribbed urn finial, 36cm. high.(Robert W. Skinner Inc.) $300

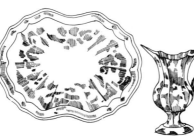

Mid 18th century Continental pewter ewer and basin, 21cm. high.(Sotheby's) $765

Swiss or South German Ringschraubflasche of mid 18th century. (Phillips) $1,000

PIANOS

Mahogany Art Nouveau upright piano by Arthur Wilson & Co., circa 1900, 57¼in. wide. (Sotheby's Belgravia)$385

George III mahogany square piano by Thos. Haxby, York, 1776. (Woolley & Wallis) $1,540

Fine 19th century boudoir upright pianoforte in satinwood with marquetry inlay, 4ft.7in. (Taylor Lane & Creber) $1,310

Robert Warnham painted satinwood grand piano on tapering legs with castors, circa 1910. (Sotheby's Belgravia) $9,800

Boudoir grand pianoforte by Collard & Collard in painted and lacquered ebonised case, 62in. long. (Dacre, Son & Hartley) $1,735

German painted satinwood grand piano, circa 1900, on square tapering legs. (Sotheby's Belgravia) $3,170

Grand piano by John Broadwood & Son, circa 1928, in polished ebonised case, 48½in. wide.(Coles, Knapp & Kennedy) $1,745

Arts and Crafts oak piano by Vose & Sons, Boston, Massachusetts, circa 1910, 60½in. wide. (Robert W. Skinner Inc.) $3,400

Grand pianoforte by John Broadwood & Son, London, 1798, 7ft. 5½in. long. (Sotheby's) $9,520

Late 18th century square piano by Schrader & Hartz, London, 1ft.5½in. wide. (Sotheby's) $3,095

Baby grand pianoforte by Monington & Weston, in gilt and black lacquered case decorated with chinoiserie scenes. (Geering & Colyer) $9,155

Baby grand pianoforte in figured walnut case, by Knight. (Edgar Horn) $1,430

Late 19th century American pipe set in leather case. (Robert W. Skinner Inc.) $220

Large Meerschaum pipe, 41cm. long, carved with a figure of a mother and child, circa 1860. (Christie's S. Kensington) $8,050

Meerschaum cheroot holder, carved with a figure of a man, with amber mouthpiece, 18.5cm. long. (Christie's S. Kensington)$200

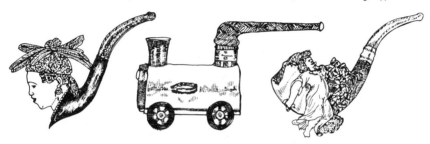

Meerschaum pipe with amber mouthpiece, 17cm. long. (Christie's S. Kensington) $2,225

Briar pipe shaped as train engine, vulcanite mouthpiece, 12cm. long. (Christie's S. Kensington)$175

Partly toned Meerschaum pipe, amber mouthpiece with metal band, 16cm. long. (Christie's S. Kensington) $610

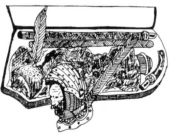

Rare Meerschaum double pipe, heads and shoulders forming covers, 12.5cm. wide, on brass stand. (Christie's S. Kensington) $1,640

Rare briar pipe with carved bowl, with separate cheroot holder, 52.3cm. long. (Christie's S. Kensington) $2,225

Meerschaum pipe, circa 1880, with figure of a lady. (Alfie's Antique Market) $545

French or Austrian Meerschaum cheroot holder, heavily carved, circa 1860, 27.2cm. long. (Sotheby's Belgravia) $935

Meerschaum pipe with bowl carved as a bearded Arab. (Christie's S. Kensington) $2,320

Late 19th/early 20th century Meerschaum pipe, bowl carved as a bulldog's head, 21.3cm. long. (Sotheby's Belgravia) $325

PIPES

Early 20th century Austrian Meerschaum pipe, bowl carved as a hare's head, 13.3cm. long. (Sotheby's Belgravia) $175

Silver mounted ivory stemmed Meerschaum Churchwarden's pipe. (Edgar Horn) $200

Late19th/early 20th century Austrian Meerschaum pipe, bowl carved with a coat-of-arms, 15.5cm. long. (Sotheby's Belgravia) $115

Late 19th century Austrian Meerschaum pipe with carved stem and flowerhead mouthpiece, 20cm. long. (Sotheby's Belgravia) $410

Late 19th century Austrian Meerschaum pipe, bowl carved as a pheasant's head, with glass eyes, 16.3cm. long. (Sotheby's Belgravia) $100

Late 19th/early 20th century Meerschaum pipe, bowl carved with a soldier's head, 15cm. long. (Sotheby's Belgravia) $195

Late 19th/early 20th century Austrian Meerschaum pipe with amber mouthpiece, 10.8cm. long. (Sotheby's Belgravia) $70

Bizarre pipe by Charles Edwards, London, 1885, 34oz., 24cm. long. (Sotheby's Belgravia) $2,340

Late 19th century Austrian Meerschaum pipe, bowl carved as the head of a young lady, 13cm. long. (Sotheby's Belgravia) $155

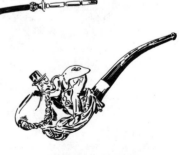

Late 19th century Austrian Meerschaum pipe, stem carved with a claw foot, 16.3cm. long. (Sotheby's Belgravia) $105

Austrian or Bavarian pipe with painted porcelain bowl, 1830's, 37cm. long. (Sotheby's Belgravia) $700

Late 19th century Austrian Meerschaum pipe with amber mouthpiece, 24.3cm. long. (Sotheby's Belgravia) $290

542

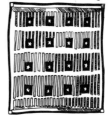

Mid 19th century American quilted patchwork coverlet, 72 x 90in. (Robert W. Skinner Inc.)$325

Patchwork quilt with central flower medallion, circa 1820, 108in. square. (Sotheby's Belgravia) $345

American patriotic coverlet in cotton sewn to give the effect of the American flag, 7ft.6in. square, circa 1880. (Robert W. Skinner Inc.) $1,200

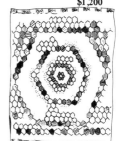

Late 19th century bedcover made from officer's uniforms, 91½ x 77in. (Sotheby's Belgravia) $395

Late 19th century American Victorian crazy quilt with matching shams, 76in. square. (Robert W. Skinner Inc.) $1,000

Early 19th century patchwork quilt in hexagons, square and triangles, 94 x 87in. (Sotheby's Belgravia) $345

Late 19th century embroidered bedspread on a midnight-blue satin ground, 99 x 85in. (Sotheby's Belgravia)$430

Late 19th/early 20th century American patchwork quilt in navy blue and white triangles, 75½in. square. (Sotheby's Belgravia) $300

18th century Portuguese coverlet, couchwork on Chinese silk, 100 x 80in. (Sotheby's Belgravia) $2,640

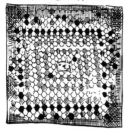

Chintz patchwork bedcover with square central medallion and broad border, 65 x 60in. (Sotheby's Belgravia) $145

Early 18th century embroidered bedcover sold with three pillowcases with white cotton ground. (Sotheby's Belgravia) $770

Mid 18th century English 'Italian quilted' bedcover in white cotton, 103 x 93½in. (Sotheby's Belgravia) $745

QUILTS

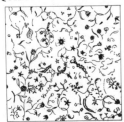

Mid 18th century American crewel-work coverlet on handwoven cotton sheeting, 94 x 98in. (Robert W. Skinner Inc.) $1,200

Late 19th century French cream linen bedcover with insets of fillet and reticella, 87½ x 65½in. (Sotheby's Belgravia) $165

Mid 19th century dated applique coverlet of white cotton squares with leaf patterns, 84in. wide. (Robert W. Skinner Inc.) $175

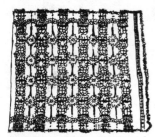

Mid 19th century American jacquard coverlet in wool on cotton ground, 88 x 78in. (Robert W. Skinner Inc.) $375

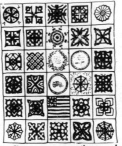

Applique commemorative coverlet of thirty quilted squares, 1853, 93in. square. (Robert W. Skinner Inc.) $2,700

Antique Baltimore friendship quilt, dated 1843, 108in. wide. (C. G. Sloan & Co. Inc.) $450

RUGS

Fine Yomut asmalyk with nut-brown field and ivory panel border, 3ft.11in. x 2ft. (Christie's) $470

Fine and unusual Qashqai rug, blood-red field with stylised flowerheads, 7ft. 6in. x 5ft.3in.(Christie's) $2,350

Antique part silk salor juval with shaded rust-brown field, 4ft.5in. x 3ft. (Christie's) $3,055

Fine Shirvan rug with royal blue field, 5ft.6in. x 4ft.3in. (Christie's) $5,405

Unusual antique Belouch rug with nut-brown field, 5ft.5in. x 3ft.10in. (Christie's) $2,350

Antique Chodor carpet with aubergine and brown field, slight damaged, 10ft.8in. x 6ft.3in.(Christie's) $4,230

544

One of a pair of Persian tribal Sou-
mac bag faces, 1ft.7½in. x 1ft.8in.
(Robert W. Skinner Inc.)
$2,200

Panderma Saph, circa 1940, 7ft.3in. x 2ft.7in.
(Sotheby's) $655

Soumak rug on a rust-red field,
slightly worn, 5ft.2in. x 6ft.3in.
(Robert W. Skinner Inc.)
$950

Antique Sarouk rug with ivory-grey
central field, 3ft.5in. x 4ft.10in.
(Robert W. Skinner Inc.)
$2,100

Fine Zile peacock rug in fair condition,
circa 1880, 6ft.3in. x 3ft.5in.
(Sotheby's) $3,615

Eastern caucasian rug with black
central field, 3ft.1in. x 4ft.11in.
(Robert W. Skinner Inc.)
$850

Baku rug in fair condition, with four borders,
circa 1880, 7ft.3in. x 4ft.1in. (Sotheby's)
$2,050

Antique shield Kazak rug
with central lozenge medallion, 5ft.7in. x 3ft.3in.
(Christie's) $1,290

Verne carpet with four rows of dragon
medallions, 10ft.10in. x 6ft.11in., circa
1900. (Sotheby's) $8,435

Tapestry carpet in muted colors ,
15ft.10in. x 12ft.4in. (Christie's)
$3,775

Samakand rug, rose field decorated with
scrolls, bats and an urn, 8ft.8in. x 4ft.6in.
(Sotheby, King & Chasemore) $440

Late 18th century Aubusson carpet woven in fresh but muted
colors , 18ft.3in. x 16ft.3in.
(Christie's) $2,260

RUGS

One of a pair of Mashhas rugs, circa 1930, 196 x 122cm. (Sotheby's) $1,080

Aubusson rug, circa 1830, 14ft.11in. x 12ft.8in. (Christie's)
$14,460

Antique Senna rug with royal blue field, 4ft.10in. x 3ft.6in. (Christie's) $3,375

Colorful Kelim rug, 9ft.10in. x 4ft.8in. (Parsons, Welch & Cowell) $1,070

Shirvan rug with all-over motifs on a brick-red ground, 5ft.4¼in. x 3ft. 11½in. (Geering & Colyer)
$2,180

Very fine Ispahan meditation rug, 1.40m. x 2.20m.(Phillips) $15,000

Kazak rug with blue field containing a rectangular white panel, 5ft.5in. x 2ft.10in. (Robert W. Skinner Inc.)
$950

Pakistan-Bokhara rug, 9ft. x 12ft. (C. G. Sloan & Co. Inc.)
$1,100

Kazak rug with central field of madder red 6ft.11in. x 3ft.3in. (Robert W. Skinner Inc.)
$1,300

Kashan rug with ivory field, circa 1940, 7ft.2in. x 4ft.4in. (Sotheby's) $1,405

Kashan rug with palmettes and flowering leafy vine, 7ft. x 4ft.6in (Christie's) $2,260

Bokhara Susani panel with ivory field, circa 1900, condition fair, 8ft.5in. x 5ft.6in. (Sotheby's)
$2,650

546

Zelli Sutlan rug with ivory field, slightly worn, 6ft.8in. x 4ft.4in. (Christie's) $1,905

Antique Kazak prayer rug, 3ft.6in x 3ft.7in. (C. G. Sloan & Co. Inc.) $1,050

Josan rug with medium blue field showing palmettes, flowerheads and vines, 7ft. 5in. x 4ft.5in. (Christie's) $3,856

Fine Sarough rug with ivory field, circa 1900, 6ft.8in. x 4ft.3in. (Sotheby's) $1,930

Fine embossed silk Kashan rug in pink, blue, gold and ivory, 10ft. 10¼in. x 7ft.11½in.(Geering & Colyer) $9,955

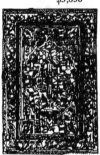

Kashan rug in fair condition, 5ft.2in. x 3ft.5in.(Sotheby's) $1,770

Baluchistan Tree of Life rug, circa 1930, 5ft.1in. x 2ft.7in. (Sotheby's) $660

Fine Teheran Tree of Life rug, circa 1920, 6ft.9in. x 4ft.8in.(Sotheby's) $1,935

Antique Shirvan rug, indigo filed with four medallions and hooked guls, circa 1860, 11ft.6in. x 4ft. 11in. (Sotheby's) $1,815

Daghestan rug with stylised floral figured honeycomb design, 7ft.5¼in. x 4ft.7¼in.(Geering & Colyer) $3,410

Kashan Tree of Life rug, in good condition, with blue ground, 6ft. x 4ft. (Smith-Woolley & Perry)$1,145

Kashan rug with curved-edge indigo foliate pole medallion, 7ft. x 4ft.4in. (Sotheby, King & Chasemore) $1,850

Esfahan Tree of Life rug, circa 1920, 6ft.6in. x 4ft.6in. (Sotheby's) $2,925

Sarough Mahal rug, circa 1930, 6ft. 7in. x 4ft.2in. (Sotheby's) $2,225

Eastern Caucasian rug with ivory field, 3ft.1in. x 5ft.8in.(Robert W. Skinner Inc.) $325

Shirvan rug with three geometrically figured star-shaped medallions, signed, 9ft.10½in. x 3ft.10½in.(Geering & Colyer) $1,075

Fine Kashan embossed silk prayer rug, 6ft.10in. x 4ft.3in. (Geering & Colyer) $5,475

Antique Kazak rug, 4ft.3in. x 6ft.6in. (C. G. Sloan & Co. Inc.) $1,100

Anatolian yastik with central medallion, restored, 2ft.2in. x 3ft.6in. (Robert W. Skinner Inc.) $125

Persian rug with blue ground and diamond-shaped center panel, 6ft. 3in. x 4ft.6in. (Honiton Galleries) $325

Anatolian saddle bags in tapestry weave, 3ft.8in. x 1ft.4in. (Robert W. Skinner Inc.) $700

One of a pair of Kashan rugs, circa 1930, 6ft.7in. x 4ft.6in., with vine and spearhead border. (Sotheby's) $4,095

Bokhara Susani door hanging in fair condition, circa 1900, 7ft.2in. x 5ft.5in. (Sotheby's) $1,255

Turkish needlework prayer panel in fair condition, circa 1850, 5ft. 1in. x 2ft.8in. (Sotheby's) $770

Peking rug with indigo field, circa 1920, 6ft.7in. x 4ft. (Sotheby's) $770

Kazakh rug, madder field three rows of seven guls, pale indigo star. (Sotheby, King & Chasemore) $2,015

Soumakh rug with indigo field, in fair condition, circa 1880, 8ft.3in. x 4ft.11in. (Sotheby's) $1,880

Persian rug with ivory ground and flowering decoration, 7ft. x 4ft.5in. (Morphets) $1,085

Perepedil rug with royal blue field, 5ft.9in. x 3ft.10in. (Christie's) $1,785

Unusual Turkman embroidered panel in fair condition, 6ft.3in. square, circa 1880. (Sotheby's)$1,445

Talish rug with dark blue field and outer trefoil border, 3ft.11in. x 8ft. 4in. (Robert W. Skinner Inc.) $1,600

Zile horsecover, pale blue field with animals, circa 1880, in fair condition, 5ft.3in. x 4ft. 7in. (Sotheby's)$2,050

Seychour rug, slightly worn, with parts restored, 6ft.4in. x 4ft.11in. (Christie's) $1,665

Shirvan rug, field with three medallions, in fair condition, circa 1880, 7ft.11in. x 4ft. 7in. (Sotheby's)$1,685

Shirvan Gelim rug with ivory field, circa 1880, in fair condition, 10ft. 6in. c 6ft.1in. (Sotheby's) $1,205

Teheran rug, field with indigo pole medallion, circa 1920, in fair condition 6ft.3in. x 4ft. 5in. (Sotheby's) $3,135

English gold fob seal with domed
fluted base and flower-chased
border, circa 1830, 3.5cm. high.
(Sotheby's) $620

Mid 19th century gold and hardstone swivel
desk seal, 3.5cm. high. (Sotheby's)
                                      $1,425

Gadrooned and chased English fob
seal, 5cm. high, circa 1830.
(Sotheby's) $830

Ivory triple desk seal in the form
of a hand. (Christie's S. Kensington) $1,215

Early 19th century English fob seal in gold,
2.8cm. high, sold with another. (Sotheby's)
                                      $525

English gold, hardstone, mother-
of-pearl triple seal, circa 1835,
6cm. high. (Sotheby's)$855

Gold and jasper table seal formed as
a dove alighting on a nest, 41mm.
high. (Christie's) $1,200

Gold and turquoise desk seal, circa 1840,
8.5cm. high. (Sotheby's) $1,905

Mid 19th century French parcel-
gilt silver desk seal, 6.9cm. high.
(Sotheby's Belgravia) $425

19th century English two-color
gold desk seal, handle in the form
of a Corinthian column, 7cm. high.
(Sotheby's) $1,955

Early 19th century pierced gold fob seal
of bell form, 3.8cm. high, sold with
another. (Sotheby's) $300

19th century gold fob seal with
urn-shaped handle, 3.8cm. high.
(Sotheby's) $530

19th century Shibayama tusk vase, decorated in mother-of-pearl, gilt and lacquer, 50cm. high. (Taylor Lane & Creber) $1,145

Silver and Shibayama rectangular vessel, 33cm. high. (Phillips) $11,040

Late 19th century Shibayama decorated ivory vase with silver mounts. (Grays Antique Mews) $4,840

Japanese silver and Shibayama globular vase and cover, center band of mother-of-pearl, 16cm. high. (H. Spencer & Sons) $2,600

One of a pair of Shibayama bezique counters decorated with birds and insects, circa 1900, 9cm. high. (Sotheby's Belgravia) $510

Shibayama box and cover, circa 1900, 12cm. high, cover with peony knop. (Sotheby's Belgravia) $730

Enamelled, oxidised silver and Shibayama vase, circa 1900, 19.5cm. high. (Sotheby's Belgravia) $1,270

Enamelled silver and Shibayama garniture, circa 1900, 16.5cm. high. (Sotheby's Belgravia) $1,905

Late 19th century silver mounted ivory tusk vase inlaid in Shibayama style, 23.4cm. high. (Christie's) $1,755

One of a pair of richly decorated hexagonal Shibayama vases, 31cm. high. (Lambert & Symes) $4,600

Late 19th century Shibayama elephant with ivory body, 23cm. high. (Sotheby's Belgravia) $4,025

One of a pair of Masayuki Shibayama tusk vases, circa 1890, 17.4cm. high. (Sotheby's Belgravia) $2,805

551

19th century American moulded copper fish sign, gold leafed, 36in. long. (Robert W. Skinner Inc.) $1,350

Rolled brass LNWR nameplate. (Christie's S. Kensington) $1,315

One of six lithographic Guinness posters, 30in. high, dating from 1934. (Sotheby's Belgravia) $80

18th century English painted tin trade sign and iron bracket, 17¼in. high. (Robert W. Skinner Inc.)$900

Large decorative lithographic poster by John Hassall for Veritas, 120in. high. (Sotheby's Belgravia) $155

Decorative lithographic advertising poster by H. de Faurencin for Priceless Oil, 63in. high.(Sotheby's Belgravia) $115

18th century tobacconist's sign of Red Indian figure. (Boardmans) $985

Poster advertising Omega bicycles printed by P. Dupont, Paris, circa 1885, 47in. high. (Robert W. Skinner Inc.) $250

Large decorative lithographic poster for a circus, showing acrobats, balancers and horses, 118in. high. (Sotheby's Belgravia) $170

Antique carved walnut tobacconist's sign modeled as a rotund Turk, 22in. high. (C. G. Sloan & Co. Inc.) $1,200

19th century enameled metal sign, 76cm. high. (Bonham's) $600

Early 19th century carved wooden mermaid Tavern sign, 55cm. long. (Robert W. Skinner Inc.) $1,500

American locksmith's sign in the form of a carved wooden key, circa 1900, 76in. long. (Robert W. Skinner Inc.) $300

One of two 19th century framed stoneware price lists, Vermont, 13½in. high. (Robert W. Skinner Inc.) $300

Reproduction cigar store Indian advertising figure, 38½in. high. (Sotheby's Belgravia) $60

Early film poster for Keystone Comedies, framed and glazed, 43in. high.(Sotheby's Belgravia) $355

Colour lithograph for Nestle's Milk, 74in. high, published by Waterlow & Sons Ltd., London. (Robert W. Skinner Inc.) $400

Mid 19th century carved wooden figure of a tradesman, 31in. high.(Sotheby's Belgravia) $430

Rare advertising plaque by T. J. & J. Mayer for Huntley & Palmer's. (Phillips) $1,870

Double sided tavern sign 'The Bell', 40in. high. (Vernon's) $300

18th century painted tin trade sign with decanter set in a laurel wreath. (Robert W. Skinner Inc.)$250

One of six painted tin swifts, probably English, circa 1900, 35½in. high. (Sotheby's Belgravia) $450

ARGYLES

Capstan-shaped argyle with slight skirt base, circa 1775, 14cm. high. (Sotheby's) $360

Inverted baluster-shaped argyle with base heater and stepped domed cover, circa 1775, 17.5cm. high. (Sotheby's) $315

Vase-shaped argyle with wood loop handle, by Peterson & Podio, circa 1790, 18.5cm. high. (Sotheby's) $315

BASKETS

Shaped circular fruit basket by R. F. Mosley & Co. Ltd., Sheffield, 1907, 18.8oz., 26cm. diam. (Sotheby's Belgravia) $395

Late 19th century German hallmarked silver cake basket with pierced border, 14oz. (Robert W. Skinner Inc.) $300

George III silver sugar basket, London, 1797, 5.6oz., 5½in. wide. (Thomas Watson & Son) $750

Presentation shaped circular cake basket by John Watson & Son, Sheffield, 1839, 26.7oz., 27cm. diam. (Sotheby's Belgravia) $655

George III bread basket by John Wakelin and William Taylor, London, 1790, 36oz.10dwt., 25.4cm. diam. (Christie's) $1,100

George III boat-shaped cake basket by Hester Bateman, 1786, 36.7cm. long, 32oz. (Christie's) $2,820

One of a pair of silver sweetmeat baskets by Goldsmiths & Silversmiths Ltd., London, 1907, 10oz. (Sotheby, King & Chasemore) $650

George II shaped oval cake basket on mask and scroll feet, by S. Herbert & Co., 1759, 14¼in. long, 37oz. (Christie's) $3,135

Cast and pierced sugar basket with swing handle, by J. C. Edington, London, 1862, 11oz., 11.5cm. high.(Sotheby's Belgravia) $750

554

Dutch two-handled oval basket by
Martinus Logerath, Amsterdam, 1795,
24.9cm. long, 19oz.8dwt.(Christie's)
$5,245

Late 19th century Russian silver
enameled sweetmeat basket,
12cm. diam. (Robert W. Skinner
Inc.) $700

English openwork oval two-handled
cake basket by D. & J. Wellby, London, 1902, 33cm. wide, 22.8oz.
(Sotheby's Belgravia) $815

George III circular sweetmeat
basket by William Wooller,
London, 1774, 6oz.13dwt.,
13cm. high. (Sotheby Beresford Adams) $855

George II shaped oval cake basket with pierced
sides by John Swift, London, 1739, 37.8cm.
long, 63oz. (Christie's) $7,680

George III silver sugar basket
with circular tapered body by
Samuel Massey, London,
1783, 6.2oz. (Thomas Watson
& Son) $820

George III sugar basket by Charles
Chesterman I, 1788, 8oz.
(Phillips) $780

English sterling silver two-part covered
basket, 39oz.16dwt., 27.5cm. long.
(C. G. Sloan & Co. Inc.) $950

Regency silver cake basket by Paul
Storr, London, 1819, 35.5cm. long,
55oz. (Christie's) $7,800

George III oval cake basket by
Robert Hennell, 1788, 37.9cm.
long, 30oz. (Christie's)
$2,000

George III shaped oval cake basket by Edward
Aldridge, 1763, 36.2cm. long, 33oz.
(Christie's) $2,890

One of a pair of Hukin & Heath
shaped oblong cake baskets, Sheffield, 1908, 24cm. long, 52.5oz.
(Sotheby's Belgravia)$1,055

BEAKERS

Small Russian silver gilt and niello beaker, Moscow, 1864, 6.7cm. high. (Christie's) $640

Novelty spirit beaker in the form of a tooth, by H. W. Dee, London, 1875, 5.7cm. high. (Sotheby's Belgravia) $470

Charles II silver beaker by CT, London, 1670, 9.8cm. high, 4oz.10dwt. (Christie's) $1,500

Early 17th century Scandinavian beaker with cylindrical stem, 9.2cm. high, 4oz.2dwt. (Christie's) $5,280

Continental silver gilt beaker of tapering cylindrical shape on three bud feet, circa 1600, 12.5cm. high, 4oz.13dwt. (Christie's) $1,390

French parcel gilt beaker of shaped oval form, by Joachim-Frederic Kirstein 1, Strasbourg, 1756, 8.5cm. high, 4oz.15dwt. (Christie's) $2,965

Russian parcel gilt beaker by Afanacii Kubakov, Moscow, 1742, 3½in. high, 3oz.18dwt. (Christie's) $1,570

Silver gilt presentation beaker by C. T. & G. Fox, London, 1890, 11oz., 13.3cm. high. (Sotheby's Belgravia) $935

Early 17th century German parcel gilt beaker, Hamburg, 3½in. high. (Phillips) $14,960

BELLS

Victorian silver table bell by GG, 1886, 5oz.8dwt. (Christie's) $1,095

Mappin & Webb table bell, London, 1923, 8cm. high, 5.2oz. (Sotheby's Belgravia) $545

George III silver gilt table bell by William Plummer, 1773, 5oz. 11dwt. (Christie's) $1,495

556

Circular rosebowl by Charles Stuart Harris, London, 1894, 31.7oz., 25.5cm. diam. (Sotheby's Belgravia) $820

Circular two-handled punchbowl by Johnson, Walker & Tolhurst, London, 1896, 38cm. wide, 49.6oz. (Sotheby's Belgravia) $1,200

Compressed circular 'Armada' pattern rosebowl by Elkington & Co. Ltd., London, 1896, 30cm. wide, 42.3oz. (Sotheby's Belgravia) $1,520

Large late Victorian silver gilt jardiniere. (Christie's S. Kensington) $3,840

William Hutton & Sons Ltd., circular rose bowl, 23.5cm. diam., London, 1899, 19.8oz. (Sotheby's Belgravia) $480

Shaped oval fruit bowl by Horace Woodward & Co. Ltd., London, 1893, 17.6oz., 27.3cm. long. (Sotheby's Belgravia) $490

Small circular rose bowl by Wm. Hutton & Sons Ltd., London, 1899, 18.5cm. diam., 14.6oz. (Sotheby's Belgravia)$430

Two-handled oval fruit jardiniere by Edward & Sons, Glasgow, 1899, 106.8oz., 51cm. wide. (Sotheby's Belgravia) $3,160

Gorham sterling silver punchbowl with lion mask and loose ring handles, 25cm. high, 78oz. (C. G. Sloan & Co. Inc.) $2,000

Gorham sterling silver bowl with over-turned lip, 45cm. long, 110oz.8dwt. (C. G. Sloan & Co. Inc.) $2,600

Circular silver fruit bowl with broad everted rim, by Redlich & Co., New York, 76.4oz. (Sotheby's Belgravia) $1,215

Circular presentation rosebowl by Henry Wilkinson & Co. London, 1877, 33.3oz., 26.5cm. diam. (Sotheby's Belgravia) $935

Oval fruit bowl with plain glass liner
by Wilhelm Binder, circa 1910,
16.7oz. (Sotheby's Belgravia)
$275

George III punchbowl by R. Keay,
Perth, 1817, 27cm. high, 46oz.15dwt.
(Sotheby's) $2,650

Circular fruit bowl by Martin, Hall
& Co. Ltd., Sheffield, 1919, 21cm.
diam., 17oz. (Sotheby's Belgravia)
$255

Regency silver bowl by Edward Farrell,
London, 1818, 25oz., 17cm. diam.
(Christie's) $1,100

Early George II silver sugar bowl,
unmarked, circa 1730.(Sotheby's)
$6,425

George III circular punchbowl by
Charles Wright, London, 1773, 26.5cm.
diam., 58oz.2dwt. (Sotheby's)
$2,415

Silver gilt bowl of bulbous form,
Moscow, 1883, 7.4cm. high.
(Sotheby's) $665

Komei Koku silver and enamel bowl, circa
1900, 25cm. diam., with wavy rim.
(Sotheby's Belgravia) $1,870

Pedestal fruit bowl/cake dish by
W. G. K., Birmingham, 1902,
29.8cm. diam., 20.7oz.
(Sotheby's Belgravia)$375

German silver dessert bowl, 1925,
16.5cm. high, 15oz.16dwt.
(Sotheby Beresford Adams)
$285

Silver gilt mounted mother-of-pearl bowl,
early 17th century, 4¾in. diam.
(Sotheby's) $2,735

Maltese oval covered sugar bowl by
Gaetano Offenaghel, circa 1790,
7oz.5dwt., 13.3cm. high.(Sotheby
Beresford Adams) $855

Late 18th century French silver bowl. (Parsons, Welch & Cowell) $240

Guild of Handicrafts Ltd. silver twin loop handled dish, London, 1900, 24.25cm. wide. (Sotheby's Belgravia) $1,405

W. H. Haseler silver, enamel and copper bowl, Birmingham, 1903, 19.5cm. (Sotheby's Belgravia) $840

George II sugar bowl by Humphrey Payne, London, 1732, 14.3cm. diam., 9oz.10dwt. (Christie's) $3,500

Green glass bowl in WMF stand. (Alfie's Antique Market) $350

Twin handled rosebowl with half fluted body by T. Smith & Son, Glasgow, 1897, 52oz. (Taylor Lane & Creber) $1,075

George II plain circular punchbowl, Newcastle, 1725, 29.8cm. diam., .65oz. (Christie's) $6,385

Large Jensen coupe with bell-shaped bowl, 1936, 19cm. high. (Sotheby's Belgravia) $1,405

Silver bowl of squat baluster form, Birmingham, 1905, 21cm. high, 53oz. (Sotheby, King & Chasemore) $1,250

George IV silver gilt bowl by Edward Farrell, 1824, 15.3cm. diam., 16oz. 9dwt. (Christie's) $2,170

Early 20th century German oval two-handled fruit bowl, 49.2cm. wide, 63.3oz. (Sotheby's Belgravia) $935

Silver gilt kovsh, embossed center, Moscow, circa 1755, 30cm. wide. (Sotheby's) $6,665

BOXES

George III engraved Freedom snuff box. (Sotheby Bearne) $2,620

One of two George I ambassadorial circular seal boxes by John Bridge, London, 1824-25, 37oz. (Sotheby's) $4,485

Silver and niello vesta case with tinder compartment, circa 1895, 5.6cm. wide. (Sotheby's) $225

Large rectangular silvered and ebonised wood casket, circa 1870, 44cm. long. (Sotheby's Belgravia) $1,295

German rectangular silver box, importer's mark John Smith, London, 1899, 5.6oz., 10.5cm. long. (Sotheby's Belgravia) $350

Jewel casket in silver by W. W. Harrison & Co., Sheffield, 1884, 24cm. wide. (Sotheby Beresford Adams) $1,190

Mid 20th century oval plique a jour box in silver-colored metal, 16cm. long. (Sotheby's Belgravia) $4,740

Jewish religious silver spice box, London, 1916, 13½in. high. (Grays Antique Market) $845

Silver tobacco box set with oval enamel plaque, Birmingham, 1890, 7.5cm. long. (Grays Antique Market) $655

Late 17th century Dutch marriage casket by Theodorus Huigen, 6.8cm. long, 3oz.14dwt. (Christie's) $5,545

Rectangular vesta case by Sampson Mordan, London, 1881, 4.7cm. high.(Sotheby's Belgravia) $225

French electroplated copper electrotype mounted oak liqueur box, circa 1860, 38cm. wide.(Sotheby's Belgravia) $450

Oval silver box, London, 1902, 12.4cm. long. 5.8oz. (Sotheby's Belgravia) $470

17th century silver box, 16.5cm. wide. (Robert W. Skinner Inc.) $650

George III plain oval spice box on shell and scroll feet, 1763, 18cm. long, 16oz.6dwt. (Christie's)$5,040

Rectangular gilt-metal and mother-of pearl 'Palais — Royal' casket in the form of a writing box, circa 1820, 17.9cm. wide. (Sotheby's) $405

Silver and lacquer vanity box by George Stockwell, 1932, 5.1cm. high. (Sotheby's Belgravia) $50

Silver and niello cigar case by M. F. Sokolov, Moscow, 1878, 11.2cm. wide. (Sotheby's) $620

17th century silver box, engraved top and bottom, 13.5cm. wide. (Robert W. Skinner Inc.) $900

Danish silver spice box by Jurgen Joachim Jurgensen, 1824, 12.4cm. high. (Sotheby Beresford Adams) $1,095

German rectangular silver snuff box with cased lid, circa 1730, 7.3cm. wide. (Sotheby's) $1,140

Late 19th century rectangular silver-mounted box miniature, 7.9cm. wide. (Sotheby's) $2,500

19th century Viennese silver-gilt and enamel jewel box, 132mm. high. (Christie's) $3,360

Victorian silver cigar box in the form of an Officer's shako, with hinged top, by E. H. Stockwell, London, 1874. (Sotheby Bearne) $3,055

Rectangular silver gilt box by Charles Dumenil, London, 1914, 18.6cm. long, 11.4oz. (Sotheby's Belgravia) $585

20th century sterling silver and enamel thimble case of egg shape, 4cm. high. (Robert W. Skinner Inc.) $185

Large silver cheroot box by Rawlings & Sumner, London, 1837, 12.7oz., 12cm. long. (Sotheby's Belgravia) $820

Dutch silver tobacco box, 17th century, with repousse decoration, 6½in. long. (Robert W. Skinner Inc.) $650

Late 19th century circular silver gilt and enamel powder box, by Faberge, 4.8cm. diam. (Sotheby's) $4,525

Dutch rectangular box by Y. T. van Erp, Leeuwarden, 1915, 5.8oz., 14.6cm. long. (Sotheby's Belgravia) $350

Silver rectangular casket by Wm. Hutton & Sons, London, 1902, 18.5cm. long, 460gm. (Sotheby's Belgravia) $280

Silver and mother-of-pearl spectacle case. (Sotheby's) $435

Biscuit box in the form of a sedan chair by Edward & Sons, Glasgow, 1900, 22.5oz., 19cm. high. (Sotheby's Belgravia) $890

Indian parcel gilt and frosted rectangular address casket, circa 1920, 41.5cm. wide, 171oz. (Sotheby's Belgravia) $2,125

French gilt metal and dark blue velvet trinket box set with pietra dura plaques, 19cm. long, circa 1880. (Sotheby's Belgravia) $420

Unusual trinket box in the form of a slumbering pig, 16cm. long, London, 1914, 17.2oz. (Sotheby's Belgravia) $1,450

George II brandy saucepan, London, 1729, 2in. high, 2oz.11dwt. (Sotheby's) $475

George IV saucepan and cover by Paul Storr, London, 1820, 20cm. diam., 40oz.10dwt. (Christie's) $4,200

George II brandy saucepan by John Newton, London, 1737, 4oz., 7½in. long. (Christie's) $1,000

George III baluster covered saucepan by Robert Gaze, London, 1810, 12oz.12dwt., 14cm. high. (Sotheby's) $1,070

George I baluster brandy saucepan by William Fleming, London, 1718, 2¼in. high, 3oz.15dwt. (Sotheby's) $900

Regency silver covered saucepan by Rebecca Emes and Edward Barnard, London, 1818, 20oz., 25.5cm. (Christie's) $2,000

BUCKLES

Large Art Deco rose-diamond, enamel, gold and silver gilt buckle by Cartier. (Christie's) $1,580

Rare early 19th century Swiss buckle, enameled with white and black flowers. (Taylor Lane & Creber) $300

Silver belt buckle in two sections, Birmingham, 1902, 2.4oz., 12cm. long.(Sotheby's Belgravia) $255

Silver belt buckle by Theodor Fahrner, circa 1900, 6.5cm. long. (Sotheby's Belgravia) $700

Faberge oval silver gilt mounted enamel belt buckle, St. Petersburg, 1899-1908, 7cm. long. (Christie's) $1,550

Liberty & Co. enameled silver waist clasp, Birmingham, 1906, 6.3cm. long. (Sotheby's Belgravia) $795

563

One of a pair of German two-light candelabra, Augsburg, 1823, 51cm. high, 64oz. (Christie's) $4,200

Large four-light candelabrum by Hunt & Roskell, London, 1858, 54.7cm. high. (Sotheby's Belgravia) $2,360

Five-light candelabrum by Goldsmiths & Silversmiths Ltd., London, 59cm. high, circa 1909-10. (Sotheby's Belgravia) $1,870

One of a pair of Regency Sheffield three-light candelabra, 45cm. high. (C. G. Sloan & Con. Inc.) $450

Five-light candelabrum by R. & S. Garrard & Co'., London, 1904, 41.7cm. high, 47oz. (Sotheby's Belgravia) $1,640

Six-light candelabrum with triform base, by Benjamin Smith, London, 1845, 155.5oz., 75.5cm. high. (Sotheby's Belgravia) $3,510

Victorian three-light candelabrum by Barnard & Co., 1838, 67.3cm. high, 165oz. (Christie's) $4,580

Victorian four-light candelabrum by Robert Garrard, 1841, 30½in. high, 249oz. (Christie's) $5,665

One of a pair of George III three-light candelabra by Richard Cooke, London, 1799, 175oz.10dwt., 21½in. high. (Sotheby's) $20,520

Victorian candelabrum centrepiece by Robert Garrard, 1863, 77.5cm. high, 294oz.(Christie's) $7,050

One of a pair of 18th century George III Sheffield silver candelabra, by John Green, 1797-98. (Robert W. Skinner Inc.) $3,500

One of a pair of Empire ormolu six-light candelabra, 83cm. high. (Christie's) $2,620

One of a pair of George III two-light candelabra by Matthew Boulton, Birmingham, 1792, 16½in. high.(Christie's) $5,435

One of a pair of Sheffield plate three-light candelabra, circa 1840, 53.5cm. high. (Sotheby's Belgravia) $635

One of a set of three Victorian candelabra by Barnard & Co., 1843 and 1844, 372oz. (Christie's) $10,870

One of a pair of George III Sheffield plate three-branch candelabra, 50cm. high. (Dacre, Son & Hartley) $445

One of a pair of heavy Victorian five-light candelabra by Robert Garrard, London, 1866, 596oz.3dwt., 32in. high. (Sotheby's) $26,180

One of a pair of silver plated three-light candelabra, 56cm. high. (C. G. Sloan & Co. Inc.) $950

Large early Victorian five-light candelabrum table centerpiece by Mortimer & Hunt, 1842, 216oz. 17dwt. (Sotheby Beresford Adams) $4,045

One of a pair of George III two-light candelabra by Benjamin Laver, 1786, 17½in. high, 98oz. (Christie's)$7,055

Regency seven-light candelabrum on triangular base, by Philip Rundell, 1819, 66cm. high, 501oz. (Christie's)$10,030

One of a pair of Sheffield plate three-light candelabra, circa 1845, 60.4cm. high. (Sotheby's Belgravia) $820

One of a pair of George III four-light candelabra by William Fountain, London, 25in. high, 330oz.2dwt.(Sotheby's) $13,325

One of a pair of Louis XVI silver candelabra by Pierre-Francois Coguely, Paris, 1784, 133oz. (Sotheby's) $27,000

CANDLESTICKS

Small late 19th century German table candlestick, 12.2cm. high, 3.5oz. (Sotheby's Belgravia) $130

One of a pair of George II table candlesticks by J. Marsh, London, 1750, 38oz.16dwt., 21cm. high. (Sotheby's)$2,415

One of a set of four table candlesticks by Hawksworth, Eyre & Co., Sheffield, 27.5cm. high. (Sotheby's Belgravia) $1,535

One of a pair of George II table candlesticks by Michael Fowler, Dublin, circa 1757, 25cm. high, 50oz.1dwt.(Sotheby's) $2,415

One of a pair of George I cast silver Irish candlesticks, by Thomas Slade, Dublin, 1723, 15cm. high, 22oz. (Aldridges) $3,160

One of a pair of table candlesticks by Hawksworth, Eyre & Co., Sheffield, 1892, 27.6cm. high. (Sotheby's Belgravia) $815

One of a set of four Victorian silver pillar candlesticks, 24cm. high, by H. Wilkinson & Co., Sheffield, 1840. (Clifford Dann & Partners) $2,806

George I taperstick on octagonal base by James Seabrook, 1717, 13cm. high, 4oz.10dwt. (Christie's) $2,280

One of a rare pair of William III Scottish table candlesticks by Patrick Murray, Edinburgh, 1697, 7¾in. high, 39oz.12dwt. (Sotheby's) $10,950

One of a pair of George III table candlesticks by Ebenezer Coker, London, 1765, 10½in. high, 40oz.6dwt. (Sotheby's)$4,385

One of a pair of George I table candlesticks by David Willaume I, London, 1715, 7¾in. high, 40oz.10dwt. (Sotheby's)$12,375

One of a pair of George III enamel table candlesticks, circa 1770, 29.8cm. high.(Christie's) $1,200

566

One of a pair of silver table candlesticks by Walker & Hall, Sheffield, 32.3cm. high, 1901. (Sotheby's Belgravia) $710

One of a set of four George II table candlesticks by John Cafe, London, 1751, 22.5cm. high, 89oz.8dwt. (Sotheby's) $6,670

One of four George III table candlesticks by John Smith, Sheffield, 1779, 31cm. high. (Christie's) $4,800

One of a pair of Queen Anne candlesticks by David Willaume, London, 1706, 7in. high, 29oz.4dwt. (Sotheby's) $7,615

One of a set of six George III candlesticks by H. Tudor and T. Leader, Sheffield, 1780, 30.5cm. high. (Christie's) $6,025

One of a pair of William IV candlesticks by Paul Storr, 1836, 24.7cm. high. (Christie's) $7,710

One of a pair of table candlesticks by Walker & Hall, Sheffield, 1896, 32.3cm. high. (Sotheby's Belgravia) $750

One of a pair of George II candlesticks by John Quantock, London, 1752. (Phillips) $1,840

One of a pair of George II table candlesticks by Robert Gordon, Edinburgh, 1758, 57oz.12dwt., 33cm. high. (Sotheby's) $3,495

One of a pair of table candlesticks by Hawksworth, Eyre & Co., Sheffield, 1891, 24.3cm. high. (Sotheby's Belgravia) $565

One of a pair of George I candlesticks on stepped bases by Thomas Folkingham, 1725, 16.5cm. high, 31oz. (Christie's) $6,000

One of a pair of table candlesticks by Roberts & Belk Ltd., Sheffield, 1964, 31cm. high. (Sotheby's Belgravia) $560

One of a pair of French silver candlesticks on turned supports, 30oz.12dwt., 23cm. high.(C. G. Sloan & Co. Inc.) $750

One of a pair of George II candlesticks by A. Craig and J. Neville, 1740, 17.2cm. high, 29oz. (Christie's)$3,840

One of a pair of table candlesticks by I. S. Greenberg, Birmingham, 1902. (Sotheby's Belgravia) $610

One of four Austrian table candlesticks, Vienna, 1858, 26.7cm. high, 39.6oz. (Sotheby's Belgravia) $990

One of two Corinthian column candlesticks, Sheffield, 1892, 22.5cm. high. (Andrew Grant) $240

One of a large pair of George III table candlesticks by Matthew Boulton, Birmingham, 1813, 34cm. high.(H. Spencer & Sons) $2,065

One of a set of four George II cast candlesticks by Wm. Cafe, 1746, 22cm. high, 101.25oz. (Phillips) $7,130

One of a pair of Hawksworth, Eyre & Co., candlesticks, 23cm. high, Sheffield, 1898. (Sotheby's Belgravia) $710

One of a pair of table candlesticks in George II style, by Wm. Hutton & Sons Ltd., Sheffield, 1908, 30.5cm. high. (Sotheby's Belgravia) $655

One of a set of four George II table candlesticks by Eliza Godfrey, London, 1744, 67oz.1dwt., 19.5cm. high. (Sotheby Beresford Adams) $8,090

One of a pair of William III candlesticks by John Eckfourd, 1701, 15.3cm. high, 25oz. (Christie's) $6,750

One of a pair of table candlesticks in George II style by Walter Latham & Sons, Sheffield, 1922, 22.8cm. high. (Sotheby's Belgravia) $670

One of a pair of George III Adam style silver candlesticks by J. Green & Co., Sheffield, 30cm. high. (May Whetter & Grose) $1,345

One of a pair of table candlesticks by Elkington & Co. Ltd., Birmingham, 1901, 26.5cm. high. (Sotheby's Belgravia) $700

George I taperstick by J. Bird, London, 1718, 11.8cm. high, 4oz. (Christie's) $1,600

One of a pair of table candlesticks by Henry Wilkinson & Co., Sheffield, 1851, 29cm. high. (Sotheby's Belgravia) $625

One of a pair of George I silver candlesticks, 1716, 6in. high. (Christie's) $4,510

One of a pair of Victorian table candlesticks, London, 1862, 28cm. high.(Sotheby Beresford Adams) $1,380

One of a pair of Queen Anne table candlesticks by William Denny, London, 1705, 27oz.14dwt., 19.5cm. high.(Sotheby's) $6,190

One of a set of four George III cast silver candlesticks, 92oz. (Edgar Horn)$200

One of a pair of George III table candlesticks by John Carter, London, 1773, 41oz.9dwt., 11.5cm. high. (Sotheby Beresford Adams) $3,330

One of a set of four table candlesticks by Hawksworth, Eyre & Co., Sheffield, 1888, 27cm. high. (Sotheby Beresford Adams) $1,475

One of a set of six table candlesticks by Martin, Hall & Co. Ltd., 27.8cm. high, Sheffield, 1891. (Sotheby's Belgravia) $1,890

One of a pair of George III table candlesticks by John Scofield, London, 1783, 32oz.11dwt., 11¼in. high. (Sotheby's) $3,080

CARD CASES

Parcel gilt electroplated copper electrotype card case by Elkington & Co., circa 1860, 9.7cm. long. (Sotheby's Belgravia) $50

Elaborately engraved Victorian card case, Birmingham, 1864. (Andrew Grant) $135

Silver shaped rectangular card case by Edward Smith, Birmingham, 1850, 9.7cm. long. (Sotheby's Belgravia) $130

Shaped rectangular card case by Wheeler & Cronin, Birmingham, 1842, 9.8cm. high. (Sotheby's Belgravia) $295

Rectangular silver card case by Rawlings & Sumner, London, 1868, 9.8cm. long. (Sotheby's Belgravia) $110

Shaped rectangular card case by Nathaniel Mills, Birmingham, 1844, 10cm. high. (Sotheby's Belgravia) $475

Rectangular card case by Edward Barnard & Sons, London, 1880, 9.5cm. high. (Sotheby's Belgravia) $95

Unusual shaped rectangular card case, maker's mark E.T., Birmingham, 1852, 10.2cm. high. (Sotheby's Belgravia) $310

Shaped rectangular card case by Hilliard & Thomason, Birmingham, 1885, 9.8cm. high. (Sotheby's Belgravia) $170

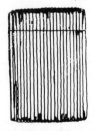

Silver oblong card case by George Unite, Birmingham, 1892, 9.9cm. long. (Sotheby's Belgravia)$90

Late 19th century Indian electroplated rectangular card case, 10.9cm. long. (Sotheby's Belgravia) $50

Mid 19th century English mother-of-pearl veneered card case, 9.9cm. long. (Sotheby's Belgravia)$95

570

George I dredger by John Albright, London, 1723, 2oz.10dwt., 8.2cm. high. (Christie's) $1,400

George I silver caster by Samuel Welder, London, 1724, 7oz., 16.5cm. high. (Christie's) $2,000

George I dredger by James Stone, London, 1726, 2oz. 8.2cm. high. (Christie's) $1,200

One of a set of three William III casters by Christopher Canner I, London, 1700, 20oz. (Christie's) $22,000

One of a pair of sugar casters by Crichton Brothers, London, 1928, 17.8cm. high, 21.8oz. (Sotheby's Belgravia) $560

Dutch silver caster, Leiden, 1723, 5oz., 14.4cm. high. (Christie's) $1,300

One of a pair of cylindrical sugar casters by Lambert & Co., London, 1906, 18.3cm. high, 22.7oz. (Sotheby's Belgravia) $585

Silver caster by Zachariah Bridgden, Boston, Massachusetts, 1734-87, 5¾in. high, 4 troy oz. (Robert W. Skinner Inc.) $750

James II silver caster by WB, London, 1685, 12oz., 19cm. high.(Christie's) $6,000

One of a set of three George II fluted pear-shaped casters by Henry Hayens, 1754, 39oz. (Christie's) $3,080

Sugar caster by Garrard & Co. Ltd., London, circa 1925, 11.7oz., 18cm. high. (Sotheby's Belgravia) $270

One of a pair of silver pepperettes, London, 1747, by Samuel Wood, 12cm. high. (Sotheby, King & Chasemore) $735

CENTERPIECES

Victorian silver presentation centerpiece with three candle sconces, Birmingham, 1860. (Jose Collins & Harris) $2,400

Sterling silver centerpiece by Bailey, Banks & Biddle, 37.5cm. diam., 41oz. (C. G. Sloan & Co. Inc.) $975

Silver gilt centerpiece by Smith, Nicholson & Co., London, 1852, 67oz., 56.4cm. high. (Sotheby's Belgravia) $780

Shaped circular Austrian table centerpiece in Art Nouveau style, circa 1900, 37oz.8dwt., 33cm. diam. (Sotheby Beresford Adams) $905

French dessert dish with fluted and waved edge glass bowl, circa 1880, 32cm. high, 30oz. (Sotheby, King & Chasemore) $465

Electroplated table centerpiece with glass bowl. (Sotheby, King & Chasemore) $1,055

Victorian silver table garniture by Robert Garrard, 1872-73, 328oz. (Christie's) $11,570

Shaped circular Austrian table centerpiece in Art Nouveau style, circa 1900, 37oz. 8dwt., 33cm. diam. (Sotheby Beresford Adams) $905

Unusual late 19th century sterling silver and cut-glass flower center, 7¼in. high, Eastern United States. (Robert W. Skinner Inc.) $300

Victorian silver centerpiece by Stephen Smith, London, 1882, 52.5cm. high, 171oz.5dwt. (Sotheby's) $4,820

572

Electroplated three-branch center-piece, 53cm. high, by Elkington, Mason & Co., 1857. (Sotheby's Belgravia) $1,170

Unusual water-lily table centerpiece by R. F. Mosley & Co. Ltd., Sheffield, 1910, 46.5oz., 48cm. long. (Sotheby's Belgravia) $6,085

Three-light centerpiece by Henry Wilkinson & Co., Sheffield, 1872, 112.2oz., 50.8cm. high. (Sotheby's Belgravia) $2,040

Large and heavy early 20th century rosebowl centerpiece by Marius Hammer, Bergen, 273.4oz. (Sotheby's Belgravia)$7,020

Russian silver table centerpiece by P. Sazikov, St. Petersburg, 1882, 58cm. high.(Sotheby's Belgravia) $5,150

One of a pair of Victorian fruit stands by F. B. Thomas, London, 1876, 154oz. (Phillips) $5,150

Parcel gilt centerpiece and two fruit stands by Elkington, Birmingham, 129oz. (Sotheby's Belgravia) $2,620

Three-piece table suite of a centerpiece and two fruit dishes, by Fenton Bros., Sheffield, 1874, 86.3oz. (Sotheby's Belgravia) $1,680

Fruit dish stand with triform base by E. Barnard & Sons, London, 1865, 47.8cm. high, 44.4oz.(Sotheby's Belgravia) $1,440

Heavy table suite of jardiniere and two flower holders by Asprey & Co. Ltd., 1913, 64.4oz., 26cm. high. (Sotheby's Belgravia) $10,765

Six-light candelabrum centerpiece by Hunt & Roskell, London, 1854, 62.5cm. high, 203.5oz.(Sotheby's Belgravia) $4,720

CHAMBERSTICKS

William II rare chamberstick by William Gamble, London, 1699, 7.5cm. diam., 3oz.10dwt. (Christie's) $4,500

George IV silver chamberstick complete with snuffer. (Sotheby's) $750

One of a pair of George III chamber candlesticks by John Hutson, London, 1809, 19oz. 6dwt., 5½in. diam. (Sotheby's) $1,945

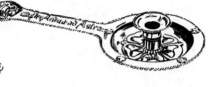

One of a pair of shaped circular chamber candlesticks by R. & S. Garrard & Co., London, 1860, 19.1oz., 15cm. diam. (Sotheby's Belgravia) $1,355

Guild of Handicrafts silver chamber candlestick, London, 1920, 31cm. long. (Christie's) $480

Early 19th century Sheffield plate chamberstick complete with glass shade. (Vernon's) $150

CHOCOLATE POTS

Early George II tapered cylindrical chocolate pot by John Eckfourd, Jun., 1731, 9½in. high, 31oz.5dwt. (Sotheby's) $4,105

Louis XV chocolate pot, circa 1770, possibly Strasbourg, 20oz.10dwt., 22.8cm. high. (Christie's)$1,400

George I Irish chocolate pot by Thomas Walker, Dublin, 1717, 27oz.10dwt., 11in. high. (Sotheby's) $11,230

Queen Anne tapered cylindrical chocolate pot by Simon Pantin, London, 1709, 27oz.10dwt., 9½in. high. (Sotheby's) $7,895

George I plain octagonal chocolate pot, 1716, 10in. high, 23oz. (Christie's) $9,440

German pear-shaped chocolate pot by Johann Georg Kloss, Augsburg, 1755-57, 26.3cm. high, 19oz. (Christie's) $5,245

Silver gilt and cloisonne enamel cigarette case, Moscow, 1896, 10.7cm.
wide. (Sotheby's) $570

Silver gilt and cloisonne enamel cigarette case, Moscow, 1894, 9cm. wide.
(Sotheby's) $595

Rectangular cloisonne enamel cigarette case, Moscow, 1908-1917,
11cm. wide. (Sotheby's)$665

Early 20th century oblong enameled
cigarette case by Max Fleischmann,
8.7cm. long. (Sotheby's Belgravia)
$1,025

Silver samorodok cigarette case with
a vesta and tinder compartment,
10.2cm. wide, 1899-1908, St.
Petersburg. (Sotheby's) $760

Early 20th century German enamel
and silvered metal cigarette case,
9cm. high. (Sotheby's Belgravia)
$880

Silver gilt and cloisonne enamel cigarette case, Moscow, 1908-1917,
10.8cm. wide. (Sotheby's)$620

Silver and niello cigarette case of
rectangular form, Moscow, circa
1890, 9.5cm. wide. (Sotheby's)
$285

Silver and niello cigarette case, Moscow, 1887, 11.5cm. wide.(Sotheby's)
$475

Shaped rectangular cigarette case
by George Unite, Birmingham,
1882, 10cm. high. (Sotheby's
Belgravia) $100

French Art Deco lacquered cigarette
case in sunburst design, 1920's, 8.2cm.
long. (Sotheby's Belgravia) $420

Oblong silver cigarette case engraved on both sides, London, 1883,
2oz., 8.6cm. high. (Sotheby's
Belgravia) $50

575

CLARET JUGS

Victorian silver mounted claret jug, London, 1881, 29cm. high. (May Whetter & Grose) $910

Mid Victorian claret jug in the form of a duck, with electroplate mounts, 14in. high. (Christie's S. Kensington) $530

One of a pair of presentation claret jugs by Hunt & Roskell, London, 1874, 20.7cm. high, 69.1oz. (Sotheby's Belgravia)$3,540

Cut-glass claret jug with silver mounts, by Grachev Brothers, St. Petersburg, 27.7cm. high, 1899-1908. (Sotheby's) $620

Silver gilt mounted clear glass claret jug, 1880, 25.4cm. high. (Sotheby's Belgravia) $650

Faberge tall cut-glass claret jug, Moscow, 1908-1917, 38.8cm. high. (Christie's) $2,735

Silver mounted cut-glass claret jug, Birmingham, 1902, 9in. high. (Burrows & Day) $470

Glass and silver claret jug.(Woolley & Wallis) $1,070

Late Victorian silver mounted glass claret jug, Birmingham, 1899, 9¾in. high. (Burrows & Day) $245

Victorian silver gilt mounted glass claret jug, 1899, 41.3cm. high. (Christie's) $3,375

Victorian silver mounted cut-glass claret jug, with floral engraving, London, 1858. (Sotheby, King & Chasemore) $720

Victorian claret jug of baluster form, with bright-cut engraving and foliate handle. (Taylor Lane & Creber) $1,055

One of a pair of George III wine coasters by Richard Morton & Co., Sheffield, 1776, 12.5cm. diam. (Sotheby Beresford Adams) $1,285

William IV plain wine wagon on four wheels by Robert Garrard, London, 1836, 33oz. (Christie's) $4,080

One of a pair of George III circular wine coasters by Peter and Anne Bateman, London, 1796, 4¾in. diam. (Sotheby's) $975

One of a set of four Georgian silver coasters, London, 1797, with pierced silver sides and turned wood bases. (Butler & Hatch Waterman) $2,160

One of a pair of 'jolly boat' decanter stands, circa 1820, 12¾in. long. (Sotheby's) $2,850

One of a set of four George III silver gilt coasters, by Matthew Boulton and John Fothergill, 1773. (Christie's) $3,530

One of a set of four Regency silver gilt coasters by Robert Garrard, 1818. (Christie's) $20,200

One of a pair of Regency silver gilt circular wine coasters by Robert Garrard, 1818. (Christie's) $2,350

One of a pair of George III circular coasters by Robert Breading, Dublin, 1803, 12cm. diam. (Sotheby's) $1,655

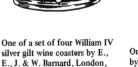

One of a set of four William IV silver gilt wine coasters by E., E., J. & W. Barnard, London, 1836, 6in. diam. (Sotheby's) $6,910

One of a pair of George IV wine coasters by Matthew Boulton & Co., Birmingham, 1827, 20cm. diam. (Sotheby Beresford Adams) $1,905

One of a set of four early Victorian wine coasters by Henry Wilkinson & Co., Sheffield, 1837, 17cm. diam. (Sotheby Beresford Adams) $3,570

COFFEE POTS

George III baluster coffee pot by Thomas Wallis, London, 1769, 11in. high, 27oz.8dwt.(Sotheby's) $4,505

George III oval coffee pot by George Brasier, London, 1801, 28cm. high, 25oz.16dwt. (Sotheby's) $1,496

George III coffee pot with hinged lid, scroll handle and embossed decoration, by S. A., London, 1789, 20oz. (Mallams) $1,405

George III baluster coffee pot by James Young, London, 1773, 34oz.9dwt., 28cm. high. (Sotheby Beresford Adams) $2,975

George I coffee pot by Richard Watts, London, 1716, 28oz.10dwt., 25.5cm. high. (Christie's) $5,600

Silver coffee pot by Edward Feline, London, 1741, 31oz. (Irelands) $5,190

Early George III Scottish pot by Adam Graham, Glasgow, circa 1765, 12¼in. high, 36oz.7dwt. (Sotheby's) $3,555

Monster coffee pot and hot milk jug on double lampstand by Carrington & Co., London, 1900, 186.2oz. (Sotheby's Belgravia) $6,240

George III vase-shaped coffee pot by John Denziloe, London, 1796, 30oz.13dwt., 27.3cm. high. (Sotheby's) $2,875

George III coffee pot by Smith & Sharp, London, 1765, 25oz.17dwt., 24cm. high. (Sotheby Beresford Adams) $1,905

Silver coffee pot by William Grundy, London, 1771, 38oz. (H. Spencer & Sons) $2,790

George III coffee pot by Thomas Pratt and Arthur Humphreys, London, 1784, 27oz., 30.5cm. high. (Christie's) $1,600

George III silver gilt coffee jug with stand and burner, 13¾in. high, 39oz., London 1776. (Sotheby's) $2,370

George III baluster coffee pot by Smith & Sharp, London, 1769, 26cm. high, 28oz.13dwt. (Sotheby's) $4,025

Sterling silver coffee pot by R. & W. Wilson, Philadelphia, 22oz. 18dwt., 29cm. high. (C. G. Sloan & Co. Inc.) $525

George III silver coffee pot, London 1765. (Parsons, Welch & Cowell) $1,665

George III baluster coffee pot, London, 1816, 12in. high, 37oz.3dwt. (Sotheby's) $2,140

George II tapered cylindrical shaped coffee pot by George Smith, London, 1739, 22oz. 5dwt. (Sotheby, King & Chasemore) $2,400

Lidded presentation jug and cover by Richard Hennell, London, 1863, 32oz.10dwt., 24cm. high. (Messenger, May & Baverstock) $1,590

Baluster coffee pot by Edward Barnard & Sons, 1895, 18.8cm., high, 20.6oz. (Sotheby's Belgravia) $455

George III coffee pot by John Swift, 1763, 30cm. high, 32.75oz. (Phillips) $6,210

Circular coffee pot by Edward Hutton, London, 1881, 23oz., 23.5cm. high. (Sotheby's Belgravia) $505

George III coffee jug by Henry Chawner, London, 1792, 12¾in. high, 24oz.17dwt. (Sotheby's) $1,895

George II plain coffee pot engraved with a coat-of-arms, by Ayme Videau, 1743, 21.5cm. high, 24oz. (Christie's) $4,340

579

COFFEE POTS

Baluster coffee pot by George Angell, London, 1852, 16cm. high, 16.6oz. (Sotheby's Belgravia) $515

Baluster coffee pot with leaf-capped silver handle, by Hunt & Roskell, London, 1854, 24.5cm. high, 31.6oz. (Sotheby's Belgravia) $1,055

Tapering cylindrical coffee pot by Edward Barnard & Sons, London, 1870, 24.1oz., 24cm. high. (Sotheby's Belgravia) $890

Sterling silver coffee pot by R. & W. Wilson, Philadelphia, 22oz.18dwt., 29cm. high. (C. G. Sloan & Co. Inc.) $525

George II coffee pot by Peter Archambo, 1731, 28oz., 21.5cm. high. (Neales) $2,270

George III baluster coffee pot by Emick Homer, London, 1760, 10¾in. high, 30½oz. (H. C. Chapman & Son) $2,050

Baluster coffee jug by D. & J. Wellby, London, 1882, 26.1oz., 28.6cm. high. (Sotheby's Belgravia) $935

Early George III silver coffee pot by John Scofield, London, 1784, 27oz. (Graves, Son & Pilcher) $1,650

Sheffield plate coffee pot with baluster body, 1830's, 29cm. high. (Sotheby's Belgravia) $515

Early George III baluster coffee pot by B. Brewood, London, 1761, 24oz.17dwt., 10in. high.(Sotheby's) $2,445

One of a pair of silver jugs for coffee and hot milk by Carrington & Co., London, 1912-13, 64.4oz., 26cm. high.(Sotheby's Belgravia) $1,685

George II tapered cylindrical coffee pot by P. Archambo and P. Meure, London, 1752, 23oz.7dwt., 8¾in. high.(Sotheby's) $3,100

George II cream jug by George Greenhill Jones, London, 1731, 8cm. high, 2oz. 10dwt. (Christie's) $750

Russian silver gilt and niello milk jug by V. Semenov, Moscow, 1870, 5.4cm. high. (Christie's)$500

Louis XV French provincial silver side-handle cream pitcher, circa 1775-81, 16cm. high. (C. G. Sloan & Co. Inc.) $1,450

George III Irish covered cream jug by William Homer, Dublin, circa 1760, 5oz.10dwt. (Christie's) $3,200

George III helmet-shaped cream jug by Peter and Jonathan Bateman, London, 1790, 2oz.19dwt., 5¾in. high. (Sotheby's) $1,600

George II Irish cream jug by Edward Raper, Dublin, circa 1755, 7oz. 10dwt., 11cm. high. (Christie's) $1,500

George III helmet-shaped silver milk jug by Hester Bateman, London, 1796, 17cm. high, 4oz. (May Whetter & Grose) $1,010

Victorian silver cream jug by Edward and John Barnard, London, 1851, 6oz.8dwt. (Sotheby, King & Chasemore) $235

Victorian cream jug by J. S. Hunt, London, 1865, 5oz., 9.5cm. high. (Christie's) $700

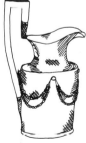

George I octagonal milk jug by Thos. Tearle, circa 1725, 3oz.4dwt., 2¾in. high. (Sotheby's) $4,045

French provincial silver milk jug, 1798-1809, 13oz., 20.5cm. high. (Christie's) $500

Spherical milk jug with reeded neck by A., F. & A. Pairpoint, London, 1927, 10.1oz. (Sotheby's Belgravia) $165

George III navette-shaped cruet frame by James Young, London, 1783, 31cm. wide, 19oz.4dwt.(Sotheby Beresford Adams) $855

George III silver cruet stand with bright cut engravings, London, 1800. (Parsons, Welch & Cowell) $720

George III silver cruet frame with six cut-glass bottles, London, 1809, by J. W. Story and Wm. Elliott. (Sotheby, King & Chasemore) $960

George IV silver cruet, fitted with six bottles. (Parsons, Welch & Cowell) $1,115

George III silver cruet, 25.5cm. high, base with beaded borders, on wooden base. (H. Spencer & Sons)$685

Victorian silver set of six egg cups and spoons in a stand, London, 1837-40. (Vincent & Vanderpump) $864

Large Victorian oval cruet frame by Atkin Bros., Sheffield, 1866, 49oz. 10dwt., 28cm. high. (Sotheby Beresford Adams) $1,045

Shaped circular egg cruet, complete with six egg cups, 24.7cm. high, by John Tapley, London, 1843, sold with six spoons, 47.4oz. (Sotheby's Belgravia) $1,130

George III Warwick frame by Samuel Wood, London, 1760, 39oz.6dwt., 23cm. high. (Sotheby's) $3,215

George III shaped oblong cruet by Thomas Richard, 1817, 40oz. (Christie's S. Kensington)$1,350

George IV silver four-egg cruet. stand. (Phillips) $240

Georgian silver eight position cruet with original cut-glass bottles, London, 1815, 32oz. (Burtenshaw Walker) $1,495

Beaded quatrefoil cruet stand by C. T. & G. Fox, London, 1878, 13.3cm. high, 14.1oz. (Sotheby's Belgravia) $935

Silver egg cruet for six, by Robert Hennell, London, 1851, 33oz., 23.8cm. long. (Sotheby's Belgravia) $1,285

Late 19th century American papier-mache and mother-of-pearl castor set. (Robert W. Skinner Inc.) $150

CUPS

17th century English sterling silver caudle cup with two scroll handles, 12oz., 11cm. diam. (Robert W. Skinner Inc.) $1,400

George III two-handled cup and cover by Wm. Frisbee, 1807, 17¼in. high, 83oz. (Christie's) $1,275

Russian silver gilt covered cup, Moscow, circa 1841, 21oz.14dwt., 17cm. high. (C. G. Sloan & Co. Inc.) $950

Danish silver cup with shell-shaped bowl, 24cm. high, circa 1860, 18.4oz., by Anton Michelsen, Copenhagen. (Sotheby's Belgravia) $820

Parcel gilt four-piece christening set by Wakely & Wheeler, London, 1892, 10.5oz. (Sotheby's Belgravia) $515

Two-handled presentation campana-shaped cup by Chas. Boyton, London, 1863, 23.7oz., 27.3cm. high. (Sotheby's Belgravia) $360

Silver presentation cup, body heavily embossed, sold by Black, Starr & Frost, New York, 1876, 9in. high, 17 troy oz. (Robert W. Skinner Inc.) $550

One of a pair of German wager cups, importer's mark of Thomas Glaser, London, 1894, 24.5cm. high, 25.7oz. (Sotheby's Belgravia) $1,520

Two-handled presentation cup and cover by Chas. Gordon, London, 1838, 29cm. high, 38.9oz. (Sotheby's Belgravia)$1,055

CUPS

George IV stirrup cup by Edward Thomason, Birmingham, 1825, 6in. long, 5oz.1dwt. (Sotheby's) $4,045

Charles II tumbler cup by Thomas Mangy, York, 1669, 5 oz., 9.5cm. diam. (Christie's) $1,300

William and Mary small two-handled caudle cup, London, 1690, 6.4cm. high, 2oz.10dwt. (Christie's) $500

Early George I two-handled cup with bell-shaped body by J. M. Stockar, London, 1715, 12oz., 11.2cm. high. (Sotheby Beresford Adams) $1,145

Martele sterling silver loving cup, Rhode Island, circa 1920, 30 troy oz., 7¾in. high. (Robert W. Skinner Inc.) $1,100

George III thistle-shaped cup by Robert Gray & Sons, Edinburgh, 1813, 34oz., 26cm. high. (Sotheby's) $700

Chinese silver presentation cup and cover, dated 1876, 54cm. high, 3,617gm. (Sotheby's Belgravia) $2,150

William IV silver gilt ovoid two-handled cup and cover by Joseph Angell, London, 1830, 114oz.1dwt., 17¼in. high. (Sotheby's) $3,800

George III vase-shaped silver gilt christening cup and cover by Thomas Heming, London, 1771, 35.5cm. high, 79oz.12dwt. (Sotheby's) $6,190

Late 19th century German parcel gilt standing cup, 16.6cm. high, 3.9oz. (Sotheby's Belgravia) $285

Rare George I spout cup and cover by Timbrell & Bell, London, 1719, 7oz.15dwt., 14.5cm. high.(Sotheby Beresford Adams) $1,095

Two-handled cup and cover by Johnson, Walker & Tolhurst Ltd., London, 1913, 23.1oz., 21.5cm. wide. (Sotheby's Belgravia) $430

One of a pair of fox mask stirrup cups by William Plummer, London, 1790, 9cm. high. (Andrew Grant)$3,980

Charles II tumbler cup, York, 1675, 5.7cm. high, 5oz.7dwt. (Christie's) $1,085

One of a pair of silver cups and saucers, French export mark for 1840, 6½oz. (Robert W. Skinner Inc.) $125

William and Mary two-handled caudle cup by Timothy Ley, London, 1692, 7oz.10dwt., 9.2cm. high. (Christie's N. York) $1,500

Large Charles II porringer and cover, 1676, 18cm. high, 32oz. (Phillips) $9,200

Rare silver electrotype cup by Elkington & Co., 16oz., 10.8cm. high. (Sotheby's Belgravia) $1,415

George III two-handled cup and cover by Robert Sharp, 1793, 44.5cm. high, 97oz. (Christie's) $5,520

One of a pair of George III vase-shaped two-handled cups by Michael Homer, Dublin, 1789, 29oz.17dwt. (Sotheby's) $1,060

Silver gilt cup by William Bateman, 113oz. (Worsfolds)$2,835

Australian silver-mounted emu egg cup, 21cm. high, circa 1870. (Sotheby's Belgravia)$1,130

One of a pair of George II two-handled cups and covers by David Willaume II, 23.5cm. high, 119oz. (Christie's)$9,600

New Zealand two-handled cup by C. Young, Dunedin, 75oz., 38cm. high. (Christie's)$7,295

Dublin hallmarked dish ring with glass liner by Joseph Jackson, circa 1780. 9cm. high. (Sotheby, King & Chasemore) $3,480

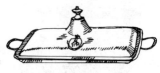

George III two-handled bacon dish and cover by Henry Green, London, 1787, 21.6cm. wide, 15oz.10dwt. (Christie's) $2,200

One of a set of four George III silver gilt cushion-shaped entree dishes and covers by Robert Sharp, London, 1792, 194oz. 14dwt., 10½in. wide. (Sotheby's) $23,800

Large two-handled circular fruit stand by Mappin & Webb, London, 1910, 44cm. wide, 98.7oz. (Sotheby's Belgravia) $2,160

German silver gilt two-handled shaped oval dish, circa 1760, 32.5cm. long, 21oz. (Christie's) $2,530

One of a set of Jensen silver fruit dishes, London, 1928, largest 30cm. high. (Sotheby's Belgravia) $4,680

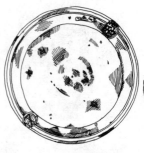

Rare James I small circular spice dish, London, 1617, 4½in. diam., 2oz. 14dwt. (Sotheby's) $9,045

One of a pair of George III plain circular two-handled vegetable dishes and covers by Richard Cooke, 1805, 22.5cm. diam., 99oz. (Christie's) $5,760

George III silver gilt circular dish by William Pitts, 1787, 19cm. diam., 10oz.5dwt. (Christie's) $1,640

Early Victorian bacon dish by E., E., J. & W. Barnard, London, 1840, 61oz. 4dwt., 13¾in. wide. (Sotheby's) $2,500

One of a pair of George III butter shells by Aldridge & Green, London, 1777, 4¼in. wide, 6oz. 2dwt. (Sotheby's) $665

George II silver gilt rectangular toasted cheese dish by Robert Sharp, London, 1792, 11¼in. wide, 33oz. 2dwt. (Sotheby's) $4,285

One of a pair of Dutch 20th century oval two-handled fruit dishes, 33.2oz., 25.7cm. wide. (Sotheby's Belgravia) $1,060

Circular fruit dish, Birmingham, 1899, 26cm. diam., 39oz. (Sotheby's Belgravia) $1,060

One of a pair of George III entree dishes and covers by Robert Gaze, London, 1776, 61oz. 10dwt., 31.8cm. long. (Christie's N. York) $2,200

One of a set of four George IV plain two-handled oblong entree dishes and covers by William Eaton, 1823, 29.8cm. long, 215oz. (Christie's) $9,600

One of a pair of George III circular entree dishes and covers, London, 1810, 10¾in. diam., 123oz. 8dwt. (Sotheby's) $13,805

One of a set of three George III oblong entree dishes and covers by John Foskett, London, 1810, 177oz. 2dwt. (Sotheby's) $3,680

Circular rosewater dish by Paul Storr, London, 1815, 37oz., 37cm. diam. (Osborne, King & Megran) $8,720

WMF silvered metal dish, circa 1900, 23.6cm. diam. (Sotheby's Belgravia) $700

Late 19th/early 20th century German shaped oval fruit dish, 11oz., 24.5cm. wide. (Sotheby's Belgravia) $355

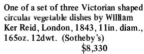

Oval silver dessert dish by William Comyns, London, 1906, 39cm. long, 99.5oz. (Sotheby's Belgravia) $2,350

Early 20th century American sterling silver compote by S. Kirk, 25cm. diam., 19oz. (Robert W. Skinner Inc.) $250

One of a set of three Victorian shaped circular vegetable dishes by William Ker Reid, London, 1843, 11in. diam., 165oz. 12dwt. (Sotheby's) $8,330

DISHES

Parcel gilt two-handled oval fruit dish by Lazarus Posen Wwe, Frankfurt, circa 1900, 30.3oz. (Sotheby's Belgravia) $600

One of a set of six silver mounted shaped circular hardstone dishes by D. & J. Wellby, London, 1868, 15.7cm. diam. (Sotheby's Belgravia) $1,905

Large silver gilt and enamel kovsh by Alexander B. Lybavin, St. Petersburg, 35cm. long, in oak case. (Sotheby's) $6,665

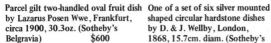

Russian glass dish with silver handle. (Parsons, Welch & Cowell) $685

William III brazier by Anthony Nelme, London, 1700, 32cm. long, 19oz.2dwt. (Sotheby's) $3,570

One of a pair of trefoil vegetable dishes and covers by Elkington & Co. Ltd., Birmingham, 1898, 112.4oz., 29.5cm. across.(Sotheby's Belgravia) $2,925

Ming silvered alloy tripod censer and cover, 16th/17th century, 25.5cm. high. (Christie's) $420

Pair of George III shaped oblong entree dishes and covers by William Burwash, London, 1816, 32cm. wide, 128oz.13dwt. (Sotheby Beresford Adams) $3,810

One of a pair of George III oblong entree dishes and plated heater bases, by William Burwash, London, 1819, 119oz. (Sotheby's) $2,820

Cast and pierced oval fruit dish with glass liner, by Dobson & Sons, London, 1901, 34.2cm. long, 40.9oz. (Sotheby's Belgravia)$1,170

One of a pair of rare James I shaped circular sweetmeat dishes, London, 1617, 12oz.4dwt., 20cm. diam. (Sotheby's) $5,950

One of a set of four George III oblong entree dishes and covers by Richard Cooke, London, 1803, 230oz.5dwt., 11½in. wide. (Sotheby's) $8,650

Parcel gilt flagon and four goblets by S. Smith & Son, London, 1870, 113.2oz. (Sotheby's Belgravia) $4,915

George I six-sided lidded flagon by Samuel Wastell, London, 20cm. high, 1714, 46oz. (Aldridges) $8,660

FRAMES

Large shaped rectangular photograph frame by Elkington & Co. Ltd., Birmingham, 1905, 40.8oz.(Sotheby's Belgravia) $1,265

Early 20th century French rectangular gilt metal photograph frame with laurel leaf borders, 40.7cm. high. (Sotheby's Belgravia) $560

Art Nouveau style silver photograph frame by J. & A. Zimmerman, 29cm. high. (Sotheby's Belgravia) $450

Silver gilt and white enamel photograph frame, by I. Brizin, St. Petersburg, 1899-1908, 17.6cm. high. (Sotheby's) $4,045

Shaped rectangular silver gilt and enamel photograph frame, 12.3cm. high, St. Petersburg, 1908-1912. (Sotheby's) $2,620

Silver gilt and enamel photograph frame by Faberge, 1899-1908, 16.4cm. high. (Sotheby's) $5,475

FLASKS

George III pocket flask with detachable beaker by Phipps & Robinson, 1796, 8oz.12dwt., 18.5cm. high. (Sotheby Beresford Adams) $525

Large silver spirit flask with detachable beaker base, by FP, London, 1876, 19.5cm. high, 24oz. (Sotheby's Belgravia) $750

One of a pair of large Victorian silver gilt pilgrim bottles, by George Fox, 1895, 346oz., 54.6cm. high. (Christie's) $19,975

FLATWARE

Pair of Old English pattern serving spoons by Peter and Ann Bateman, London, 1793, 23cm. long. (Andrew Grant) $215

Part of a large set of Jensen tableware, 1930's, 4.407gm. (Sotheby's) $5,150

Part of a canteen of silver Old English cutlery in mint condition. (Locke & England) $2,420

Sterling silver punch ladle by William Gale & Son, New York, circa 1850-60, 6½oz. (Robert W. Skinner Inc.) $325

Fish slice by Faberge, Moscow, 1898-1908, with monogrammed handle. (Sotheby's) $785

Guild of Handicraft Ltd. silver spoon designed by C. R. Ashbee, London, 1905, 19.3cm. long. (Sotheby's Belgravia) $750

Charles I gilded seal top spoon, London, 1637, by Charles Punge. (Sotheby, King & Chasemore) $480

One of a set of four Russian silver-gilt and niello spoons by V. Akimov, Moscow, 1890, 170mm. long. (Christie's) $1,320

Part of a set of eighteen silver-gilt ice-cream spoons by Wakely & Wheeler, London, 1888, 19.5oz., 13.2cm. long. (Sotheby's Belgravia) $710

Early George II punch ladle by Richard Richardson, Chester, 1733, with turned wood handle. (Sotheby Beresford Adams) $1,000

One of a pair of Scottish toddy labels. (Andrew Grant) $170

Three from a set of twelve George I silver gilt teaspoons and a mote spoon, circa 1725, 7oz.10dwt. (Christie's) $2,800

Part of a George IV and Victorian silver table service for twelve persons. (Russell, Baldwin & Bright) $6,875

Part of a twenty-four-piece silver dessert service by Faberge, Moscow, circa 1890. (Christie's) $4,200

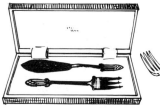

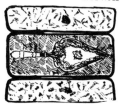

Cased set of Sybil Dunlop silver fish servers with Gothic pierced decoration, London, 1927, 8oz. (Smith-Woolley & Perry) $250

Silver gilt four-piece christening set by John Hunt and Robert Roskell, London, 1880, 11.5oz. (Sotheby's Belgravia) $850

Alexander Clark Manufacturing Co. Ltd., presentation trowel, Sheffield, 1901, 41.5cm. long. (Sotheby's Belgravia) $1,680

Seal top spoon by William Rawson, circa 1650. (Sotheby, King & Chasemore) $840

James I silver gilt seal top spoon, London, 1607. (Christie's) $480

17th century Dutch silver and ivory domestic knife and sheath, 23cm. long. (Phillips) $3,000

James I provincial seal top spoon, impressed for Lincoln, circa 1617. (Sotheby, King & Chasemore) $765

Early Charles II silver spoon, York 1661. (Woolley & Wallis) $2,000

Regency caddy spoon by Joseph Willmore, Birmingham, 1814, 7.5cm. long. (Christie's N. York) $1,300

One of a set of six silver gilt teaspoons by Paul Storr, London, 1833, 8oz.15dwt.(Sotheby's) $1,240

Early George II punch Ladle by George Jones, London, 1730, with wooden handle. (Sotheby Beresford Adams) $310

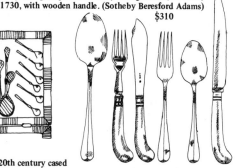

Part of a set of forty-five pieces of King's pattern table silver by J. & W. Marshall, Edinburgh, 87oz. (Sotheby's)$2,410

Early 20th century cased set of fifteen Norwegian enameled spoons by Marius Hammer. (Sotheby's Belgravia) $315

Part of a canteen of rat-tail pattern table silver by William Comyns & Sons, London, 1967-69, 193.6oz. (Sotheby's Belgravia) $6,000

Russian silver and enamel decorated serving piece with scalloped lip, 15cm. long. (C. G. Sloan & Co. Inc.) $275

Part of a German silver dessert set, circa 1880, 77.3oz. (Sotheby's Belgravia) $1,355

Part of a set of twelve silver gilt teaspoons by Elkington & Co., Birmingham, each 13cm. long. (Sotheby's Belgravia)$255

One of two mid 18th century cutlery boxes containing a silver gilt dessert service, 35cm. high, circa 1770. (Sotheby's) $4,760

Part of a large set of sterling silver flatware by Whiting Manufacturing Co., Rhode Island, early 20th century. (Robert W. Skinner Inc.) $4,900

Selection from a canteen of Gorham Manufacturing Co. tableware, Birmingham, 1911, 401.9oz. (Sotheby's Belgravia) $7,920

Canteen of silver tableware by E. Vander, Sheffield, 1932, 170oz. (McCartney, Morris & Barker) $4,115

Set of six silver gilt apostle spoons and a sugar sifter by H. Holland & Son, London, 1870, 19.5oz. (Sotheby's Belgravia) $375

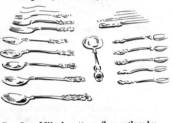

Set of King's pattern silver cutlery by Mary Shawley, London, 1838, 144oz (Warren & Wignall) $4,470

Part of a ninety-six-piece Jensen service in silver coloured metal. (Sotheby's Belgravia) $5,615

Fiddle thread shell pattern table silver by Spink & Son, London, 1900, 143.1oz. (Sotheby's Belgravia) $3,040

Part of a canteen of table silver by Viners Ltd., Sheffield, circa 1949-51, kept in bow-fronted wood cabinet. (Sotheby's Belgravia)$6,320

One of a pair of George III bell-shaped goblets by Godbehere & Wigan, London, 1795, 6½in. high, 15oz.17dwt. (Sotheby's) $1,310

One of a set of four goblets by Elkington & Co., London, 1877, 38oz., 13cm. high. (Sotheby's Belgravia) $2,105

One of a pair of George III bell-shaped goblets by Henry Green, London, 1788, 5½in. high, 13oz. 7dwt. (Sotheby's) $1,905

One of a set of six small Russian silver gilt and niello vodka goblets, Moscow, 1841, 10cm. high. (Christie's) $1,255

One of a pair of embossed Victorian goblets by Richard Hennell, London, 1861. (Phillips) $980

One of a pair of Irish goblets by Michael Homer, Dublin, 1787. (Christie's S. Kensington) $1,390

German silver gilt chalice, mid 19th century, 24.2cm. high, 18.1oz. (Sotheby's Belgravia) $290

Austrian silver parcel gilt wine goblet, Vienna, 1847, 21cm. high, 8oz.18dwt. (Sotheby Beresford Adams)$380

Silver presentation goblet by Ramsden & Carr, London, 1905, 13cm. high, 206gm. (Sotheby's Belgravia) $375

INKSTANDS

Soft metal inkwell in form of an owl, 18.5cm. high, circa 1890. (Sotheby's) $155

Single well inkstand by Hunt & Roskell, London, 1843, 15.5cm. high, 25.1oz. (Sotheby's Belgravia) $680

Liberty & Co. silver and enamel ink-well, Birmingham, 1900, with clear glass liner, 6.5cm. high. (Sotheby's Belgravia) $280

A Newlyn silver and enameled inkstand, 24cm. square, London, 1911. (Christie's) $420

Royal shaped oval two-bottle inkstand by Elkington & Co., Birmingham, 1856, 31.8oz., 37cm. long. (Sotheby's Belgravia) $1,125

Shaped rectangular two-bottle inkstand by Lambert & Co., London, 1908, 31cm. long, 56.4oz. (Sotheby's Belgravia) $1,215

Shaped rectangular two-bottle inkstand by Edward Barnard & Sons, London, 1860, 55.9oz., 33.5cm. long. (Sotheby's Belgravia) $1,650

Shaped oblong two-bottle inkstand by John Walton, Newcastle, 1844, 31.6cm. long, 42.8oz. (Sotheby's Belgravia) $890

Large presentation two-bottle inkstand on ebonised wood plinth, by Hukin & Heath, Birmingham, 1898, 41cm. long. (Sotheby's Belgravia) $1,870

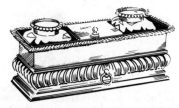

Coffer-shaped double inkwell by Carrington & Co., London, 1921, 23.8cm. long, 44.6oz. (Sotheby's Belgravia) $840

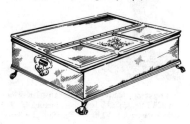

Early 20th century electroplated rectangular treasury inkstand, 29cm. long. (Sotheby's Belgravia) $395

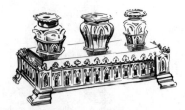

Rectangular two-bottle inkstand by Joseph & John Angell, London, 1838, 43.9oz., 27.5cm. long. (Sotheby's Belgravia) $935

Shaped rectangular two-bottle inkstand by Henry Wilkinson & Co., Sheffield, 1844, 31.5cm. long, 21.2oz. (Sotheby's Belgravia) $625

George III plain oblong inkstand by William Plummer, 1787, 28cm. long, 28oz. (Christie's) $1,735

Rectangular silver inkstand, London, 1915, 32cm. wide. (Lambert & Symes) $870

German inkstand in the form of a tortoise, importer's mark for B. Muller & Son, Chester, 1900, 33.1oz., 30cm. long. (Sotheby's Belgravia) $2,225

Victorian silver oval desk stand, London, 1859, 31oz. 1ft.2in. long. (Messenger May & Baverstock) $1,525

George II inkstand by Edward Feline, London, 1740, 23.8cm. long, 26oz. (Christie's) $11,000

Victorian standish with three bottles, centre bottle with candlestick and snuffer, by George Fox, 1864, 21oz. (Taylor Lane & Creber) $1,075

William IV shaped oblong inkstand by J. & J. Angell, London, 1834, 28oz.6dwt. (Sotheby's) $1,905

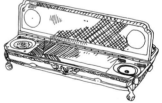

George III oblong treasury inkstand by William Pitts and William Preedy, London, 1794, 14½in. long, 107oz.17dwt. (Sotheby's) $9,995

George III silver inkstand by Michael Plummer, London, 1797, 10oz.10dwt., 20.2cm. long. (Christie's) $1,500

Silver gilt two-bottle inkstand by Hunt & Roskell, London, 1850, 25.7cm. long, 21.8oz. (Sotheby's Belgravia) $1,640

Silver hot water jug, Birmingham 1895. (Christie's S. Kensington) $450

Silver hot water jug by Walker & Hall, Sheffield, 1899, 23.5cm. high, 23oz. (Sotheby's Belgravia) $560

George IV baluster ewer by Benjamin Smith, London, 1825, 11¾in. high, 39oz.2dwt. (Sotheby's) $2,620

One of a pair of lidded baluster jugs with domed hinged lids by Robert Breading, Dublin, 1798, 41oz., 18cm. high. (Lambert & Symes) $21.960

One of a pair of Chinese silver vase-shaped jugs, mid 19th century, 35.5cm. high, 87oz. (Christie's) $1,920

George II large plain pear-shaped jug with scroll handle by John White, 1728, 24.7cm. high, 37oz. (Christie's) $3,855

Italian helmet-shaped ewer on circular foot, Naples, 1770, 23.5cm. high, 21oz. (Christie's) $3,120

Early Victorian silver wine ewer.(Woolley & Wallis) $1,960

Large George III silver beer jug by Francis Crump, London, 1768, 30.8cm. high, 59oz.10dwt. (Christie's) $7,500

Elizabeth I silver gilt mounted tiger-ware jug, 1579, 20.3cm. high. (Christie's) $4,140

American presentation silver water pitcher by B. Gardiner, New York, circa 1830, 26oz.14dwt., 31cm. high. (C. G. Sloan & Co. Inc.) $500

Silver gilt jug with baluster body, St. Petersburg, 1882, 8.9cm. high. (Sotheby's) $835

Plain water jug by Goldsmiths & Silversmiths Ltd., London, 1911, 18cm. high, 18.7oz. (Sotheby's Belgravia) $505

Unusual George III cider jug by Peter and Anne Bateman, London, 1796, 30oz., 23cm. high. (Christie's) $10,000

Silver beer jug and cover, London, 1872. (Christie's S. Kensington) $1,815

Ribbed and fluted William IV hot water jug by Jonathan Hayne, London, 1833, 12½in. high, 42oz.4dwt. (Sotheby's) $2,500

Géorge III hot water jug by Hester Bateman, London, 1785, 32.5cm. high, 24oz.10dwt. (Christie's) $2,000

Victorian silver plated Renaissance style ewer, 42.5cm. high. (C. G. Sloan & Co. Inc.) $425

Fine 19th century Austrian silver gilt ewer with hexagonal body, 31.5cm. high. (Phillips) $7,360

Victorian ewer and basin by James Garrard, 1885, 142oz. (Christie's) $7,750

Queen Anne shaving jug by Anthony Nelme, 1713, 20cm. high, 23oz. (Phillips) $6,670

Heavy silver gilt ewer, by Garrard, 1838.(Sotheby's) $9,120

Late 19th century Gorham sterling silver water pitcher, 10¼in. high, 40 troy oz. (Robert W. Skinner Inc.) $625

George III silver jug by John Scofield, 1783, 29cm. high. (Grays Antique Mews) $1,965

JUGS

Silver gilt ewer by George Angell, London, 1859, 26.7cm. high, 24.5oz., also with French marks. (Sotheby's Belgravia) $3,040

Silver presentation jug by WJ, London, 1884, 25cm. high, 37.7oz. (Sotheby's Belgravia) $1,520

Electrogilt copper electrotype jug, cylindrical body decorated with cherubs, 23cm. high, circa 1870. (Sotheby's Belgravia) $560

Victorian rococo revival coin silver water pitcher by Jones Ball & Poor, Boston, circa 1852, 33 troy oz., 11in. high. (Robert W. Skinner Inc.) $1,100

'Cellini' pattern ewer by George Fox, London, 1873-76, 53.1oz., 42.5cm. high. (Sotheby's Belgravia) $2,225

Parcel gilt 'Armada' pattern wine ewer by J. Smyth, Dublin, 1871, 36.7cm. high, 42.9oz. (Sotheby's Belgravia) $2,150

LIGHTERS

George III cigar lighter in the form of Aladdin's lamp by Digby Scott and Benjamin Smith, London, 8oz.17dwt. (Sotheby Beresford Adams) $2,095

Novelty table lighter by JB, London, 1886, 7cm. high. (Sotheby's Belgravia) $165

George III silver cigar lighter by John Emes, London, 1806, 11.7cm. long, 5oz.10dwt. (Christie's) $1,500

MATCH CASES

Rectangular silver matchbox by Stephen Smith & Son, London, 1878, 4.7oz., 7.2cm. long. (Sotheby's Belgravia) $130

Enamelled sentry-box vesta case by Sampson Mordan, London, 1886, 5.7cm. high. (Sotheby's Belgravia) $425

Unusual niello vesta/fusee case with folding lid and striker, 1872, 4.9cm. high. (Sotheby's Belgravia) $285

Rare George II Scottish dog collar in silver by Robert Luke, Glasgow, circa 1740, 5½in. diam., 5oz.1dwt. (Sotheby's) $1,785

Auctioneer's silver gavel by George Unite, Birmingham, 1876, 10.6cm. long, 5.9oz. (Sotheby's Belgravia) $1,030

Faberge silver mounted desk barometer. (Phillips) $22,610

Circular silver magnifying glass, circa 1790, 10.8cm. long. (Sotheby's) $405

Silver Holy Water stoup, late 17th century, Augsburg. 14.5cm. high. (May, Whetter & Grose) $190

Beehive honey pot by Asprey & Co. Ltd., Sheffield, 1970, 29.6oz., 13.5cm. high. (Sotheby's Belgravia) $720

Parcel gilt and pearl finished posy holder by George Unite, Birmingham, 1887, 14.7cm. high, 2.7oz. (Sotheby's Belgravia) $315

George III wax-jack by Crouch & Hannam, London, 1787, 14cm. high, 5oz.(Christie's) $1,500

Jensen cocktail shaker designed by Harold Nielsen, in three sections, 28cm. high, 1930's. (Sotheby's Belgravia) $1,405

Chased gilt metal plaque applied with twelve carved shell cameos, Italian, circa 1880. (Sotheby's Belgravia) $570

George I miniature tea service and table by David Clayton, circa 1725, 12.9cm. long. (Christie's) $3,360

Italian chased gilt metal plaque applied with seven Roman mosaics, circa 1880. (Sotheby's Belgravia) $640

Silver group of pigs by Rosa Bonheur. (Bonham's) $1,870

Late 19th/early 20th century German silver model of a sedan chair, 16.4cm. high, 265gm. (Sotheby's Belgravia) $395

One of a pair of late 19th century silver peacocks, 14oz., 27.5cm. long. (Robert W. Skinner Inc.)$350

Persian silver standing figure of a Ruler, 35oz., 40cm. high. (C. G. Sloan & Co. Inc.) $1,200

Unusual early 20th century silver colored metal model of a gunboat, 24cm. wide. (Sotheby's Belgravia) $710

Cast bust of Queen Victoria by Wilson & Sharpe, Edinburgh, 1908, 15.3cm. high, 16oz. (Sotheby's Belgravia)$350

Cast silver figure of a Royal Fusilier in tropical kit, London, 1915, 21oz., 16.5cm. high. (May Whetter & Grose) $550

Pair of German equestrian figures by B. Neresheimer & Sohne, Hanau, 1920, 91.1oz. (Sotheby's Belgravia) $3,160

Silver model of a soldier by Elkington & Co., Birmingham, 1862, 36.5cm. high. (Sotheby's Belgravia) $1,415

Large Victorian equestrian centerpiece by Elkington & Co., Birmingham, 1863, 241oz.4dwt. (Sotheby Beresford Adams) $6,425

Silver group of a mounted jockey and an Indian groom, by Elkington & Co., Birmingham, circa 1880, 21.5cm. long. (Sotheby's Belgravia) $980

One of a pair of silver gilt female figures by Elkington & Co., Birmingham, 1888, 111.6oz., 21.7cm. long. (Sotheby's Belgravia) $2,125

Tapering cylindrical mug, inscribed on one side, by Charles Boyton, London, 1861, 16.4oz., 12.2cm. high. (Sotheby's Belgravia) $630

Spool-shaped child's can by Charles Reily and George Storer, London, 1851, 10.5cm. high, 5.9oz. (Sotheby's Belgravia) $470

Christening mug of baluster form by Thomas Wynne, London, 1769, 5oz. (Sotheby, King & Chasemore) $310

Victorian child's mug by George Adams, London, 1867, 10cm. high, 5oz.9dwt. (Sotheby Beresford Adams) $355

Victorian child's mug by E. C. Brown, London, 1879, 9cm. high, 5oz.6dwt. (Sotheby Beresford Adams) $260

One of a pair of George I plain mugs by William Fleming, 1714, 11.4cm. high, 22oz. (Christie's) $2,530

American silver cylinder-shaped mug by R. & W. Wilson, circa 1835, 7oz. 10dwt., 10cm. high. (C. G. Sloan & Co. Inc.) $350

Victorian silver child's mug by Creswick & Co., Sheffield, 1858, 10.5cm. high, 7oz.11dwt. (Sotheby Beresford Adams) $620

Early George III baluster mug by Francis Crump, London, 1763, 14oz.15dwt., 13cm. high. (Sotheby Beresford Adams) $1,045

George II plain mug by Paul de Lamerie, 1734, 10.2cm. high, 10oz. 10dwt. (Christie's) $3,615

Victorian child's mug by George Adams London, 1875, 9cm. high. (Sotheby Beresford Adams) $260

Footed silver cann by Samuel Bartlett, Boston, circa 1790, 14 troy oz., 5¾in. high. (Robert W. Skinner Inc.) $2,300

MUGS

George III silver baluster-shaped cann, Newcastle, circa 1760-68, by John Langlands, 13oz.3dwt., 13.5cm. high. (C. G. Sloan & Co. Inc.) $700

George III baluster-shaped silver cann, by Charles Hougham, London, 1785, 12.5cm. high, 13oz. (C. G. Sloan & Co. Inc.) $700

George I silver cann by John East, London, 1722-23, 12oz.12dwt., 11cm. high. (C. G. Sloan & Co. Inc.) $1,300

MULLS

Small hoof table snuff box with Victorian silver mount, 1858. (Neales) $165

Scottish silver mounted ram's head snuff mull, late 19th century, 52cm. wide. (Sotheby's) $965

Scandinavian silver and ivory double-ended snuff mull, circa 1760, 7.5cm. high. (Sotheby's) $1,945

Scottish silver mounted cow horn snuff mull, cover with central agate plaque, circa 1800, 11½in. long. (Christie's) $635

Scottish early horn flask converted to a snuff mull, circa 1623, 8in. long. (Christie's) $800

Scottish ram's horn snuff mull. (Wallis & Wallis) $685

 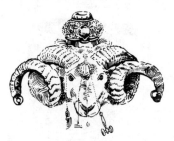 

Silver and tortoiseshell snuff mull. mid 18th century, 60cm. high. (Christie's) $3,120

Ram's head snuff mull with silver mounts, Edinburgh, 1891, 42.5cm. long.(Sotheby's) $1,325

Silver mounted horn vinaigrette in the form of a snuff mull, Birmingham, 1885, 5.7cm. long. (Sotheby's Belgravia)$225

Silver mustard pot by E. J. & B. W. Barnard, London, 1841, 4oz., 4.5cm. high. (Allen & May) $410

George I kitchen pepper by Isaac Callard, 1719, 7cm. high, 2oz. (Sotheby's) $1,430

Heath & Middleton silver preserve pot and cover with blue glass liner, Birmingham, 1900, 7.25cm. (Sotheby's Belgravia) $325

Rectangular mustard pot with fluted decoration by Finley & Taylor, London, 1883, 2.9oz. (Sotheby's Belgravia) $105

Pair of Continental silver pepperettes modelled as Great Auks. (Christie's S. Kensington) $645

Tapering cylindrical mustard pot and spoon by Robert Hennell, London, 1848-51, 6.4oz.(Sotheby's Belgravia) $185

Six-piece silver condiment set by Hardy Brothers, Ltd., London, 1948, 24.9oz. (Sotheby's Belgravia)$650

Twelve-piece condiment set plus spoons by W. Lister & Sons Ltd., London, 1917-26, 33.6oz. (Sotheby's Belgravia) $1,405

C. T. & G. Fox owl pepperette, London, 1870, 7.7cm. high, 1.8oz. (Sotheby's Belgravia) $260

Early 20th century pair of German pepperettes, 12cm. high, 10.1oz., in silver coloured metal. (Sotheby's Belgravia) $450

Silver mustard pot by Hester Bateman, 1785, 13.5cm. high, 3.5oz. (Phillips) $1,335

MUSTARDS & PEPPERS

Five-piece condiment set, stamped Jays, Oxford St., London, 14.5oz. (Sotheby's Belgravia) $285

NEFS

Continental parcel gilt nef by Berthold Muller, 28in. high, 201oz. (Christie's) $4,180

Large and impressive German nef by B. Muller & Son, Chester, 1898, 93cm. high, 325oz. (Sotheby's Belgravia) $24,780

Large Hungarian silver gilt nef, decorated with blue enamel, London, 1974, 56.8cm. high. (Sotheby's Belgravia) $3,510

Early 20th century electroplated three-masted nef, probably German, 60cm. high. (Sotheby's Belgravia) $650

NUTMEGS

Parcel gilt nef by Heinrich Winterstein, Augsburg, circa 1600, 29.3cm. high. (Sotheby's) $17,290

Continental parcel gilt three-masted nef on four wheels, 24½in. high, 151oz. (Christie's) $4,180

Early 19th century George III silver nutmeg grater with hinged cover, by John Robins, London, 5cm. long. (Robert W. Skinner Inc.) $300

19th century George IV silver nutmeg grater by Reily & Storer, London, 1833, 6cm. long. (Robert W. Skinner Inc.) $300

18th century George III silver nutmeg grater of box form, by Phipps & Robinson, London, 4.5cm. long. (Robert W. Skinner Inc.) $350

Early 20th century silver prize quaich with engraved inscription, 3oz.5dwt. (Vernon's) $40

Charles II two-handled porringer, circa 1684-87, 9.4cm. high, 9oz.1dwt. (Christie's) $3,080

Early 18th century hemispherical quaich by Robert Ker, Edinburgh, 6oz.15dwt. (Sotheby's) $1,640

American silver porringer by Edward Winslow, Boston, circa early 18th century, 12cm. diam. (Robert W. Skinner Inc.) $800

Fine James II porringer and cover, London, 1686, 7½in. high, 32oz.2dwt. (Sotheby's) $49,980

Late 18th century American silver porringer with dome bottom and pierced handle, 5¼in. diam. (Robert W. Skinner Inc.)$950

Small Commonwealth porringer and cover, maker's mark ET, 1657, 10cm. diam., 10.75oz. (Phillips) $16,100

American silver porringer by Paul Revere Snr., engraved handle, 19cm. long. (C. G. Sloan & Co. Inc.) $3,900

James II porringer and cover, London, 1685, 30oz.14dwt., 18.5cm. high. (Sotheby's) $6,190

Silver porringer, London, 1694, 10½oz. (Honiton Galleries) $930

William III two-handled porringer by Anthony Nelme, London, 1694, 6oz., 8cm. high. (Sotheby Beresford Adams) $1,380

Commonwealth two-handled porringer by GS, 1658, 5.6cm. high, 3oz. 11dwt. (Christie's) $955

605

One of a set of four compressed circular salt cellars by Charles Stuart Harris, London, 1876, 15.9oz., 7cm. diam. (Sotheby's Belgravia) $700

Pair of Victorian silver salts by F. D., London, 1845, 12oz. (Alfie's Antique Market) $785

One of a pair of George II trencher salt cellars by David Chapman, London, 1729, 5oz., 8.2cm. long. (Christie's) $1,600

One of a pair of George IV salt cellars by Emes & Barnard, London, 1824, 8oz.14dwt., 3½in. diam. (Sotheby's) $570

One of a pair of German silver gilt salt cellars, circa 1870, 8.5cm. wide, 17.9oz. (Sotheby's Belgravia) $255

One of a set of six George IV shaped circular salt cellars by Emes & Barnard, London, 1825, 25oz. 18dwt., 9cm. diam. (Sotheby's) $905

One of a set of six George II cast salt cellars by Paul Crespin, London, 1734, 55oz. (Andrew Grant) $2,225

Set of four escallop shell salt cellars by Edward Farrell, London, 1840, with four spoons. (Sotheby's Belgravia) $2,225

One of a pair of shell salt cellars by W. W., London, 1860, 11cm. long, 12.8oz. (Sotheby's Belgravia) $1,055

Electroplated parcel gilt mustard pot, mustard spoon, four salt cellars and spoons in case, by Elkington & Co., Birmingham. (Sotheby's Belgravia)$630

One of a pair of Victorian silver gilt salt cellars by Hunt & Roskell, 1855, 37oz. (Christie's) $5,875

One of a pair of large German salt cellars by Johann Martin Schott, Frankfurt, circa 1815, 25oz. (Christie's) $1,900

606

18th century Irish silver sauceboat, one of a pair, by Robert
Calderwood, Dublin, 32oz.,
21cm. long. (Robert W. Skinner
Inc.) $3,600

One of a pair of George I sauceboats by
Peter Archambo I, London, 1726, 19.5cm.
long, 25oz.10dwt. (Christie's)
                                 $11,000

One of a pair of George IV fluted
oval sauceboats, London, 1827.
(Phillips) $4,655

One of a pair of George II sauceboats by Thomas Heming, London, 1756, 7¼in. wide, 21oz.10dwt.
(Sotheby's) $3,200

Very large sauceboat by Edmund Johnson, Dublin, 1902, 35.7cm. long,
30.2oz. (Sotheby's Belgravia)
                                 $935

One of a pair of George III plain
sauceboats by J. Wakelin and W.
Taylor, 1784, 31oz. (Christie's)
                                 $4,340

One of a pair of oval sauceboats,
by Joshua Vander, London, 1902,
19oz., 18cm. long. (Sotheby's
Belgravia) $450

One of a pair of early George III plain
sauceboats, circa 1770, 43oz. (Irelands)
                                 $7,080

One of a pair of George II oval sauceboats by Christian Hillan, London,
1738, 7¾in. wide, 32oz.4dwt.
(Sotheby's) $9,995

One of a pair of large George II
sauceboats by John Pollock, London, 1755, 28oz.10dwt., 31.5cm.
long. (Christie's) $2,800

George II sauceboat by Christian Hillan,
1740, 5oz.19dwt. (Christie's)
                                 $3,135

One of a pair of George II oval
sauceboats by William Grundy,
London, 1755, 7¼in. wide, 39oz.
16dwt. (Sotheby's)$8,090

SCENT BOTTLES

Daum scent flask with silver gilt mounts. (Christie's S. Kensington) $415

Silver mounted Vernis Martin scent bottle case by Nicolas-Gabriel Saltret, 7cm. high, 1756-1762. (Sotheby's) $760

Mid 19th century gold mounted blue glass scent bottle, 7cm. high. (Christie's) $1,500

Unusual silver mounted Webb glass scent bottle modeled as a fish, 1884. (Phillips) $450

Silver gilt mounted enamel scentflask/smelling salts bottle, by Thomas Johnson, London, circa 1875, 13.7cm. long. (Sotheby's Belgravia) $140

Small porcelain scent bottle, modeled as a cat, 6.4cm. high. (Clarke Gammon) $485

Late Victorian scent bottle of teardrop form, with silver cap, 1889. (Phillips) $225

Early 18th century silver and mother-of-pearl scent flask of shaped baluster form, 7.8cm. high. (Sotheby's) $310

Victorian ceramic scent bottle with silver cap by Sampson Mordan, 1885. (Phillips) $180

Late 17th century German silver gilt cast scent bottle of pear shape. (Phillips) $605

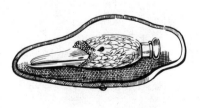

Parcel gilt silver swan's head scent flask by S. Mordan & Co., London, 1884, 14.8cm. long. (Sotheby's Belgravia) $610

18th century German silver perfume box, circa 1760, 5cm. high. (Phillips) $190

Oblong silver gilt snuff box by Frederick Marson, Birmingham, 1860, 7.7cm. long, 1.8oz. (Sotheby's Belgravia) $155

Circular tortoiseshell pique snuff box, Birmingham, 1745-1750, 6cm. diam. (Sotheby Beresford Adams)$130

Silver gilt and engine-turned oblong snuff box by Rawlings & Sumner, London, 1863, 2.9oz., 8.7cm. long. (Sotheby's Belgravia) $215

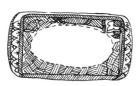

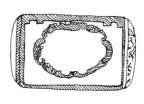

Oblong silver gilt snuff box by George Unite, Birmingham, 1870, 2.8oz., 8.5cm. long. (Sotheby's Belgravia) $215

Parcel gilt and niello snuff box of navette form, Veliki Ustiug, circa 1800, 6.9cm. wide. (Sotheby's) $1,072

Oblong silver gilt snuff box by George Unite, Birmingham, 1867, 8.6cm. long, 2.8oz. (Sotheby's Belgravia)$225

Shaped rectangular presentation snuff box by Nathaniel Mills, Birmingham, 1849, 8.4cm. long. (Sotheby's Belgravia) $540

William IV fox mask snuff box by Joseph Willmore, Birmingham, circa 1835, 3½in. long. (Sotheby's) $1,545

Rectangular snuff box by Edward Smith, Birmingham, 1842, 8cm. long. (Sotheby's Belgravia) $470

Rectangular snuff box with chased borders by Edward Smith, Birmingham, 1838, 9.5oz., 10.7cm. long. (Sotheby's Belgravia) $680

Shaped rectangular presentation snuff box by Edward Smith, Birmingham, 1859, 8.5cm. long. (Sotheby's) $420

Rectangular presentation snuff box by Francis Clark, Birmingham, 1839, 8.5cm. long. (Sotheby's Belgravia) $540

Mid 18th century English silver and hardstone snuff box of cartouche form, 6.5cm. wide. (Sotheby's) $415

French Vernis Martin snuff box, lid painted with flowers, circa 1755, 8.5cm. diam. (Sotheby's) $920

Mid 18th century English silver and hardstone snuff box, lid inset with agate, 7.4cm. wide. (Sotheby's) $415

Frederick Marson shaped rectangular snuff box, Birmingham, 1858, 3.7oz., 7.8cm. long. (Sotheby's Belgravia) $380

Mid 18th century English circular gilt metal snuff box, lid inset with tortoiseshell, 5.5cm. diam. (Sotheby Beresford Adams) $165

Oblong silver gilt snuff box by Cartwright, Woodward & Co., Birmingham, 1853, 2.2oz., 8.7cm. long. (Sotheby's Belgravia) $225

Unusual silver mounted tortoiseshell snuff box, silver gilt lined, 8.5cm. wide, circa 1775. (Sotheby's) $1,105

German hardstone snuff box with silver gilt cagework mounts, 7cm. wide, circa 1750.(Sotheby's) $620

German rectangular silver gilt snuff box with chased lid, circa 1730, 7.3cm. wide. (Sotheby's) $1,140

Mother-of-pearl and gilt metal snuff box, 7.2cm. wide, circa 1760. (Sotheby's) $345

Silver and niello snuff box of navette form, Veliki Ustiug, circa 1800, 6.9cm. wide. (Sotheby's) $475

18th century English snuff box with portrait of Frederick the Great. (Woolley & Wallis) $1,980

Mid 18th century circular English gilt metal snuff box, 7cm. diam. (Sotheby's) $415

Silver gilt double opening snuff box, one side with a verge watch by Iohan Georg Gugel of Brin, 91mm. diam., circa 1720. (Sotheby's) $6,550

Silver-mounted narwhal-tusk root snuff box by William Tiebzsch, London, 1879, 16.5cm. wide. (Sotheby's Belgravia) $520

Rectangular silver gilt snuff box by Ledsham Vale & Wheeler, Birmingham, 1827, 77mm. long. (Christie's) $1,440

Early 18th century cartouche-shaped silver-mounted ivory snuff box, probably Dieppe, 70mm. long. (Christie's) $2,640

Early 18th century English tortoiseshell pique snuff box, 6.5cm. wide. (Sotheby's) $310

Mid 18th century gilt metal and hardstone snuff box of oval form, 7.8cm. wide. (Sotheby's) $830

Louis XV pointed oval silver snuff box, Paris, 1763, 90mm. long. (Christie's) $1,800

Silver-gilt oval snuff box by R. & S. Garrard & Co., London, 1913, 8.1cm. long, 3.3oz. (Sotheby's Belgravia)$285

William IV oblong snuff box with scroll borders, Birmingham, 1836, 6oz.3dwt., 10cm. wide. (Sotheby Beresford Adams) $760

Early 18th century cartouche-shaped silver snuff box, possibly German, 84mm. long. (Christie's) $1,080

18th century oval pinchbeck snuff box, 74mm. long. (Christie's) $670

George III dish cross by S. Herbert & Co. London, 1760, 16oz. 10dwt., 31.8cm. long. (Christie's) $1,300

Oblong fruit stand on spreading base, by Frank Cogg & Co., Sheffield, 1965, 42cm. long, 34.2oz. (Sotheby's Belgravia) $960

George II dish cross by William Plummer, London, 1758, 24oz., 33.3cm. long. (Christie's) $900

Triform dish stand with rococo base, by Edward Barnard & Sons, London, 1855, 65.3oz., 27.8cm. high. (Sotheby's Belgravia) $1,990

Victorian electroplated cotton-reel stand, 37.5cm. high. (Christie's S. Kensington) $265

Late 19th century Tiffany & Co. standing fruit bowl, New York, 10¼in. diam., 28 troy oz.(Robert W. Skinner Inc.) $600

One of a pair of circular dessert stands, German, circa 1870, 28.5cm. high, 68oz.16dwt. (Sotheby Beresford Adams) $1,330

Viennese gilt metal and mother-of-pearl candle shade and stand, 32cm. high, circa 1815. (Sotheby's) $1,310

WMF silver metal tazza modeled as a young-woman, circa 1900, 37.5cm. high. (Sotheby's Belgravia) $700

Circular fruit stand by James Dixon & Sons, Sheffield, 1901, 32cm. diam., 43.8oz. (Sotheby's Belgravia) $850

Teapot stand with spirit burner by Paul Storr, 19oz.8dwt., 12cm. diam. (Sotheby, King & Chasemore)$745

Victorian shaped circular dessert stand with domed base, London, 1872, 22.5cm. diam., 27oz. 15dwt. (Sotheby Beresford Adams) $640

George III baluster tankard by James Sutton, London, 1780, 7½in. high, 24oz.2dwt. (Sotheby's) $2,110

Charles II plain cylindrical tankard by Thomas Jenkins, 1674, 6in. high, 29oz. (Christie's) $38,380

Queen Anne tankard by Colin McKenzie, Edinburgh, 1711, 8½in. high, 40oz. (Christie's)
$10,100

Queen Anne tapered cylindrical tankard by Nathaniel Locke, London, 1712, 21oz.18dwt., 7½in. high. (Sotheby's)
$2,350

George III tapered cylindrical tankard by John Robertson, Newcastle, 1797, 27oz.18dwt., 7¾in. high. (Sotheby's)
$1,090

James II large plain cylindrical tankard, 1688, 6¼in. high, 29oz. (Christie's) $3,920

George III cylindrical tankard on rim foot, by B. & J. Smith, 1811, 7½in. high, 45oz. (Christie's)
$3,530

One of a pair of George II pint tankards by Humphrey Payne, London, 1748, 26oz. (Taylor Lane & Creber)
$3,195

Scandinavian silver peg tankard by J. J. Reimers, Bergen, 6½in. high, 17oz.7dwt. (Christie's)
$5,290

Cylindrical tankard in 17th century style, by S. W. Smith & Co., London, 1913, 31.6oz., 18cm. high. (Sotheby's Belgravia)
$585

George II plain cylindrical tankard by Francis Spilsbury, 1729, 7in. high, 27oz. (Christie's) $2,350

American silver tankard by Benjamin Burt, Boston, circa 1770, 26oz.8dwt., 22.5cm. high. (C. G. Sloan & Co. Inc.)$4,000

613

Queen Anne cylindrical tankard
by David King, Dublin, 1702,
17.5cm. high, 23oz.17dwt.
(Sotheby's) $3,795

Victorian silver tankard by Robert
Harper, London, 1845, 11½oz.
(Clifford Dann & Partners)
$560

George III baluster tankard by
John Scofield, London, 1776,
19cm. high, 25oz. 7dwt.
(Sotheby's) $2,115

George III tapered cylindrical
tankard by Thomas Wallis, London, 1771, 18.5cm. high, 23oz.
10dwt. (Sotheby's) $1,795

George III baluster-shaped pint
tankard by John Denwell, London, 1773, 11oz. (Andrew Grant)
$480

One of a pair of silver tankards
with ribbed bands, by Septi-
mus and James Crespell, 61oz.,
London, 1770. (Irelands)
$7,550

George I silver tankard by
William Pearson, 9½in. tall,
44oz. (Robert W. Skinner
Inc.) $1,700

Charles II cylindrical tankard by A. B.,
London, 1676, 20cm. high, 32oz.18dwt.
(Sotheby's) $10,950

One of a pair of silver tankards
with hinged lids, Dublin, 1798,
by Robert Breading, 17.5cm.
high. (Lambert & Symes)
$21,780

Georgian tankard by A. B., London,
1799, with later embossing, 11oz.
(Clifford Dann & Partners) $610

Charles II plain cylindrical tankard
with scroll handle, 1681, 17.8cm.
high, 30oz. (Christie's)
$5,280

George III Irish tankard by
Thomas Jones, Dublin, 1783,
24.5cm. high. (Phillips)
$5,060

George III tapered cylindrical
tankard, 19cm. high, 23oz.1dwt.
(Sotheby's) $1,195

Late 16th century German gilt
tankard by Ulrich Beck,
Augsburg, circa 1590, 15.25cm.
high, 15½oz. (Phillips)
$18,400

William and Mary tankard,
London, 1694, 25oz.12dwt.,
17cm. high. (Sotheby
Beresford Adams)
$4,520

William III tapered cylindrical tankard by Humphrey Payne, London,
1701, 6½in. high, 20oz.2dwt.
(Sotheby's) $3,690

Russian silver cylindrical
tankard, Moscow, circa
1899-1908, 27.4cm.
high. (Sotheby's) $1,905

William IV tankard and cover
by Paul Storr, London, 1836,
31oz., 20cm. high. (Christie's)
$6,000

Queen Anne cylindrical tankard
by Joseph Walker, Dublin, 1706,
7¾in. high, 34oz.19dwt.
(Sotheby's) $5,450

Queen Anne plain cylindrical
tankard by Richard Green,
1710, 17.2cm. high, 22oz.
(Christie's) $3,600

George II silver baluster tankard and cover by John Jones I,
London, 1742, 21cm. high,
30oz. (Sotheby, King &
Chasemore) $2,040

George I tapered cylindrical
tankard by Matthew Lofthouse,
London, 1718, 17cm. high,
20oz.19dwt. (Sotheby's)
$2,855

17th century leather blackjack
with silver-mounted rim, 39cm.
high. (Christie's) $840

George III tankard by Henry
Chawner, 1786, 19oz., with
scroll handle. (Taylor, Lane
& Creber) $1,120

George II silver tea caddy, heavily embossed. (Parsons, Welch & Cowell) $825

George III oval tea caddy by Aaron Lestourgeon, London, 1776, 9cm. high, 10oz.1dwt. (Sotheby's) $1,655

One of a pair of George I octagonal tea caddies by Edward Gibbon, London, 1723, 13oz.18dwt., 4¾in. high. (Sotheby's) $1,975

George III tea caddy by John Parker and Edward Wakelin, London, 1768, 14oz., 14.5cm. high. (Christie's) $1,700

Silver tea caddy by Hester Bateman. (Bradley & Vaughan) $1,450

George I octagonal tea caddy by Sarah Holliday, 1725, 7oz. (Taylor Lane & Creber) $985

Late Victorian tortoiseshell and silver mounted tea caddy. (Christie's S. Kensington) $580

Three George III caddies, two tea and one sugar, by Samuel Taylor, London, 1750, 27oz. (Andrew Grant) $2,340

19th century French Louis XVI style silver tea caddy, 15cm. high, 8½oz. (Robert W. Skinner Inc.) $450

George III tea caddy, London, 1798, 16.5cm. high, 16oz. (Christie's) $1,700

One of a set of three George III tea caddies by Elizabeth Godfrey, London, 1754, 5¼in. high, 56oz.19dwt (Sotheby's) $9,280

George III plain oval tea caddy by A. Fogelberg and F. Gilbert, 1786, 13oz. 1dwt. (Christie's) $1,455

One of a pair of Queen Anne tea caddies by Simon Pantin, 1702, 22oz.5dwt.(Neales)$1,945

George III tea caddy by Aldridge & Green, 1779, 12cm. high, 13.5oz. (Phillips) $2,300

Drum-shaped tea caddy and cover by Hunt & Roskell, London, 1856, 10.7cm. high, 13.7oz. (Sotheby's Belgravia) $610

One of a set of three George III plain oblong tea caddies by Matthew Boulton and John Fothergill, 1774, 3½in. high, 33oz. (Christie's) $4,705

Silver tea caddy by W. & P. Cunningham, Edinburgh, 1797, 10oz. (Biddle & Webb) $1,210

One of three George III tea caddies by Thomas Heming, London, 1748, 5½in. high, 48oz.11dwt. (Sotheby's) $5,950

One of a pair of Dutch silver tea caddies, 1713, 12cm. high, 6oz. 16dwt. (Christie's)$2,235

Pair of George III chinoiserie tea caddies and mixing bowl in a shagreen case. (Bonhams) $2,730

One of a pair of George III tea caddies of inverted pear form by Samuel Taylor, 1763, 16.7cm. high, 23oz. (Christie's) $3,015

George I plain octagonal tea caddy by Thomas Tearle, 1725, 11oz. 4dwt. (Christie's) $1,800

Victorian silver tea caddy by J. S. Hunt, London, 1861, 16cm. long, 25oz. (Christie's) $1,700

George III silver tea caddy by Crispin Fuller, London, 1796, 16cm. high, 10oz.6dwt. (Sotheby, King & Chasemore) $1,200

617

Puiforcat five-piece tea service, 1920's, 17.25cm. high milk jug. (Sotheby's Belgravia) $3,275

Small three-piece teaset by Edward Barnard & Sons Ltd., London, 1881, 16.2oz. (Sotheby's Belgravia) $700

George IV inverted pear-shaped three-piece teaset by Hyam Hyams, London, 1825-27, 46oz.6dwt. (Sotheby's) $1,265

William IV three-piece inverted pear-shaped teaset by Elder & Co., Edinburgh, 1834-36, 54oz.7dwt. (Sotheby's) $1,265

Four-piece Jensen silver tea service with ivory side handles, circa 1926-29. (Sotheby's Belgravia) $4,445

Four-piece tea and coffee set by Martin, Hall & Co. Ltd., Sheffield, 1874, 77.2oz. (Sotheby's Belgravia) $2,060

Five-piece tea and coffee set in Moorish taste by Mappin & Webb, London, 1871, 142.3oz. (Sotheby's Belgravia) $2,690

Fine Edwardian four-piece tea and coffee service by Elkington & Co., Birmingham, 1901, 88oz. (Locke & England) $2,370

George III three-piece teaset, sold with sugar tongs, 52oz. 16dwt. (Sotheby's) $1,735

Unusual four-piece teaset by A. E. Jones, Birmingham, 1907, 33oz.8dwt. (Sotheby Beresford Adams) $880

Victorian four-piece tea and coffee set, London, 1874-75, 75oz.12dwt. (Sotheby's) $1,795

WMF Art Nouveau silver plated tea service of three pieces. (Smith-Woolley & Perry) $190

Victorian three-piece teaset by James Howden & Co., Edinburgh, 1846, 46oz. (Sotheby's) $1,395

George IV compressed circular three-piece teaset by J. McKay, Edinburgh, 1823, 50oz.18dwt. (Sotheby's) $1,610

Tea and coffee set with tray and twelve tea glass holders by Bruder Frank, Vienna, circa 1925, 289.5oz.(Sotheby's Belgravia) $4,915

Four-piece tea and coffee service and shaped oval salver, Sheffield, 1976, 114oz. (Sotheby's Belgravia) $2,040

TEA & COFFEE SETS

Three-piece teaset by Elkington & Co. Ltd., London, 53.5oz., circa 1900. (Sotheby's Belgravia)
$1,320

Late 19th century Art Nouveau silver teaset of three pieces. (Frank H. Fellows)
$715

Solid silver four-piece tea and coffee service, Birmingham, 1932 and 1933, 50oz. (Locke & England)
$1,030

Four-piece tea and coffee service in Queen Anne style, by William Comyns & Sons, London, 1910, 57oz. (Sotheby's Belgravia)
$1,800

American three-piece teaset with faceted bodies, circa 1830, by N. J. Bogert, 74.1oz. (Sotheby's Belgravia)
$1,390

William IV silver gilt tea and coffee service by William Eley II, 15.2cm. high, 39oz. (Christie's)
$2,850

Mid 20th century four-piece tea and coffee service by Birks, Canada, 99.9oz. (Sotheby's Belgravia)
$1,730

Four-piece tea and coffee set by Reily & Storer, London, 1845, 81.5oz. (Sotheby's Belgravia)
$2,830

Victorian 'plantagenet' pattern three-piece teaset, London, 1851, 51oz.5dwt. (Sotheby Beresford Adams) $1,140

Four-piece teaset and matching tray by E. Viner, Sheffield, 1957, 121oz.10dwt. (Sotheby Beresford Adams) $1,810

Three-piece teaset by Garrard & Co. Ltd., 1922, 41.2oz. (Sotheby's Belgravia) $960

Four-piece tea and coffee set by Martin, Hall & Co., Sheffield, 1865, 74.7oz. (Sotheby's Belgravia) $2,360

Three-piece teaset by Charles Reily and George Storer, London, 1839, 53.3oz. (Sotheby's Belgravia) $1,440

Matching three-piece coffee set by Walker & Hall, Sheffield, 1892, 43.6oz. (Sotheby's Belgravia) $1,055

Victorian four-piece silver tea and coffee set by James Dixon & Sons, Sheffield, 1848, 67½oz. (Parsons, Welch & Cowell) $1,650

Small late 19th century three-piece teaset, 21.5oz. (Sotheby's Belgravia) $565

TEA & COFFEE SETS

Late 19th century German five-piece teaset and tray, 132.5oz. (Sotheby's Belgravia) $3,480

George IV three-piece silver tea service, 40oz.12dwt. (Geering & Colyer) $1,090

George V tea and coffee service of vase shape, Birmingham, 1929, 63oz. (H. Spencer & Sons) $730

Three-piece teaset by Joseph Angell, London, 1855, 44oz. (Sotheby's Belgravia) $1,170

Victorian four-piece teaset by Roberts & Slater, Sheffield, 1853, 78oz.10dwt. (Sotheby Beresford Adams) $2,855

Victorian three-piece teaset of small size by Frederick Elkington, London, 9oz.9dwt. (Sotheby Beresford Adams) $690

English electroplated three-piece teaset and tray, unmarked, circa 1885. (Sotheby's Belgravia) $365

Three-piece teaset by A. B. Savory & Sons, London, 1840-41, 56.4oz. (Sotheby's Belgravia) $1,405

Three-piece teaset by Elkington & Co. Ltd., London, 1904, 39oz. (Sotheby's Belgravia) $615

Three-piece silver teaset, Sheffield, 1901, 45oz. (Sotheby, King & Chasemore) $1,055

Georgian silver four-piece teaset. (Biddle & Webb) $2,905

Five-piece silver tea and coffee service by Walker & Hall, Sheffield, 1885, 93oz. (Sotheby, King & Chasemore) $2,640

Four-piece silver tea and coffee service by Savory, London, 1833. (Sotheby, King & Chasemore) $3,720

William IV three-piece teaset by John, Henry and Charles Lias, London, 1836, 60oz. (Thomas Watson & Son) $1,920

Three-piece silver teaset, Birmingham 1906, 24oz. (Honiton Galleries) $545

Four-piece teaset by Atkin Brothers, Sheffield, with shaped rectangular bodies, circa 1890. (Sotheby's Belgravia) $865

623

TEA & COFFEE SETS

Shaped oblong teapot and pedestal sugar basin by Charles Stuart Harris & Sons Ltd., London, 1916, 25.2oz. (Sotheby's Belgravia) $730

Victorian three-piece teaset with sugar tongs by Barnard & Co. London, 1874, 29oz. (Sotheby, King & Chasemore) $665

19th century French gold-washed silver teaset, 70 troy oz. (Robert W. Skinner Inc.) $1,000

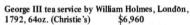

George III tea service by William Holmes, London, 1792, 64oz. (Christie's) $6,960

Seven-piece sterling silver tea and coffee service, New York, circa 1890, 297 troy oz. (Robert W. Skinner Inc.) $8,400

Gorham repousse sterling silver teaset, Rhode Island, circa 1891, 116 troy oz. (Robert W. Skinner Inc.) $4,200

Victorian silver three-piece teaset, London, 1886. (Sotheby, King & Chasemore) $495

Four-piece tea and coffee service with matching kettle on stand by William Aitken, Birmingham, 1900, 105oz. (Sotheby's Belgravia) $2,150

Three-piece silver tea service, Birmingham, 1934, 29oz. (Honiton Galleries) $420

Late 19th century Indian silver-colored metal tea service and tray, 1.284gm. (Sotheby's Belgravia) $840

Three-piece teaset by Elkington & Co., Birmingham, 1918, 40.9oz. (Sotheby's Belgravia) $590

Lobed three-piece teaset by Edward Barnard & Sons, 49.7oz. (Sotheby's Belgravia) $1,150

Four-piece teaset by Roberts & Belk Ltd., Sheffield, 1936, 50.8oz. (Sotheby's Belgravia) $1,150

Victorian silver three-piece teaset by George Fox, London, 1873, 40oz. (Sotheby, King & Chasemore) $1,125

Five-piece tea and coffee set by G. Richards, London, 1853, 89.8oz. (Sotheby's Belgravia) $4,245

20th century four-piece tea and coffee set by A. Aucoc. (Sotheby's Belgravia) $1,920

TEA KETTLES

Chinese export silver kettle on stand by Wosing, 37oz., 24cm. high. (C. G. Sloan & Co. Inc.) $1,000

Early George III silver gilt tea kettle and stand by D. Smith and R. Sharp, London, 1768, 15¾in. high, 77oz. (Sotheby's) $5,450

Victorian tea kettle, stand and lamp by J. S. Hunt, London, 1860, 44.4cm. high, 109oz. (Christie's) $4,000

Victorian kettle, stand and burner in George II style, Sheffield, 1879, 36cm. (H. Spencer & Sons) $830

Electroplated tea kettle on lampstand by Elkington, Mason & Co., Birmingham, 1851, 44cm. high. (Sotheby's Belgravia) $610

George II inverted pear-shaped tea kettle on lampstand by Shaw & Priest, London, 1753, 62oz.2dwt., 36cm. high. (Sotheby's) $2,855

George II tea kettle, stand and lamp by Wm. Grundy, London, 1754, 37cm. high, 76oz.10dwt. (Christie's)$2,000

Large tea kettle on stand by Richard Hennell, London, 1865, 17in. high, 87oz.10dwt.(Messenger May & Baverstock) $1,930

George II tea kettle, stand and lamp by Thos. Whipham, 1756, 30.5cm. high, 71oz. (Christie's) $2,890

Silver tea kettle with spirit burner, Sheffield, 1921, 43oz. (Taylor Lane & Creber) $865

English sterling silver kettle on stand of globular form, 77oz., 40cm. high. (C. G. Sloan & Co. Inc.) $2,200

Lobed oval tea kettle on lampstand by Elkington & Co., Birmingham, 1880, 81.7oz., 35cm. high. (Sotheby's Belgravia) $1,535

626

Compressed circular teapot engraved with Queen Victoria's cypher, by J. & J. Angell, London, 11.2cm. high, 17.4oz. (Sotheby's Belgravia) $750

Hallmarked silver teapot by Peter and Anne Bateman, London, 1832, 14oz. (Biddle & Webb) $895

George II bullet-shaped teapot by John Swift, London, 1738, 14oz.18dwt., 4¾in. high. (Sotheby's) $2,435

American coin silver teapot by Shepherd & Boyd, Albany, circa 1815, 36oz.6dwt., 25cm. high. (C. G. Sloan & Co. Inc.) $650

18th century Dutch rococo silver teapot with turned wood finial, 4in. high, 8 troy oz. (Robert W. Skinner Inc.) $1,700

Shaped circular teapot by Reily & Storer, London, 1847, 18.7cm. high, 27.1oz. (Sotheby's Belgravia) $585

Ornate silver teapot by Rebecca Emes and Edward Barnard, London, 1828, 31oz. (Sotheby, King & Chasemore)$1,105

Inverted pear-shaped teapot by Hayne & Cater, London, 1848, 25.6oz. (Sotheby's Belgravia) $585

Circular teapot by Stephen Smith, London, 22cm. high, 26.7oz. (Sotheby's Belgravia) $660

Ribbed baluster teapot by J. & A. Savory, London, 1852, 24.1oz. (Sotheby's Belgravia)$700

Chinese export silver teapot, 4½in. high, 21 troy oz. (Robert W. Skinner Inc.) $650

George III teapot of inverted pear shape, by James Wildgoose, Aberdeen, circa 1770, 23oz. (Christie's) $4,040

George III oval silver teapot by Hester Bateman, London, 1785, 13.5cm. high, 14oz. (Geering & Colyer) $1,525

Shaped oval teapot by H. & H. Lias, London, 1870, 14.4oz. (Sotheby's Belgravia) $540

George III miniature teapot by James Phipps, London, 1774, 7.5cm. high, 5oz. (Christie's) $500

Fine George I silver teapot by Joseph Ward, London, 1716, 6¼in. high, 20oz. (Christie's) $16,000

Coin silver footed teapot by C. Bard & Son, Pennsylvania, circa 1850, 36oz., 27.5cm. high. (Robert W. Skinner Inc.) $850

Georgian silver teapot by Duncan Urqhart and Naphtali Hart, London, 1799, 15cm. high, 14oz. (Allen & May) $640

George II bullet teapot by John Got-helf-Bilsings, Glasgow, circa 1730, 21oz. 13dwt., 14cm. high. (Sotheby's) $1,565

George III inverted pear-shaped teapot by SW, 1762, 17oz. 10dwt. (Christie's) $1,205

Plain compressed circular teapot by E., E., J. & W. Barnard, London, 1845, 11.6cm. high, 18.5oz. (Sotheby's Belgravia) $670

George III oval teapot by Hester Bateman, London, 1790, 10oz. 4dwt., 11.7cm. high. (Sotheby Beresford Adams) $950

George I octagonal teapot by Thomas Farren, London, 1719, 6½in. high. 13oz. 10dwt. (Sotheby's) $6,185

George III silver teapot and stand. (Phillips) $1,475

Compressed circular teapot by
A. B. Savory & Sons, Ltd.,
London, 1845, 12.3cm. high,
19.7oz. (Sotheby's Belgravia)
$650

Georgian silver melon teapot by Joseph
Wilson, London, 1824, 9cm. high, 11oz.
(Allen & May) $295

George III teapot by Charles
Wright, London, 1774, 15oz.,
13cm. high. (Christie's)
$1,300

Dutch silver teapot, Haarlem, 1711,
14cm. high, 9oz.10dwt. (Sotheby
Beresford Adams) $1,905

George IV demi-fluted teapot
with floral cashed border, by
John Angell, London, 1823,
25oz. (Graves Son & Pilcher)
$640

American silver teapot by Steven
Burdet, New York, circa 1730,
15oz., 12.7cm. high. (Christie's)
$5,500

Plain spherical teapot by D. &
C. Houle, London, 1876, 12.3cm.
high, 16.3oz. (Sotheby's Belgravia)
$565

George III teapot by Stephen Adams,
London 1806, 16oz. 10dwt., 17cm.
high. (Sotheby, King & Chasemore)
$670

Circular teapot with beaded collar
by R. Martin & E. Hall, Sheffield,
1895, 24.3oz., 13cm. high.
(Sotheby's Belgravia) $490

Dutch circular teapot on fluted
foot, Sneek, 1736, 9oz. 7dwt.
(Christie's) $1,995

George I teapot by Humphrey Payne,
London, 1714, 13oz., 15.2cm. high.
(Christie's) $8,500

George III silver teapot by Fuller
White, London, 1763, 16.5cm.
high, 28oz.10dwt. (Christie's)
$850

TOAST RACKS

George III nine-bar toast rack by
Robert Hennell, London, 1788,
5oz.11dwt., 16.5cm. wide.
(Sotheby Beresford Adams)
$380

Victorian silver toast rack by George
Fox, London, 1865, 16cm. long,
11oz. (Christie's) $420

Heath & Middleton silver toast rack,
London, 1881, 12.5cm. high.
(Sotheby's Belgravia) $935

TOILET REQUISITES

French oval tortoiseshell necessaire with
gilt metal inlay, circa 1860, 12.2cm.
long. (Sotheby's Belgravia) $585

Antique English brass inlaid rosewood necessaire de voyage, 14in.
wide. (C. G. Sloan & Co. Inc.)
$750

Rectangular 'Palais-Royal' mother-of-
pearl and gilt metal musical necessaire,
circa 1815, 16.5cm. wide, with two
keys. (Sotheby's) $950

Crocodile skin gentleman's traveling dressing case by
Mappin & Webb, London, 1923, 1936. (Sotheby's
Belgravia) $1,320

Silver mounted six-piece dressing table set by Levi &
Salaman, Birmingham, 1909-10. (Sotheby's Belgravia)
$1,055

Victorian dressing case by JH, London,
1866, fully fitted. (Sotheby's)
$905

Italian silver soap box, circa 1740,
9oz., 10cm. high. (Christie's)
$2,000

Brass bound mahogany traveling
dressing case, fully fitted. (Sotheby's
Belgravia) $680

Mother-of-pearl and gilt metal 'Palais-Royal' necessaire of shell form, circa 1820, 14.2cm. wide. (Sotheby's) $855

Silver mounted shagreen traveling necessaire of trefoil shape, 6cm. high, circa 1780. (Sotheby's) $425

Gilt metal and mother-of-pearl 'Palais-Royal' necessaire in the form of a wheelbarrow, circa 1810, 26.4cm. long. (Sotheby's) $760

Fine 19th century rosewood inlaid brass toilet case, completely fitted, 34cm. wide. (May Whetter & Grose) $580

Fitted dressing case by Paul Storr, larger pieces marked 1892. (Bonham's) $17,005

Brass bound hardwood traveling dressing case by T. W., London, 1876. (Sotheby's Belgravia) $685

20th century Italian dressing table set with silver mounts. (Sotheby's Belgravia) $935

Silver gilt dressing case, by John Harris, 1855. (Edgar Horn) $3,035

Asprey & Son traveling dressing case fitted with silver gilt items, 1879, case 34.4cm. wide. (Sotheby's Belgravia) $1,830

French necessaire, 'Palais-Royal', circa 1830, 10.5cm. long. (Christie's) $550

TRAYS & SALVERS

Shaped circular salver by D. & C. Houle, London, 1852, 40.5cm. diam., 56.1oz. (Sotheby's Belgravia) $1,320

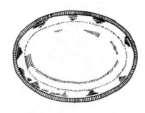

George III silver meat dish by William Fountain, London, 1802, 30.5cm. long, 25oz.10dwt. (Christie's) $1,100

Early George III silver salver by Richard Rugg, London, 1775, 41cm. diam., 58oz. (Sotheby, King & Chasemore) $1,465

George II shaped circular salver by Paul de Lamerie, London, 1736, 6in. diam., 7oz.8dwt. (Sotheby's) $4,520

George I octagonal dish by Paul de Lamerie, London, 1719, 11in. wide, 19oz.2dwt. (Sotheby's) $9,520

One of a set of twelve George II shaped circular dinner plates by Thomas Heming, London, 1751, 9¾in. diam., 229oz.13dwt. (Sotheby's) $9,005

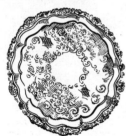

George IV shaped circular salver by Robert Gray & Son, Glasgow, 1827, 28cm. diam., 31oz.8dwt. (Sotheby's) $805

One of a pair of George II silver gilt waiters by Christian Hillan, 1742, 28oz., 19cm. diam. (Christie's) $6,815

Large shaped circular salver by Elkington & Co. Ltd., Birmingham, 1919, 46cm. diam., 81.7oz. (Sotheby's Belgravia) $1,800

George II shaped circular salver by Paul de Lamerie, London, 1736, 8½in. diam., 16oz.12dwt. (Sotheby's) $6,665

George III two-handled oval tray by William Bennett, 1803, 51.6cm. long, 81oz. (Christie's) $3,360

George III silver salver by Crouch & Hannam, London, 1799, 36cm. diam., 47oz.3dwt. (Sotheby's) $2,990

Shaped circular salver by James Deakin & Sons Ltd., Sheffield, 1899, 32cm. diam., 38.5oz. (Sotheby's Belgravia) $680

Victorian two-handled tray by Robert Garrard, London, 1856, 64.8cm. wide, 150oz. (Christie's) $6,500

Large Victorian shaped circular salver, 1868, 196oz., 62.8cm. diam. (Christie's) $6,385

George III silver salver by John Carter, London, 1773, 66oz.10dwt., 42cm. diam. (Christie's) $3,500

George IV shaped oval meat dish by Paul Storr, London, 1829, 41cm. wide, 49oz. (Sotheby's) $2,760

Shaped circular salver by Martin Hall & Co. Ltd., Sheffield, 1925, 32cm. diam., 28.8oz. (Sotheby's Belgravia), $650

Shaped circular salver by John Watson, Newcastle, 1844, 39.5cm. diam., 46.4oz. (Sotheby's Belgravia) $1,010

American Gorham sterling silver tray with beaded rim, 46oz., 47cm. long, circa 1898. (Robert W. Skinner Inc.) $225

One of two George IV shaped circular salvers by Barnard & Co., 1829, 42.5cm. diam., 141oz. (Christie's) $3,735

Shaped circular salver by Edward Barnard & Sons, London, 1843, 33.2cm. diam., 30.8oz. (Sotheby's Belgravia) $630

Regency two-handled oblong tray on four feet, by Benjamin Smith III, 1819, 46.4cm. long, 92oz. (Christie's) $3,190

Shaped circular salver by Goldsmiths Alliance Ltd., London, 1875, 25.5cm. diam., 18.7oz. (Sotheby's Belgravia) $525

George II shaped circular second course dish by George Methuen, London, 1757, 54oz.2dwt., 39cm. diam. (Sotheby Beresford Adams) $5,235

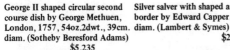

Silver salver with shaped and gadrooned border by Edward Capper, 1766, 35cm. diam. (Lambert & Symes) $2,660

Shaped circular salver by Edward Barnard & Sons, London, 1859, 33.1cm. diam., 29.6oz.(Sotheby's Belgravia) $610

Shaped oval two-handled tea tray by Charles Boyton & Son, London, 1897, 176.4oz., 81cm. wide. (Sotheby's Belgravia)$4,445

One of a pair of early Victorian shaped circular salvers by E. E. J. & W. Barnard, London, 1840, 30oz. 1dwt., 25cm. diam. (Sotheby's Belgravia) $1,190

Oval pierced trellis pattern two-handled silver bread tray by Daniel Smith and Robert Sharp, 60oz. (Irelands) $17,110

Shaped circular salver by Samuel Walker, Sheffield, 1839, 52.5cm. diam., 105.9oz. (Sotheby's Belgravia) $2,105

Italian plain shaped circular salver on foot, Naples, 1716, 31cm. diam., 32oz. (Christie's) $3,120

Parcel gilt presentation quatrefoil salver by S. Smith & Son, London, 1871, 71.1oz., 47.5cm. diam. (Sotheby's Belgravia)$1,755

George III oval tea tray by William Bennett, London, 1800, 191oz. 7dwt., 32¾in. wide. (Sotheby's) $8,090

Victorian circular shaped salver by Barnard & Co., London, 1861, 45cm. diam., 76oz. (Sotheby, King & Chasemore) $1,920

George III oval tea tray by Crouch & Hannam, London, 1795, 26in. wide, 92oz.2dwt. (Sotheby's) $4,740

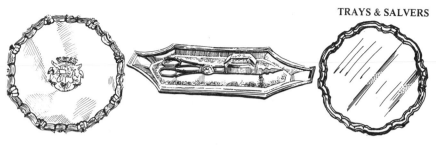

George II shaped octagonal salver by Robert Abercromby, London, 1745, 15¾in. diam., 57oz.16dwt. (Sotheby's) $4,760

One of a pair of George III silver candle snuffers and trays.(Biddle & Webb) $2,055

18th century George II sterling silver footed salver, 21oz., 23cm. diam. (Robert W. Skinner Inc.) $900

George I octagonal salver by William Penstone, London, 1717, 13in. wide, 22oz.16dwt. (Sotheby's) $14,280

Shaped circular salver by C. S. Harris & Sons, Ltd., London, 1900, 66.5oz., 40.6cm. diam. (Sotheby's) $1,125

George III shaped oval tea tray by Paul Storr, London, 1815, 27½in. long, 151oz.3dwt. (Sotheby's) $18,960

Shaped circular salver by C. S. Harris, London, 50cm. diam., 94.5oz. (Sotheby's Belgravia) $1,520

Oval silver tea tray by Marshall & Sons, Edinburgh, 1885, 68.5cm. long, 158.1oz. (Sotheby's Belgravia) $2,810

Engine-turned shaped circular waiter by W. W. W., London, 1869, 6.1oz., 16cm. diam. (Sotheby's Belgravia) $280

George III oval tea tray by William Bennett, London, 1804, 96oz.12dwt., 65cm. wide. (Sotheby Beresford Adams) $4,045

Round silver waiter with Chippendale molding by Deakin & Francis, Birmingham, 25cm. diam., 14oz. (Biddle & Webb) $215

George III plain two-handled oval tray with reeded border, by John Hutson, 1800, 51.4cm. long, 67oz.(Christie's) $3,600

TUREENS

Oval soup tureen with domed cover, circa 1820, 42.3cm. wide. (Sotheby Beresford Adams) $810

George IV silver vegetable tureen and cover, by Richard Sibley, 1822, 150oz. (Harrods) $11,225

George III oval soup tureen by Smith & Sharp, London, 1784, 45cm. long, 99oz.2dwt. (Sotheby's) $6,900

One of a pair of George IV two-handled sauce tureens and covers by Philip Rundell, London, 1822, 56oz. 10dwt., 16.5cm. long. (Christie's) $2,800

Shaped oval melon pattern soup tureen and cover by Walker, Knowles & Co., circa 1840, 40cm. wide. (Sotheby Beresford Adams) $1,045

Floral repousse sterling silver soup tureen by S. Kirk & Son, 72oz.14dwt., 64cm. long. (C. G. Sloan & Co. Inc.) $2,500

One of a pair of Sheffield plate turkey covers by Matthew Boulton, with scroll handles, 33cm. long. (C. G. Sloan & Co. Inc.) $650

George III two-handled soup tureen and cover by J. Parker and E. Wakelin, 1771, 31.6cm. long, 85oz. (Christie's) $10,080

George III soup tureen and cover by Daniel Smith and Robert Sharp, London, 1788, 33.5cm. long, 107oz. 10dwt. (Christie's) $4,200

George III plain oval two-handled soup tureen and cover by W. Burwash and R. Sibley, 1809, 31.4cm. long, 100oz. (Christie's) $9,120

636

George III shaped oval soup tureen and cover by William Homer, Dublin, circa 1765, 90oz.10dwt., 38cm. wide. (Sotheby's) $6,670

18th century George III silver covered tureen by James Young, London, 1792-93, 52cm. long.(Robert W. Skinner Inc.) $5,000

One of two George III heavy oval soup tureens and covers by Thomas Robins, London, 1808, 355oz. 10dwt., 15¾in. wide. (Sotheby's) $26,070

Early 20th century circular two-handled soup tureen and cover, German, 31cm. wide, 81.2oz. (Sotheby's Belgravia) $1,730

Sheffield plated soup tureen and cover with cast fruit finial. (Taylor Lane & Creber) $410

Large silver tureen and cover by J. Crichton, Edinburgh, 1876, 126oz. (Biddle & Webb) $1,815

Danish silver two-handled soup tureen and cover, 45cm. wide, 128oz. (Sotheby's Belgravia) $2,575

George III oval soup tureen and cover by Paul Storr, London, 1809, 153oz.7dwt., 42.5cm. wide. (Sotheby's) $15,470

George III plain two-handled oval soup tureen by J. Wakelin and W. Taylor, 1789, 33.5cm. long, 85oz. (Christie's) $8,435

George III plain oval two-handled soup tureen and cover with beaded border by Henry Greenway, 1778, 324cm. long, 96oz.(Christie's)$10,050

A fine Sheffield plate vase-shaped tea urn with scrolled handles and gadrooned borders. (Vernon's) $600

19th century plated tea urn with half fluted body, 15½in. high. (Phillips) $200

Sheffield Regency hot water urn with domed cover, 45cm. high. (C. G. Sloan & Co. Inc.) $600

George III vase-shaped tea urn by John Edwards, London, 1810, 185oz., 17¼in. high. (Sotheby's) $3,450

Regency two-handled circular vase-shaped tea urn by B. & J. Smith, 1810, 15½in. high, 157oz. (Christie's) $4,310

George II two-handled tea urn with square base, by D. Whyte and W. Holmes, 1767, 52cm. high, 82oz. (Christie's) $3,305

18th century George III silver hot water urn by Thomas Chawner, London, 1784-85, 52cm. high, 83 troy oz. (Robert W. Skinner Inc.) $2,000

Elkington, Mason & Co. electroplated pear-shaped tea urn, dated for 1855, 47cm. high. (Sotheby's Belgravia) $695

George III two-handled tea urn by Abraham Peterson and Peter Podio, London, 1786, 55.4cm. high, 110oz.10dwt. (Christie's) $2,200

Late 18th century Sheffield plated tea urn, 20in. high. (Taylor Lane & Creber) $265

One of two Sheffield plate George III style covered urns and covers, 50cm. high. (C. G. Sloan & Co. Inc.) $700

George IV inverted pear-shaped tea urn by J. McKay, Edinburgh, 1822, 17½in. high, 163oz.6dwt. (Sotheby's) $4,700

George III circular sugar vase by
Hester Bateman, 1776, 7oz.13dwt.
(Christie's) $1,295

Replica of the Warwick vase, by Barnard
& Co., London, 1901. (Sotheby, King &
Chasemore) $4,400

One of a pair of silver bottle vases,
circa 1890. (Alfie's Antique
Market) $105

Art Nouveau sterling silver vase by
Goff, Washbourne & Dunn, New
York, circa 1900, 20 troy oz., 13in.
high. (Robert W. Skinner Inc.)
                    $325

Slender silver vase and cover by Ramsden
& Carr, on oak plinth, London, 1913,
43.2cm. high, 744gm. (Sotheby's
Belgravia) $935

Liberty & Co. 'Cymric' silver and
enamel vase designed by Harry
Silver, Birmingham, 1904,
18.25cm. high. (Sotheby's
Belgravia) $6,550

Early 20th century Italian two-handled
amphora-shaped vase, 38cm. high,
53oz. (Sotheby's Belgravia)
                    $1,055

Large German trumpet-shaped
vase, 38.5oz., 33.3cm. high.
(Sotheby's Belgravia)
                    $980

Late 19th century Sanju enameled
silver vase, signed Sanju saku,
20.5cm. high. (Sotheby's Belgravia)
                    $750

WMF silver metal vase with twin
whiplash handles, 23.5cm. high,
circa 1900. (Sotheby's Belgravia)
                    $770

Rare George III covered vase containing a hot
water jug, by John Emes, London, 1803,
41oz.10dwt. (Christie's) $24,000

Continental silver swirl fluted
vase of tapering form, 27cm.
high, 13oz.7dwt. (C. G. Sloan
& Co. Inc.) $200

VINAIGRETTES

Taylor & Perry book-shaped vinaigrette, Birmingham, 1838, 2.5cm. long. (Sotheby's Belgravia) $330

Rectangular silver gilt vinaigrette by John Bettridge, Birmingham, 1829, 39mm. long. (Christie's) $600

Edward Smith shaped oval vinaigrette, Birmingham, 1862, 3.3cm. long. (Sotheby's Belgravia) $260

Small shaped rectangular vinaigrette by Edward Smith, Birmingham, 1855, 2.6cm. long. (Sotheby's Belgravia) $155

Early 19th century Scottish silver gilt mounted agate vinaigrette, by George Jamieson, Aberdeen, 58mm. high. (Christie's) $1,095

Silver gilt shaped rectangular vinaigrette by Yapp & Woodward, Birmingham, 1852, 3.5cm. long. (Sotheby's Belgravia) $165

Shaped rectangular vinaigrette by Edward Smith, Birmingham, 1854, 3.4cm. long. (Sotheby's Belgravia) $190

19th century rectangular vari-colored gold vinaigrette, probably Swiss, 32mm. long. (Christie's) $1,870

Early 19th century Scottish oblong gold mounted Cairngorm vinaigrette, 38mm. long. (Christie's) $2,160

Rectangular vinaigrette by Joseph Taylor, Birmingham, 1839, 4.3cm. long. (Sotheby's Belgravia) $795

Finely pierced circular vinaigrette in original presentation case, 2.5cm. diam. (Andrew Grant) $100

Rectangular vinaigrette by Nathaniel Mills & Son, Birmingham, 1840, 3.1cm. long. (Sotheby's Belgravia) $200

Large shaped rectangular vinaigrette by George Unite, Birmingham, 1853, 4.5cm. long. (Sotheby's Belgravia) $260

Silver gilt mounted tapering oval enamel vinaigrette scentflask, 9.9cm. high, circa 1875. (Sotheby's Belgravia) $395

Rectangular vinaigrette by Nathaniel Mills, Birmingham, 1838, 4.1cm. high. (Sotheby's Belgravia) $590

One of a pair of Old Sheffield plated wine coolers. (Christie's S. Kensington) $970

Victorian silver two-handled wine cooler. (Russell, Baldwin & Bright)$1,215

One of a pair of late 19th century Continental silvered metal wine coolers, 38cm. high. (Pearsons) $4,140

One of a pair of George III bell-shaped wine coolers by George Ashforth, Ellis Hawksworth & Best, Sheffield, 1801, 126oz. 5dwt. (Sotheby's)$10,475

Pair of George III wine coolers by Paul Storr, London, 1815, 8in. high, 184oz. (Sotheby's) $23,700

One of a pair of Regency two-handled wine coolers and covers by W. & P. Cunningham, Edinburgh, 1818, 13in. high, 165oz. (Christie's) $10,100

One of a pair of 19th century campana-shaped wine coolers, 10in. high. (Taylor Lane & Creber) $1,240

Pair of George III wine coolers by Philip Rundell, London, 1819, 8in. high, 180oz. (Sotheby's) $13,035

One of a pair of Sheffield plate wine coolers, 1840's, 24.5cm. high. (Sotheby's Belgravia) $1,215

One of a pair of George III bell-shaped wine coolers by Robert Sharp, London, 1795, 140oz., 9¼in. high.(Sotheby's) $9,520

One of a pair of Victorian two-handled wine coolers by Edward Farrell, London, 1837, 9¼in. high, 114oz. (Christie's) $17,500

Silver gilt wine cooler by Robinson Edkins & Aston, Birmingham, 1837, 27cm. high. (Lambert & Symes) $3,145

641

WINE FUNNELS

George III silver wine funnel with
filter, London, 1800, 5oz.
(Sotheby's) $350

Silver wine funnel by Charles Fowler,
Elgin, circa 1790. (Christie's &
Edmiston's) $1,625

Silver wine funnel by Paul Storr,
6in. high, London, 1830, 4oz.
12dwt. (Sotheby's) $620

WINE LABELS

Rare George III Scottish provin-
cial wine label by John Sid,
Perth, circa 1806, 4cm. wide.
(Phillips) $210

George III wine label by Hester Bateman,
circa 1775, 4.5cm. wide. (Phillips)$170

Rare George III Irish provincial
cup and leaf festooned wine
label by Carden Terry & Jane
Williams, Cork, circa 1808.
(Phillips) $145

One of a set of twelve George III
large silver gilt wine labels by
Benjamin Smith, 1807, 27oz.
(Christie's) $13,690

One of a pair of George III neck rings
by William Bateman, 1808, 7.5cm.
wide. (Phillips) $425

One of a set of three George III
large wine labels by Paul Storr,
1811, 6oz.13dwt. (Christie's)
$3,895

WINE TASTERS

Charles I wine taster, London, 1648,
3¾in. diam., 1oz.18dwt.(Sotheby's)
$1,975

Charles II two-handled circular wine
taster, 1660, 9.4cm. diam., 1oz.9dwt.
(Christie's) $1,150

Charles I wine taster by PH, London, 1641, 8.2cm. diam., 1oz.
10dwt. (Christie's)$4,200

Imperial yellow glass snuff bottle, each side carved with a dragon, 1780-1850. (Sotheby's)$715

Rare early rock crystal inside-painted snuff bottle by Chen Chuan, signed. (Sotheby's) $140

Qianlong moulded snuff bottle with original stopper, covered overall in coral-red glaze. (Sotheby's) $310

'Han' jade snuff bottle and stopper of sage green tone, carved on the front. (Sotheby's) $665

Rare blue and white porcelain snuff bottle of the Xianfeng period. (Sotheby's) $240

Chalcedony snuff bottle and stopper of upright rectangular form, in dark amber color. (Sotheby's)$180

Tortoiseshell snuff bottle and stopper carved with warriors on horseback. (Sotheby's) $215

Imperial yellow glass snuff bottle and stopper of rounded double gourd shape. (Sotheby's) $180

Fine and unusual rock crystal snuff bottle of disc shape with green glass stopper and red glass collar. (Christie's) $1,145

Overlay glass disc-shaped snuff bottle with green glass stopper. (Christie's) $240

18th century Peking glass snuff bottle in the form of a fish. (Sotheby's) $240

Hornbill snuff bottle and stopper carved on both sides with oxen and trees. (Sotheby's) $165

Chalcedony snuff bottle and stopper, carved on the front. (Sotheby's) $225

Glass snuff bottle in the form of an eggplant with green stalk-shaped stopper. (Sotheby's) $85

Agate snuff bottle with banding of russet and pale brown with white rivering. (Sotheby's) $155

Chalcedony snuff bottle and stopper of flattened upright form in honey-colored stone with two darker splashes. (Sotheby's) $165

Chalcedony snuff bottle and stopper carved with a tethered horse. (Sotheby's) $285

Attractive moss agate snuff bottle and stopper in mottled honey-color with white and green rivering. (Sotheby's) $190

Inside-painted glass flattened baluster snuff bottle, signed Wang Xisan, dated 1975, with jade stopper. (Christie's) $430

Pale grey agate rounded square snuff bottle with green glass stopper. (Christie's) $240

Rock crystal inside-painted snuff bottle of pear shape, with stopper. (Sotheby's) $355

Rock crystal inside-painted snuff bottle of faceted hexagonal section. (Sotheby's) $165

Glass inside-painted snuff bottle and stopper, dated 1974, of flattened pear shape. (Sotheby's) $140

White jade snuff bottle and stopper of tapering cylindrical form, carved in relief. (Sotheby's) $190

Chinese carved grey stone figure of a reclining Buddha, 78cm. long. (C. G. Sloan & Co. Inc.) $700

Late period Egyptian fragmentary grey stone figure of a Sphinx, 15in. (Sotheby's) $2,575

George IV coadestone sphinx, signed ***ggon Late Coade, 1823, 108cm. wide. (Sotheby's) $2,620

Large 20th century Continental stoneware figure of a putto, 83cm. high. (Sotheby's Belgravia) $240

Rare stoneware commemorative jug, circa 1830, 9in. high. (Sotheby's Belgravia) $235

Painted stoneware figure of a rustic with a basket of vegetables, circa 1790-1820. (Alfie's Antique Market) $470

10th century glazed grey stoneware oviform bottle with slender conical neck, 30cm. high. (Christie's) $470

One of a pair of grey stone carvings of horses, 26cm. long. (Sotheby's) $5,125

One of a pair of 19th century ormolu mounted granite pot-pourri vases with domed lids, 24in. high. (Christie's) $2,410

2nd-3rd century A.D. East Roman sandstone column capital, 12in. high. (Christie's) $1,045

Carved stone group by A. Gennarelli, 1920's, 59.25cm. wide. (Sotheby's Belgravia) $420

Late 2nd/early 3rd century A.D. East Roman limestone head of a bearded man, 7in. high. (Christie's) $2,320

TAPESTRIES

Late 16th century South German needlework tapestry panel, dated 1592, 3ft. x 8ft.10in. (Geering & Colyer) $14,935

Late 16th century Brussels game park tapestry, 10ft.8in. x 12ft.7in. (Sotheby's) $18,720

Mid 17th century Brussels Verdure tapestry woven in muted colors, 8ft.9in. x 10ft.5in. (Christie's) $5,235

17th century Aubusson Verdure tapestry woven with a crane and swans, 14ft.8in. x 9ft.8in. (Christie's) $3,570

Good Charles I tent-stitch picture, circa 1640, 14½in. x 19in. (Sotheby's) $1,685

Late 17th century Mortlake tapestry, 7ft.4in. x 9ft.1in. (Christie's) $4,285

Early 17th century Flemish feuille de choux tapestry fragment, 6ft.8in. x 3ft.8in. (Christie's) $7,710

Allegorical tapestry, possibly Diana and Vulcan, 206cm. wide. (Sotheby's Belgravia) $1,270

17th century Brussels tapestry woven in muted blues, greens and yellows, 7ft.10in. x 8ft.7in. (Christie's) $5,710

Brussels Renaissance tapestry, circa 1540, 11ft.4in. high x 15ft.6in. wide. (Sotheby's) $14,040

17th century Brussels Teniers tapestry, 14ft.11in. x 10ft. (Christie's) $11,570

19th century French tapestry panel of the Lady and the Unicorn, 8ft. x 7ft.9in. (Geering & Colyer) $3,585

Early 18th century Brussels mythological tapestry, 11ft.4in. x 16ft.9in. (Christie's) $28,920

Mid 18th century Teniers tapestry by Pieter and Frans van Borcht, Brussels, 7ft.5in. x 9ft.4in. wide. (Sotheby's) $9,360

17th century Flemish tapestry fragment woven with a Queen and her attendants, 6ft.7in. x 6ft.3in. (Christie's) $3,810

17th century Flemish tapestry fragment of a seated Queen, 6ft.3in. x 5ft.4in. (Christie's) $5,000

TOYS

Britain's Skinner's Horse, mounted with officer. (Sotheby's Belgravia)$50

Meccano two-seater non-constructional sports car in original cardboard box, circa 1934, 8¾in. long. (Sotheby's Belgravia) $580

Britain's Chinese Infantry 'boxers' charging with swords, no. 241.(Sotheby's Belgravia) $135

Two from a set of six Britain's Argentine Infantry, no. 1837. (Sotheby's Belgravia) $95

Late 19th century mechanical duck in felt-covered papier-mache, 12in. high. (Robert W. Skinner Inc.) $325

French laundress tinplate toy by F. Martin, circa 1899, in poor condition, 7½in. high. (Sotheby's Belgravia) $540

Lehmann female circus tightrope walker, circa 1905, 15cm. high. (Christie's S. Kensington) $1,190

Britain's set, no. 1316, full silver band of the Salvation Army, 1936. (Phillips) $3,335

German tinplate toy frog by Kellerman, circa 1930, 4¼in. high. (Sotheby's Belgravia) $250

Unusual late 19th century miniature horse, covered in hide, 44cm. long. (Sotheby's Belgravia) $310

Early 20th century German monkey pull toy by Steiff, 9in. long. (Robert W. Skinner Inc.) $125

Large dapple-grey rocking horse with brass-buttoned saddlecloth, 66in. long. (Morphets)$715

One from a set of eight Britain's United States Aviation men in peaked caps. (Sotheby's Belgravia) $70

Andre Citroen 'C Six' tinplate motor car, French, circa 1929, 15¾in. long. (Sotheby's Belgravia) $670

20th century German ride-on lion with glass eyes, probably Steiff, 25½in. long. (Robert W. Skinner Inc.) $175

Mid 19th century rooster in felt and rabbit hair, 6in. high. (Robert W. Skinner Inc.) $150

Clockwork tinplate airliner, with lithograph detail, circa 1940. (Sotheby, King & Chasemore) $230

American carved wood and painted carousel horse on fitted base, 47in. high. (C. G. Sloan & Co. Inc.) $1,000

Exploding bottle of Mason's O.K. sauce, circa 1910, 15cm. high.(Phillips) $240

Edwardian rocking horse in iron swing frame, in good condition. (Butler & Hatch Waterman) $390

Early 19th century painted wood doll's house, circa 1820, with a collection of furniture, 29½in. high. (Sotheby's Belgravia) $745

German Bucking Bronco tinplate cowboy toy by Lehmann, circa 1935, 6¼in. long. (Sotheby's Belgravia) $395

Unusual mid 19th century roulette game in painted wooden box, 18½in. wide. (Sotheby's Belgravia) $145

19th century articulated wooden toy 'Tom Gilpin's Ride'. (Christie's S. Kensington) $345

German tut-tut tinplate car by Lehmann, circa 1910, 18cm. long. (Sotheby's Belgravia) $435

Two from a set of twelve late 19th century carpet bowls, 8.2cm. diam. (Sotheby's Belgravia) $190

Child's large German tinplate gas stove and pans, circa 1920, in box 29in. wide. (Sotheby's Belgravia) $380

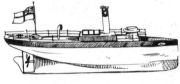

Early Bing tinplate torpedo boat in original box, 37.5cm. long. (Sotheby's Belgravia) $965

Orobr tinplate airship, German, circa 1925, 10½in. long. (Sotheby's Belgravia) $455

Two from a set of thirteen Britain's United States Infantry in Federal dress. (Sotheby's Belgravia) $145

19th century compendium of Chinese ivory puzzles and games, in black lacquered box. (May Whetter & Grose) $430

Three of a set of seventeen Britain's boy scouts with scoutmaster. (Sotheby's Belgravia) $155

Part of a set of Britain's General Staff Officers, all in service dress, set no. 1907. (Sotheby's Belgravia) $120

German tinplate Alfa Romeo racing car, circa 1925, in need of repair. (Sotheby's Belgravia) $480

W. Gamage set of conjuring tricks, circa 1915, 17¼in. wide. (Sotheby's Belgravia) $285

Two of an eight-piece set of Britain's Prussian Infantry, marching at slope.(Sotheby's Belgravia) $70

American Zilotone tinplate musical toy, by Wolverine Supply & Manufacturing Co., 19cm. wide. (Sotheby's Belgravia) $335

Lehmann 'naughty nephew' tinplate toy, circa 1910, German, 5in. long. (Sotheby's Belgravia) $285

Part of a set of eleven pieces of Britain's Bulgarian Infantry. (Sotheby's Belgravia)$135

Jep tinplate fire engine, French, circa 1935-40, 9¼in. long, with six crew members. (Sotheby's Belgravia)$95

Britain's bi-plane, complete with pilot, finished in silver, no. 1521. (Sotheby's Belgravia) $1,080

Sample box, by W. Edwards, possibly for use in a schoolroom, circa 1880, 41cm. wide. (Sotheby's Belgravia) $335

Two from a set of sixteen Britain's United States Marines, some in blue uniforms, some in active service dress. (Sotheby's Belgravia) $190

Lehmann 'stubborn donkey' tinplate toy, circa 1925, 7in. wide. (Sotheby's Belgravia) $480

Part of a set of Britain's Bikanir Camel Corps, set no. 123. (Sotheby's Belgravia) $95

Britain's covered lorry with gun and limber, set no. 1462. (Sotheby's Belgravia) $215

German Marklin field gun in cast iron and cast brass, circa 1905, 40.5cm. long. (Sotheby's Belgravia) $240

German tinplate landaulette, possibly by Carette, circa 1912, 28cm. long. (Sotheby's Belgravia) $915

Part of a set of twenty-three Britain's Royal Marines. (Sotheby's Belgravia) $145

Jep tinplate landaulette, French, circa 1925-30, 14in. long. (Sotheby's Belgravia) $355

TOYS

Clockwork tinplate Mercedes Berline de Voyage chaffeur driven limousine, circa 1910, 38cm. long. (Phillips) $1,800

Scale model of a set of three-abreast galloping horses roundabout, 84in. diam.(Christie's) $1,435

Steam traction engine by Bing, 23cm. long. (Phillips) $160

Britain's set no. 26 Boer Infantry, in original box, circa 1899. (Phillips) $415

Set of Hornby vehicles in original box.(Sotheby King & Chasemore) $3,475

Britain's model of H.I.H. The Emperor of Germany, circa 1895, in original box. (Sotheby's Belgravia) $240

Part of a nineteen-piece set of Britain's Green Howards.(Sotheby's Belgravia) $430

Marx 'Tidy Tim' clockwork dustbin man pushing a bin, 1934.(Phillips) $80

Britain's British Army tank with personnel and machine gun, set no. 1203.(Sotheby's Belgravia) $145

Lehmann's 'Paddy and the Pig' toy, tinplate with clockwork mechanism, 14cm. long.(Sotheby, King & Chasemore) $440

Bing printed tinplate tourer.(Christie's S. Kensington) $840

Four-seater model clockwork car by Bing, 22cm. long.(Phillips) $2,645

Scale model of The R.A.E., SE5A, frame of brass and steel, 27cm. long. (Thomas Watson & Son) $1,520

Fine Lehmann auto-hutte tinplate garage and cars, German, circa 1930-35.(Sotheby's Belgravia) $670

Small collection of Britain's and Mignot's lead soldiers and waggons.(Bradley & Vaughan) $1,695

Band of the 1st King's Dragoon Guards with mechanical bandmaster by Heyde.(Phillips) $1,950

Britain's Black Watch Pipe Band, twenty-pieces in all, in original box. (Sotheby's Belgravia) $670

'Halloh' clockwork gyroscopic action man riding a motorcycle by Lehmann, circa 1918, 22cm. long. (Phillips) $875

Britain's no. 1439, a roundabout with six riders, 1938. (Phillips) $415

Clockwork 'B-type' motorbus by Bing, circa 1903, 29cm. long.(Phillips) $1,520

TOYS

Fully furnished Georgian doll's house. (Graves, Son & Pilcher) $2,620

Good Lehmann Panne tinplate open tourer, No. 687, circa 1920, 6¾in. long. (Sotheby's Belgravia) $495

20th century German ride-on brown bear with wheels, by Steiff, 20in. high. (Robert W. Skinner Inc.) $375

Early and unusual Austrian 'Little Artist' child's game, circa 1775, 5in. wide. (Sotheby's Belgravia) $395

Early tinplate automobile with clockwork mechanism, circa 1890, 10½in. long. (Sotheby's Belgravia) $60

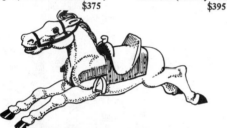

English carved wood carousel galloper with leather saddle and bridle, 66in. long, circa 1920. (Sotheby's Belgravia) $415

Small wooden carousel galloper, 41in. long, circa 1930. (Sotheby's Belgravia) $395

French tinplate piano player toy by F. Martin, circa 1905, 5in. wide, with clockwork mechanism. (Sotheby's Belgravia) $580

Tumbling Clowns toy, probably Bavarian, circa 1860, 10¼in. (Sotheby's Belgravia) $725

Painted wood doll's house with furniture and chattels. (Christie's S. Kensington) $1,580

Champion Scullers tinplate toy, German, circa 1908, with clockwork mechanism, 15in. long.(Sotheby's Belgravia) $725

German tinplate limousine by Hans Eberl, circa 1910, 9½in. long. (Sotheby's Belgravia) $1,345

19th century horse-drawn hearse. (Biddle & Webb) $3,660

Four cylinder Wolseley eight saloon, 1947, 918cc., 7ft.5in. (Sotheby's) $995

Four cylinder Austin Seven saloon with four speed gearbox, wheelbase 6ft.9in., 1933. (Sotheby's) $3,790

Old basketwork Bath chair with steering handle. (Morris, Marshall & Poole) $155

Dursley-Pedersen pedal cycle, circa 1905, with three speed gearing. (Sotheby's) $1,945

Clement-Bayard 8CV type 4M 10h.p. two-seater car, 1913. (Sotheby's) $13,745

Standard Flying Ten saloon, 1937, wheelbase. 7ft. 6in. (Sotheby's) $1,540

Morris Oxford 13.9h.p. saloon, 1924, with four cylinder engine, wheelbase 8ft 6in (Sotheby's) $22,515

Fiat model 59B 15/20h.p. shooting brake, 1912, wheelbase 9ft. (Sotheby's) $14,220

Royal Enfield T.S. 225cc. solo motorcycle, circa 1927, with two speed gearbox. (Sotheby's) $1,470

M.G. type ZB magnette saloon, 1958, with four speed syncromesh gearbox. (Sotheby's) $1,775

Mercedes-Benz 220SE two-door coupe, 1964, with six cylinder engine. (Sotheby's) $615

Morris Minor 1000 two-door saloon, 1959, wheelbase 7ft.2in. (Sotheby's) $1,185

American Victorian penny-farthing bicycle, circa 1880, 5ft. high. (Robert W. Skinner Inc.) $1,000

Swift pedal tricycle with steering by twin hand grips, 1880. (Sotheby's) $4,385

Morris Isis Six saloon car, 1930. (Phillips) $17,600

Triumph two-litre Vitesse MK 1 convertible, 1970, with four speed gearbox. (Sotheby's)$1,895

Unregistered Austin Seven van, 1932, wheelbase 6ft.9in. (Sotheby's) $5,225

Standard Fulham 8.9h.p. 'nine' fabric saloon, 1928, wheelbase 7ft.8in. (Sotheby's) $4,030

Early 20th century Reading caravan painted red, blue and beige. (Vernon's) $5,000

Bentley S2 series B standard steel saloon with v-eight engine, wheelbase 10ft.3in. (Sotheby's)
$10,900

Aston Martin 15/98 short chassis two-litre close-coupled four-seater open sports car, 1937. (Sotheby's)
$10,430

Calthorpe 245cc. solo motorcycle, 1921, final drive by chain and belt. (Sotheby's)
$1,280

Ford Model 'T' saloon, circa 1919, wheelbase 8ft.4in. (Sotheby's)
$10,665

TRAYS

George III mahogany and satinwood oval tea tray with serpentine gallery, 31in. wide, with later stand. (Christie's)
$4,180

Sheraton mahogany oval tray with satinwood conch shell inlaid centre, 81cm. wide. (Jackson-Stops & Staff)
$730

One of a pair of rectangular black lacquer trays by Vishniakov, 19.5cm. wide, circa 1870. (Sotheby's)
$525

American decorated Tole tea tray with rolled rim, circa 1850, 26in. wide. (Robert W. Skinner Inc.)
$300

Gilt metal mounted oval Roman mosaic tray, circa 1870, 40.5cm. long. (Sotheby's Belgravia)
$1,510

20th century Tuthill glass tray, signed, 13½in. long. (Robert W. Skinner Inc.)
$525

Large iron tsuba, inlaid in copper and gold takazogan, with inlaid soft metal reserve. (Sotheby, King & Chasemore) $285

Small circular Shakudo-Nanako tsuba, 6.1cm. high. (Christie's) $355

Circular Sentoku Migaki-Ji tsuba, signed with a kao, Nara School, 7.6cm. high. (Christie's) $525

Late 17th century oval iron tsuba, signed Nishigaki Kampei, 7.5cm. high. (Christie's) $525

19th century unsigned Shakudo Mokko tsuba decorated with a dragon, 8cm. high. (Christie's) $570

Unsigned 19th century oval Shibuichi tsuba with gilt and silver detail, 6.3cm. high.(Christie's) $335

Oval iron tsuba inscribed Soheishi Nyudo Soten Sei, 7.7cm. high. (Christie's) $380

Oval iron tsuba of the Edo period, signed Suihan no shi Shigenaga saku, 8.2cm. high. (Christie's) $430

Unsigned 18th century oval Shakudo-Nanako tsuba decorated with flowers, 6.7cm. high. (Christie's) $450

Rounded-square Sentoku and Shinchu Hariawase tsuba, inscribed Hamano Yasuyuki, 8.2cm. high. (Christie's) $835

Iron Migaki-Ji tsuba, unsigned, Shoami School, 8.2cm. high. (Christie's) $380

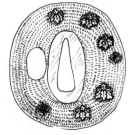

17th century oval Shakudo-Nanako tsuba, unsigned, Hirata School, 6.6cm. high. (Christie's) $810

INDEX

662